# EFFORTLESS E-COMMERCE with PHP and MySQL

SECOND EDITION

LARRY ULLMAN

**Effortless E-Commerce with PHP and MySQL, Second Edition**
Larry Ullman

New Riders
www.newriders.com
To report errors, please send a note to: errata@peachpit.com

New Riders is an imprint of Peachpit, a division of Pearson Education.



**Project Editor**: Nancy Peterson
**Copyeditor**: Liz Welch
**Proofreader**: Scout Festa
**Technical Reviewer**: Chris Cornutt
**Production Coordinator and Compositor**: David Van Ness
**Cover Designer**: Aren Straiger
**Indexer**: Karin Arrigoni



ISBN 13: 978-0-321-94936-3
ISBN 10: 0-321-94936-6

9 8 7 6 5 4 3 2 1

Printed and bound in the United States of America

*This book is dedicated to all the friends, family, and coworkers who have been so helpful, supportive, understanding, and generous with their time over the past few years. It's a long list, in no particular order: Roxanne, Nicole, Sarah, Meredith, Paula, Barb, Christina, Shirley, Cyndi, Sommar, Brian, Gary, Heather, Rich, Gina, Mike, Kay, Janice, David, and everyone at Peachpit Press.*

# A BUSHEL—THAT'S FOUR WHOLE PECKS—OF THANKS TO...

Nancy, for managing the project, for being great to work with, and for assembling such a top-notch team.

Chris, for joining in at the last minute to provide an excellent technical review.

David, for magically converting a handful of random materials into something that walks and talks like a book.

Liz and Scout, for the sharp eyes in improving my muddled words, grammar, and syntax.

Karin, the indexer who makes it easy for readers to find what they need to know without wading through all of my blather.

Aren, for the snazzy cover design.

All the readers who requested that I write this book and provided detailed thoughts as to what they would and would not want this book to be. I hope it's what you were looking for!

To all the readers who liked the first edition and made suggestions for how I could improve this one.

Gary at Kona Earth coffee (www.konaearth.com) for the ton of feedback. And for the truly excellent coffee!

Templates.com (www.templates.com) for permission to use their template in the book's Coffee example.

Jon, for permission to use his "Architecture by Hand" stencil for some of the book's figures (www.jonathanbrown.me).

Rashelle, for always entertaining the kids so that I can get some work done, even if I'd rather not.

Zoe and Sam, for being the kid epitome of awesomeness.

Jessica, for doing everything you do and everything you can.

# CONTENTS

# INTRODUCTION

Electronic commerce has been an important and viable part of the Internet for well over 15 years now. From the behemoths like Amazon.com to the mom-and-pop online stores to the boutiques run through Etsy, e-commerce is performed in a number of ways. Despite the dozens, or hundreds, of failures for every single commercial success, e-commerce can still be an excellent business tool when done properly. And yet, surprisingly, there are very few books dedicated to the subject.

Using two concrete examples, plus plenty of theory, this book covers the fundamentals of developing e-commerce websites using PHP and MySQL. Emphasizing security, a positive customer experience, and modular, extendable programming, this book presents tons of detailed solutions to today's real-world e-commerce demands. Whether you've been creating dynamic websites for years or just weeks, you're bound to learn something new over the course of the next 15 chapters.

## WHAT IS E-COMMERCE?

In the broadest sense, the term *e-commerce* covers the gamut of possible online commercial transactions. Any website with the intention of making money for a business could fall under the "e-commerce" label. Of course, such a liberal definition encompasses the vast majority of existing websites. On the opposite end of the scale, e-commerce can be defined as strictly the online act of taking money directly from customers. And that's the kind of e-commerce this book addresses.

There are two key differences between a site hoping simply to *make* money and one intending to *take* money:

- How comfortable the customer needs to be
- How secure the site needs to be

A site can make money from selling ads, in which case all that's required of the customer is that she visits. Or a site could make money from referrals, where the hope is that the customer will use a link on the site to purchase something from another site. In both cases, what's being asked of the user is insignificant. But when a site wants a customer to provide her full name, address, and credit card information, that becomes serious business. In order for the site to succeed, the customer must be respected, her questions answered, her concerns addressed, and her fears mitigated. And, of course, the site has to have something the customer wants to spend money on there and not somewhere else.

When it comes to e-commerce, I can't overstress the importance of security. To protect both the business and its customers, a site must be designed and programmed so as to establish and maintain an appropriate level of security. As you'll see, especially in Chapter 2, "Security Fundamentals," the overall security of a website is impacted not just by the code you write but also by some of the initial decisions that you make, such as the chosen hosting environment. With this in mind, security concerns are presented in the book from the big picture and the general theories down to the nuances of specific code. You can rest assured that the book's examples have no known security holes. Moreover, there's plenty of discussion as to how you can make specific processes even more secure, as well as warnings about what you shouldn't do, from a security perspective.

# ABOUT THIS BOOK

The goal of this book is to portray the widest possible range of what e-commerce can be, in terms of PHP code, SQL and MySQL, and a site's user interface. To that end, the book is broken into four parts, cleverly named Part 1, Part 2, Part 3, and (drumroll) Part 4.

Part 1, "Fundamentals," has just two chapters, which examine

- Fundamental theories and issues surrounding an e-commerce business
- Decisions you need to make up front
- Critical aspects of online security

In Part 2, "Selling Virtual Products," you develop an entire e-commerce site. This site sells virtual products, namely access to content. With virtual products, there's no inventory management and nothing to ship. The business just needs to accept payment from customers and ensure that access is denied to nonpaying customers. For this example, PayPal is used to handle customer payments. PayPal is a wise choice for beginning e-commerce sites because it has a name that almost all customers will be familiar with (and therefore trust), and it minimizes the security risks taken by the site itself.

Part 3, "Selling Physical Products," creates an entire e-commerce site for the sake of selling physical products. This involves inventory management, an online catalog, shopping carts, order history, and more. For that example, the Authorize.net payment gateway is integrated directly into the website, creating a more seamless and professional experience.

Part 4, "Extra Touches," is entirely new in this edition of the book. Part 4 explores dozens of features, techniques, approaches, and so forth that you can apply to the two example sites or to e-commerce in general. One chapter makes specific recommendations regarding the virtual product example site. Another chapter gives the same treatment to the second example site (which sells physical products). The third new chapter singles out JavaScript and Ajax as a great way to enhance the e-commerce experience. And the fourth new chapter explains how to use Stripe, a revolutionary way to process payments.

By using two examples with different goals and features, the book presents a smorgasbord of ideas, database designs, HTML tricks, and PHP code. The intention is that, after completing the book, you'll feel comfortable implementing any number or combination of features and approaches on your own e-commerce sites.

## Technologies Used

This book, as its title implies, uses the PHP scripting language (www.php.net) and the MySQL database application (www.mysql.com) as the foundation of the websites. When writing the book, I was using version 5.5 of PHP and version 5.6 of MySQL, although you should have no problems with any of the code as long as you're using PHP 5.3 or greater and MySQL 5.0 or greater. In places where newer versions of these technologies are required, you'll see alternative ways to accomplish the same tasks.

As with any modern website, HTML is involved (of course), as is CSS. The book does not explain either in great detail, but it does show some best practices in terms of their use.

In Part 4, you'll encounter JavaScript and the jQuery framework (www.jquery.com). JavaScript, jQuery, and Ajax are used to enhance the sites and add some functionality. I explain the code in some detail, but if you're entirely unfamiliar with JavaScript, it might be daunting. JavaScript knowledge isn't necessary for either of the book's examples, however.

Part 3 also taps into some of what the Apache web server (http://httpd.apache.org) can do. As with the JavaScript, the Apache particulars aren't required knowledge, but it's worth your time to become familiar with them.

## What's New in This Edition

The biggest and most obvious addition in this edition is Part 4. It consists of four chapters:

- Chapter 12, "Extending the First Site"
- Chapter 13, "Extending the Second Site"
- Chapter 14, "Adding JavaScript and Ajax"
- Chapter 15, "Using Stripe Payments"

These chapters present more ways you can implement e-commerce, from specific features you could add, to alternative coding techniques, to improving the security. And the last chapter presents a new way of taking payments online.

Besides the obvious new material, I've updated all the code in the two sites to keep them current and secure, reflecting changes in technologies or approaches since the first edition was written. For example, there are new and better ways of communicating with PayPal and Authorize.net. There's also a greatly improved and more secure technique for storing and verifying passwords in PHP. And I've changed the client-side foundation of the first e-commerce site from using a third-party template to implementing the Twitter Bootstrap framework (version 3; www.getbootstrap.com).

Finally, I've gone through all the code and fixed anything that was suboptimal, or outright wrong, in the first edition of the book. In a couple of the more complicated places, I've lengthened, clarified, or just flat-out improved the explanation of what's happening and why.

## Getting Help

If you have any problems with, or questions about, what is said or done in this book, there are several resources to which you can turn, starting with the book's website, www.LarryUllman.com. There you can find all the files, code, and SQL commands used in this book.

At www.LarryUllman.com/forums/ you'll find a support forum dedicated to this book. If you post a question or comment there, you'll get a relatively prompt reply, from others or from me.

# WHAT YOU'LL NEED

Just as e-commerce is a transaction between a customer and a website, a book can be viewed as a transaction between the writer and the reader (just not one that takes place in real time). I've already presented a synopsis of this book, but who do I imagine you to be and what will you need?

## Some Fundamental Skills

The goal of this book is to demonstrate the application of PHP and MySQL to the task of creating an e-commerce site. Although I expect that even a seasoned web developer will learn a lot, the book does not teach the fundamentals of either PHP or MySQL. If you're not already comfortable with these two technologies, this is not the book for you. If you have no problems executing a MySQL query using PHP and then handling those query results, you'll be fine.

The same must be said for the secondary technologies involved, namely HTML and CSS. If the definition of an HTML form is foreign to you, you should learn those basics before getting immersed in this book's material.

As for the JavaScript, jQuery, and Apache work that you'll come across, no previous experience with them is expected, although those sections will certainly be easier to follow if you have some.

## A Web Server

To develop a site using PHP and MySQL, you'll need a web server, a computer running PHP through a web server application (such as Apache, nginx, or IIS [Internet Information Services]), and the MySQL database application server. Fortunately, you can install all of these on your own computer, at absolutely no cost. The easiest way to do so is to use an all-in-one package, such as XAMPP (www.apachefriends.org) or MAMP (www.mamp.info). If you already have a website being hosted on a live server, that will work as well.

## And a Bit More

A web server will let you *run* a dynamic website, but you need additional tools to *develop* one: At the very least, you'll need a decent text editor or integrated development environment (IDE). A commercial IDE like PhpStorm (www.jetbrains.com/phpstorm/) is fine, as is an open source IDE like Aptana Studio (www.aptana.com) or a plain-text editor such as SublimeText (www.sublimetext.com). Just use something with more features than Notepad!

It doesn't matter what web browser you're using, as long as you use one with great debugging tools.

And that's it! If you've already done some PHP and MySQL development (which is a requirement for following along with this book), you probably already have everything you need. So let's get started!

# PART ONE
# FUNDAMENTALS

# 1 GETTING STARTED

Just as you don't begin building a house by grabbing a hammer, creating an e-commerce site doesn't start with your computer. Well, you'll probably use your computer for research, but actual coding is a step that comes much later. In this chapter, you'll learn how to commence developing your e-commerce site. The goal of the chapter is to explain two things:

- The steps you'll need to take
- This book's perspective on e-commerce

Although the point of this book is to provide concrete answers and usable code, there will be some subjects, especially over the next few pages, for which I can't tell you what to do. In such cases, I instead try to identify what questions you'll need to answer and how you might go about doing so.

At a root level, the success of any website, regardless of whether it's intended to make money, depends on its usability, reliability, and performance: If people are attempting to use the site, can they? In this chapter, you'll encounter many of the decisions you'll need to make that impact your site's availability. The choices you make aren't permanent, but as with most things, not having to make big changes further down the road is preferable.

The success of an e-commerce site further depends on security. This chapter touches on a few security issues, but security is addressed in more detail in the next chapter, and then throughout the rest of the book.

The last thing to note is that you may be creating an e-commerce site under one of two scenarios: for yourself or for others. When creating a site for yourself, you'll need to make most of the decisions. When creating a site for others, they'll be the ones making most of these decisions and your part in the process is, at best, advisory. Take, for example, the business's goals....

# IDENTIFYING YOUR BUSINESS GOALS

Before you do anything, anything at all—mock up a web design, identify your web host, or even buy the domain name—you need to identify your business goals. For an e-commerce site, the goal is to make money, which you can do in different ways:

- Selling goods or services directly
- Advertising on the site
- Promoting goods or services that can be purchased elsewhere

In this book, I'm using the term *e-commerce* to refer to sites that directly accept money from end users. I've limited myself to that scope, because handling money directly demands a level of security well beyond other types of sites.

Say you wanted to create a site that reviews music: You might give all the content away for free but hope to make money by displaying ads on your site and/or by using affiliate links to other sites that actually sell music. In either case, the security issues you'd have are no bigger than those for most other non-e-commerce sites. As another example, my blog, www.LarryUllman.com, supports and augments the books I write, which ideally increases the sales of the books; however, the blog itself does not take money directly. The goal in this book is to create sites that sell goods or services directly to customers.

**tip**

A good way to get people to your site is to offer something, almost anything, for free!

Achieving a business's goals involves many components. The focus of this book is strictly on manufacturing the online experience; you'll need to follow through on your own with the other facets of running a business, such as

- Creating a legal business entity
- Properly handling business taxes
- Doing the company accounting
- Coordinating with vendors
- Marketing your business

- Managing employees and payroll
- Controlling physical inventory
- Managing shipping and returns

In short, just creating the website isn't all you'll need to do. Most importantly, know from the outset that even if you make a *fantastic* e-commerce website, that alone is no guarantee of business success.

**tip**

Give people a reason to visit your site even when they're not shopping, so they might buy something on impulse or think of your site first when they do want to make a purchase.

So stop reading right now and write down your business goals. What do you hope to achieve? What are your short-term goals? What are your long-term goals? Try to be realistic about them.

Next, write down (on a large piece of paper!) everything you think you'll need to do and have in order to achieve those goals. How much money can you invest up front? How much time? Who will help you? How will the helpers be compensated? From where will you get more money when you suddenly need more money? Who is going to handle the bookkeeping? How will you get people to visit your site? If you're selling physical products, where will they be stored? How will you ship the merchandise?

Clearly, you'll need to answer a lot of questions, even for the most basic of goals. But there's one key question I *can* answer for you: How do you create a good, secure e-commerce site? Answer: Read this book!

# RESEARCHING LEGAL ISSUES

Whenever you're dealing with other people's money, and whenever you're creating your own business, you have to take into account legal issues. This is a big area in which I can be of little assistance: I'm not a lawyer, and I don't know in which country, state, province, territory, or city you live. But this doesn't mean I can't point you in the right direction.

## National and International Laws

The legal issues involved differ when the website is for your business and when you're creating it for a client. When working for a client, you must have a sound, legal contract. In particular, the contract should limit the liability you personally have should something go wrong. As a general rule, good contracts limit your liability to the amount of money you made on the project itself, should you be at fault. Also, you should define a process for how to handle change requests. One approach is to provide one round of requests after the initial version of the site is complete. Secondary requests, or any additions unreasonably beyond the original scope of the contract, must be renegotiated.

If you have your own business and there is no client, you still have tons of other legal issues to investigate that have nothing to do with the e-commerce site itself. For these, start by contacting every applicable governmental department to see what you must know and do. Many cities and states have small business branches dedicated to helping people like you navigate the maze of legal necessities.

In either case, you must be knowledgeable about legal issues specifically addressing online commerce. Again, your local and national governments should be able to provide you with this information. The particulars will differ greatly from one country to the next. They may even depend on where you're located, where the client is located, where the customers are, where the site is physically hosted, where the associated bank can be found, and so forth. In the United States, the Federal Trade Commission (FTC) oversees many aspects of e-commerce. On the FTC website, www.ftc.gov, you'll find excellent guidelines for e-commerce, international sales, security, and more.

As another example, in the United Kingdom, the government has exact requirements as to what information should be available on the website, as well as on order forms and in emails. This includes

- The company's physical address
- The company's registration number
- Any trade associations
- The value added tax (VAT) number

Because you'll be storing information about the customers, other laws are involved. The European Union has specific regulations as to how personal data is stored and used. The United States also has precise rules about the use of customer email addresses for advertising, promotional emails, and the handling of disclosures. All these laws apply to basic personal information; if you're storing credit card data (and you really shouldn't), even more laws apply.

You'll also need to know whether Internet sales should be taxed and, if so, at what rate. In the United States, this is still being debated and varies from state to state. And if you're shipping physical products, there are rules about when you can charge the customer based on when the order ships. If part of the order ships, you can only charge the customer part of the order total at that time.

tip

All laws aside, treat your customers and their personal information as you would hope sites treat you and your information.

Should the worst happen—say your system is hacked and the data is breached—laws may apply as well. The state of California, for example, has strict laws as to what you must do once you find a security violation. Part of planning—a big part, really—is preparing yourself should the worst happen so that you're not scrambling to find answers in the middle of a crisis.

I understand that the number and complexity of laws that may apply can be overwhelming, but take that as an indicator of how important it is that you pursue these issues to the fullest extent. When you're building a business, and when you're trying to make money via e-commerce, instituting proper and complete compliance with all laws is the only way to go.

## PCI Compliance

Another legal issue on which you should be extremely well versed is PCI DSS, short for Payment Card Industry Data Security Standard (www.pcisecuritystandards.org). This is a specific set of rules for ensuring secure, proper handling of credit cards by all commercial vendors. Any company that processes, stores, or transmits credit card information must follow these guidelines, thereby being *PCI compliant*.

tip

Many payment gateways allow for recurring payments, meaning you can charge a customer multiple times, still without storing their payment information yourself.

By following the code in this book, you'll neither store nor process any credit cards yourself, which is for the best. *You absolutely do not want to store the user's credit card information!* There are companies that do that, yes, but that's their full-time job and they have the knowledge, resources, and money to do that properly. Still, even taking credit card information on your site and passing it off to another company means you need to be PCI compliant. The specific requirements differ based on what you do with credit cards and how many transactions per year you process. I'll get into those requirements in the next chapter.

tip

The credit card companies, Visa in particular, have loads of documentation on their websites regarding secure handling of credit cards, what to do if your system is compromised, and more.

If your site is not PCI compliant and there's a security breach, several bad things could happen (beyond the effects of the security breach itself). First, the credit cards companies will likely escalate your security requirements to a higher level, such as requiring external security scans of your system. This means more work for you and higher expenses. Second, the credit card companies that created the PCI DSS—such as Visa, MasterCard, American Express, Discover, and JCB (Japan Credit Bureau)—could make you pay any damages they incur because of your security breach. They may even fine you as well. Third, those same companies could deny you the option of accepting their cards, which will pretty much shut down your business.

Technically, the PCI DSS isn't a law, but some parts of the specification may also be an applicable law in your country, state, province, or territory. And the potential penalties that the credit card companies can impose can be just as scary as any legal repercussion.

# CHOOSING WEB TECHNOLOGIES

Over the past 20 years, the web has changed in many ways. It has changed significantly in just the past five! But some things remain the same. For starters, there's HTML (HyperText Markup Language). Whatever else has changed—whatever image types, video options, and server-side technologies you use—the end user first interacts with HTML. This book does not, and cannot, teach HTML. If you need more information about HTML, pick up a book on that subject, such as the de facto standard, Elizabeth Castro and Bruce Hyslop's *HTML and CSS: Visual QuickStart Guide, 8th Edition* (Peachpit Press, 2013).

This book doesn't teach HTML, CSS, JavaScript, PHP, SQL, or MySQL; instead, it demonstrates real-world application of these technologies.

With modern web browsers, most of a site's layout and design comes from CSS (Cascading Style Sheets). I'll be using CSS in this book, too, and just like with HTML, I don't explain it in much detail. Still, I won't be using CSS in any super-fancy way, so you shouldn't have a problem following along.

When I first began doing web development in the late 1990s, there was this annoying little thing called JavaScript. At that time, JavaScript was largely used for petty and cutesy tricks. In short, JavaScript was almost entirely unnecessary. Today, thanks to Ajax, Web 2.0, and other marketing terms that people throw around, things are quite different. Now, JavaScript, when properly used, greatly improves the user experience. Many website features that people appreciate, such as being able to present lots of content in a limited space, being able to add something to a cart without leaving the page, and so forth, require JavaScript. Although JavaScript is valuable, it's really an "extra." With that in mind, this book will make use of some JavaScript to implement some extras. If you're not comfortable with JavaScript already, might I selfishly recommend my own book, *Modern JavaScript: Develop and Design* (Peachpit Press, 2012)?

On the server side of the equation, unlike in the client, you have a vast range of web technology to consider. This book uses PHP as the programming language of choice and MySQL as the database application. These are among my personal favorite server-side technologies, and if you're reading this book, I assume you think so as well. But if you aren't already well versed in PHP and MySQL, you will have difficulty with some of this book's code. Consider reading my *PHP and MySQL for Dynamic Web Sites: Visual QuickPro Guide, Fourth Edition* (Peachpit Press, 2011) to learn more about these technologies.

After this chapter, I'll stop recommending other books to buy, I promise!

## EASY E-COMMERCE ALTERNATIVES

In this book, you'll learn how to write an e-commerce application from scratch, using a combination of HTML, CSS, JavaScript, PHP, SQL, and MySQL. There are, however, faster, less custom approaches you can take.

If you just want to get an e-commerce site online quickly, or if you don't know any of the listed technologies, you can use "turnkey" e-commerce sites that Yahoo, Google, and others provide. By answering some questions and using the chosen company's interface, you can create a basic e-commerce site in a day. It'll even be tied automatically into a payment system. But make no mistake: Although you'll get up and running in no time, the end result will be rather amateurish and very limited.

A middle-ground solution between using an entire third-party system and creating your own is to use an off-the-shelf e-commerce package, such as ZenCart (www.zen-cart.com), FoxyCart (www.foxycart.com), or osCommerce (www.oscommerce.com). They provide all the functionality, from creating a catalog or a shopping cart to administration, which can then be tied to one of several payment systems. These tools have been around for years; they're quite solid and well supported, but they'll still have some limitations compared to writing your own e-commerce site, especially when it's time to add features that will be uniquely yours. At the same time, these packages will also be bogged down with lots of features that you might not ever use.

# SELECTING A WEB HOST

**tip**

You may need to put your site on a hosted server in order to test it with a payment gateway.

I strongly advocate that you *develop* your entire site using just your personal computer or other development environment that you have readily available. You can install all the necessary tools—a web server, PHP, and MySQL—on your own computer, then develop the database, write the code, test, and so on. Developing on your personal computer is faster (because you don't have to upload files), cheaper (because you're not paying for hosting during this time), and more secure (because incomplete, potentially unsecure code won't be online).

After getting the project nearly complete, you'll need to move it to your web host. Let's look at how you choose one.

## Hosting Options

With regard to hosting, you can generally say that you get what you pay for, and I say that as a person who's inclined to go the cheapest route whenever possible. Over the years, I've used probably five or six hosts for my own websites and dealt with many others for clients. The old adage says that you have to spend money to make money; selecting a cheap host is a bad way to go about making money.

Hosting plans vary based on

- Price
- Features
- Performance
- Amount of control

The *price* is directly related to the quality of the other three attributes. If you spend more, you'll get more.

To be honest, the *features* don't really matter. Well, some do and many don't. Most hosting plans will offer some 56 features, of which you'll need 10. This even goes for disk space and bandwidth limitations: Hosting plans will offer you more of these than you'll ever need, thereby tempting you with trivialities. The minimally required features are PHP, MySQL, a mail server (to send and receive email), and security software, such as a firewall, a virus detector, and so forth. Additionally, beneficial features include regular backups and excellent—truly excellent—customer support. When it comes time to compare one hosting option to another, decide what really counts—like uptime, backups, security, and customer service—and ignore the rest.

The *performance* of a server will depend on the type of hosting involved, the server's specific hardware—amount of RAM, disk types, processor types, the number of processors, and the server's network connection. As I mentioned earlier, the site's performance is hugely important, but it's unfortunately something that's not easily determined in advance.

The *amount of control* you have over the server will depend on the hosting type. Different web-hosting companies offer different plans, but the basic hosting options are

- Free
- Shared
- Virtual private server (VPS)
- Dedicated or colocation (colo)

**tip**

You'll eventually come to regret using free or very cheap hosting plans for your website, so save yourself that headache!

*Free* hosting plans are harder to come by now than they used to be, but you shouldn't even consider them for an e-commerce site. You may have a free site possibility with some account you have, or from your ISP, but you probably can't even use your domain name on them.

*Shared* hosting plans are the most common and the cheapest (of the paid choices). Shared hosting involves putting tens of clients and possibly hundreds of websites on a single server. Shared hosting is inexpensive—decent plans range from $10 to $20 (all prices in the book will be in U.S. dollars) per month and may be a reasonable way to start. However, because there are multiple users on each server, your website will only be as secure as the weakest security link in any site on the server. The performance of the site will also suffer, as the demands are so high. Finally, you'll have little to no control over how the server runs. You won't be able to use a particular version of PHP, enable certain PHP settings or features, or tweak how MySQL runs. Shared hosts aren't likely to make any changes that might adversely impact the other clients on the same server. Still, shared hosting may be appropriate for smaller, less demanding sites without higher security concerns.

A happy medium between shared hosting and dedicated is the *virtual private server* (it's what I've personally used for several years). Instead of having tens of clients on a single server, there may be only a couple or a handful, with each client running her own virtual operating system. Although all the servers' hardware is still being shared, limitations can be placed so that you'll always get a minimum amount of RAM, thereby guaranteeing some performance no matter what happens to the other sites on the server. From a security perspective, each virtual server is a separate entity: The actions that the other clients take on their VPS instances can't impact yours. And since the VPS is yours alone, you can do whatever you want with it in terms of installing and configuring software. VPS hosting plans run from as cheap as $30 per month to around $100 per month.

**tip**

When using dedicated or colocated hosting, make sure that the hosting company will still provide some maintenance and security assistance.

A *dedicated* or *colocated* server is on the other end of the hosting spectrum. This kind of hosting puts an entire computer—its software and hardware—under your command, but the server is physically housed at the hosting company's location. That location should have multiple, fast connections to the Internet; redundant power supplies with battery backups; secure physical access to the server rooms; climate control; and so on. (The technical difference between dedicated and colocated hosting is that the host typically owns a *dedicated* server, whereas you typically own a *colocated* one.)

The other hosting types can't match the amount of control, the number of features, or possibly the performance of running your own entire server. But the cost of a dedicated or colocated server will be much, much higher—from a couple of hundred dollars per month to several hundred. Just as important is the fact that, depending on the particulars of the hosting plan, you may be responsible for all the maintenance and security of the server. You'll need to decide if you think you're better suited to handle server security than someone who does that full time and has likely been doing it for years. Also, the web-hosting company will have people monitoring your server 24 hours a day, whereas you've got to sleep sometime.

### CLOUD COMPUTING

Another hosting option has come up in the past few years: *cloud hosting*. Cloud computing sounds ethereal, but it's just moving some server functionality—processing of data, storing of data, handling of emails, or whatever—to a different computer (or bank of computers) not under your control and on a different network. One benefit to cloud computing is that it can automatically scale to your needs without you having to take extra steps. If, for some freak, benevolent reason, you go from processing an average of 100 sales per day to 10,000, the cloud will be able to handle the increased traffic, which might otherwise have crashed a basic hosting plan. But there are extra security concerns with cloud computing, and you'd need to be prepared to pay the price. For example, if your site gets hit with a denial-of-service (DoS) attack (discussed in Chapter 2, "Security Fundamentals"), you'll have to foot the bill for the extra cloud computing, but the attack itself will have generated no extra revenue.

A cloud hosting option, such as Amazon's Web Services, is fantastic in many ways. You can expand easily and still only pay for what you use. But cloud hosting is implemented differently than any other type of hosting, and those differences present another hurdle to overcome when you're just starting out. On the other hand, you can start with a traditional hosting scenario and later add extended networking (for example, a content delivery network) to gain some of the benefits of cloud hosting.

This book doesn't discuss cloud computing beyond what I've just said. But be aware of this potential avenue, and you may want to look into vendors and pricing if you suspect that cloud computing could be a good fit for your site and situation.

## My Hosting Recommendation

As a reader, you're probably looking for as many definitive answers as possible, so my recommendation is to select a quality shared or VPS hosting plan to begin, depending on the project itself and your budget. You absolutely don't want to host the site on your personal computer; you absolutely don't want to use free hosting; and you most likely shouldn't go with dedicated hosting to start, unless you have money to waste.

One important thing to know is that you're not permanently locked into a given hosting plan or even a web host. A good web host should be able to upgrade or expand your hosting plan with little or no downtime. Start with a plan that's reasonably basic, and should you have the good fortune of profound success, you can scale up your plan to meet the increased demands over time.

It's possible to change web hosts as well, just not as easily. It's best to start with a great host that you'll be able to stick with for years and years. This means not only someone reliable, but also a host that's established in such a way to allow for your site's expansion. For example, a really cheap host probably does only shared hosting. You'd never be able to move to a dedicated server with them, and you probably wouldn't want to. Conversely, the hosting company I use provides only VPS and dedicated hosting plans. The VPS works for me for now, and I can move to one or more dedicated servers with this same company when I have that need.

**tip**

You can save yourself some money by developing the entire site on your own computer before you purchase a hosting plan.

My final piece of advice is not to spend dramatically more than you need to earlier than you need to. By that I mean, you many think you've got a site that will someday have millions of users, and therefore you'll need dozens of servers, but today you've got no site and no users, so a single server (or hosting plan) will be more than sufficient.

## Finding a Good Host

The final question, then, is how do you know if a web host is good? First, go online and search using terms like *web host review* or *best web host*. In the search results, *ignore* every site whose sole purpose is to rate and review web hosts. Yes, that's right: ignore those. They're unreliable and built on advertising, and you'll never know what kind of relationship they may have with the companies they're "ranking." Plus, in my experience, such sites are ranking web hosts for the masses, for those who don't know any better. If you want to find a couple of recommendations this way, mostly as a basis of comparison, that's fine, but these rankings should not be used to make a decision.

**note**

All of the lousy web hosts I've used over the years were found by listening to "official" rankings of the best web hosts!

The best way to find a good host is to get real-world feedback and comments from real people. One way to do so is by finding forums where people talk about their hosting experiences. In the past, I've also emailed people to ask them if they're happy with their host, prior to making a decision. You can also get recommendations through mailing lists and the like.

If you're curious, I personally use ServInt (www.servint.net) and have for years. I've also heard good things about DreamHost (www.dreamhost.com) but have no personal experience with them.

Once you've got a few potential candidates, start by excluding those that are really cheap. You don't want to try to save money by skimping on web hosting. It's not a good long-term plan. Cheaper hosting options than the one I use are out there, but my site is always available. I've got peace of mind, and you can't put a price on that. Interestingly, my current host doesn't even offer a free month of hosting, as many companies do. Their argument, which I buy into, is that providing a free month invites malicious people to temporarily get a server just to send spam or do other harmful or annoying activities. You don't want to be part of a network where that's happening.

You should also rule out those companies that try to do too much: better to have a host that excels at one or two things than one that is average at several. One of the worst hosting experiences I ever had, if not the worst, was with a company whose primary function was as a domain registrar. They were fine as registrars but *terrible* as hosts.

Don't let your registrar host your site, and don't let your host register your domain name!

As I already said, all web hosts will offer tons of features and more disk space, bandwidth, and add-ons than you'll ever need. And it's almost impossible to compare performance from one host to the next. For me, then, I focus on a host's security approach and customer service. If your hosting company strives for top-level security, that minimizes the chances of a problem occurring in the first place. If your hosting company also offers great customer service, they'll provide a quick fix should a problem arise.

# USING A PAYMENT SYSTEM

As with your choice of a web-hosting company, the payment system you use for your e-commerce site will have a significant impact on the end result. This is not to say that the site will be married to a single payment system for eternity, but as with any divorce, ending a relationship with a payment system can be tedious and costly for your business. Furthermore, it's possible, if not common, to use more than one payment system at the same time (for example, PayPal and another).

The payment system is the differentiating element between a standard website and an e-commerce one. The whole point of a payment system is to transfer money between the customers and the business.

When I wrote the first edition of this book in 2010, there were only two broad types of payment systems. These are frequently known by a variety of names but can be described as either a *payment processor* or a *payment gateway*.

In the years since I wrote this book, a third approach has arisen. For lack of an existing label, I'm going to call this option "the middle way," for reasons to be explained shortly.

Some companies, like PayPal, offer more than one type of payment system.

In this book, I'll demonstrate an example of each of the three types, but here, I'll outline their pros and cons.

## Payment Processors

A *payment processor* is a delayed payment system that normally goes through a third-party site (**Figure 1.1**). The best example is the *Payments Standard* option at PayPal (www.paypal.com). If you want to accept payment through PayPal using their basic service, you'll send the customer to PayPal's site along with your PayPal identification and some other information. The customer then uses PayPal to authorize the transfer of that amount of money. PayPal (hopefully) returns the customer to your site, and at some later point in time PayPal will make the funds available to you, minus their fees.

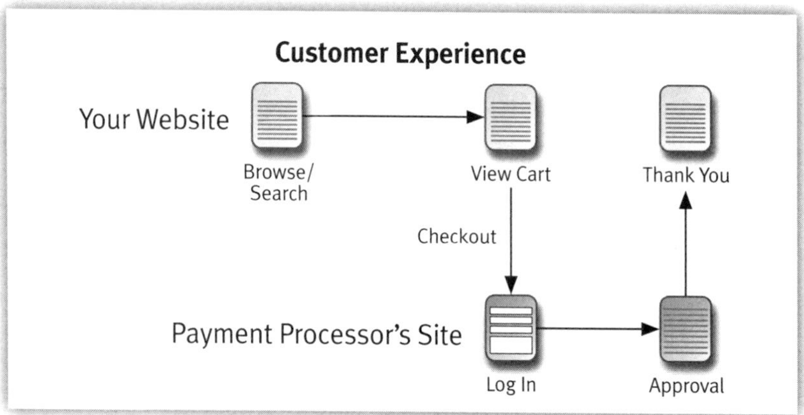


**Figure 1.1**

Using a payment processor like PayPal Payments Standard or Google's Checkout may be easy to establish, has little-to-no up-front costs, and taps into a service that many customers will be familiar with (customers are especially comfortable with PayPal). On the other hand, these systems aren't as integrated into your site as the alternatives, and sending customers away from your site is a risky e-commerce move, increasing the odds of losing the sale. Also, the per-transaction costs tend to be a bit higher, and deposits most likely won't be automatically made into your business's bank account (that is, you may need to go into the payment processor's system in order to accept and then transfer your credits).

In this book, I'll demonstrate how you can integrate PayPal, which is perhaps the most common payment processor, into your site. However, it can be a real chore to work with, even for experienced developers. But I'll help you navigate that morass in the first e-commerce example in this book, which I'm calling "Knowledge Is Power."

## Payment Gateways

A *payment gateway* is a real-time payment system that can be directly integrated into your own site, resulting in a process that's more professional and seamless. Instead of sending users away in the hopes they'll come back, transaction data is transmitted behind the scenes, and the customer won't leave your site at any point in the entire process (**Figure 1.2**). Also, a gateway offers much better fraud prevention, among other extra features (more on fraud protection in the next section). The gateway will deposit your monies into a *merchant account* automatically, normally charging less per transaction than payment processors do.

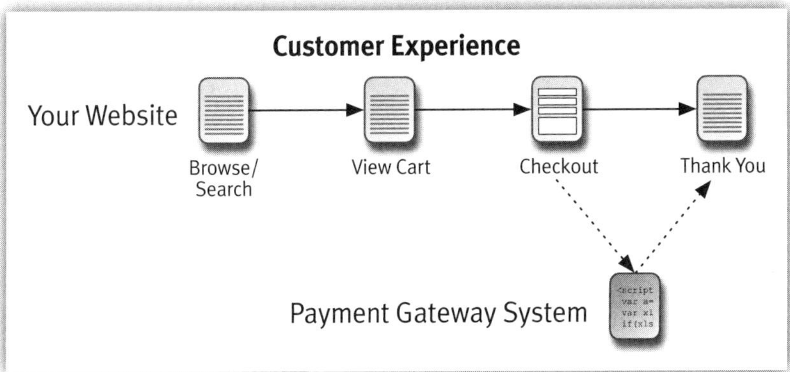


**Figure 1.2**

On the other side of the equation, a payment gateway may have higher setup costs and will require more programming to integrate the system into your site. Payment gateways also require a *merchant account*, which is an account into which credit card charges can be deposited and refunded (for customer returns). You may or may not be able to use your business bank as your merchant account, depending on your bank.

Further, because your site will be temporarily handling the customer's payment information, you'll need to maintain PCI compliance. This means more work and more money. PCI compliance will also dictate what hosting options are viable for you: shared hosting, for example, would be unacceptable.

Tons of payment gateways are available. Moreover, some gateway systems are resold through other vendors, giving you the ability to shop around for the best deal. Authorize.net (www.authorize.net) is perhaps the best-known payment gateway, and it will be used in the book's second example, which I'm simply calling "Coffee."

## The Middle Way

In the three years since I wrote the first edition of this book, a new type of payment option has arisen. I have yet to see a label applied to this approach, so I'll refer to it as "the middle way," because it offers the best aspects of both traditional models (payment processors and payment gateways).

With the middle way approach, customers enter their payment information on your site, as when using a payment gateway. But the payment information will be directly sent to the payment company (using JavaScript) and never touch your server. This simple difference greatly reduces the steps required for you to be PCI compliant, while simultaneously offering an optimal customer experience. For the developer, the middle way approach is surprisingly simple to set up and integrate. For the business, the fees are competitive, generally comparable to PayPal's fees, without any monthly or setup fees. And the middle way is a "full-stack" solution, which means you don't need to find and use a merchant account.

**note**

Both PayPal and Authorize.net offer "middle way" solutions as well.

The most popular middle way payment options available at the time of this writing are as follows:

- Stripe (https://stripe.com)
- Braintree (www.braintreepayments.com)
- Paymill (www.paymill.com)

These aren't perfect solutions, of course. The fees may be higher than other payment options, and there may be a longer delay in getting the money transferred to your bank account than you'd prefer. From a technological perspective, the middle way route tends to require JavaScript. Although only a very small percentage of web users have JavaScript disabled (between 1 and 3 percent), this requirement could be a factor.

In my experience, the biggest negative to these options is that they may not be available yet in your country. These are new approaches, by new companies, and although each company is expanding quickly, they may not be able to service your country quite yet.

New in this edition of the book, I'll demonstrate how to use Stripe as a payment option. As a disclaimer, as of this writing, I'm employed by Stripe (as a Support Engineer). Although I'm clearly biased toward Stripe, know that I'm working for Stripe because I love what they're doing, not the other way around. I started using Stripe, and writing about Stripe, long before they hired me.

## Which Should You Use?

If I were to start an e-commerce site today, I'd use one of these middle way companies, if available. Obviously I'm biased here, as I work for one of them, but whether or not you use Stripe, I think that the middle way approach offers the best of all the possible pros and cons.

tip

Payment systems will provide test accounts, dummy credit card numbers, and false processing systems through which you can test your site before going live.

That being said, many customers prefer to use PayPal, and having more payment options is always better. You might consider using a middle way approach *and* PayPal.

If you can't or don't want to use a middle way approach, you'll need to select the best traditional payment gateway. When selecting among payment providers, you should first determine if your business bank or web-hosting company has an arrangement with any payment companies. By choosing a preapproved vendor for this important service, you'll minimize some of the potential headaches and hopefully have an expert to turn to when you need technical support.

Another factor is geography: Different providers will work in your part of the world and will be limited as to what other regions they support. Also, you'll want to check that the currency the provider uses matches your business's currency, and that of your customers.

tip

Make sure your payment solution provider is in full PCI compliance and can assist in guiding your site's compliance, too.

There are many features to weigh when making your selection:

- Tools for fraud prevention
- Ability to perform recurring billing
- Acceptance of eChecks
- Automatic tax calculation
- Automatic shipping calculation and processing
- Digital content handling
- Integrated shopping cart

Clearly, many of these features can greatly simplify the development of your e-commerce site and result in a more professional web application, but I'd like to highlight fraud prevention. You may not have given much thought to the subject, but excellent fraud prevention is in the best long-term interest of your site. If someone can use a credit card at your site that isn't valid or isn't theirs, you'll have a false sale and later have some cleanup to perform to undo the transaction. Further, the person whose credit card was fraudulently used will think poorly of your business for allowing the fraud in the first place. For these

tip

Some gateways offer virtual terminals where the merchant can process credit card payments manually. These can be used to issue returns, for example.

reasons, using a gateway with sophisticated fraud-prevention tools is a must. The two most common techniques are to verify the billing address and the card verification value (CVV; those numbers on the back of the card).

**tip**

If the price of your transactions will be small—less than $10 on average—find a payment provider that supports *micropayments*, which have smaller transaction fees.

A final, obvious factor that I didn't list earlier is cost. You'll need to consider the initial setup costs, the monthly fees, and the individual transaction expenses. If you require features that come at an extra cost, factor those in as well.

# THE DEVELOPMENT PROCESS

After you've finalized your business plan, researched the laws, decided on a hosting company, and selected a payment system, it's time to start putting down HTML tags, SQL commands, and **`if-then`** statements. The development process itself is the point of this book, so let's take a look at it in detail (**Figure 1.3**).

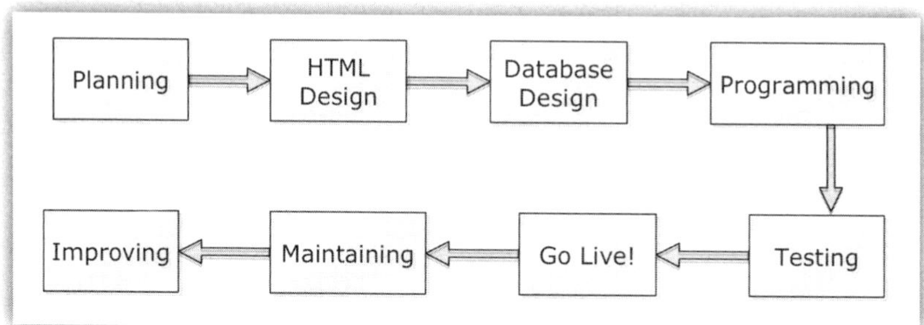


**Figure 1.3**

The development process occurs in phases. If each phase is approached deliberately and the end results are properly generated, you'll develop a great e-commerce site as efficiently as possible. If, on the other hand, you jump around, rush the process, skip steps, and make omissions, the whole procedure will take much longer, and the end result will be buggier.

At the end of the development process, you'll hopefully have created the best possible e-commerce site, but that site will undoubtedly need to be changed next week (as clients always want), next month, or next year. If the first goal is a smooth, optimal process, then the second is output—specifically PHP code and a MySQL database—that's flexible and scalable. When those inevitable changes need to be made, you should be able to do so without breaking or rewriting the entire system.

## Site Planning

The first step in the development process is planning a generic site. This is much like establishing your business goals, but specifically with the site itself. What should the site do? What should it look like? Who are the target users? What browsers and/or devices should the site support? Use pen and paper, or any application in which you can make notes, and be as inclusive as you possibly can. It'll be much better, further down the road, if you considered an idea and ruled it out than if you never thought of it in the first place.

**tip**

As a model for how to do e-commerce well, you can't do much better than examining Amazon.com in detail.

The best thing you can do at this point is look online. The web is a rich tapestry of both the good and the bad, so look at the sites you like and use. What do they do well? What would you do differently? What fonts, colors, and designs appeal to you? There's an old adage about writing: *good writers plagiarize; great ones steal*. That's kind of true for websites, too.

## HTML Design

The next thing you should do in the development process is mock up the HTML designs for the site. I, for one, have absolutely no design skills whatsoever. If you can say the same, here are two simple solutions:

- Hire a qualified designer to create the HTML templates.
- Use an off-the-shelf design that you tweak a bit.

**tip**

The HTML design process will, rightfully, include a few iterations of feedback, followed by updated designs.

I've taken both approaches several times; which you use depends on the site and your budget. If you're hiring someone, at a minimum, you'll want her to create a few templates:

- The home page
- An inner, basic content page
- A styled form

From these you can easily generate the appearance of most of your site. If you're developing an e-commerce site that sells products, you'll also want *representative browsing* (that is, showing multiple products at once) and detailed listing pages.

**tip**

As I'm not a web designer, I've relied on a design framework and an available third-party template for the two e-commerce sites in this book.

If you don't have the budget or time to purchase a custom design, you can take an existing one and modify it to your needs. Both free and commercial designs are available, although you'll need to abide by the licensing where applicable. For example, some designs are free to use as long as you give credit to the designer in the footer. Other designs are free for noncommercial use but require licenses for commercial endeavors. In any case, you can take the existing template and then adjust the HTML and CSS to personalize the design for your or your client's tastes.

 tip

Your site's design should include obvious links for contacting the administrator, finding the site's return policy, and viewing the privacy policy.

The goal at this point is to get the client (or you) to sign off on the look of the site. Moreover, the design also implies much of the functionality; getting approval of that is even more critical to the process. Think about: How will the look and function of the site be different if the user is logged in? How will navigation be handled? How are items added to the cart? How will the cart contents be shown? Also pay attention to the fundamentals of the user interface: simplicity, ease of use, proper navigation, breadcrumbs, obvious access to the cart, and so on.

## Database Design

Designing the database is a key step, largely because changes to the database at a later date have far larger implications and potential complications than changing any other aspect of the site. Adding functionality through database changes is a steep challenge, and fixing database flaws is excruciating. Make every effort you can to get the database design right the first time.

 note

This is absolutely the last reference I make to another book, I promise. Unless I think of another....

Good database design begins, naturally, with *normalizing* the database. If you aren't familiar with normalization, see any good resource on the subject, including my *MySQL: Visual QuickStart Guide, 2nd Edition* (Peachpit Press, 2006). Normalization and performance mean that you also

- Use the smallest possible column types.
- Avoid storing **NULL** values as much as possible.
- Use numeric columns as much as possible.
- Use fixed-length columns when you can.
- Provide default values for columns, if applicable.

 tip

If MySQL is running with the `--log-long-format` feature enabled, the database will write to the log any queries that aren't using indexes.

Performance is also greatly affected by using indexes properly. Declaring indexes is somewhat of an art, but here are some general rules:

- Index columns that will be involved in **WHERE** and **ORDER BY** clauses.
- Avoid indexing columns that allow **NULL** values.
- Apply length restrictions to indexes on variable-length columns, such as indexing only the first 10 characters of a person's last name.

- Use **EXPLAIN** queries to confirm that indexes are being used.
- Revisit your indexes after some period of site activity to ensure they're still appropriate to the real-world data.

A final consideration in your database design, which gets less attention, is the storage engine (or table type) in use. One of MySQL's strengths is its support for multiple storage engines, meaning you can select the one whose features best match your needs. For example, you can create MySQL tables in memory, which will perform exceptionally well but provide no data permanence. The two most common MySQL storage engines are *InnoDB* and *MyISAM*. The InnoDB engine is now the default for MySQL, and it's an excellent fail-safe in sensitive situations.

The **--log-slow-queries** option in MySQL can be used to help you catch detrimental queries.

If you have administrative-level control over your database, you should know about a number of configurations that impact MySQL's performance. To start, there's **back_log**, **key_buffer_size**, **max_connections**, and **thread_cache_size**. You can use a configuration file to change these settings from their defaults to values more appropriate to your server and site. See the MySQL manual for more information for the version of MySQL that your server is running—assuming that you have that kind of control over your server, of course.

Should you get to a point where your site is so active that multiple servers are appropriate, you can consider *replicating* the database. Database replication stores the same data on more than one server, with that data automatically synced among them. By adopting replication, you'll get improved security, reliability (if one server fails, the data still lives on elsewhere), and performance.

## Programming

The primary focus of this book is the PHP programming, where PHP acts as the glue between the user/browser and, well, pretty much everything else: the database, email, payment systems, and more. From a programming perspective, you'll want to create code that's not only functional but also reusable, extendable, and secure.

To make reusable, extendable code, it must be well organized and thoroughly documented. I can't stress this enough: Document your code to the point of overkill. As you program, begin with your comments and revisit them frequently. When you make any changes to your code, double-check that the comments remain accurate. You should also use flowcharts, UML (Unified Modeling Language) diagrams, and other tools to outline and represent your site in graphical and noncode ways.

Formal PHP documentation can be achieved using phpDocumentor (www.phpdoc.org).

**note**

Because this book is one giant comment on entire sites of PHP code, the scripts displayed in the book won't be as documented as yours should be.

The security of your code is based on so many factors that the next chapter will start discussing just this one subject. Secure programming is even more critical in e-commerce sites, however, so the topic will be reinforced time and again throughout the entire book.

Depending on the circumstances, you may also want to look into version-control software such as Subversion (http://subversion.tigris.org) or Git (http://git-scm.com). Version-control software makes site updates a smoother process, allowing you to accurately implement all site changes or roll back problems to previously sound states. If you're developing a site with a team of people, version control will almost certainly be mandatory.

With PHP, unlike with many other languages, you have a choice of using an *object-oriented* or *procedural* approach. I'm perfectly comfortable doing either, and I don't believe one approach is clearly better than the other. I advise against buying into the myth that object-oriented programming (OOP) is more extendable or secure than procedural code. Poorly written OOP will cause you endless headaches, whereas well-written procedural code won't hamper your site's long-term development in any way.

When asking for reader input on this book, there was a moderately heated discussion as to which approach I should use and to what extent. Some feel that OOP is the hallmark of professional programming; others don't know or care for it and wouldn't get much value out of an OOP-based book. In the end, I decided to use a mostly procedural approach, as it's the common denominator of all PHP programmers, and procedural code can more easily be turned into OOP than vice versa. New in this edition of the book, however, is Chapter 16, "An OOP Example." It demonstrates how key components of an e-commerce site would be programmed using OOP.

Similarly, there was some discussion as to whether I should incorporate a framework. Again, my heart is not set one way or the other on frameworks. Sometimes I use them; sometimes I don't. In the end, I decided against using any framework in this book, because those chapters would inherently be more about the framework than the underlying example—an e-commerce site, the real focus of the book.

All that being said, when it comes to your own projects, you'll need to make the decision on procedural versus object-oriented, frameworks or not, and if using a framework, which one. Know up-front that these decisions will neither adversely affect nor guarantee the success of your e-commerce site. The only thing you want to avoid doing is starting off on one path only to later change course. That's a recipe for frustration and a likely guarantee of disaster.

## Testing

Testing your website isn't a onetime, standalone step, but rather something you'll need to do often. You can't test your site too much! Unfortunately, it's hard for the site developer to perform a truly good test of the site: He created it, so he knows how it should work and uses it accordingly. A better test is what happens when your family, coworkers, and annoying friends give the site a whirl. And I specify the *annoying* friends, because they're the ones who will attempt to do things you never would have imagined. When these people, who aren't web developers themselves, purposefully or accidentally misuse the site, what happens? From these experiences you can improve the user interface and security of the whole application. Improving those two things will go a long way toward a successful e-commerce venture. Still, there are steps you can take to effectively test your site yourself.

Relatively new to PHP is the concept of *test-driven development* and *unit testing* (although unit testing generally requires that you're using OOP). You define concrete and atomic tests of your code, and then run the tests to confirm the results. Each test should be concise and clear. As you write more code, you define more tests and continue to check each test to ensure that what you just did didn't break any other functionality. Test-driven development and unit testing are big enough subjects that I recommend you research both further on your own, when you're ready.

A different type of site testing you could address is *performance*. If you want to start with the big picture—how well the server copes with demand—software like ApacheBench (https://httpd.apache.org/docs/2.2/programs/ab.html) and Siege (www.joedog.org/index/siege-home) will run benchmarks on your web server, reporting on how many requests can be handled per second. Requests per second (RPS) is the standard measuring tool for a site's performance. Once you start checking your site's performance, you'll find that big, systemwide changes you make will have the greatest impact. These include

- Changing the server hardware: increasing memory, installing faster hard drives, and using faster processors
- Changing the demands on the server: disabling unnecessary features, putting fewer users or sites on a single server, and balancing loads across multiple servers
- Caching the PHP output
- Caching the PHP execution
- Caching the database results

**tip**

Look online for specifics on implementing any of these caching techniques.

If you think about the process involved for handling the request of a PHP-MySQL based page, you'll see three areas where caching can be applied (**Figure 1.4**). First, if the database or PHP is caching the results of a database query, then that query won't need to be executed with each request. Second, by default, each request of a PHP script requires that the PHP code be executed as if it had never been run before. By applying an *opcode* cache such as the Alternative PHP Cache (APC; www.php.net/apc), the PHP code itself is cached by the system, making that execution faster. Finally, the end result is that HTML is sent to the web browser. If you can cache the dynamically generated HTML, then no PHP code will be executed at all, no database queries are required, and the request itself becomes as fast as a request for a static HTML page.

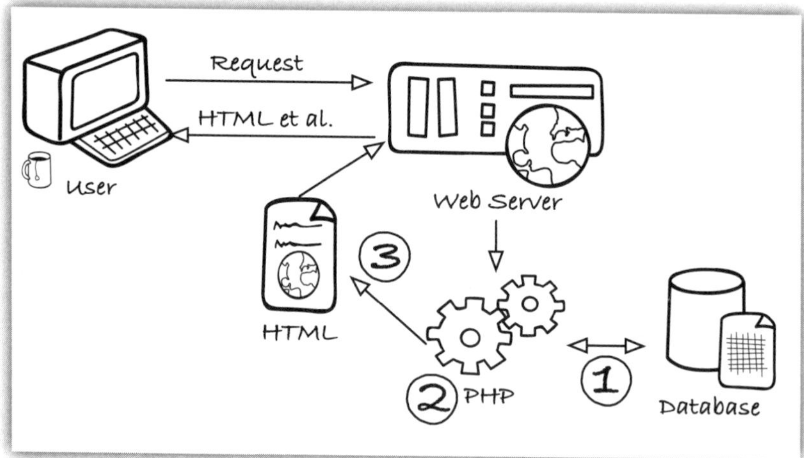


**Figure 1.4**

You can also spend some time profiling your code, using tools like Xdebug (www.xdebug.org) or the Advanced PHP Debugger (APD; www.php.net/apd) to see where potential bottlenecks are in the PHP itself. Bottlenecks usually occur when PHP interacts with the filesystem, whether that means literal files on the server (like reading and writing text files or using sessions) or through the database application. I caution you against spending too much time worrying about profiling individual sections of code, because the improvements you can make that way will be relatively minor and possibly not worth your time. Better to learn good programming habits so that you don't have to worry about profiling after the fact.

## Going Live

Once a site has been completely developed and tested, then updated to include the latest bug fixes and customer requests, it's time to go live. Before doing so, you should revisit all the legal and security issues to make sure the site is in full compliance. Second, have a plan in place for what should be done when something goes wrong (notice I said *when*, not *if*). Third, if any assumptions were made in the code, or any dummy processes installed, remove those. By "assumptions," I mean things such as using the test version of the payment system, not requiring real authentication to the administration pages, and so forth.

Brick-and-mortar stores normally have what's called a *soft opening*. During this period, the business is open and fully functioning but not promoting itself actively. The hope is that the arrival of some traffic will catch issues and allow for improvements, without attempting to do so under the burden of a full user base. This is something you may want to consider as well, although in truth, pretty much every website that doesn't have millions of dollars of advertising behind it has a soft opening.

## Maintaining

Depending on the situation, going live may or may not be the end of your involvement with the project. If it's not, such as when it's your site, you'll need to have a plan in place for maintaining the project. Site maintenance begins and ends with creating good, frequent backups of your site's data. This is something the hosting company should be doing for you (check when you are researching hosts) and something you should be doing as well. Make sure that backups are kept in multiple locations, too, so that a natural or man-made disaster doesn't wipe out both your server and your backups. Keep in mind that laws will likely apply if you're storing customer information in your backups (which, presumably, you will be).

**tip**

For security purposes, safely store your backups, such as in a locked safe or a bank deposit box.

The maintenance of a site also requires that you keep an eye on the data itself. Check and optimize your database tables to improve their performance. Watch your database logs for slow and underperforming queries. Review your web server logs for *file not found* errors, high loads, and potential security problems. Analyze your data to find sales trends and places where you can make improvements. In short, collect and examine as much information as you can. And keep making backups!

**note**

The running of the site—dealing with customers, handling inventory, processing orders, reviewing customer feedback, and so on—is a whole separate way that a site has to be maintained.

## Improving

The final step in the development process is improving what you've created. Improvements may stem from the client, from customer feedback, or from changes in available technologies. Improving a site is a subroutine of this entire development process: Think about what you want to change, plan its implementation, mock up the design, retool the database, write the code, test the end result, go live, and maintain the updated version of the site.

Although it's best to treat the development process as a linear progression of discrete steps, when you factor in repeated places for feedback, and the high potential for the process to be revisited for improvements, the real design process is best represented by **Figure 1.5**.

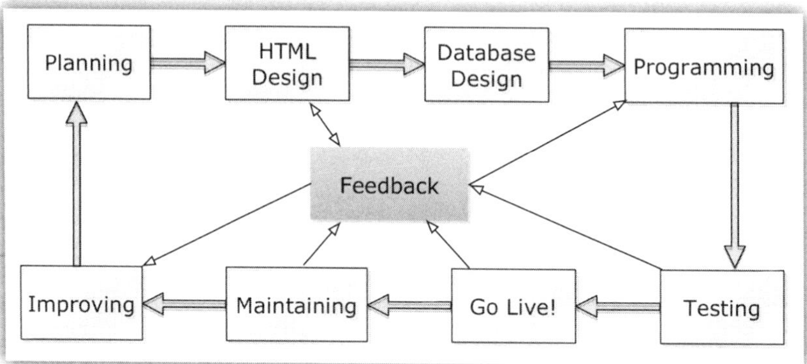


**Figure 1.5**

# 2 SECURITY FUNDAMENTALS

Although every chapter in the rest of the book will include recommendations for improving the security of your website, security is such an important subject that this chapter focuses on it alone. There are three broad topics:

- Exploring general theory and background information
- Creating a secure environment
- Recognizing and combating common vulnerabilities

Some of the topics discussed here will be implemented in real-world code in subsequent chapters. A few of the other recommendations are steps to implement a single time. And a handful of tips will apply only if you have administrative-level influence over the server. Still, it's only by grasping the whole picture that you can implement security on a high level.

## SECURITY THEORY

Before getting into security specifics, let's think about what it means to be secure. I want to start with two simple, but perhaps heretical, ideas:

- No website is completely secure.
- Maximum security isn't the goal.

These two statements probably sound so absurd that I've lost all credibility, but in no way am I saying that security isn't important. In fact, when it comes to e-commerce sites, security is the most vital criterion. I'm just saying that you may need to think about security differently than you currently do. I'll explain....

## No Website Is Secure

The first fact you have to accept about any type of security is that security isn't a binary thing, where a site, application, or computer is either secure or not. Security is measured on a spectrum (**Figure 2.1**). The code, software, environment, people involved, and other factors move the security rating up and down that scale. No matter what you know or do, you'll never create a website that's *absolutely secure*; the only thing you can do is attempt to make it *more secure*.

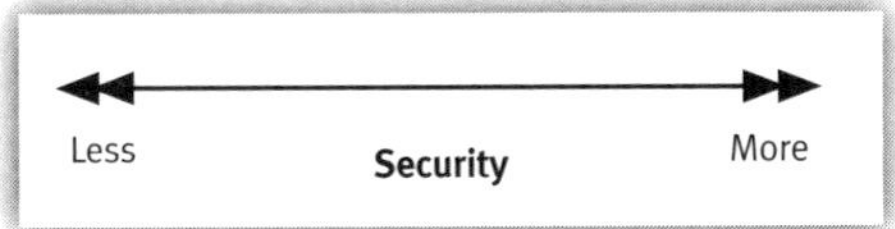


Figure 2.1

**note**

Accepting that you can't create absolute security doesn't mean you shouldn't try but rather that you should never stop trying.

I've had people—well, one person—say this approach is wrong and dangerous, but I think quite the contrary is true. When you begin to believe that your site is absolutely secure, that's when it's the most vulnerable, because you've let your guard down. What you should be doing is taking steps so that your site is *secure enough*.

As an analogy, think about a car. If you drive somewhere and get out but don't lock the car, it still may be relatively secure, depending on the time of day, the type of car, the area in which it's parked, and the length of time you'll leave it there. Just leaving a car unlocked doesn't mean it's guaranteed to be broken into, just as locking it doesn't mean it won't be. It's certainly harder to break into a locked car, but it's not impossible. If you leave the car in your garage, it's much, much less likely to get broken into, until you leave the garage door open or someone breaks into the garage. And, of course, never taking a car out of the garage defeats the whole point of having a car.

The same is true for a website. Doing X, Y, and Z will make it harder—but not impossible—to break into, because there's always a potential flaw just around the corner. Even if the server isn't turned on and is sitting in a locked hosting cage somewhere, people who work for that hosting company can still access the machine. Simply put, there's nothing you can do to guarantee absolute security.

I say that no website is completely secure for two reasons. First, I want to promote eternal vigilance when it comes to your site's security. *Complacency is dangerous.* The second reason is...

## Maximum Security Isn't the Goal

Again, this may sound blasphemous, but it's really not. You have to first accept that security comes at a cost. Making something—pretty much anything—more secure requires more time and money. Also, anything that's more secure is inherently less usable and, in terms of computers, slower (**Figure 2.2**).

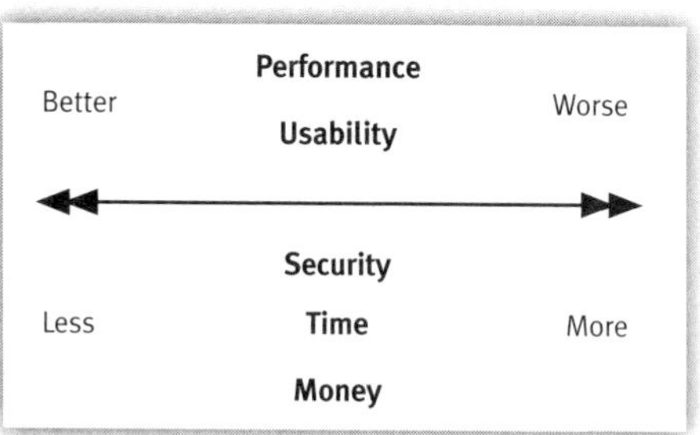


Figure 2.2

tip

The success of a site will increase its risks, because the extra attention will make it a bigger target for hackers.

Returning to my car analogy, if you live in a city, you likely lock the car when you drive it somewhere and park. But when you park it in your garage, you probably don't lock it. The same might be true if you live in a small town or if your car is a total beater. In some situations, maybe you use a secondary antitheft device, like a steering wheel lock. What you're doing with your car, consciously or not, is adjusting the security measures in place based on the perceived level of risk and the potential loss (for example, an expensive car versus a cheap one).

The same is true of websites: Different types of sites require different levels of security. A site on which I list my favorite books is at a different point on the security spectrum than one that stores user information. Even that is on a less critical plateau than a site that handles credit cards. Even beyond that high-security level are sites for online banking, sensitive government and/or military data, and so forth (**Figure 2.3**).

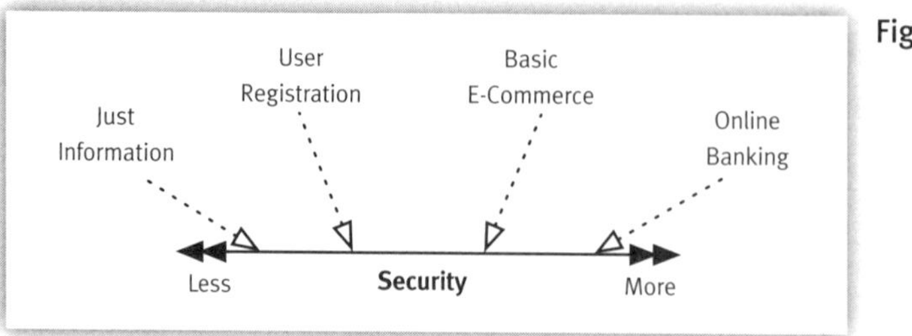


Figure 2.3

The goal, then, isn't to implement the highest level of security but rather the *highest level of security that's appropriate for the site*. Let's look at two examples of what I mean.

You may already know that Secure Sockets Layer (SSL) is an essential part of the e-commerce system. SSL provides the first line of defense for protecting user-submitted information; when the time comes to take the customer's credit card, SSL must be used. But this doesn't mean that SSL must be used for every page on your site. SSL puts a strain on the server, and only a fraction of SSL requests can be handled simultaneously compared to non-SSL requests. As a compromise between security and performance, you may choose to use SSL only for the checkout process and use a non-SSL connection for the bulk of your site.

As server capabilities have improved, the performance hit for using SSL has decreased.

As another example, a shared host is going to be less secure than a dedicated host simply because more people have access to, and more software is running on, the server. On the other hand, a shared host will cost a tenth or less of what a dedicated host costs. You can increase the security by purchasing a more expensive hosting plan, but that may not be necessary, let alone prudent.

All this being said, I don't want you thinking that I'm cavalier about security or that you should be. In this chapter, you'll learn the fundamentals for creating a secure website, but it's not reasonable to think that your site has to be secure to the *n*th degree. There are many baseline recommendations—in terms of code and server environments—that you should ideally implement for any site. But you'll be presented with plenty of choices for which you must weigh all the pros and cons before coming to a decision. The goal is to hit the appropriate mark on the security spectrum for the given situation (as in Figure 2.3). Then, give your site a nudge just a wee bit to the right on that spectrum, just to be safe.

When making security decisions, always err on the side of being overprotective.

## Security for Customers

E-commerce sites and websites in general have a client-server relationship: two parties equally participating in an event. There are two sides to security as well: one you implement as the site developer and/or server administrator and one the customer is aware of. Now let's take a couple of pages to talk about security from the customer's perspective.

The success of an e-commerce site partly depends on a customer's comfort in spending money there.

There's an old expression that says cleanliness is next to godliness. My house wouldn't suggest that I live by that expression, but it leads me to an analogy I have for website security:

**Security Is Next to Godliness.**

Think of security the way you might think about cleanliness. Say you go to eat at a restaurant. The restaurant may or may not *look* clean, and it may or may not *be* clean. But if the restaurant doesn't look clean, then it probably isn't actually clean, and you don't want to eat there. The same goes for a website's security: If it doesn't give the appearance of being secure, it probably isn't secure, and potential customers won't want to use the site (and shouldn't). So how does a site look secure to the lay user?

- It's professional in appearance.
- It's honest and transparent with respect to what the business is, what its policies are, how customer information will be used, and so on.
- It uses SSL.
- It doesn't do anything that may make the customer feel the site isn't secure.

**tip**

Having friends and family test your site is a good way to get feedback on potentially confusing or problematic parts.

This last quality is the most important, as the common person may not know the difference between a secure-looking and unsecure-looking site. A successful e-commerce site gives customers every reason to complete their sale and absolutely no reason not to. If a customer goes to a site and sees technical error messages, alerts from their browser (for example, because of poor JavaScript or improper use of SSL), and so forth, she'll likely (or hopefully) take her business elsewhere. If the website does something that makes the customer say "Huh?," think of it like seeing a rodent scurry across the restaurant floor: It's time for the customer to go.

The second part of this analogy is that though it's important for a restaurant to *look* clean (so people will eat there), it's more important that it's *actually* clean (so that patrons don't get sick, so that the inspector doesn't shut it down, and so on). Your website must be secure so that nothing bad can happen to the customers or your client.

**tip**

If you're creating a site for a client, put a plan in place so that someone continues to maintain the site's security after you're done with the project.

The final reason I believe this analogy works is that it also supports the two maxims I already put forth. Security, like cleanliness, isn't an absolute, and the amount of effort you put into it should depend on the situation. The place where a restaurant keeps its garbage doesn't need to be that clean, but the kitchen sure does. Maybe you're the kind of person who would thoroughly clean monthly, weekly, or daily. Maybe you're the kind who will take cleaning to the disinfecting level. There's no right answer in these situations: There's better and there's worse, and there's what's right for you and your situation. The same goes for security. Most importantly, just because you cleaned today doesn't mean it will stay clean forever. And the website that went live today without any issues could become vulnerable tomorrow, even if that's through no fault of your own.

# PCI REQUIREMENTS

In Chapter 1, "Getting Started," I mention that you'll need to be aware of *PCI compliance*. Compliance means abiding by all 12 requirements outlined in the PCI DSS. Depending on your level of involvement in the e-commerce project, some of these may not be applicable to you personally, but you should still be aware of them and pass them along to those who are responsible.

Extra precautions apply if wireless technology will be used on your business's internal network.

Taken verbatim from www.pcisecuritystandards.org, the requirements are as follows:

**Build and Maintain a Secure Network**

*Requirement 1:* Install and maintain a firewall configuration to protect cardholder data.

*Requirement 2:* Do not use vendor-supplied defaults for system passwords and other security parameters.

**Protect Cardholder Data**

*Requirement 3:* Protect stored cardholder data.

*Requirement 4:* Encrypt transmission of cardholder data across open, public networks.

**Maintain a Vulnerability Management Program**

*Requirement 5:* Use and regularly update anti-virus software or programs.

*Requirement 6:* Develop and maintain secure systems and applications.

**Implement Strong Access Control Measures**

*Requirement 7:* Restrict access to cardholder data by business need to know.

*Requirement 8:* Assign a unique ID to each person with computer access.

*Requirement 9:* Restrict physical access to cardholder data.

**Regularly Monitor and Test Networks**

*Requirement 10:* Track and monitor all access to network resources and cardholder data.

*Requirement 11:* Regularly test security systems and processes.

Depending on the level of PCI compliance that applies to your business, you may be required to perform annual validation tests.

**Maintain an Information Security Policy**

*Requirement 12:* Maintain a policy that addresses information security for all personnel.

If you go to the PCI website, you can download a 70-plus-page PDF that explains each of these regulations in more detail. The document also discusses how to test each condition and provides a worksheet to annotate your results. You should read this PDF at some point, but I want to add a few notes of my own here.

 **tip**

The PCI DSS has lots of useful security recommendations, applicable to even non-e-commerce sites.

First, some of these rules, such as using a firewall and antivirus software, may be beyond your role and server authority, but they still need to be done. In fact, you should use a firewall and antivirus software on any server. Changing the default passwords is also a must, but the second requirement goes well beyond just changing passwords, into areas such as disabling unnecessary software.

As for requirements 3 and 4, the best advice I can give is *not to store credit card information at all,* but if you do, ratchet your security up many, many levels. Also know that there are key pieces of data that you're not allowed to store, such as the card verification value (CVV) or its PIN. Storing credit card information is not for the beginning developer or the small business, so please design your site and use payment gateways in such a way to relieve you of that burden.

Requirement 6—develop and maintain secure systems and applications—is what this book is all about. That's a big topic whose bottom line is to program securely.

Requirements 7–9 are impacted by both the business and the hosting company. But one rule you can use in just the programming facet is requirement 8: providing unique identifiers to each administrator. Unless you'll have only one person administering your site, create a system and get in the habit of defining multiple users with appropriate permissions. In this book's first e-commerce example (paid access to content), one administrator type might only be able to manage the site's content. Another administrator might be able to do that and access the noncommercial customer data. The highest level of access might also allow for viewing payment data (in this case, a record of payments made, not the actual customer information charged for payments). Extra security can be achieved by forcing regular password changes, adding password requirements (length, use of capital and nonletters), and disabling inactive accounts.

The remaining three requirements are ongoing tasks, necessary even if none of the site's code changes. I talk about this some in the first chapter—keeping a close eye on the server to catch something bad, and having a plan in place when it does.

These 12 requirements are excellent and appropriately encompassing. When you read the full PCI DSS document, you'll get tons of specific recommendations, each of which will improve your site's security that much more.

Some people feel that the PCI DSS is too demanding, although I think it's better to overdo security than to take risks. An opposite complaint about the PCI DSS is that it can fool people into thinking that their site or system is secure just because they've abided by these requirements. Remember that the PCI DSS establishes a *baseline* for the *minimum* you must do toward improving security. If your situation warrants, there are always more steps you can take.

# SERVER SECURITY

Most of the rest of the book will address security as affected by the PHP code you write, but let's first look at many of the server-based factors that play into the overall security of your e-commerce site. The approach to server security is simple:

1. Deny
2. Authorize
3. Record

**tip**

A public website page has an opposite security model: anyone and everyone is allowed to view it.

You should first deny everybody and everything you can. Then allow limited capability only after proper authorization and authentication. Finally, record pretty much everything so that you know what people might be trying to do (but failing) and what they did do.

## Hosting Implications

**note**

An organization's own employees can be a weak security link. Be aware of the potential for "inside jobs."

The biggest question with respect to server security will be the hosting of the site. A shared host will be less secure than a VPS or dedicated hosting plan just by the virtue of having more people with access to the server itself. Further, any hosting that gives you some administrative-level control over the server *can* be more secure, as you'll be able to customize how the server runs and better lock it down. I would argue, however, that unless you're an expert in server administration, using a managed server is better than trying to do it all by yourself. Whatever your situation, do your best to limit the number of people who have physical and network access to the server.

Per the PCI DSS, the server should also be running a firewall and an antivirus program. The antivirus program has to be kept up to date if it's to be any good at all. But the same can be said for all the software on the server. Quite frequently, security holes are introduced when a design flaw (a bug) is found in common applications, like the Apache web server, DNS, or an email system. Upgrading and patching these tools when new versions are released is a key component to your server's security.

**tip**

Subscribe to software mailing lists so that you're contacted when new versions are released.

And, of course, you should create very secure passwords for accessing the server and change them regularly.

Finally, use the server's logs to track who accesses a site and when. This way you have a record of who could've done something bad. You may also want to be notified (via email or text message) when anyone logs into the server at all.

## PHP and Web Security

A secondary level of security is controlled by how the web server (for example, Apache, nginx, IIS, and so on) and PHP are configured. First, keep both up to date, along with any related software. Specific security issues will depend on the web server in use, so research and stay abreast of security factors surrounding your particular web server. By learning more about Apache, for example, you'll find that the **DocumentRoot** directive, which limits the web server to working only with files found within that directory, can be a great security asset.

**tip**

The PHP manual lists other security recommendations depending on PHP's relationship to the web server (CGI binary versus Apache module).

You can make a number of adjustments to affect how PHP runs. View the current settings by invoking the **phpinfo()** function (**Figure 2.4**). You'll find each setting listed with two columns: Local Value and Master Value. The Local Value column indicates settings that are being overridden within the current directory.

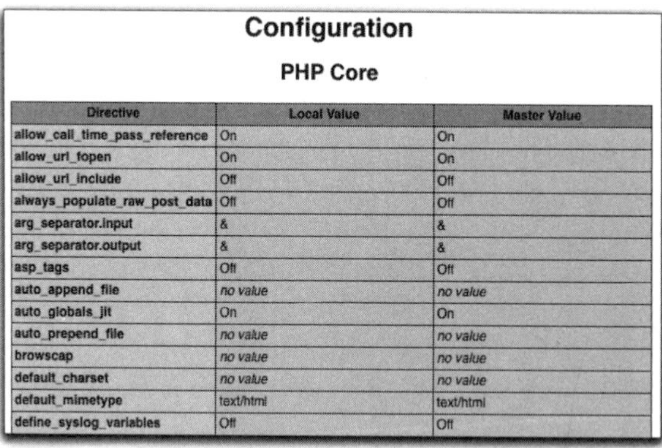

**Configuration**

**PHP Core**

| Directive | Local Value | Master Value |
|---|---|---|
| allow_call_time_pass_reference | On | On |
| allow_url_fopen | On | On |
| allow_url_include | Off | Off |
| always_populate_raw_post_data | Off | Off |
| arg_separator.input | & | & |
| arg_separator.output | & | & |
| asp_tags | Off | Off |
| auto_append_file | *no value* | *no value* |
| auto_globals_jit | On | On |
| auto_prepend_file | *no value* | *no value* |
| browscap | *no value* | *no value* |
| default_charset | *no value* | *no value* |
| default_mimetype | text/html | text/html |
| define_syslog_variables | Off | Off |

Figure 2.4

**tip**

Don't leave a **phpinfo()** script publicly available on your server. It displays too much information about your server!

To modify how PHP runs, edit the **php.ini** configuration file. The **phpinfo()** function also reveals its location. You can modify some PHP settings within a PHP script, although in terms of security, it's best to make such changes on a global basis (otherwise, if you forget to make the change in any given script, you'd create a security hole). After making changes to the web server or PHP configuration, restart the web server to enact those changes.

In terms of specifics, you should start by using the **open_basedir** setting, which limits the directories from which PHP can open files. If you set this value to your web directory, or the parent of the web directory, malicious PHP code can't be used to read important system files located in other places.

On a similar note, you should, if you can, take advantage of non-web directories as a place to store sensitive information. For example, your URL, www.example.com, might point to the actual server directory **/var/www/username/htdocs**, so that loading http://www.example.com/home.php executes (through the web browser) **/var/www/username/htdocs/home.php** (**Figure 2.5**). In this case, the **htdocs** folder is called the *web root directory*. Anything placed within that directory is theoretically accessible via the HTTP protocol. For example, the **image.png** file stored in the **images** subdirectory is available via http://www.example.com/images/image.png. Anything stored above the **htdocs** directory—**/var/www/username**, the parent of the web directory—isn't available via HTTP (and, therefore, not available over a network using a browser). Files and folders placed there can still be accessed by PHP running on the server, but they cannot be directly accessed remotely via HTTP.

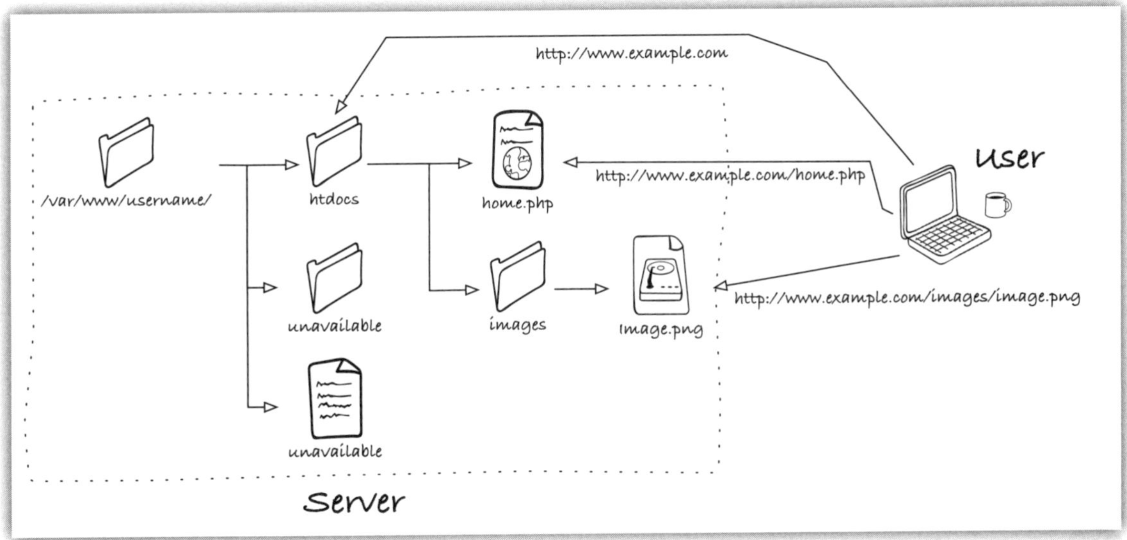


**Figure 2.5**

How errors are handled can often undermine the security, and the professionalism, of a website. A common attack is for hackers to supply problematic data in the hopes that generated errors will be revealing. To safeguard against this type of attack, start by developing your site under the error level of **E_ALL | E_STRICT**. By doing so, any potential problem will be reported to you via email or a log. Then, before the site goes live, disable **display_errors** so that no PHP problem will be shown to the user. Instead, use a custom error handler that displays appropriate messages to end users and reports detailed, technical messages only to you. You'll see specific code for doing this in the example chapters.

**tip**

*nix is a common abbreviation for Unix and Unix-like operating systems, such as Linux.

If you're using a shared host, another recommendation I'd make is to change the session directory. By default, PHP will write all session data to a common, temporary directory, such as `/tmp` on *nix systems. But this directory is readable and writable by anyone on the server, meaning that any user on the server—and a shared host may have dozens—can read the session data stored there. A better alternative is to create a writable directory within your own private area of the server (but not within the web directory) that only your site will use for the sessions. Or you could use a database to store the session data.

My final PHP recommendation isn't a setting but involves practices you won't see me do anywhere, but I want it to be clear now. You should absolutely avoid using functions that execute code on the server, such as `system()` and `exec()`. Also, be careful when using any function that manipulates server files and directories, whether that means creating, opening, reading, or writing. When you must manipulate server files and directories, be 100 percent certain that you're using thoroughly validated data in these function calls, not user-supplied data that hasn't been validated.

## Database Security

**tip**

See the MySQL manual, or my *MySQL: Visual QuickStart Guide, 2nd Edition* (Peachpit Press, 2006), for instructions on creating MySQL users.

Even if your website won't be storing the most dangerous customer information—credit card data—the database still needs to be thoroughly protected. The breach of any customer information is a huge business liability.

The front line of database defense is MySQL's access privileges system. MySQL allows you to create specific users that have limited permissions on only particular databases. Users are identified by the combination of their name, password, and host (that is, which computer the user is on). To start, create unique, secure usernames with unique, extremely secure passwords. And, as with pretty much everything, it's best to change those passwords regularly. Also, be certain to change the root user's password on a new MySQL installation.

**note**

Delete any databases whose names begin with "test," because MySQL allows any user to connect to them.

Next, every MySQL user should be restricted to connecting to MySQL only from *localhost* or 127.0.0.1 (that is, from the same server). If MySQL is running on a machine separate from the web server, you can create a MySQL user who has permission to connect only from that other server's IP address. An added benefit of restricting users to just 127.0.0.1 and specific IP addresses (if other IP addresses are absolutely necessary) is that you can then run MySQL with the `--skip-name-resolve` and `--skip-networking` options. This is more secure and will improve performance, because MySQL won't need to resolve hostnames.

You should also create separate MySQL users for different types of activity. For example, the administrator user for the site will need **SELECT**, **INSERT**, and **UPDATE** permissions. An administrator may also need **DELETE** privileges, but it's best not to allow that unless absolutely necessary. Conversely, almost everything a customer will do on an e-commerce site will only require a MySQL user with **SELECT** privileges. Browsing and searching the catalog are simple **SELECT** queries. It may not be until the user starts to complete an order—actually check out—that an **INSERT** is required. An **UPDATE** would be needed if customers can change their password or other personal information. **DELETE** permissions would never be appropriate for the public users, customer or not. In theory, you could create three distinct types of MySQL users with specific permissions:

- Public: **SELECT**
- Customer: **SELECT, INSERT, UPDATE**
- Admin: **SELECT, INSERT, UPDATE, DELETE**

By taking this approach, you ensure that any potential vulnerability that exists in the bulk of the site couldn't damage the database. The MySQL users with more privileges might only be connecting in areas of the site that require customer or administrator login and an SSL connection. Those restricted realms would offer additional built-in safety.

**tip**

Simplifying MySQL user permissions will also improve performance, because permissions have to be checked with each query.

Avoid giving **PROCESS, FILE, SHUTDOWN, GRANT, RELOAD, DROP, ALTER,** or **CREATE** privileges to any MySQL user who will be connecting from a website. If that site can be hacked, the cracker will have too much database power. Instead, create a database administrator, for one or a limited number of databases, and use that account only to create and manage the database through a command-line interface, if at all possible.

To get data to and from the MySQL server in the most secure way possible, you can use SSL. This is only necessary when MySQL and PHP are running on separate machines, of course, and when the data is particularly sensitive. See the MySQL manual for instructions on setting up MySQL with SSL for your server's operating system and MySQL version. Understand that there will be performance degradation when using SSL with MySQL, due to the extra encryption and decryption work involved.

For the purposes of security, separation of site logic, and performance, consider putting as much functionality in the database as possible. This includes using *view tables*, *stored procedures*, *triggers*, and so forth. The Coffee site example in Part 3, "Selling Physical Products," will demonstrate this point concretely.

As a final note, the MySQL server itself (the process known as **mysqld**) is a system process that's run by a specific operating system user (that is, the server process doesn't run as one of the MySQL database users). Although it used to be common to run the **mysqld** process as the computer's root user, you shouldn't do this. There are MySQL commands that manipulate the filesystem; if MySQL is running with ultimate authority, it can manipulate any file on the server. Instead, run **mysqld** as a different, limited computer user.

# SECURE TRANSACTIONS

**note**

Transmitted data will pass through any number of computers between the client and the server, which is why SSL is necessary.

**tip**

SSL should be used any time the data being transmitted shouldn't be seen by others.

Secure Sockets Layer (SSL) defines a protocol for protecting data transmitted over public networks. SSL over HTTP results in HTTPS. HTTPS is an absolute must for e-commerce sites and for many non-e-commerce sites as well. SSL provides encryption and decryption of data passed back and forth between the server and the client, making it safe from potentially prying eyes. If your site properly uses HTTPS (and therefore, SSL), users will see a closed lock icon in their browser (**Figure 2.6**). If the site improperly uses HTTPS, such as serving a mixture of HTTPS and HTTP content, users will see a broken lock icon (or one with a warning, as shown in **Figure 2.7**). Each browser behaves a bit differently, but for those users who pay attention to such things (and you do, don't you?), this visual indicator is a reassurance that it's safe to provide critical personal information.

Figure 2.6

Figure 2.7

**note**

In cases where sensitive form data is submitted, you should display *and* handle the form using an SSL connection.

The process works like this:

1. The browser makes an SSL request of a server.
2. The server sends a digital certificate to the browser.
3. The browser indicates what encryption it supports.
4. The server selects the best encryption possible.
5. Encryption keys are generated by the browser and server for the session.

These steps are required only the first time the browser makes an SSL request from that server; subsequent requests will use the encryption keys already created.

**tip**

SSL can be used to secure lots of connection types, not just HTTP, but also FTP, SMTP, and so forth.

To use SSL, you must first buy a certificate. In terms of *actual* security, the digital certificate acts as the public key used for the encryption. In terms of *perceived* security, a certificate is intended to reassure the end user that SSL is properly in place, that the underlying business is legitimate—that it's been verified—and that the site is therefore safe to use. Browsers provide a way for users to view the certificate's details (**Figure 2.8**), although I don't know how often most people do this. If there's a mismatch between the certificate and how it's being used, or if you use a less secure certificate (like a self-signed one), the browser may even directly warn the user of the potential danger. **Figure 2.9**, which shows a Firefox response, is explicitly telling the user not to trust the site, and the user has to take extra steps in order to proceed. If your site displayed this message to the user, it would be very bad for your business.

Failing to provide all the content on an HTTPS page—the HTML, the media, the JavaScript, the CSS, and so on—through the HTTPS protocol can create a broken lock icon in the browser.

Figure 2.8

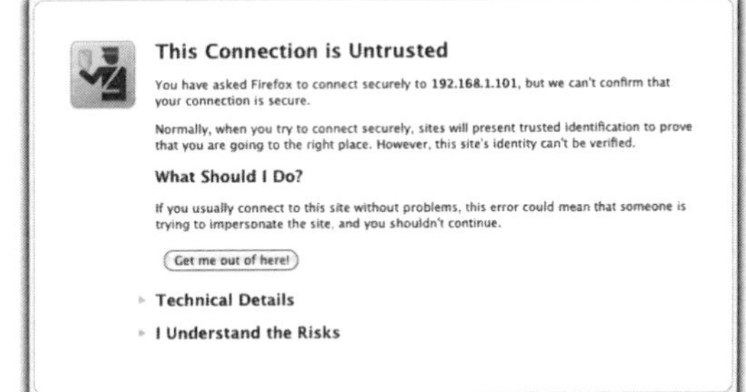


Figure 2.9

A certificate can be purchased from any number of Certifying Authorities (CA), from security specialists like Thawte (www.thawte.com) and VeriSign (www.verisign.com) to simple resellers such as GoDaddy (www.godaddy.com), to possibly your own hosting company. Built into all major browsers is a list of 50-plus major CAs that are to be trusted. When you purchase a certificate from a major company, you're buying, in part, the assurance that the user's browser isn't going to warn the user about the validity of the certificate (as in Figure 2.9). That's a legitimate reason to purchase a high-quality certificate instead of using a cheaper one. Each of these companies also sells levels of certificates at different prices, which is the next consideration.

Cookies can be restricted so that they're sent over secure connections only.

In terms of actual (not perceived) security, one thing that may cost more is the maximum level of encryption used, from 40-bit to 256-bit. The higher the encryption, the better, although the maximum actual encryption level used will depend on the web server and the browser involved in the transaction. A 128-bit security is fine for most sites; 256-bit is the online-banking level.

Fairly active sites may require only one web server but multiple database servers, in which case the one certificate might still suffice.

Next, some certificates come with warranties to reimburse you in case of a failure. The cheapest GoDaddy certificates might insure you for up to $2000; expensive VeriSign ones cover up to $250,000. That's a big difference, although I've never personally known of an SSL certificate failure.

**tip**

If you spend more money on a certificate, you'll also get better technical support.

You'll also pay more for a flexible certificate. A valid certificate for a single domain is cheaper than one for all subdomains (www.example.com, shop.example.com, and admin.example.com); a single certificate valid for multiple domains (example.com and example.net) costs even more. Another consideration is the ability to use the same certificate on multiple servers. Only very active sites require multiple servers, but if you do, you'll need to buy the more expensive certificate.

Conversely, you should not use certificates tied to a given host or that are shared by multiple sites on the same server. These kinds of certificates may be free or cheap with your hosting, but they'll be a red flag to customers.

**tip**

Certificates can be self-signed and cost nothing, but these aren't appropriate for e-commerce sites.

More expensive certificates also mean that the issuer has done more extensive checks into who the purchaser is. A cheap certificate basically says someone bought this certificate. An expensive certificate says someone bought this certificate for this domain and it has been validated that the person owns that domain. Moreover, it's been validated that the purchaser is a valid company operating in X country. Someone has spoken to the purchaser on the phone, and read a letter from the purchaser's accountant, and so on (and I'm not making all that up). Finally, you can buy high-end certificates that enable the "green address bar" effect in some web browsers, also called extended validation (EV). This is an obvious, visual cue to users that they've got a really secure connection, and it's safe for them to do whatever they're about to do.

# COMMON VULNERABILITIES

To wrap up this chapter, I want to talk about some of the common vulnerabilities that websites are prone to and that you'll need to watch out for. You'll see some redundancies with the information already presented, but reinforcing good security approaches is never a bad thing.

Security is all about protecting data: protecting it from being seen, altered, or deleted by the wrong people. What most vulnerabilities have in common is that they provide potential holes through which hackers can see or manipulate data to which they shouldn't have access. The following sections cover the most common security hacks and attacks, and what you need to do to prevent them.

## Protecting Information

Dynamic websites deal with lots of information, from just content to user-supplied data to transaction histories. This data will be received by PHP scripts, passed to a MySQL database, and later retrieved from the database to again make it available in PHP. To strengthen this process, start by taking only the minimum amount of information needed: You don't need to worry about protecting something you don't have.

Next, validate the user-supplied data to the utmost degree. PHP's *Filter* functions (www.php.net/filter), formerly found in PECL (PHP Extension Community Library, http://pecl.php.net) and part of the language core as of PHP 5.2, provide excellent tools for validating and sanitizing values. Always assume that user input is wrong, and then verify that it's right.

 **tip**

The security measures you can take will also depend on the versions of software in use—another reason to keep software up to date!

Third, store only the minimum amount of data. For example, you may need to take 12 pieces of information about a customer, and then pass 7 of those along to a payment gateway while storing only 5 in your own database.

Fourth, if PHP and MySQL are on separate servers, use SSL to protect the data during transmission.

Fifth, retrieve from the database only the information you actually need.

These just-mentioned techniques for handling data in PHP and MySQL can also be applied to the client-server relationship. Be very careful about what you store in the browser (in cookies), pass to the browser in HTML, or display as part of the URL. PayPal, with an amazing lack of foresight, was once set up to accept the total price being charged in the URL, where it's available for anyone to easily—really easily—change! You also need to validate and/or sanctify cookie and URL data, treating it the same as any other user-supplied data (such as from a form), because cookies and URL parameters are under the user's control.

For sensitive data being stored on the server, but not stored in a database, use the web root directory's parent folder (see Figure 2.5) or any other directory that's not publicly accessible. Also make sure your server isn't giving away anything with error messages that are too revealing or that are lingering in **`phpinfo()`** scripts.

Finally, to protect all the server data, perform regular backups. If you use a RAID array of hard drives, you'll also be protected should a single drive fail.

## Protecting the User

Protecting the user, aka the customer in an e-commerce site, is the primary goal, because the trust of the customer is what makes your business thrive. Protecting customer information is part of protecting customers, but there's another way that your site may cause harm: through *cross-site scripting* (XSS) attacks. In an XSS attack, malicious person Alice injects JavaScript into your site. Most commonly this is done through forms intended for user input, such as a comments or reviews area (that is, Alice includes JavaScript as part of her comments). When Bob loads your page in his web browser (for example, when he looks at the product reviews), the malicious JavaScript in Alice's comment is executed (as if it were something you put there), to Bob's detriment. The JavaScript might be used to read Bob's cookies or execute code found on Alice's site. Bob is the victim, but your site was an accomplice.

**tip**

If you want to allow some HTML in user content, the second argument to the **`strip_tags()`** function lets you dictate what specific tags are acceptable.

As scary as XSS may sound, preventing it is quite simple. As always, you must validate user input. Admittedly, in a case like comments or reviews, you can't come up with a strict model for what the submission should contain (compared to, say, an email address that has a precise format). However, you do know that it *shouldn't* contain JavaScript. By applying the **`strip_tags()`** function, which removes any HTML, JavaScript, or PHP from a string, to any user-provided input that will be redisplayed in the web browser, you can prevent XSS attacks.

**note**

As a site would logically have fewer constraints on administrator-supplied content, it's that much more critical that you can trust those with admin access.

The same rules apply to filtering output. If data being displayed on a page comes from a less secure source (for example, a comments form submission stored in a database), you can run it through **`strip_tags()`** before adding it to your page's HTML.

Another way to protect users is to educate them about common scams potentially involving your site. The website associated with my personal bank does an excellent job of sending out emails indicating fake scams making the rounds. They also make it clear that they would never ask for certain types of personal information through email, stating that you should never send such information in any email reply.

**tip**

Notifying customers of security issues not only protects them but also makes you look good.

Another recommendation for protecting users involves protecting their account. When people attempt to log in to your site, using a combination of a username or email address and a password, you have a choice as to how mistakes are reported. Indicating that just the password is wrong verifies that a submitted username or email address does exist in the database. This gives any potential hacker half of the equation; from there the hacker can continue trying common passwords in order to access the user's actual account. Instead of acknowledging the validity of the username or email address, just indicate that the *combination* doesn't match the database.

## Protecting the Site

The website itself is the agent between the customer and the data, and it, too, has vulnerabilities. The first kind of attacks to be aware of are *denial-of-service* (DoS) attacks. These are brute-force attacks where many zombie or slave servers, all around the world, attempt to connect to your site simultaneously.

Consequently, your server will be so overwhelmed that it won't be able to handle legitimate requests. Unfortunately, there's not much you can do to prevent a DoS attack. Even if you have lots and lots and lots of servers, all around the world, service denial can still happen (it has happened to even the biggest sites). But by closing unused server ports, using a firewall, and monitoring network activity, you can minimize the potential. Fortunately, you have to be pretty successful to even be a target, so you could look at a DoS attack as a sign that you've made it (in a lemons-to-lemonade kind of way).

Whereas DoS attacks are relatively rare and hard to prevent, *SQL injection* attacks are quite common and easy to prevent. The premise behind a SQL injection attack is that the user submits dangerous SQL to a site in the hope that a problematic SQL command will be executed without proper filtering. The hope is that the resulting query would either reveal sensitive information or damage the database. For example, a login form might run a query like this:

```
SELECT * FROM users WHERE email='$email' AND pass=SHA1('$pass')
```

The **$email** and **$pass** values presumably come from the login form. If the user were to submit *';DROP TABLE users;* as the password, and if steps weren't taken to prevent this, the resulting query would be

```
SELECT * FROM users WHERE email='whatever@example.edu' AND
➥pass=SHA1('';DROP TABLE users;')
```

In theory, the one SQL command becomes three separate ones. First, there's a syntactically invalid **SELECT**, which would do nothing other than create an error; then the **DROP TABLE** command would be run, followed by a third meaningless, syntactically invalid query. If these three queries were executed, that would be bad.

There are many ways of stopping these attacks from being productive. First, you should validate data to expected values as much as possible (that is, an email address has an exact format, and certain values must be positive integers). Second, run all strings, even those you've validated, through a database-specific escaping function, such as **mysqli_real_escape_string()**:

```
$pass = mysqli_real_escape_string($dbc, $_POST['pass']);
```

Next, you should typecast all values that should be numeric to force them to be numbers:

```
$id = (int) $_GET['id'];
```

With that code, if the user manipulated **$_GET['id']** to be ***';DROP TABLE users;***, that string would be typecasted to an integer with a value of 0. When used in a query, it will probably return no results, but it won't do any harm.

An alternative is to use *prepared statements*, in which specific values get separated from the query and are recombined on the database level. You must still validate data used in prepared statements—there's no purpose in running a query with data that's known to be bad, but the query will always be safe.

To compare and contrast these two approaches—using an escaping function and using prepared statements—the first example site will initially use an escaping function. In Chapter 12, "Extending the First Site," you'll see how to use prepared statements instead.

Hackers will supply bad data to achieve three other goals:

- Remote file inclusion
- Local file inclusion
- System calls

In a remote file inclusion (RFI) attack, the hacker attempts to get a site to include a file found on another server (probably theirs). PHP, when it calls **fopen()**, **require()**, **include()**, and the like, will execute any PHP code in the included file as if that code were part of the original file. If Chuck can get your site to open and execute his code, he can start manipulating your server, with disastrous results. Again, prevention is simple: Don't use unvalidated user data in these function calls.

**tip**

Using PHP's *open_basedir* directive can also help prevent RFI and LFI attacks.

A local file inclusion (LFI) attack is similar, but the hopes are that a sensitive document on the same server, like a password file, will be read and displayed.

The same steps used to prevent RFI and LFI attacks apply if your site uses **exec()** and other functions that run commands on the server itself. It's best that your servers not use these functions, but if they do, you absolutely can't use unvalidated user data in them. Further, you can use PHP's **escapeshellcommand()** function to make user-supplied data safer in such calls.

Moving on, if your site accepts file uploads from users, that system can be used to attempt a *malicious file execution* on your server. The hacker's hope is that he can upload, for example, his own PHP script to your system, and then execute that PHP script by loading it directly in his browser. Say your site allows users to upload images of themselves. You should validate that the upload is of a given type—GIF, JPEG, PNG—but that can easily be faked. If you were to store the uploaded files in the web directory (for example, the **images** folder in Figure 2.5), then the hacker can later run the script by going to http://www.yoursite.com/images/scriptname.php. But if you store user submissions outside the web directory (such as the **unavailable** folder in Figure 2.5), then uploaded files can't be directly executed through the web browser.

Another prevention technique involves changing the name of the uploaded file: If hackers don't know what it's called on the server, they can't invoke it.

In both Parts 2 and 3 of the book, you'll see techniques for securely handling file uploads.

The last type of attack you should know about is the *cross-site request forgery* (CSRF). This attack attempts to execute unauthorized commands from an authorized user. The success of these attacks is predicated upon the site trusting users as they have previously been authenticated. For example, say your site has a page that adds credits to user accounts: There's a form for selecting a user and the number of credits; when the form is submitted, the credits are processed. Now say that Jane is an administrator who went to your site, was authenticated, and did whatever (it doesn't matter whether or not she used the add credit system). If Jane doesn't log out, there's still a cookie in her browser indicating that she's an authenticated user of your site. Next, Jane comes across some page in which hacker Marc has identified a PHP script as the source for an image tag:

```
<img src="http://www.yoursite.com/add_credits.php?
➥user=12&credits=100" />
```

This might be a public forum, or a review system, or any site that allows users to post images in some way.

When Jane loads the page with that image tag, her browser will make a request for the **add_credits.php** script on your site, passing along the user and credits numbers. This request will look, to the server, exactly the same as if Jane had consciously gone to the **add_scripts.php** page. That page will first confirm that the requesting user is authenticated, which Jane is. The page would then, in theory, perform whatever action is the result of receiving those two values in the URL.

This is a *blind attack* in that the original hacker, Marc, will never see the results of the request being made: He's just putting this out there in the hopes that, in this case, his account at your site gets credited when some authenticated user stumbles upon this code. Know that just authenticating the user won't prevent this kind of attack, because it's that trust that makes this kind of attack plausible.

To prevent a CSRF attack, start by teaching your administrators to log out. Then, restrict the lifetime of an authentication cookie so that it will expire some minutes after they've stopped being active on your site (online banks may only allow 10–15 minutes of user inactivity). This will narrow the window of CSRF danger to just that brief cookie lifetime.

CSRF attacks are more successful against very popular sites that use long-lasting cookies.

Not making sensitive information (like a user ID value) public is also important, but just relying on a hacker not knowing about something isn't real security (that concept is called *security through obscurity*). Although it's possible to perform CSRF requests via the POST method, relying on posted data for sensitive requests is more secure (and is in keeping with the approach that POST is to be used when a request will result in site changes).

The true CSRF prevention comes from guaranteeing that sensitive requests, like the transfer of credits, are actually prompted by your own site. You cannot reliably use a browser's "referrer" value (that is, what page the browser was on before this one), though. Instead, create your own tie between the HTML form and the page that handles its request. The tie itself will be a secret token, uniquely generated for each request. Here's what you'd do on the page that displays the form (with much of the code implied):

```
<?php // form.php
...
$csrf_token = uniqid(); // or uniqid(rand(), true);
session_start();
$_SESSION['csrf_token'] = $csrf_token;
...
echo '<input type="hidden" name="csrf_token" value="' .
➥$csrf_token . '" />';
...
?>
```

On the page that handles the request, validate the token:

```
<?php // handle_form.php
...
session_start();
if ( ($_SERVER['REQUEST_TYPE'] === 'POST') // only POST is allowed
&& (isset($_SESSION['csrf_token'], $_POST['csrf_token']))
➥// make sure the token exists
&& ($_SESSION['csrf_token'] === $_POST['csrf_token']) ) {
➥// OK!
...
} else { // Invalid request!
}
...
?>
```

Now the request will be processed *only* if Jane is still logged in (that is, her cookie is still live), if the request is via the POST method, if a **csrf_token** element exists in both **$_SESSION** and **$_POST**, and if the two values match. That's pretty good security!

# PART TWO
# SELLING VIRTUAL PRODUCTS

# 3 FIRST SITE: STRUCTURE AND DESIGN

The first e-commerce site being developed in this book, "Knowledge Is Power," will provide content to paid subscribers. It will have these primary features:

- Straightforward application of HTML, PHP, and MySQL
- Dependency on user accounts
- Ability for administrators to add HTML and PDF content
- Payments processed via PayPal

This will be a relatively standard e-commerce example, applicable to most small to medium-sized businesses. By comparison, the more complex project, developed in Part 3, "Selling Physical Products," will use HTML, PHP, and MySQL in more advanced ways, won't require user accounts, will sell products that get shipped later (that is, the customer won't be billed immediately), and will integrate a different payment system. This is not to say that what you'll learn in this part of the book won't be applicable to real-world situations—just that it should be easier to implement for most developers than that in Part 3.

The user account system will have several pieces: registering, logging in, logging out, retrieving forgotten passwords, and changing existing passwords. As a bonus, the user's password will be handled with extra security, in a way that you perhaps haven't yet seen.

The available content that the customer is paying to see will be in two formats: HTML and PDF. For the former, you'll integrate a WYSIWYG editor into an HTML form that will allow administrators to easily create HTML without knowledge of

HTML. For the latter, you'll write a *proxy script* that serves protected files not available over HTTP or to unvalidated users.

In this chapter, you'll set the stage for developing the site. This includes the database design, the organization of files on the server, the HTML template, plus a couple of necessary helper files that every other PHP script will use. The entire code for the site is also downloadable from www.LarryUllman.com.

# DATABASE DESIGN

The database I've designed for this example is simple yet appropriate, with only five tables (**Figure 3.1**). The name of the database itself is **ecommerce1**.

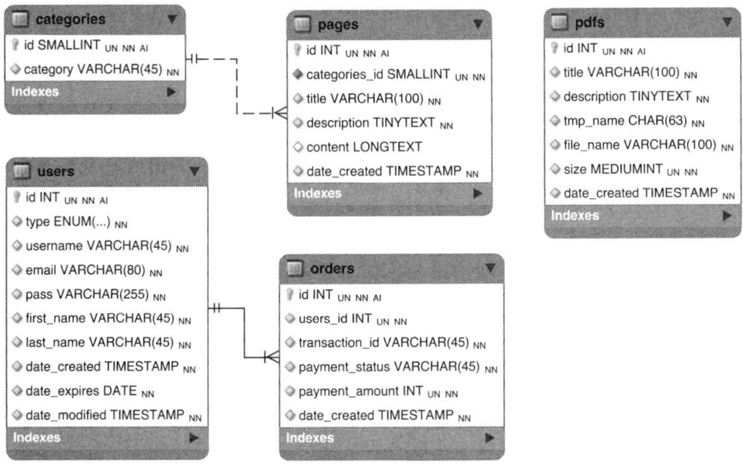


**Figure 3.1**

The **categories**, **pages**, and **pdfs** tables represent the "products" side of this e-commerce example. The **categories** table just lists the categories into which the HTML content will be organized. Each category will contain one or more pages, but each page will be in only one category.

The **pages** table stores the actual HTML content. For each HTML page, there are three important columns: **title**, **description**, and **content**. The **title** column is used as a link to each page and is also used as the browser's title. The **description** column is a short block of text that, um, describes the page's content. This value is viewable to any user and to search engines. The **content** column stores the actual HTML content. You'll see all of this in action in Chapter 5, "Managing Site Content."

**tip**

I'm a programmer, so I start a new site by sketching the database and working my way to the HTML design. You may prefer to start with the user interface and work your way down to the database instead.

The **pdfs** table lists the particulars for each PDF file the site has, including a title for the PDF, like the HTML page title; a short description, viewable by anyone; the name of the actual PDF file; and its size in kilobytes. When a PDF file is uploaded to the site, it'll be stored under a nonobvious, random name (for example, *ce0347c00456588459672150 25e56d53d31b4c6a-51fa6740714da8.33955614*). This generated filename must be stored in the database as well, in order to find the file on the server. But when the PDF is served to the user, its original filename will be provided. The PDFs aren't being associated with the various categories of information, like the HTML content.

**note**

Most of the tables have a column that reflects when a record was added. The **users** table also has a field indicating when a record was last modified.

The **users** table stores a minimum amount of information about the site's customers. Each customer can create a username, and the system will also store the user's email address, a password, her first name, and her last name. The password will be stored as a *hash*, which is a representation of a value (as opposed to being an encrypted version that could be decrypted). Hashes always have exact lengths, so that column *could be* declared as a fixed **CHAR**. However, the particular tool I'll be using for hashing passwords recommends leaving the column as a **VARCHAR**, which will allow for later changes in the algorithm (although later changes would require users to re-register their passwords).

The site will have two types of users—members and administrators. An **ENUM** column (that is, an enumerated list of options) stores the type, with a default value of **member**. Although administrators will never have to pay for access to the site, I thought it would make sense for administrators to use the same login system the nonadministrators use. Thus, the administrators must be registered in the database, too. The **users** table also has a **date_expires** column that stores the date through which a user's account is active (that is, paid). When the user first subscribes and pays, the account will be set to expire in a year. When the user renews his membership, the account will be updated to one year later. Users whose accounts have expired will still be able to log in, but they won't be able to view any content and will be notified that they need to renew.

**tip**

With databases, it's generally better to save more information than you end up needing than to later discover you haven't been storing something you do need.

All payments will be handled through PayPal. Even though PayPal will provide detailed logs of every transaction, it's wise to record the basics of each transaction in this system as well. The **orders** table stores every transaction that goes through PayPal, associated with the ID of the user (as taken from the **users** table). Each order is associated with exactly one user, but each user can have one or more records in the **orders** table. Three pieces of information from the PayPal transaction are recorded, too: the **transaction_id**, which is a unique identifier; the **payment_status**, which is a confirmation code; and the **payment_amount**. The payment amount is stored as an integer, which computers handle better than decimals. In the code, prices need to be converted from decimals to integers and back as needed.

Storing this basic data will allow you to create a simple admin interface for viewing the total number of orders, amount of money taken in, and so on, without going to PayPal for that information. The **transaction_id** is the most sensitive piece of data stored in the database; through it, many details are accessible, but only to the authorized owner of the associated PayPal account.

**tip**

In Part 4, "Extra Touches," I'll discuss a couple more tables you can create to expand this example.

I assume that you know how to create a database and its tables using a tool like phpMyAdmin, the command-line mysql client, and so forth. If you don't, see one of my MySQL-related books, search online, or just ask in my support forum. You can download the SQL commands from my website, but here they are as well:

```
CREATE TABLE `categories` (
  `id` SMALLINT UNSIGNED NOT NULL AUTO_INCREMENT,
  `category` VARCHAR(45) NOT NULL,
  PRIMARY KEY (`id`),
  UNIQUE INDEX `category_UNIQUE` (`category` ASC)
) ENGINE = InnoDB DEFAULT CHARSET=utf8;
CREATE TABLE `orders` (
  `id` INT UNSIGNED NOT NULL AUTO_INCREMENT,
  `users_id` INT UNSIGNED NOT NULL,
  `transaction_id` VARCHAR(45) NOT NULL,
  `payment_status` VARCHAR(45) NOT NULL,
  `payment_amount` INT UNSIGNED NOT NULL,
  `date_created` TIMESTAMP NOT NULL DEFAULT CURRENT_TIMESTAMP,
  PRIMARY KEY (`id`),
  INDEX `date_created` (`date_created` ASC),
  INDEX `transaction_id` (`transaction_id` ASC),
  CONSTRAINT `fk_orders_users1` FOREIGN KEY (`id`)
    REFERENCES `users` (`id`)
    ON DELETE NO ACTION ON UPDATE NO ACTION
) ENGINE = InnoDB DEFAULT CHARSET=utf8;
CREATE TABLE `pages` (
  `id` INT UNSIGNED NOT NULL AUTO_INCREMENT,
  `categories_id` SMALLINT UNSIGNED NOT NULL,
  `title` VARCHAR(100) NOT NULL,
  `description` TINYTEXT NOT NULL,
  `content` LONGTEXT NULL,
  `date_created` TIMESTAMP NOT NULL DEFAULT CURRENT_TIMESTAMP,
  PRIMARY KEY (`id`),
  INDEX `date_created` (`date_created` ASC),
```

*(continues on next page)*

```
  INDEX `fk_pages_categories_idx` (`categories_id` ASC),
  CONSTRAINT `fk_pages_categories` FOREIGN KEY (`categories_id`)
    REFERENCES `categories` (`id`)
    ON DELETE NO ACTION ON UPDATE NO ACTION
) ENGINE = InnoDB DEFAULT CHARSET=utf8;
CREATE TABLE `pdfs` (
  `id` INT UNSIGNED NOT NULL AUTO_INCREMENT,
  `title` VARCHAR(100) NOT NULL,
  `description` TINYTEXT NOT NULL,
  `tmp_name` CHAR(63) NOT NULL,
  `file_name` VARCHAR(100) NOT NULL,
  `size` MEDIUMINT UNSIGNED NOT NULL,
  `date_created` TIMESTAMP NOT NULL DEFAULT CURRENT_TIMESTAMP,
  PRIMARY KEY (`id`),
  UNIQUE INDEX `tmp_name_UNIQUE` (`tmp_name` ASC),
  INDEX `date_created` (`date_created` ASC)
) ENGINE = InnoDB  DEFAULT CHARSET=utf8;
CREATE TABLE `users` (
  `id` INT UNSIGNED NOT NULL AUTO_INCREMENT,
  `type` ENUM('member','admin') NOT NULL DEFAULT 'member',
  `username` VARCHAR(45) NOT NULL,
  `email` VARCHAR(80) NOT NULL,
  `pass` VARCHAR(255) NOT NULL,
  `first_name` VARCHAR(45) NOT NULL,
  `last_name` VARCHAR(45) NOT NULL,
  `date_created` TIMESTAMP NOT NULL DEFAULT CURRENT_TIMESTAMP,
  `date_expires` DATE NOT NULL,
  `date_modified` TIMESTAMP NOT NULL DEFAULT CURRENT_TIMESTAMP
    ON UPDATE CURRENT_TIMESTAMP,
  PRIMARY KEY (`id`),
  UNIQUE INDEX `username_UNIQUE` (`username` ASC),
  UNIQUE INDEX `email_UNIQUE` (`email` ASC),
  INDEX `login` (`email` ASC, `pass` ASC)
) ENGINE = InnoDB  DEFAULT CHARSET=utf8;
```

**tip**

If you're not familiar with foreign key constraints, see one of my MySQL-related books, search online, or just ask in my support forum.

You'll see that almost every column is defined as **NOT NULL**, which is ideal, in terms of performance and normalization standards. Default values are also set, as appropriate. Indexes have been established on the primary key columns, on columns whose values must be unique, and on columns that will be used in joins, **WHERE** clauses, and **ORDER BY** clauses. As is almost always the case, you could certainly add a couple more indexes here and there.

Foreign key constraints exist in two tables: **pages** and **orders**. The constraints require that a corresponding value for a foreign key must exist as a primary key in the related table. For example, an order with a **users_id** value of 23890 can only be recorded if there's already a **users** record with an **id** of 23890. No actions are set for when an associated primary key record (for example, the **users** record with an **id** of 23890) is updated or deleted, as I wouldn't put that functionality into the site (that is, you'd never delete a record or change a primary key value).

The **InnoDB** table type will be used consistently, which is the current default storage engine for MySQL. The database and the site as a whole will use the UTF-8 character set, thereby supporting any possible written language.

# SERVER ORGANIZATION

Before creating any HTML documents or PHP scripts, let's look at how the server should be organized. The standard structure for most sites would be to have folders for the following purposes within the web root directory:

- Administration files
- CSS
- Images
- Other media
- PHP includes
- JavaScript

**tip**

For marginally improved security, give your includes and administration directories nonobvious names.

For large sites, with multiple public areas, it may make sense to have subdirectories for each area as well: store, forums, blog, account, and so forth. This particular example is comparatively small, with only around a dozen public pages, all of which will go within the web root directory.

This site won't place the administration pages—only two are being developed in this book—in a separate directory, so you don't have to worry about that folder. Also, the barebones HTML template used by the site won't need images or other media folders. Thus, the web root directory has just three subfolders to start, which I'll cleverly name **css**, **includes**, and **js**.

**tip**

In Chapter 7, "Second Site: Structure and Design," you'll learn other ways to protect your site's directories.

The **css** directory will contain two files, from the site template, named **bootstrap.min.css** and **sticky-footer-navbar.css** (more on the template later in this chapter).

The **includes** directory will store PHP scripts that will be included by other scripts. In other words, the **includes** directory is for files that won't be executed on their own. Over the next three chapters, you'll create six documents for the **includes** directory:

- **config.inc.php** is a script that defines the site's general behavior and various constants.
- **footer.html** represents half of the HTML template.
- **form_functions.inc.php** defines a function used by every form.
- **header.html** is the first half of the HTML template.
- **login.inc.php** handles the login process.
- **login_form.inc.php** contains the login form.

As you can tell, I'm breaking out much of the site functionality into separate files to make the site easy to maintain.

The **js** folder contains one file required by the template: **bootstrap.min.js**. Again, the template will be discussed later in the chapter. The **js** folder will also store the WYSIWYG editor files.

Along with all the PHP scripts that represent specific pages, such as registering, logging out, and so on, the site needs one more PHP script, named **mysql.inc.php**. This script will connect to the database. Because that script defines sensitive information, it should ideally be stored outside the web root directory.

**note**

The **robots.txt** file shown in the figures won't be formally developed in this book but is available for viewing in the downloadable code.

The site also needs a folder to store PDFs that are available to paid subscribers. The PDFs will be placed in this folder by a script that handles the upload. In order to do that, the permissions on the folder must allow the web server to write to it. Since that openness creates a potential security hole, it's best to place the folder outside the web root. Furthermore, moving the PDFs out of the web directory stops unpaid visitors from accessing them directly. The PDFs will only be made available, to paid subscribers, through a proxy script that validates the user.

**Figure 3.2** shows the server organization, where the **html** folder is the web root directory (www.example.com points there).

If you can't put anything below the web root directory, which is common on shared hosts, you should use a structure like that shown in **Figure 3.3**. It shows that the **`mysql.inc.php`** script and the **`pdfs`** folder have been moved into the **`includes`** directory. Then, as a precaution, use the web server's tools to restrict access to the **`includes`** directory (for example, use Apache's **`.htaccess`** files to deny all access to it). Doing so will prevent users from loading anything in the **`includes`** directory (and the **`pdfs`** subfolder) in their browsers, but the PHP scripts on the server will still be able to access those contents. Chapter 7 will discuss ways of denying access to directories in detail.

Figures 3.2 and 3.3 together show every file and folder that will be created over the next four chapters.

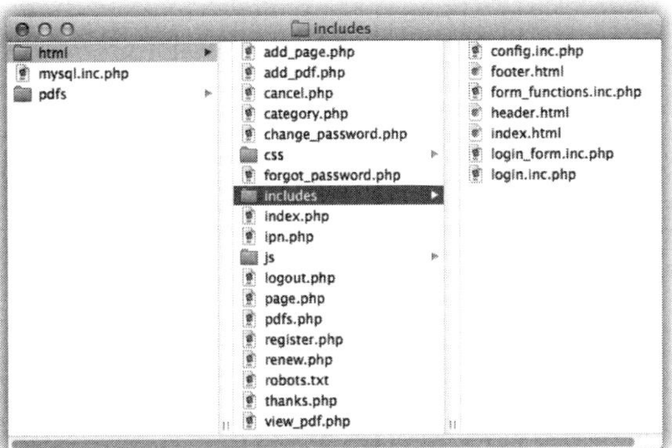


Figure 3.2

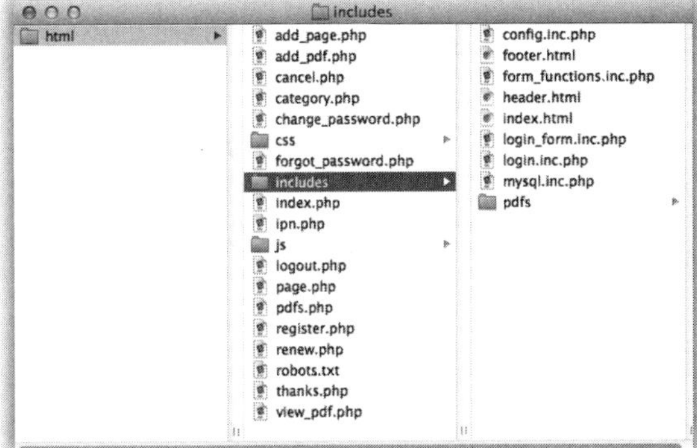


Figure 3.3

## FILE EXTENSIONS

When a user requests a page that uses the **`.html`** extension, the server will pass along the page's contents directly to the browser without any additional server processing. But when the user requests a page with a **`.php`** extension, the server will first run the page's content (that is, the code) through the PHP interpreter, which will then execute the code. (These are the standard settings; servers can be set up to treat extensions in other ways.) With this in mind, it's important that the site's primary pages—those that the user will directly access—use the **`.php`** extension in order for the code to be processed. Pages that are included by other PHP scripts and not run directly in the browser aren't handled by the server directly, so you have your choice of what extension to use.

I use the **`.html`** extension for files that are primarily HTML, such as the header and footer. For pages that are primarily PHP, but are intended as included files, I use a combination: **`.inc.php`**. The **`.inc`** part indicates that it's a file to be included, but the **`.php`** prevents the code from being revealed should the file somehow be run directly in a web browser. If you were to use just **`.inc`**, the server would probably not send the contents through the PHP interpreter, thereby sending potentially sensitive information to the browser. That's a security risk that's not worth taking.

# CONNECTING TO THE DATABASE

**note**

Since the site will be using the UTF-8 character set, your text editor or IDE must be set to encode each page also using UTF-8.

Every PHP script in the site will require a connection to the database, so let's create a separate file for that purpose.

1. Create a new PHP script in your text editor or IDE to be named **mysql.inc.php**.

   See Figures 3.2 and 3.3 for indications of where this file should be placed.

2. Define the constants for accessing the database:

```
<?php
DEFINE ('DB_USER', 'username');
DEFINE ('DB_PASSWORD', 'password');
DEFINE ('DB_HOST', 'localhost');
DEFINE ('DB_NAME', 'ecommerce1');
```

   You'll need to replace these values with those that are correct for your server. For my setup, I created a database called *ecommerce1* and created a MySQL user with **SELECT**, **INSERT**, and **UPDATE** privileges on that database. You *must* use a more secure username and password than these!

**note**

Any connection errors that occur will be handled by the custom error handler defined in the configuration file (in just a couple of pages).

3. Connect to the database:

```
$dbc = mysqli_connect (DB_HOST, DB_USER, DB_PASSWORD, DB_NAME);
```

   The **mysqli_connect()** function is used to connect to the database. The connection is assigned to the **$dbc** variable, which will be used by many functions in other scripts.

4. Establish the character set:

```
mysqli_set_charset($dbc, 'utf8');
```

   This function indicates what character set should be used for communications between PHP and the database. The database tables, the HTML pages, and the PHP-MySQL connection must all use the same character set.

5. Begin defining a function for making data safe to use in queries:

```
function escape_data ($data, $dbc) {
```

   This function will take a piece of data as its first argument and return a version of that data that's safe to use in database queries. In other words, this function will prevent SQL injection attacks from succeeding (see Chapter 2, "Security Fundamentals"). The function does three things:

   - Removes extra slashes when Magic Quotes is enabled

- Trims extra spaces from the data
- Runs the data through the **mysqli_real_escape_string()** function

This last task is the most important, because the function **mysqli_real_escape_string()** will make a value safe to use in a query. Moreover, the function will do so while taking into account the database's configuration and character set in use. The function needs the database connection, which is passed along as the second argument.

6. Strip the extra slashes if Magic Quotes is on:

```
if (get_magic_quotes_gpc()) $data = stripslashes($data);
```

Magic Quotes was created to provide a blanket level of security on incoming data, but it's not as secure as using **mysqli_real_escape_string()**. Hopefully, Magic Quotes is disabled (or nonexistent) on your server, but if Magic Quotes is enabled, then incoming data will already have slashes applied to potentially problematic characters that might break a query. Those slashes would be a problem, because **mysqli_real_escape_string()** will also apply slashes, thereby creating two slashes when there should be only one. To prevent that from happening, this line of code checks the Magic Quotes setting and calls the **stripslashes()** function if Magic Quotes is on.

Magic Quotes as a feature has been deprecated as of PHP 5.3 and removed as of PHP 5.4.

7. Return a trimmed, secure version of the data:

```
return mysqli_real_escape_string ($dbc, trim ($data));
```

The difference between **mysqli_real_escape_string()** and something like Magic Quotes or **addslashes()** is that **mysqli_real_escape_string()** identifies what characters could be problematic based on the database, the character set in use, and so forth.

8. Complete the **escape_data()** function:

```
} // End of the escape_data() function.
```

9. Save the file.

You may notice that you're not being instructed to include the closing PHP tag here. This is acceptable and, in many situations, actually better. If you were to use the closing tag and then inadvertently leave an extra space or blank line after that tag, the inclusion of this file by other scripts will result in headers being sent to the web browser. If the including (that is, parent) script later attempts to send a cookie, start a session, or redirect the browser, you'll get a "headers already sent" error message. By omitting the closing tag, you ensure that can't happen (at least not when this script is included). Furthermore, there are arguments that omitting the closing PHP tag (when possible) results in better performance.

The **mysql.inc.php** file found in the downloadable source code for this book contains additional code discussed in later chapters.

# THE CONFIG FILE

The next PHP script to be created is a configuration, or config, file. Like the **mysql.inc.php** script, this one will be used by every script in the site (although some sites will have pages that don't require a database connection, every PHP script in every site should always use the config file). The config file has four purposes:

- Define systemwide settings that may be changed easily
- Define useful constants that may be used by multiple scripts
- Start the session
- Establish how errors will be handled

Let's start defining the config file now, and later in the chapter, more code will be added to it.

1. Create a new PHP script in your text editor or IDE to be named **config.inc.php** and stored in your **includes** directory, as in Figures 3.2 and 3.3.

2. Define the **LIVE** and **CONTACT_EMAIL** constants:

   ```
   <?php
   if (!defined('LIVE')) DEFINE('LIVE', false);
   DEFINE('CONTACT_EMAIL', 'you@example.com');
   ```

   The **LIVE** constant is the most important setting because it'll dictate how errors will be handled. Depending on the payment gateway, this variable could also be used to switch from just testing the payment processing to actually using it. However, PayPal is a bit different, so that won't be the case in this example.

   The **CONTACT_EMAIL** constant specifies the email address to which error messages will be sent when the site goes live. It could also be used for contact forms, or you could define different email addresses for different purposes.

   In case you're wondering why I've added the **IF** clause to the first line, I've done so to allow the live setting to be set on a single page as well. For example, I might want to debug a specific page without impacting the live setting for the entire site. To do so, I'd use this code on the page to be debugged:

   ```
   DEFINE('LIVE', true);
   require('./includes/config.inc.php');
   ```

3. Define the other constants:

```
define ('BASE_URI', '/path/to/dir/');
define ('BASE_URL', 'www.example.com/');
define ('MYSQL', BASE_URI . 'mysql.inc.php');
```

These are the first three constants the site will use, and you'll need to change the values to fit your environment. The first constant should point to the *parent* of the web root directory, if your site can use that folder. Understand that this is a reference to the directory on the server using the filesystem. On a Mac this might be **/Users/<your-username>/Sites/ecom1/**. On Windows, this might be **C:\xampp\htdocs\ecom1**.

With the **BASE_URI** value set, using the layout in Figure 3.2, **BASE_URI . pdfs** will store the PDFs and **BASE_URI . mysql.inc.php** will contain the MySQL connection script. If you can't access folders above the web root directory, then assign to **BASE_URI** the web root directory itself. So, in Figure 3.3, **BASE_URI . 'includes/pdfs'** will be where the PDFs are stored.

The second constant is the base URL of the site, without the protocol, such as **www.example.com/**. In other words, this is the main part of the site's address that you'd use to access it in your browser. I've specifically left off the *http://* part, because some pages will use *https://*.

The third constant points to the MySQL connection script just created. You can use **BASE_URI** to help create this full path, although you don't have to.

Constants like these are used for a couple of reasons. First, if you reference certain values in multiple scripts in multiple directories, it can be hard getting the references consistently correct. By using absolute references, they'll always be right. Second, if you change anything big about the site—its domain name or its hosting—just changing these values is all you'll need to do. For example, during development on your own computer, **BASE_URL** may be **localhost/ecom1/**, but the production value would be **www.example.org/**.

**note**

Both the **BASE_URI** and **BASE_URL** end with a slash.

4. Start the session:

```
session_start();
```

The site will use sessions to track logged-in users. Since every page will require the config file, starting the session here will make sure that every page has access to the session data. Plus, if you want to customize the session, like its name or how long it lasts, you can do that in one place.

On the other hand, this also means that sessions will be started in some situations where they're not actually necessary, such as when someone views the home page or a content listing page, without going further.

5. Begin defining an error-handling function:

```
function my_error_handler($e_number, $e_message, $e_file,
➥$e_line, $e_vars) {
```

PHP allows you to define your own functions for handling errors. By doing so, you can precisely control what errors get reported, how, and in what detail. Every time a PHP error occurs, or one is triggered using **trigger_error()**, this function will be called by a script that will be created shortly. The only errors that can't use the customer error handler are parse and other serious PHP errors that would prevent this script from being executed in the first place.

An error-handling function can be defined to take anywhere from two to five arguments. Here I'm using all five. The first is a numeric error identifier that might be assigned a value such as 2, which represents an **E_WARNING**. The second argument is the received error message. The next argument is the name of the file in which the error occurred, and the fourth is on which line. The fifth argument is an array of every variable that existed when the error occurred. This can be useful debugging information (and when it comes to debugging, more information is almost always better than less).

**note**

For extra security and professionalism, you could also define a custom *exception* handler, in case any part of your code or an included library throws an exception.

6. Begin creating a detailed error message:

```
$message = "An error occurred in script '$e_file' on line
➥$e_line:\n$e_message\n";
```

The detailed error message will start with the name of the file in question, the line number, and the message string.

7. Add the backtrace information:

```
$message .= "<pre>" .print_r(debug_backtrace(), 1) . "</pre>\n";
```

A *backtrace* is essentially everything that happened up until the point of the error. This will include files that were executed, functions that were called, arguments passed to the functions, and variables that existed. You can get the backtrace information by calling the **debug_backtrace()** function, which returns an array. To add that array to the error message, pass it (or the function call that creates the array) as the first argument to **print_r()** and use **1** or **true** as the second value in **print_r()**. Providing a positive second argument to **print_r()** tells the function to return the value instead of printing it. I'm wrapping this code in HTML preformatted tags, **<pre>...</pre>**, to make it easier to read.

If you don't want the detailed backtrace, you could just append the list of variables and values to the message, like so:

```
$message .= "<pre>" . print_r ($e_vars, 1) . "</pre>\n";
```

8. If the site isn't live, show the error message in the browser:

```
if (!LIVE) {
   echo '<div class="alert alert-danger">' . nl2br($message)
   ➥. '</div>';
```

For a nonlive site, it's best to immediately be notified of any problems. Here, the error message will be printed within a DIV that's been assigned the classes **alert** and **alert-danger**. (These classes map to those defined in the CSS file.)

To turn the newlines (the \n) into HTML break tags, the **nl2br()** function is applied. **Figure 3.4** shows the first part of a sample detailed error message in the browser.

```
An error occurred in script '/Users/larryullman/Sites/ex1/html/index.php' on line 27:
Undefined variable: var
Array
(
    [0] => Array
        (
            [file] => /Users/larryullman/Sites/ex1/html/index.php
            [line] => 27
            [function] => my_error_handler
```

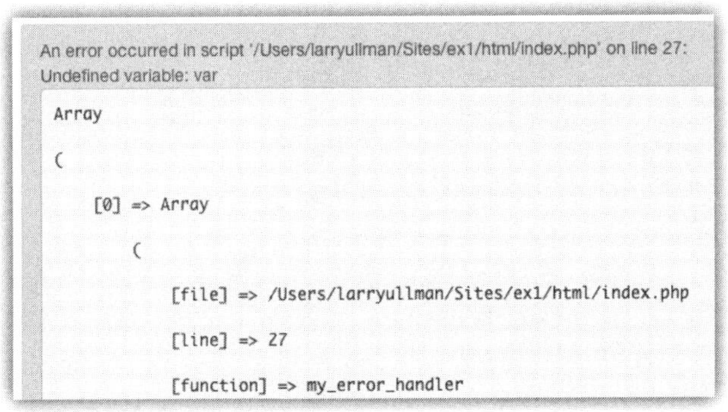

Figure 3.4

9. If the site is live, send the error in an email:

```
} else {
   error_log($message, 1, CONTACT_EMAIL,
   ➥'From:admin@example.com');
```

The **error_log()** function can log errors in different ways. Its first argument is the error message itself. The second is a destination type, with 1 meaning email (the default of 0 would send the message to the operating system's log). The third argument is the destination; with an email, this is the "to" email address. The fourth argument is only for sending emails and is for adding any additional headers, such as the "from" email address.

10. If the site is live, show a generic message, if the error isn't a notice:

```
if ($e_number != E_NOTICE) {
   echo '<div class="alert alert-danger">A system error
   ➥occurred. We apologize for the inconvenience.</div>';
}
```

**note**

Hopefully, in a fully tested, live site, customers will never see even the generic error message, because all the bugs will have been squashed already.

If the site is live, the user should not see the detailed error message (that would be a terrible security violation); instead the user will see a nondescript response. But some errors that occur may not be actual problems, just technical oversights that have no impact on the functionality. Such errors are raised as *notices*, so an error will be reported only if it's not on the notice level. In fact, the error indicated in Figure 3.4 wouldn't be reported if the site were live. **Figure 3.5** shows what the user might see with a different type of error.

A system error occurred. We apologize for the inconvenience.

Figure 3.5

**11.** Complete the `my_error_handler()` function:

```
    } // End of $live IF-ELSE.
    return true;
} // End of my_error_handler() definition.
```

The error-handling function should return a nonfalse value to indicate that the error has been handled. If the function returns false, then PHP's default error handler will also be invoked (which would be bad on a live site).

**12.** Apply the error handler:

```
set_error_handler('my_error_handler');
```

This line tells PHP to use the custom function for handling errors. If you don't execute this function call, PHP will still use its default handler. This is also why a parse error won't go through your own error handler: The parse error prevents the PHP script from being executed.

**13.** Save the file.

# THE HTML TEMPLATE

**tip**

Feel free to use your own design or tweak my generated theme to your tastes instead.

To create the browser side of the site, start by designing one or more HTML templates that portray what the final, dynamic site should look like. For this site, I wanted to use an elegant design that wouldn't detract from what the site is selling: its content. I'm incapable of creating such a design. In the end, I decided to use the popular Twitter Bootstrap framework (http://getbootstrap.com) as the basis of this site. I started with the "Sticky footer with fixed navbar" example (by Martin Bean and Ryan Fait, available at http://examples.getbootstrap.com), and then modified it to my needs. You can find the end result by downloading the code from my website (see the **template.html** file).

On the left side of the screen, I wanted the site to show a login form if the user isn't logged in (**Figure 3.6**). If the user is logged in, the form won't appear, but some account management links will be added at the top of the page (**Figure 3.7**). If the logged-in user is an administrator, she'll see an additional group of options (**Figure 3.8**).

The site's content will be organized in categories, listed on the left as well. Visitors who aren't paid subscribers will just be able to see what content is available (titles and short descriptions); paid subscribers will be able to see the content itself.

**tip**

I don't explain Twitter Bootstrap in any detail in this book, but the framework is well documented online.

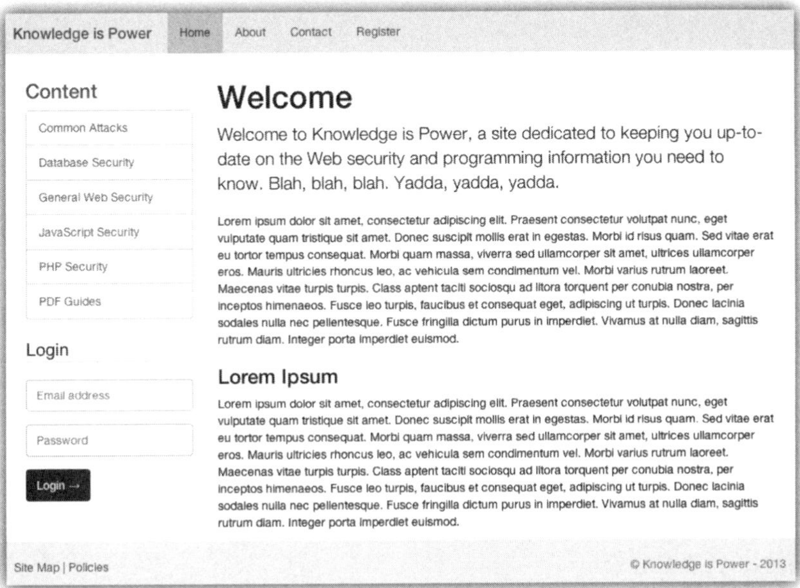


**Figure 3.6**

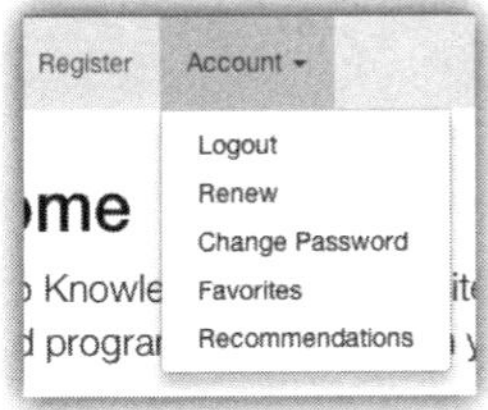

**Figure 3.7** **Figure 3.8**

To incorporate this HTML design into every page in the site, I'll use a standard technique whereby the template is broken down into a header file and a footer file. Each page will include the header, then display the page-specific content, and then include the footer. Once you've finalized the basic template (or templates), you can start creating the individual files.

**tip**

If your site uses more than one template, just create multiple header and footer files and then include the proper ones for each specific page.

## Creating the Header

The header needs to begin the HTML page, include any necessary CSS, and code the body of the page up until the point where the page-specific content begins.

1. Open your designed template file in your text editor or IDE, if it isn't already open.

   Again, the **template.html** file, found in the downloadable files from my website, has the entire design.

2. Copy all the HTML from the template file, from the first line up to the page-specific content.

   For my template, the header begins with the doctype:

   ```
   <!DOCTYPE html>
   ```

   The header file ends with the creation of a DIV with a class value of **col-9** (that is, an area that's nine columns wide in a grid system):

   ```
   <div class="col-9">
     <!-- CONTENT -->
   ```

3. Create a new file to be named **header.html** and stored in the **includes** directory.

4. Paste in the copied code.

5. Save the file.

## Adding Dynamic Functionality to the Header

The next series of steps add dynamic functionality to the HTML template by incorporating PHP within the HTML. You'll want to do this for anything that might change on a page-by-page basis or otherwise won't be static. For the header file, several areas should be dynamic:

- The browser page title
- The highlighting of the top navigation link (see the first tab in Figure 3.6)
- The existence of two additional drop-down menus (Figures 3.7 and 3.8)
- The specific items in the content list
- The existence of the login form

Assuming you're working with the same template that I am, I'll explain the modifications required for each of those dynamic components.

1. In **header.html**, use an **if-else** clause to define the page title:

```
<title><?php if (isset($page_title)) {
   echo $page_title;
} else {
   echo 'Knowledge is Power: And It Pays to Know';
}
?></title>
```

The page's title shows at the top of the browser window, in bookmarks, and in the browser's history; it should be different from one page to the next. The aptly named **$page_title** variable will be available to the header file to represent that value. However, proper programming says that you shouldn't assume that a variable exists. For that reason, this code first checks if that variable is set (that is, has a value). If it is, that value will be printed as the page's title. If the **$page_title** variable isn't set, a default title will be used.

2. Remove the list items that constitute the top navigation tabs:

```
<li class="active"><a href="index.php">Home</a></li>
<li><a href="about.php">About</a></li>
<li><a href="contact.php">Contact</a></li>
<li><a href="register.php">Register</a></li>
```

The navigation tab for the currently viewed page has a specific CSS class applied to it (**active**, see above), which changes how it appears. You could use JavaScript to create this effect, but for easy, all-browser compatibility, I'll make this happen in PHP.

3. In place of the list items, begin a PHP code block:

```
<?php
```

4. Create an array of pages:

```
$pages = array (
   'Home' => 'index.php',
   'About' => '#',
   'Contact' => '#',
   'Register' => 'register.php'
);
```

This array represents the main navigation items. The key for each element is the text to be displayed on the tab. The value for each element is the corresponding page (that is, what page that tab will be linked to).

5. Determine which page is currently being viewed:

```
$this_page = basename($_SERVER['PHP_SELF']);
```

A few of the pages linked in the header and footer won't actually be created in this book but will be quite easy for you to create, when necessary.

To dynamically apply a class to the current page, the script needs to know what the current page is, which happens to be the value PHP assigns to **$_SERVER['PHP_SELF']**. If the user is viewing **http://www.example.com/dir/file.php**, then **$_SERVER['PHP_SELF']** will have a value of **/dir/file.php**. To get just the **file.php** part of that, apply the **basename()** function.

6. Loop through each page:

```
foreach ($pages as $k => $v) {
   echo '<li';
```

This loop will run once for each item in the array. Within the loop, the **$k** and **$v** values can be used to create the navigation tabs. The first line of code within the loop begins a new HTML list item.

I generally recommend that programmers use curly brackets for all conditionals. When you don't (I don't when I'm saving space in this book!), place the entire construct on one line to be clear, as in step 7.

7. Add the class if it's the current page:

```
if ($this_page == $v) echo ' class="active"';
```

The link for the current page needs to use the HTML: **<li class="active">**. This code will generate that.

8. Complete the list item started in step 6:

```
echo '><a href="' . $v . '">' . $k . '</a></li>
';
```

First the opening **<li>** tag is closed. Then a link is created to the specific page, represented by **$v**. Next, the displayed text is written within SPAN tags, and the link and list item tags are completed. The **echo** statement concludes on the next line so that a newline is added to the HTML source of the page (**Figure 3.9**).

```
<li><a href="index.php">Home</a></li>
        <li><a href="#">About</a></li>
        <li><a href="#">Contact</a></li>
        <li class="active"><a href="register.php">Register</a></li>
```

**Figure 3.9**

Have your PHP code create tidy HTML output in case you need to examine it.

9. Complete the **foreach** loop and the PHP code block:

```
} // End of FOREACH loop.
```

10. Next, begin an **if** conditional for showing menus to logged-in users:

```
if (isset($_SESSION['user_id'])) {
```

The page will know that the user is logged in if **$_SESSION['user_id']** is set.

11. Add the account links using PHP:

```
echo '<li class="dropdown">
<a href="#" class="dropdown-toggle" data-
toggle="dropdown">Account <b class="caret"></b></a>
  <ul class="dropdown-menu">
    <li><a href="logout.php">Logout</a></li>
    <li><a href="renew.php">Renew</a></li>
    <li><a href="change_password.php">Change Password</a></li>
    <li><a href="favorites.php">Favorites</a></li>
    <li><a href="recommendations.php">Recommendations</a></li>
  </ul>
</li>';
```

This PHP code creates the same links as in the original template. The linked pages will be created in subsequent chapters.

Most of the HTML comes from Twitter Bootstrap and is how drop-down menus are created.

12. Display administration options, if the user is also an administrator:

```
if (isset($_SESSION['user_admin'])) {
  echo '<li class="dropdown">
  <a href="#" class="dropdown-toggle" data-toggle="dropdown">
  ➥Admin <b class="caret"></b></a>
    <ul class="dropdown-menu">
      <li><a href="add_page.php">Add Page</a></li>
      <li><a href="add_pdf.php">Add PDF</a></li>
      <li><a href="#">Something else here</a></li>
    </ul>
  </li>';
}
```

If the user is logged in and is of type **admin**, she should get extra options. This code will create a secondary panel of links in the sidebar. You'll develop the **add_page.php** and **add_pdf.php** scripts in Chapter 5.

13. Complete the **$_SESSION['user_id']** conditional:

```
}
?>
```

To be clear, this closing PHP tag is required, because this closes a PHP block dropped within a larger body of HTML.

14. Later in the file, in place of the static HTML category links, dynamically generate them:

```
<?php
$q = 'SELECT * FROM categories ORDER BY category';
$r = mysqli_query($dbc, $q);
while (list($id, $category) = mysqli_fetch_array($r,
➥MYSQLI_NUM)) {
   echo '<a href="category.php?id=' . $id . '"
   ➥class="list-group-item" title="' . $category . '">' .
   ➥htmlspecialchars($category) . '
   </a>';
}
?>
```

This is basic PHP and MySQL: A query is run, its results are fetched, and one list item is created for each returned record. The links pass along the category ID in the URL that will be used by **category.php**, which you'll write in Chapter 5.

To prevent XSS attacks, the category is run through the function **htmlspecialchars()** first. (This isn't necessary with the **id** column, as that can only be an integer.)

The link to the PDFs page is separate because that's not a content category in the database.

If your content categories aren't likely to change often, it'd be better to hardcode the category links as HTML and save yourself the overhead of the extra database query.

15. After the list of content links, include the login form if the user isn't logged in:

```
<?php
if (!isset($_SESSION['user_id'])) {
   require('includes/login_form.inc.php');
}
?>
```

The login form itself will be created in the next chapter.

16. Save the file.

And that's it for the header and the dynamic functionality.

## Creating the Footer

The footer file takes over after the page-specific content. It creates the sidebar items and the page footer (such as the copyright and other tertiary links), and completes the HTML page.

1. Open the designed template file in your text editor or IDE, if it isn't already open.

2. Copy all the HTML from the template file, from the page-specific content to the end, like so:

```
            <!-- END CONTENT -->
            </div><!--/col-9-->
        </div><!--/row-->
    </div><!--/container-->
    </div><!--/wrap-->
    <div id="footer">
        <div class="container">
        <p class="text-muted credit"><span class="pull-left">
        ➥<a href="site_map.php">Site Map</a> | <a href=
        ➥"policies.php">Policies</a></span> <span class=
        ➥"pull-right">&copy; Knowledge is Power - 2013</span></p>
        </div>
    </div>
    <script src="//ajax.googleapis.com/ajax/libs/jquery/1.10.2/
    ➥jquery.min.js"></script>
    <script src="js/bootstrap.min.js"></script>
    </body>
</html>
```

   The footer code mostly closes the existing DIVs, adds a footer, and includes two JavaScript files. The first JavaScript file is the jQuery library, hosted on Google's content distribution network (CDN). The second is a Twitter Bootstrap file. Both are required to create the drop-down menu (as well as many other dynamic components in the Twitter Bootstrap framework).

3. Create a new file to be named **footer.html** and stored in the **includes** directory.

4. Paste in the copied code.

5. Save the file.

## Creating the Home Page

To put it all together, you'll next create the home page, which will combine the four files—configuration, header, MySQL connection, and footer—into one complete page.

1. Create a new PHP script in your text editor or IDE to be named **index.php** and stored in the web root directory.

2. Include the config file:

```
require('./includes/config.inc.php');
```

The config file defines system settings, handles errors, and starts the session, so it should always be the first (noncomment) code in your pages.

**tip**

The parentheses with **require** and **include** aren't required, but you'll see me use them in this book.

**tip**

In the downloadable version of **index.php**, you'll see a bit of extra code, which you'll add in Chapter 4.

3. Require the database connection:

```
require(MYSQL);
```

The database connection script can be included by referring to the **MYSQL** constant, defined in the config file. This means that even if you change the name or location of **mysql.inc.php**, you have to change only one line in the config file and all your pages will still include that script properly.

The database connection is required before the header file, as the header file runs a query.

4. Include the header file:

```
include('./includes/header.html');
```

5. Create the page-specific content:

```
?><h3>Welcome</h3>
<p class="lead">Welcome to Knowledge is Power, a site dedicated
➥to keeping you up-to-date on the Web security and programming
➥information you need to know. Blah, blah, blah. Yadda, yadda,
➥yadda.</p>
```

6. Include the footer file:

```
<?php
include('./includes/footer.html');
?>
```

7. Save the file.

8. Load the file in your web browser to test the result.

Since this is PHP, you must run **index.php** through a URL (such as http://something), not through **file://**.

9. To test what it looks like when logged in, add this line after including the config file:

```
$_SESSION['user_id'] = 1;
```

10. To test what the page looks like when logged in as an administrator, add the following line of code after including the config file:

```
$_SESSION['user_admin'] = true;
```

## REQUIRE AND INCLUDE

In the home page, I use both **require** and **include** to bring in the four scripts. These two control structures (they're not technically functions) serve the same purpose but differ in how they fail. Failure to *include* a file results in a warning; failure to *require* a file results in a fatal error. Because the configuration and MySQL files are critical to the site's functionality, failure to incorporate them should be fatal. Conversely, failure to incorporate the header or footer is just a cosmetic issue, not that you'd want that to happen either.

You may notice that I did not use **require_once** or **include_once**. These two control structures run checks to ensure that the same file isn't incorporated multiple times by the same script. Because of those repeated checks, using them has an adverse effect on the site's performance. In this site, which is straightforward, a repeated inclusion of a file is highly unlikely, so it's best to go with the more direct **require** and **include**. If you have a very complex site, with lots of included files that include other files, using the **_once** variants may be necessary. You will see a couple of appropriate uses of **include_once** in later chapters.

# DEFINING HELPER FUNCTIONS

Before getting into the primary scripts in the next chapter, there are two helper functions that you should define. The first will redirect the browser should the user not meet the requirements for accessing a particular page. The second will greatly facilitate handling some of the site's forms.

Here are some benefits to using these custom functions:

- You keep complex logic from cluttering up other code.
- You allow the same logic to be used in multiple scripts.
- You can make changes to the logic in a snap.

The last two benefits are the key points: If you separate out processes, they can be used by different parts of a site without having to repeat the code. And if you later decide you need to tweak the process, you can do so in one place.

## Redirecting the Browser

The first helper function will be used to restrict access to certain pages to proper users. For example, a couple of public pages should only be viewable by current users, and the two administrative pages should be viewable by administrators only. If the current user doesn't meet the page's criteria, the browser should be redirected elsewhere, and the current page should be terminated (**Figure 3.10**). By writing this process in a function, any page that requires authorization will need to invoke only this function, without any additional logic.

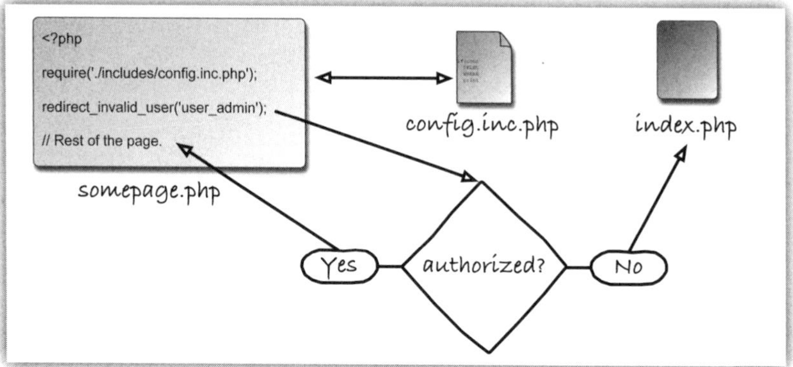


Figure 3.10

Since the config file, **config.inc.php**, will be included by every script in the site, it makes sense to define this function there:

**tip**

In a site that uses cookies, the same function could verify the user against **$_COOKIE** instead of **$_SESSION**.

```
function redirect_invalid_user($check = 'user_id', $destination =
➥'index.php', $protocol = 'http://') {
  if (!isset($_SESSION[$check])) {
    $url = $protocol . BASE_URL . $destination;
    header("Location: $url");
    exit();
  }
}
```

The function takes three arguments, all of which are optional. The first is the session array element to validate against; the default is **user_id**. In other words, if **$_SESSION['user_id']** isn't set, the user hasn't logged in and shouldn't be looking at this page. In Chapter 5, the same function will be used to restrict access to scripts to administrators.

The second argument to the function is the page to which the user should be redirected. By default, this will be the home page, but you could send the user to the registration page or any other page by changing the value passed to this function as the second argument.

The third argument is the protocol to use; the default is **http://**. I've included this option so that users can be redirected to SSL or non-SSL pages.

Within the function, a conditional checks the session variable. If it's not set, a redirection URL is defined by concatenating the protocol and destination to the **BASE_URL** constant (also defined in the config file). Then a **header()** call performs the actual redirection. Finally, the **exit()** function (language construct, technically) will terminate the script (the one that called this function). This is necessary because PHP will continue to execute a script after a **header()** call, even if the browser has already moved on.

When creating the login script in the next chapter, you'll have to keep in mind how this redirection function works. Specifically, authorization is based on a value being set, not on what that value is. For example, a logged-in user just has any **user_id** value and an administrator will also have any **user_admin** value.

I imagine this function only being called immediately after including the config file (see Figure 3.10), so the function doesn't check that headers haven't already been sent, which would prevent the browser from being redirected. If you want to account for that possibility, just use the **headers_sent()** function in a conditional within the function. If it returns false, redirect the user; if it returns true, include the header and footer and display an error message:

```
if (!headers_sent()) {
   // Redirect code.
} else {
   include_once('./includes/header.html');
   trigger_error('You do not have permission to access this page.
   ➥Please log in and try again.');
   include_once('./includes/footer.html');
}
```

**tip**

I use **include_once()** instead of **include()** in this block of code because if the headers have been sent already, that's possibly because the header file was included prior to calling this function.

## Creating Form Inputs

The functionality provided by the scripts in the next chapter is almost entirely form based: The user must complete a registration, login, change password, or forgot password form. All these forms use just three types of form inputs—text, password, and email (not counting the submit buttons). An input starts off with this simple HTML:

```
<input type="type" name="name" id="name">
```

For example:

```
<input type="type" name="username" id="username">
```

**tip**

The Twitter Bootstrap framework adds additional properties to inputs (such as classes), as you'll see in subsequent code.

In cases where the form was submitted but not properly completed, the user will be presented with the form again. As a convenience, the form should remember the entered values (that is, it should be *sticky*). To achieve that effect, you need to add **`value="whatever value"`** to each input. In PHP code, that would be

```
<input type="text" name="username" id="username"
value="<?php echo $_POST['username']; ?>">
```

**tip**

You can add sizes to the inputs, if you want. I chose not to size them, so they would all be equally sized to the browser's default.

However, the first time the form is loaded, **`$_POST['username']`** won't be set, so the code should really be

```
<input type="text" name="username" id="username"
value="<?php if (isset($_POST['username']))
➥echo $_POST['username']; ?>">
```

If the user, for whatever reason, used quotation marks in a value, the quotation marks will mess up the HTML. **Figure 3.11** shows the result if the user enters *Jeff "The Dude" Lebowski* as the username.

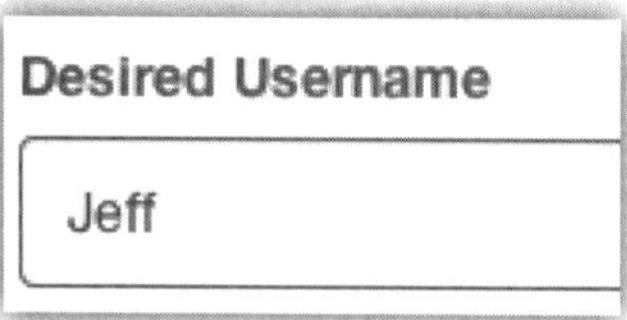


**Figure 3.11**

To protect against that, you can apply the **`htmlspecialchars()`** function (**Figures 3.12** and **3.13**):

```
<input type="text" name="username" id="username"
value="<?php if (isset($_POST['username']))
➥echo htmlspecialchars($_POST['username']); ?>">
```

Desired Username

Jeff "The Dude" Lebowski

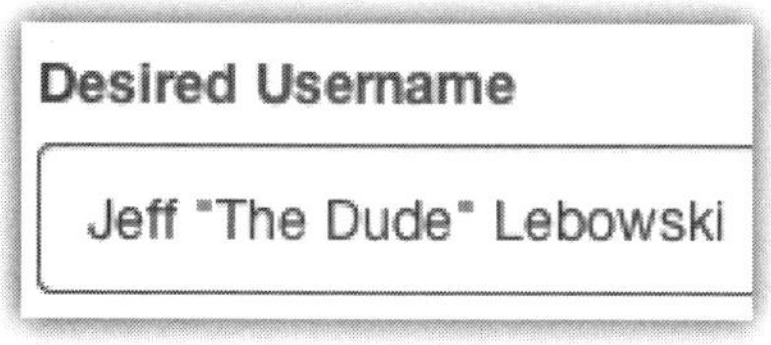

Figure 3.12

```
<label for="username" class="control-label">Desired Username</label>
<input type="text" name="username" id="username" class="form-control" value="Jeff &quot;The Dude&quot; Lebowski">
```

Figure 3.13

And, if Magic Quotes is enabled, the **stripslashes()** function should be applied to the value. I'll add that code shortly, but first, there's one more complication: If the form isn't completed properly, it'd be nice to add a CSS class to the input so that it's displayed with a red border. Here's how that's done using Twitter Bootstrap (version 3):

```
<div class="form-group<?php if (/* error on this input */)
➥echo ' class="has-error"'; ?>">
<label for="username" class="control-label">Desired Username</label>
<input type="text" name="username" id="username"
➥class="form-control" value="<?php if (isset($_POST['username']))
➥echo htmlspecialchars($_POST['username']); ?>">
<span class="help-block">Please enter a desired name!</span>
</div>
```

Also, in that case, the error message should be added after the input (**Figure 3.14**):

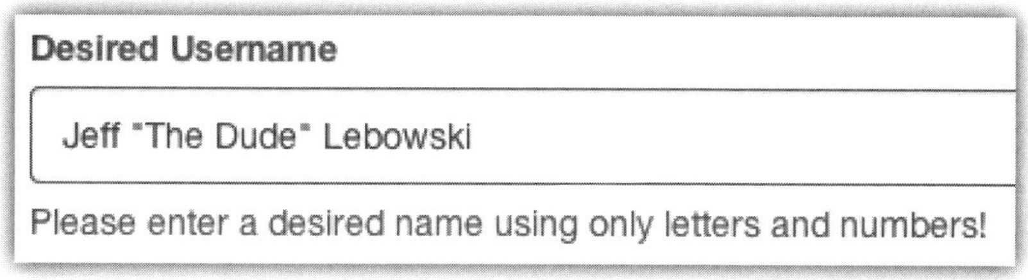

Desired Username

Jeff "The Dude" Lebowski

Please enter a desired name using only letters and numbers!

Figure 3.14

```
<div class="form-group<?php if (/* error on this input */)
➥echo ' has-error'; ?>">
<label for="username" class="control-label">Desired Username</label>
<input type="text" name="username" id="username"
➥class="form-control" value="<?php if (isset($_POST['username']))
➥echo htmlspecialchars($_POST['username']); ?>">
<?php if (/* error on this input */) echo '<span class=
➥"help-block">Please enter a desired name!</span>'; ?>
</div>
```

As you can tell, there's a lot of logic going into these inputs and their error handling, and those examples haven't even addressed Magic Quotes yet. The code above is just a mess to look at, it'll need to be used a dozen times, and if you later decide to handle things differently, you'll be editing code all day. Instead of doing all that manually for each form input in the example, let's write one function that does all this automatically. In Chapter 5, forms will also contain textareas, so this function will be flexible enough to handle those, too.

I'm using the plural, *functions*, in the filename even though only one function is being defined. Other functions might be added to it later (in theory).

1. Create a new PHP file in your text editor or IDE to be named **form_functions.inc.php**.

   This file should be stored in the **includes** directory.

2. Begin defining the function:

   ```
   <?php
   function create_form_input($name, $type, $label = '',
   ➥$errors = array(), $options = array()) {
   ```

   The function takes up to five arguments, although only two are required. The first argument is the name that will be given to the element. The second is the element type, which will be either **text**, **password**, or **email** in this chapter, and **textarea** in the next. The third argument is a label value. The fourth will be an array of errors. And the fifth will allow for additional options to be passed to the function. For example, this will allow you to pass a placeholder value.

3. Check for and process the value:

   ```
   $value = false;
   if (isset($_POST[$name])) $value = $_POST[$name];
   if ($value && get_magic_quotes_gpc())
   ➥$value = stripslashes($value);
   ```

   First, the function assumes that no value exists. Then, if a value does exist for this input in **$_POST**, that value is assigned to the **$value** variable.

The third step strips extraneous slashes from the value, but only if Magic Quotes is enabled.

This function assumes that the form uses the POST action. You could create another argument that accepts POST or GET and checks the corresponding superglobal for the value, if you want to make the function even more flexible.

**tip**

I recommend writing conditionals over multiple lines and always using curly brackets, but this book will have some single-line conditionals to save space.

4. Create the DIV that surrounds the element:

```
echo '<div class="form-group';
if (array_key_exists($name, $errors)) echo ' has-error';
echo '">';
```

This code is strongly tied to the syntax for creating form elements when using Twitter Bootstrap 3. In that framework, each element and its label are surrounded by a DIV with the class **form-group**. That's created on the first line.

Next, I want to also add the class **has-error** if there's an error associated with the element being created. An array of errors will be passed to the **$errors** parameter when the function is called. That array will contain every form error that occurred, indexed by the input's name (you'll see this in the scripts that handle the forms). Hence, if the array has a key with the same name as this input, the **has-error** class should be added to the DIV.

If no such array element exists, the input is completed without any additional class styling (on the last line of that code).

5. Create the label, if one was provided:

```
if (!empty($label)) echo '<label for="' . $name . '"
➥class="control-label">' . $label . '</label>';
```

The label is optional, but if provided, it will be created by this code (again, using syntax recommended by Twitter Bootstrap 3).

6. Create a conditional that checks the input type:

```
if ( ($type === 'text') || ($type === 'password') ||
➥($type === 'email')) {
```

This function will create text inputs, password inputs, email inputs, and textareas. The first three are virtually the same in syntax, except for the **type** value used in the HTML. The function starts by handling those three types.

**note**

The template uses HTML5, which defines an *email* input type.

7. Begin creating the input:

```
echo '<input type="' . $type . '" name="' . $name . '"
➥id="' . $name . '" class="form-control"';
```

This is the initial shell of the HTML input, with its **type**, **name**, **id**, and **class** properties.

8. Add the input's value, if applicable:

```
if ($value) echo ' value="' . htmlspecialchars($value) . '"';
```

If the **$value** variable has a value, it should be added to the input, after running it through **htmlspecialchars()**.

9. Check for any additional options:

```
if (!empty($options) && is_array($options)) {
   foreach ($options as $k => $v) {
      echo " $k=\"$v\"";
   }
}
```

This additional touch allows you to add placeholders or other element attributes.

10. Complete the element:

```
echo '>';
```

11. Show the error message, if one exists:

```
if (array_key_exists($name, $errors)) echo '<span
➥class="help-block">' . $errors[$name] . '</span>';
```

The code first checks the **$errors** variable to see if an error exists. If so, the error message is added after the input (see Figure 3.14).

12. Check if the input type is a textarea:

```
} elseif ($type === 'textarea') {
```

The syntax of textareas is different, so they'll be generated differently by this function.

13. Display the error first:

```
if (array_key_exists($name, $errors)) echo '<span class=
➥"help-block">' . $errors[$name] . '</span>';
```

Unlike with the text and password inputs, where the error message will be displayed below the input itself, for textareas, I want to display the error message above the textarea, so that the error is more obvious.

14. Begin creating the textarea:

```
echo '<textarea name="' . $name . '" id="' . $name . '"
class="form-control"';
```

Here, the textarea's opening tag is created, providing dynamic **name** and **id** values.

**15.** Check for any additional options:

```
if (!empty($options) && is_array($options)) {
   foreach ($options as $k => $v) {
      echo " $k=\"$v\"";
   }
}
```

This would allow you to set the number of rows and columns, for example.

**16.** Complete the opening tag:

```
echo '>';
```

**17.** Add the value to the textarea:

```
if ($value) echo $value;
```

The value for textareas is written between opening and closing textarea tags. Step 16 closed the opening tag, and step 18 will create the closing one, so the value should just be printed here.

**18.** Complete the textarea:

```
echo '</textarea>';
```

**19.** Complete the function:

```
   } // End of primary IF-ELSE.
   echo '</div>';
} // End of the create_form_input() function.
```

Be certain to close the DIV that surrounds the entire element (begun in step 4).

**20.** Save the file.

Again, I'm not using a closing PHP tag, for reasons explained earlier.

# 4 USER ACCOUNTS

The next step in the evolution of the "Knowledge Is Power" e-commerce site is to create a system of user accounts. When the site is complete, PayPal will be the crucial part in the registration process, but just to understand the user account system on its own, as well as to be able to create an administrative user for the next chapter, let's look at user accounts as a separate entity first.

There are four primary facets to the implementation of user accounts in this chapter. First, a new user registers. Second, a registered user logs in. Third, the logged-in user logs out (in theory, many people, including me, don't always do so). Fourth, users need to be able to retrieve a forgotten password and change an existing password.

Although this example won't be storing any sensitive e-commerce data, security will still be taken seriously, for the benefit of the customers and the site itself. In a few places, I'll make recommendations as to how you can increase security even further, and the chapter ends with even more suggestions. Chapter 12, "Extending the First Site," makes even more suggestions—security-related and otherwise.

# PROTECTING PASSWORDS

How secure a user account system is will depend largely on how passwords are handled. Passwords can be stored on the server in three ways:

- In plain text, which is a terrible thing to do
- In an encrypted format, which *can* be decrypted
- In a hashed format, which *can't* be decrypted

If you store passwords in an encrypted format, it's safe from prying eyes and can be retrieved when necessary. But if someone gets onto your server and can find your code for performing the decryption, that person will be able to view every user's password. And it turns out that you don't need passwords to be decryptable: It doesn't matter whether or not anyone can ever see the plain text in its original form again.

**note**

The discovery of a user's password is a huge security violation because many people use the same email and password combination at many sites.

An alternative is to create a *hash* of the password. A hash is a representation of data. For example, MD5 is a hashing algorithm that's been around for years. The MD5 hash of the word "password" is **`5f4dcc3b5aa765d61d8327deb882cf99`**; the MD5 hash of the word "omnivore" is **`04f7696e917f292f99925f80fcdb1db1`**. You can create a hash out of any piece of data, and, in theory, no two pieces of data have the same hash.

Storing the hash version of a password is more secure in that it can't be decrypted. If hackers get your data, the best they can do is create hashes of common words in the hopes that they find the matching hash (this is called a *dictionary attack*). But storing a hash still makes logging in possible: When a user logs in, the hashed version of the user's login password just needs to equal the already stored hashed version. If the two hashes equate, the submitted password is correct.

Once you've decided to hash the passwords, you'll need to choose what hashing *algorithm* (or formula) to use and where the hashing should take place. By the latter I mean that you can hash the password in either the database or in your PHP code. Normally I recommend having the database do as much as possible, but PHP has more sophisticated hashing functions available than MySQL.

MD5 is a common legacy hashing algorithm, but not very secure. An improvement is SHA or SHA1, which are fine for some applications, although not e-commerce. For improved security, I'm going to turn to PHP's very new **password_hash()** function. This function was added to the language as of PHP 5.5. This means you must have a current version of PHP in order to use it (as of this writing, the most current version is only 5.5.3).

If you aren't running PHP 5.5 or greater, you can use an external library found at https://github.com/ircmaxell/password_compat. This library was created by Anthony Ferrara (http://blog.ircmaxell.com/) and is the basis for the version implemented in PHP 5.5. The library requires PHP 5.3.7 or greater.

To test whether you can use the library:

1. Download the zip file from the GitHub URL just mentioned.
2. Unzip the downloaded file to create a folder of goodies (**Figure 4.1**).

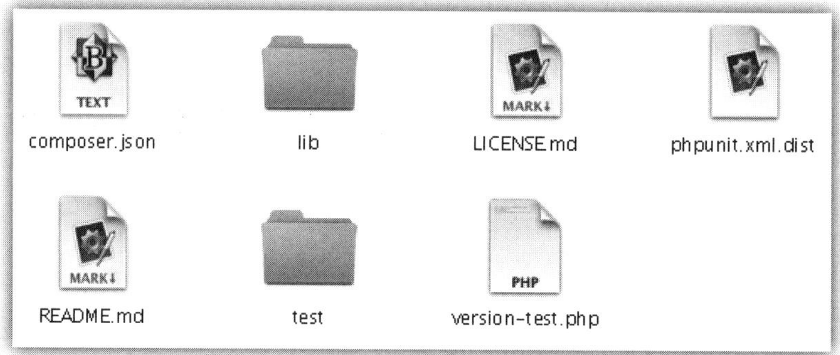


**Figure 4.1**

3. Copy the **version-test.php** file to your server's web directory.
4. Run the **version-test.php** in your browser (**Figure 4.2**).

Test for functionality of compat library: Pass

**Figure 4.2**

If you're not using PHP 5.5 or greater, and if the **password_compat** library indicates that it *can't* be used, you should upgrade your PHP version. If that's not possible either, post a message in my support forums (www.LarryUllman.com/forums/) for alternative hashing approaches.

To hash passwords with this new function, you'll use this code:

```
$hash = password_hash($password, PASSWORD_BCRYPT);
```

That will work if you have PHP 5.5 or later. If you're using the **password_compat** library, you must first include that library. Copy the **lib** directory from the downloaded file (see Figure 4.1) into your **includes** folder. Then include the library prior to invoking **password_hash()**:

```
include('./includes/lib/password.php');
$hash = password_hash($password, PASSWORD_BCRYPT);
```

That's all there is to it! It's very simple and yet highly secure.

To verify a password upon login, use the **password_verify()** function. Its first argument is the submitted, unhashed password. The second is the stored, hashed password:

```
if (password_verify($password, $hash)) {
   /* Valid */
} else {
   /* Invalid */
}
```

Again, if you're using the **password_compat** library you'll need to include it prior to calling **password_verify()**.

**tip**

The **password_hash()** function will automatically generate and use a secure salt for each password.

**tip**

For more information on using the **password_hash()** function, see the PHP manual.

# REGISTRATION

The registration form needs to present fields for everything being stored in the database. Plus, it's common to have users confirm their password, just to make sure they know what it is (since password inputs don't display the entered text, it's easy to unknowingly make a mistake). The same PHP script will display the form and handle its results. Therefore, if the registration form is incomplete, it can be shown again, with the existing values in place, along with detailed error messages (**Figure 4.3**).

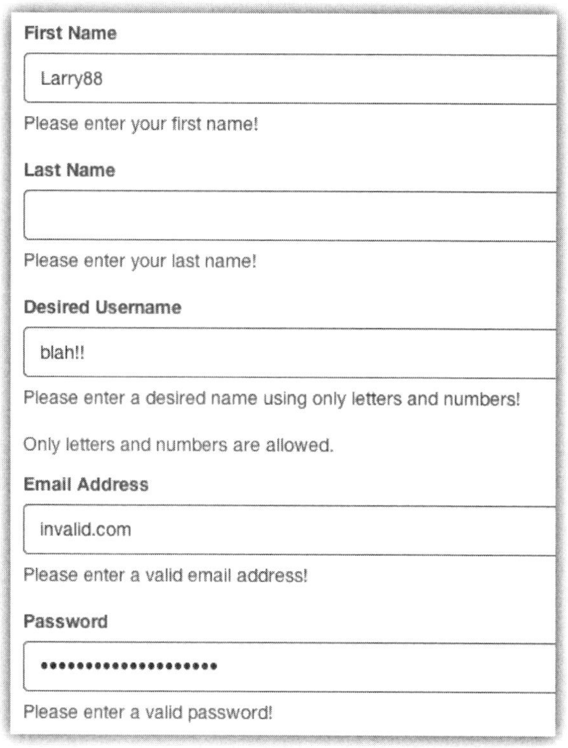

First Name

Larry88

Please enter your first name!

Last Name

Please enter your last name!

Desired Username

blah!!

Please enter a desired name using only letters and numbers!

Only letters and numbers are allowed.

Email Address

invalid.com

Please enter a valid email address!

Password

••••••••••••••••••••

Please enter a valid password!

Figure 4.3

The registration script I came up with, which you can download from www.LarryUllman.com, is about 160 lines total, including comments. Rather than walk you through the entire script in one long series of steps, let's look at this script as its three distinct parts.

## Creating the Basic Shell

Every PHP page in the site—every script that a user will access directly and that won't be included by other PHP scripts—has the same basic structure. First, it includes the configuration file; then the MySQL connection script; and then the HTML header (likely setting the page title beforehand). Next comes the page-specific content, and finally, the footer is included. Here, then, is what you can start with for `register.php`:

```
<?php
require('./includes/config.inc.php');
require(MYSQL);
$page_title = 'Register';
include('./includes/header.html');
?>

<h1>Register</h1>
<p>Access to the site's content is available to registered users
➥at a cost of $10.00 (US) per year. Use the form below to begin
➥the registration process. <strong>Note: All fields are required.
➥</strong> After completing this form, you'll be presented with
➥the opportunity to securely pay for your yearly subscription via
➥<a href="http://www.paypal.com">PayPal</a>.</p>

<?php include('./includes/footer.html'); ?>
```

For the registration page, it's important that you give the customer a sense of the process. You may want to graphically indicate the steps involved using a progress bar (or progress meter), although the process of registering for this site has only two steps. Also indicate how all the data will be used (for example, explain that the user won't be spammed), and maybe refer the user to whatever site policies exist (I've created a link to a policy file in the footer). Just do everything you can to reassure the user that it's safe to proceed.

## Creating the Form

The registration form contains six inputs: four text and two password (plus the submit button). I've already defined a function for creating these inputs, so the first thing the registration form needs to do is include the **form_functions.inc.php** file. Do this just before the page-specific content:

```
require_once('./includes/form_functions.inc.php');
?><h3>Register</h3>
```

As a complication, the **form_functions.inc.php** script may already have been included by the header file (to make the login form). To ensure that **form_functions.inc.php** is also available here, without seeing an error for possibly including it a second time, the **require_once()** function is the appropriate way to include that file before the registration form.

The form itself looks like this:

```
<form action="register.php" method="post" accept-charset="utf-8">
<?php
create_form_input('first_name', 'text', 'First Name', $reg_errors);
create_form_input('last_name', 'text', 'Last Name', $reg_errors);
create_form_input('username', 'text', 'Desired Username',
➥$reg_errors);
echo '<span class="help-block">Only letters and numbers are
➥allowed.</span>';
create_form_input('email', 'email', 'Email Address', $reg_errors);
create_form_input('pass1', 'password', 'Password', $reg_errors);
echo '<span class="help-block">Must be at least 6 characters long,
➥with at least one lowercase letter, one uppercase letter, and one
➥number.</span>';
create_form_input('pass2', 'password', 'Confirm Password',
➥$reg_errors);
?>
<input type="submit" name="submit_button" value="Next &rarr;"
➥id="submit_button" class="btn btn-default" />
</form>
```

**tip**

In theory, the user's name may be used to greet them personally on the site or in emails sent to them.

You'll see that with the aid of the **create_form_input()** function, all the code for creating each input and handling all the errors is extremely simple. As an example, for the first name input, the function is called indicating that the input should have **name** and **id** values of **first_name**, should be of **text** type, and should use **First Name** as the label. The fourth argument to the function is an array of errors named **$reg_errors**. In a few pages, this array will be added to the registration script so that it's already defined prior to this point. The same function is called for all six inputs, changing the arguments accordingly.

**tip**

Many sites these days are forgoing the confirmation of the password, taking it just the one time.

For the username and passwords, the user is being presented with a clear indication of what's expected of them. It drives me crazy when sites complain that I didn't complete a form properly (such as by not using at least one number or capital letter in a password) when no such instructions were included.

## Processing the Form

The bulk of the **register.php** script is the validation of the form and the insertion of the new record into the database. That part of the script is over one hundred lines of code, so I'll walk through it more deliberately.

**Figure 4.4** shows a flowchart of how this entire page will be used and may help you understand what's going on with the code. Note that all the code in the steps that follow gets placed after the MySQL connection script is included—because you'll need access to the database—but before the **form_functions.inc.php** include and the page-specific content. Again, see the downloadable scripts if you're confused about the order of things.

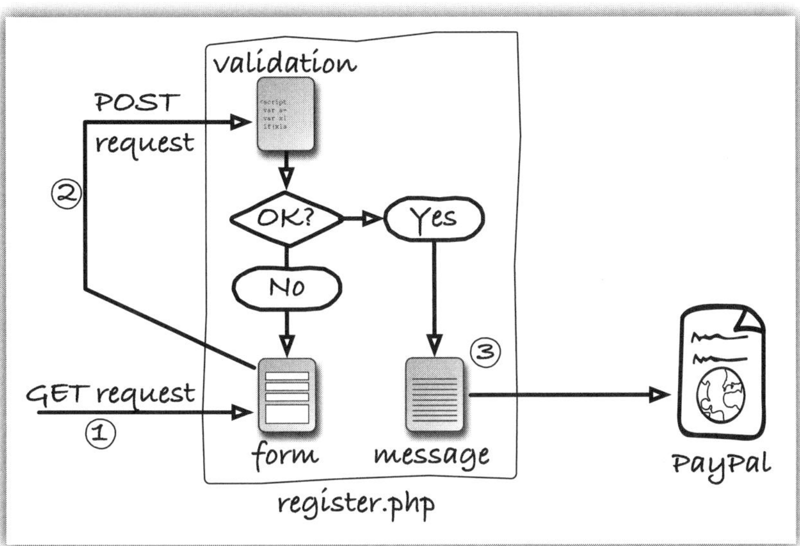


**Figure 4.4**

1. Create an empty array for storing errors:

   ```
   $reg_errors = array();
   ```

   This array will be used to store any errors that occur during the validation process. Normally, I might include this line within the section that begins the validation process (see Step 2), but because the **create_form_input()** function calls are going to use **$reg_errors** the very first time the page is loaded, you need to create this empty array at this point.

2. Check for a form submission:

   ```
   if ($_SERVER['REQUEST_METHOD'] === 'POST') {
   ```

   The first time the user goes to **register.php** (that is, when the user loads the form), it will be a GET request. In that case, this conditional, and all the code to follow, won't apply. When the user clicks submit, a POST request will be made of **register.php**, and this code will be executed.

3. Check for a first name:

```
if (preg_match ('/^[A-Z \'.-]{2,45}$/i', $_POST['first_name'])) {
   $fn = escape_data($_POST['first_name'], $dbc);
} else {
   $reg_errors['first_name'] = 'Please enter your first name!';
}
```

Names are difficult to validate, so I'm using a *regular expression* that's neither too strict nor too lenient. The pattern insists that the submitted value be between 2 and 45 characters long and only contain a combination of letters (case-insensitive), the space, a period, an apostrophe, and a hyphen. If the value passes this test, the escaped version of that value is assigned to the **$fn** variable. If the value doesn't pass this test, a new element is added to the **$reg_errors** array. The element uses the same key as the form input so that the **create_form_input()** function can properly display the error.

Alternatively, you could just check that this value isn't empty, and then run it through **strip_tags()** to make sure it doesn't contain anything it shouldn't.

**tip**

If you're not comfortable with Perl-compatible regular expressions (PCREs), search online for tutorials or see my *PHP and MySQL for Dynamic Web Sites: Visual QuickPro Guide* book.

4. Check for a last name:

```
if (preg_match ('/^[A-Z \'.-]{2,45}$/i', $_POST['last_name'])) {
   $ln = escape_data($_POST['last_name'], $dbc);
} else {
   $reg_errors['last_name'] = 'Please enter your last name!';
}
```

This is the same code as for the first name, but with a longer maximum length.

5. Check for a username:

```
if (preg_match ('/^[A-Z0-9]{2,45}$/i', $_POST['username'])) {
   $u = escape_data($_POST['username'], $dbc);
} else {
   $reg_errors['username'] = 'Please enter a desired name using
   ➥only letters and numbers!';
}
```

The username, per the instructions indicated in the form, is restricted to just letters and numbers. The username has to be between 2 and 45 characters long.

**tip**

Size restrictions in regular expressions should match the restrictions on those same values in the database columns.

6. Check for an email address:

```
if (filter_var($_POST['email'], FILTER_VALIDATE_EMAIL)) {
   $e = escape_data($_POST['email'], $dbc);
} else {
   $reg_errors['email'] = 'Please enter a valid email address!';
}
```

Unlike names, email addresses have to adhere to a fairly strict syntax. The simplest and most fail-safe way to validate an email address is to use PHP's **filter_var()** function, part of the Filter extension added in PHP 5.2. Its first argument is the variable to be tested, and its second is a constant representing a validation model.

If you're not using a version of PHP that supports the Filter extension, you'll need to use a regular expression instead (you can find good patterns online and in my books).

**note**

Technically, a valid email address wouldn't contain any characters that could be used in a SQL injection attack, but it's still best to run the email address through the escaping function.

7. Check for a password and match against the confirmed password:

```
if (preg_match('/^(\w*(?=\w*\d)(?=\w*[a-z])(?=\w*[A-Z])\w*)
➥{6,}$/', $_POST['pass1']) ) {
   if ($_POST['pass1'] === $_POST['pass2']) {
      $p = $_POST['pass1'];
   } else {
      $reg_errors['pass2'] = 'Your password did not match the
      ➥confirmed password!';
   }
} else {
   $reg_errors['pass1'] = 'Please enter a valid password!';
}
```

**tip**

The strength of a user account system will depend on how secure you require your users' passwords to be.

OK, so, um, here's a little magic for you. Good validation normally uses regular expressions, with which not everyone is entirely comfortable. And, admittedly, I often have to look up the proper syntax for patterns, but this one requires a high level of regular expression expertise. For the password to be relatively secure, it needs to contain at least one uppercase letter, one lowercase letter, and one number. In other words, it can't just be a word out of the dictionary, all in one case. Creating a regular expression that confirms that these characters exist in the password, but in any position in the string, requires what's called a *zero-width positive lookahead assertion*, represented by the *?=*. The positive lookahead makes matches based on what follows a character. Rather than reading a page of explanation as to how this pattern works beyond that simple definition, you can test it for yourself

**note**

The technical editor, among others, prefers to avoid variables with very short names, as their meaning isn't as obvious as variables with longer names.

to confirm that it does and research zero-width positive lookahead assertions online if you're curious.

Note that the password doesn't need to be run through the **escape_data()** function. The password itself won't be used in a query, but rather the hash of the password will be.

8. If there are no errors, check the availability of the email address and username:

```
if (empty($reg_errors)) {
   $q = "SELECT email, username FROM users WHERE email='$e' OR
   ➥username='$u'";
   $r = mysqli_query($dbc, $q);
   $rows = mysqli_num_rows($r);
   if ($rows === 0) {
```

**tip**

In truth, I just added the username field to demonstrate how to guarantee both unique email addresses and usernames.

If the **$reg_errors** array is still empty, no errors occurred (because even one error would add an element to this array, making it no longer empty). Next, a query looks for any existing record that has the submitted email address or username. In theory, this query could return up to two records (one for the email address and one for the username); if it returns no records, it's safe to proceed.

9. Add the user to the database:

```
$q = "INSERT INTO users (username, email, pass, first_name,
➥last_name, date_expires) VALUES ('$u', '$e', '"  .
➥password_hash($p, PASSWORD_BCRYPT) .  "', '$fn', '$ln',
➥ADDDATE(NOW(), INTERVAL 1 MONTH) )";
$r = mysqli_query($dbc, $q);
```

**tip**

As a security measure, the user's type can only ever be **member** after going through the registration process. You must go into the database and change a user's type manually in order to create an administrator.

The query uses the submitted values to create a new record in the database. Note that for the password value, the **password_hash()** function is called. If you're not using PHP 5.5 or later, you'll need to install and include the **password_compat** library prior to this first line.

The user's type doesn't need to be set because if no value is provided for an **ENUM** column, the first enumerated value—here, **member**—will be used.

Until PayPal is integrated (see Chapter 6, "Using PayPal"), I'm setting the account expiration date to a month from now. Once PayPal has been integrated, the expiration will be set to yesterday. In that case, when PayPal returns an indication of successful payment, the user's account will subsequently be set to expire in a year.

**10.** If the query created one row, thank the new customer and send out an email:

```
if (mysqli_affected_rows($dbc) === 1) {
   echo '<div class="alert alert-success"><h3>Thanks!</h3>
   ➥<p>Thank you for registering! You may now log in and access
   ➥the site\'s content.</p></div>';
   $body = "Thank you for registering at <whatever site>.
   ➥Blah. Blah. Blah.\n\n";
   mail($_POST['email'], 'Registration Confirmation', $body,
   ➥'From: admin@example.com');
   include('./includes/footer.html');
   exit();
```

First, a Thanks! page is displayed (**Figure 4.5**). The next step would be to send the user off to PayPal, which will be added in Chapter 6. Also, an email can be sent to the user saying whatever you want, although you shouldn't include the user's password in that email. Finally, the footer is included and a call to **exit()** stops the page. This is necessary so that the registration form isn't shown again, thereby confusing the user.

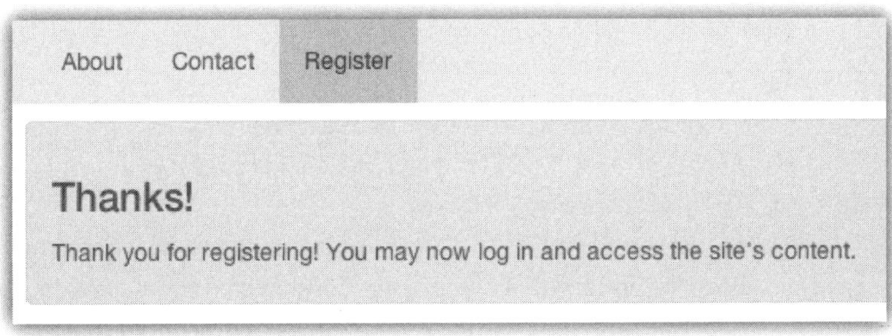


**Figure 4.5**

**11.** If the query didn't work, create an error:

```
} else {
   trigger_error('You could not be registered due to a system
   ➥error. We apologize for any inconvenience. We will correct
   ➥the error ASAP.');
}
```

At this point, if the query didn't create a new row, there was a database or query error. In that case, the **trigger_error()** function is used to generate an error that will be managed by the error handler in the config file. On a live, already tested site, this would likely occur only if the database server is down or overloaded.

12. If the email address or username is unavailable, create errors:

```
if ($rows === 2) {
   $reg_errors['email'] = 'This email address has already been
   ➥registered. If you have forgotten your password, use the
   ➥link at left to have your password sent to you.';
   $reg_errors['username'] = 'This username has already been
   ➥registered. Please try another.';
```

The **else** clause applies if the **SELECT** query returns any records. This means that the email address and/or the username have already been registered. If so, the next step is to determine which of the two values is the culprit.

If two rows were returned, both have already been registered. The assumption would be that the same customer already registered (because her email address is in the system) and another customer already has that username (because it's associated with a different email address). The error messages are added to the **$reg_errors** array, indexed at **email** and **username**, so that the errors can appear beside the appropriate form input when the form is redisplayed.

13. Confirm which item has been registered:

```
} else {
   $row = mysqli_fetch_array($r, MYSQLI_NUM);
   if( ($row[0] === $_POST['email']) && ($row[1] ===
   ➥$_POST['username'])) {
      $reg_errors['email'] = 'This email address has already
      ➥been registered. If you have forgotten your password, use
      ➥the link at left to have your password sent to you.';
      $reg_errors['username'] = 'This username has already been
      ➥registered with this email address. If you have forgotten
      ➥your password, use the link at left to have your password
      ➥sent to you.';
   } elseif ($row[0] === $_POST['email']) {
      $reg_errors['email'] = 'This email address has already
      ➥been registered. If you have forgotten your password, use
      ➥the link at left to have your password sent to you.';
   } elseif ($row[1] === $_POST['username']) {
      $reg_errors['username'] = 'This username has already been
      ➥registered. Please try another.';
   }
} // End of $rows === 2 ELSE.
```

## ACTIVATING ACCOUNTS

On a site that doesn't require payment, I normally include an activation process:

1. When the user registers, a random code is stored in the **users** table.
2. An email is sent to the registered email address, which includes a link to an activation page on the site. The link passes the user's email address and the specific code to the PHP page: **`https://www.example.com/activate.php?x=email@example.com&y=`*`CODE`***

   (For even better security, you could pass a hash of the email address.)
3. The PHP page confirms that there's a record in the table with that combination of email address and code, then presents the opportunity to log in.
4. When the user logs in, the query must confirm that the email and password combination is correct, and that the code matches, too.
5. Upon successful login, the code column in the table is set to **NULL**, to indicate that the account is now active.
6. Subsequent logins will require that the email address and password are correct, and that the code column has a **NULL** value.

This is called a "closed-loop" confirmation process and prevents fake registrations. In this "Knowledge Is Power" site, using PayPal will prevent fake registrations, because hackers don't typically spend money in their hack attempts.

If only one row was returned, the code needs to figure out if the username matched, the email address matched, or both matched in the same record. Three conditionals test for each possibility, with appropriate error messages assigned (**Figures 4.6** and **4.7**).

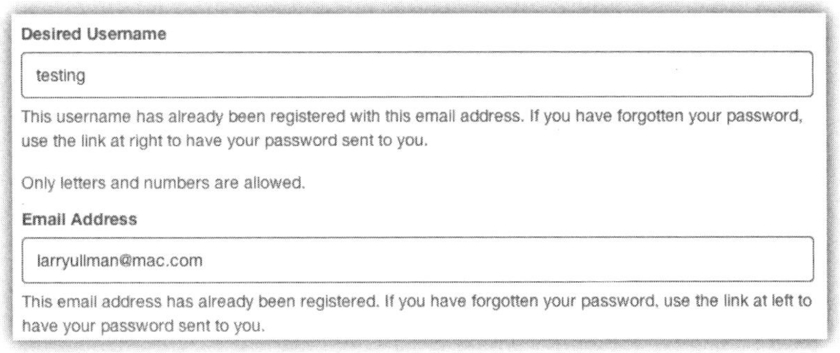

Desired Username

testing

This username has already been registered with this email address. If you have forgotten your password, use the link at right to have your password sent to you.

Only letters and numbers are allowed.

Email Address

larryullman@mac.com

This email address has already been registered. If you have forgotten your password, use the link at left to have your password sent to you.

Figure 4.6

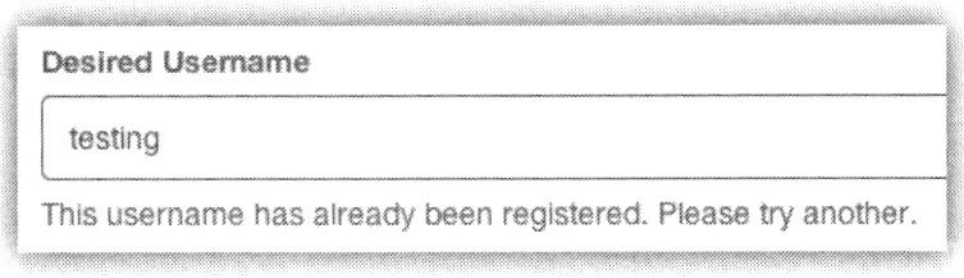

Desired Username

testing

This username has already been registered. Please try another.

Figure 4.7

14. Complete the conditionals:

```
        } // End of $rows === 0 IF.
    } // End of empty($reg_errors) IF.
} // End of the main form submission conditional.
```

15. Save and test the registration script.

# LOGGING IN

Logging in to the site is a two-step process: completing the form and validating the submitted values against the database. The login form is not its own page—it's shown in the sidebar to all non-logged-in users. For this reason, the login form can't use the same single-script approach as in **register.php**. The question then becomes: where should the user end up when he successfully logs in and when he doesn't? In both cases, I decided the user should end up back on the home page; for this reason, the login form gets submitted to **index.php**. Hence, the index page needs to be updated with the code for handling the form. Rather than writing that code directly into the home page, it's better to include it as a separate file, just after the database connection but prior to the inclusion of the header file:

 **tip**

By including the login processing code, instead of writing it to the **index.php** file, I'm maintaining better separation of code.

```
if ($_SERVER['REQUEST_METHOD'] === 'POST') {
   include('./includes/login.inc.php');
}
```

This is feasible because normally **index.php** will be requested via GET. If it's a POST request, the login form has been submitted, and this script includes the file that will test the login credentials.

## Processing the Form

I think it will be easier to follow the login process if I talk about the form last, so let's first look at the code that handles the login form. That process needs to do the following in this order:

1. Validate the submitted email address and password.
2. Compare the submitted values with those in the database.

3. Define errors if the values are incorrect.
4. Store data in a session if the values are correct.

Here's how all of that works in actual code:

1. Create a new PHP script in your text editor or IDE to be named `login.inc.php`.

   This will be stored in the **includes** directory.

2. Create an empty array for recording errors:

```
<?php
$login_errors = array();
```

   This errors array will be used just like **$reg_errors** in the registration script.

3. Validate the email address:

```
if (filter_var($_POST['email'], FILTER_VALIDATE_EMAIL)) {
   $e = escape_data($_POST['email'], $dbc);
} else {
   $login_errors['email'] = 'Please enter a valid email
   ➥address!';
}
```

   This code replicates that in the registration process, using PHP's Filter extension to validate the email address.

4. Validate the password:

```
if (!empty($_POST['pass'])) {
   $p = $_POST['pass'];
} else {
   $login_errors['pass'] = 'Please enter your password!';
}
```

   To validate the password, I'm just making sure it's not empty. Part of the reason is performance—this will be faster than the zero-width positive lookahead regular expression used in the registration process—and part of the reason will be explained later in the chapter.

   In theory, you don't need to validate the submitted values because the database query will be confirming whether the submitted values are correct. However, database queries are expensive (in terms of server resources and performance), so it's best not to run one unless necessary.

**tip**

It's best to give variables in included files unique names so they don't overwrite any variables created by the parent script.

5. If there are no errors, query the database:

```
if (empty($login_errors)) {
   $q = "SELECT id, username, type, pass, IF(date_expires >=
   ➥NOW(), true, false) AS expired FROM users WHERE email='$e'";
$r = mysqli_query($dbc, $q);
```

   The basic query selects five values from the **users** table: the user's ID, username, type, password, and account expiration. The **WHERE** clause checks that the email address matches the submitted email address. The password will be checked in the PHP code.

   For the account expiration, I'm doing something that may be new to you. I don't care *when* the user's account expires, only whether it's valid right now. One way of accomplishing this would be to select the expiration value, which is a date, and then use PHP to convert it into a timestamp and compare it to the current timestamp. That's a lot of code and logic to put onto PHP. Instead, I'm doing an **IF** conditional within my MySQL query. That syntax is just

```
IF(date_expires >= NOW(), true, false)
```

   The first expression is the condition being tested; the second is what's returned if the condition is true; the third value is what's returned if the condition is false. Thus, if the expiration date is greater than or equal to this moment, the value **true** will be selected.

6. If one row was returned by the database query, fetch the data:

```
if (mysqli_num_rows($r) === 1) {
   $row = mysqli_fetch_array($r, MYSQLI_ASSOC);
```

   This conditional will be true if the email address exists in the database.

7. Compare the password against the stored password:

```
if (password_verify($p, $row['pass'])) {
```

   This code was explained at the beginning of the chapter, and it lets you verify a submitted password against a stored one. Again, you'll need to include the **password_compat** library before this line if you're using a version of PHP prior to 5.5.

8. If the user is an administrator, create a new session ID, just to be safe:

```
if ($row['type'] === 'admin') {
   session_regenerate_id(true);
   $_SESSION['user_admin'] = true;
}
```

If the user is an administrator, two things must be done. First, the session identifier ought to be changed as a security measure. Doing so prevents session fixation attacks (where a hacker sets a user's session ID to match the hacker's own session ID, then gets the administrator to log in, thereby giving the hacker administrative authority). The **session_regenerate_id()** function serves this purpose.

 **tip**

For stricter security, you could regenerate the session ID whenever anyone logs in.

Next, I only want to create a **$_SESSION['user_admin']** element with a true value if the user's type equals **admin**. Understand that I don't want to create a **$_SESSION['user_admin']** element equal to false if the user's type is **member**. This is because the function that will validate a user's access to pages—**redirect_invalid_user()** in **config.inc.php**—will check only if a session variable is set, not what its actual value is.

**9.** Store the other data in the session:

```
$_SESSION['user_id'] = $row['id'];
$_SESSION['username'] = $row['username'];
if ($row['expired'] === 1) $_SESSION['user_not_expired'] = true;
```

First, the user's ID and name are stored in the session, but given **user<*something*>** names so that they won't possibly conflict later on with anything else I might store in the session.

For the expiration, I only want to store a value indicating that the account hasn't expired. MySQL will return the number 1 for the Boolean value **true**, so if **$row['expired']** (which is the value in the array for the expiration status) equals that, I create a new element in **$_SESSION**. Again, I'm not assigning a value if the account has expired.

**10.** If the password didn't match, or if no database row was returned, create an error message:

```
    } else {
        $login_errors['login'] = 'The email address and password
        ➥do not match those on file.';
    }
} else {
    $login_errors['login'] = 'The email address and password do
    ➥not match those on file.';
}
```

The same error message will be used if the user supplied a valid email address but the password didn't match that stored in the database, or if the email address wasn't found in the database at all. For security purposes, the script doesn't indicate which of the two values is incorrect, or if the email address has been registered at all.

**11.** Complete the script:

```
} // End of $login_errors IF.
```

As with all other scripts that will be included by other scripts, I'm omitting the closing PHP tag.

**12.** Save the file.

## Creating the Form

The next script to discuss, `login_form.inc.php`, is the first step in the process. It needs to do just two things: present a form and report any errors that occurred when the form was submitted. The form contains two inputs: one for the email address and one for the password. Both are created using the same `create_form_input()` function, which means that the `form_functions.inc.php` script must be included. The function needs to take an array of errors—`$login_errors`—as its fourth argument. That array is created in `login.inc.php`. However, if the user is just loading the login form for the first time, `$login_errors` won't exist, so this script should initialize an empty array in that case.

Here's the complete `login_form.inc.php`:

```
<?php
if (!isset($login_errors)) $login_errors = array();
require('./includes/form_functions.inc.php');
?>
<form action="index.php" method="post" accept-charset="utf-8">
<fieldset>
<legend>Login</legend>
<?php
if (array_key_exists('login', $login_errors)) {
   echo '<div class="alert alert-danger">' . $login_errors['login']
   ➥. '</div>';
}
create_form_input('email', 'email', '', $login_errors,
➥array('placeholder'=>'Email address'));
create_form_input('pass', 'password', '', $login_errors,
➥array('placeholder'=>'Password'));
?>
<button type="submit" class="btn btn-default">Login &rarr;</button>
</fieldset>
</form>
```

By default, all errors are reported via the **`create_form_input()`** function. However, this form is a bit different in that **`login.inc.php`** could create an error (that is, an element in the **`$login_errors`** array) not associated with a particular form input. That error results when both fields are properly filled out but the values don't, together, match a record in the database. In that case, the **`$login_errors['login']`** element is assigned an error message. Therefore, the form first checks if that array element exists in **`$login_errors`**, in which case the error message will be displayed just before the two inputs (**Figure 4.8**). Other error messages are associated with the offending form input (**Figure 4.9**).

**tip**

You could also change the header file so that the register tab is not shown to users who are logged in.

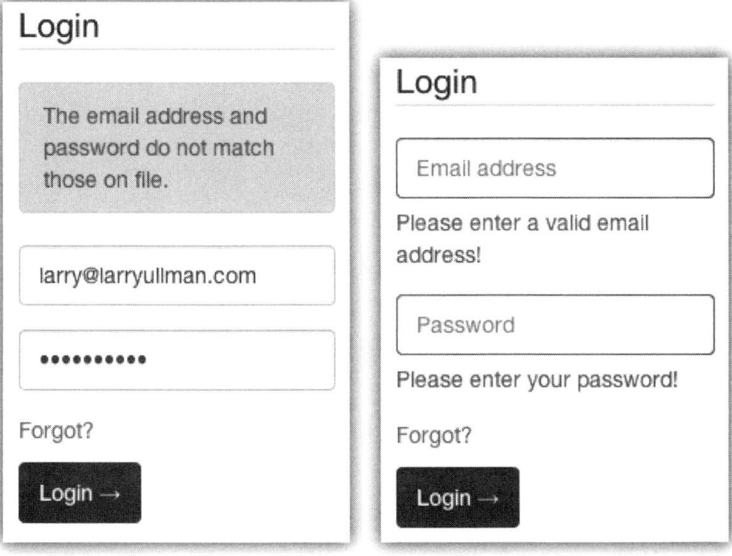


**Figure 4.8** **Figure 4.9**

After you've done all this, you can now test the login process.

# LOGGING OUT

Logging out is the simplest part of the process. The `logout.php` page starts off as a standard script, including the config file, the header, the MySQL connection, and the footer. Only logged-in users should be able to access this page, though, so a call to `redirect_invalid_user()` is included just after the config file is defined.

To wipe out the session, three steps are required. First, clear out the `$_SESSION` array that represents the variables available to this script:

```
$_SESSION = array();
```

Next, the `session_destroy()` function removes the data stored on the server:

```
session_destroy();
```

Finally, modify the session cookie in the user's browser so it no longer has a record of the session ID:

```
setcookie(session_name(), '', time()-300);
```

That line sends a cookie with the same session name, but no value (no session ID) and an expiration of five minutes ago.

Here's the complete `logout.php`:

```
<?php
require('./includes/config.inc.php');
redirect_invalid_user();
$_SESSION = array();
session_destroy();
setcookie (session_name(), '', time()-300);
require(MYSQL);
$page_title = 'Logout';
include('./includes/header.html');
echo '<h1>Logged Out</h1><p>Thank you for visiting. You are now
➥logged out. Please come back soon!</p>';
include('./includes/footer.html');
?>
```

**Figure 4.10** shows the result.



**Figure 4.10**

# MANAGING PASSWORDS

The site will have two pages for managing user passwords. One will be used to recover a forgotten password, and the other will change an existing password. Both pages are simple forms, but whereas users wouldn't be logged in when recovering a forgotten password, they must be logged in to change their password.

## Recovering Passwords

Because the user passwords aren't being stored in an encrypted format, they can't be decrypted and recovered. When users forget or lose their password, an option is to create a new password and send it to them in an email. The form to start this process is simple: it just takes an email address (**Figure 4.11**).

Reset Your Password

Enter your email address below to reset your password.

Email Address

Reset →

**Figure 4.11**

I will say in advance that there are two arguments against using this approach. I'll discuss those at the end of the sequence. In Chapter 12, you'll see an alternative approach that doesn't involve emailing passwords.

1. Create a new PHP script in your text editor or IDE to be named **forgot_password.php** and stored in the web root directory.

2. Include the standard stuff:

```
<?php
require('./includes/config.inc.php');
require(MYSQL);
$page_title = 'Forgot Your Password?';
include('./includes/header.html');
```

3. Create an array for storing errors:

```
$pass_errors = array();
```

4. Validate the email address:

```
if ($_SERVER['REQUEST_METHOD'] === 'POST') {
   if (filter_var($_POST['email'], FILTER_VALIDATE_EMAIL)) {
      $q = 'SELECT id FROM users WHERE email="'.
      ➥escape_data($_POST['email'], $dbc) . '"';
      $r = mysqli_query($dbc, $q);
      if (mysqli_num_rows($r) === 1) {
         list($uid) = mysqli_fetch_array($r, MYSQLI_NUM);
      } else {
         $pass_errors['email'] = 'The submitted email address
         ➥does not match those on file!';
      }
```

If the page is accessed via a POST request, then the form has been submitted. In that case, the first thing the script should do is validate that a proper email address was provided. This is a two-step process. First, the **filter_var()** function confirms that the submitted value adheres to the email syntax. Then a query specifically confirms that this email address exists in the database. If it does, the user ID value is retrieved. If the email address doesn't exist in the database, an error message is assigned to the array.

5. Complete the **filter_var()** conditional:

```
} else {
   $pass_errors['email'] = 'Please enter a valid email address!';
} // End of $_POST['email'] IF.
```

This error applies if the user doesn't provide a syntactically valid email address.

**tip**

Because the random generated password won't meet the criteria of the user-generated password, neither the login form nor the change password form applies the zero-width positive lookahead expression to the current password.

6. Generate a new password:

```
if (empty($pass_errors)) {
   $p = substr(md5(uniqid(rand(), true)), 10, 15);
```

To generate the password, call the **uniqid()** function, which returns a unique ID. If it's passed some value as its first argument, that value will be used as the prefix, thereby expanding the returned string. For the prefix value, invoke the **rand()** function. When a second argument of true is passed to **uniqid()**, a more random unique ID will be returned. This value will be sent through **md5()**, which will create a string 32 characters long, consisting of letters and numbers. From that string, take a substring starting with the eleventh character (because indexes start at 0) and going for 15 characters. The end result will be a completely random and unique password like *6e968eff0833110*.

7. Update the new password in the database:

```
$q = "UPDATE users SET pass='" .  password_hash($p,
➥PASSWORD_BCRYPT) . "' WHERE id=$uid LIMIT 1";
$r = mysqli_query($dbc, $q);
if (mysqli_affected_rows($dbc) === 1) {
```

The query uses the user ID value just fetched from the database to know which record to update. The generated password must also be run through the **password_hash()** function, because all passwords are stored in a hashed format.

tip

To make the generated password more secure, insert one or more random capital letters into it.

8. Send the new password to the user:

```
$body = "Your password to log into <whatever site> has been
➥temporarily changed to '$p'. Please log in using that password
➥and this email address. Then you may change your password to
➥something more familiar.";
mail($_POST['email'], 'Your temporary password.', $body,
➥'From: admin@example.com');
```

This is a simple email message (**Figure 4.12**). You should make it more interesting.

From: admin@example.com Hide
Subject: Your temporary password.
Date: August 2, 2013 2:27:03 PM EDT
To: Larry Ullman

Your password to log into <whatever site> has been temporarily changed to 'f023f69d43af9d9'. Please log in using that password and this email address. Then you may change your password to something more familiar.

**Figure 4.12**

9. Print a message and wrap up:

```
echo '<h1>Your password has been changed.</h1><p>You will receive
➥the new, temporary password via email. Once you have logged
➥in with this new password, you may change it by clicking on the
➥"Change Password" link.</p>';
include('./includes/footer.html');
exit();
```

As with any process, you want to indicate to the user what should happen next (**Figure 4.13**). The **exit()** line terminates the script so that the form is not shown again.

Your password has been changed.

You will receive the new, temporary password via email. Once you have logged in with this new password, you may change it by clicking on the "Change Password" link.

Figure 4.13

**10.** If the database update couldn't run, generate an error:

```
} else { // If it did not run OK.
   trigger_error('Your password could not be changed due to a
   ➥system error. We apologize for any inconvenience.');
}
```

This **else** clause applies if the database query didn't work, indicating a system error.

**11.** Complete the processing section of the script:

```
   } // End of $uid IF.
} // End of the main Submit conditional.
```

**12.** Create the form:

```
require_once('./includes/form_functions.inc.php');
?><h1>Reset Your Password</h1>
<p>Enter your email address below to reset your password.</p>
<form action="forgot_password.php" method="post"
➥accept-charset="utf-8">
<?php create_form_input('email', 'email', 'Email Address',
➥$pass_errors); ?>
<input type="submit" name="submit_button" value="Reset &rarr;"
➥id="submit_button" class="btn btn-default" />
</form>
```

The form uses the same **create_form_input()** function to generate the single text input.

**13.** Complete the page:

```
<?php include('./includes/footer.html'); ?>
```

**14.** Save and test the forgotten password script.

As I mentioned at the beginning of this sequence, there are two arguments against the approach taken here. First, it allows anyone to reset anyone's password. Second, it sends a less secure password in an email (which is a less secure protocol). That being said, this approach may be sufficiently secure for some sites, and it's certainly easy to implement.

In Part 4 of this book, I'll present another solution. That approach sends the user an access link without changing the user's existing password. That approach doesn't have either of the above-mentioned issues, but it requires a bit more effort to implement.

## Changing Passwords

Changing a password is kind of like a combination of the login and registration processes. The user should enter his current password as an extra precaution, then his new password, and finally a confirmation of the new password (**Figure 4.14**). The user must be logged in to perform this task.

**Figure 4.14**

1. Create a new PHP script in your text editor or IDE to be named **change_password.php** and stored in the web root directory.

2. Include the standard stuff:

```
<?php
require('./includes/config.inc.php');
redirect_invalid_user();
require(MYSQL);
$page_title = 'Change Your Password';
include('./includes/header.html');
```

You'll notice that just before the MySQL connection script is included, the script invokes the **redirect_invalid_user()** function so that only logged-in users can access the page.

3. Create an array for storing errors:

```
$pass_errors = array();
```

4. Check for the current password:

```
if ($_SERVER['REQUEST_METHOD'] === 'POST') {
   if (!empty($_POST['current'])) {
      $current = $_POST['current'];
   } else {
      $pass_errors['current'] = 'Please enter your current
      ➥password!';
   }
```

As with the login form, this conditional only checks that there's a password value. If the user is changing her password from a legitimate system-generated one, the current password wouldn't pass the more strict regular expression.

5. Validate the new password:

```
if (preg_match('/^(\w*(?=\w*\d)(?=\w*[a-z])(?=\w*[A-Z])\w*)
{6,}$/', $_POST['pass1']) ) {
   if ($_POST['pass1'] == $_POST['pass2']) {
      $p = $_POST['pass1'];
   } else {
      $pass_errors['pass2'] = 'Your password did not match the
      ➥confirmed password!';
   }
} else {
   $pass_errors['pass1'] = 'Please enter a valid password!';
}
```

This code is almost exactly like that in the registration script, except that errors are assigned to the **$pass_errors** array.

6. If everything is fine, validate the current password against the database:

```
if (empty($pass_errors)) {
   $q = "SELECT pass FROM users WHERE id={$_SESSION['user_id']}";
   $r = mysqli_query($dbc, $q);
   list($hash) = mysqli_fetch_array($r, MYSQLI_NUM);
   if (password_verify($current, $hash)) {
```

   To confirm that the current password is correct, a database query is run, similar to the login query except that it uses the user's ID (from the session), instead of the email address.

7. Update the database with the new password:

```
$q = "UPDATE users SET pass='" . password_hash($p,
➥PASSWORD_BCRYPT) . "' WHERE id={$_SESSION['user_id']} LIMIT 1";
if ($r = mysqli_query($dbc, $q)) {
```

   This query is almost exactly like that in **forgot_password.php**.

8. Indicate to the user the successful change:

```
echo '<h1>Your password has been changed.</h1>';
include('./includes/footer.html');
exit();
```

   The message is printed, the footer is included, and then the script is terminated using **exit()** so that the form isn't shown again (**Figure 4.15**). You may also want to email the user to indicate the password change (without actually emailing the new password to the user).

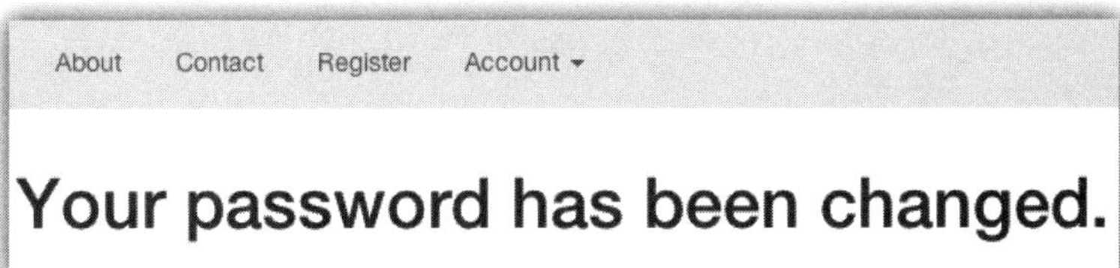


**Figure 4.15**

9. If there was a problem, trigger an error:

```
} else {
   trigger_error('Your password could not be changed due to a
   ➥system error. We apologize for any inconvenience.');
}
```

   This **else** clause applies if the database update failed, which shouldn't happen on a live, tested site.

10. Complete the processing section of the script:

```
        } else { // Invalid password.
          $pass_errors['current'] = 'Your current password is
          ➥incorrect!';
        }
      } // End of empty($pass_errors) IF.
    } // End of the form submission conditional.
```

This **else** clause applies if the supplied current password doesn't match the one in the database for the current user. In that case, an error is created that will be displayed next to the current password input.

11. Display the form:

```
require_once('./includes/form_functions.inc.php');
?><h1>Change Your Password</h1>
<p>Use the form below to change your password.</p>
<form action="change_password.php" method="post"
➥accept-charset="utf-8">
<?php
create_form_input('current', 'password', 'Current Password',
➥$pass_errors);
create_form_input('pass1', 'password', 'Password',
➥$pass_errors);
echo '<span class="help-block">Must be at least 6 characters
➥long, with at least one lowercase letter, one uppercase
➥letter, and one number.</span>';
create_form_input('pass2', 'password', 'Confirm Password',
➥$pass_errors);
?>
<input type="submit" name="submit_button" value="Change &rarr;"
➥id="submit_button" class="btn btn-default" />
</form>
```

The form has three password inputs. Each is generated using the **create_form_input()** function.

12. Complete the page:

```
<?php include('./includes/footer.html'); ?>
```

13. Save and test the change password script.

# IMPROVING THE SECURITY

The user accounts system in this example demonstrates a good approach to security. For starters, users are forced to use both letters and numbers in their password and at least one letter in each case. You could improve the security by requiring at least one nonalphanumeric character and by increasing the minimum length. Security is inversely proportional to convenience, so you would make these changes knowing that you'll annoy some of your potential customers. I also chose not to implement a "remember me" option because requiring that users log in each time they visit the site makes for better security (although, again, that requirement is an inconvenience).

**tip**

There's no reason to limit a password's length, as longer passwords are inherently more secure.

As another safeguard, the passwords are securely hashed before being sent to the database. And the only user account type that can be created through the registration process is the standard member; there's no way to trick the system into creating an administrative account.

Another obvious and relatively easy way you can improve the security of the site is to implement SSL for the registration and login processes. To do so, change the link to the registration page to `'https://' . BASE_URL . 'register.php'`. That form will be loaded via HTTPS, and the form data will be posted back to the server via HTTPS, too. In fact, with nothing but relative links in the site, everything will be HTTPS from that point forward until you create a link that returns to an HTTP connection.

Serving the login form over HTTPS is trickier, because the form is included by other pages. Your options are to serve every page over HTTPS, which isn't ideal, or to create a separate login page.

**tip**

Part 3, "Selling Physical Products," will demonstrate switching the use of SSL as appropriate.

As mentioned before, you could implement an activation process as part of the registration, in which case the customer would be sent to PayPal after activating the account, not after first registering. You could also send an email when a password change is requested and only by clicking the link in that email would the user have her password reset. I'll explain this approach in Part 4.

Because this system relies on a login to authenticate the user, much of its security depends on using sessions and a cookie (for storing the session ID in the browser). Limiting the life of the cookie, changing the session name (which is also the cookie's name), and tweaking the other cookie parameters can all increase the site's security. You can even send the cookie only over SSL, but that would require using SSL for every page once the user logged in.

**tip**

Storing session IDs in cookies is preferred, security-wise, to storing them in links and forms.

For the session itself, one recommendation that I had in Chapter 2, "Security Fundamentals," was to change the session storage directory when using a shared host. You can also shorten how quickly the session expires, as well as how quickly the session cookie expires.

**tip**

An even more secure way to store session data is to put it into the database.

Another nice security feature is the prevention of session fixation attacks when an administrator logs in. To recap that scenario and code, a session fixation attack is when a malicious user, Alice, starts her own session on your site, quite legitimately. She then gets administrator Bob to visit the site using that same session ID, normally by getting Bob to click a link with the session ID embedded. When Bob logs in to the site, that same session will now be associated with an administrative account, giving Alice administrative access through her browser and existing session.

Preventing such attacks is quite simple: Change the session ID using the **session_regenerate_id()** function:

```
if ($row['type'] === 'admin') {
   session_regenerate_id(true);
   $_SESSION['user_admin'] = true;
}
```

By doing so, when Bob logs in, his session ID will change, meaning Alice's legitimate session won't be updated to reflect Bob's administrative status.

You'll need to call **session_regenerate_id()** before storing any session data, because by passing a value of **true** as the first argument to the function, any existing session data is also destroyed. Arguably, this same approach could be used to heighten security when any user logs in. You could also regenerate the session ID when major account changes occur, such as resetting the password.

A last consideration is that access to site content in this example will be determined by dates without times. With the sessions as written, the worst thing that could happen would be that a user whose account expires today is allowed to continue accessing site content for some minutes or hours into tomorrow. But even that is only true if the user keeps his session active. Not a huge concern, in my opinion.

# 5 MANAGING SITE CONTENT

If you're reading this book in order—and I certainly hope you are—then you've got a site where users can register, log in, change their password, and log out, but there's nothing for them to look at! On the other hand, they haven't paid anything yet either, so....

In this chapter, you'll create the content management side of the equation, with two kinds of content: HTML pages and PDFs. I'll explain how to write the code for creating and displaying the content.

But first, you'll need to create an administrative user.

## CREATING AN ADMINISTRATOR

Even though administrators will use the same login system and the same underlying **users** table as regular users, for security reasons you can't create an administrator through the site itself (not as the code thus far has been written, that is). Thanks to that design, no possible flaw in the site could result in administrators being created. And since administration accounts won't be created often, it makes sense not to implement that feature anyway. But you still need at least one administrator, so let's create one now.

1. Register the administrator using the same registration page.

   This would likely be the first user who gets registered anyway, just to test the system. Enter the administrator's email address and give the administrator a logical username, such as **`admin`**.

**tip**

The system, as written, allows for any number of administrators, all with the same powers (which is not many).

2. Access your database using a third-party interface.

   On a hosted server, you most likely have a phpMyAdmin interface for manipulating your database, accessible only after logging in to a control panel. Or you could use the command-line MySQL client, if you prefer.

3. Change the user's type value.

   You can change the type by running a query such as

   ```
   UPDATE users SET type='admin' WHERE email='theEmailAddress'
   ```

   Or, if you're using phpMyAdmin:

   **A.** Browse the **`users`** table.

   **B.** Click the pencil icon next to the record you want to change (**Figure 5.1**).

**tip**

As of this writing, the most current version of phpMyAdmin allows for inline record editing, on the "browse" page of results.

**Figure 5.1**

   **C.** Use the editor form to change the user type (**Figure 5.2**).

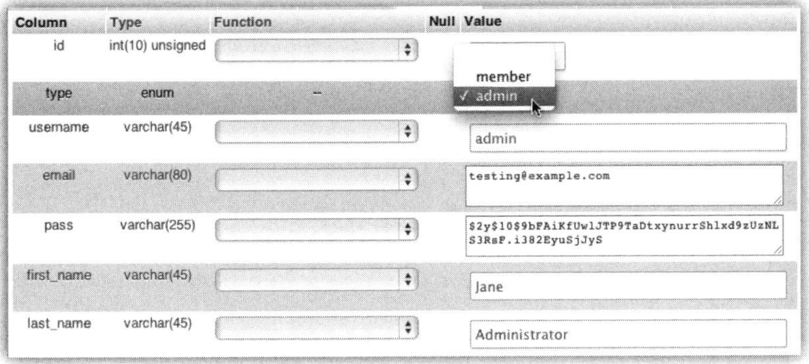


**Figure 5.2**

   **D.** Click Go.

# ADDING PAGES

As I've said (several times over by now), the site will have two kinds of content. The first kind will be HTML, but the site's not going to assume that the administrator knows how to create an HTML page. Instead, there will be an interface for doing so. The administrator will use a simple, single page that displays and handles an HTML form. To create the HTML content, a What You See Is What You Get (WYSIWYG) editor will be incorporated into the form (**Figure 5.3**).

Figure 5.3

## Creating the Basic Script

To start, you'll create the PHP script that displays and handles the form. Then you'll integrate the WYSIWYG editor in a separate series of steps.

1. Create a new PHP script in your text editor or IDE to be named **add_page.php** and stored in the web root directory.

2. Include the configuration file:

```
<?php
require('./includes/config.inc.php');
```

3. Redirect nonadministrators:

```
redirect_invalid_user('user_admin');
```

The **redirect_invalid_user()** function, defined in **config.inc.php** (in Chapter 4, "User Accounts"), will redirect invalid users to another page. That function's first argument is the session variable to check for. In this case, the session variable that identifies administrators is **user_admin**, because **$_SESSION['user_admin']** is set only if the user is an administrator.

4. Require the database connection:

```
require(MYSQL);
```

5. Include the header file:

```
$page_title = 'Add a Site Content Page';
include('./includes/header.html');
```

It's important that the redirection (in Step 3) take place before you include the header file.

6. Create an array for storing errors:

```
$add_page_errors = array();
```

Just like the registration, login, and password forms, this script will use one array for representing any problems with the user-supplied form data.

7. Validate the page title:

```
if (!empty($_POST['title'])) {
   $t = escape_data(strip_tags($_POST['title']), $dbc);
} else {
   $add_page_errors['title'] = 'Please enter the title!';
}
```

Simply by restricting access to this page to administrative users, you guarantee less risk of it being abused. For that reason, the validation routines don't need to be quite as strict as those on the public pages. For the page's title, you're confirming only that it isn't empty, as opposed to validating it using a regular expression. The **strip_tags()** function is still applied to the title, because no HTML should be there when the content is listed or displayed (as you'll see shortly).

**tip**

Validation of administrator-generated content doesn't need to be as strict as public content as long as there's restricted access to the admin pages.

8. Validate the category:

```
if (filter_var($_POST['category'], FILTER_VALIDATE_INT,
➥array('min_range' => 1))) {
  $cat = $_POST['category'];
} else { // No category selected.
   $add_page_errors['category'] = 'Please select a category!';
}
```

Each HTML page is in a single category. That association is made by attaching to each page record a foreign key to the proper value in the **categories** table. To confirm that the category value is an integer greater than, or equal to, 1, I'm again turning to PHP's Filter extension.

9. Validate the description:

```
if (!empty($_POST['description'])) {
   $d = escape_data(strip_tags($_POST['description']), $dbc);
} else {
   $add_page_errors['description'] = 'Please enter the
   ➥description!';
}
```

The description is being treated in the same manner as the title. I'm again stripping out any HTML or PHP tags.

For all these validation routines, failures result in messages being added to the errors array.

10. Validate the content:

```
if (!empty($_POST['content'])) {
   $allowed = '<div><p><span><br><a><img><h1><h2><h3><h4><ul>
   ➥<ol><li><blockquote>';
   $c = escape_data(strip_tags($_POST['content'], $allowed),
   ➥$dbc);
} else {
   $add_page_errors['content'] = 'Please enter the content!';
}
```

The content is the heart of the page and is expected to contain *some* HTML. However, you probably don't want to allow just *any* HTML. For example, allowing the script tag opens the door for cross-site scripting (XSS) attacks, and allowing the table tag lets the administrator potentially mess up the layout of the page. The **strip_tags()** function takes an optional second argument, which is a string of allowed tags. I've defined several allowed tags, but you might want to expand the list.

**11.** If there are no errors, add the record to the database:

```
if (empty($add_page_errors)) {
   $q = "INSERT INTO pages (categories_id, title, description,
   ➥content) VALUES ($cat, '$t', '$d', '$c')";
   $r = mysqli_query($dbc, $q);
   if (mysqli_affected_rows($dbc) === 1) {
      echo '<div class="alert alert-success"><h3>The page has
      ➥been added!</h3></div>';
```

Most of this should be fairly standard stuff for you. The last line, though, clears the **$_POST** array so that the already-inserted values aren't redisplayed in the sticky HTML form (**Figure 5.4**).

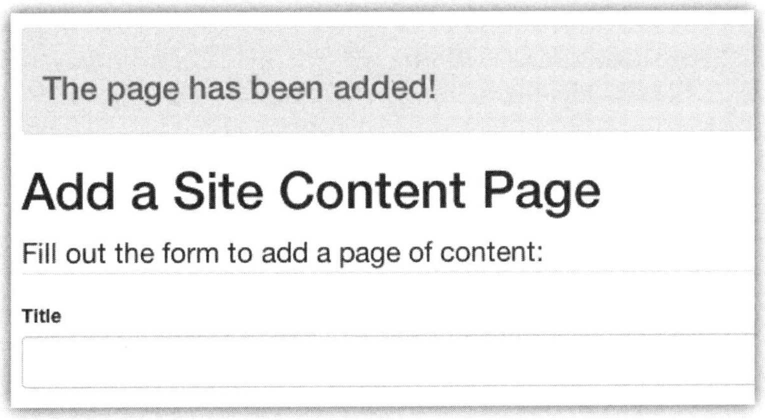

Figure 5.4

**12.** Trigger an error if the query failed:

```
      } else { // If it did not run OK.
         trigger_error('The page could not be added due to a
         ➥system error. We apologize for any inconvenience.');
      }
   } // End of $add_page_errors IF.
} // End of the main form submission conditional.
```

**13.** Include the **form_functions.inc.php** script:

```
require('includes/form_functions.inc.php');
?>
```

As with the public forms, this form and **add_pdf.php** will use the helper function defined in **form_functions.inc.php**.

**tip**

Depending on the experience of the site administrator, you may want to add better instructions to this page.

14. Begin the form:

```
<h1>Add a Site Content Page</h1>
<form action="add_page.php" method="post" accept-charset=
➥"utf-8">
<fieldset><legend>Fill out the form to add a page of content:
➥</legend>
<?php
create_form_input('title', 'text', 'Title', $add_page_errors);
```

The form contains one text input, one drop-down menu, and two textareas. The text input and textareas will be created using the `create_form_input()` function.

15. Add the category menu:

```
echo '<div class="form-group';
if (array_key_exists('category', $add_page_errors)) echo '
➥has-error';
echo '"><label for="category" class="control-label">Category
➥</label>
<select name="category" class="form-control">
<option>Select One</option>';
$q = "SELECT id, category FROM categories ORDER BY category
➥ASC";
$r = mysqli_query($dbc, $q);
while ($row = mysqli_fetch_array($r, MYSQLI_NUM)) {
   echo "<option value=\"$row[0]\"";
   if (isset($_POST['category']) && ($_POST['category'] ==
   ➥$row[0]) ) echo ' selected="selected"';
   echo ">$row[1]</option>\n";
}
echo '</select>';
if (array_key_exists('category', $add_page_errors)) echo
➥'<span class="help-block">' . $add_page_errors['category'] .
➥'</span>';
echo '</div>';
```

The `create_form_input()` function wasn't written to handle select menus. In part, this is because select menus are too different from inputs and textareas, and in part because there's only one select menu on the site. So this code has to replicate all that function's logic, including making the form sticky and displaying errors (**Figure 5.5**).

**tip**

For the query and query result, I prefer short variables names—`$q` and `$r`, accordingly—but you may want to use something more verbose, such as `$query` and `$result`.

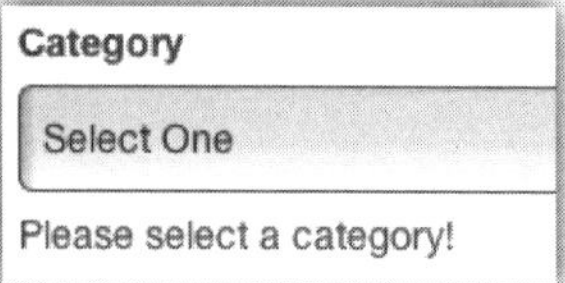


**Figure 5.5**

**16.** Complete the form:

```
create_form_input('description', 'textarea', 'Description',
➥$add_page_errors);
create_form_input('content', 'textarea', 'Content',
➥$add_page_errors);
?>
<input type="submit" name="submit_button" value="Add This Page"
➥id="submit_button" class="btn btn-default" />
</fieldset>
</form>
```

The two textareas are also generated by the **create_form_input()** function, although textareas will display their errors before the textarea box (**Figure 5.6**), not after, as with the text inputs.

Figure 5.6

**17.** Complete the page:

```
<?php include('./includes/footer.html'); ?>
```

**18.** Save the file and load it in your browser.

At this point, the form will look like that in Figure 5.3, except the content textarea will look like the description's textarea (because it will be lacking the WYSIWYG editor).

## Adding a WYSIWYG Editor

Web-based WYSIWYG editors are so common these days that you have many to choose from. To create a WYSIWYG editor, you install the editor code on your site, create a textarea in a form, and then indicate that the editor should be used for that textarea. The two most common WYSIWYG editors are probably CKEditor (formerly FCKEditor, although FCKEditor is still available; www.ckeditor.com) and TinyMCE (www.tinymce.com). I've used these in different projects, and they're more similar than not. Both are written in JavaScript, are open source, and have a slew of plug-ins for adding features such as spell check or fancy lists. The documentation for these projects is fair, and if you can follow the right syntax outlined there, you should have no trouble installing and customizing these tools.

**tip**

Free third-party file management plug-ins are available, but I haven't found them to be as good as the commercial ones.

For no particular reason, I choose to use TinyMCE for this project. I'll walk you through the steps for integrating TinyMCE here. But first, there's one thing you should know: A WYSIWYG editor can make it easy to create styled and formatted HTML, containing any valid tag, from lists to links to font-related elements. A WYSIWYG editor can also make it easy to add any kind of media, most commonly images and video. However, TinyMCE and CKEditor require a plug-in to manage file uploads, and in both cases, the plug-ins are created by the same companies and are commercial products. For this reason, I'm not integrating that functionality into this example. When the time comes that you need this functionality, just check out the corresponding documentation for the WYSIWYG editor of your choice.

1. Download the latest version of TinyMCE from www.tinymce.com.
2. Extract the files from the download.

**note**

There are two *tinymce* folders. You'll want to copy the innermost one to your site's JavaScript folder.

3. Copy the `tinymce` subfolder from the extracted files to your web directory's `js` folder.

   When you extract the files in Step 2, the result will be a folder called `tinymce`. Within it is a `js` folder. Within `js` is the `tinymce` folder that contains the files you need.

4. Open `add_page.php` in your text editor or IDE, if it isn't already open.

**tip**

Web pages will load more quickly if JavaScript is placed at the end of the document.

5. After the closing form tag, add

   ```
   <script type="text/javascript" src="js/tinymce/tinymce.min.js">
   ➥</script>
   ```

   The first thing you'll need to do is include the main `tinymce.min.js` file, which is what this line does.

6. On the next line, begin customizing TinyMCE:

   ```
   <script type="text/javascript">
   tinyMCE.init({
      selector : "#content",
      width : 800,
      height : 400,
      browser_spellcheck : true,
   ```

This JavaScript code will turn a textarea into a WYSIWYG editor. To do so, the **tinyMCE** class's **init()** function is called, sending it several name-value pairs. You can find these all detailed in the TinyMCE documentation, of course, but I'll highlight the most important.

The **selector** value, **#content**, indicates that the element with an **id** value of **content** should be converted. This matches the **id** value already given to the content textarea. The **width** and **height** properties change the size of the editor. Finally, the editor is told to use the browser's spell-check ability.

**tip**

You can't use the same **<SCRIPT>** tag to both include a separate JavaScript file and write inline JavaScript code.

7. Identify the plug-ins to use:

```
plugins: "paste,searchreplace,fullscreen,hr,link,anchor,image,
➥charmap,media,autoresize,autosave,contextmenu,wordcount",
```

TinyMCE has a slew of plug-ins. Here I'm choosing to enable 13 of them.

8. Customize the editor's buttons:

```
toolbar1: "cut,copy,paste,|,undo,redo,removeformat,|hr,|,
➥link,unlink,anchor,image,|,charmap,media,|,search,replace,|,
➥fullscreen",
toolbar2: "bold,italic,underline,strikethrough,|,alignleft,
➥aligncenter,alignright,alignjustify,|,formatselect,|,bullist,
➥numlist,|,outdent,indent,blockquote,",
```

Each line indicates a row of buttons to create in the editor (**Figure 5.7**). TinyMCE uses specific names to create specific buttons, most of which are obvious. Using the pipe character (|) creates separators within a line so that you may group related buttons.

**tip**

Match the allowed tags in the ***strip_tags()*** function to the buttons in the editor.

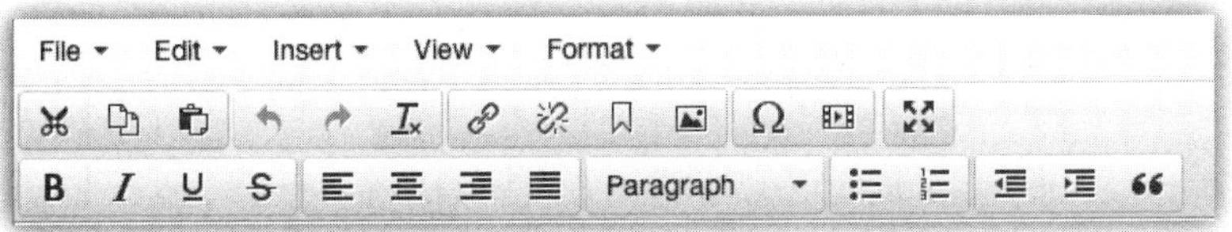


**Figure 5.7**

**tip**

By restricting what's possible in a WYSIWYG editor, you can keep administrators from making ugly, unruly content.

9. Complete the customization:

```
content_css : "css/bootstrap.min.css",
```

You can associate your site's CSS file with the editor so that content created within it will look the same as it will within a site page. That's what this line does. The reference to the CSS file can be absolute, or relative to the page that uses TinyMCE (not relative to the **TinyMCE** folder).

You'll need to change this value to match your setup. For example, if you've put your site in a subdirectory, you'll need to add that subdirectory to the path to the CSS script.

10. Complete the script block:

```
});
</script>
```

11. Save the file.

12. Reload the web page in your browser to see the result (see Figure 5.3).

    If the editor doesn't show, or it doesn't reflect your customizations, make sure you have refreshed the browser. If there's still a problem, the cause is probably a syntax error in your JavaScript. Check your error console to confirm this.

13. Create several pages of content.

    Or, if you'd rather, you can use the SQL commands from my website (www.LarryUllman.com/) to populate the database for you.

# DISPLAYING PAGE CONTENT

Now that you have several pages of pretend content in the database, it's time to create the scripts to display that content. There are two:

- **category.php** lists the specific pages under a category.
- **page.php** shows the actual content.

For marketing purposes, **category.php** will be available to any user. The **page.php** script will also be available to any user, but if the user is not logged in with a valid account, she'll only see the same description of the content that's displayed on the category page. Only current customers can see the full content.

## Creating category.php

The **category.php** script receives an ID value in the URL (from the links that appear in the sidebar, created by the header file). The script should validate the ID value, then select the category's information from the database. By doing so, the category's name can be used as the browser's title. Next, the script retrieves and lists all the pages that exist within that category (**Figure 5.8**).

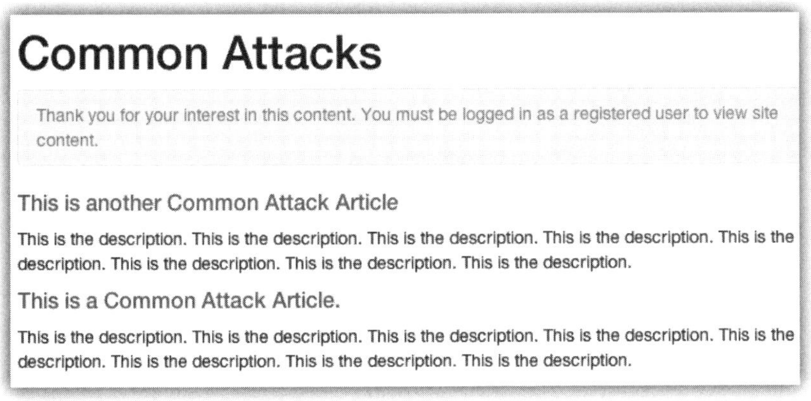

Common Attacks

Thank you for your interest in this content. You must be logged in as a registered user to view site content.

This is another Common Attack Article

This is the description. This is the description. This is the description. This is the description. This is the description. This is the description. This is the description. This is the description.

This is a Common Attack Article.

This is the description. This is the description. This is the description. This is the description. This is the description. This is the description. This is the description. This is the description.

Figure 5.8

1. Create a new PHP script in your text editor or IDE to be named **category.php** and stored in the web root directory.

2. Include the configuration file:

```
<?php
require('./includes/config.inc.php');
```

3. Require the database connection:

```
require(MYSQL);
```

4. Validate the category ID:

```
if (filter_var($_GET['id'], FILTER_VALIDATE_INT,
➥array('min_range' => 1))) {
   $cat_id= $_GET['id'];
```

The **filter_var()** function is being used to validate the category ID, the same as in the **add_page.php** script.

5. Get the category title:

```
$q = 'SELECT category FROM categories WHERE id=' . $cat_id;
$r = mysqli_query($dbc, $q);
```

This query serves two purposes. First, it confirms not only that the supplied ID value is a valid integer, but also that it corresponds to a value from the database. Second, it will retrieve the category's name to use as the browser's title and as a page heading (see Figure 5.8).

6. If one row was not returned, report the problem:

```
if (mysqli_num_rows($r) !== 1) {
   $page_title = 'Error!';
   include('./includes/header.html');
   echo '<div class="alert alert-danger">This page has been
   ➥accessed in error.</div>';
   include('./includes/footer.html');
   exit();
}
```

The results shown in Figure 5.9 will only be seen by users attempting things they shouldn't.

If the query doesn't return exactly one row, then an invalid category ID was provided. In that case, a default page title is created, the header is included, an error message is displayed, the footer is included, and the script is terminated. **Figure 5.9** shows the end result.

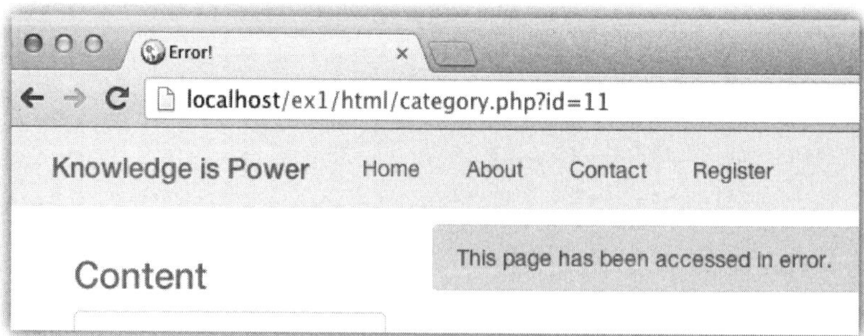


Figure 5.9

The `list()` function assigns parts of an array to individual variables.

7. Fetch the category title and use it as the page title:

```
list($page_title) = mysqli_fetch_array($r, MYSQLI_NUM);
include('./includes/header.html');
echo '<h1>' . htmlspecialchars($page_title) . '</h1>';
```

If the previous query did return one record, the selected column is fetched directly into the `$page_title` variable; then the header is included and a page header is displayed.

8. Print a message if the user doesn't have an active account:

```
if (isset($_SESSION['user_id']) && !isset($_SESSION['user_not_
➥expired'])) {
   echo '<div class="alert"><h4>Expired Account</h4>Thank you for
   ➥your interest in this content. Unfortunately your account has
   ➥expired. Please <a href="renew.php">renew your account</a> in
   ➥order to access site content.</div>';
} elseif (!isset($_SESSION['user_id'])) {
   echo '<div class="alert">Thank you for your interest in this
   ➥content. You must be logged in as a registered user to view
   ➥site content.</div>';
}
```

   Three types of users could be looking at this page: guests (people not logged in), logged-in users whose accounts have expired, and logged-in users whose accounts haven't expired. In the last case, no error messages need to be displayed.

   In the second case, `$_SESSION['user_id']` will be set, but `$_SESSION['user_not_expired']` won't be. This latter element would've been assigned a value of true if the user's account was still good when the user logged in. When that's the case, the user is told that he needs to renew his account.

   If the user isn't logged in at all, a message says that he needs to be registered and logged in to view the content.

9. Get the pages associated with this category:

```
$q = 'SELECT id, title, description FROM pages WHERE
➥categories_id=' . $cat_id. ' ORDER BY date_created DESC';
$r = mysqli_query($dbc, $q);
if (mysqli_num_rows($r) > 0) {
   while ($row = mysqli_fetch_array($r, MYSQLI_ASSOC)) {
      echo '<div><h4><a href="page.php?id=' . $row['id'] . '">' .
      ➥htmlspecialchars($row['title']) . '</a></h4><p>' .
      ➥htmlspecialchars($row['description']) . '</p></div>';
   } // End of WHILE loop.
```

   Each returned record will be displayed on the page as its own DIV. The page title will be put within H4 tags and linked to **page.php**, passing along the page ID in the URL. After the title, the page's description is added. The **htmlspecialchars()** function is used liberally to prevent XSS attacks.

**tip**

Because the PHP script finished using the results of the first query, it's safe to use the same **$q** and **$r** variables here.

**10.** Print a message if no pages are available:

```
} else { // No pages available.
   echo '<p>There are currently no pages of content associated
   ➥with this category. Please check back again!</p>';
}
```

On a live site, hopefully there won't be any categories in the database that don't have content. But, so as not to make any assumptions, if the **pages SELECT** query doesn't return any rows, a message will be shown to the user to check back again (**Figure 5.10**).

PHP Security

There are currently no pages of content associated with this category. Please check back again!

**Figure 5.10**

**11.** If no valid ID was received by the page, display an error:

```
} else {
   $page_title = 'Error!';
   include('./includes/header.html');
   echo '<div class="alert alert-danger">This page has been
   ➥accessed in error.</div>';
}
```

This is a replication of the code executed if the category **SELECT** doesn't return one record. This clause applies if no category ID was passed to this page, or if one was, but it wasn't an integer greater than or equal to 1.

**12.** Include the HTML footer and complete the page:

```
include('./includes/footer.html');
?>
```

**13.** Save and test the category script.

**tip**

The script as written doesn't paginate the page listings. If a category might have more than, say, 15 or 20 pages associated with it, you may want to add pagination, discussed in my *PHP and MySQL for Dynamic Web Sites: Visual QuickPro Guide* book.

## Creating page.php

Like **category.php**, the **page.php** script also receives an ID value in the URL (from the links in **category.php**). The script should validate the ID value, then select the page's information from the database. The page's title will be used as the browser's title and displayed as a page header. What comes next will depend on the person viewing the page:

- Logged-in users with current accounts will see the content (**Figure 5.11**).
- Logged-in users with expired accounts will see the content's description, along with a recommendation to renew their account.
- Guests will see the content's description, along with a recommendation to register (**Figure 5.12**).

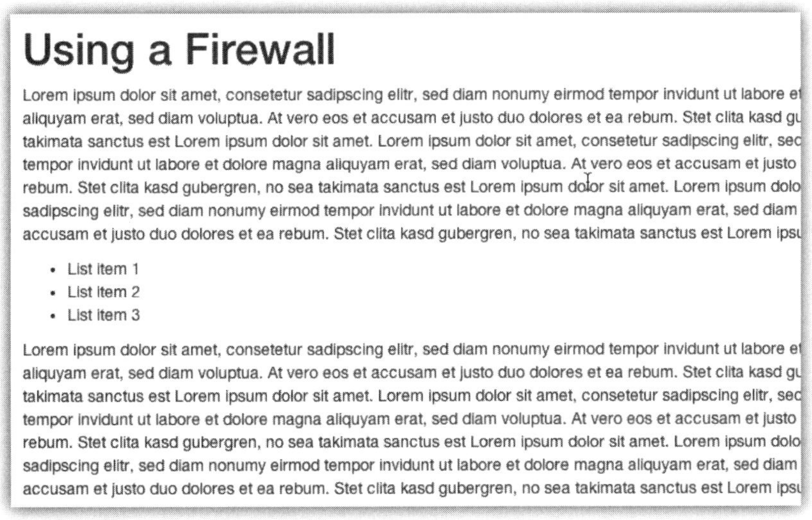

**Figure 5.11**

**Figure 5.12**

As you'd expect, much of this functionality will be like that in the **category.php** script.

1. Create a new PHP script in your text editor or IDE to be named **page.php** and stored in the web root directory.

2. Include the config file:

```
<?php
require('./includes/config.inc.php');
```

3. Require the database connection:

```
require(MYSQL);
```

4. Validate the page ID:

```
if (isset($_GET['id']) && filter_var($_GET['id'],
➥FILTER_VALIDATE_INT, array('min_range' => 1))) {
   $page_id = $_GET['id'];
```

This is the same validation used with the category ID.

5. Get the page info:

```
$q = 'SELECT title, description, content FROM pages WHERE
➥id=' . $page_id;
$r = mysqli_query($dbc, $q);
```

A simple query retrieves three fields from the **pages** table for one record.

6. If no rows were returned, print an error:

```
if (mysqli_num_rows($r) !== 1) {
   $page_title = 'Error!';
   include('./includes/header.html');
   echo '<div class="alert alert-danger">This page has been
   ➥accessed in error.</div>';
   include('./includes/footer.html');
   exit();
}
```

Again, as with **category.php**, if the supplied ID value is an integer but doesn't correlate to any database record, a complete page is created that indicates a problem (similar to Figure 5.9).

7. Fetch the page info:

```
$row = mysqli_fetch_array($r, MYSQLI_ASSOC);
$page_title = $row['title'];
include('includes/header.html');
echo '<h1>' . htmlspecialchars($page_title) . '</h1>';
```

The page's title will be used as the browser's title and as a header on the page.

8. Display the content if the user's account is current:

```
if (isset($_SESSION['user_not_expired'])) {
   echo "<div>{$row['content']}</div>";
} elseif (isset($_SESSION['user_id'])) {
   echo '<div class="alert"><h4>Expired Account</h4>Thank you for
   ➥your interest in this content, but your account is no longer
   ➥current. Please <a href="renew.php">renew your account</a> in
   ➥order to view this page in its entirety.</div>';
   echo '<div>' . htmlspecialchars($row['description']) .
   ➥'</div>';
} else {
   echo '<div class="alert">Thank you for your interest in this
   ➥content. You must be logged in as a registered user to view
   ➥this page in its entirety.</div>';
   echo '<div>' . htmlspecialchars($row['description']) .
   ➥'</div>';
}
```

This conditional dictates what is shown on the page, based on the user viewing it. Only logged-in users with current accounts—those who have a `$_SESSION['user_not_expired']` value—can see the content itself. The other user types see only the description, along with a message appropriate to the user's status.

9. Complete the ID conditional:

```
} else { // No valid ID.
   $page_title = 'Error!';
   include('includes/header.html');
   echo '<div class="alert alert-danger">This page has been
   ➥accessed in error.</div>';
} // End of primary IF.
```

If no integer ID value greater than or equal to 1 was received by this page, the user will see this error message.

**10.** Complete the page:

```
include('./includes/footer.html');
?>
```

**11.** Save and test the **page.php** script.

To test it, you'll need to click a link on **category.php**. You should also test it as three different user types—guest, expired member, and active member—to get the full effect.

# ADDING PDFS

The second administrative page for this example will handle uploading PDF files to the site. Although the administrator needs to provide only three pieces of information—a title, a description, and the PDF file itself—the process for handling the form is tricky, largely because I wanted to make the form *sticky*, like the others in the site. As you may know, the file form input can't be made sticky in the same way that a text input can, so I had to use some logic to fake the concept (**Figure 5.13**).

Add a PDF

Fill out the form to add a PDF to the site:

Title

JavaScript Cheat Sheet

Description

Please enter the description!

PDF

Choose File No file chosen

Currently: "About Stacks.pdf"

PDF only, 5MB Limit

**Figure 5.13**

Also, allowing users—even administrators—to upload files to your server is a potential security hole, so several techniques need to be applied to make this process as safe as possible. But first, the server needs to be set up to allow for file uploads.

## Setting Up the Server

Server permissions on files and directories comes down to *who* can do *what*. As for the *what*, the options are read, write, and execute. The *who* is either the specific server user or groups of users.

Before a PHP script can put files onto the server, there must be a folder on the server to which the PHP script can *write*, or alter the directory's contents. As PHP is run through the web server, the *who* is the web server user. So the goal is to create a folder that the web server user can write to.

How you go about doing this will depend on how your server is set up, the operating system in use, and how PHP is running with respect to the web server. At the end of the day, what this normally means is that you'll create a directory and give "everyone" permission to write to it. In Unix terms, this is represented by the number 755. Normally, your web host provides a control panel through which you can change a folder's permissions, or you may be able to do it through your FTP application (**Figure 5.14**).

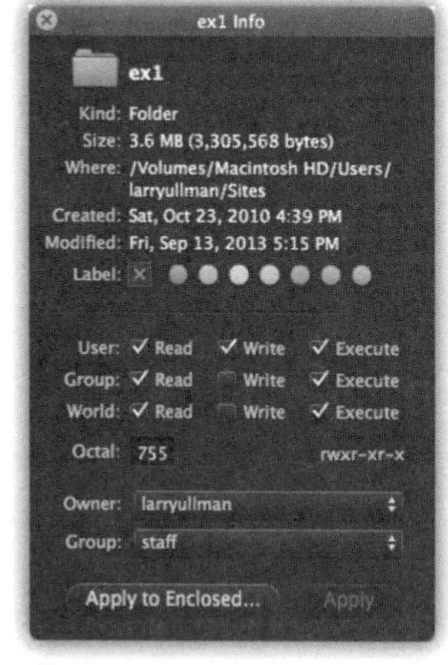

Figure 5.14

Although allowing everyone to do everything with a directory may sound extremely dangerous, it's not. What is meant by "everyone" is every user on the server. By "user" I mean a user account registered with the server. For example, there may be a `mysql` user that runs the database and the web server may run as the user **nobody**. With *open* permissions, both of these users, as well anyone with FTP or SSH access to the server, can read from, write to, or execute the files in the directory. That's not insignificant, but being available to everyone does not mean that anyone on the Internet can write files to that directory; a recognized server user is still required.

All that being said, it doesn't mean that you should be blasé about creating an open directory like this. If you're on a shared server, everyone with a user account on that server may be able to manipulate this directory—assuming they know it exists, of course, which is a big *if*. And if there's a security hole in a website, that vulnerability could be used to manipulate the directory—in this case, by users over the Internet—as the web server user would be the active agent.

There are many instances in which an open directory is necessary for the functioning of a site. The question becomes how to make the system as secure as possible. The answer is found by thinking like a hacker. If a hacker can't break into a server, the next goal will be to have the server execute some dangerous code for him. One way of doing so is trying to get PHP (or whatever) to open, require, or include—thereby executing—some dangerous code found on another server. I talk about this exploit in Chapter 2, "Security Fundamentals."

A second route is to get the dangerous code onto the server somehow and then execute it directly. That's a two-step process. Protecting against such an attempt is also, therefore, a two-step process:

1. Do everything you can to prevent dangerous code from being placed on the server.
2. Make it difficult, if not impossible, to directly execute dynamically added content.

 tip

Ways to use the web server to protect directories is discussed in Chapter 7, "Second Site: Structure and Design."

For the first step, it's largely a matter of validating uploaded content: making sure it's of an acceptable type. For the second step, the best solution is to store uploaded content in a directory outside the web root directory. In such a case, if bad person Bob (on the Internet, not on your server) can trick your system into uploading some dangerous script, he still could not execute that script, since there would be no way to invoke it if it's not in the web root directory.

If that's not possible (for example, some shared hosts don't allow you to put content above the web directory), you should create a nonobvious folder within the web directory. This folder will still require the open permissions, but you should password-protect the directory so that it's only available (over HTTP) to authorized users. You can do this using your web host's control panel.

 tip

In Chapter 3, "First Site: Structure and Design," I talk about the server's organization and where the **pdfs** directory should ideally go.

Once you've created the **pdfs** directory with open permissions and protected it appropriately if you had to place it in the web root directory, you can create the PHP script that will upload a PDF file to that folder. But first, I recommend creating another constant in the configuration file that's an absolute path to this folder:

```
// In config.inc.php:
define ('PDFS_DIR', BASE_URI . 'pdfs/');
```

Change the value of the constant to be correct for the location of your **pdfs** destination directory.

## Creating the PHP Script

This PHP script has the same basic structure as all the other scripts with forms: The form is first displayed; the data is validated after the user submits the form; and the form is displayed again with its current values indicated should there be any errors. But this particular process will be trickier than the other form-handling scripts in that it's also dealing with an uploaded file. The file input can't be made sticky, and more important, the actual file on the server must be addressed when the form is being redisplayed because of other errors. I'll explain all the corresponding logic in the following steps.

1. Create a new PHP script in your text editor or IDE to be named **add_pdf.php** and stored in the web root directory.

2. Include the configuration file:

```
<?php
require('./includes/config.inc.php');
```

3. Redirect nonadministrators:

```
redirect_invalid_user('user_admin');
```

4. Require the database connection:

```
require(MYSQL);
```

5. Include the header file:

```
$page_title = 'Add a PDF';
include('./includes/header.html');
```

6. Create an array for storing errors:

```
$add_pdf_errors = array();
```

7. If the form was submitted, validate the title and description:

```
if ($_SERVER['REQUEST_METHOD'] === 'POST') {
  if (!empty($_POST['title'])) {
    $t = escape_data(strip_tags($_POST['title']), $dbc);
  } else {
    $add_pdf_errors['title'] = 'Please enter the title!';
  }
  if (!empty($_POST['description'])) {
    $d = escape_data(strip_tags($_POST['description']), $dbc);
  } else {
    $add_pdf_errors['description'] = 'Please enter the
    ➥description!';
  }
```

The validation routines just check for any value for both of these inputs. If they're not empty, the values are run through the **strip_tags()** function and then the custom escaping function. If either value is empty, an error message is added to the array.

8. Check for a PDF:

```
if (is_uploaded_file($_FILES['pdf']['tmp_name']) &&
➥($_FILES['pdf']['error'] === UPLOAD_ERR_OK)) {
   $file = $_FILES['pdf'];
```

The first time the form is submitted, there should be data in the special **$_FILES** array, thanks to the file input whose name is *pdf*. This conditional checks that there's an uploaded file and that no error exists (because you can have an uploaded file but also an error). If both conditions are true, the **$file** variable is turned into a shorthand version of **$_FILES['pdf']**, for later use.

**tip**

As written, only one error will be associated with the file input, so if the uploaded file is both too large and not a PDF, the user will see only the second error.

9. Validate the file information:

```
$size = ROUND($file['size']/1024);
if ($size > 5120) {
   $add_pdf_errors['pdf'] = 'The uploaded file was too large.';
}
```

First, the file's size is calculated in kilobytes. This value will first be used to make sure the file isn't too large. On the public side, this value will be displayed to the end user, indicating how big the PDF is (a nice feature). If the file is larger than 5 megabytes (or 5120 kilobytes), an error message is created. Since the **MAX_FILE_SIZE** hidden form input is a recommendation that's easy to circumvent, it's best to check the file's size using PHP, too.

10. Validate the file's type:

```
$fileinfo = finfo_open(FILEINFO_MIME_TYPE);
if (finfo_file($fileinfo, $file['tmp_name']) !==
➥'application/pdf') {
   $add_pdf_errors['pdf'] = 'The uploaded file was not a PDF.';
}
finfo_close($fileinfo);
```

Next, the file's type is validated. The most secure way of doing so is to use PHP's Fileinfo extension, added in PHP 5.3. See the PHP manual for details if this code is entirely unfamiliar to you.

11. If there were no errors, create the file's new name and destination:

```
if (!array_key_exists('pdf', $add_pdf_errors)) {
   $tmp_name = sha1($file['name']) . uniqid('',true);
   $dest =  PDFS_DIR . $tmp_name . '_tmp';
```

For security purposes, the uploaded file should be renamed to something random and unpredictable. To do so, the **sha1()** function will create a 40-character hash from the file's name. Appended to this will be a unique identifier. The result will be a unique, somewhat random string that's exactly 63 characters long.

The destination value is the absolute path to where the file will be stored on the server—its final resting place, including the file's new name. The **PDFS_DIR** constant added to **config.inc.php** earlier in the chapter is used for part of that destination. At this point, I'm also adding **_tmp** to the file's name to indicate that the file is on the server but not associated with a database record as of yet.

tip

Renaming uploaded files is generally recommended so that hackers won't know what an uploaded file is called on the server.

**12.** Move the file:

```
if (move_uploaded_file($file['tmp_name'], $dest)) {

   // Store the data in the session for later use:
   $_SESSION['pdf']['tmp_name'] = $tmp_name;
   $_SESSION['pdf']['size'] = $size;
   $_SESSION['pdf']['file_name'] = $file['name'];

   // Print a message:
   echo '<div class="alert alert-success"><h3>The file has been
   ➥uploaded!</h3></div>';

} else {
   trigger_error('The file could not be moved.');
   unlink ($file['tmp_name']);
}
```

The **move_uploaded_file()** function will transfer only files uploaded via HTTP POST, so it can't be manipulated to move other files around on the server. Its first argument is the file to move, which is represented by the file's temporary name (something like **/tmp/php4902**). The second argument is the file's destination, which includes both the directory and filename.

Next, three pieces of information about the file are stored in the session for later reference. This includes the file's new name (without the additional **_tmp**), its size, and its original name. Then a message is displayed indicating that the file has been handled.

If the file could not be moved, an error message is triggered and the uploaded file is removed (so it's not cluttering up the temporary directory).

**13.** If there was no uploaded file, look for an error:

```
    } // End of array_key_exists() IF.
} elseif (!isset($_SESSION['pdf'])) {
    switch ($_FILES['pdf']['error']) {
        case 1:
        case 2:
            $add_pdf_errors['pdf'] = 'The uploaded file was too
            ➥large.';
            break;
        case 3:
            $add_pdf_errors['pdf'] = 'The file was only partially
            ➥uploaded.';
            break;
        case 6:
        case 7:
        case 8:
            $add_pdf_errors['pdf'] = 'The file could not be uploaded
            ➥due to a system error.';
            break;
        case 4:
        default:
            $add_pdf_errors['pdf'] = 'No file was uploaded.';
            break;
    } // End of SWITCH.
} // End of $_FILES IF-ELSEIF-ELSE.
```

The PHP manual lists all the file upload-related error codes. This script shouldn't be too descriptive in its error reporting to the user, so each code is turned into a more generic message. As some codes, such as 1 and 2 or 6, 7, and 8, have the same net meaning, I'm using a *fall-through* in the **switch**, where multiple cases have the same effect.

**tip**

There is no error code 5 (that's not a typo in the book).

**14.** Add the PDF to the database:

```
if (empty($add_pdf_errors)) {
    $fn = escape_data($_SESSION['pdf']['file_name'], $dbc);
    $tmp_name = escape_data($_SESSION['pdf']['tmp_name'], $dbc);
    $size = (int) $_SESSION['pdf']['size'];
    $q = "INSERT INTO pdfs (title, description, tmp_name, file_
    ➥name, size) VALUES ('$t', '$d', '$tmp_name', '$fn', $size)";
    $r = mysqli_query($dbc, $q);
```

If there were no errors, the next step is to insert the PDF data into the database. To do so, the three pieces of information about the file, already stored in the session, are made safe to use in the query (the title and description were already run through `mysqli_real_escape_string()` by this point).

**15.** If the query worked, rename the file:

```
if (mysqli_affected_rows($dbc) === 1) {
   $original = PDFS_DIR . $tmp_name . '_tmp';
   $dest = PDFS_DIR . $tmp_name;
   rename($original, $dest);
```

To make the upload permanent, the file will have the `_tmp` removed from its name.

**16.** Indicate the success to the user and clear the values:

```
echo '<div class="alert alert-success"><h3>The PDF has been
➥added!</h3></div>';
$_POST = array();
$_FILES = array();
unset($file, $_SESSION['pdf']);
```

All these values need to be cleared so that the form doesn't display any existing values.

**17.** If there was a problem with the query, trigger an error:

```
} else { // If it did not run OK.
   trigger_error('The PDF could not be added due to a system
   ➥error. We apologize for any inconvenience.');
   unlink ($dest);
}
```

There shouldn't be a database query error on a live, tested site, but just in case, an error will be triggered and the file will be deleted (so that there's no file on the server without a corresponding database reference).

**18.** Complete the processing part of the script:

```
} else {
   unset($_SESSION['pdf']);
} // End of the submission IF.
```

The **else** clause applies if this is a GET request. In that case, the script should clear any potential value that might be in `$_SESSION['pdf']`. This is only necessary in cases where the administrator uploaded a file but had other errors, then clicked the Add PDF link again.

19. Begin the form:

```
require('includes/form_functions.inc.php');
?><h1>Add a PDF</h1>
<form enctype="multipart/form-data" action="add_pdf.php"
➥method="post" accept-charset="utf-8">
<input type="hidden" name="MAX_FILE_SIZE" value="5242880">
<fieldset><legend>Fill out the form to add a PDF to the site:
➥</legend>
```

This form will use the same **create_form_input()** function for the title and the description. The form must use the **enctype** property and the POST method in order to handle the file data. The **MAX_FILE_SIZE** value is a suggestion to the browser and may or may not be ignored.

20. Create the first two elements:

```
<?php
create_form_input('title', 'text', 'Title', $add_pdf_errors);
create_form_input('description', 'textarea', 'Description',
➥$add_pdf_errors);
```

21. Start creating the file input:

```
echo '<div class="form-group';
```

There's no file input generation in the **create_form_input()** function because there's only one file input in the entire site (and because file inputs are quite different than text, password, email, or textareas). Because a fair amount of PHP logic will be required to properly handle the file input, the initial DIV is begun by a PHP **echo** statement. The statement doesn't close the DIV element yet so that a **has-error** or other class may be added (in the next step).

22. Check for an error or successful upload:

```
if (array_key_exists('pdf', $add_pdf_errors)) {
   echo ' has-error';
} else if (isset($_SESSION['pdf'])) {
   echo ' has-success';
}
```

If there was an error, the **has-error** class is added to the surrounding DIV—to highlight it in red. If there was no error, then the input is closed.

If there was no error but the PDF information has been stored in the session, that means the file was successfully uploaded but the form wasn't otherwise filled out completely. In that case, a different class is added to the DIV to highlight the file input in green.

23. Add the file input:

```
echo '"><label for="pdf" class="control-label">PDF</label>
➥<input type="file" name="pdf" id="pdf">';
```

24. Check for an error to be displayed:

```
if (array_key_exists('pdf', $add_pdf_errors)) {
   echo '<span class="help-block">' . $add_pdf_errors['pdf'] .
'</span>';
```

This code adds the error message after the file input.

25. If the file already exists, indicate that to the user:

```
} else { // No error.
   if (isset($_SESSION['pdf'])) {
      echo '<p class="lead">Currently: "' . $_SESSION['pdf']
      ➥['file_name'] . '"</p>';
   }
} // end of errors IF-ELSE.
```

This **else** clause applies if there was no error with this input. That would be the case if the form was loaded for the first time or if it has been submitted but there were errors with the other form elements. In this latter case, a file has been uploaded already and the form should indicate the existence of that file to the user (see Figure 5.13).

tip

If the user sees the form again because of an error and then completes the form while submitting a new PDF, the new PDF file will be used in place of the old.

26. Complete the file input DIV:

```
echo '<span class="help-block">PDF only, 5MB Limit</span>
</div>';
?>
```

27. Complete the form and the page:

```
<input type="submit" name="submit_button" value="Add This PDF"
➥id="submit_button" class="btn btn-default" />
</fieldset>
</form>
<?php include('./includes/footer.html'); ?>
```

28. Save the script and test the PDF upload process.

**note**

Through incomplete use of this script, it's possible to end up with extraneous files on the server, but their names will end with `_tmp` and can be deleted manually.

**Figure 5.15** shows the result of successfully adding a new PDF.

The file has been uploaded!

The PDF has been added!

Add a PDF

Fill out the form to add a PDF to the site:

Figure 5.15

# DISPLAYING PDF CONTENT

Just as with the HTML content, displaying the PDF content on the site requires two scripts. The first, **`pdfs.php`**, just lists every PDF in the catalog, along with a link to view the PDF itself. The second, **`view_pdf.php`**, retrieves and displays a specific PDF, but only after validating the user.

## Creating pdfs.php

The **`pdfs.php`** page works much like **`category.php`**, except that it does not receive an ID value in the URL. It just displays every PDF (**Figure 5.16**).

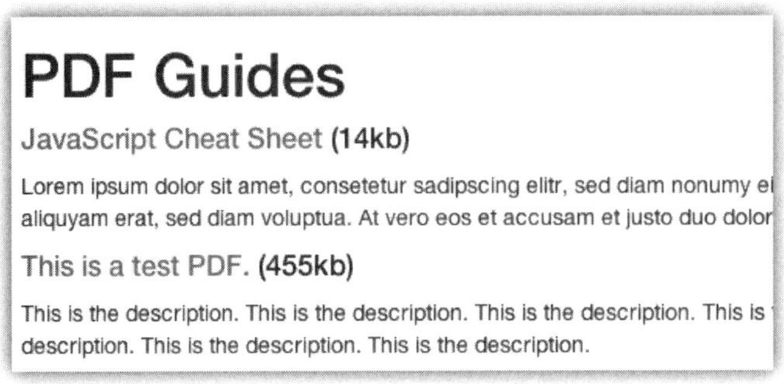

PDF Guides

JavaScript Cheat Sheet (14kb)

Lorem ipsum dolor sit amet, consetetur sadipscing elitr, sed diam nonumy e
aliquyam erat, sed diam voluptua. At vero eos et accusam et justo duo dolor

This is a test PDF. (455kb)

This is the description. This is the description. This is the description. This is
description. This is the description. This is the description.

Figure 5.16

1. Create a new PHP script in your text editor or IDE to be named **pdfs.php** and stored in the web root directory.

2. Include the configuration file:

```
<?php
require('./includes/config.inc.php');
```

3. Require the database connection:

```
require(MYSQL);
```

4. Include the header file and display a page header:

```
$page_title = 'PDFs';
include('./includes/header.html');
echo '<h1>PDF Guides</h1>';
```

5. Print a message if the user isn't active:

```
if (isset($_SESSION['user_id']) && !isset($_SESSION['user_not_
➥expired'])) {
   echo '<div class="alert"><h4>Expired Account</h4>Thank you for
   ➥your interest in this content, but your account is no longer
   ➥current. Please <a href="renew.php">renew your account</a> in
   ➥order to view any of the PDFs listed below.</div>';
} elseif (!isset($_SESSION['user_id'])) {
   echo '<div class="alert">Thank you for your interest in this
   ➥content. You must be logged in as a registered user to view
   ➥any of the PDFs listed below.</div>';
}
```

The messages differ slightly from those in **category.php**, but the checks on the user's status are the same.

6. Get the PDFs:

```
$q = 'SELECT tmp_name, title, description, size FROM pdfs
➥ORDER BY date_created DESC';
$r = mysqli_query($dbc, $q);
if (mysqli_num_rows($r) > 0) {
```

The query returns the temporary name, title, and description for each PDF in the database, in order from newest to oldest.

7. Fetch and display every PDF:

```
while ($row = mysqli_fetch_array($r, MYSQLI_ASSOC)) {
    echo '<div><h4><a href="view_pdf.php?id=' .
    ➥htmlspecialchars($row['tmp_name']) . '">' .
    ➥htmlspecialchars($row['title']) . ' </a>
    ➥(' . $row['size'] . 'kb)</h4><p>' .
    ➥htmlspecialchars($row['description']) . '</p></div>';
}
```

Each record is displayed as its own DIV, with the title as a linked H4, followed by the size of the file. The file's description comes next. Each link points to **view_pdf.php**, passing along the temporary name—the 63-character hash—in the URL.

8. Complete the page:

```
} else { // No PDFs!
    echo '<div class="alert alert-danger">There are currently no
    ➥PDFs available to view. Please check back again!</div>';
}
include('./includes/footer.html');
?>
```

This message will be shown if there are no PDFs in the database, which will hopefully never be the case.

9. Save the script and test **pdfs.php** in your web browser.

You obviously can't test any of the links until you create **view_pdf.php** first.

## Creating view_pdf.php

The user arrives at this final script after clicking a link in **pdfs.php**. This page's sole purpose is to display the PDF to the user, provided that the user's account is active.

1. Create a new PHP script in your text editor or IDE to be named **view_pdf.php** and stored in the web root directory.

2. Include the configuration file and the database connection:

```
<?php
require('./includes/config.inc.php');
require(MYSQL);
```

3. Create a flag variable:

```
$valid = false;
```

This script will have many tests before getting to the point of displaying the PDF, so it will start by assuming that something's wrong.

4. Validate the PDF ID:

```
if (isset($_GET['id']) && (strlen($_GET['id']) === 63) &&
➥(substr($_GET['id'], 0, 1) !== '.') ) {
  $file = PDFS_DIR . $_GET['id'];
  if (file_exists ($file) && (is_file($file)) ) {
```

The PDF identifier should come into this script through the URL. The ID won't be an integer, but it must be exactly 63 characters long, making that quality a good first thing to look at.

Next, a common way to hack a system such as this would be for the malicious user to submit `../path/to/something/useful` as the value, where the `..` moves up a directory. The intention would be to have the PHP script grab and display a sensitive document, such as a server password file. To prevent that from happening, the third part of the conditional checks that the first character isn't a period.

**tip**

As an extra security measure, you could again use the Fileinfo extension to confirm that the file is a PDF.

If all three conditions are true, then an absolute path to the file is defined. Next, the file is tested to confirm that it exists and is a file (as opposed to a directory).

5. Get the PDF information from the database:

```
$q = 'SELECT id, title, description, file_name FROM pdfs WHERE
➥tmp_name="' . escape_data($_GET['id'], $dbc) . '"';
$r = mysqli_query($dbc, $q);
if (mysqli_num_rows($r) === 1) {
  $row = mysqli_fetch_array($r, MYSQLI_ASSOC);
  $valid = true;
```

The query fetches the PDF's title, description, and original filename. The first two pieces of information will be used if the current viewer doesn't have permission to see the PDF itself.

If one row was returned, the data is retrieved and the **`$valid`** variable is changed to **`true`**.

6. Only display the PDF to a user whose account is active:

```
if (isset($_SESSION['user_not_expired'])) {
   header('Content-type:application/pdf');
   header('Content-Disposition:inline;filename="' .
   ➥$row['file_name'] . '"');
   $fs = filesize($file);
   header("Content-Length:$fs\n");
   readfile ($file);
   exit();
```

**note**

Different browsers will use the filename disposition differently.

If the user's account is active, the PDF should be loaded in the browser. To do that in PHP, start by sending a header indicating the content type. Then indicate the content's disposition—*inline*, meaning show the file in the browser—and what its filename is. For the file's name, the original filename is provided. Next, the size of the file is indicated, using the actual file's size, not the database-stored approximation. Finally, the **readfile()** function reads in all the binary data and sends it to the browser. The script is then terminated.

7. For inactive users, show the content's description:

```
} else { // Inactive account!
   $page_title = $row['title'];
   include('./includes/header.html');
   echo "<h1>$page_title</h1>";
   if (isset($_SESSION['user_id'])) {
      echo '<div class="alert"><h4>Expired Account</h4>Thank
      ➥you for your interest in this content, but your account
      ➥is no longer current. Please <a href="renew.php">renew your
      ➥account</a> in order to access this file.</div>';
   } else { // Not logged in.
      echo '<div class="alert">Thank you for your interest in
      ➥this content. You must be logged in as a registered user
      ➥to access this file.</div>';
   }
   echo '<div>' . htmlspecialchars($row['description']) .
   ➥'</div>';
   include('./includes/footer.html');
} // End of user IF-ELSE.
```

If the user is logged in but inactive (that is, the user's account has expired), she'll be asked to renew her account (**Figure 5.17**). If the user isn't logged in, she'll be asked to log in (**Figure 5.18**).

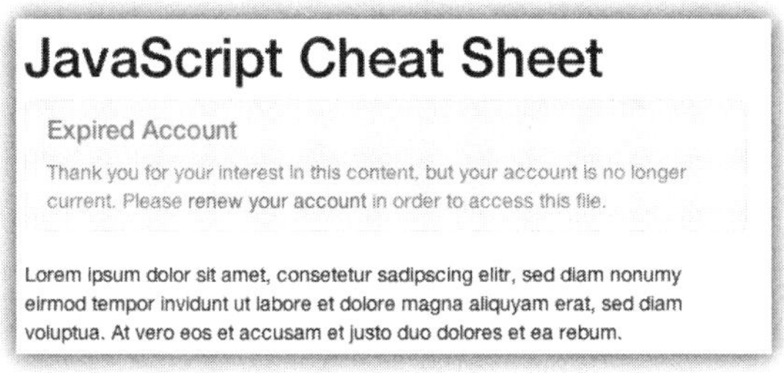

**Figure 5.17**

**Figure 5.18**

**8.** Complete the conditionals:

```
        } // End of mysqli_num_rows() IF.
    } // End of file_exists() IF.
} // End of $_GET['id'] IF.
```

**9.** Indicate a problem and complete the page:

```
if (!$valid) {
    $page_title = 'Error!';
    include('./includes/header.html');
    echo '<div class="alert alert-danger">This page has been
    ➥accessed in error.</div>';
    include('./includes/footer.html');
}
?>
```

If the page didn't receive an ID value corresponding to a database record and an actual file on the server, the user will see an error message like that in Figure 5.9.

**10.** Save the file and test it by clicking a link on **pdfs.php**.

Now the site has the ability for the administrator to create new content, in both HTML and PDF format. And users (which is to say, customers) can view that content. In order to turn as many visitors as possible into paying customers, all of the content is available in a preview format—title and description, with ample opportunities to register or renew accounts.

# 6 USING PAYPAL

The final yet most important step in the "Knowledge Is Power" site is to integrate PayPal so that the site may actually make money. Using PayPal isn't necessarily that hard, but it's such a critical step that I want to give it extra attention. And, as with many technologies, wading through all the documentation and possible uses can be the biggest challenge.

In this chapter, you'll learn about the current state of PayPal and what payment options PayPal offers. The next step is to begin using PayPal for testing purposes. After that, you can complete the PHP scripts required by the site and completely test the end result. Once you're satisfied that everything is working properly with your test accounts, you'll repeat some of these steps for a live PayPal account and quickly update a couple of pages, and then you've completed your e-commerce site!

## ABOUT PAYPAL

PayPal is probably the biggest payment solution provider around, and there are some good reasons to consider using it with your e-commerce sites. From a development standpoint, choosing PayPal has its benefits, such as freeing you from the hardships of PCI compliance. From the customer's point of view, PayPal is a trusted name, which makes a big difference in a user's willingness to part with his money.

One frequent misconception about PayPal is that customers must also have a PayPal account. If a customer *does* have a PayPal account, she can make a payment using it. But both PayPal users and non-PayPal users can also pay with their credit cards through PayPal's system. A second misconception is that PayPal transactions always require that the customer leave your site and go to the PayPal site. This used to be the case, but PayPal has three primary payment solutions now, two of which allow you to handle customer transactions without the user leaving your site at all.

**tip**

PayPal has tons of documentation and videos explaining the various programs, features, and fees. Almost too much, really....

PayPal offers

- No setup fees
- No monthly costs for the basic payment option
- Fraud protections
- Shipping calculators and shipping label service
- Tax calculators
- Availability in 190 countries and with 24 currencies
- Currency conversions
- International tax and shipping calculators
- Ability to send invoices
- Inventory management
- A virtual terminal to manually process transactions
- Integration with popular third-party e-commerce systems, such as FoxyCart, Magento Go, and Zen Cart

**note**

All the information about PayPal in this chapter is current as of this writing and is virtually guaranteed to change over time.

What PayPal doesn't do, however, is transfer money directly into your bank account. The funds received from transactions get applied to *your PayPal account*. You can then go into your PayPal account and transfer money to your registered bank account. A couple of days later, you'll have your money.

**tip**

PayPal's "Log In with PayPal" feature makes it possible to let users log in to your site using their PayPal account.

At the PayPal website, you can also view monthly reports, search through your transaction history, and even allow different types of users to access the PayPal account (for example, a low-level user may only be allowed to print shipping labels without seeing any payment details).

There are, of course, arguments *against* using PayPal. First, PayPal can be much trickier to implement than the alternatives. This is due, in no small part, to PayPal's documentation: overwhelming in quantity and frequently inconsistent. Second, PayPal has a reputation for freezing accounts and taking other poorly communicated actions, although I've not personally witnessed these behaviors. Third—and this may not be an issue for you—PayPal has several financial limits, such as a $10,000 per charge cap. Still, many users prefer PayPal, and e-commerce is, at heart, all about making users happy.

### PAYPAL IN 2013

As of this writing, in the fourth quarter of 2013, PayPal is in the process of undergoing several significant changes. First, PayPal historically created payment buttons as part of forms that you'd embed in your site. Those forms would be submitted to the PayPal site. This can be called the "classic" PayPal approach. While I was writing this chapter, PayPal was developing an alternative solution that instead uses JavaScript to create the PayPal button. Try as I could to explain this new approach in this chapter, I found it to be too buggy and poorly documented to recommend, particularly when the classic approach is still available and works fine. If, in the time after the book is published, PayPal gets its JavaScript solution to a viable point, I'll explain how to use it on my blog (www.LarryUllman.com).

The second most significant change is in PayPal's Developer site, which is crucial to the testing process. As of this writing, the PayPal Developer site is in beta, and it's an ugly beta. I'm referencing and explaining it in this chapter to the best of my ability, and to reflect its current state, but it's extremely buggy. I can only hope that it's fixed and more usable by the time you read this.

Third, while I was writing this book, PayPal purchased another major payments provider, Braintree Payments. It is unclear how this acquisition will affect PayPal (or Braintree), but the initial statements from the company suggest that the two will be left as autonomous as possible.

Regardless of what changes occur between the time I'm writing this and when you're reading it, you can always refer to the PayPal documentation to find the latest information. If you have trouble with the documentation, or have any other problems, you can always contact me through my support forums (www.LarryUllman.com/forums/).

## Payment Solutions

PayPal offers three base payment solutions, named *PayPal Payments Standard*, *PayPal Payments Advanced*, and *PayPal Payments Pro*. Each solution allows you to accept payment from PayPal users or via credit cards. Each also allows you to use a shopping cart, whether a custom one of your own devising or a third-party system.

There's no guarantee a user will immediately return to your site after completing the PayPal process.

The Standard option is what people historically think of as PayPal: The customer starts off on your site and then heads to the PayPal site to complete the transaction, after which she can return to your site. There's no monthly fee for this option, and it's pretty easy to set up: You just need your own PayPal account. Although you can customize the PayPal experience to some degree, it will be clear to the customer that she's no longer on your site, and the charge on the customer's credit card statement will use a combination of PayPal and your business's name.

The Pro payment solution is like other, non-PayPal payment gateways in that the customer doesn't need to leave your site to complete the transaction (that is, to pay you). The Pro system is $30 per month and you have to complete a credit application to qualify (you'll need your own PayPal account as well, of course). The Pro system will also let you customize the fraud protection, but stricter PCI compliance will be required on your part.

**note**

All prices in this chapter and book are in United States dollars.

The Advanced option falls somewhere between the Standard and Pro payment solutions. The customer doesn't leave your website, but you also won't have complete control over the look of the checkout page. It has a monthly cost of $5.

The transaction fees, regardless of the solution type, are 30 cents per transaction. You'll also pay a percentage of the transaction total, depending upon how much business you do per month (**Table 6.1**). International transactions have varying rates as well (for example, when your customer is in another country).

**tip**

If your transactions normally average less than $10 each, you can save money by using PayPal's *micropayments* rates.

### Table 6.1 PayPal Fees

| Monthly Sales | Per-Transaction Fee |
|---|---|
| $0 to $3,000 | 2.9% + $0.30 |
| $3,000.01 to $10,000 | 2.5% + $0.30 |
| $10,000.01 to $100,000 | 2.2% + $0.30 |
| Over $100,000 | Call PayPal to see |

In this chapter, you'll use the PayPal Payments Standard solution. You can assume that most of what I say and do throughout the rest of this chapter applies only to it. The next e-commerce site, *Coffee* (which you'll begin developing in Chapter 7, "Second Site: Structure and Design"), will use another payment gateway. That process and code is comparable to using the PayPal Payments Pro solution. In Chapter 15, "Using Stripe Payments," you'll see how to use a newer type of payment approach, which is incomparable to PayPal's current options (although it is comparable to Braintree Payments).

**note**

Currency conversions and payments from other countries have extra fees.

## Payment Buttons

The PayPal Payments Standard system relies on using PayPal's tools to generate HTML code specific for your e-commerce situation. By filling out a form and answering a few questions, PayPal will create some HTML that you can drop into the right spot on your website. The code itself creates an HTML button that, when clicked, takes the user to PayPal.

 **tip**

Buttons you've created can be customized later—for example, to change the price charged for an item.

There are different types of default buttons for different situations:

- *Buy Now*, for selling single items
- *Add to Cart*, for selling multiple items
- *Subscribe*, for selling subscriptions
- *Donate*, for accepting donations

You've no doubt seen examples of these buttons many times over (**Figure 6.1**). The Buy Now and Add to Cart buttons also let you set different attributes for products and adjust the price based on the selected attributes. For example, if you sell software through your site, the customer might be allowed to select the number or type of licenses to purchase.

**Figure 6.1**

 **tip**

You could create a script that emails any user whose account is about to expire within the next week. Then execute the script once or twice a week.

You can start with one of these default buttons, customize it to your situation, and even use a different image for the button itself. As a security feature, the button only passes identifiers—an indicator of your account and a button ID—to the PayPal website. All the particulars, such as the price to be charged, are stored within PayPal's system, meaning that a hacker can't manipulate those values. For this project, you'll use the subscribe option, because the site is selling subscriptions to its content.

 **tip**

Users can see what automatic billings they have agreed to in the *My preapproved payments* area, under the *My money* section of their PayPal Profile page.

Once the user subscribes via PayPal, she'll automatically be billed again when the time period you establish is up. From a business perspective, a recurring payment is great, because you continue to get your money until the customer cancels the recurring payment. You should indicate this to the user, though, and perhaps let the user know when her account is about to expire and that she'll be billed again prior to that occurring (or else you'll have to be prepared to process some refunds).

# TESTING PAYPAL

As part of the process of testing a new website, you most certainly want to test the payment-handling system. PayPal, like most payment solutions, offers a playground environment that can pretend to handle transactions without any real money changing hands.

There are three primary PayPal sites you'll use for testing purposes (see the accompanying sidebar). The entire testing process goes like this:

1. Create a real PayPal account.
2. Create two or more test PayPal accounts.
3. Create a test PayPal button.
4. Implement and test the button.

With PayPal, you still need a real PayPal account in order to test the process, so let's start by setting that up.

## THE MANY FACES OF PAYPAL

There are multiple PayPal-related sites that you'll deal with. The first and most obvious is the real PayPal, at www.paypal.com. To test a payment process, or to implement a live one, you'll need a PayPal account there, representing your e-commerce site. Once your site is live, you'll use the real PayPal site to create a real payment button, view payments, transfer money to your own bank account, and so forth.

Next, there are two sites involved in the development and testing process. The first is PayPal Developer, at http://developer.paypal.com. This site has some documentation, provides useful tools, and can be used to create JavaScript-based PayPal buttons (both live or test ones). You can't create classic PayPal buttons at the Developer site. Also, you'll want to log in at the primary PayPal site before making much use of the Developer site. As of this writing, the Developer site is in beta format and has more than its fair share of bugs.

The last site you'll use is the Sandbox Test Site at www.sandbox.paypal.com. This site looks and functions exactly like the real PayPal, except that it says "Test Site" and "Sandbox" here and there. You can't log in to the Sandbox site using a real PayPal account; you *must* use a test PayPal account, created at the Developer site.

Unfortunately, the Sandbox can often appear exactly the same as the real PayPal, and what you can do in the Developer site may or may not also be possible in the real PayPal site. As you read the rest of this chapter, pay close attention to which PayPal site I reference at each step. Also, it's common enough that you'll be in the PayPal Sandbox and clicking a link will take you to the real PayPal. Considering these potential traps, make sure that the URL in your browser matches each instruction appropriately.

## Registering at PayPal

The very first thing you'll need to do is register with PayPal (the main site), to create a business or premier account. If you already have a personal account, you can upgrade it to one of these other types. Or you can do what I do: have a personal account under one email address and register a new business or premier account using a different email address. (This approach also helps to separate my personal spending from my business accounting.)

If you already have a business or premier PayPal account, just log in, and then proceed to the next sequence of steps. If you don't have one of those account types yet, follow this sequence first.

1. Go to www.paypal.com.
2. Click Sign Up.
3. On the resulting page, select your country or region as well as your language, and then click Get Started under the business option (**Figure 6.2**).

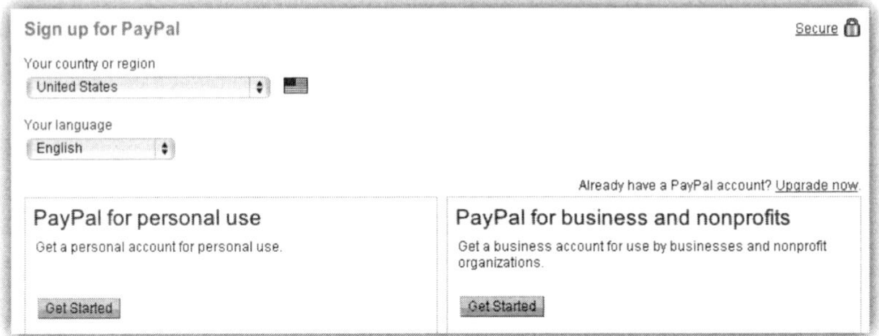


Figure 6.2

**note**

Undoubtedly the steps to create a new account will change over time.

4. On the next page, click Get Started under the appropriate PayPal payments solution type.

   For the purposes of this chapter, I'll use the Standard option, but the choice is up to you.
5. On the next page, click Create New Account.

6. Complete the first registration form (**Figure 6.3**).

   The first thing you'll need to do is enter your account access information (email address, password, and so forth).

   **Figure 6.3**

7. Complete the second registration form.

   The second form is where you enter more information about your business: your URL, the types of transactions you'll perform, your address, and more.

8. Check your email.

   After registering, you'll receive an email with a link that you must click to activate your account.

9. Click the link in the email to activate the account.

10. Log in to PayPal using your password.

## Creating Test Customer Accounts

> **note**
>
> Historically, you'd have had to create a test business account, too, but PayPal will now do that for you.

Once you've registered and logged in to PayPal, the next step is to create one or more test customer accounts. You do this on the PayPal Developer site, after logging in at PayPal proper.

1. Log in to PayPal, if you haven't already done so.
2. Change your browser URL to https://developer.paypal.com.

   As of this writing, the Developer pages are in beta format, and there's no direct link from PayPal to those pages.
3. Click the Applications link.

   As of this writing, there are only four main areas of the Developer site: Documentation, Applications, Dashboard, and Support.
4. Click Sandbox Accounts.

   On the resulting page, you should see one email address already, which is a variation on the email address with which you registered. This is your test business account. You can create other test business accounts, if you'd like, or use that one.
5. Click Create Account.
6. Complete the resulting form (**Figure 6.4**).

   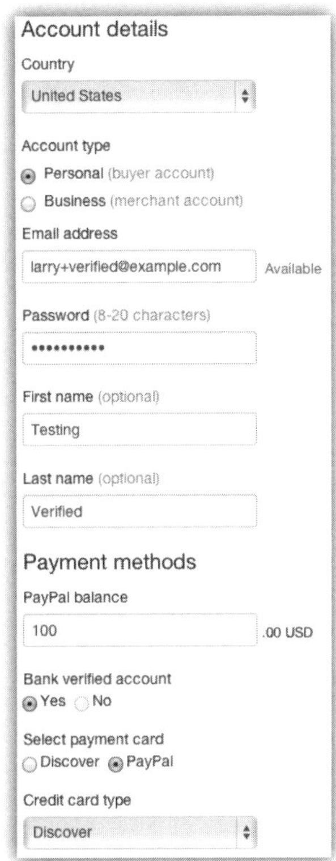
   

   **Figure 6.4**

   > 
   >
   > **tip**
   >
   > Write down every password, because you'll need them for the test account.

   Unfortunately there's not much documentation as to what you should do here, but the good news is that you're reading a book that will explain such things! First, select the Personal account type. For the address, enter any email address you want. The email address doesn't have to exist; it just has to be unique within the PayPal Developer system (unique across all developers). *No email* will ever be sent to this email address. I recommend making each email address somewhat descriptive, which will allow you to more easily test the system using various types of users (verified, unverified, different balances, and so on).

   The password should be easy to remember and enter. The name fields don't matter.

   For the Payment Methods (see Figure 6.4), you should create at least one verified account with a positive PayPal balance. As I'm about to recommend, you'll create other accounts, too. The payment card options (Discover and PayPal in Figure 6.4) is where you set whether the consumer will use a credit card or her PayPal balance. If you choose Discover, the credit card type menu can be used to select the specific card type (not that it matters much).

7. Click the Create Account button.

   Doing so will take you back to the list of Sandbox accounts.

8. Repeat Steps 5–7 to create more buyer accounts.

   For the test buyer accounts, you'll need to create one or more with a positive bank account balance and/or a credit card. For full testing, you can create a buyer with insufficient funds, too, or buyers from other countries.

   Each account you create will be listed on the Sandbox accounts page (**Figure 6.5**).

| Email address | Type | Country | Date created |
|---|---|---|---|
| larry-facilitator@larryullman.com | Business | US | 22 Aug 2013 |
| buyNSF_1281297388_per@mac.com | Personal | US | 19 Apr 2011 |
| larryu_1299204016_per@mac.com | Personal | US | 03 Mar 2011 |
| larryu_1297383583_per@mac.com | Personal | US | 10 Feb 2011 |
| larryu_1288483696_per@mac.com | Personal | US | 30 Oct 2010 |
| larryu_1288483603_per@mac.com | Personal | US | 30 Oct 2010 |
| buyBA_1281297335_per@mac.com | Personal | US | 08 Aug 2010 |
| buyCC_1281297278_per@mac.com | Personal | US | 08 Aug 2010 |
| seller_1281297018_biz@mac.com | Business | US | 08 Aug 2010 |

**Figure 6.5**

**tip**

If you create a buyer account without a credit card or bank account, or with insufficient funds, that buyer account will pay using pretend e-checks.

**tip**

Once created, an account's details can be updated after logging in to the Sandbox Test Site (using that account), as if it were a real PayPal account.

## Creating a Button

Once you've created one or more test buyer accounts, you can add a fake PayPal button to your website to simulate the e-commerce transactions. This is arguably the most important sequence of steps, because you'll perform these same actions for real when you take your site live.

Note that although PayPal has created a way to make buttons using JavaScript, I'm explaining the older, classic approach here:

1. Log in to the PayPal Sandbox using your test business account.

   In order for me to do this, I had to first click Profile under the account's name in the list of Sandbox test accounts (Figure 6.5) to update the password to something I knew.

2. Click the Merchant Services tab.

3. Click the Create Payment buttons for your website.

4. Under the list of options, click Subscriptions.
5. On the Create PayPal payment button page, enter an item name (**Figure 6.6**).

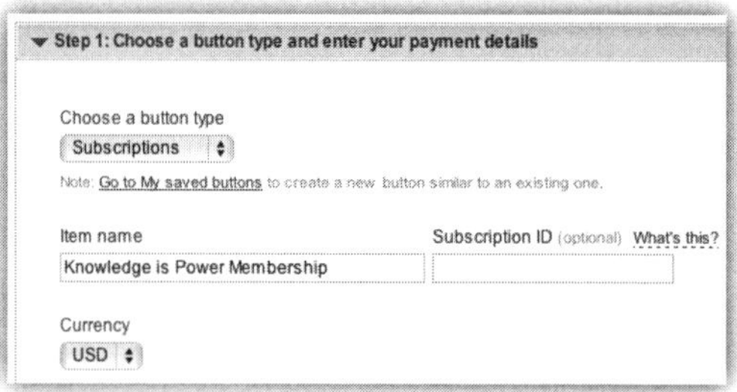


Figure 6.6

The button type should be selected automatically (as a subscription). You may or may not want to change the currency, too.

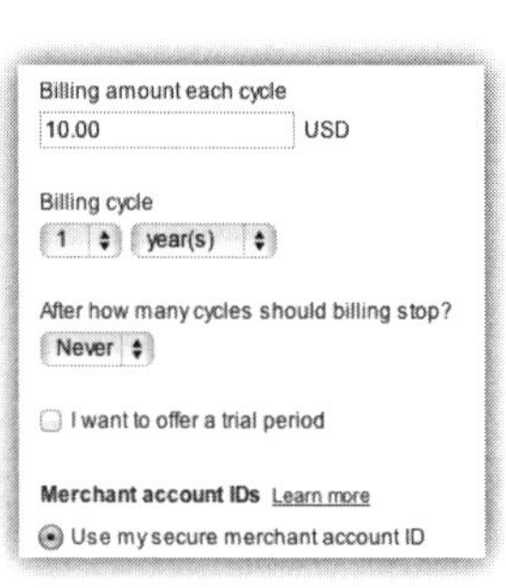


Figure 6.7

6. Further down under Step 1 of the form, enter a billing amount and cycle period (**Figure 6.7**).

   The billing amount is obviously the most important consideration. The billing cycle is for how long that billing amount covers. You can choose to have automatic billing stop after two or more cycles, or never.
7. Opt to use your secure merchant account ID (see Figure 6.7).
8. Under Step 2 of the form, make sure that the Save Button At PayPal option is selected (**Figure 6.8**).

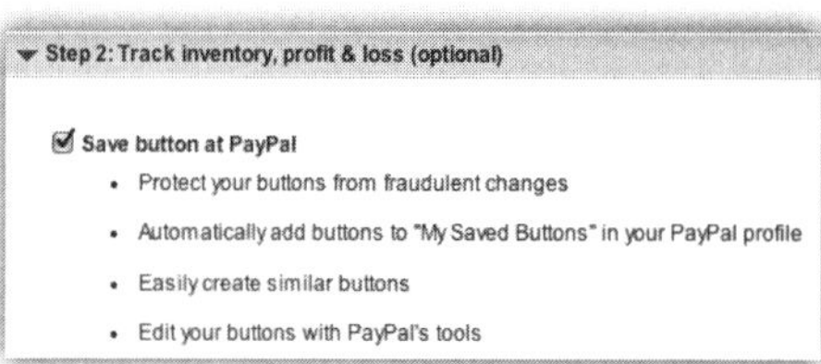


Figure 6.8

9. Under Step 3 of the form, indicate that you don't need the customer's shipping address.

   If you were selling a physical product, you'd want the user to confirm the shipping address in PayPal. You could then use PayPal to generate the shipping label for you, taking the shipping cost out of the money already transferred to your account.

**10.** Also under Step 3 of the form, supply the "cancel" and "finish" URLs, and select the corresponding check boxes (**Figure 6.9**).

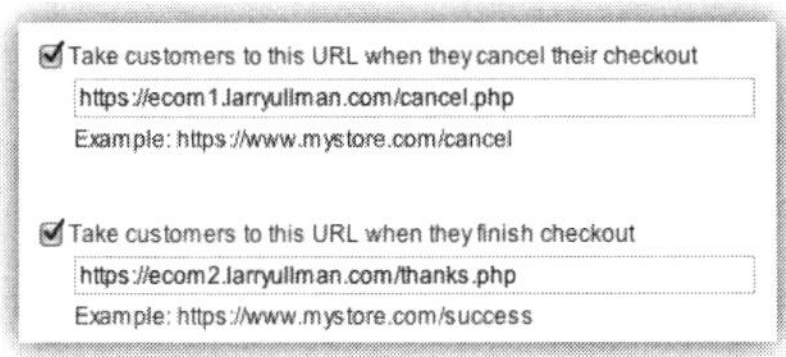


**Figure 6.9**

These two values must point to pages on your server, available via HTTPS. You'll create the two scripts, to be named **cancel.php** and **thanks.php**, later in this chapter.

**11.** Click Create Button.

**12.** On the next page, copy the generated code (**Figure 6.10**).

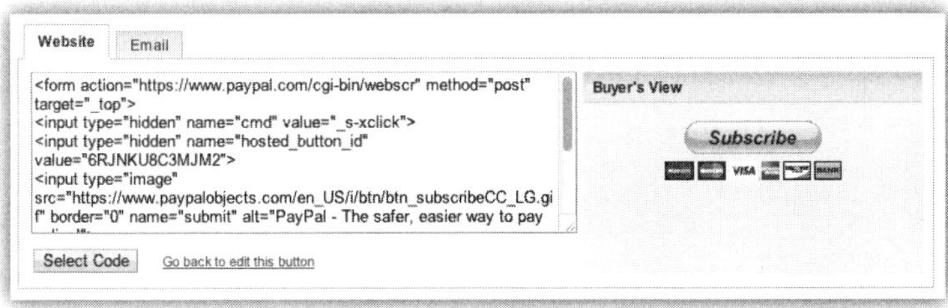


**Figure 6.10**

This is the code to be integrated into the site, which you'll do next. The value of the form action will be to either www.paypal.com or www.sandbox.paypal.com, depending upon whether you created a real or test button.

# INTEGRATING PAYPAL

Once you've created the test accounts and the PayPal button, you can tie your site into the fake PayPal. Doing so is a snap:

**1.** Add the button code where appropriate.

**2.** Create the **thanks.php** page.

**3.** Create the **cancel.php** page.

Inevitably, there will be a couple of catches, however, so after you integrate and test PayPal on the most basic level, you'll learn a way to improve the initial system.

## Updating the Registration Page

Remember that you can download all the source code for this example from www.LarryUllman.com.

With this particular website, the user should go to PayPal (by clicking the button) after successfully completing the registration process. To pull that off, start by changing the thank-you message in **register.php** so that it tells the user what to do next:

```
echo '<div class="alert alert-success"><h3>Thanks!</h3><p>Thank
➥you for registering! To complete the process, please now click the
➥button below so that you may pay for your site access via PayPal.
➥The cost is $10 (US) per year. <strong>Note: When you complete
➥your payment at PayPal, please click the button to return to this
➥site.</strong></p></div>';
```

Next, drop in the PayPal-generated code in order to add the button (**Figure 6.11**):

Figure 6.11

```
echo '<form action="https://www.sandbox.paypal.com/cgi-bin/webscr"
➥method="post">
<input type="hidden" name="cmd" value="_s-xclick">
<input type="hidden" name="hosted_button_id" value="8YW8FZDELF296">
<input type="image" src="https://www.sandbox.paypal.com/en_US/i/btn/
➥btn_subscribeCC_LG.gif" border="0" name="submit" alt="PayPal - The
➥safer, easier way to pay online!">
<img alt="" border="0" src="https://www.sandbox.paypal.com/en_US/i/
➥scr/pixel.gif" width="1" height="1">
</form>
';
```

The previous code should be placed just after the thank-you message and before the footer is included.

You have two more changes to make. First, the original **INSERT** query gave the new user access for the next month. Now you should change it so that the user's access is good until yesterday (that is, the account isn't active):

```
$q = "INSERT INTO users (username, email, pass, first_name,
➥last_name, date_expires) VALUES ('$u', '$e', '"  .
➥password_hash($p, PASSWORD_BCRYPT) .  "', '$fn', '$ln',
➥SUBDATE(NOW(), INTERVAL 1 DAY) )";
```

Second, you'll store the user's new ID value in a session so that his record may be updated when he returns from PayPal. To do so, just add the following code anywhere after you confirm that **mysqli_affected_row($dbc)** equals 1:

```
$uid = mysqli_insert_id($dbc);
$_SESSION['reg_user_id']  = $uid;
```

I'm specifically naming this **reg_user_id** instead of **user_id** so as not to confuse the system into thinking the user has logged in when he hasn't (the login process creates **$_SESSION['user_id']**). You'll see **$_SESSION['reg_user_id']** used in **thanks.php**.

## Creating thanks.php

The customer ends up at the **thanks.php** page after completing the PayPal order and clicking a button to return to this site. This page needs to update the database, adding a year of access to the user's account (**Figure 6.12**). Here's how it might be defined:

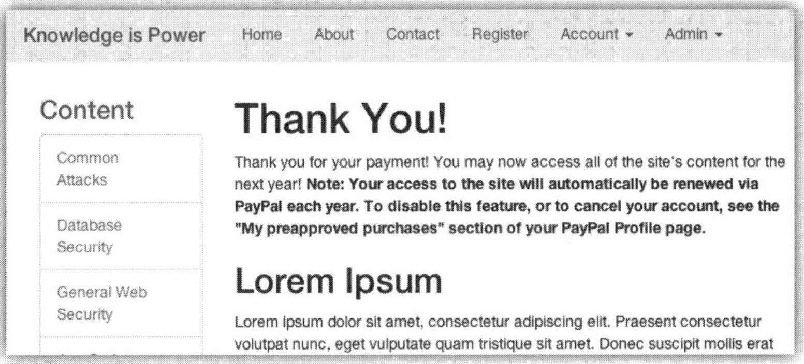


**Figure 6.12**

```
<?php
require('./includes/config.inc.php');
redirect_invalid_user('reg_user_id');
require(MYSQL);
$page_title = 'Thanks!';
include('./includes/header.html');
if (filter_var($_SESSION['reg_user_id'], FILTER_VALIDATE_INT,
➥array('min_range' => 1))) {
$q = "UPDATE users SET date_expires = ADDDATE(date_expires, INTERVAL
➥1 YEAR) WHERE id={$_SESSION['reg_user_id']}";
$r = mysqli_query($dbc, $q);
}
unset($_SESSION['reg_user_id']);
?><h1>Thank You!</h1>
<p>Thank you for your payment! You may now access all of the site's
➥content for the next year! <strong>Note: Your access to the site
➥will automatically be renewed via PayPal each year. To disable
➥this feature, or to cancel your account, see the "My preapproved
➥purchases" section of your PayPal Profile page.</strong></p>
<?php include('./includes/footer.html'); ?>
```

The key lines are highlighted. First, this script should be accessed only if the **reg_user_id** element exists in the session, meaning the page is accessible only after registering. If that session element doesn't exist, the user will be redirected thanks to this line:

```
redirect_invalid_user('reg_user_id');
```

As a courtesy, the customer is told that payments will automatically recur and what she can do to prevent that.

Second, the query runs an **UPDATE** command on the **users** table, adding one year to the expiration date for this user.

Third, the **$_SESSION['reg_user_id']** element is unset after the query. By taking this step, the page can be loaded only once, as the customer will be redirected if she were to access the page a second time. That check prevents hackers from adding years to their account by just reloading this page.

From a security standpoint, there's one big problem with this script: It assumes that the user has paid, but you don't actually know that for certain. If you register a new account and then change the URL to **thanks.php** without going through PayPal, the net effect will be the same. That would be bad.

From a customer standpoint, there are three problems. First, the customer will only be credited for her purchase if she returns to this page. This puts the responsibility on the customer for making sure she's credited, whereas the responsibility is yours to make sure customers get what they've paid for. Second, there's no confirmation that the **UPDATE** query worked properly (that is, that one row was affected). And third, there's no record anywhere associating the customer's PayPal order with the account on this site. Due to that omission, debugging potential problems would be hard.

All four of these issues will be remedied in a few pages by using something called *IPN*. But first, let's implement the cancellation page.

## Creating cancel.php

If the customer cancels the PayPal transaction, she will end up at the **cancel.php** page (because that's how the button was configured when it was created in PayPal). This page should just indicate to the customer where the account now stands (**Figure 6.13**). Here's how that script might look:

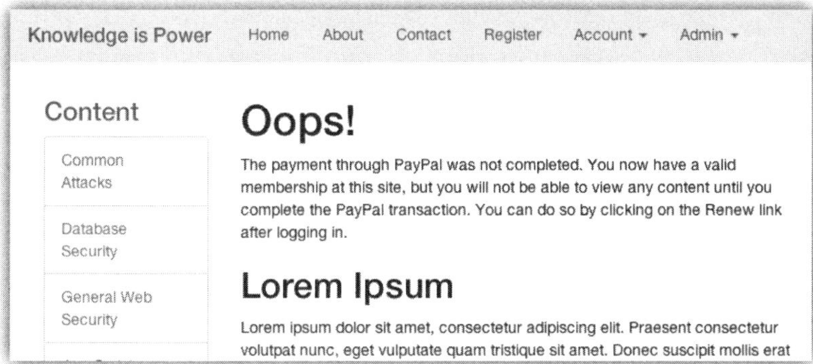


Figure 6.13

```
<?php
require('./includes/config.inc.php');
require(MYSQL);
$page_title = 'Oops!';
include('./includes/header.html');
?><h1>Oops!</h1>
<p>The payment through PayPal was not completed. You now have a
➥valid membership at this site, but you will not be able to view any
➥content until you complete the PayPal transaction. You can do so by
➥clicking on the Renew link after logging in.</p>
<?php include('./includes/footer.html'); ?>
```

tip

The renew process will be implemented toward the end of this chapter.

The important thing is for this page to indicate that

1. The customer has successfully registered at the site.
2. The customer still can't access any content.
3. To change #2, the customer should log in and click Renew.

# TESTING THE SITE

By this point in time, the site is very close to being a complete and real-world e-commerce project. To verify this, let's test the system as it currently stands.

1. Log in to PayPal.

   To use any of the test accounts you created, you'll need to be actively logged in to PayPal.

2. Successfully register with the "Knowledge Is Power" site.

   If you want, after registering and before Step 3, you could take a look at the database (using phpMyAdmin or another tool) to confirm that the user was registered but with a **`date_expires`** value in the past. You could also log in to the "Knowledge Is Power" site with this new account (in a different browser) to confirm this.

3. Click the PayPal button shown on the registration page.
4. On the PayPal site, use one of the test-buyer accounts to log in (**Figure 6.14**).

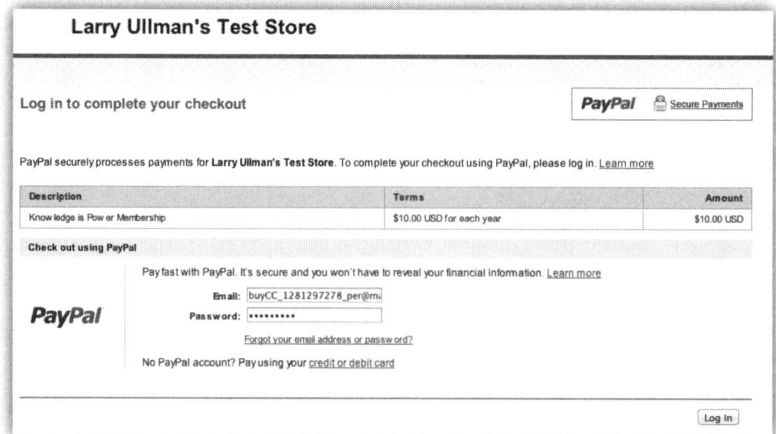


Figure 6.14

5. On the next page, click the Agree And Pay button (**Figure 6.15**).

   If you click the Cancel And Return link, you'll be taken to the site's cancel page.

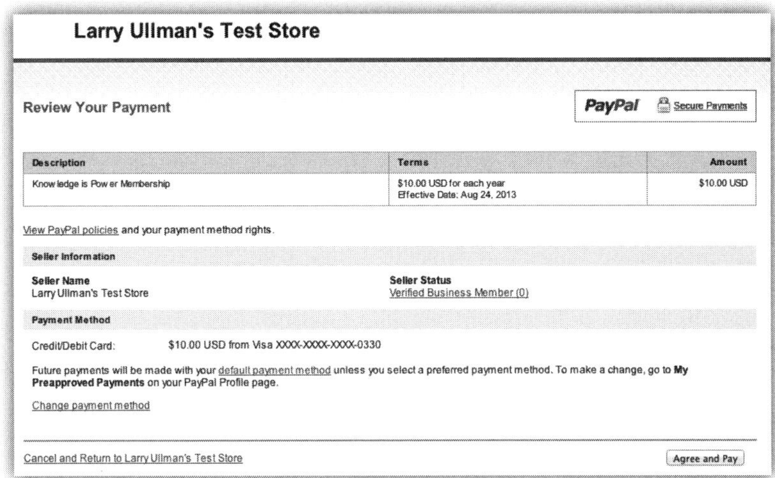


Figure 6.15

6. Once the purchase has been completed, click the Return To... button to return to the "Knowledge Is Power" site (**Figure 6.16**).

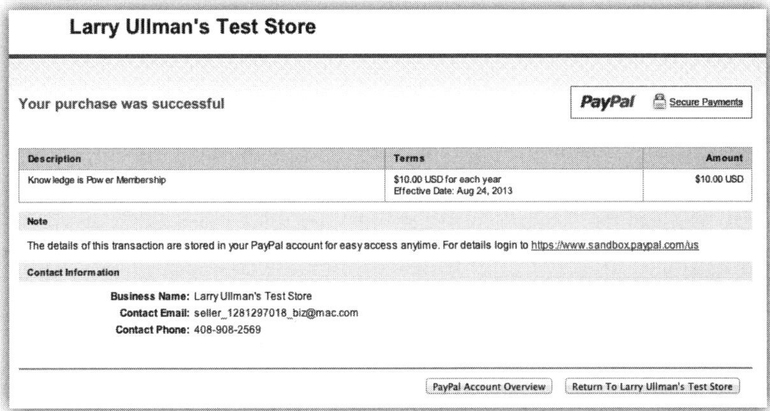


Figure 6.16

7. Look at the database again, or log in, to confirm that the expiration date has been updated.

8. If you want, log in to the PayPal Sandbox using the seller account to view the orders.

9. You can view a buyer's transactions by clicking the Notifications link under an email address in the list of Sandbox test accounts on the Developer site (**Figure 6.17**).

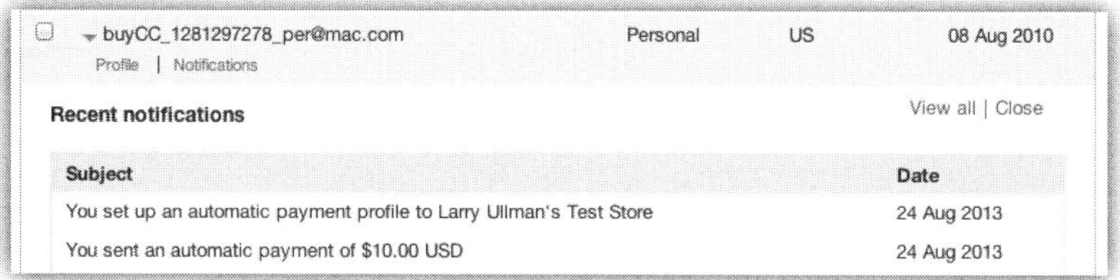


**Figure 6.17**

The PayPal Sandbox won't send emails, but the emails that would have been sent are viewable by clicking the corresponding items that appear in the notifications list.

# USING IPN

**note**

The most important aspect of IPN to remember is that it happens behind the scenes, without you or the customer being aware of it.

The PayPal system as written will work, but unfortunately the site only reacts to a user action: If the user doesn't, for whatever reason, return to your site (before the session expires), he won't be credited with a year of access. This is pretty bad form, because the user's action of sending you money via PayPal should be sufficient to immediately get what the user paid for. Granted, you can go into PayPal's system and see every credit you've received, but then it would be up to you to follow through and the user still can't access the site's content until the circuit has been completed.

Fortunately, PayPal thought of this and created something called *Instant Payment Notification* (IPN). IPN, when set up, will notify a website when a payment has been processed. This isn't "notify" in the sense of sending you an email—PayPal will already do that (if you want)—but is rather a server-to-server communication that neither the customer nor the site's administrator will witness. Through these communications, the e-commerce site can verify the transaction and update the database accordingly. More importantly, this communication will take place automatically no matter what the customer does after completing his order within PayPal.

**tip**

IPN is triggered for any kind of transaction, including purchases, refunds, disputes, and more.

Integrating IPN is a two-part process: enabling it on a PayPal account and creating the listening script on the server.

## Enabling IPN

The first part of the two-part process of integrating IPN is to enable IPN in your PayPal account.

1. Log in to the PayPal Sandbox using the steps already outlined.

   You'll need to log in using your merchant account.

2. Click Profile > My Selling Tools.

3. Click the Update link to change the Instant Payment Notifications settings.

4. On the subsequent page, enter the notification URL (**Figure 6.18**).

   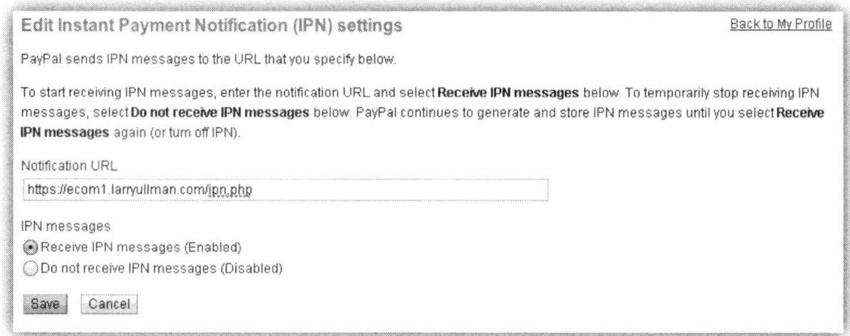
   

   **Figure 6.18**

   The notification URL needs to be a page on your site accessed via HTTPS. I'm naming it **`ipn.php`**, but you may want to use a more original name than that.

5. Select the Receive IPN Messages (Enabled) option.

   You can disable IPN through these preferences by selecting the Do Not Receive IPN Messages (Disabled) option.

6. Click Save.

## Updating the Registration Script

Yes, yes: I said that integrating IPN was a two-part process and here I am introducing a third. I stand by my two-part statement because this third step may or may not be necessary. I'll explain....

For the user to be properly credited, there needs to be a way to tie the user's account on the e-commerce site to the PayPal purchase. In the original **`register.php`**-PayPal-**`thanks.php`** system, the tie-in was accomplished by storing the user's ID value in a session and then using it on the **thanks.php** page. Since this new version of the process won't rely on the **thanks.php** page to perform the update, the user must be tracked in another way. To track the user now, the updated site will use IPN to pass all sorts of information back to the e-commerce site.

One theoretical option would be to use the customer's email address to update the account. This is information that the IPN will return in the **$_POST['payer_email']** variable. I say "theoretical," because if the customer registered with one email address but signed in to PayPal with another, this won't work. My more foolproof solution is to pass the user's ID along to PayPal so that PayPal may return it as part of the IPN data. Here's how **register.php** should be altered to implement this technique:

1. Remove the line that stores the user ID in the session:

   ```
   $_SESSION['reg_user_id'] = $uid;
   ```

2. Add the following code to the PayPal form:

   ```
   <input type="hidden" name="custom" value="' . $uid . '">
   ```

This code is output by an **echo** statement as part of the larger form and PayPal button. The code creates a hidden form input with a **name** of **custom**. You must use that exact name for the input, as **custom** is a special way to pass any data to PayPal with the express intent of having it returned to the site. The value is the user's ID, already determined by calling **mysqli_insert_id()** earlier in the script.

While you're expanding the code and functionality, go ahead and pass the user's email address to PayPal as well so that the PayPal login form will be prepopulated with it (and this may also be usable as a fallback way to connect site users with PayPal transactions). There are many hidden-form inputs that PayPal will recognize, like **first_name**, **last_name**, and **email**. Here's the new **echo** statement in **register.php**:

```
echo '<form action="https://www.sandbox.paypal.com/cgi-bin/webscr"
➥method="post">
<input type="hidden" name="cmd" value="_s-xclick">
<input type="hidden" name="custom" value="' . $uid . '">
<input type="hidden" name="email" value="' . $e . '">
<input type="hidden" name="hosted_button_id" value="8YW8FZDELF296">
<input type="image" src="https://www.sandbox.paypal.com/en_US/i/btn/
➥btn_subscribeCC_LG.gif" border="0" name="submit" alt="PayPal - The
➥safer, easier way to pay online!">
```

```
<img alt="" border="0" src="https://www.sandbox.paypal.com/en_US/i/
➥scr/pixel.gif" width="1" height="1">
</form>
';
```

For the **email** value, you'll see that I'm using the **$e** variable, which would've just been used in the **INSERT** query.

## Creating the IPN Script

The next part of the process of implementing IPN is creating the listener script. The IPN listener script—the file on the e-commerce site with which PayPal will automatically and behind-the-scenes communicate—is clearly important and is accordingly complex. The process goes like this:

1. When the IPN page is requested, it must immediately confirm the request with PayPal. This keeps the script from being fraudulently used.
2. The IPN page reads in the response from PayPal.
3. The IPN page thoroughly validates the response and other data.
4. If the data is valid, the IPN page updates the database.

Once IPN notifications have been enabled, PayPal will continue calling the IPN script until the notification is acknowledged.

The process can be implemented in different ways. In the first edition of this book, I used PHP's **fsockopen()** function to have the IPN script communicate with PayPal. In the most recent PayPal integration I personally performed, I used PHP's **libcurl** for the communication. Another option is to use the **file_get_contents()** function along with a PHP stream. Of just these three possible approaches (and there are no doubt others), I'm going to explain the **libcurl** route here. I think it's the cleanest option without being overly complex. The only requirement is that you must have a version of PHP with **libcurl** enabled, which is fairly standard now.

What this script doesn't have to do is generate any HTML, because it's not intended to be run through a web browser. As a reminder, neither you nor the customer will ever see this script's regular execution.

1. Create a new PHP script in your text editor or IDE to be named **ipn.php** (or something more original) and stored in the web root directory:

   ```
   <?php
   require('./includes/config.inc.php');
   ```

   This script needs access to the configuration file for the purposes of error reporting and connecting to the database. The script also needs to be

You cannot test the IPN process from localhost.

publicly accessible. Where you store this file must match the URL you provided to PayPal for it.

2. Check that the script is being accessed properly:

```
if (($_SERVER['REQUEST_METHOD'] === 'POST') && isset($_POST
➥['txn_id']) && ($_POST['txn_type'] === 'web_accept') ) {
```

Just in case this script might be accessed improperly (by a hacker, or by mistake), the code will first check for several conditions before attempting to do anything else. First, the code confirms that a POST request is being made. That is how PayPal will access the IPN script. Next, the conditional confirms that a transaction ID value is present among the information posted to this script. Much more than a transaction ID is required, but without a transaction ID, there's no point in continuing. Finally, the script confirms that the transaction type is **web_accept**. That's the value when a payment has been made.

3. Initialize a cURL request handler:

```
$ch = curl_init();
```

If you've never worked with cURL before, understand that it's a command-line utility used to transfer data using URL syntax. The process of using cURL in PHP, through the **libcurl** library, begins by initializing cURL. The result is assigned to a variable for later use, in much the same way that a file handler (a pointer to an opened file) will be used by subsequent file-related functions.

**tip**

Instead of using one call to **curl_setopt_array()**, you could call **curl_setopt()** once for each setting.

4. Configure the cURL request:

```
curl_setopt_array($ch,
array (
    CURLOPT_URL => 'https://www.sandbox.paypal.com/cgi-bin/
    ➥webscr',
    CURLOPT_POST => true,
    CURLOPT_POSTFIELDS => http_build_query(array('cmd' =>
    ➥'_notify-validate') + $_POST),
    CURLOPT_RETURNTRANSFER => true,
    CURLOPT_HEADER => false
));
```

These lines are where you dictate the behavior of the cURL request. The **curl_setopt_array()** function takes the handler as its first argument, and an array of name-value pairs as its second (the pairs can be in any order). All of the options are explained in the PHP manual, but I'll cover these most important five here.

First, the **CURLOPT_URL** option is where you set the URL to be requested. In this case, the URL is the file on PayPal's system to which the confirmation request must be made. In test mode, that value is **https://www.sandbox.paypal.com/cgi-bin/webscr**.

When the site goes live, the request will be made to just **https://www.paypal.com/cgi-bin/webscr**.

Second, setting **CURLOPT_POST** to true indicates that a POST request is to be made (that is, this script will make a POST request back to PayPal).

The third option, **CURLOPT_POSTFIELDS**, is where you provide data to be posted as part of the request (data to be sent to PayPal). PayPal expects to receive all of the data posted to this IPN script, plus **cmd=_notify-validate**. This value indicates the command being made to PayPal (that is, the purpose for the communication).

There are a couple of ways to include all the POST data in the request. The **http_build_query()** function is perfect for this, and easy to use. The alternative would be to build up a string using a loop:

```
$req = 'cmd=_notify-validate';
foreach ($_POST as $key => $value) {
   $value = urlencode($value);
   $req .= "&$key=$value";
}
```

After that code, you'd then assign **$req** to **CURLOPT_POSTFIELDS**.

The fourth setting, **CURLOPT_RETURNTRANSFER**, is set to **true**, indicating that the result of the cURL request should be returned as a string, not immediately displayed. You'll see how this plays out shortly.

Finally, **CURLOPT_HEADER** is set to **false** to indicate that the header shouldn't be included in the output (the result of the request).

**tip**

Alternatively, you could define the live and test URLs in the configuration file, so the URL is automatically changed when the site goes live.

5. Perform the cURL request:

```
$response = curl_exec($ch);
```

This is where the actual request of PayPal is performed. The result of that request will be assigned to the **$response** variable.

6. Get the status code of the cURL response:

```
$status = curl_getinfo($ch, CURLINFO_HTTP_CODE);
```

To verify the response, the script will look at the HTTP status code returned by PayPal. That value is fetched using this code.

**tip**

You could write every IPN transaction to a text file as a backup. The **ipn_log.php** example file in the downloadable scripts does this.

7. Close the cURL request:

```
curl_close($ch);
```

8. Check that the status code was 200 and the response equals **VERIFIED**:

```
if ($status === 200 && $response === 'VERIFIED') {
```

The HTTP status code is checked to confirm that the PayPal communication worked. If the status code was 404 or some such, the wrong URL was most likely used.

The response, which is assigned to the variable when the request is made, needs to equal **VERIFIED** (case-sensitive) to confirm that the request was valid.

 **tip**

Validating the values posted to the script is key to preventing users from defrauding your site.

9. Check for the right values:

```
if ( isset($_POST['payment_status'])
   && ($_POST['payment_status'] === 'Completed')
   && ($_POST['receiver_email'] ===
   ➥'seller_1281297018_biz@mac.com')
   && ($_POST['mc_gross'] === 10.00)
   && ($_POST['mc_currency']  === 'USD')
   && (!empty($_POST['txn_id']))
) {
```

Just looking for a verified response isn't sufficient. For the transaction to be official enough to warrant updating the site's database, several other qualities should exist. For starters, **payment_status** needs to equal **Completed**, because there will be other possible statuses that don't warrant changes (such as **Pending**). You should confirm that the payment was received by the proper email address (the one that matches the e-commerce site's merchant PayPal account). This check prevents the site from taking action based on a payment that didn't go to that merchant (because someone attempted a hack).

**note**

Make sure you use your actual PayPal-associated email address for the ***receiver_email*** comparison.

Next, the **mc_gross** and **mc_currency** values should match the gross cost and currency for the transaction. This keeps someone from trying to pay you just one cent or 10.00 Thai baht (equivalent to 31 cents as I write this). Finally, you want to make sure that the transaction ID isn't empty.

All these values are available in **$_POST**, because they're part of the original request of this script.

 **tip**

If you change any of your site's parameters, such as the cost of a subscription, you'll need to change this script, too.

**10.** Check for this transaction in the database:

```
require (MYSQL);
$txn_id = escape_data($_POST['txn_id'], $dbc);
$q = "SELECT id FROM orders WHERE transaction_id='$txn_id'";
$r = mysqli_query($dbc, $q);
if (mysqli_num_rows($r) === 0) {
```

It's possible, through nefarious actions or normal operations, that the IPN script might get a repeated request for the same transaction. To prevent such an occurrence from crediting a user's account again, this query checks if the transaction ID is already listed in the **orders** table. If the query returns no records, then this is a new, proper transaction.

To prevent SQL injection attacks, potentially problematic data is run through the escaping function.

**11.** Add this transaction to the **orders** table:

```
$uid = (isset($_POST['custom'])) ? (int) $_POST['custom'] : 0;
$status = escape_data($_POST['payment_status'], $dbc);
$amount = (int) ($_POST['mc_gross'] * 100);
$q = "INSERT INTO orders (user_id, transaction_id,
➥payment_status, payment_amount) VALUES ($uid, '$txn_id',
➥'$status', $amount)";
$r = mysqli_query($dbc, $q);
if (mysqli_affected_rows($dbc) === 1) {
```

First, three more values are made safe to use in a query. You'll see here a reference to **$_POST['custom']**, which is the user's ID originally stored in the **register.php** script, then passed to PayPal, and now returned home like a loyal pet. This value gets passed back to the site, via IPN, whether or not the customer immediately returns to the site. If, for some reason, the user ID ends up with a value of 0, then the order is still recorded and the administrator would have to pursue the matter to see what customer ought to be credited.

The **orders** table also records the transaction ID, payment status, and payment amount. Note that the payment amount in the database is stored in cents, so the received amount must be multiplied times 100.

**tip**

As an extra check, you could confirm that **$_POST['custom']** is a valid integer.

**tip**

As written, the script is logging only successful, new transactions in the **orders** table, but you could easily modify the script to log every IPN request but still update the **users** table only for successful, new ones.

12. Update the **users** table:

```
if ($uid > 0) {
   $q = "UPDATE users SET date_expires = IF(date_expires >
   ➥NOW(), ADDDATE(date_expires, INTERVAL 1 YEAR),
   ➥ADDDATE(NOW(), INTERVAL 1 YEAR)), date_modified=NOW()
   ➥WHERE id=$uid";
   $r = mysqli_query($dbc, $q);
   if (mysqli_affected_rows($dbc) !== 1) {
      trigger_error('The user\'s expiration date could not be
      ➥updated!');
   }
} // No user ID.
```

By this point, the script is ready to update the user's account, assuming a valid user ID was provided. To do that, an **UPDATE** query is run, providing a new value for both the **date_expires** column and **date_modified**. I improved the updating of the **date_expires** value to allow for users whose accounts lapsed and were later renewed. I'll explain.

In the original **thanks.php**, the query added a year to the current **date_expires** value. But if the **date_expires** value is in the past, the user would be credited a year from that date in the past: not a full year at all. So instead, the new value for **date_expires** will be a year from its current value, if its current value is greater than **NOW()**; otherwise, it will be a year from now.

If one row wasn't affected by the query, an error is triggered. This is important, as it would imply that a payment went through but no user was credited.

13. Complete several conditionals:

```
      } else { // Problem inserting the order!
         trigger_error('The transaction could not be stored in
         ➥the orders table!');
      }
   } // The order has already been stored, nothing to do!
} // The right values don't exist in $_POST!
```

The **else** clause applies if the order couldn't be inserted into the **orders** table, in which case an error needs to be triggered. (Again, that would mean a payment was made but no account was credited.) The two other curly brackets close earlier **IF** conditionals but take no further actions.

**14.** If the PayPal response isn't valid, or the status code wasn't 200, log the request:

```
} else { // Bad response!
   // Log for further investigation.
}
```

If this is an invalid request, as opposed to a verified one, you may want to trigger an error or log the request so that you can investigate whether someone is trying to manipulate the system.

**15.** Complete the first conditional (that checks for a POST request and more):

```
} else {
   echo 'Nothing to do.';
}
```

To be clear, the script doesn't have to do anything at this point. If the page wasn't requested via POST, or a transaction ID wasn't provided, or the transaction type didn't equal **web_accept**, there's nothing for this script to do. However, I like to add this little statement for one simple reason: It gives me the opportunity to run the script to test it for parse errors (**Figure 6.19**). If you someday make an edit to this script but create a parse error, you'd never know that the IPN notifications were not being acknowledged.

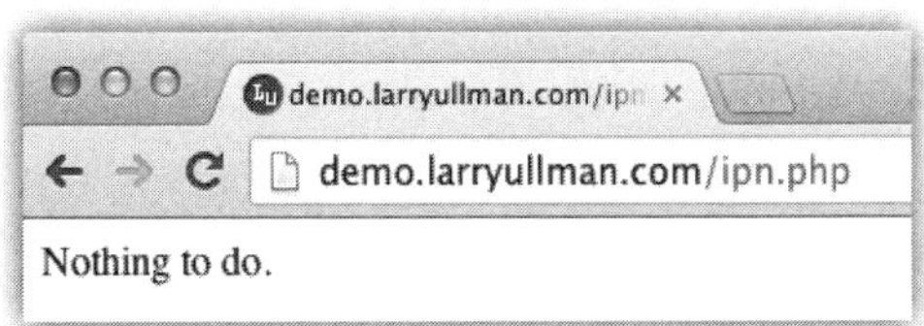


Figure 6.19

**16.** Complete the script:

```
?>
```

**17.** Save the file.

You can put the file onto your server and run it in your browser if you want. You should see the same as Figure 6.19. You can also test it using PayPal's IPN simulator (see the accompanying sidebar). However, before thinking that you're done with the site, there's still one more step in this *two-step* incorporation of IPN!

### PAYPAL'S IPN SIMULATOR

A very welcome addition in PayPal's upgraded Developer site is the IPN simulator. This is available under Tools, on the Applications tab. The simulator is simple to use: Enter the URL for your IPN script and select a transaction type. You can test any type of transaction, but a successful payment is a **web_accept** transaction (as reflected in the IPN script). Depending on the transaction type, you'll then be presented with a form you can fill out to configure the transaction.

To confirm that the IPN script in this chapter is working for completed payments, you'd want to set the **txn_id**, **payment_status**, **receiver_email**, **mc_gross**, and **mc_currency** fields to values your script is expecting. You can even pass other information in the **custom** field (as the site uses it to pass along the user ID).

After filling in the form, click Send IPN. You should see that the request was sent, although you won't see the response. To confirm that the IPN script is working, you'd then check your database (if a database change should have occurred), or have the IPN script log all requests to a text file for you to view later. The **ipn_log.php** script available in the downloadable code does just that.

## Updating the Thanks Script

And now there's Step 4 in the two-part series on integrating IPN (math is not my strong suit). With the current version of **thanks.php**, if the customer successfully goes through PayPal and returns to the site, her expiration date will be updated twice: once in **thanks.php** and once in **ipn.php**. To fix that, remove or comment out the following lines of code:

```
redirect_invalid_user('reg_user_id');
if (isset($_SESSION['reg_user_id']) && filter_var($_SESSION
➥['reg_user_id'], FILTER_VALIDATE_INT, array('min_range' => 1))) {
$q = "UPDATE users SET date_expires = ADDDATE(date_expires, INTERVAL
➥1 YEAR) WHERE id={$_SESSION['reg_user_id']}";
$r = mysqli_query($dbc, $q);
}
unset($_SESSION['reg_user_id']);
```

Now you can test the new system by repeating the steps outlined in the "Testing the Site" section of this chapter.

## USING PDT WITH PAYPAL

The chapter's first system for handling the PayPal response was built into **thanks.php** and relied on the customer coming immediately back from PayPal. The second (and final in this chapter) solution used IPN to update the database and didn't care whether or not the user came back from PayPal. This does mean it's theoretically possible that the customer returns to your site before the IPN script is triggered, allowing for the potential that the customer has just paid but must still wait (even momentarily) for the expiration date to be extended by the IPN script. A solution to that possible (but improbable) problem can be found by implementing PDT (Payment Data Transfer).

The PDT process is quite similar to the IPN process, but PDT is invoked only when the user returns to your site. Implementing PDT and IPN provides great "belt and suspenders" protection, but extra logic has to be added so that the effect of the purchase (the extending of the account) only occurs once. I'll explain exactly how to do that in Chapter 12, "Extending the First Site."

# RENEWING ACCOUNTS

The last addition to the site that must be created is the ability to renew an account. Given the recurring payment system setup in PayPal, there are only two situations in which a customer might need to renew her account:

- The customer registered but didn't complete payment at PayPal.
- The customer registered and completed payment at PayPal, but later canceled the recurring payment and now wants to renew the account some time after it has expired.

A renewal page should only be accessible to logged-in users and should display the same PayPal button code that the registration page does. Everything else about the process would be exactly the same. Here's **renew.php**:

```
<?php
require('./includes/config.inc.php');
redirect_invalid_user();
$page_title = 'Renew Your Account';
require(MYSQL);
include('./includes/header.html');
```

*(continues on next page)*

```
?><h1>Thanks!</h1><p>Thank you for your interest in renewing your
➥account! To complete the process, please now click the button
➥below so that you may pay for your renewal via PayPal. The cost
➥is $10 (US) per year. <strong>Note: After renewing your membership
➥at PayPal, you must logout and log back in at this site in order
➥process the renewal.</strong></p>
<form action="https://www.sandbox.paypal.com/cgi-bin/webscr"
➥method="post">
<input type="hidden" name="cmd" value="_s-xclick">
<input type="hidden" name="custom" value="<?php echo
➥$_SESSION['user_id']; ?>">
<input type="hidden" name="hosted_button_id" value="8YW8FZDELF296">
<input type="submit" name="submit_button" value="Renew &rarr;"
id="submit_button" class="btn btn-default" />
</form>
<?php include('./includes/footer.html'); ?>
```

To show you something different and to make the button more like the rest of the site, I changed the button itself from an IMG tag, pointing to a file on PayPal's server, to a submit input with the same class used for other submit buttons on the e-commerce site. **Figure 6.20** shows the result. This change doesn't affect the PayPal system at all, because the button is used only as something for the user to click; the true functionality is in the hidden inputs. Speaking of which, you should note that the custom value is coming from the session in this case, as the renew script is available only to users who are logged in.

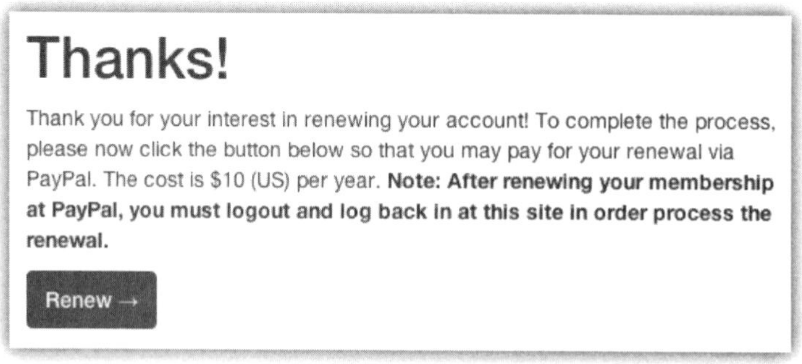

Figure 6.20

# GOING LIVE

When you've thoroughly tested how your site works with PayPal and you're ready to take the whole project live, you need to perform just a few simple steps:

1. Log in to PayPal using your real merchant account (your business or premier account).
2. Customize the PayPal experience (see the accompanying sidebar).
3. Using the real PayPal account, create the button code to be used on your e-commerce site.
4. Replace the button code in **register.php** and **renew.php** with the new, real PayPal-generated button code (variations of the same code can be used for both).
5. Also in PayPal, enable IPN for the account (see the steps earlier in the chapter).
6. Update the **ipn.php** script.

   You'll want to:

   - Change the **CURLOPT_URL** value to use the real PayPal.
   - Make sure the right email address is being used for comparison to **$_POST['receiver_email']**.
   - Make sure the right payment amount is being used for comparison to **$_POST['mc_gross']**.
   - Make sure the right currency abbreviation is being used for comparison to **$_POST['mc_currency']**.
7. Change the value of the **$live** variable in **config.inc.php** to **true**.

**tip**

The four **ipn.php** factors listed could be defined in the configuration file instead to make them easier to change.

Me being me, after doing all this I would probably execute a couple of real transactions, just to confirm that the system is working. By doing so you'll cost yourself a few bucks (in the transaction fees, because the money will be going from you to you), but you'll get peace of mind. Also, be certain to routinely compare the transactions in your PayPal history with those in your **orders** table so that you know no customer is being cheated or is cheating you.

## CUSTOMIZING THE PAYPAL EXPERIENCE

Although using the PayPal Payments Standard system means the customer will leave your site and spend some time at PayPal, the experience doesn't need to be too jarring. If you log in to PayPal and click Profile, there's quite a lot you can do under the My Selling Tools option. This is where you can establish tax and shipping policies. You can also view and update your buttons there. More important from a customer-experience point of view, you can create a specific Customer Service Message and define templates to act as Custom Payment Pages. Custom Payment Pages can use your own images and colors—to some degree—so that the PayPal interface looks similar to your own website. How you go about doing this is well documented in links found on PayPal's Custom Payment Pages document.

# PART THREE
## SELLING PHYSICAL PRODUCTS

# 7 SECOND SITE: STRUCTURE AND DESIGN

The second e-commerce project that you'll develop with the help of this book will sell physical products: coffee (beans, not brewed!) and coffee-related goodies. The Coffee site will have these primary features:

- Browsable catalog
- Sale items
- Shopping cart
- Customer wish list
- On-site payment processing via Authorize.net
- Administrative ability to create products, discount items, manage inventory, and process orders

The five chapters in Part 3, "Selling Physical Products," will walk you through the implementation of this combination of common e-commerce features. To make the resulting project more maintainable and secure, and to demonstrate a broader range of what "e-commerce" means, this example will use several concepts and approaches that are significantly more advanced than those found in Part 2, "Selling Virtual Products."

Less experienced developers may find some of these implementations to be confusing. Other developers may not be able to replicate one or more of my approaches, due to server (or hosting) limitations. For these reasons, when I introduce particularly complex or advanced concepts, I'll also present alternative solutions that you could implement instead. Chapter 13, "Extending the Second Site," will present even more alternatives, in terms of both techniques and features.

# ABOUT THE SITE

Because this coffee shop example will be much more complex than the content management one, I want to talk about its goals and functionality in some detail before getting into the actual implementation.

## What's Being Sold

The aim of this book is to present the widest possible range of what it means to perform e-commerce, so the first goal of the Coffee site example is to sell a physical product. Selling physical products requires a different approach than selling virtual content. One implication is that the Coffee site will need to be prudent about when customers are charged for orders relative to when the orders actually ship. Selling physical products also requires using SKUs (Stock-Keeping Units): unique identifiers for each item sold. Without SKUs, there's no inventory management. Without SKUs, there's no certainty that a customer is receiving the exact item she wanted.

**note**

Selling virtual products may also require SKUs, although you don't have to consider inventory management.

Physical products come in two broad categories:

- Single, individual items, such as works of art
- Variations on a theme, such as a book that's available in hardcover, paperback, or electronic format

The distinction between these categories is important. For example, if you're selling books, you'll want the customer to be able to select the format from among the available options, all on the same page. But each available format still needs its own unique identifier. Conversely, a work of art or any product that's not available in different formats or with different attributes is much easier to present to the customer and to manage as inventory. Hopefully you've already inferred that how you handle SKUs and other product attributes differs between these two types. The Coffee e-commerce store sells both categories of physical products: goodies, such as mugs, biscotti, and so on, which are treated individually (**Figure 7.1**), and coffee that has common generic properties but is purchased in specific formats (for example, 8oz. or 1lb., ground versus whole beans, **Figure 7.2**).

**Figure 7.1**

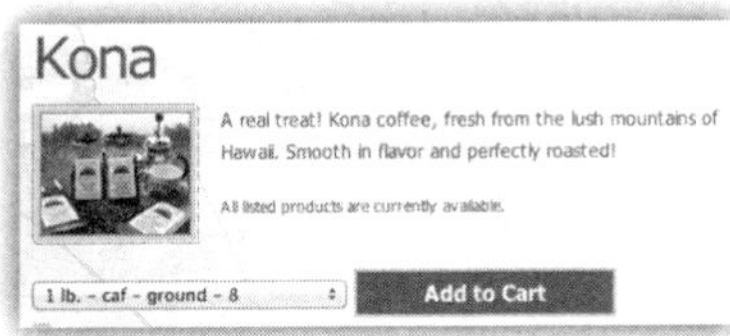


**Figure 7.2**

tip

To simplify the example a bit, I've opted to ignore some coffee bean variables and entirely ignore the issues that arise with selling perishable goods.

Most of the work and code in this part of the book will involve using SKUs in the database, in the displayed catalog of products, in the shopping cart, and in the administrative interface. In your own e-commerce projects, you can apply these same theories and code to sell music in different formats, clothes in different sizes and colors, and so forth.

The database and code is further complicated by supporting the ability to offer products at a discounted price. This is a nice feature, and one that can go a long way toward increasing business.

## No Customer Registration

Another way in which the Coffee e-commerce project differs from the "Knowledge Is Power" site is that this site doesn't obligate customers to register in order to make purchases. Required registration, which is mandatory in a content access example, has actually been proven to hurt sales (although truth be told, Amazon.com gets away with required registration just fine). This site will focus on the purchases, not on the customer. This approach will have some interesting ramifications in terms of the database and how the site operates, as you'll learn in this chapter.

If you'd rather, you could provide your customers with the option of registering or not. In such a case, you would take the code from the "Knowledge Is Power" example and modify it to add registration and login capability to your site.

## Implementing MVC

tip

MVC is an example of a *design pattern*: an accepted and standard way to programmatically solve a problem.

For this coffee shop site, I've decided to implement somewhat of an MVC approach. MVC, which stands for *Model-View-Controller*, is a popular way to design more complex web (and other) applications. Within MVC, a project's code and files are divided into their discernible parts:

- **Model** is used to access and work with the data involved.
- **View** is the presentation layer (what the user sees).
- **Controller** is the logic that ties everything together and reacts to user activity.

tip

Advanced programmers develop not just for today's expectations but also for what can reasonably be expected down the line.

By implementing MVC, you'll have a project that's easier to develop—especially when working on a team—and easier to maintain, with cleaner code. Further, the site will potentially be more scalable. *Scalability* is the ability to handle an increased load implicitly through an increase in resources. A website may start with one server and be able to handle up to X number of concurrent visitors.

If the site can "scale well," then it will also be able to handle, say, four times the concurrent visitors by just adding another web server or two database servers. Conversely, a site that doesn't scale well couldn't properly handle four times the concurrent load even if you were to throw four or eight more servers at the problem. With the hope that an e-commerce site will take off, the ability for the site to scale well is a reasonable consideration.

But what does MVC mean in terms of real code? It's simple in theory, although I'm applying MVC in a casual manner. The controller is represented by PHP code, which handles user behavior and reacts accordingly, often as an agent between the model and the view. The data, with few exceptions, is managed entirely by the database. The view is HTML. To keep these three things separate, the Coffee shop site first moves much of the model functionality into the database, using something called *stored procedures* (discussed at the end of the chapter). Second, the site stores almost all the HTML in separate files, included as appropriate by the PHP scripts. The end result will be little to no SQL or HTML intermingled with PHP. In fact, many of the PHP scripts will be quite short.

**tip**

OOP and frameworks generally use MVC and other design patterns by their very nature.

Another benefit of this MVC approach is that you'll be able to look at and edit any facet of the site without having to wade through unrelated code. For example, you can adjust an SQL query without seeing any PHP; you can tweak the PHP without mucking about in HTML. You can also address performance issues by focusing on individual pieces. If you look back at Figure 1.4, in which I point out the three areas in which caching can be applied to improve performance, you'll see that the MVC approach isolates these same three areas of the process. This means that when your site takes off and multiple servers are appropriate, each server can focus on a specific aspect: say two or three for just the database (that is, the models) and one or two for the PHP and HTML. You can also offload specific parts to cloud computing, if you want to go that route.

There are a couple of obvious downsides to using an MVC approach. First, you'll end up with *a lot* more files. Whereas one PHP script could query the database and generate the HTML output, now you'll have one PHP script, one stored procedure in the database, and one or more HTML files to accomplish the same task. Second, MVC requires that assumptions be made about what has happened previous to certain points (for example, a view file assumes that it receives some data to display). Third, pushing model functionality into the database will require a level of database access that not everyone necessarily has.

**tip**

If you find that you can't follow or don't appreciate the MVC approach used in this example, feel free to use the more direct PHP-MySQL-HTML approach demonstrated in Part 2.

## Heightened Security

The most significant distinction between the two e-commerce examples in this book is the level of required security. Because this site will briefly handle credit card information and permanently store more user information, extra precautions will be taken. To start, the site will be more exacting about using SSL (in the "Knowledge Is Power" content management example, SSL was used to send the user to PayPal and back, but otherwise ignored). The first checkout page in the Coffee site will use SSL, and SSL will continue to be required throughout the checkout process and on every administration page.

The second security distinction will be the placement of every administration page in a separate, password-protected directory. Third, as previously mentioned, the site will use *stored procedures*, which is a more secure way to interact with the database.

# DATABASE DESIGN

Since the Coffee site is more complex than the "Knowledge Is Power" example, the database is correspondingly more involved. I've come up with 12 tables, evenly split between those for representing the catalog of products and those associated with the customers and orders.

## Product Tables

Six product-related tables represent the specifics about all the products available on the Coffee site (**Figure 7.3**).

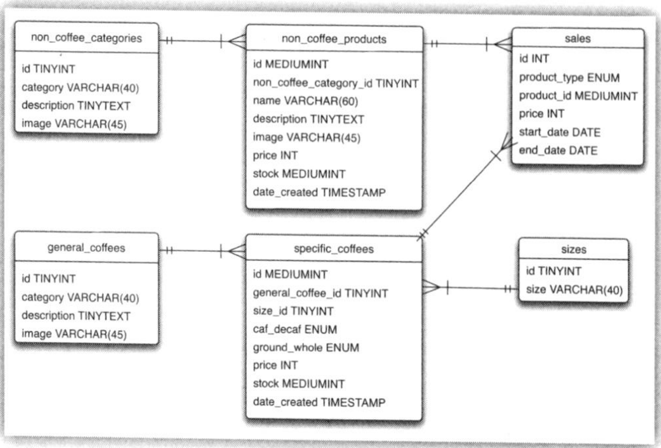


**Figure 7.3**

The **non_coffee_categories** table stores the general types of non-coffee products that will be sold: books, mugs, edibles, and so on. This table has columns for the category name, a description, and an image (the image will display on a page that lists the categories). The **non_coffee_products** table has a many-to-one relationship with **non_coffee_categories**. Each product will be in one category and each category will have multiple products (Figure 7.3). The **non_coffee_products** table has foreign key, name, description, image, price, stock, and creation-date columns. This table represents the specific non-coffee products that customers will purchase, and its **id** field will become part of the product's SKU. The **stock** field contains an indication of the quantity of the item in stock, not a simple *Yes/No*.

**tip**

All prices in the database are stored in integer fields and will represent the price in cents.

The **general_coffees** and **specific_coffees** tables have a parallel relationship to the two non-coffee tables. The **general_coffees** table is defined exactly like **non_coffee_categories** and will represent the primary types of coffee sold. For those types, I'm using a somewhat pedestrian organization, mixing roasts, bean types, and flavors: original, dark roast, vanilla, Kona, and so on. If the customer knew he wanted to purchase Kona coffee, he'd look into that coffee "category." The **specific_coffees** table lists the actual items the customer would purchase, which is a combination of the coffee "category," a size, ground or whole beans, and caffeinated or decaffeinated. Each combination of these qualities gets its own record in this table, and therefore its own SKU, price, and quantity in stock. This allows the customer to purchase a pound of ground Kona coffee or two pounds of decaffeinated whole beans. The available sizes come from the **sizes** table.

**tip**

If you're selling variations on a product, like clothing in different sizes and colors, you'd use a structure similar to the coffee tables.

The sixth table pertaining to products is **sales**. A sale is defined by overriding the price of an item. The easy way to do this would be to change the price in one of the products tables, but then you wouldn't have any indication that the new price is a sale price, as opposed to just the new default price. The **sales** table has a price column, plus start- and end-date columns, with the end date allowed to be **NULL**, indicating an open-ended sale. To associate the price override with a specific product, the product's type and ID numbers are stored. If the **product_type** is **coffee**, the **product_id** will be the **id** value from the **specific_coffees** table. If the **product_type** is **goodies**, the **product_id** will be the **id** value from the **non_coffee_products** table.

## Customer Tables

Four customer-related tables will represent an individual order, starting with **customers**, which stores the customer's name, mailing address, email address, and phone number (**Figure 7.4**).

**note**

Figure 7.4 loosely reflects the relationships between the product-related tables—**sales, specific_coffees,** and **non_coffee_products**—and the order-related tables: **order_contents, carts,** and **wish_lists**.

**note**

Because no customer registration is required, or allowed, the same customer may be repeated multiple times in the **customers** table.

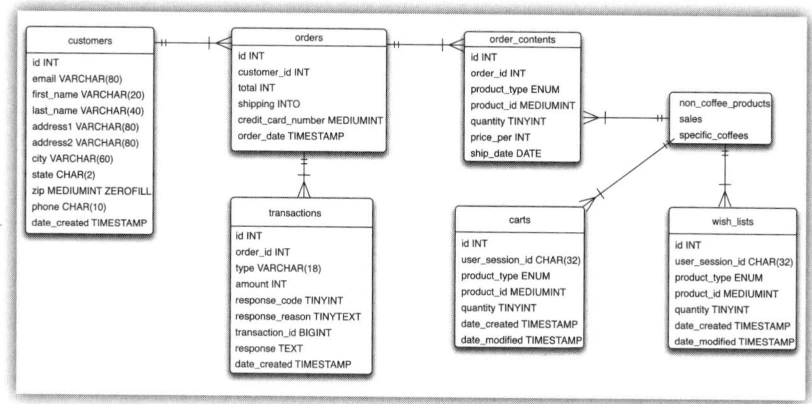


Figure 7.4

The **orders** table will store individual, completed orders. It stores a foreign key to the **customers** table, the total of the order, the cost of shipping, the date and time the order was entered, and part of the customer's credit card number. Note that the site won't be storing the full credit card number, just the last four digits (so that the site can indicate the card used, as in *####).

The **order_contents** table represents the actual items purchased in an order. It has a foreign key to the **orders** table, plus the **product_type** and **product_id** columns as in the **sales** table. The **quantity** and **price** columns indicate the number ordered and the price paid per item. This is necessary because there may be a sale price and, over time, the prices in the two products tables will change. Finally, the **ship_date** column is **NULL** by default, indicating that the item hasn't shipped. When the item ships, this column's value will be set to that ship date and the customer will be billed for that part of the order.

The **transactions** table will be used to record every interaction between this web application and the payment gateway, Authorize.net. The first four columns are for internal use, tying the transactions to a specific order and recording exactly what was being attempted. The bulk of the columns then store parts of the Authorize.net response. You'll see how this table is used in Chapter 10, "Checking Out."

The **carts** and **wish_lists** tables have mirrored definitions and require a bit of explanation. I decided that this project wouldn't use sessions at all, in part because the user isn't logging in and out and therefore isn't being tracked. But if I forgo formal PHP sessions and move session-like functionality to the database, the site can still have some data permanence. By storing the customer's shopping cart contents and wish-list items in the database, the customer can leave and return (in a day, a week, or a month) and still have her previous actions recorded and available, without ever logging in. This is a nice feature that only requires a single cookie. To accomplish all this, the **carts** table records everything that's in the customer's cart (the items the customer intends to purchase now) and the **wish_lists** table records everything that the customer has saved for later (items the customer intends to purchase down the road). Each item gets listed as its own record, indicating the quantity, product type, and product ID. Each item stored is associated with a **user_cookie_id**, which will be a unique representative value that's stored in the user's cookie.

From a marketing standpoint, this system means that customers could be emailed to

- Remind them to complete an order (gently: you want to be careful about this)
- Let them know that an item they are interested in has just gone on sale
- Let them know about similar items they may like
- Warn them that a sale item is about to go off sale

Of course to do any of these, the site would need to get the customer's email address at some point and store it in the **carts** and **wish_lists** tables. The site should also require the customer to formally opt in to such communications.

## The SQL

Here are the complete SQL commands for creating the tables:

**tip**

Because no customer registration is required, or allowed, the same customer may be repeated multiple times in the **customers** table.

```
CREATE TABLE `carts` (
   `id` INT(10) UNSIGNED NOT NULL AUTO_INCREMENT,
   `user_session_id` CHAR(32) NOT NULL,
   `product_type` ENUM('coffee','goodies') NOT NULL,
   `product_id` MEDIUMINT(8) UNSIGNED NOT NULL,
   `quantity` TINYINT(3) UNSIGNED NOT NULL,
   `date_created` TIMESTAMP NOT NULL DEFAULT CURRENT_TIMESTAMP,
   `date_modified` TIMESTAMP NOT NULL DEFAULT '0000-00-00 00:00:00',
   PRIMARY KEY (`id`),
   KEY `product_type` (`product_type`,`product_id`),
   KEY `user_session_id` (`user_session_id`)
) ENGINE=InnoDB  DEFAULT CHARSET=utf8;
```

*(continues on next page)*

```
CREATE TABLE `customers` (
   `id` INT(10) UNSIGNED NOT NULL AUTO_INCREMENT,
   `email` VARCHAR(80) NOT NULL,
   `first_name` VARCHAR(20) NOT NULL,
   `last_name` VARCHAR(40) NOT NULL,
   `address1` VARCHAR(80) NOT NULL,
   `address2` VARCHAR(80) DEFAULT NULL,
   `city` VARCHAR(60) NOT NULL,
   `state` CHAR(2) NOT NULL,
   `zip` MEDIUMINT(5) UNSIGNED zerofill NOT NULL,
   `phone` CHAR(10) NOT NULL,
   `date_created` TIMESTAMP NOT NULL DEFAULT CURRENT_TIMESTAMP,
   PRIMARY KEY (`id`),
   KEY `email` (`email`)
) ENGINE=InnoDB  DEFAULT CHARSET=utf8;
CREATE TABLE `general_coffees` (
   `id` TINYINT(3) UNSIGNED NOT NULL AUTO_INCREMENT,
   `category` VARCHAR(40) NOT NULL,
   `description` TINYTEXT,
   `image` VARCHAR(45) NOT NULL,
   PRIMARY KEY (`id`),
   UNIQUE KEY `type` (`category`)
) ENGINE=InnoDB  DEFAULT CHARSET=utf8;
CREATE TABLE `non_coffee_categories` (
   `id` TINYINT(3) UNSIGNED NOT NULL AUTO_INCREMENT,
   `category` VARCHAR(40) NOT NULL,
   `description` TINYTEXT NOT NULL,
   `image` VARCHAR(45) NOT NULL,
   PRIMARY KEY (`id`),
   UNIQUE KEY `category` (`category`)
) ENGINE=InnoDB  DEFAULT CHARSET=utf8;
CREATE TABLE `non_coffee_products` (
   `id` MEDIUMINT(8) UNSIGNED NOT NULL AUTO_INCREMENT,
   `non_coffee_category_id` TINYINT(3) UNSIGNED NOT NULL,
   `name` VARCHAR(60) NOT NULL,
   `description` TINYTEXT,
   `image` VARCHAR(45) NOT NULL,
   `price` INT(10) UNSIGNED NOT NULL,
   `stock` MEDIUMINT(8) UNSIGNED NOT NULL DEFAULT '0',
   `date_created` TIMESTAMP NOT NULL DEFAULT CURRENT_TIMESTAMP,
```

```
  PRIMARY KEY (`id`),
  KEY `non_coffee_category_id` (`non_coffee_category_id`)
) ENGINE=InnoDB  DEFAULT CHARSET=utf8;
CREATE TABLE `orders` (
  `id` INT(10) UNSIGNED NOT NULL AUTO_INCREMENT,
  `customer_id` INT(10) UNSIGNED NOT NULL,
  `total` INT(10) UNSIGNED DEFAULT NULL,
  `shipping` INT(10) UNSIGNED NOT NULL DEFAULT 0,
  `credit_card_number` MEDIUMINT(4) ZEROFILL UNSIGNED NOT NULL,
  `order_date` TIMESTAMP NOT NULL DEFAULT CURRENT_TIMESTAMP,
  PRIMARY KEY (`id`),
  KEY `order_date` (`order_date`),
  KEY `customer_id` (`customer_id`)
) ENGINE=InnoDB  DEFAULT CHARSET=utf8;
CREATE TABLE `order_contents` (
  `id` INT(10) UNSIGNED NOT NULL AUTO_INCREMENT,
  `order_id` INT(10) UNSIGNED NOT NULL,
  `product_type` ENUM('coffee','goodies') DEFAULT NULL,
  `product_id` MEDIUMINT(8) UNSIGNED NOT NULL,
  `quantity` TINYINT(3) UNSIGNED NOT NULL,
  `price_per` INT(10) UNSIGNED NOT NULL,
  `ship_date` DATE DEFAULT NULL,
  PRIMARY KEY (`id`),
  KEY `ship_date` (`ship_date`),
  KEY `product_type` (`product_type`,`product_id`)
  KEY `order_id`
) ENGINE=InnoDB  DEFAULT CHARSET=utf8;
CREATE TABLE `sales` (
  `id` INT(10) UNSIGNED NOT NULL AUTO_INCREMENT,
  `product_type` ENUM('coffee','goodies') DEFAULT NULL,
  `product_id` MEDIUMINT(8) UNSIGNED NOT NULL,
  `price` INT(10) UNSIGNED NOT NULL,
  `start_date` DATE NOT NULL,
  `end_date` DATE DEFAULT NULL,
  PRIMARY KEY (`id`),
  KEY `start_date` (`start_date`),
  KEY `product_type` (`product_type`,`product_id`)
) ENGINE=InnoDB  DEFAULT CHARSET=utf8;
```

*(continues on next page)*

```
CREATE TABLE `sizes` (
  `id` TINYINT(3) UNSIGNED NOT NULL AUTO_INCREMENT,
  `size` VARCHAR(40) NOT NULL,
  PRIMARY KEY (`id`),
  UNIQUE KEY `size` (`size`)
) ENGINE=InnoDB  DEFAULT CHARSET=utf8;
CREATE TABLE `specific_coffees` (
  `id` MEDIUMINT(8) UNSIGNED NOT NULL AUTO_INCREMENT,
  `general_coffee_id` TINYINT(3) UNSIGNED NOT NULL,
  `size_id` TINYINT(3) UNSIGNED NOT NULL,
  `caf_decaf` ENUM('caf','decaf') DEFAULT NULL,
  `ground_whole` ENUM('ground','whole') DEFAULT NULL,
  `price` INT(10) UNSIGNED NOT NULL,
  `stock` MEDIUMINT(8) UNSIGNED NOT NULL DEFAULT '0',
  `date_created` TIMESTAMP NOT NULL DEFAULT CURRENT_TIMESTAMP,
  PRIMARY KEY (`id`),
  KEY `general_coffee_id` (`general_coffee_id`),
  KEY `size` (`size_id`)
) ENGINE=InnoDB  DEFAULT CHARSET=utf8;
CREATE TABLE `transactions` (
  `id` INT(10) UNSIGNED NOT NULL AUTO_INCREMENT,
  `order_id` INT(10) UNSIGNED NOT NULL,
  `type` VARCHAR(18) NOT NULL,
  `amount` INT(10) UNSIGNED NOT NULL,
  `response_code` TINYINT(1) UNSIGNED NOT NULL,
  `response_reason` TINYTEXT,
  `transaction_id` BIGINT(20) UNSIGNED NOT NULL,
  `response` TEXT NOT NULL,
  `date_created` TIMESTAMP NOT NULL DEFAULT CURRENT_TIMESTAMP,
  PRIMARY KEY (`id`),
  KEY `order_id` (`order_id`)
) ENGINE=InnoDB  DEFAULT CHARSET=utf8;
CREATE TABLE `wish_lists` (
  `id` INT(10) UNSIGNED NOT NULL AUTO_INCREMENT,
  `user_session_id` CHAR(32) NOT NULL,
  `product_type` ENUM('coffee','goodies') DEFAULT NULL,
  `product_id` MEDIUMINT(8) UNSIGNED NOT NULL,
  `quantity` TINYINT(3) UNSIGNED NOT NULL,
  `date_created` TIMESTAMP NOT NULL DEFAULT CURRENT_TIMESTAMP,
  `date_modified` TIMESTAMP NOT NULL DEFAULT '0000-00-00 00:00:00',
  PRIMARY KEY (`id`),
```

```
  KEY `product_type` (`product_type`,`product_id`),
  KEY `user_session_id` (`user_session_id`)
) ENGINE=InnoDB  DEFAULT CHARSET=utf8;
```

The table definitions and column types should be easily understood, given the descriptions of the tables already provided. I want to point out that every table uses the *InnoDB* storage engine. This is the default table type for MySQL, giving the best performance and data integrity. InnoDB also supports database transactions, meaning that a series of commands that populate both tables can be set to either completely succeed or entirely roll back.

**tip**

As an extra measure, you could add foreign key constraints for better data integrity.

As previously mentioned, all prices are stored in integer columns, as cents. Every table uses the UTF8 character set, as will the HTML pages.

# SERVER SETUP

There are a few more server needs in the Coffee e-commerce example than in the "Knowledge Is Power" site, so let's look at those in detail.

## Server Organization

The server organization—how the files and folders are laid out—is represented in **Figure 7.5**. One file, the MySQL connection script, is stored outside the web root directory. Within the web root directory are folders for the CSS, images, and JavaScript. All the administrative pages will go in the **admin** directory, which you should rename to something less obvious. The **includes** directory will contain PHP and HTML scripts only included by other PHP scripts. For example, this is where the configuration file, the HTML header, and the HTML footer will go.

**tip**

For extra security, you could put the administration pages in a subdomain, such as **https://admin.example.com**.

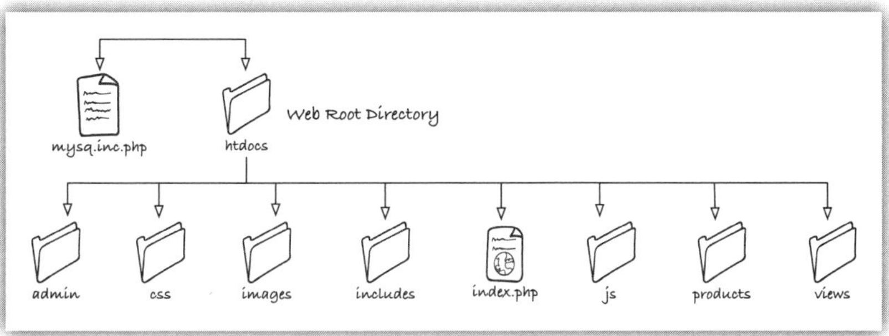


**Figure 7.5**

The **products** directory is a special case in that it'll store the images for the products sold on the site. Those products will be added via PHP, so this directory needs to be writable by the web server. For even more security, you could place this directory outside the web root and use a proxy script to serve every image (just like the PDF handling in Part 2). However, the admin script will have plenty of precautions to prevent abuse of this open directory. As an extra security technique to keep people from browsing the contents of this directory, place a blank **index.html** file in the **products** and **includes** folders. By doing so, you ensure that the web server won't provide a list of the folder's files to a nosy visitor.

The **views** directory will store files that represent individual snippets of HTML. These snippets will be used to display site components such as these:

- The contents of the home page
- The shopping cart
- The wish list
- A listing of categories
- A listing of products

The **views** directory is part of the MVC breakdown that the site uses. Next, you'll see how to protect this and the other sensitive directories from prying eyes.

## Customizing the Server Behavior

For this site, you need to customize how your server runs in four ways. Your ability to perform any of these alterations will depend on your hosting situation, although most hosts will allow at least two of the four alterations. The specific steps involved also depend on your hosting situation as well as your web server application (Apache, nginx, IIS, etc.). Here, I'll provide instructions for Apache, still the most common web server.

### APPLYING PASSWORD PROTECTION

Figure 7.6

The administration directory needs to be password protected so that only authenticated users can access its contents. If you want to get your hands dirty, you can accomplish this by connecting to your server via a command-line interface and executing the proper commands (search online for what those would be). Or, most likely, your web host provides a way to password-protect a directory through the site's control panel (**Figure 7.6**).

The control panel should take you to a form where you can indicate what directory to protect, as well as what message should be provided to someone attempting to access that directory (**Figure 7.7**). This message will appear in the browser's login prompt (**Figure 7.8**). Depending on your control panel, you might use another form to establish the username and password required to access the protected directory (**Figure 7.9**).

As always, use obscure and secure usernames, passwords, and directory names for administrative folders.

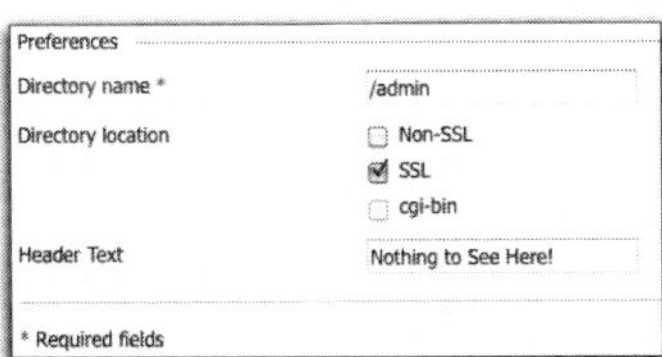


**Figure 7.7**

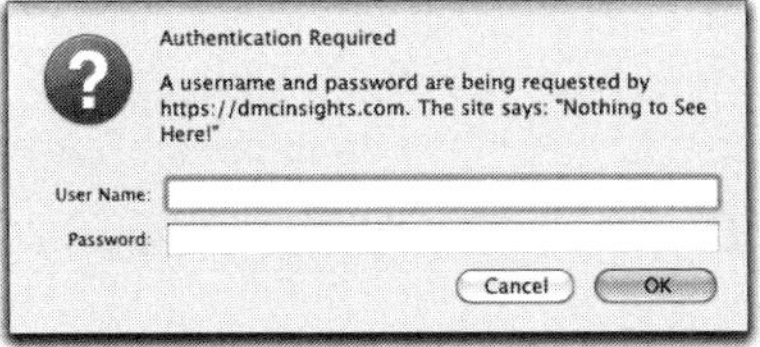


**Figure 7.8**

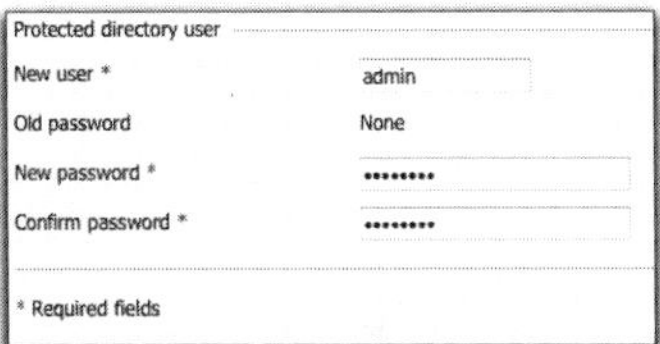


**Figure 7.9**

## PROTECTING OTHER DIRECTORIES

Beyond password protection, there are other ways you can keep a folder safe from unwanted visitors. The process of password-protecting a directory creates (or modifies) an **.htaccess** file. The **.htaccess** file alters how the Apache web server treats that directory and its contents (other web servers use other approaches). This file, literally named **.htaccess** and placed in the directory you want to affect (or a parent directory), has a specific syntax for achieving different effects.

For example, you can use the **.htaccess** file to make a directory entirely unavailable through a web browser. Here's the syntax for doing that:

```
# Disable indexing:
Options All -Indexes
# Ignore every file:
IndexIgnore *
# Prevent access to any file:
<FilesMatch "^.*$">
Order Allow,Deny
Deny from all
</FilesMatch>
```

As the comments indicate (comments in an **.htaccess** file are preceded by a **#**), the first command allows every option except for indexing, which is to say the web server shouldn't create an index of the directory. The second command says that every file should be ignored by any indexing (this is an extra precaution).

The final block applies a set of rules to a group of files consisting of every file in the directory (`^.*$`). The **`Order Allow,Deny`** command indicates that all *allow* rules should be checked first; then all *deny* rules are applied. Next, the **`Deny from all`** command says that no one should be allowed access.

If you create a file with a name of **`.htaccess`** that contains that code and place it in both your **`includes`** and **`views`** directories, no one will be able to see the contents of those directories, or a specific file within either folder, through a browser (**Figure 7.10**).

**Forbidden**

You don't have permission to access /includes/footer.html on this server.

**Figure 7.10**

**tip**

This section packs a lot of information about **`.htaccess`** files and Apache configuration into a small area. Look online to expand your knowledge of these important subjects.

Most likely, your web host won't have a control panel tool for editing **`.htaccess`** files, but you might be able to create one in any text editor, and then FTP it to the web server. Or you could create one on the server via a command-line interface, an SSH connection, and a command-line text editor like vi or Emacs.

Understand that using **`.htaccess`** files will work only if the web server is configured to allow changes on a directory basis. This setting is dictated by the server's primary configuration file, which is likely outside your influence, unless you have your own server.

## USING MOD_REWRITE

The next server alteration, which also requires **`.htaccess`** files, is to use Apache's mod_rewrite feature.

As mentioned in Chapter 5, "Managing Site Content," one way to improve the search engine rankings of your site is to use descriptive URLs. Accomplishing this—creating so-called "pretty" URLs—requires using mod_rewrite, which is Apache's rewrite module. This tool can transform URLs from one format to another, behind the scenes, so that the browser (that is, the user) is unaware of the change.

## PROBLEMS WITH URLS AND MOD_REWRITE

With the first edition of the book, the use of mod_rewrite resulted in the most confusion and number of questions in my support forums. To hopefully nip that in the bud, I'll first say that using mod_rewrite to change the URLs is entirely optional. The site can work without it; you'll just need to change some of the PHP and HTML accordingly. I'll explain what changes you'd make when the time is right. That being said, if you're implementing mod_rewrite, I'll go ahead and identify a couple of the most common problems and solutions here.

One problem you might find is that when you go to run the site in your browser, your images don't appear or your page isn't formatted properly (as if the CSS file weren't included). The problem is actually in your HTML; it's not an Apache issue. This is most likely due to where you put your files relative to the web root directory. See the sidebar "Using a Subdirectory" later in this chapter to learn more.

When you go to test the site, if you find that the links aren't working, that could be because of the HTML or mod_rewrite. Again, you'll want to see the "Using a Subdirectory" sidebar if you haven't placed the files in the web root directory. If the files are in the web root directory, then your mod_rewrite may not be working for some reason. Start by confirming that mod_rewrite is enabled and working in the most minimal way. One way to do that is to test a simple rule:

```
RewriteRule ^test/?$ index.php
```

With that rule in place, attempts to go to http://www.example.com/test/ should result in the index page being displayed. Running this test should help you see whether the problem is with mod_rewrite not working at all or not working for the specific links in the Coffee example.

Finally, you may also have problems where the browser is being redirected to the correct page but the values don't seem to be passed in the URL (there's nothing in **`$_GET`**). It's likely that the solution to that problem is to begin your **`.htaccess`** file like so:

```
<IfModule mod_rewrite.c>
Options -MultiViews
RewriteEngine on
```

That code disables Apache's MultiViews feature. MultiViews is an Apache tool that will try to find the best possible match for a URL. For example, with MultiViews enabled, Apache might automatically provide the page **`sales.php`** when you go to /sales/ in the browser, even without a rewrite rule in place. This useful tool can be a problem with mod_rewrite, so you may need to disable it, as the previous code does.

For the Coffee site, two public URLs need to be rewritten: **shop.php** and **browse.php**. The shop page will list the general coffee and non-coffee product categories. To know which to display, the page needs to receive a **type** value in the URL. Instead of having URLs like **shop.php?type=coffee**, let's use **shop/coffee/**. To accomplish this, create an **.htaccess** file in the web root directory that starts off with

```
<IfModule mod_rewrite.c>
RewriteEngine on
</IfModule>
```

These lines say that if the **mod_rewrite** module exists, turn on the rewrite engine. After turning on the rewrite engine and before the closing **IfModule**, you define rules. Here's the complete set of rules that will be defined; I'll explain them subsequently in detail:

```
<IfModule mod_rewrite.c>
RewriteEngine on

# For sales:
RewriteRule ^shop/sales/?$ sales.php

# For the primary categories:
RewriteRule ^shop/(coffee|goodies)/?$ /shop.php?type=$1

# For specific products:
RewriteRule ^browse/(coffee|goodies)/([A-Za-z\+\-]+)/([0-9]+)/?$
➥browse.php?type=$1&category=$2&id=$3

</IfModule>
```

**tip**

The rewrite rules apply to the part of the URL after the hostname. In www.example.com/shop/coffee, the matching begins after www.example.com/.

For the **shop.php** script, the rule is

```
RewriteRule ^shop/([A-Za-z\+]+)/?$ shop.php?type=$1
```

A rewrite rule is written using this syntax:

```
RewriteRule <URL to match> <file to actually serve> [additional
➥settings]
```

For the URL to match, regular expressions are in use, so if you're unfamiliar with them, the rules may seem like hieroglyphics to you. I'll explain them in pieces, starting with the rule that matches the primary categories:

```
RewriteRule ^shop/(coffee|goodies)/?$ shop.php?type=$1
```

The middle chunk (between **RewriteRule** and **shop.php?type=$1**) identifies the URLs to match. That regular expression matches any URL that has text beginning (indicated by the caret ^) with **shop** followed by a slash. That needs to be followed by either the word **coffee** or the word **goodies**. The pipe (|) is the *or* operator in regular expressions, and it applies to the whole word (or grouping) on either side of it. Those two words, and the pipe, reside within parentheses to make a *grouping,* which will be relevant at the end of the rule. That grouping is followed by an *optional* slash. This slash is optional because it's followed by the question mark, which is a *quantifier modifier* in regular expressions. The question mark says that zero or one of the things it follows is acceptable. At the point of just **^shop/(coffee|goodies)/?**, the pattern matches **shop/coffee**, **shop/coffee/**, **shop/goodies**, or **shop/goodies/**.

Next is the dollar sign, which concludes the matching rule. The dollar sign marks the end of the string. This means that if any characters follow what's been matched to this point, the match is invalidated. Put another way, the final dollar sign still allows for **shop/coffee** or **shop/coffee/** but doesn't allow for **shop/coffee/a** or **shop/coffee/123**.

When a match is made, the URL will be rewritten to **shop.php?type=$1**. The **$1** represents whatever string matched the first grouping: **(coffee|goodies)**. This is called *backreferencing* because it refers back to something already found. The end result is that **shop/coffee** and **shop/coffee/** become **shop.php?type=coffee** and **shop/goodies** becomes **shop.php?type=goodies**. In both cases, **$_GET['type']** will be available to the **shop.php** script because the rewrite module will create it and assign it a value.

Next in the **.htaccess** file, you'll find this:

```
RewriteRule ^shop/sales/?$ /sales.php
```

Whereas viewing the all product categories will be done through **shop.php**, the sale items will be listed on the **sales.php** script. But to make the URLs consistent, this rule is added. This rule specifically matches either **shop/sales** or **shop/sales/** and rewrites that as **sales.php**.

Continuing along, the **browse.php** page will list specific products in a general category: all the Kona coffees available or all the mugs. The browse script needs to know the category type and the specific category ID. For search engine optimization (SEO) purposes and to make the URL more accessible to the customer as well, the URL will be in the format **browse/*type*/*CategoryName*/*id***, such as **browse/coffee/Kona/3**.

Here's the rule to handle this:

```
RewriteRule ^browse/(coffee|goodies)/([A-Za-z\+\-]+)/([0-9]+)/?$
➥browse.php?type=$1&category=$2&id=$3
```

This rule matches any URL that begins with **browse**, followed by a slash, followed by either **coffee** or **goodies**, using code already explained. One of those two words must then be followed by a slash: **browse/coffee/** or **browse/goodies/**.

This bit is followed by some combination of letters, the plus sign, and a hyphen: **([A-Za-z\+\-])+**. The square brackets create a *class* of characters. The specific class matches upper- and lowercase letters and the plus sign, which is how spaces are represented in URLs (for example, *Kona Coffee* in a URL is *Kona+Coffee*). I've also allowed for a hyphen (\-). I preface both the plus sign and the hyphen with a backslash to prevent confusion (because both have other meanings in parts of regular expressions).

This class is followed by the plus sign, which is a quantity modifier that matches one or more of whatever the plus sign follows. So **browse/coffee/Kona+Coffee** matches **^browse/(coffee|goodies)/([A-Za-z\+\-]+)**, but just **browse** doesn't and neither does **browse/coffee/123**.

The class and plus sign quantity modifier is wrapped in parentheses to make the second grouping in this pattern. This grouping is followed by a *required* slash.

Finally, the pattern ends by matching one or more numbers: **[0-9]+**. This represents the ID value. This is the third grouping, and it can also be followed by an optional slash.

Now that the (somewhat complex) regular expression has been defined, a match can be made, and the rule just needs to indicate what file should be served for that URL. The incoming URL will be in the format **browse/*type*/*CategoryName*/*id***, such as **browse/coffee/Kona/3**, and should be handled by **browse.php**, passing along the type, category, and ID values in the URL:

```
browse.php?type=$1&category=$2&id=$3
```

That code makes use of **$1**, **$2**, and **$3**, which represent the first, second, and third matched groupings. Hence, **www.example.com/browse/coffee/Kona/3** becomes (behind the scenes): **www.example.com/browse.php?type=coffee&category=Kona&id=3**.

Whew!

## USING A SUBDIRECTORY

All the instructions and code in Part 3 assume that the website resides in the root directory. This means that http://localhost or http:// example.com point to the directory where the **index.php** file can be found.

If you place your site in a subdirectory of your web server, you'll need to make some additional changes to the **.htaccess** file and to your HTML code. This would be the case if your site URL is something like http://example.com/ex2/ or http://localhost/ecom/ex2/html/.

If you use a URL like that (because of your server setup and where you've put the files), the mod_rewrite rules won't work, your HTML links won't work, your images won't show up, and your CSS script won't be included. The solutions, however, are easy.

For the sake of simplicity, let's say you're using http://example.com/ex2/ as the URL, which means the site files are stored within the **ex2** folder of the web root directory. To fix the mod_rewrite, change the initial code to this:

```
<IfModule mod_rewrite.c>
RewriteEngine on
RewriteBase /ex2/
```

This additional lines tell mod_rewrite that all the rules apply as if they began with **/ex2/**. The alternative would be to update each rule to begin with **^/ex2/** (as in **^/ex2/shop/sales/**).

When you get to your HTML, you'll just need to preface all references to images, CSS, JavaScript, and links with **/ex2/**:

```
<link href="/ex2/css/style.css" rel="stylesheet" type="text/css" />
```

And:

```
<a href="/ex2/cart.php"><img alt="" src="/ex2/images/icon-cart.gif" /></a>
```

Those simple changes should make everything work perfectly for you when you've stored the site files within a web root subdirectory.

## ENFORCING SSL

While the site is already making use of mod_rewrite, let's utilize it further to enforce SSL for several pages:

- The entire administration directory
- **checkout.php**
- **billing.php**
- **final.php**

To do this, you must have SSL enabled (see the "Enabling SSL" sidebar), and add this code to your **.htaccess** file, within the same **<IfModule mod_rewrite.c>** block:

```
RewriteCond %{HTTPS} off
RewriteRule ^(checkout\.php|billing\.php|final\.php|admin/(.*))$
➥https://%{HTTP_HOST}/$1 [R=301,L]
```

The first line checks for the condition where HTTPS is off: **%{*something*}** refers to a server environmental variable. Then the rule attempts to match **checkout.php**, **billing.php**, **final.php**, or **admin/*anything***. If a match is made, the URL is rewritten to **https://*hostname*/$1**, where **$1** is the matched item.

The **R=301,L** part says that this should be a permanent redirection type, associated with the server code 301, and that this should be the last rule evaluated.

By adding this rule, you ensure that the server won't allow the browser to load any of those pages over a nonsecure connection. Obviously if you don't have SSL enabled on your machine (which means you're not handling or processing any credit cards, because you can't do that without SSL), then don't include these two new lines.

## ENABLING SSL

Enabling SSL on your server is an important step to take for any e-commerce project, but unfortunately one for which I can't provide you with specific directions. There are just too many factors involved, from the hosting company, to the server type, to where you get your SSL certificate. In Chapter 2, "Security Fundamentals," I talked about some of the sites that offer digital certificates and what features you should consider. If you buy one through your hosting company, the company will likely install it for you, which is a benefit. If you buy one through a third party, you may save money but have to install it yourself (although the third party should provide some instructions). In that case, you may be able to install the certificate through your web-hosting control panel. If that's not an option, then installation is a matter of using the command line to put the right files in the right places and then editing the server's configuration files. There are plenty of tutorials online that will explain the steps in detail.

# HELPER FILES

The Coffee site will use several helper files, not including the HTML templates and views. The first two discussed in this chapter are largely the same, in syntax and usage, as the corresponding scripts in Part 2, but let's look at them individually, just to be thorough.

## Connecting to the Database

The first helper script will connect to the database. This file, named **mysql.inc.php**, should ideally be stored outside the web directory (see Figure 7.5). Here's how it's defined:

```
<?php
// Set the database access information as constants:
DEFINE('DB_USER', 'username');
DEFINE('DB_PASSWORD', 'password');
DEFINE('DB_HOST', 'localhost');
DEFINE('DB_NAME', 'ecommerce2');

// Make the connection:
$dbc = mysqli_connect(DB_HOST, DB_USER, DB_PASSWORD, DB_NAME);

// Set the character set:
mysqli_set_charset($dbc, 'utf8');

// Omit the closing PHP tag to avoid 'headers already sent' errors!
```

This code is pretty much the same as that in Chapter 3, "First Site: Structure and Design," except that the connection constants will have different values, and there's no need for the **escape_data()** function. That function isn't required because stored procedures and prepared statements will be used instead (covered near the end of this chapter).

**note**

Make sure you're using unique and secure usernames and passwords, unlike my purposefully obvious ones!

To improve the security of this example, you could create different MySQL users that have different permissions on specific tables. The most common MySQL user would have **SELECT** permissions on all the non-customer-related tables; another MySQL user would have **SELECT** plus **INSERT**, **UPDATE**, and **DELETE** permissions on the **carts** and **wish_lists** tables; and a third would have only **INSERT** permissions on the order-related tables. To switch the MySQL user on a page-by-page basis, you'd indicate the user type prior to including the MySQL connection script:

```
$user = 'general';
require (MYSQL);
```

Then, in the connection script, you'd have

```
DEFINE('DB_HOST', 'localhost');
DEFINE('DB_NAME', 'ecommerce2');
if (isset($user) && ($user === 'general')) {
   DEFINE('DB_USER', 'username');
   DEFINE('DB_PASSWORD', 'password');
} elseif (isset($user) && ($user === 'cart')) {
   DEFINE('DB_USER', 'otherUser');
   DEFINE('DB_PASSWORD', 'otherPassword');
} elseif…
```

## The Configuration File

The configuration file in this site does pretty much what the configuration file in the "Knowledge Is Power" site did: define site settings, define constants, and declare an error handler. The Coffee site won't use sessions, though, so that's omitted from the configuration file, as is the redirection function.

```
<?php
// Are we live?
if (!defined('LIVE')) DEFINE('LIVE', false);

// Errors are emailed here:
DEFINE('CONTACT_EMAIL', 'you@example.com');

// Determine location of files and the URL of the site:
define('BASE_URI', '/path/to/html/dir/');
define('BASE_URL', localhost/');
define('MYSQL', BASE_URI . 'mysql.inc.php');

function my_error_handler($e_number, $e_message, $e_file, $e_line,
➥$e_vars) {

   // Build the error message:
   $message = "An error occurred in script '$e_file' on line
   ➥$e_line:\n$e_message\n";

   // Add the backtrace:
   $message .= "<pre>" .print_r(debug_backtrace(), 1) . "</pre>\n";

   // Or just append $e_vars to the message:
   // $message .= "<pre>" . print_r ($e_vars, 1) . "</pre>\n";
```

```
  if (!LIVE) { // Show the error in the browser.

    echo '<div class="error">' . nl2br($message) . '</div>';

  } else { // Development (print the error).

    // Send the error in an email:
    error_log ($message, 1, CONTACT_EMAIL,
    ➥'From:admin@example.com');

    // Only print an error message in the browser, if the error
    ➥isn't a notice:
    if ($e_number != E_NOTICE) {
      echo '<div class="error">A system error occurred. We
      ➥apologize for the inconvenience.</div>';
    }

  } // End of $live IF-ELSE.

  return true; // So that PHP doesn't try to handle the error, too.

} // End of my_error_handler() definition.

// Use my error handler:
set_error_handler ('my_error_handler');

// Omit the closing PHP tag to avoid 'headers already sent' errors!
```

I should point out an inconsistency introduced by the error handler that may become apparent in the next few chapters. Every PHP script in this site uses *view files*—separate HTML pages—to display content. Technically, a separate view file should be created for displaying errors, too. Without such a file, you may see errors displayed in odd places. I've omitted a dedicated error view file here so as not to complicate things even further, but you can find it among the downloadable code available at www.LarryUllman.com.

Also, be certain to change the values of the constants to be correct for your setup. In particular, the **BASE_URI** and **BASE_URL** must be correct:

```
define('BASE_URI', '/path/to/html/dir/');
define('BASE_URL', 'localhost/');
```

**tip**

If you're unsure about any of the code in the helper files, see Part 2, where it's explained in detail.

The **`BASE_URI`** constant represents an absolute path to the web root directory using the filesystem. This might be, for example, **`C:\xampp\htdocs\ex2`** or **`/Applications/MAMP/htdocs/larry/ex2`**. On a hosted site, you'd need to check with your hosting company, but it might be something like **`/var/www/domain.com/httpdocs`**.

The **`BASE_URL`** is the domain and path that's used in the browser, without the scheme (http, https) but ending with a slash. This could be as simple as *localhost/* or *example.com/*, or it could have an additional folder reference if your files aren't in the web root directory: *localhost/ex2/* or *example.com/larry/ex2/*.

# THE HTML TEMPLATE

I feel that the HTML design for the Coffee site needs to be more graphically interesting than that used in the "Knowledge Is Power" site. Selling physical products requires that you appeal to the user's eye: Customers want to see what they're buying. Once again, designing something like that is well beyond my abilities. This time around, I'm turning to the Coffee template (**Figure 7.11**) offered by Templates.com (www.templates.com).

Figure 7.11

There's nothing particularly fancy from a PHP perspective in the HTML template, so rather than walking through the files in detail, I'll just present them in their entirety. You'll see that what follows is only moderately modified from the Templates.com original.

## The HTML Header

The HTML header file begins the page and uses the same dynamic system for setting the page title as used in Part 2 of this book. The header file also has the main navigation links.

```
<!DOCTYPE html PUBLIC "-//W3C//DTD XHTML 1.0 Strict//EN" "http://
➥www.w3.org/TR/xhtml1/DTD/xhtml1-strict.dtd">
<html xmlns="http://www.w3.org/1999/xhtml" xml:lang="en" lang="en">
<head>
<title><?php // Use a default page title if one wasn't provided...
if (isset($page_title)) {
   echo $page_title;
} else {
   echo 'Coffee - Wouldn\'t You Love a Cup Right Now?';
}
?></title>
<meta http-equiv="Content-Type" content="text/html; charset=utf-8"
/>
<meta name="description" content="Place your description here" />
<meta name="keywords" content="put, your, keyword, here" />
<meta name="author" content="Templates.com - website templates
➥provider" />
   <link href="/css/style.css" rel="stylesheet" type="text/css" />
<!--[if lt IE 7]>
   <script type="text/javascript" src="/js/ie_png.js"></script>
   <script type="text/javascript">
      ie_png.fix('.png, .logo h1, .box .left-top-corner, .box
      ➥.right-top-corner, .box .left-bot-corner, .box .right-
      ➥bot-corner, .box .border-left, .box .border-right, .box
      ➥.border-top, .box .border-bot, .box .inner, .special dd,
      ➥#contacts-form input, #contacts-form textarea');
   </script>
<![endif]-->
</head>
```

*(continues on next page)*

```
<body id="page1">
  <!-- header -->
  <div id="header">
    <div class="container">
    <div class="wrapper">
      <ul class="top-links">
      <li><a href="/index.php" class="first"><img alt=""
      ➥src="/images/icon-home.gif" /></a></li>
      <li><a href="/cart.php"><img alt=""
      ➥src="/images/icon-cart.gif" /></a></li>
      <li><a href="/contact.php"><img alt=""
      ➥src="/images/icon-mail.gif" /></a></li>
      <li><a href="/sitemap.php"><img alt=""
      ➥src="/images/icon-map.gif" /></a></li>
      </ul>
      <div class="logo">
      <h1><a href="/index.php">Coffee</a><span>Wouldn't you love a
      ➥cup right now?</span></h1>
      </div>
      </div>
      <ul class="nav">
      <!-- MENU -->
      <li><a href="/shop/coffee/">Coffee</a></li>
      <li><a href="/shop/goodies/">Goodies</a></li>
      <li><a href="/shop/sales/">Sales</a></li>
      <li><a href="/wishlist.php">Wish List</a></li>
      <li><a href="/cart.php">Cart</a></li>
      <!-- END MENU -->
    </ul>
    </div>
  </div>
  <!-- content -->
  <div id="content">
    <div class="container">
      <div class="inside">
```

## The HTML Footer

The footer file completes all the DIV tags, prints a small copyright, and links to Templates.com, which created the original template.

```
        </div>
      </div>
    </div>
    <!-- footer -->
    <div id="footer">
      <div class="container">
        <div class="indent">
          <div class="fleft"> &copy; - Clever Coffee, Inc.</div>
          <div class="fright">Site designed by: <a href=
          ➥"http://www.templates.com">Templates.com</a></div>
        </div>
      </div>
    </div>
</body>
</html>
```

## Adjusting Your References

An important aspect to note about both files is that every link, image, CSS script, and JavaScript file must be referenced from the web root directory. Because the URLs for some of the pages will be ***/something/other_thing***, such as **shop/coffee**, it will seem as if, on that page, the browser is accessing a file within the ***something/other_thing*** directory, when that's not actually the case. If you were to use a reference like **images/filename.gif** or **css/style.css**, the browser would look for **shop/coffee/images/filename.gif** and **shop/coffee/style.css**. Those obviously don't exist.

If you're not using mod_rewrite, you don't need to begin references with a slash.

The solution is to start all of the references with a slash, which says to begin in the web root directory (as in the above code). This will work as long as your site files are also in the web root directory. If you've placed them in a subdirectory, you must also add that to your references: **/ex2/images/filename.gif** or **/larry/ex2/style.css**.

I've also slightly modified the CSS file, which you can download from www.LarryUllman.com.

The use of mod_rewrite has complicated the HTML a bit, but the simple fact is that if your links aren't working, your images aren't appearing, or your CSS isn't being included, your references are incorrect and need to be adjusted for your setup.

## Creating Constants for HTML

Before leaving the template, I want to add two more constants to make the final view files easier to read. I like the template used by this example, but it's got a lot of HTML in it, particularly a lot of DIVs to create the fancy boxes. Here's an example:

```
<!-- box begin -->
<div class="box alt">
    <div class="left-top-corner">
        <div class="right-top-corner">

        </div>
    </div>
    <div class="border-left">
        <div class="border-right">
            <div class="inner">
            <h2>Your Shopping Cart</h2>
            <p>Your shopping cart is currently empty.</p>
            </div>
        </div>
    </div>
    <div class="left-bot-corner">
        <div class="right-bot-corner">
            <div class="border-bot"></div>
        </div>
    </div>
</div>
<!-- box end -->
```

Almost all of that code will be repeated verbatim in each view file. To save a lot of typing, to save you a lot of reading, and to save precious book pages, I'm going to represent the repeating HTML in two constants. You should add these to the configuration file:

**tip**

Arguably, to maintain the MVC approach, the beginning and ending of the HTML boxes should go in view files that would be included where necessary.

```
define('BOX_BEGIN', '<!-- box begin --><div class="box alt">
➥<div class="left-top-corner"><div class="right-top-corner">
➥<div class="border-top"></div></div></div><div class="border-left">
➥<div class="border-right"><div class="inner">');
define('BOX_END', '</div></div></div><div class="left-bot-corner">
➥<div class="right-bot-corner"><div class="border-bot"></div>
➥</div></div></div><!-- box end -->');
```

With those two constants defined, the previous code now becomes

```
<?php echo BOX_BEGIN; ?>
<h2>Your Shopping Cart</h2>
<p>Your shopping cart is currently empty.</p>
<?php echo BOX_END; ?>
```

To be entirely truthful, in a live site I may or may not do this, as all the HTML gets buried in view files and is generally out of site, out of mind. But in the book, all of that HTML is too much of a distraction and takes up too much space.

# MAKING THE MOST OF MYSQL

For improved security and to separate some database activity from the PHP code, this project will tap into a couple of more advanced features when it comes to using MySQL. I'm specifically speaking of *prepared statements* and *stored procedures*. In this chapter, I want to talk about the benefits of each feature as well as provide you with alternative approaches should you not meet the minimum requirements. That way, when you see the actual implementation of these features in subsequent chapters, you'll already know how you'll need to change your code if you're not using these approaches.

In terms of support for these features, if you have PHP 5+ and MySQL 5+, you should be fine. However, on a hosted site, you may not be able to use stored procedures; you'll need to check with your host to confirm.

## Prepared Statements

In database-based applications, many times the same query will be executed repeatedly using just slightly different parameters. For example, a query that paginates some results varies in its **LIMIT** clause:

```
SELECT * FROM tablename LIMIT 0, 20
SELECT * FROM tablename LIMIT 20, 20
SELECT * FROM tablename LIMIT 40, 20
```

An **INSERT** query varies in the values being inserted:

```
INSERT INTO tablename (column1, column2) VALUES ('value1', 'value2')
INSERT INTO tablename (column1, column2) VALUES ('valueX', 'valueY')
```

Unlike those five queries, which have both the table references and the data to be used hardcoded into them, a prepared statement separates the static content from the dynamic values, using placeholders for the latter:

```
SELECT * FROM tablename LIMIT ?, 20
INSERT INTO tablename (column1, column2) VALUES (?, ?)
```

The database is then asked to "prepare" the statement, at which point the database will confirm that the query is syntactically valid (assuming that values will later be provided for each placeholder). There can be a performance benefit to this approach, since the database can cache the preparation of the query, making subsequent uses of the same prepared statement faster.

After the statement is "prepared," the next steps are to provide a value for all the placeholders and then execute the query.

**tip**

This query comes from Chapter 4.

In terms of your PHP code, I'll explain how you go about using a prepared statement. Start by defining the query, using question marks to indicate the values to be provided later. For example, if the site had a login functionality, its query might look like

```
$q = 'SELECT id, username, type, pass, IF(date_expires >= NOW(),
➥true, false) AS expired FROM users WHERE email=?';
```

It's very important that you don't quote any placeholders, even if their values will be strings.

Then, call the **mysqli_prepare()** function, providing it with the database connection and the query:

```
$stmt = mysqli_prepare($dbc, $q);
```

This function returns a **MySQLi_STMT** object, to be used by later functions.

If you want to see any errors that might have occurred, you could next do this:

```
if (!$stmt) echo mysqli_stmt_error($stmt);
```

The next step is to *bind* the variables, which is how you associate each placeholder with a PHP variable:

```
mysqli_stmt_bind_param($stmt, 's', $email);
```

The first argument is the statement representative variable. The next is an indicator of the formats of the various placeholders, using one symbol for each placeholder. The available symbols are in **Table 7.1**.

**Table 7.1 Bound Value Types**

| Letter | Represents |
|---|---|
| d | Decimal |
| i | Integer |
| b | BLOB (binary data) |
| s | All other types |

For this query, there is one placeholder and it will be a string (that is, not a decimal, integer, or BLOB). The **mysqli_stmt_bind_params()** function then takes one variable for each placeholder. These variables can have any valid name and they wouldn't necessarily be existing variables prior to this point, because it's after this point that each variable is often assigned a value:

```
$email = $_POST['email'];
```

Finally, execute the statement:

```
mysqli_stmt_execute($stmt);
```

To clarify a common point of confusion, the variables bound to the placeholders must have their appropriate values when the **mysqli_stmt_execute()** function is called. As you'll see in a later chapter, this means that you can prepare and bind a statement, and then assign values to use within a loop or other control structure.

Also, and more importantly, you don't need to take any extra steps to prevent SQL injection attacks because the prepared statements already prevent them simply by separating the values from the rest of the query.

For **UPDATE** and **INSERT** queries, you can confirm that a record was affected using

```
if (mysqli_stmt_affected_rows($stmt) === 1) {
```

For **SELECT** queries, to count the number of returned rows, do this:

```
mysqli_stmt_store_result($stmt);
if (mysqli_stmt_num_rows($stmt) >= 1) {
```

Once you're finished with the prepared statement, you can close it and free up the resources:

```
mysqli_stmt_close($stmt);
```

All the previous code demonstrates *inbound* prepared statements, in which the values used in a query come from variables. You can also use *outbound* prepared statements—with or without inbound parameters—in which case the query's results are assigned to variables. Assuming the earlier query returned a row, you could then use

```
mysqli_stmt_store_result($stmt);
if (mysqli_stmt_num_rows($stmt) === 1) {
mysqli_stmt_bind_result($stmt, $id, $username, $type, $pass,
➥$expired);
mysqli_stmt_fetch($stmt);
```

At this point, the **$id**, **$username**, **$type**, **$pass**, and **$expired** variables have the values returned by the database.

tip

Chapter 11, "Site Administration," will use prepared statements exclusively.

If your server configuration doesn't support prepared statements, the solution is simple: Use **mysqli_query()** and the other standard functions as you normally would. Just make sure you use an escaping function and other techniques to prevent SQL injection attacks.

## Stored Procedures

note

Both *stored procedures* and *stored functions* fall under the general category of *stored routines*.

Stored procedures are a way to define blocks of code within the database itself. Instead of running a query on the database, you call the corresponding stored procedure, which will do the querying for you.

Stored procedures can offer the following benefits:

- Improved security
- Better performance
- Cleaner model-controller separation
- Increased application portability

note

I'm just introducing the concept of stored procedures here; later chapters will present much more context and syntax.

The most important of these is security. Because routines are stored within the database itself, the programming interface—PHP in this case—won't have direct access to the underlying tables and data. In fact, the interface wouldn't even need to know what tables and columns exist when stored procedures are used.

tip

I ran a few informal benchmarks and saw this book's stored procedures running significantly faster than the literal queries.

You can get better performance with a stored procedure in two ways. First, as you'll see, stored procedures require that less data be sent to the database, because you'll mostly be sending just values without any SQL (this is another security benefit). Second, stored procedures can be cached and managed so that the database executes them as efficiently as possible.

The cleaner model-controller separation is obvious: More logic goes into the database, removing SQL from the PHP code.

Stored procedures are associated with a specific database and become part of its definition.

As for the increased application portability, this is both true and not true. Because the logic will be stored in the database, other interfaces, like a Java application or the command line, can invoke the stored procedures in exactly the same way (this may or may not be beneficial to you). On the other hand, with the logic stored in the database, you could not as easily change the database application in use.

As stored procedures transfer more of the processing load from the web server to the database server, you may find that the database server becomes overloaded more quickly.

Stored procedures are created using this SQL command:

```
CREATE PROCEDURE name(arguments)
BEGIN
  CODE
END
```

The procedure's name can contain letters, numbers, and the underscore, but avoid using the same name as an existing MySQL function, keyword, database name, or table name.

Banks and other extremely secure environments rely on stored procedures for increased security.

For the procedure's arguments, give each argument a name and a MySQL-defined type, with multiple arguments separated by a comma:

```
CREATE PROCEDURE do_this(age INT, name VARCHAR(20)...
```

Again, stick to letters, numbers, and the underscore, and avoid using existing names and keywords for the argument names. Note that these are MySQL stored procedure variables, not PHP ones, so there are no dollar signs. The variable types are also basic, omitting extra qualities such as **UNSIGNED** or **NOT NULL**.

The **BEGIN** and **END** blocks aren't required with only a single command, but I think it's best to still use them.

The **BEGIN** and **END** blocks aren't required with only a single command, but you should always keep them in there. First, doing so clearly separates the procedure's logic from the rest of the syntax. Second, you won't create errors if you later add additional commands but forget to add **BEGIN** and **END**.

The ***CODE*** part is where the magic happens. In this section you can execute SQL queries, create and manipulate variables, use control structures (conditionals and loops), and so forth. In layman's terms, whatever is the result of the ***CODE*** section will be what's returned by the stored procedure (that is, what you'd have to work with after invoking the stored procedure in PHP).

You must use parentheses for the procedure's arguments, even if there are none.

There is, however, one little catch: Because MySQL, by default, uses the semicolon to terminate SQL commands, any use of a semicolon within the procedure's definition will terminate the *definition* itself. The workaround is to change the delimiter prior to the definition:

As with prepared statements, don't quote the arguments used *within* a stored procedure query, even if they are strings.

```
DELIMITER $$
CREATE PROCEDURE name(arguments)
BEGIN
  CODE
END$$
```

**Figure 7.12** shows a stored procedure being defined using the command-line MySQL client.

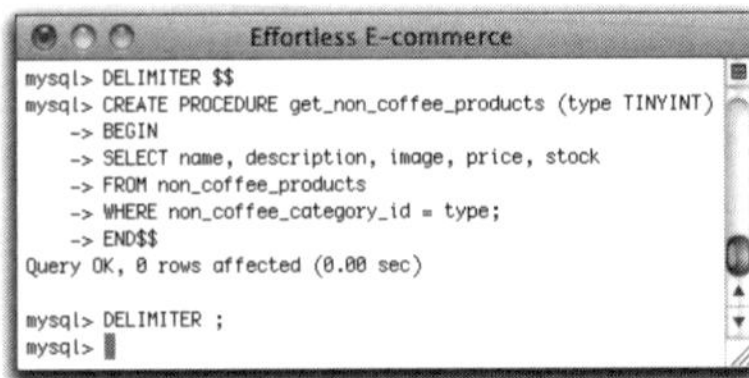


Figure 7.12

To execute a stored procedure, use **CALL** ***name (arguments)*** (**Figure 7.13**).

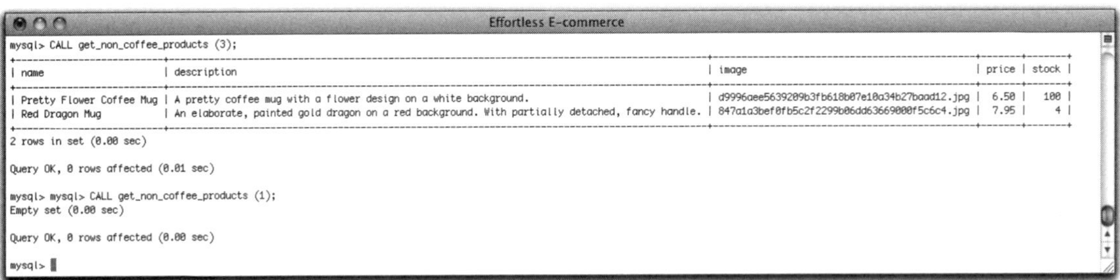


Figure 7.13

In PHP, you can use the **mysqli_query()** function to execute a stored procedure:

```
$r = mysqli_query("CALL get_non_coffee_products($id)");
```

Then you can use the **mysqli_fetch_array()** function to get the results.

The last thing you should know is that you can create stored procedures, using phpMyAdmin, the mysql command-line client, or whatever, just as you can execute any other query, provided that you're connected to the database as a user with that permission. The MySQL user you're connecting as must have **CREATE ROUTINE** permissions, which will normally also mean that the MySQL user also has **ALTER ROUTINE** and **EXECUTE** permissions. Unfortunately, I can't say how common it is for different web hosts to allow stored procedures. You'll need to check with yours to see.

MySQL permissions with respect to stored procedures are more complicated than I'm presenting it. See the MySQL manual if you want all the details.

If your server environment makes using stored procedures impossible, you'll need to move all the logic and SQL back into your PHP scripts and execute the SQL commands as you would standard queries. In case it's not obvious how to do that, Chapter 13 explains some of the conversions.

# 8 CREATING A CATALOG

After preparing the server for the site (see the previous chapter), the next step is to start creating the catalog, because the customer can't shop without it. To do so, you'll need to prepopulate the database with some products, since you won't develop the administrative scripts for adding products until Chapter 11, "Site Administration." Then you can write the two PHP scripts for generating the catalog: one for browsing by category and a second for listing specific products.

After that, the chapter demonstrates better ways to show the availability of products and any applicable sale prices. From there, you'll write new PHP scripts for showing the sale items on their own.

If you have intermediate PHP and MySQL experience, nothing in this chapter should be too challenging for you, although you'll learn some new tricks. On the other hand, the SQL queries in this chapter are some of the most complex in the book, and they'll be wrapped inside stored procedures to boot. You'll also see a real-world way of implementing the MVC design pattern in a moderately complex site.

# PREPARING THE DATABASE

The code in this chapter will use half of the database tables. To see any results in the browser, you'll need to insert some records into these tables first. For three of them—**general_coffees**, **non_coffee_categories**, and **sizes**, there will be no administration page created in the book. The data in all three tables should be fairly stable, and if you want administrative capability over them, it's easy enough for you to create corresponding administrative pages yourself. For the other three tables—**specific_coffees**, **non_coffee_products**, and **sales**—you'll create administrative scripts, but not until Chapter 11. For now, you'll populate these tables using just SQL, and then create the three stored procedures used by the PHP scripts in this chapter.

tip

See Chapter 7, "Second Site: Structure and Design," for a discussion of the database's tables.

## Populating the Tables Using SQL

You can populate any database table via any interface to the MySQL database. The two most common are the web-based phpMyAdmin and the command-line **mysql** client. With phpMyAdmin—which is what your web host likely provides (perhaps indirectly through another control panel)—you can use the SQL tab or the SQL query window to enter SQL commands.

tip

All of the SQL commands can be downloaded from www.LarryUllman.com.

Because this is an intermediate-level book, I'm going to assume that you already know how to communicate directly with the database. Once you've accessed the database via any interface, you can start populating the tables (assuming you've already defined them).

tip

Chapter 13, "Extending the Second Site," has additional code and ideas for augmenting what you'll do in this and the next three chapters.

1. Populate the **sizes** table:

```
INSERT INTO `sizes` (`size`) VALUES
('2 oz. Sample'), ('Half Pound'), ( '1 lb.'), ('2 lbs.'),
➥('5 lbs.');
```

   The **sizes** table is used by the **specific_coffees** table to indicate in what quantities someone can buy coffee. The table has only a primary key column and a **size** column. This query adds five values to the table.

2. Populate the **non_coffee_categories** table:

```
INSERT INTO `non_coffee_categories` (`category`, `description`,
➥`image`) VALUES
('Edibles', 'A wonderful assortment of goodies to eat. Includes
➥biscotti, baklava, lemon bars, and more!', 'goodies.jpg'),
('Gift Baskets', 'Gift baskets for any occasion! Including our
➥many coffees and other goodies.', 'gift_basket.jpg'),
```

*(continues on next page)*

tip

phpMyAdmin also provides an insert option, which presents forms through which you can add multiple records to a table.

```
('Mugs', 'A selection of lovely mugs for enjoying your coffee,
➥tea, hot cocoa or other hot beverages.', '781426_32573620.jpg'),
('Books', 'Our recommended books about coffee, goodies, plus
➥anything written by Larry Ullman!', 'books.jpg');
```

The **non_coffee_categories** table represents the categories of non-coffee items the site will sell—in short, the goodies. The three nonprimary key columns are **category**, **description**, and **image**. For the images, you'll need to create a representative image for each category, with a matching image name. The images should be placed in the **products** directory (see Figure 7.5). You can, of course, just copy the images available in the downloadable code from the book's corresponding website.

3. Populate the **general_coffees** table:

```
INSERT INTO `general_coffees` (`category`, `description`,
➥`image`) VALUES
('Original Blend', 'Our original blend, featuring a quality
➥mixture of bean and a medium roast for a rich color and smooth
➥flavor.', 'original_coffee.jpg'),
('Dark Roast', 'Our darkest, non-espresso roast, with a full
➥flavor and a slightly bitter aftertaste.', 'dark_roast.jpg'),
('Kona', 'A real treat! Kona coffee, fresh from the lush
➥mountains of Hawaii. Smooth in flavor and perfectly roasted!',
➥'kona.jpg');
```

This table has the same structure as **non_coffee_categories**. Again, grab the images from the downloadable files and place them in your **products** folder.

4. Populate the **non_coffee_products** table:

```
INSERT INTO `non_coffee_products` (`non_coffee_category_id`,
➥`name`, `description`, `image`, `price`, `stock`,
➥`date_created`) VALUES
(3, 'Pretty Flower Coffee Mug', 'A pretty coffee
➥mug with a flower design on a white background.',
➥'d9996aee5639209b3fb618b07e10a34b27baad12.jpg',
➥650, 100, NOW()),
(3, 'Red Dragon Mug', 'An elaborate, painted gold dragon on
➥a red background. With partially detached, fancy handle.',
➥'847a1a3bef0fb5c2f2299b06dd63669000f5c6c4.jpg', 795, 4, NOW());
```

In Chapter 11, you'll create a PHP script that does all the heavy lifting for you, so let's just create a couple of records in this table for now. Each product has a **non_coffee_category_id** of 3, which is **Mugs**. A specific name and description is provided, along with an image's name (also to be placed in the **products** directory). Next come the price and the quantity in stock. To test how stock availability will be handled, one product has plenty of stock and another very little.

For the prices, remember that they'll always be stored as integers: a stored value of 650 represents a price of 6.50, and 795 is 7.95.

5. Populate the **specific_coffees** table:

```
INSERT INTO `specific_coffees` (`general_coffee_id`, `size_id`,
➥`caf_decaf`, `ground_whole`, `price`, `stock`, `date_created`)
➥VALUES
(3, 1, 'caf', 'ground', 200, 20, NOW()),
(3, 2, 'caf', 'ground', 450, 30, NOW()),
(3, 2, 'decaf', 'ground', 500, 20, NOW()),
(3, 3, 'caf', 'ground', 800, 50, NOW()),
(3, 3, 'decaf', 'ground', 850, 20, NOW()),
(3, 3, 'caf', 'whole', 750, 50, NOW()),
(3, 3, 'decaf', 'whole', 800, 20, NOW()),
(3, 4, 'caf', 'whole', 1500, 30, NOW()),
(3, 4, 'decaf', 'whole', 1550, 15, NOW()),
(3, 5, 'caf', 'whole', 3250, 5, NOW());
```

To create specific coffee products to sell, you're creating multiple products of one coffee type (**Kona**, with a **general_coffee_id** of 3). The products come in varying sizes and combinations of caffeinated, decaffeinated, ground beans, and whole beans. The products have different prices and quantities in stock. Again, the prices are integers, in cents.

6. Populate the **sales** table:

```
INSERT INTO `sales` (`product_type`, `product_id`, `price`,
➥`start_date`, `end_date`) VALUES
('goodies', 1, 500, '2013-08-16', '2013-08-31'),
('coffee', 7, 700, '2013-08-19', NULL),
('coffee', 9, 1300, '2013-08-19', '2013-08-26'),
('goodies', 2, 700, '2013-08-22', NULL),
('coffee', 8, 1300, '2013-08-22', '2013-08-31'),
('coffee', 10, 3000, '2013-08-22', '2013-09-30');
```

**tip**

If you want, you can run some basic **SELECT** queries to confirm the database's contents.

Finally, let's put some items on sale by discounting their prices. For each sale item, you need to indicate a product type, the item's product ID (from the corresponding **specific_coffees** or **non_coffee_products** tables), the new price, and the starting date for the sale. The ending date is optional. Unless you're reading this book as I'm writing it, which would freak me out, you'll need to change the dates to be current for you.

## Looking at the Stored Procedure Queries

The three stored procedures about to be created will use six queries, four of which are relatively complex:

- All the specific coffee products when given a general coffee category
- All the specific non-coffee products when given a general non-coffee category
- All the sale items
- A few random sale items to be listed on the home page

**tip**

For help with complex SQL, search online, see the MySQL manual, or check out my *MySQL: Visual QuickStart Guide* (2nd Edition, Peachpit Press).

Before moving on to the stored procedures, let's look at these queries in detail. Truth be told, these queries are pretty complex and make the most of the database application. If you have any problems understanding any of these queries (after my explanations), break them down into their simplest forms, execute them, and then add additional pieces, reexecuting as you go. That way, you'll be able to see the impact of each **JOIN**, concatenation, and so forth.

### SELECTING EVERY COFFEE PRODUCT

The query for selecting every coffee product looks like this:

```
SELECT gc.description, gc.image, CONCAT("C", sc.id) AS sku,
CONCAT_WS(" - ", s.size, sc.caf_decaf, sc.ground_whole,
➥CONCAT("$", FORMAT(sc.price/100, 2))) AS name,
sc.stock
FROM specific_coffees AS sc INNER JOIN sizes AS s ON s.id=sc.size_id
INNER JOIN general_coffees AS gc ON gc.id=sc.general_coffee_id
WHERE general_coffee_id=<some_category_id> AND stock>0
ORDER by name ASC;
```

**Figure 8.1** shows the MySQL output for the query, when replacing **<some_category_id>** with the number 3 (for Kona coffee).

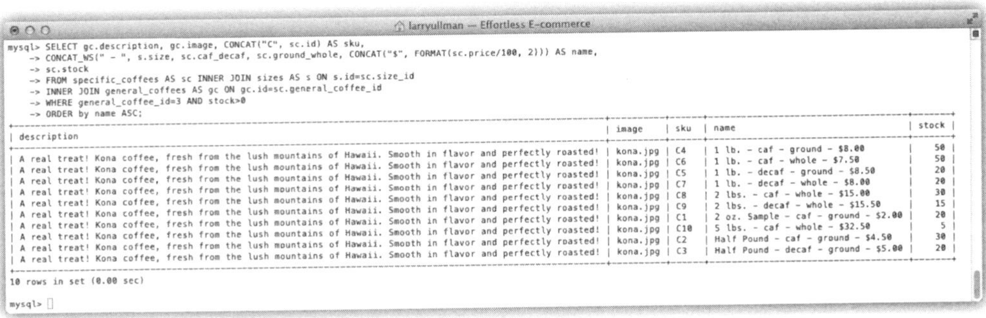

```
mysql> SELECT gc.description, gc.image, CONCAT("C", sc.id) AS sku,
    -> CONCAT_WS(" - ", s.size, sc.caf_decaf, sc.ground_whole, CONCAT("$", FORMAT(sc.price/100, 2))) AS name,
    -> sc.stock
    -> FROM specific_coffees AS sc INNER JOIN sizes AS s ON s.id=sc.size_id
    -> INNER JOIN general_coffees AS gc ON gc.id=sc.general_coffee_id
    -> WHERE general_coffee_id=3 AND stock>0
    -> ORDER by name ASC;
+-------------------------------------------------------------------------------+-----------+-----+--------------------------------------+-------+
| description                                                                   | image     | sku | name                                 | stock |
+-------------------------------------------------------------------------------+-----------+-----+--------------------------------------+-------+
| A real treat! Kona coffee, fresh from the lush mountains of Hawaii. Smooth in flavor and perfectly roasted! | kona.jpg | C4  | 1 lb. - caf - ground - $8.00         |    50 |
| A real treat! Kona coffee, fresh from the lush mountains of Hawaii. Smooth in flavor and perfectly roasted! | kona.jpg | C6  | 1 lb. - caf - whole - $7.50          |    50 |
| A real treat! Kona coffee, fresh from the lush mountains of Hawaii. Smooth in flavor and perfectly roasted! | kona.jpg | C5  | 1 lb. - decaf - ground - $8.50       |    20 |
| A real treat! Kona coffee, fresh from the lush mountains of Hawaii. Smooth in flavor and perfectly roasted! | kona.jpg | C7  | 1 lb. - decaf - whole - $8.00        |    20 |
| A real treat! Kona coffee, fresh from the lush mountains of Hawaii. Smooth in flavor and perfectly roasted! | kona.jpg | C8  | 2 lbs. - caf - whole - $15.00        |    30 |
| A real treat! Kona coffee, fresh from the lush mountains of Hawaii. Smooth in flavor and perfectly roasted! | kona.jpg | C9  | 2 lbs. - decaf - whole - $15.50      |    15 |
| A real treat! Kona coffee, fresh from the lush mountains of Hawaii. Smooth in flavor and perfectly roasted! | kona.jpg | C1  | 2 oz. Sample - caf - ground - $2.00  |    20 |
| A real treat! Kona coffee, fresh from the lush mountains of Hawaii. Smooth in flavor and perfectly roasted! | kona.jpg | C10 | 5 lbs. - caf - whole - $32.50        |     5 |
| A real treat! Kona coffee, fresh from the lush mountains of Hawaii. Smooth in flavor and perfectly roasted! | kona.jpg | C2  | Half Pound - caf - ground - $4.50    |    30 |
| A real treat! Kona coffee, fresh from the lush mountains of Hawaii. Smooth in flavor and perfectly roasted! | kona.jpg | C3  | Half Pound - decaf - ground - $5.00  |    20 |
+-------------------------------------------------------------------------------+-----------+-----+--------------------------------------+-------+
10 rows in set (0.00 sec)

mysql>
```

Figure 8.1

To understand what's happening in this query, you'll find it helpful to see how the data is being used in a web page (**Figure 8.2**). For the coffee products, the general coffee type's **image** and **description** will be used, so those need to be selected. The product's SKU will be a combination of the capital letter "C" (for *coffee*) and the product's ID value, so these are concatenated together in the query. The SKUs are used as the values for each option in the drop-down menu, as in **Figure 8.3**.

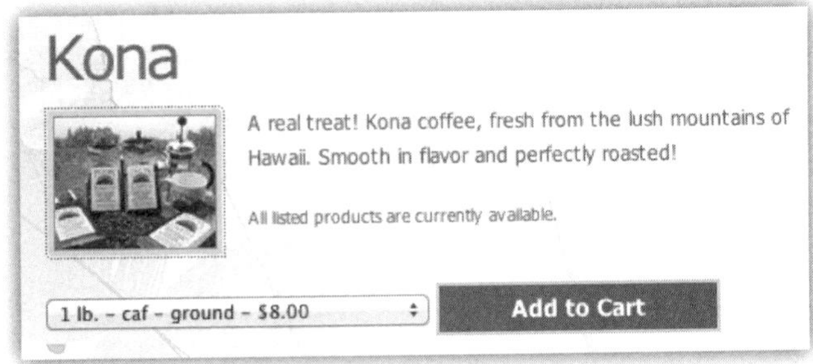


Figure 8.2

```
<option value="C4">1 lb. - caf - ground -
<option value="C6">1 lb. - caf - whole -
<option value="C5">1 lb. - decaf - ground
<option value="C7">1 lb. - decaf - whole -
<option value="C8">2 lbs. - caf - whole -
<option value="C9">2 lbs. - decaf - whole
<option value="C1">2 oz. Sample - caf - gr
<option value="C10">5 lbs. - caf - whole -
<option value="C2">Half Pound - caf - grou
<option value="C3">Half Pound - decaf - gr
```

Figure 8.3

The select menu's label—what the customer sees—is the concatenation of the coffee's size, caffeinated/decaffeinated status, ground/whole bean status, and price. You can see this in Figures 8.1 and 8.2. To generate this value, use the **CONCAT_WS()** function, short for *concatenation with separator*, where the first argument provided will be used in between each concatenated value. This whole construct is given the alias of **name**.

As the price is stored as an integer, it must first be divided by 100 to display it as a decimal. To format that calculation as exactly *two* decimals, you apply the MySQL **FORMAT()** function. This result is concatenated with a dollar sign to create a price in the format $7.95.

The product's **stock** value is selected as well, to be used later.

**tip**

If you'd rather, you could just select the raw price from the database and format it in PHP.

**tip**

If your records in the **sizes** table are in ascending size order, you could select the coffee products ordered by **size_id** first.

The query uses a **JOIN** across three tables: **specific_coffees**, **general_coffees**, and **sizes**. The **WHERE** conditional restricts the results to a general coffee type and retrieves only those products that are currently in stock. And the whole record set is returned in order by name so that similar products will appear near each other.

## SELECTING EVERY NON-COFFEE PRODUCT

Here's the query for selecting every non-coffee product:

```
SELECT ncc.description AS g_description, ncc.image AS g_image,
CONCAT("G", ncp.id) AS sku, ncp.name, ncp.description, ncp.image,
CONCAT("$", FORMAT(ncp.price/100, 2)) AS price, ncp.stock
FROM non_coffee_products AS ncp INNER JOIN non_coffee_categories
➥AS ncc
ON ncc.id=ncp.non_coffee_category_id
WHERE non_coffee_category_id=<some_category_id>
ORDER by date_created DESC;
```

**tip**

Ending a query with **\G** instead of a semicolon returns the query results as a vertical list (as in Figure 8.4) rather than a horizontal table. This is sometimes easier to read.

**Figure 8.4** shows the output for the query when replacing **<some_category_id>** with the number 3 (for **Mugs**). **Figure 8.5** shows how this data will be used in the site.

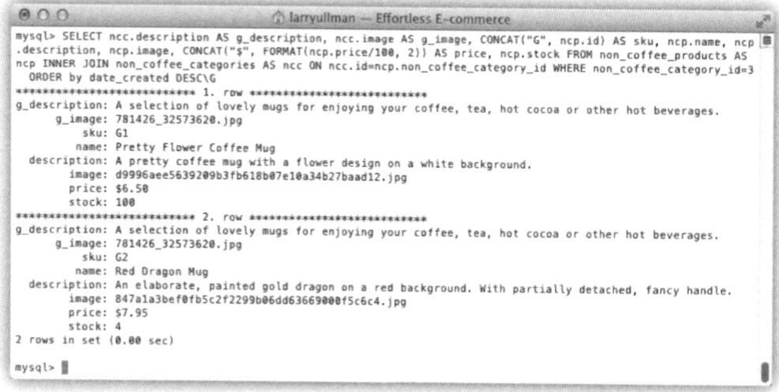


Figure 8.4

Figure 8.5

This query is more straightforward, because it performs a **JOIN** across only two tables. The query selects the **description** and **image** values from the **non_coffee_categories** tables, aliasing them as **g_description** and **g_image** accordingly (the **g_** is short for *general*). Again, the product's SKU is created in the query, by concatenating the capital letter "G" (for *goodie*) to the product's ID value. The specific product's **name**, **description**, **image**, **price**, and **stock** values are also retrieved. As with the coffee query, the price is formatted within the query itself. The only condition in this query is for restricting the results to a specific category, and the results are ordered from newest items to oldest.

## SELECTING EVERY SALE ITEM

Next is the query for selecting every sale item:

```
SELECT CONCAT("G", ncp.id) AS sku, sa.price AS sale_price,
➥ncc.category,
ncp.image, ncp.name, ncp.price AS price, ncp.stock, ncp.description
FROM sales AS sa
INNER JOIN non_coffee_products AS ncp ON sa.product_id=ncp.id
INNER JOIN non_coffee_categories AS ncc ON
➥ncc.id=ncp.non_coffee_category_id
WHERE sa.product_type="goodies" AND
((NOW() BETWEEN sa.start_date AND sa.end_date) OR (NOW() >
➥sa.start_date AND sa.end_date IS NULL) )
UNION
SELECT CONCAT("C", sc.id), sa.price, gc.category, gc.image,
CONCAT_WS(" - ", s.size, sc.caf_decaf, sc.ground_whole), sc.price,
➥sc.stock, gc.description
FROM sales AS sa
INNER JOIN specific_coffees AS sc ON sa.product_id=sc.id
INNER JOIN sizes AS s ON s.id=sc.size_id
INNER JOIN general_coffees AS gc ON gc.id=sc.general_coffee_id
WHERE sa.product_type="coffee" AND
((NOW() BETWEEN sa.start_date AND sa.end_date) OR
➥(NOW() > sa.start_date AND sa.end_date IS NULL) );
```

**tip**

Because of the order of the two **SELECT** queries, the non-coffee products will be returned first, followed by the coffee products.

**Figure 8.6** shows the output for the query.

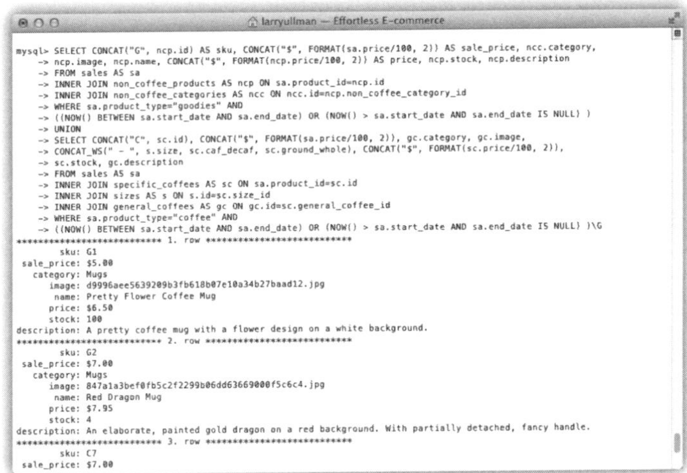

**Figure 8.6**

This query is relatively complex, because it performs a **UNION** of two **SELECT** queries, one of which is a **JOIN** across three tables and the other of which is a **JOIN** across four! The complexity derives from the fact that some records in the **sales** table will relate to the **specific_coffees** table (when the **sales** table's **product_type** value is **coffee**), and other records will relate to the **non_coffee_products** table (when the **sales** table's **product_type** value is **goodies**). To perform both of these **JOIN**s at one time requires the **UNION** statement, which is a way of combining two similar but unrelated queries to create one result set.

The individual **SELECT** queries are similar to those just explained, but without a **WHERE** condition on the category. However, both **SELECT** queries do require a conditional that confirms the item is currently on sale:

```
((NOW() BETWEEN sa.start_date AND sa.end_date) OR (NOW() >
➥sa.start_date AND sa.end_date IS NULL) )
```

An item's sale price is applicable if the current moment is between the start and end dates of that sale, or if the current moment is after the start date and there's no end date.

For both **SELECT** queries, the SKU is manufactured (as in the other queries), and the product's category, image, name, regular price, stock, and description are also returned. For the non-coffee products, the name will simply be the **name** value from the **non_coffee_products** table, and the **image** and **description** will come from there as well. For the coffee products, **name** will be the concatenation of several values, and **image** and **description** will come from the **general_coffees** table. Again, all prices are formatted by the query.

## SELECTING A FEW RANDOM SALE ITEMS

The last complex query selects up to four random sale items:

```
(SELECT CONCAT("G", ncp.id) AS sku, CONCAT("$",
➥FORMAT(sa.price/100, 2)) AS sale_price, ncc.category,
ncp.image, ncp.name
FROM sales AS sa
INNER JOIN non_coffee_products AS ncp ON sa.product_id=ncp.id
INNER JOIN non_coffee_categories AS ncc ON ncc.id=ncp.non_coffee_
➥category_id
WHERE sa.product_type="goodies" AND
((NOW() BETWEEN sa.start_date AND sa.end_date) OR (NOW() >
➥sa.start_date AND sa.end_date IS NULL) )
ORDER BY RAND() LIMIT 2)
```

```
UNION
(SELECT CONCAT("C", sc.id), CONCAT("$", FORMAT(sa.price/100, 2)) AS sale_price, gc.category, gc.image,
CONCAT_WS(" - ", s.size, sc.caf_decaf, sc.ground_whole)
FROM sales AS sa
INNER JOIN specific_coffees AS sc ON sa.product_id=sc.id
INNER JOIN sizes AS s ON s.id=sc.size_id
INNER JOIN general_coffees AS gc ON gc.id=sc.general_coffee_id
WHERE sa.product_type="coffee" AND
((NOW() BETWEEN sa.start_date AND sa.end_date) OR (NOW() > sa.start_date AND sa.end_date IS NULL) )
ORDER BY RAND() LIMIT 2);
```

**Figure 8.7** shows the output for the query, running it twice to see the variety of results (although with only a few sale items in the database, the differences aren't that pronounced).

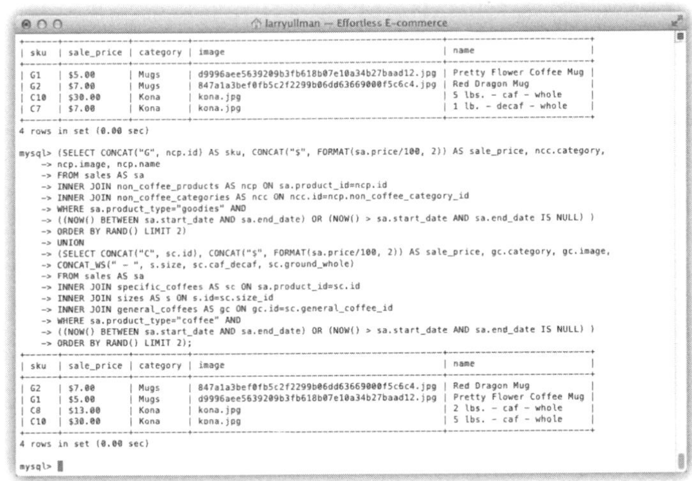


Figure 8.7

This **UNION** contains the same two **SELECT** queries as are used to find every sale item, with the addition of **ORDER BY RAND() LIMIT 2**. This query will be used on the home page, where only a couple of sale products can be advertised. For that reason, each **SELECT** query returns up to two randomly selected items: two random non-coffee products and two random coffee products. Because the **ORDER BY** and **LIMIT** clauses can confuse the **UNION** statement, both **SELECT** statements are individually wrapped in parentheses, making the general structure: **(SELECT...) UNION (SELECT...)**.

**tip**

To sort the entire result set, use this structure: **(SELECT... UNION SELECT...) ORDER BY...**

**tip**

Procedure names are case-insensitive and can be up to 64 characters long.

**note**

A common problem with stored procedures is that you must have a MySQL user with permission to create stored routines.

**tip**

I've included indentations in the procedures here for improved legibility, but you may need to remove the indents when pasting these commands into the `mysql` client.

**note**

Because this is a MySQL stored procedure, not PHP code, the syntax for both the conditional itself and the equality condition (note the single equals sign, not a double) differs slightly.

# Creating Stored Procedures

This project will primarily use stored procedures, at least on the public side of the site. For the functionality being developed in this chapter, three stored procedures are required, each of which runs one of two **SELECT** queries. You can create stored procedures using most MySQL interfaces, although you must be connecting to the database as a MySQL user with **CREATE ROUTINES** permissions.

If you're using a hosted account that doesn't grant you permission to create and use stored procedures, you can skip this section. You'll then need to adjust the subsequent PHP scripts to run the queries directly instead of invoking the stored procedures. Chapter 13 explains some of the ways you'd perform that conversion.

1. Create the `select_categories()` procedure:

```
DELIMITER $$
CREATE PROCEDURE select_categories (type VARCHAR(7))
BEGIN
  IF type = 'coffee' THEN
    SELECT * FROM general_coffees ORDER by category;
  ELSEIF type = 'goodies' THEN
    SELECT * FROM non_coffee_categories ORDER by category;
  END IF;
END$$
DELIMITER ;
```

   The first line changes the delimiter from the default semicolon to something else. This change prevents the semicolons within the procedure from causing problems. The procedure itself is named `select_categories()`, which is a clear indication of what the procedure does.

   The procedure takes one argument, named **type** and of MySQL data type **VARCHAR(7)**. The procedure executes one of two possible **SELECT** queries, depending on the value of **type**. An **IF-ELSE IF** conditional accomplishes this.

   The last line reverts the delimiter back to the default semicolon. If you're going to be creating multiple procedures at once, as in these steps, you have to change the delimiter before the first definition only and change it back after the last, but I'm changing it with each definition to avoid confusion and possible errors.

2. Create the **select_products()** procedure:

```
DELIMITER $$
CREATE PROCEDURE select_products(type VARCHAR(7), cat TINYINT)
BEGIN
  IF type = 'coffee' THEN
    SELECT  gc.description, gc.image, CONCAT("C", sc.id) AS sku,
    CONCAT_WS(" - ", s.size, sc.caf_decaf, sc.ground_whole,
    CONCAT("$", FORMAT(sc.price/100, 2))) AS name, sc.stock
    FROM specific_coffees AS sc
    INNER JOIN sizes AS s ON s.id=sc.size_id
    INNER JOIN general_coffees AS gc ON
    ➥gc.id=sc.general_coffee_id
    WHERE general_coffee_id=cat AND stock>0
    ORDER by name ASC;
  ELSEIF type = 'goodies' THEN
    SELECT ncc.description AS g_description, ncc.image AS
    ➥g_image,
    CONCAT("G", ncp.id) AS sku, ncp.name, ncp.description,
    ➥ncp.image,
    CONCAT("$", FORMAT(ncp.price/100, 2)) AS price, ncp.stock
    FROM non_coffee_products AS ncp
    INNER JOIN non_coffee_categories AS ncc
    ON ncc.id=ncp.non_coffee_category_id
    WHERE non_coffee_category_id=cat
    ORDER by date_created DESC;
  END IF;
END$$
DELIMITER ;
```

This procedure takes two arguments: a **type** and a **category**. If **type** equals **coffee**, then a **SELECT** runs to retrieve every specific coffee product. If **type** equals **goodies**, then a **SELECT** runs to retrieve every non-coffee product. These are the same queries already explained, just compressed (that is, the breaks have been removed).

3. Create the **select_sale_items()** procedure:

```
DELIMITER $$
CREATE PROCEDURE select_sale_items (get_all BOOLEAN)
BEGIN
  IF get_all = 1 THEN
```

*(continues on next page)*

**note**

Your stored procedure arguments shouldn't have the same name as any column or table in the database, or as any MySQL keyword.

**tip**

Queries in stored procedures, when written as I have in these examples, are just as safe as prepared statements, so you don't need to worry about using the arguments in the queries.

**note**

To improve legibility, I haven't used backticks around table and column names in the stored procedure queries, but you may prefer to use them.

```
    SELECT CONCAT("G", ncp.id) AS sku, CONCAT("$",
    FORMAT(sa.price/100, 2)) AS sale_price, ncc.category,
    ncp.image, ncp.name, CONCAT("$", FORMAT(ncp.price/100, 2))
    AS price, ncp.stock, ncp.description
    FROM sales AS sa
    INNER JOIN non_coffee_products AS ncp
    ON sa.product_id=ncp.id
    INNER JOIN non_coffee_categories AS ncc
    ON ncc.id=ncp.non_coffee_category_id
    WHERE sa.product_type="goodies" AND
    ((NOW() BETWEEN sa.start_date AND sa.end_date) OR
    (NOW() > sa.start_date AND sa.end_date IS NULL) )
    UNION
    SELECT CONCAT("C", sc.id), CONCAT("$", FORMAT(sa.price/100,
    2)), gc.category, gc.image, CONCAT_WS(" - ", s.size,
    sc.caf_decaf, sc.ground_whole), CONCAT("$",
    FORMAT(sc.price/100, 2)), sc.stock, gc.description
    FROM sales AS sa
    INNER JOIN specific_coffees AS sc
    ON sa.product_id=sc.id
    INNER JOIN sizes AS s ON s.id=sc.size_id
    INNER JOIN general_coffees AS gc
    ON gc.id=sc.general_coffee_id
    WHERE sa.product_type="coffee" AND
    ((NOW() BETWEEN sa.start_date AND sa.end_date) OR
    (NOW() > sa.start_date AND sa.end_date IS NULL) );
  ELSE
    (SELECT CONCAT("G", ncp.id) AS sku, CONCAT("$",
    FORMAT(sa.price/100, 2)) AS sale_price, ncc.category,
    ncp.image, ncp.name
    FROM sales AS sa
    INNER JOIN non_coffee_products AS ncp
    ON sa.product_id=ncp.id
    INNER JOIN non_coffee_categories AS ncc
    ON ncc.id=ncp.non_coffee_category_id
    WHERE sa.product_type="goodies" AND
    ((NOW() BETWEEN sa.start_date AND sa.end_date) OR
    (NOW() > sa.start_date AND sa.end_date IS NULL) )
    ORDER BY RAND() LIMIT 2)
    UNION
    (SELECT CONCAT("C", sc.id), CONCAT("$",
```

```
        FORMAT(sa.price/100, 2)), gc.category, gc.image,
        CONCAT_WS(" - ", s.size, sc.caf_decaf, sc.ground_whole)
        FROM sales AS sa
        INNER JOIN specific_coffees AS sc
        ON sa.product_id=sc.id
        INNER JOIN sizes AS s ON s.id=sc.size_id
        INNER JOIN general_coffees AS gc
        ON gc.id=sc.general_coffee_id
        WHERE sa.product_type="coffee" AND
        ((NOW() BETWEEN sa.start_date AND sa.end_date) OR
        (NOW() > sa.start_date AND sa.end_date IS NULL) )
        ORDER BY RAND() LIMIT 2);
    END IF;
END$$
DELIMITER ;
```

This stored procedure uses the two sales-related queries already explained. It takes only one argument: a Boolean value indicating whether or not every sale item should be returned (that is to say, is this the sales page or the home page?).

4. Test the stored procedures by calling them:

```
CALL select_categories('coffee');
CALL select_categories('goodies');
CALL select_products('coffee', 3);
CALL select_products('goodies', 3);
CALL select_sale_items(false);
CALL select_sale_items(true);
```

The results of these procedure calls should be exactly as those shown in the earlier figures (in which the same queries are run directly).

# SHOPPING BY CATEGORY

With the stored procedures and the overall HTML template in place (that is, two parts of an MVC-like approach have been written), the PHP script that lists the available categories becomes quite simple. All this file has to do is

- Validate the received type
- Invoke the stored procedure
- Include the HTML template and specific view files

**tip**

See Chapter 7 for an explanation of mod_rewrite and how the Coffee site uses it.

As a reminder, the PHP script for listing the product categories is called **shop.php**, and it's linked in the header as either **/shop/coffee/** or **/shop/goodies/**. The server's mod_rewrite module will convert that URL (unbeknownst to the user) into either **shop.php?type=coffee** or **shop.php?type=goodies**. If you're not using mod_rewrite, then your URLs should just be those.

Let's write the PHP script first, and then the view files it uses.

## Creating the PHP Script

In keeping with the MVC-like approach, this PHP script should have little-to-no HTML (technically, none) and as little SQL as possible. The end result is a smattering of logic and the inclusion of several files.

1. Create a new PHP script in your text editor or IDE to be named **shop.php** and stored in the web root directory.

2. Include the configuration file:

```
<?php
require('./includes/config.inc.php');
```

3. Validate the product type:

```
if (isset($_GET['type']) && ($_GET['type'] === 'goodies')) {
   $page_title = 'Our Goodies, by Category';
   $type = 'goodies';
} else {
   $page_title = 'Our Coffee Products';
   $type = 'coffee';
}
```

   The product type can be one of only two values: **goodies** or **coffee**. The default product type to display will always be **coffee**, so the first part of the conditional just checks if **$_GET['type']** is set and if it equals **goodies**.

   For each condition, the page's title is determined, and the **$type** variables is assigned appropriate values.

4. Include the header file and the database connection:

```
include('./includes/header.html');
require (MYSQL);
```

5. Call the stored procedure:

```
$r = mysqli_query($dbc, "CALL select_categories('$type')");
```

This one line is all you need to invoke the stored procedure for either type. Because the **$type** value will be a string, it must be quoted when you pass it to the stored procedure.

The core SQL command is the same that would be run in the **mysql** client or phpMyAdmin:

```
CALL select_categories('coffee')
```

or

```
CALL select_categories('goodies')
```

For debugging purposes, you could include this line next, although you wouldn't want to use it on a live site:

```
if (!$r) echo mysqli_error($dbc);
```

This line will print any MySQL errors that occurred, if **$r** doesn't have a positive value.

**note**

The MySQL user that the PHP script is connecting as must have **EXECUTE** permissions in order to call a stored procedure.

6. If records were returned, include the view file:

```
if (mysqli_num_rows($r) > 0) {
   include ('./views/list_categories.html');
```

You can use the **mysqli_num_rows()** function to confirm that results were returned by this stored procedure, as if the script had executed a standard **SELECT** query. If some rows were returned, the **list_categories.html** file, found within the **views** directory, will be included. That file will handle the actual retrieval and display of the returned rows.

7. If no records were returned, include the error view:

```
} else {
   include ('./views/error.html');
}
```

The **error.html** view file will be included any time a query didn't return sufficient results. You could also, at this point, write an error message to a log or send it to an email address.

8. Complete the PHP page:

```
include ('./includes/footer.html');
?>
```

9. Save the file.

## Creating the View Files

The **shop.php** script uses one of two possible view files: **list_categories.html** or **error.html**. Remember that these view files represent just a snippet of HTML: a subset of the entire page, presenting a small portion of what the user sees. Each view file uses an **.html** extension to indicate its basic nature and should have a bare minimum of PHP code and logic.

Looking at the **error.html** file, all it needs to do is display a message within the context of the HTML template. For the Coffee template, the context is a box generated by several DIV tags. As a reminder, because the HTML template is quite verbose (to create the fancy box), I've assigned the two bits of oft-repeated HTML to PHP constants. This was explained in Chapter 7. The end result is a very short and simple **error.html**:

```
<?php echo BOX_BEGIN; ?>
   <h2>Error!</h2>
   <p>Unfortunately a system error has occurred. Please use the
   ➥links at the top of the page to continue shopping. We apologize
   ➥for the inconvenience.</p>
<?php echo BOX_END; ?>
```

Should the stored procedure not return any results, the user will see the message shown in **Figure 8.8**. This would occur only if the database wasn't available, if it wasn't populated, or if the connecting MySQL user doesn't have **EXECUTE** permissions (the right to run a stored procedure).

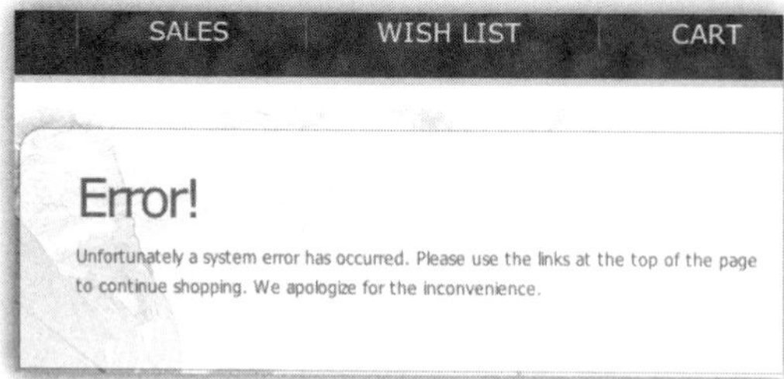


Figure 8.8

The **list_categories.html** file is a bit more complicated, but only slightly (view files shouldn't be truly complex). It uses a loop to run through the query results and outputs the results within the proper context.

1. Create a new HTML file in your text editor or IDE to be named **list_categories.html** and stored in the **views** folder.

2. Begin with the contextual HTML:

```
<?php
echo BOX_BEGIN;
echo '<ul class="items-list">';
```

For the Coffee template that I'm using, everything goes within a series of DIV tags that create a box. These lines start that box and conclude by starting an unordered list.

3. Begin a **while** loop:

```
while ($row = mysqli_fetch_array($r, MYSQLI_ASSOC)) {
```

As you saw in Chapter 7, the MVC approach requires that assumptions are made, such as the assumption here that there are records to be fetched. As an extra precaution, you could add a conditional before the loop:

```
if ($r) {...
```

That being said, this **while** loop is as complicated as the view gets.

4. Print each item:

```
echo '<li><h3>' . $row['category'] . ' </h3>
<p><img alt="' . $row['category'] . '" src="/products/' .
➥$row['image'] . '" />' . $row['description'] . '<br />
<a href="/browse/' . $type . '/' . urlencode($row['category']) .
➥'/' . $row['id'] . '" class="h4">View All ' . $row['category'] .
➥' Products</a></p>
</li>';
```

The goal is to generate HTML that looks like this (as a single example):

```
<li><h3>Gift Baskets</h3>
   <p><img alt="Gift Baskets" src="/products/imagename.ext" />
   ➥Actual Description<br />
   <a href="/browse/goodies/Gift+Baskets/2" class="h4">View All
   ➥Gift Baskets Products</a></p>
</li>
```

For the image's **src** and the link's **href** attributes, the paths must begin with a slash. This is necessary because the current page might be **www.example.com/shop/goodies/**, in which case the references to files in the **products** folder must start at the root directory. If you're not using mod_rewrite, references don't need to begin with a slash. If you've placed your files within a subdirectory, references must begin with that subdirectory: **/ex2/products/imagename.ext**.

tip

For extra security, output all the database values through **htmlspecialchars()**.

**tip**

There's a lot of PHP and HTML interspersed, so be careful of the syntax.

The link to view all the products in the category is to ***/browse/type/category/ID***, where **type** comes from **shop.php** (and, therefore, the URL), and **category** and **ID** come from the returned database record. The **browse.php** page will use these values.

5. Complete the **while** loop:

```
}
```

6. Complete the HTML:

```
echo '</ul>';
echo BOX_END;
```

7. Save the file and test it in your browser (**Figures 8.9** and **8.10**).

   You can test this by clicking either shopping link—*coffee* or *goodies*—although clicking the links displayed on the **shop.php** page won't work, because **browse.php** hasn't been written yet.

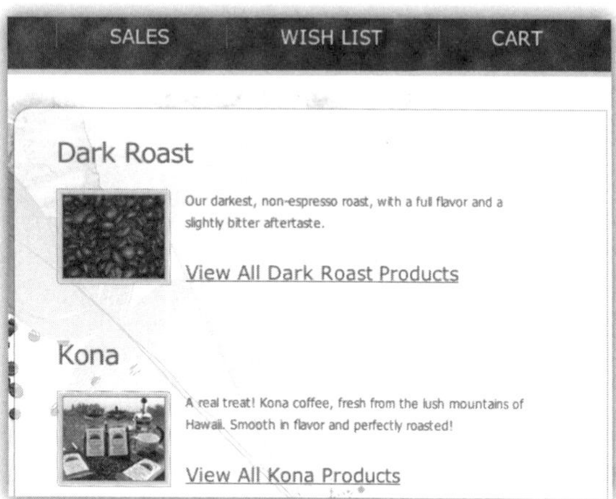


Figure 8.9

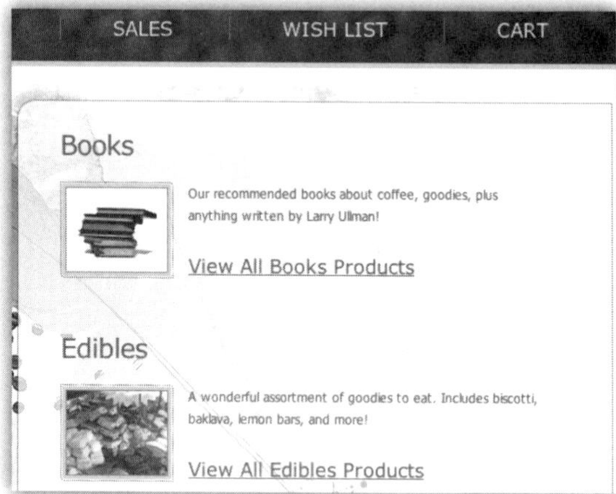


Figure 8.10

# LISTING PRODUCTS

Now that customers can shop by type—coffee and goodies—they need to be able to browse through the actual products they can purchase, within each type. The page for doing that, **browse.php**, is written in a similar manner to **shop.php**, although it uses a different view file to display each product type.

## Creating the PHP Script

The primary difference between **shop.php** and **browse.php** is that the latter has three values to validate—type, category, and ID—instead of just one. Still, even with lots of spacing and comments, the result is only about 70 lines long.

1. Create a new PHP script in your text editor or IDE to be named **browse.php** and stored in the web root directory.

2. Include the configuration file:

```
<?php
require('./includes/config.inc.php');
```

3. Start validating the required values:

```
$type = $sp_cat = $category = false;
if (isset($_GET['type'], $_GET['category'], $_GET['id']) &&
➥filter_var($_GET['id'], FILTER_VALIDATE_INT,
➥array('min_range' => 1))) {
   $category = $_GET['category'];
   $sp_cat = $_GET['id'];
```

To start the validation process, three necessary variables are initially set to `false`, requiring the script to prove that everything's OK. Next, the condition checks for the presence of three variables in the URL—**type**, **category**, and `id`—and that the ID value is an integer greater than or equal to 1.

If all of these conditions are true, then two variables are assigned values from the URL. The **category** value will be used as a header in the HTML page. The **$sp_cat** variable will be used in the stored procedure. You don't need to worry about these variables having inappropriate values here. The ID will have already been validated using `filter_var()`, and the **category** value has to match the rewrite rule in the **.htaccess** file (see Chapter 7).

4. Validate the product type and complete the validation conditional:

```
   if ($_GET['type'] === 'goodies') {
      $type = 'goodies';
   } elseif ($_GET['type'] === 'coffee') {
      $type = 'coffee';
   }
}
```

Similar to the **shop.php** script, the validation routine creates a **$type** variable, to be used in the stored procedure. Unlike **shop.php**, this script doesn't assume a default type: If an invalid type is somehow used, the customer will see an error page (because, frankly, he's probably the one who deliberately did something to cause the problem).

5. If there's a problem, display the error page:

```
if (!$type || !$sp_cat || !$category) {
   $page_title = 'Error!';
   include('./includes/header.html');
   include('./views/error.html');
   include('./includes/footer.html');
   exit();
}
```

If any of the four variables still has a **false** value, an error page should be displayed and the script terminated.

 tip

The double pipe characters (||) are an alternative way of saying "or" in a PHP conditional.

6. Create a page title and include the header file:

```
$page_title = ucfirst($type) . ' to Buy::' . $category;
include('./includes/header.html');
```

The page title will be something like *Coffee to Buy::Kona* or *Goodies to Buy::Mugs*. It will appear at the top of the browser window.

7. Include the database connection and execute the stored procedure:

```
require(MYSQL);
$r = mysqli_query($dbc, "CALL select_products('$type', $sp_cat)");
```

The stored procedure is **select_products()**, which takes two arguments: the product type and a category value. The former is quoted, because it's a string; the latter is an unquoted integer.

8. If records were returned, include the view file:

```
if (mysqli_num_rows($r) > 0) {
   if ($type === 'goodies') {
      include('./views/list_goodies.html');
   } elseif ($type === 'coffee') {
      include('./views/list_coffees.html');
   }
```

As long as some rows were returned, the view file (which will display the results) will be included. There are two different view files: one for non-coffee products and one for coffee products.

9. If no records were returned, include the "no products" view:

```
} else { // Include the "noproducts" page:
   include('./views/noproducts.html');
}
```

This will be a new view file, which neither indicates an error nor attempts to list any products, because there aren't any.

10. Complete the PHP page:

```
include('./includes/footer.html');
?>
```

11. Save the file.

# Creating the View Files

The **browse.php** script references three new files: **list_goodies.html**, **list_coffees.html**, and **noproducts.html**. There are two different products-listing files because the customer will buy a category of coffee in a specific format (based on the size, caffeine, and bean type; see Figure 8.2) but will purchase other products individually (Figure 8.5). For each product type, the page should display general information about the category as a whole; hence, each view uses a trick to show that information only once.

## CREATING THE PRODUCTS LIST

This view file should first show the general category information, then each specific product. It will create two HTML boxes (from the original template) to do so (again, see Figure 8.5).

1. Create a new HTML file in your text editor or IDE to be named **list_goodies.html** and stored in the **views** folder.

2. Begin by creating a flag variable:

```
<?php
$header = false;
```

   This variable will be used to know whether or not the initial information has been printed (so that it's printed only once). By default, the value is **false**.

3. Create the **while** loop and check the **$header** value:

```
while ($row = mysqli_fetch_array($r, MYSQLI_ASSOC)) {
   if (!$header)
```

   The loop will be executed once for each returned row. If you look at the query results shown in Figure 8.4, you'll see that the general category information is included in each returned row. This information will be used to create the header only for the first record fetched. To test for that situation, a conditional sees if **$header** is still **false**.

**tip**

Instead of fetching the general category information with each specific product, you could run two queries: one for the general category info and another for all the products in that category.

4. Add the header box:

```
echo BOX_BEGIN;
echo '<h2>' . $category . '</h2>
<div class="img-box"><p><img alt="' . $category . '" src="/
➥products/' . $row['g_image'] . '" />'. $row['g_description'] .
➥'</p></div>';
echo BOX_END;
echo '<p><br clear="all" /></p>';
```

This box will be at the top of the page, displaying the category's name, image, and description. The **$category** variable, used as a caption, is defined in the **browse.php** page; the other two values come from the returned row.

5. Begin the next box and complete the **$header IF**:

```
   echo BOX_BEGIN;
   $header = true;
} // End of $header IF.
```

All the products will be displayed within another box, which is begun as part of the **$header** conditional (so that the box is created only once). Then, in a new PHP block, the **$header** variable is set to **true**, indicating that the header has already been displayed.

6. Print each item:

```
echo '<h3>' . $row['name'] . '</h3>
   <div class="img-box"><p><img alt="' . $row['name'] . '"
   ➥src="/products/' . $row['image']  . '" />' .
   ➥$row['description'] . '<br />
   <strong>Price:</strong> ' . $row['price'] . '<br />
   <strong>Availability:</strong> ' . $row['stock'] . '</p>
   <p><a href="/cart.php?sku=' . $row['sku'] . '&action=add"
   ➥class="button">Add to Cart</a></p></div>';
```

The goal is to generate HTML that looks like this (as a single example):

```
<h3>Red Dragon Mug</h3>
<div class="img-box"><p><img alt="Red Dragon Mug"
➥src="/products/imagename.ext" />Actual Description<br />
   <strong>Price:</strong> $4.50<br />
   <strong>Availability:</strong> 67</p>
   <p><a href="/cart.php?sku=023&action=add"
   ➥class="button">Add to Cart</a></p></div>
```

**tip**

Make your Add to Cart buttons big and obvious!

As with **list_categories.html**, the image's **src** and the link's **href** attributes use paths that begin with a slash. You'll need to change these references if your files aren't in the web root directory.

For now, the quantity in stock is just displayed; you'll improve on this later. The link is a button to add the item to the cart. It passes the SKU and an **action** value to the **cart.php** page, to be written in the next chapter.

7. Complete the **while** loop and the PHP:

```
}
```

8. Complete the HTML:

```
echo '<p> <br clear="all" /></p>';
echo BOX_END;
```

9. Save the file and test it in your browser.

   You can test this view by clicking any category listed on the "goodies" shopping page (again, Figure 8.5 is a representative image of this page).

## CREATING THE COFFEES LIST

The **list_coffees.html** view should display the general coffee name, image, and description, and then provide a drop-down menu from which the user can select a coffee to order (see Figure 8.1). Unlike **list_products.html**, this view creates only one HTML box.

1. Create a new HTML file in your text editor or IDE to be named **list_coffees.html** and stored in the **views** folder.

2. Begin by creating a flag variable:

```
<?php
$header = false;
```

   This variable will be used the same way here as in **list_goodies.html**.

3. Create the **while** loop and check the **$header** value:

```
while ($row = mysqli_fetch_array($r, MYSQLI_ASSOC)) {
   if (!$header) {
```

   This is still the same as in **list_goodies.html**.

4. Create the start of the box and the general information:

```
echo '<h2>' . $category . '</h2>
    <div class="img-box">
    <p><img alt="' . $category . '" src="/products/' .
    ➥$row['image'] . '" />' . $row['description'] . '</p>
    <p><small>All listed products are currently available.
    ➥</small>';
```

The header for the coffees page includes the start of the HTML box, the coffee category as a caption (this comes from **browse.php**), and the general coffee's image and description from the first returned row.

5. Begin the form and complete the header:

```
echo '<form action="/cart.php" method="get">
    <input type="hidden" name="action" value="add" />
    <select name="sku">';
    $header = true;
} // End of $header IF.
```

The form uses the GET method and will be submitted to **cart.php**. The form contains a hidden input, named **action**, with a value of **add**. In Chapter 9, "Building a Shopping Cart," you'll create the script that handles this form. Next, a select menu, named *sku*, is begun.

6. Print each item:

```
echo "<option value=\"{$row['sku']}\">{$row['name']}</option>\n";
```

The goal here is to generate an **OPTION** tag, whose value is the SKU and whose label is the concatenated name (Figure 8.3).

7. Complete the **while** loop and the PHP block:

```
}
```

8. Complete the HTML:

```
echo '</select> <input type="submit" value="Add to Cart"
➥class="button" /></p></form></div>';
echo BOX_END;
```

The rest of the HTML closes the SELECT tag and creates the Add to Cart button.

9. Save the file and test it in your browser.

You can test this by clicking any category listed on the "coffee" shopping page (again, Figure 8.2 is a representative image of this page).

## Creating the "No Products" View

The **noproducts.html** view is similar to **error.html**—it primarily displays a static message, but it includes the name of the category involved (**Figure 8.11**), generated in **browse.php**. Here are that file's contents:

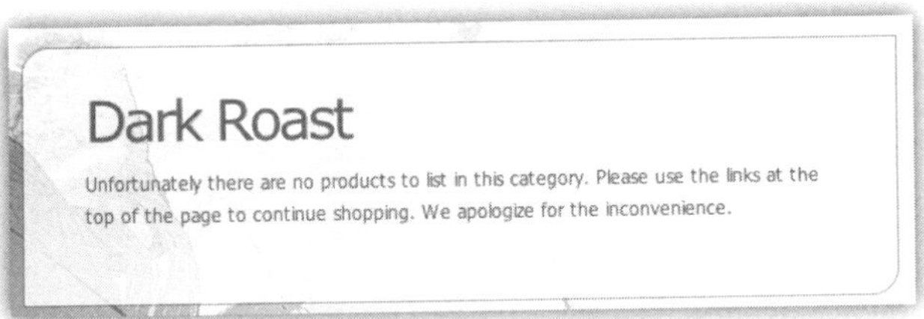


Figure 8.11

```
<?php echo BOX_BEGIN; ?>
    <h2><?php echo $category; ?></h2>
    <p>Unfortunately there are no products to list in this category.
    ➥Please use the links at the top of the page to continue
    ➥shopping. We apologize for the inconvenience.</p>
<?php echo BOX_END; ?>
```

# INDICATING AVAILABILITY

For the list of coffee products, the stored procedure only retrieves those currently in stock. For the other products, though, the stock is currently represented as the quantity on hand (see Figure 8.5), which you may not want to show the customer. Instead, let's create a function that will display the availability in a friendlier, and purchase-encouraging, manner. The function will be defined in a new script named **product_functions.inc.php**.

1. Create a new PHP script in your text editor or IDE to be named **product_functions.inc.php** and stored in the **includes** directory.

   ```
   <?php
   ```

2. Begin defining the function:

   ```
   function get_stock_status($stock) {
   ```

   The function takes one argument, assigned to the variable **$stock**.

3. Return different messages based on the value of **$stock**:

   ```
   if ($stock > 5) {
       return 'In Stock';
   ```

*(continues on next page)*

```
} elseif ($stock > 0) {
   return 'Low Stock';
} else {
   return 'Currently Out of Stock';
}
```

In reality, the amount of concern to be conveyed regarding an item's quantity in stock depends on how quickly the item sells. Having 4 of an item that gets purchased a couple of times a year isn't an issue, whereas having 10 of a product that averages 15 purchases a day will be problematic. Still, for representative purposes, this function returns a different message based on the value of **$stock**.

4. Complete the function:

```
} // End of get_stock_status() function.
```

5. Save the file.

   As with all PHP scripts included by other pages, this one doesn't use a closing PHP tag.

To use this function, you'll need to include the PHP file in the **list_goodies.html** script:

```
include('./includes/product_functions.inc.php');
```

Note that the reference to the file is relative to **browse.php**—the PHP script that includes **list_goodies.html**—because it's **browse.php** that will be executing this code.

Next, also in **list_goodies.html**, change the availability indication to

```
<strong>Availability:</strong> ' . get_stock_status($row['stock']) .
➥'</p>
```

The complete echo statement should now be

```
echo '<h3>' . $row['name'] . '</h3>
   <div class="img-box"><p><img alt="' . $row['name'] . '"
   ➥src="/products/' . $row['image']  . '" />' .
   ➥$row['description'] . '<br />
   <strong>Price:</strong> ' . $row['price'] . '<br />
   <strong>Availability:</strong> ' .
   ➥get_stock_status($row['stock']) . '</p>
   <p><a href="/cart.php?sku=' . $row['sku'] . '&action=add"
   ➥class="button">Add to Cart</a></p></div>';
```

**tip**

In the downloadable code, you'll see this modified view file named **list_goodies2.html**, to avoid confusion.

And that's it! You can now test this in your browser to see how it looks (**Figure 8.12**).

**Figure 8.12**

# SHOWING SALE PRICES

Another problem with the products listings in their current formats is that they don't reflect any applicable sale prices. This is an important issue because the sale price for a product should appear everywhere the product is listed, not just on the sales page (**Figures 8.13** and **8.14**).

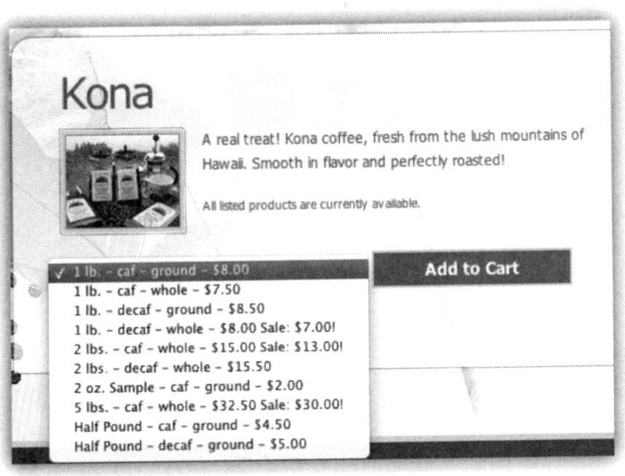


**Figure 8.13**

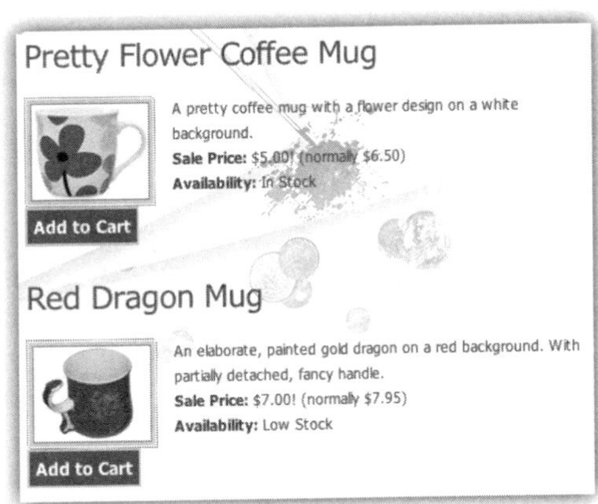


**Figure 8.14**

To make this change, you'll first need to alter the two queries in the stored procedure that fetches every product so that the sale price is also retrieved. Second, the `list_coffees.html` and `list_goodies.html` view files will need some additional logic to indicate the sale price, when one exists.

## Updating the Stored Procedure

The original stored procedure, as complex as its queries were, didn't check for any sale prices. To do that, you have to add another **JOIN** to each query to check the **sales** table. However, most items normally won't be on sale, so instead of an *inner join*, which returns only matches (records found in both joined tables), the queries will have to use an *outer join*. When you add an outer join, the query will continue to select every product currently being selected but also add in any matching rows in the **sales** table. In other words, an *inner join* is *exclusive* in that it doesn't select any records without a corresponding match, whereas an *outer join* is *inclusive*: it also selects records that do match.

Here's the first new query for the **select_products()** procedure:

**tip**

This query is a good example of how a simple thought—allowing items to be for sale without a clear ending date—can complicate queries and logic.

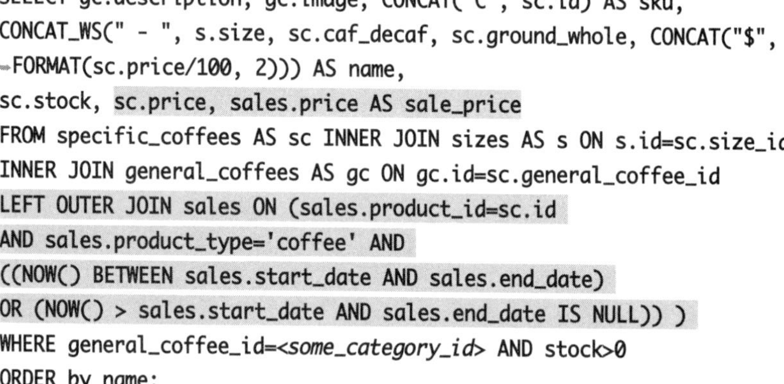

```
SELECT gc.description, gc.image, CONCAT("C", sc.id) AS sku,
CONCAT_WS(" - ", s.size, sc.caf_decaf, sc.ground_whole, CONCAT("$",
➥FORMAT(sc.price/100, 2))) AS name,
sc.stock, sc.price, sales.price AS sale_price
FROM specific_coffees AS sc INNER JOIN sizes AS s ON s.id=sc.size_id
INNER JOIN general_coffees AS gc ON gc.id=sc.general_coffee_id
LEFT OUTER JOIN sales ON (sales.product_id=sc.id
AND sales.product_type='coffee' AND
((NOW() BETWEEN sales.start_date AND sales.end_date)
OR (NOW() > sales.start_date AND sales.end_date IS NULL)) )
WHERE general_coffee_id=<some_category_id> AND stock>0
ORDER by name;
```

This query selects specific coffee products. The first alteration (highlighted in the code) is the selection of the original price and the sale price. You'll see why the price needs to be selected again—even though it already appears in the item's name—shortly. You should also notice that both prices are being selected without any formatting adjustments (that is, they'll be returned as integers representing cents, also without any initial dollar sign).

Next, the left outer join is added on the **sales** table. The condition for the **JOIN** has three parts to it:

1. The **sales.product_id** must equal the product's ID value.
2. The **sales.product_type** value must be **coffee**.
3. The dates that the product is on sale must start before right now and end after right now, or the sale's date must start before right now and be open-ended.

**Figure 8.15** shows the results of running this query, using a category ID of 3 and without selecting the description or image (to save space). The important thing to note is that the **sale_price** column will have a **NULL** value for those products not currently on sale.

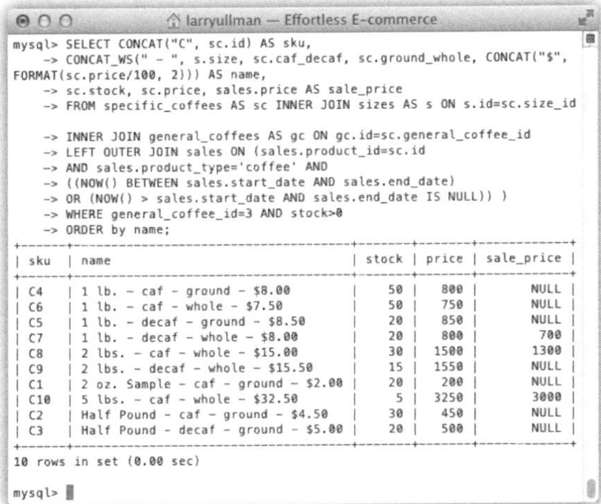


```
mysql> SELECT CONCAT("C", sc.id) AS sku,
    -> CONCAT_WS(" - ", s.size, sc.caf_decaf, sc.ground_whole, CONCAT("$",
FORMAT(sc.price/100, 2))) AS name,
    -> sc.stock, sc.price, sales.price AS sale_price
    -> FROM specific_coffees AS sc INNER JOIN sizes AS s ON s.id=sc.size_id

    -> INNER JOIN general_coffees AS gc ON gc.id=sc.general_coffee_id
    -> LEFT OUTER JOIN sales ON (sales.product_id=sc.id
    -> AND sales.product_type='coffee' AND
    -> ((NOW() BETWEEN sales.start_date AND sales.end_date)
    -> OR (NOW() > sales.start_date AND sales.end_date IS NULL)) )
    -> WHERE general_coffee_id=3 AND stock>0
    -> ORDER by name;
+------+-------------------------------------+-------+-------+------------+
| sku  | name                                | stock | price | sale_price |
+------+-------------------------------------+-------+-------+------------+
| C4   | 1 lb. - caf - ground - $8.00        |    50 |   800 |       NULL |
| C6   | 1 lb. - caf - whole - $7.50         |    50 |   750 |       NULL |
| C5   | 1 lb. - decaf - ground - $8.50      |    20 |   850 |       NULL |
| C7   | 1 lb. - decaf - whole - $8.00       |    20 |   800 |        700 |
| C8   | 2 lbs. - caf - whole - $15.00       |    30 |  1500 |       1300 |
| C9   | 2 lbs. - decaf - whole - $15.50     |    15 |  1550 |       NULL |
| C1   | 2 oz. Sample - caf - ground - $2.00 |    20 |   200 |       NULL |
| C10  | 5 lbs. - caf - whole - $32.50       |     5 |  3250 |       3000 |
| C2   | Half Pound - caf - ground - $4.50   |    30 |   450 |       NULL |
| C3   | Half Pound - decaf - ground - $5.00 |    20 |   500 |       NULL |
+------+-------------------------------------+-------+-------+------------+
10 rows in set (0.00 sec)

mysql>
```

Figure 8.15

Here's the second new query for the **select_products()** procedure:

```
SELECT ncc.description AS g_description, ncc.image AS g_image,
CONCAT("G", ncp.id) AS sku, ncp.name, ncp.description, ncp.image,
➥ncp.price, ncp.stock, sales.price AS sale_price
FROM non_coffee_products AS ncp INNER JOIN non_coffee_categories
➥AS ncc
ON ncc.id=ncp.non_coffee_category_id
LEFT OUTER JOIN sales ON (sales.product_id=ncp.id
AND sales.product_type='goodies' AND
((NOW() BETWEEN sales.start_date AND sales.end_date) OR (NOW() >
➥sales.start_date AND sales.end_date IS NULL)) )
WHERE non_coffee_category_id=<some_category_id>
ORDER by date_created DESC;
```

The update to the query that selects every non-coffee product has the same additional outer join, with similar criteria except that the product type should be **goodies**. And the sale price is selected now as well. Both it and the regular price are selected without any modification (they'll be integers).

There are a few ways you can go about updating the stored procedure: You could use an **ALTER ROUTINE** syntax; you could create the procedure using a new name; or you could just drop the routine and redefine it:

```
DROP PROCEDURE select_products;
DELIMITER $$
CREATE PROCEDURE select_products(type VARCHAR(7), cat TINYINT)
BEGIN
IF type = 'coffee' THEN
SELECT gc.description, gc.image, CONCAT("C", sc.id) AS sku,
CONCAT_WS(" - ", s.size, sc.caf_decaf, sc.ground_whole, CONCAT("$",
➥FORMAT(sc.price/100, 2))) AS name,
sc.stock, sc.price, sales.price AS sale_price
FROM specific_coffees AS sc INNER JOIN sizes AS s ON s.id=sc.size_id
INNER JOIN general_coffees AS gc ON gc.id=sc.general_coffee_id
LEFT OUTER JOIN sales ON (sales.product_id=sc.id
AND sales.product_type='coffee' AND
((NOW() BETWEEN sales.start_date AND sales.end_date)
OR (NOW() > sales.start_date AND sales.end_date IS NULL)) )
WHERE general_coffee_id=cat AND stock>0
ORDER by name;
ELSEIF type = 'goodies' THEN
SELECT ncc.description AS g_description, ncc.image AS g_image,
CONCAT("G", ncp.id) AS sku, ncp.name, ncp.description, ncp.image,
➥ncp.price, ncp.stock, sales.price AS sale_price
FROM non_coffee_products AS ncp INNER JOIN non_coffee_categories
➥AS ncc
ON ncc.id=ncp.non_coffee_category_id
LEFT OUTER JOIN sales ON (sales.product_id=ncp.id
AND sales.product_type='goodies' AND
((NOW() BETWEEN sales.start_date AND sales.end_date) OR (NOW() >
➥sales.start_date AND sales.end_date IS NULL)) )
WHERE non_coffee_category_id=cat ORDER by date_created DESC;
END IF;
END$$
DELIMITER ;
```

**tip**

Alternatively, you could remove the type logic from the stored procedure and break it into two: one procedure for coffee products and one for the goodies.

You should update the procedure, using any interface to the database, before moving forward.

## Updating product_functions.inc.php

The logic for displaying the price of a product is a bit complex to write into the view file, so it'll go into a new function, also defined in `product_functions.inc.php`.

1. Open **product_functions.inc.php** in your text editor or IDE.

2. After the **get_stock_status()** definition, begin a new function:

   ```
   function get_price($type, $regular, $sales) {
   ```

   This function takes three arguments: the type of product, its regular price, and its sale price.

3. Check if the product's type equals **coffee**:

   ```
   if ($type === 'coffee') {
   ```

   As it stands, the list of coffee products is displayed as a drop-down menu (see Figure 8.13). In that context, there's a limit as to how much additional information can be displayed, compared to how the non-coffee products are displayed. For this reason, the sale price of each product type is treated a bit differently.

4. Return the sale price, if appropriate:

   ```
   if ((0 < $sales) && ($sales < $regular)) {
      return ' Sale: $' . number_format($sales/100, 2) . '!';
   }
   ```

   The value of **$sales** will be **NULL** if no sale price exists (see Figure 8.15), so this conditional confirms that the value is greater than 0 but not greater than the regular price (on account of some sort of administrative error). If so, then the word *Sale*, followed by a colon and the sale price, is returned (for coffee products). Because these prices come in to the function as integers in cents, they must be divided by 100 to format them properly for the customer.

5. Check if the type equals **goodies**:

   ```
   } elseif ($type === 'goodies') {
   ```

   For the non-coffee products, the sale price can be displayed with more information and flair.

6. Return the appropriate price:

   ```
   if ((0 < $sales) && ($sales < $regular)) {
      return '<strong>Sale Price:</strong> $' .
      ➥number_format($sales/100, 2) . '! (normally $' .
      ➥number_format($regular/100, 2). ')<br />';
   } else {
      return '<strong>Price:</strong> $' .
      ➥number_format($regular/100, 2) . '<br />';
   }
   ```

If the sale price is greater than 0 but less than the regular price, the sale price will be returned with the regular price in parentheses (so the customer can see the extra value; Figure 8.14). Otherwise, just the regular price is returned.

7. Complete the `if-elseif` conditional and the function definition:

```
    }
} // End of get_price() function.
```

8. Save the file.

## Updating list_goodies.html

**tip**

In the downloadable code, you'll see this modified view file named `list_goodies3.html`, to avoid confusion.

For `list_goodies.html` to take advantage of the new function, you just need to replace the reference to `$row['price']` with

```
get_price($type, $row['price'], $row['sale_price'])
```

Within a larger context, `list_goodies.html` now looks like this:

```
echo '<h3>' . $row['name'] . '</h3>
<div class="img-box"><p><img alt="' . $row['name'] . '"
➥src="/products/' . $row['image']  . '" />' . $row['description'] .
➥'<br /> . get_price($type, $row['price'], $row['sale_price']) .
<strong>Availability:</strong> ' . get_stock_status($row['stock']) .
➥'</p>
<p><a href="/cart.php?sku=' . $row['sku'] . '&action=add"
➥class="button">Add to Cart</a></p></div>';
```

You can test this additional code by viewing in your browser a list of goodies available in one category (as in Figure 8.14).

## Updating list_coffees.html

For `list_coffees.html` to take advantage of the new function, you must first include the `functions` file:

```
include('./includes/product_functions.inc.php');
```

Then you need to replace this line:

```
echo "<option value=\"{$row['sku']}\">{$row['name']} </option>\n";
```

with this one:

```
echo '<option value="' . $row['sku'] . '">' . $row['name'] .
➥get_price($type, $row['price'], $row['sale_price']) . '</option>';
```

You'll notice that I purposefully switched from using double to single quotation marks here. Which quotation marks you use is a personal preference, but because a function call can't be integrated into double quotation marks anyway, I thought a switch to single quotation marks would be logical.

You can test this additional code by viewing in your browser a specific coffee (as in Figure 8.13).

**tip**

In the downloadable code, you'll see this modified view file named `list_coffee2.html`, to avoid confusion.

# HIGHLIGHTING SALES

The preceding few pages performed the important task of reflecting sale prices on the regular products listing pages, but sale items will appear in two other places:

- On the home page (**Figure 8.16**)
- On a dedicated sales page (**Figure 8.17**)

**Figure 8.16**

**Figure 8.17**

You've already completed the stored procedure for performing both tasks. Now you just need to write the PHP scripts and view files.

## Creating the Home Page

Because the home page doesn't have to perform any of the validation that the shop and browse scripts perform, it ends up being the simplest of the PHP scripts in this chapter. It uses one view file, which represents all the page's content.

### CREATING THE PHP SCRIPT

The **index.php** script, placed in the web root directory, is simple enough that there's no need to walk through it in detail. It includes the three base files: configuration, header, and footer. To retrieve some sale items, it invokes the **select_sale_items()** procedure, passing it a value of **false** to indicate that not every item should be retrieved. And it includes the **home.html** view.

```
<?php
require('./includes/config.inc.php');

$page_title = 'Coffee - Wouldn\'t You Love a Cup Right Now?';
include('./includes/header.html');

require(MYSQL);

$r = mysqli_query($dbc, "CALL select_sale_items(false)");

include('./views/home.html');

include('./includes/footer.html');
?>
```

### CREATING THE VIEW FILE

The view file for the home page should create all the content the customer sees, including an introduction to the site and a few of the sale items. With the theory that there may or may not be any current sale items, this view file will confirm that there are sales records to return as part of its logic.

1. Create a new HTML script in your text editor or IDE to be named **home.html** and stored in the **views** directory.

2. Start with the initial HTML for creating a box:

   ```
   <?php
   echo BOX_BEGIN;
   echo '<div class="wrapper">';
   ```

3. Check for any sales:

   ```
   if (mysqli_num_rows($r) > 0) {
   ```

```
    echo '<dl class="special fright">
        <dt><a href="/shop/sales/">Sale Items</a></dt>';
```

If the stored procedure called in **index.php** returns some rows, then a definition list is begun (that's how the template handles the inset products) and a header is printed. The header is linked to **/shop/sales/**, which will be turned into **sales.php**, thanks to mod_rewrite (see Chapter 7).

4. Print each sale item:

```
while ($row = mysqli_fetch_array($r, MYSQLI_ASSOC)) {
    echo '<dd><a href="/shop/sales/#' . $row['sku'] . '"
    ➥title="View This Product"><img alt="" src="/products/' .
    ➥$row['image'] . '" /><span>' . $row['sale_price'] .
    ➥'</span></a></dd>';
}
```

Each sale item on the home page is displayed within **DD** tags. The HTML is just an image and a SPAN (for the price), plus a link to view the sale item in more detail and where the customer can purchase it. The link is to */show/sales/#SKU*, where ***#SKU*** will be an anchored location on the sales page. You don't need to call the **get_price()** function, because you already know the sale price applies.

**tip**

The anchor on the sales page works without changing the mod_rewrite definition.

5. Complete the sales section of the page:

```
    echo '</dl>';
} // End of mysqli_num_rows() IF.
```

6. Complete the rest of the page's content:

```
echo '<h2>Welcome to Our Online Coffee House!</h2>
<p>We\'re so glad you made it. Have a seat. Let me get you a
➥fresh, hot cup o\' Joe. Cream and sugar? There you go.</p>
<p>Please use the links at the top to browse through our catalog.
➥If you\'ve been here before, you can find things you bookmarked
➥by clicking on your Wish List and Cart links. </p>
</div>';
echo BOX_END;
echo BOX_BEGIN;
echo '<h3>About Clever Coffee, Inc.</h3>
<p>Clever Coffee, Inc. has been selling coffee online since 1923.
➥For years, Clever Coffee, Inc. failed to make a profit, due to
➥the lack of computers and the Internet. Yadda, yadda, yadda.</p>
<p>It\'s safe to shop here, promise!</p>';
echo BOX_BEGIN;
```

The rest of the page's content is mostly bragging about the site and encouraging the customer to shop there.

7. Save the file and test the home page in your web browser (see Figure 8.16).

## Creating the Sales Page

The final web page you'll develop in this chapter displays every sale item on a single page (see Figure 8.17). Let's quickly look at this page's PHP script and corresponding view file.

### CREATING THE PHP SCRIPT

As with the **index.php** script, **sales.php** is simple: there's no validation, just the invocation of a stored procedure. In fact, this is the same stored procedure used on the home page, this time passing along a value of **true** so that every sale item is fetched from the database.

```
<?php
require('./includes/config.inc.php');

$page_title = 'Sale Items';
include('./includes/header.html');

require(MYSQL);

$r = mysqli_query($dbc, 'CALL select_sale_items(true)');

if (mysqli_num_rows($r) > 0) {
   include('./views/list_sales.html');
} else {
   include('./views/noproducts.html');
}

include('./includes/footer.html');
?>
```

One difference here is that this script checks that some records are returned by the stored procedure. If so, the **list_sales.html** view is included. If not, the previously covered **noproducts.html** view is included.

### CREATING THE VIEW FILE

The view file for the sales page just lists every product on sale. For all products, the output will be exactly like that on the pages that list non-coffee products (see Figure 8.17). This means a slightly different format for coffee products.

1. Create a new HTML script in your text editor or IDE to be named **list_sales.html** and stored in the **views** directory.

2. Include the **product_functions.inc.php** script:

```
include('./includes/product_functions.inc.php');
```

   This view will use both functions defined in this file.

3. Start the initial HTML box:

```
echo BOX_BEGIN;
echo '<h2>Current Sale Items</h2>';
```

4. Loop through each returned item:

```
while ($row = mysqli_fetch_array($r, MYSQLI_ASSOC)) {
```

5. Print each item:

```
echo '<h3 id="' . $row['sku'] . '">' . $row['category'] . '::' .
➥$row['name'] .'</h3>
  <div class="img-box">
  <p><img alt="' . $row['name'] . '" src="/products/' .
  ➥$row['image']  . '" />' . $row['description'] . '<br />' .
  get_price('goodies', $row['price'], $row['sale_price']) . '
  <strong>Availability:</strong> ' .
  ➥get_stock_status($row['stock']) . '</p>
  <p><a href="/cart.php?sku=' . $row['sku'] . '&action=add"
  ➥class="button">Add to Cart</a></p></div>';
```

   You should notice that this code is similar to that in **list_goodies.html**, at least in terms of how the product's image, description, price, availability, and Add to Cart buttons are generated. One difference is that the name for each product also reflects the category that the product is in. And by adding an **id** attribute to each H3 tag, with a value of the product's SKU, the links from the home page to a specific product on this page will work.

6. Complete the **while** loop:

```
}
```

7. Complete the HTML:

```
echo BOX_END;
```

8. Save the file and test it in your web browser.

   You can test the sales listing page in two ways: by clicking the SALES link at the top of the page or by clicking a sale item on the home page.

# 9 BUILDING A SHOPPING CART

In the previous chapter, an online catalog of products was developed, complete with buttons for adding items to the customer's shopping cart. Now it's time to implement the cart itself. A good shopping cart shows customers exactly what they have in their basket and provides ways to remove items, update the quantities, and check out. For this website, there's also a "wish-list" feature, allowing the customer to save cart items for later.

The bulk of this chapter will focus on writing the shopping cart and wish-list features. First, though, new stored procedures are required. The chapter ends with various ways to factor in shipping.

## DEFINING THE PROCEDURES

Because this site uses an MVC approach, the chapter begins by looking at the *model* aspect of the project—the database. Eight stored procedures are defined in this chapter: four for the shopping cart and four for the wish list. Only two of the queries involved come close to being as complex as those in Chapter 8, "Creating a Catalog," although the procedures themselves will use a bit more logic than the ones you've already seen. Because the **carts** and **wish_lists** tables have the same structure and because they'll be used identically, I'll just explain the stored procedures for the cart. To create the corresponding procedures for the wish-list feature, you'll just need to replace every occurrence of **cart** with **wish_list**.

As a reminder, you don't have to use stored procedures. If you don't want to, or simply can't, you'll just need to take the logic and queries written into the stored procedures and code that directly in the PHP scripts instead. Chapter 13, "Extending the Second Site," explains how you would do that.

**tip**

See Chapter 8 for instructions on creating stored procedures in your database.

## Adding Products

The **add_to_cart()** stored procedure will be invoked when the customer requests that a product be added to her shopping cart. The procedure needs to take four pieces of information—a unique user ID, the product type (**coffee** or **goodies**), the product ID, and the quantity being added. As an extra bit of logic, the procedure should *add* the product to the cart if it doesn't already exist there but *add more quantity* of the product if it's already in the cart. Here's the stored procedure definition, and I'll explain its logic next:

**tip**

You can download all the SQL and files for this project from www.LarryUllman.com.

```
DELIMITER $$
CREATE PROCEDURE add_to_cart (uid CHAR(32), type VARCHAR(7),
➥pid MEDIUMINT, qty TINYINT)
BEGIN
   DECLARE cid INT;
   SELECT id INTO cid FROM carts WHERE user_session_id=uid AND
   ➥product_type=type AND product_id=pid;
   IF cid > 0 THEN
      UPDATE carts SET quantity=quantity+qty, date_modified=NOW()
      ➥WHERE id=cid;
   ELSE
      INSERT INTO carts (user_session_id, product_type, product_id,
      ➥quantity) VALUES (uid, type, pid, qty);
   END IF;
END$$
DELIMITER ;
```

**tip**

The delimiter just needs to be changed to something other than a semicolon.

First, in keeping with how stored procedures are created, the delimiter is immediately changed to the combination of two dollar signs together. Next, the code creates the procedure's *signature*, which is the combination of its name and arguments. The first argument is the user identifier, which will be exactly 32 characters long. Next is the product type, which will be either six or seven characters long (**coffee** or **goodies**). The last two arguments are the product's ID and the quantity being added.

**note**

Variables in stored procedures must be declared immediately after the **BEGIN** statement.

To incorporate the logic that checks if the product is already in the cart, an internal variable is necessary. You can create one using **DECLARE**, followed by the variable's name and its MySQL data type. The variable created is named **cid**, short for *cart ID*.

Next, a **SELECT** query checks the **carts** table for the submitted product. If the product is already represented in the table, then its **id** value will be assigned to the **cid** variable, thanks to the **SELECT...INTO** syntax.

After the **SELECT** query, an **IF-ELSE** conditional will run either an **UPDATE** or an **INSERT** query, depending on the value of **cid**. If **cid** is greater than 0, then the product is already in the table, and the submitted quantity should be added to the existing quantity. Otherwise, a new record is inserted. The **date_modified** column is updated to the current moment only for an **UPDATE** query.

## Removing Products

**tip**

The arguments passed to a stored procedure can be used internally in queries as if the queries were prepared statements, meaning that strings needn't be quoted.

The stored procedure for removing products from the cart is the simplest of the new procedures. It requires three of the four arguments that **add_to_cart()** uses (obviously no quantity needs to be indicated when removing something). The procedure just runs a **DELETE** query:

```
DELIMITER $$
CREATE PROCEDURE remove_from_cart (uid CHAR(32), type VARCHAR(7),
➥pid MEDIUMINT)
BEGIN
  DELETE FROM carts WHERE user_session_id=uid AND product_type=type
  ➥AND product_id=pid;
END$$
DELIMITER ;
```

## Updating the Cart

**tip**

The site offers two ways to remove items from the cart: clicking a link and entering 0 for the quantity.

The stored procedure for updating the shopping cart will be invoked after the user clicks the update button on the shopping cart page (**Figure 9.1**). The procedure takes the same four arguments as **add_to_cart()**, but doesn't need to confirm that the product already exists in the database (unless the user did something tricky, the product has to exist in order to show up in the cart). However, if the user enters zero for the quantity of the item, the procedure should go ahead and remove that from the cart. Rather than write the removal functionality into this procedure, the procedure will just invoke the already defined **remove_from_cart()** procedure if the quantity is zero.

Figure 9.1

```
DELIMITER $$
CREATE PROCEDURE update_cart (uid CHAR(32), type VARCHAR(7),
➥pid MEDIUMINT, qty TINYINT)
BEGIN
   IF qty > 0 THEN
      UPDATE carts SET quantity=qty, date_modified=NOW() WHERE
      ➥user_session_id=uid AND product_type=type AND product_id=pid;
   ELSEIF qty = 0 THEN
      CALL remove_from_cart (uid, type, pid);
   END IF;
END$$
DELIMITER ;
```

**tip**

Whenever the quantity of an item in the **carts** or **wish_lists** table changes (without the product being removed), the item's **date_modified** value is automatically updated, too.

## Fetching the Cart's Contents

The fourth and final stored procedure (for the shopping cart, that is) runs a **SELECT** query to retrieve all the contents of the cart. How tricky this **SELECT** query is depends on how much information you want to display, but at its base, the query looks a lot like the sales-related queries from Chapter 8. The query is a **UNION** of two **SELECT** statements: the first is a **JOIN** across four tables and the second a **JOIN** across five. In the procedure, I've written out the query over multiple lines for clarity. This procedure only needs the user's identifier as an argument.

```
DELIMITER $$
CREATE PROCEDURE get_shopping_cart_contents (uid CHAR(32))
BEGIN
   SELECT CONCAT("G", ncp.id) AS sku, c.quantity, ncc.category,
   ncp.name, ncp.price, ncp.stock, sales.price AS sale_price
   FROM carts AS c
   INNER JOIN non_coffee_products AS ncp ON c.product_id=ncp.id
   INNER JOIN non_coffee_categories AS ncc
   ON ncc.id=ncp.non_coffee_category_id
   LEFT OUTER JOIN sales
   ON (sales.product_id=ncp.id AND sales.product_type='goodies'
   AND ((NOW() BETWEEN sales.start_date AND sales.end_date)
   OR (NOW() > sales.start_date AND sales.end_date IS NULL)) )
   WHERE c.product_type="goodies" AND c.user_session_id=uid
   UNION
   SELECT CONCAT("C", sc.id), c.quantity, gc.category,
   CONCAT_WS(" - ", s.size, sc.caf_decaf, sc.ground_whole), sc.price,
   sc.stock, sales.price
   FROM carts AS c
   INNER JOIN specific_coffees AS sc ON c.product_id=sc.id
   INNER JOIN sizes AS s ON s.id=sc.size_id
   INNER JOIN general_coffees AS gc ON gc.id=sc.general_coffee_id
   LEFT OUTER JOIN sales
   ON (sales.product_id=sc.id AND sales.product_type='coffee'
   AND ((NOW() BETWEEN sales.start_date AND sales.end_date)
   OR (NOW() > sales.start_date AND sales.end_date IS NULL)) )
   WHERE c.product_type="coffee" AND c.user_session_id=uid;
END$$
DELIMITER ;
```

**Figure 9.2** shows the result of calling this procedure. You'll notice that the query returns the default price (under the heading *price*), the quantity in stock, and the sale price, if any. This information will be needed later.

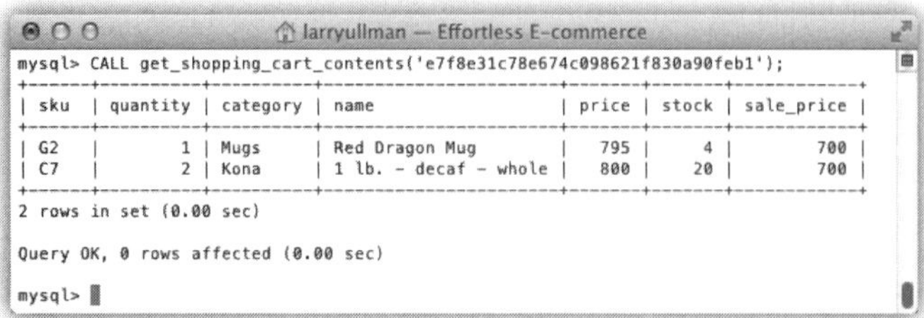


Figure 9.2

# DEFINING THE HELPER FUNCTIONS

Before getting into the shopping cart itself, there are two helper functions that will be useful to this chapter's code. The first function takes two possible prices—the regular and the sale price—and returns the appropriate price for the product:

```
function get_just_price($regular, $sales) {
   if ((0 < $sales) && ($sales < $regular)) {
      return number_format($sales/100, 2);
   } else {
      return number_format($regular/100, 2);
   }
}
```

This is similar to the **get_price()** function already defined in Chapter 8, but it just returns the numeric price (**get_price()** returned the price within some context). Again, because the price is coming from the database as an integer in cents (see Figure 9.2), the provided prices must be divided by 100.

The second function will parse a SKU—in other words, it will convert a value like C12 into **coffee** and 12, accordingly. This conversion will often be necessary, because the database uses each product's type and ID number individually. The function for parsing the SKU takes one argument—the SKU itself—and returns an array containing two elements:

```
function parse_sku($sku) {

   // Grab the first character:
   $type_abbr = substr($sku, 0, 1);

   // Grab the remaining characters:
   $pid = substr($sku, 1);

   // Validate the type:
   if ($type_abbr === 'C') {
      $type = 'coffee';
   } elseif ($type_abbr === 'G') {
      $type = 'goodies';
   } else {
      $type = NULL;
   }
```

*(continues on next page)*

```
    // Validate the product ID:
    $pid = (filter_var($pid, FILTER_VALIDATE_INT,
    ➥array('min_range' => 1))) ? $pid : NULL;

    // Return the values:
    return array($type, $pid);

} // End of parse_sku() function.
```

The two uses of **substr()** break the SKU into its parts. Next, the product type is validated based on the first character in the SKU, which must be either *C*, for *coffee*, or *G*, for *goodies*. If neither is the case, the **$type** variable is assigned the value **NULL**.

The remaining characters must be an integer greater than 1. The **filter_var()** function can test for that. If the value is an integer greater than 1, the value is assigned to **$pid**. Otherwise, the value **NULL** will be assigned.

Finally, both values are returned as an array. Because this function returns an array, you must use the **list()** function when calling it:

```
list($type, $id) = parse_sku($sku);
```

The **list()** function assigns to the variables—**$type** and **$id**—the values returned by the code on the right side of the equation.

The most appropriate place to define these two functions is within the already existing **product_functions.inc.php** script, found in the **includes** directory. Go ahead and do that before proceeding.

# MAKING A SHOPPING CART

After defining the stored procedures and the helper functions, three files must be created:

- **cart.php** will do all the work (it's the controller).
- **cart.html** is the view file for the cart.
- **emptycart.html** is the alternative view file for when there's nothing in the cart.

Let's create these files now, starting with the PHP script.

## Creating the PHP Script

As in Chapter 8, thanks to the use of stored procedures and included HTML files, the PHP script for presenting and managing a shopping cart becomes surprisingly short and quite tidy. The entire **cart.php** is only about 90 lines of code, including comments and blank lines. Most of the script is logic that invokes the correct stored procedure based on how the script is accessed.

1. Create a new PHP script in your text editor or IDE to be named **cart.php** and stored in the web root directory.

2. Include the configuration file:

```
<?php
require('./includes/config.inc.php');
```

3. Check for, or create, a user identifier:

```
if (isset($_COOKIE['SESSION']) && (strlen($_COOKIE['SESSION'])
➥=== 32)) {
  $uid = $_COOKIE['SESSION'];
} else {
  $uid = openssl_random_pseudo_bytes(16);
  $uid = bin2hex($uid);
}
```

This site needs only one cookie to handle the cart and wish-list functionality. The cookie's name is **SESSION**. Even though it's not a real PHP session, the name is indicative of how the cookie is used, and if the user sees the cookie that the site sends, this particular cookie will have an air of familiarity to it (making it less likely that the user will reject the cookie).

If the cookie *does* exist, its value is assigned to the **$uid** variable. As an added security measure, the value of the cookie is checked to have a length of 32 characters. This doesn't prevent all possible tampering but does require that whatever hacks are attempted be exactly 32 characters in length!

If the cookie doesn't exist, a new user ID must be created. A reasonably unique, usable identifier is generated using a combination of **openssl_random_pseudo_bytes()** and **bin2hex()**. The **openssl_random_pseudo_bytes()** function, added in PHP 5.3, returns a random string of bytes. Its first argument is the desired length in bytes. As I'll want a string 32 characters long, I provide 16 as the argument, as each byte represents two characters. This function returns binary data. To convert that data to a string that can be stored in a cookie, it must then be run through **bin2hex()**. The result is a string 32 characters long, with a value like **696e69455f6b3d22acdc62779a311c10**.

**tip**

See the PHP manual for details on using the **openssl_random_pseudo_bytes()** function.

**note**

Cookies must be sent prior to anything being sent to the web browser.

4. Send the cookie:

```
setcookie('SESSION', $uid, time()+(60*60*24*30), '/',
➥'www.example.com');
```

Whether the user is returning to this page or just coming here for the first time, a cookie will be sent. For new users, this is obviously necessary. For returning visitors, this call will update an existing cookie so that it lasts longer. The cookie is set to expire in 30 days from now. To improve the reliability of this cookie across all browsers, I'm providing five of the possible seven arguments.

The cookie will be sent over HTTP but will also be available over HTTPS.

Make sure you change the domain value to be correct for your site!

5. Include the header file:

```
$page_title = 'Coffee - Your Shopping Cart';
include('./includes/header.html');
```

6. Require the database connection and the functions file:

```
require (MYSQL);
include('./includes/product_functions.inc.php');
```

7. If there's a SKU value in the URL, break it down into its parts:

```
if (isset($_GET['sku'])) {
   list($type, $pid) = parse_sku($_GET['sku']);
}
```

By calling the user-defined **parse_sku()** function, the SKU, which might be present in the URL, is turned into its two components: the type and the ID.

**tip**

The **isset()** function can be used to validate that multiple variables are set in one function call.

8. Check for a product to be added to the cart:

```
if (isset($pid, $type, $_GET['action']) && ($_GET['action']
➥=== 'add') ) {
   $r = mysqli_query($dbc, "CALL add_to_cart('$uid', '$type',
   ➥$pid, 1)");
```

The logic for this script is a longish **IF-ELSEIF** conditional that checks for the various possible ways in which this script would be accessed. The first way a user might get to this page is by clicking an *Add to Cart* link, which will have a URL like **cart.php?sku=C8&action=add**. In that case, the SKU would be broken down into **$type** and **$pid** values, and **$_GET['action']** would equal **add**.

If all these conditions are true, the **add_to_cart()** stored procedure is called, passing along the user's identifier, the type of product, the product ID, and a quantity of 1.

If you're not using stored procedures, you'd just need to execute the underlying queries using standard PHP and MySQL approaches. First, you'd check if the item is in the cart. Then you'd run either an **UPDATE** or **INSERT** query accordingly.

**tip**

If you want to allow customers to add multiples of a product to the cart at one time, you just need to validate the quantity (passed in the URL) and use that as the final argument in the **add_to_cart()** call.

9. Check for a product to be removed from the cart:

```
} elseif (isset($type, $pid, $_GET['action']) &&
➥($_GET['action'] === 'remove') ) {
   $r = mysqli_query($dbc, "CALL remove_from_cart('$uid',
   ➥'$type', $pid)");
```

The **isset()** conditional is the same as that for adding products, but if **$_GET['action']** equals *remove*, the **remove_from_cart()** stored procedure will be called. This will be the case when the user clicks the *Remove from Cart* link (see Figure 9.1).

10. Check for a product to be moved into the cart:

```
} elseif (isset($type, $pid, $_GET['action'], $_GET['qty']) &&
➥($_GET['action'] === 'move') ) {
   $qty = (filter_var($_GET['qty'], FILTER_VALIDATE_INT,
   ➥array('min_range' => 1)) !== false) ? $_GET['qty'] : 1;
   $r = mysqli_query($dbc, "CALL add_to_cart('$uid', '$type',
   ➥$pid, $qty)");
   $r = mysqli_query($dbc, "CALL remove_from_wish_list('$uid',
   ➥'$type', $pid)");
```

The customer has the option of moving items back and forth between his cart and his wish list. If something is in the wish list and gets moved to the cart, the program's response should be similar to adding a product to the cart directly, with two differences. First, the quantities will be transferred over, too: If the customer has three of something in his wish list, all three will be added to the cart. Second, when this transfer occurs, the item should be removed from the wish list.

To make all this happen, the conditional checks that **$_GET['qty']** is set and that **$_GET['action']** equals **move**. The quantity value is then validated to be an integer greater than or equal to 1.

For every stored procedure call in this script, the results are assigned to the **$r** variable, even though only one of the procedure's results will be used (the procedure that returns the cart's contents). Still, I'm leaving these assignations in place for your own debugging purposes. If you have problems with the script, you could include the following line of code after a procedure call:

```
if (!$r) echo mysqli_error($dbc);
```

11. Check for a form submission:

```
} elseif (isset($_POST['quantity'])) {
```

All the previous conditions apply to GET requests, but this page can be invoked using a POST request, too. This will happen when the user submits the cart form in order to update the quantities.

12. Loop through each item:

```
foreach ($_POST['quantity'] as $sku => $qty) {
   list($type, $pid) = parse_sku($sku);
   if (isset($type, $pid)) {
      $qty = (filter_var($qty, FILTER_VALIDATE_INT,
      ➥array('min_range' => 0)) !== false) ? $qty : 1;
      $r = mysqli_query($dbc, "CALL update_cart('$uid', '$type',
      ➥$pid, $qty)");
```

`$_POST['quantity']` will be an array of elements, in the format ***SKU*** `=>` ***`quantity`***. For each element in `$_POST['quantity']`, the corresponding product in the cart must be updated. To do that, first the SKU is parsed and validated. Then the quantity is validated. If it's an integer greater than or equal to 0 (because the customer can enter a quantity of 0 to remove an item), that value will be used. If, for whatever reason, the customer enters an invalid quantity for a product, the value 1 will be used instead. Finally, the `update_cart()` stored procedure is executed, passing along the proper values.

13. Complete the primary conditional and retrieve the cart's contents:

```
}// End of main IF.
$r = mysqli_query($dbc, "CALL get_shopping_cart_
➥contents('$uid')");
```

Regardless of what action just took place, the cart's current contents will be displayed.

14. Include the appropriate view:

```
if (mysqli_num_rows($r) > 0) {
   include('./views/cart.html');
} else { // Empty cart!
   include('./views/emptycart.html');
}
```

15. Complete the page:

```
include('./includes/footer.html');
?>
```

16. Save the file.

## Creating the Views

The shopping cart uses two view files: one for displaying products and one indicating an empty cart. The latter one, named **emptycart.html**, is simple (**Figure 9.3**):

Figure 9.3

```
<?php echo BOX_BEGIN; ?>
  <h2>Your Shopping Cart</h2>
  <p>Your shopping cart is currently empty.</p>
<?php echo BOX_END; ?>
```

The second view file is more complicated, naturally. First, it must display every item retrieved by the stored procedure—every product in the cart—but it must do so as an HTML form so that the user can update the quantities. Second, each product should have its own links for removing the product from the cart or for moving it to the wish list. Third, subtotals and an order total should be calculated and displayed (**Figure 9.4** shows the initial version of the view; Figure 9.1 shows how it will be updated later).

Your Shopping Cart

Please use this form to update your shopping cart. You may change the quantities, move items to your wish list for future purchasing, or remove items entirely. The shipping and handling cost is based upon the order total. When you are ready to complete your purchase, please click Checkout to be taken to a secure page for processing.

| Item | Quantity | Price | Subtotal | Options |
|---|---|---|---|---|
| Mugs::Red Dragon Mug | 2 | $7.00 | $14.00 | Move to Wish List<br>Remove from Cart |
| Kona::2 oz. Sample - caf - ground | 1 | $2.00 | $2.00 | Move to Wish List<br>Remove from Cart |
| Kona::5 lbs. - caf - whole | 1 | $30.00 | $30.00 | Move to Wish List<br>Remove from Cart |
| | | Total | $46.00 | |

Update Quantities

Checkout

Figure 9.4

1. Create a new HTML file in your text editor or IDE to be named **cart.html** and stored in the **views** directory.

2. Begin the HTML box and the header:

```
<?php echo BOX_BEGIN; ?>
<h2>Your Shopping Cart</h2>
<p>Please use this form to update your shopping cart. You may
➥change the quantities, move items to your wish list for future
➥purchasing, or remove items entirely. The shipping and handling
➥cost is based upon the order total. When you are ready to
➥complete your purchase, please click Checkout to be taken to a
➥secure page for processing.</p>
```

   For the instructions on the cart page, you'll need to strike a balance between being informative and not being too busy. Remember that the primary purpose of the cart page is to get the customer to check out!

3. Begin the form:

```
<form action="/cart.php" method="POST">
```

   The form is submitted back to **cart.php** and uses the POST method. The action value starts with a slash to indicate that **cart.php** is in the web root directory. The slash isn't absolutely required for the **cart.php** script, but is required with many other links and references used by the site, so it's here for consistency. If you've placed these files in a subdirectory, you'll need to add that to the **action** attribute's value.

4. Begin the table:

```
<table border="0" cellspacing="8" cellpadding="6">
  <tr>
    <th align="center">Item</th>
    <th align="center">Quantity</th>
    <th align="right">Price</th>
    <th align="right">Subtotal</th>
    <th align="center">Options</th>
  </tr>
```

   In an old-school way, I'm using a standard HTML table to display the cart's contents. The table consists of five columns.

5. Begin a PHP block:

```
<?php
$total = 0;
```

   Within the PHP block, the total variable is initialized to 0 so that a proper order total can be calculated.

6. Fetch each item:

```
while ($row = mysqli_fetch_array($r, MYSQLI_ASSOC)) {
   $price = get_just_price($row['price'], $row['sale_price']);
   $subtotal = $price * $row['quantity'];
```

Within the loop, the item's price is first determined by passing the regular and sale prices to the **get_just_price()** function. Then a subtotal is calculated by multiplying the price times the quantity in the cart.

**tip**

For security purposes, the price is always coming from the database; it's not possible for the customer to manipulate it.

7. Print a table row:

```
echo '<tr><td>' . $row['category'] . '::' . $row['name'] . '</td>
   <td align="center"><input type="text" name="quantity[' .
   ➥$row['sku'] . ']" value="' . $row['quantity'] . '" size="2"
   ➥class="small" /></td>
   <td align="right">$' . $price . '</td>
   <td align="right">$' . number_format($subtotal, 2) . '</td>
   <td align="right"><a href="/wishlist.php?sku=' . $row['sku'] .
   ➥'&action=move&qty=' . $row['quantity'] .'">Move to Wish
   ➥List</a><br /><a href="/cart.php?sku=' . $row['sku'] .
   ➥'&action=remove">Remove from Cart</a></td>
</tr>
';
```

For each item, a table row is generated. The first column is the displayed name of the product. For the name, the cart shows a combination of the product's category and its specific name, as on the sales page. In the second column, the quantity is displayed. To make this value editable, it's displayed within a text input. The name for each input will be ***quantity*[sku]**, making both the SKU and the new quantity available when the form is submitted (**Figure 9.5**).

```
<tr><td>Mugs::Red Dragon Mug</td>
		<td align="center"><input type="text" name="quantity[G2]" value="2" size="2" class="small" /></td>
		<td align="right">$7.00</td>
		<td align="right">$14.00</td>
		<td align="right"><a href="/wishlist.php?sku=G2&action=move&qty=2">Move to Wish List</a><br /><a href="/cart.php?
sku=G2&action=remove">Remove from Cart</a></td>
	</tr>
	<tr><td>Kona::2 oz. Sample - caf - ground</td>
		<td align="center"><input type="text" name="quantity[C1]" value="1" size="2" class="small" /></td>
		<td align="right">$2.00</td>
		<td align="right">$2.00</td>
		<td align="right"><a href="/wishlist.php?sku=C1&action=move&qty=1">Move to Wish List</a><br /><a href="/cart.php?
sku=C1&action=remove">Remove from Cart</a></td>
	</tr>
	<tr><td>Kona::5 lbs. - caf - whole</td>
		<td align="center"><input type="text" name="quantity[C10]" value="1" size="2" class="small" /></td>
		<td align="right">$30.00</td>
		<td align="right">$30.00</td>
		<td align="right"><a href="/wishlist.php?sku=C10&action=move&qty=1">Move to Wish List</a><br /><a href="/cart.php?
sku=C10&action=remove">Remove from Cart</a></td>
	</tr>
```

**Figure 9.5**

The third and fourth columns are the price and subtotal. In the fifth column are two links. The first is to move the item to the wish list. That link passes to **wishlist.php** the SKU, the current quantity, and an action value of **move**. The second link is back to this page for removing the product.

8. Add an error message if the product isn't sufficiently stocked:

```
if ($row['stock'] < $row['quantity']) {
   echo '<tr class="error"><td colspan="5" align="center">There
   ➥are only ' . $row['stock'] . ' left in stock of the ' .
   ➥$row['name'] . '. Please update the quantity, remove the
   ➥item entirely, or move it to your wish list.</td></tr>';
}
```

If the user has more of an item in her cart than is currently in stock, she needs to be notified of the problem (**Figure 9.6**). At this point in the process, the customer is told exactly how many are left and asked to remedy the issue herself. In the next chapter, an insufficiently stocked item will be dropped from the order automatically.

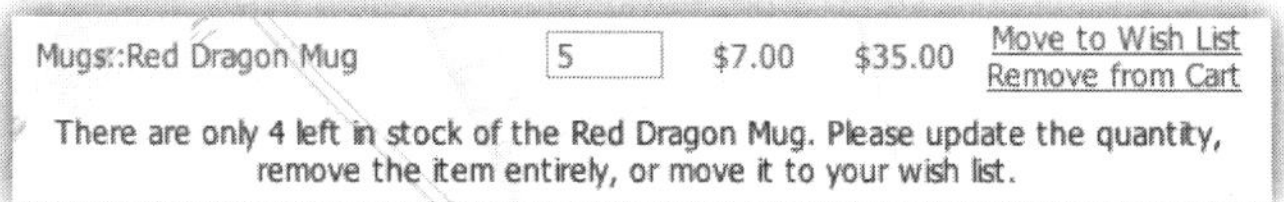


Figure 9.6

9. Add the subtotal to the total and complete the loop:

```
   $total += $subtotal;
} // End of WHILE loop.
```

10. Add the total to the table:

```
echo '<tr>
   <td colspan="3" align="right"><strong>Total</strong></td>
   <td align="right">$' . number_format($total, 2) . '</td>
   <td> </td>
</tr>
';
```

11. Complete the table and create two buttons:

```
echo '</table><br /><p align="center"><input type="submit"
➥value="Update Quantities" class="button" /></form></p><br />
➥<p align="center"><a href="https://<?php echo BASE_URL; ?>
➥checkout.php" class="button">Checkout</a></p>';
```

The first button is used to submit this form (to update the quantities). The second button is to start the checkout process. That link goes to **checkout.php**, but via an HTTPS connection. To generate that link's value, the **BASE_URL** constant is required.

**note**

The checkout process must begin on a secure page for the customer to feel safe (and to be safe)!

**12.** Complete the page:

```
echo BOX_END;
?>
```

**13.** Save the file and test the shopping cart in your web browser.

Now you should be able to test everything except for the interactions with the wish list. You can add products, update quantities, and remove items.

# MAKING A WISH LIST

Just as the stored procedures for managing the wish list are virtually the same as those for managing the shopping cart, the PHP script and HTML files involved here will be similar to the ones just written. The chapter will present all three files in entirety, but for a full description of any of the code or logic, review the previous several pages.

## Creating the PHP Script

The **wishlist.php** script, stored in the web root directory, is exactly like **cart.php** except that

- Its page title is different.
- The wish list versions of the stored procedures are called.
- Different HTML files are used for the views.
- There's no conditional checking if the user is adding an item directly.

Aside from this last difference, you can almost do a search and replace to create this script using a copy of **cart.php**. As for the last item, as written, items are added to the wish list by moving them from the cart.

```
<?php // wishlist.php
require('./includes/config.inc.php');

// Check for, or create, a user session:
if (isset($_COOKIE['SESSION']) && (strlen($_COOKIE['SESSION'])
➥=== 32)) {
   $uid = $_COOKIE['SESSION'];
} else {
   $uid = openssl_random_pseudo_bytes(16);
   $uid = bin2hex($uid);
}
```

*(continues on next page)*

```
setcookie('SESSION', $uid, time()+(60*60*24*30), '/',
➥'www.example.com');

$page_title = 'Coffee - Your Wish List';
include('./includes/header.html');
require(MYSQL);
include('./includes/product_functions.inc.php');
if (isset($_GET['sku'])) {
   list($type, $pid) = parse_sku($_GET['sku']);
}

if (isset ($type, $pid, $_GET['action']) && ($_GET['action'] ==
➥'remove') ) {
   $r = mysqli_query($dbc, "CALL remove_from_wish_list('$uid',
   ➥'$type', $pid)");
} elseif (isset ($type, $pid, $_GET['action'], $_GET['qty']) &&
➥($_GET['action'] == 'move') ) { // Move it to the wish list.
   $qty = (filter_var($_GET['qty'], FILTER_VALIDATE_INT,
   ➥array('min_range' => 1)) !== false) ? $_GET['qty'] : 1;
   $r = mysqli_query($dbc, "CALL add_to_wish_list('$uid', '$type',
   ➥$pid, $qty)");
   $r = mysqli_query($dbc, "CALL remove_from_cart('$uid', '$type',
   ➥$pid)");
} elseif (isset($_POST['quantity'])) {
   foreach ($_POST['quantity'] as $sku => $qty) {
      list($type, $pid) = parse_sku($sku);
      if (isset($type, $pid)) {
         $qty = (filter_var($qty, FILTER_VALIDATE_INT,
         ➥array('min_range' => 0)) !== false) ? $qty : 1;
         $r = mysqli_query($dbc, "CALL update_wish_list('$uid',
         ➥'$type', $pid, $qty)");
         }
      } // End of FOREACH loop.
}// End of main IF.

$r = mysqli_query($dbc, "CALL get_wish_list_contents('$uid')");
if (mysqli_num_rows($r) > 0) {
   include('./views/wishlist.html');
} else { // Empty cart!
   include('./views/emptylist.html');
}

include('./includes/footer.html');
?>
```

## Creating the Views

The **emptylist.html** view is used when the customer's wish list is empty (**Figure 9.7**).

**note**

Of course, the two view files go in the **views** directory.

Figure 9.7

```
<?php echo BOX_BEGIN; ?>
  <h2>Your Wish List</h2>
  <p>Your wish list is currently empty.</p>
<?php echo BOX_END; ?>
```

The **wishlist.html** view file displays the wish list in an HTML table. As with the shopping cart, the wish list contents can be altered:

- Their quantities can be changed.
- Items can be moved to the shopping cart.
- Items can be removed from the wish list.

Unlike the shopping cart page, the wish list doesn't display an order total or a link to checkout (**Figure 9.8**). Also, instead of indicating that insufficient quantity of a product is in stock, the wish list will indicate those items that are running low, in the hopes of inducing the customer to purchase the items now (**Figure 9.9**).

Your Wish List

Please use this form to update your wish list. You may change the quantities, move items to your cart for purchasing, or remove items entirely.

| Item | Quantity | Price | Subtotal | Options |
|---|---|---|---|---|
| Mugs::Pretty Flower Coffee Mug | 1 | $6.50 | $6.50 | Move to Cart<br>Remove from Wish List |
| Kona::1 lb. - caf - ground | 1 | $8.00 | $8.00 | Move to Cart<br>Remove from Wish List |

Update Quantities

Figure 9.8

| | | | | |
|---|---|---|---|---|
| Mugs::Red Dragon Mug | 1 | $7.00 | $7.00 | Move to Cart<br>Remove from Wish List |

There are only 4 left in stock of the Red Dragon Mug.

Figure 9.9

```
<?php echo BOX_BEGIN; ?>
<h2>Your Wish List</h2>
<p>Please use this form to update your wish list. You may change the
➥quantities, move items to your cart for purchasing, or remove items
➥entirely.</p>
<form action="/wishlist.php" method="POST">
<table border="0" cellspacing="8" cellpadding="6">
   <tr>
      <th align="center">Item</th>
      <th align="center">Quantity</th>
      <th align="right">Price</th>
      <th align="right">Subtotal</th>
      <th align="center">Options</th>
   </tr>
<?php
while ($row = mysqli_fetch_array($r, MYSQLI_ASSOC)) {
   $price = get_just_price($row['price'], $row['sale_price']);
   $subtotal = $price * $row['quantity'];
   echo '<tr>
      <td>' . $row['category'] . '::' . $row['name'] . '</td>
      <td align="center"><input type="text" name="quantity[' .
      ➥$row['sku'] . ']" value="' . $row['quantity'] . '" size="2"
      ➥class="small" /></td>
      <td align="right">$' . number_format($price, 2) . '</td>
      <td align="right">$' . number_format($subtotal, 2) . '</td>
      <td align="right"><a href="/cart.php?sku=' . $row['sku'] .
      ➥'&action=move&qty=' . $row['quantity'] .'">Move to Cart</a>
      ➥<br /><a href="/wishlist.php?sku=' . $row['sku'] .
      ➥'&action=remove">Remove from Wish List</a></td>
   </tr>
   ';
   if ( ($row['stock'] > 0) && ($row['stock'] < 10)) {
      echo '<tr class="error"><td colspan="5" align="center">There
      ➥are only ' . $row['stock'] . ' left in stock of the ' .
      ➥$row['name'] . '.</td></tr>';
   }
} // End of WHILE loop.
echo '</table><p align="center"><input type="submit"
➥value="Update Quantities" class="button" /></form></p>';
echo BOX_END;
?>
```

# CALCULATING SHIPPING

A nice feature worth adding to the shopping cart is an indication of how much the shipping will be. For many customers, the shipping and handling charges are a significant factor when deciding whether to make an online purchase. The shipping cost may be a fixed price or it may be based on these factors:

- The total weight of the order
- The distance between the origination and destination
- The physical size of the order (for example, large furniture costs extra)
- The total amount of the sale

This site will use this last criterion.

The first step is to define a function that will calculate the shipping using a formula. As an example, let's say that shipping starts with a base rate, which covers the simple fact that some employee has to be paid to assemble and box the order. Added to that should be an amount that's partly based on the amount of the order: Presumably, as the order total increases, more items are being shipped, but at the same time the site is making more money. Therefore, the bulk of the shipping cost will be proportional to the order total, and that proportion will decrease for larger orders. Here, then, is the function:

```
function get_shipping($total = 0) {

   // Set the base handling charges:
   $shipping = 3;

   // Rate is based upon the total:
   if ($total < 10) {
      $rate = .25;
   } elseif ($total < 20) {
      $rate = .20;
   } elseif ($total < 50) {
      $rate = .18;
   } elseif ($total < 100) {
      $rate = .16;
   } else {
      $rate = .15;
   }

   // Calculate the shipping total:
   $shipping = $shipping + ($total * $rate);
```

*(continues on next page)*

```
    // Return the shipping total:
    return $shipping;

} // End of get_shipping() function.
```

**note**

The database uses integers (cents) for prices but the order total will come into the shipping calculator in dollars, as the prices will have already been divided by 100.

Logically, this function should be defined in the **product_functions.inc.php** script so that it's available to multiple scripts (such as **cart.php** and **checkout.php**, which will be written in the next chapter).

To use this function in **cart.html** (the wish list doesn't display a total), add this code before displaying the total (**Figure 9.10**):

```
$shipping = get_shipping($total);
$total += $shipping;
echo '<tr>
    <td colspan="3" align="right"><strong>Shipping &amp;
    ➥Handling</strong></td>
    <td align="right">$' . number_format($shipping, 2). '</td>
    <td> </td>
</tr>
';
```

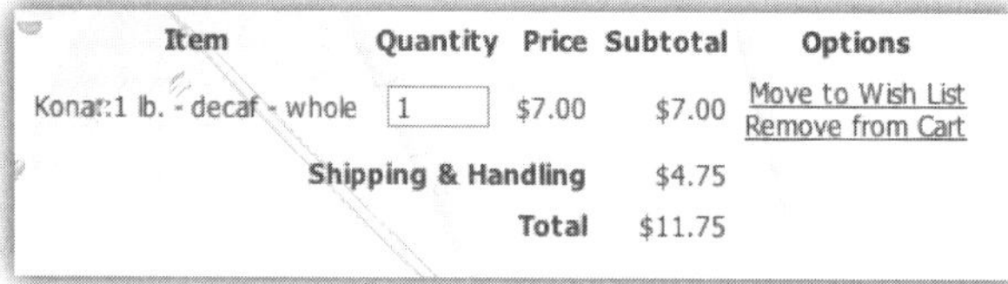


Figure 9.10

# 10 CHECKING OUT

The next step in the evolution of the Coffee site is to incorporate the payment processing system that will allow customers to complete their orders. For this project, I've chosen Authorize.net as the payment processor. The first several pages of the chapter talk about Authorize.net and walk you through setting up a test account there. Once you have a test account, you can write the entire checkout process.

The checkout process consists of four parts:

1. Take and validate the shipping information.
2. Take and validate the billing information.
3. Process the payment.
4. Wrap it up (update the database, let the customer know, and so on).

This chapter probably has the most complicated code of any in the book. But this chapter also conveys the information that many readers need the most, so ample space is dedicated to explaining the code as thoroughly as possible.

## ABOUT AUTHORIZE.NET

Authorize.net is perhaps the largest payment gateway out there and was most certainly one of the first available for e-commerce. How Authorize.net functions is different than PayPal, used in Chapter 6, "Using PayPal." PayPal fetches monies from customers' credit cards (or PayPal accounts) and deposits those amounts into your *PayPal account* (which you can later move to a bank account). By comparison, Authorize.net coordinates with several networked systems to transfer funds from credit cards to your *merchant bank account*. Authorize.net is an agent in the process, a true payment gateway, and when the transaction is completed, the money will automatically be transferred to your bank account. For this reason, you must have a merchant bank account (with an actual bank) that supports the Authorize.net system.

Authorize.net accepts all major credit cards and offers:

- Advanced fraud detection
- PCI DSS compliance
- Support for recurring payments
- International transactions
- An online virtual terminal
- Customer information management
- eCheck acceptance
- Multiple administrators with different permissions
- Good documentation and support

**tip**

If you're just testing Authorize.net, you don't need an actual merchant account.

Authorize.net provides what they call the *Merchant Interface*, where you can configure your account, manage transactions, view statements, generate reports, and so forth. This chapter will mention the Merchant Interface a few times, but keep in mind that the Merchant Interface is how a site administrator manages an Authorize.net account; it's not how the site itself communicates with the payment system.

**tip**

Authorize.net has a Verified Merchant Seal image that you can display on your website to imply your site's credibility.

As with PayPal and many other payment systems, there are multiple ways you can use Authorize.net: *Simple Checkout*, *Server Integration Method* (SIM), and *Advanced Integration Method* (AIM). When using the first two, the customer will be taken to the Authorize.net website, similar to the PayPal example in Chapter 6.

Since the first edition of the book was written, Authorize.net has created a fourth option, called *Direct Post Method* (DPM). DPM is Authorize.net's version of what I'm calling "the middle way": the customer never leaves your site, but the payment information also never touches your server. This is the same approach that companies like Stripe and Braintree Payments employ. Because Chapter 15, "Using Stripe Payments," will cover this technique in detail, and as AIM offers the highest level of customization, this chapter will demonstrate the Advanced Integration Method. Fortunately, since the first edition of this book was written, Authorize.net has created a Software Development Kit (SDK) that makes interacting with the Authorize.net system quite easy.

**tip**

AIM is the Authorize.net-recommended system, but it requires programming and web security skills.

# CREATING A TEST ACCOUNT

**tip**

If you know you'll be using Authorize.net for a real project, go ahead and create a real account with Authorize.net now.

There are two ways you can create an account for testing the Authorize.net system. First, if you create a *real* Authorize.net account, associated with your business and tied to your merchant bank account, that account will initially be in a testing mode. Once you've finished testing the account, you only need to go into the Merchant Interface to take the account live. The second option is to create a true test account: an account with limited functionality that can't later be turned into an actual account. This is the route taken in the next series of steps.

1. Go to http://developer.authorize.net/testaccount/.
2. Fill out the simple form (**Figure 10.1**) and click Sign Up.

   For this chapter, you'll need to select the Card Not Present account type (as opposed to in-person commercial transactions, where the customer is presenting you with the card).

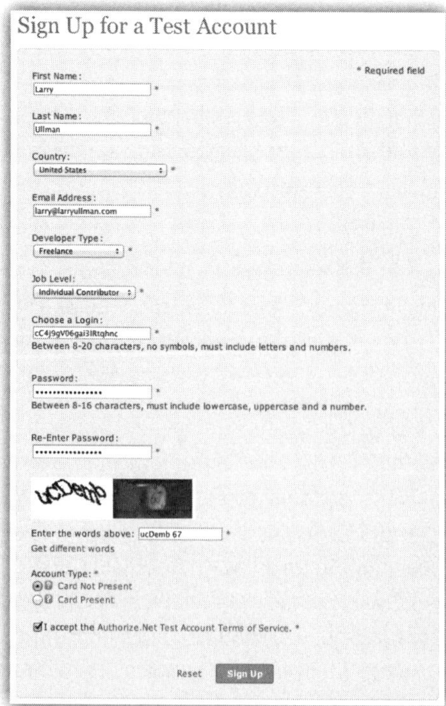


**Figure 10.1**

3. On the resulting page, make note of the API credentials provided (**Figure 10.2**).

   As a convenience, Authorize.net provides your credentials immediately, so you don't have to wait any longer to test the system. You'll also receive an email with some basic information.

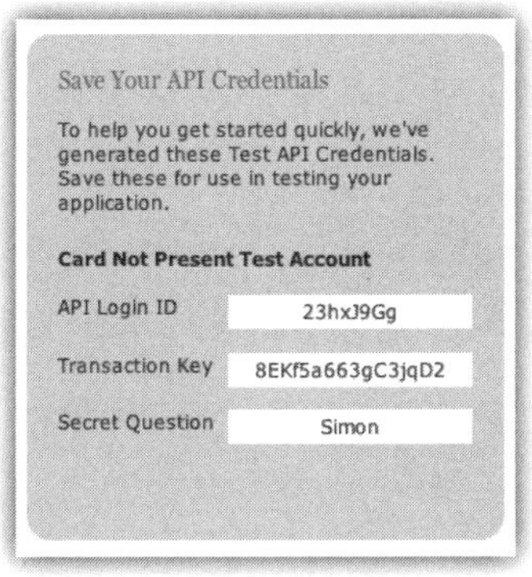

Save Your API Credentials

To help you get started quickly, we've generated these Test API Credentials. Save these for use in testing your application.

**Card Not Present Test Account**

API Login ID 23hxJ9Gg

Transaction Key 8EKf5a663gC3jqD2

Secret Question Simon

Figure 10.2

# PREPARING THE SITE

Before implementing the actual **checkout.php** script (the first in the checkout process), you have some background work to do. This includes creating the required stored procedures (for every database query), creating a modified HTML template, and defining one helper function. Let's look at the template first, because it's the simplest task to complete.

## The New HTML Template

At car dealerships, customers are able to roam around the lot and look at all the pretty, shiny vehicles. They can look at this one, then that one, and then compare those with another. But when it comes time to buy, the dealership locks the customer in a room with a salesperson whose job it is to close the sale without any distractions. With an e-commerce site, you want to metaphorically do the same thing.

At first, the customer should be free to roam about the site, eyeing the products and enjoying the "window shopping" opportunity. The online catalog, developed in Chapter 8, "Creating a Catalog," has this approach: It's designed to be easy for the customer to get around, look at products, and put them into his cart. But the checkout process should be different: The sole purpose is to get the customer to complete the sale. Toward that end, the HTML template needs to be changed for this process, discouraging the customer from doing

**tip**

A different template is also a visual cue to customers that they're in "purchase" mode instead of "browsing" mode.

anything but completing the sale. Specifically, the template should remove the shopping-related links so that the customer stays on track (**Figure 10.3**). Still, the customer shouldn't be trapped in the checkout process (car dealerships don't *literally* lock the door), so the less obvious links at the top of the page are still required.

Figure 10.3

**tip**

You can download all of this book's code from www.LarryUllman.com.

The entire checkout process will require an SSL connection. This means that any links in the template to non-checkout pages need to be absolute, to a non-SSL version (that is, to `http://whatever`).

1. Make a copy of `header.html` to be named `checkout_header.html` and stored in the `includes` directory.

2. Remove the big shopping links by deleting this code:

```
<ul class="nav">
<!-- MENU -->
<li><a href="/shop/coffee/">Coffee</a></li>
<li><a href="/shop/goodies/">Goodies</a></li>
<li><a href="/shop/sales/">Sales</a></li>
<li><a href="/wishlist.php">Wish List</a></li>
<li><a href="/cart.php">Cart</a></li>
<!-- END MENU -->
</ul>
```

3. Change the remaining links to `index.php`, `cart.php`, `contact.php`, and `sitemap.php` so that they use *HTTP* instead of *HTTPS*.

   For example, the code should be:

```
http://<?php echo BASE_URL; ?>/index.php
```

These other links, as originally defined, were *relative*. On an HTTPS page, such links would take the customer to an HTTPS version of the shopping pages, which isn't necessary (and could adversely affect the server's performance).

4. Save the file.

When viewing the pages that use this new header, the user can still return to the shopping part of the site, but it's not obvious, which is a good thing. If you want to be more generous, you could create an overt *Return to Shopping* link somewhere (just make sure it's an absolute reference using HTTP).

You don't have to change the footer for the checkout process.

**tip**

Just as the checkout process should minimize links that take the customer elsewhere, it should maximize those links and buttons that move the process onward.

## The Helper Function

For the checkout process, one helper function will be defined. Because this process involves a couple of forms (for taking the shipping and billing information), a function for creating and managing form inputs will be quite useful. In Chapter 4, "User Accounts," the **create_form_input()** function was defined. That function creates a form element, handles any existing values, and indicates errors when appropriate. That version of the function created only text, password, and textarea inputs. It also looked for existing element values only in the **$_POST** array. This site will use a new version of that function, generating both text-like inputs and select menus. The function also needs to be able to find existing values in **$_SESSION**, not just **$_POST**. Finally, because this template doesn't use the Twitter Bootstrap framework (as in the "Knowledge Is Power" example), the formatting of elements and errors will differ from the function in Chapter 4.

1. Create a new PHP script in your text editor or IDE to be named **form_functions.inc.php** and stored in the **includes** directory.

   As in Part 2, "Selling Virtual Products," this script will define only a single function, but the file's name will still be plural, in case more functions are added later.

2. Begin defining the function:

```
function create_form_input($name, $type, $errors = array(),
➥$values = 'POST', $options = array()) {
```

   The function takes five arguments, three of which are optional. The first argument is the name for the element. The second is its type (for example, **text** or **select**). The third is an array in which any errors would be found. These three arguments are the same as in the book's previous version of this function, minus the label argument, which won't be part of this function.

The fourth argument is the name of the array where existing values are to be found, for the purpose of making the form sticky. For the checkout process, the value will be either **POST** or **SESSION**. In theory, you could pass the array itself—**$_POST**, **$_SESSION** (even **$_GET** or **$_COOKIE**, if you wanted)—to the function, just as the **$errors** array is passed. But since these arrays are global in scope, they'll be available to the function without being sent along as a second copy.

The fifth argument is for passing extra HTML. This chapter will provide one value for this argument: **autocomplete="off"**. You'll see why and how later in the chapter.

3. Look for and process any existing value:

```
$value = false;
if ($values === 'SESSION') {
   if (isset($_SESSION[$name])) $value =
   ➥htmlspecialchars($_SESSION[$name], ENT_QUOTES, 'UTF-8');
} elseif ($values === 'POST') {
   if (isset($_POST[$name])) $value =
   ➥htmlspecialchars($_POST[$name], ENT_QUOTES, 'UTF-8');
   if ($value && get_magic_quotes_gpc())
   ➥$value = stripslashes($value);
}
```

First, the **$value** variable is set to **false**, thereby assuming that no value exists. A conditional then checks in which array an existing value could be found. In each case, any existing value is assigned to **$value**. Since posted values could be affected by Magic Quotes (on older versions of PHP), **stripslashes()** is applied to those values, but only if Magic Quotes is enabled.

Whether the value is coming from a session or from a form submission, the value is run through **htmlspecialchars()** to ensure that it's safe to use later in the function.

4. Determine what kind of element to create:

```
if ( ($type === 'text') || ($type === 'password') ) {
```

This version of the function will be used only to create text and select elements, but I'm leaving the password type in (as in the original version of this function), because it's defined in the same way as text inputs. Because the template I'm using doesn't use HTML5, I'm not adding support for an email input type (as in the Chapter 4 version).

**5.** Create the text input:

```
echo '<input type="' . $type . '" name="' . $name . '" id="' .
➥$name . '"';
if ($value) echo ' value="' . $value . '"';
if (!empty($options) && is_array($options)) {
   foreach ($options as $k => $v) {
      echo " $k=\"$v\"";
   }
}
if (array_key_exists($name, $errors)) {
   echo 'class="error" /> <span class="error">' . $errors[$name]
   ➥. '</span>';
} else {
   echo ' />';
}
```

All this code is similar to that explained in Chapter 4, except for how the elements are formatted and how errors are displayed. The value will be safe to use here, as it will have already been run through the **htmlspecialchars()** function.

**6.** Check for the select type:

```
} elseif ($type === 'select') {
```

The previous incarnation of this function didn't handle select menus, but this one will (four will be required by the checkout process).

**7.** If a states menu is being created, define the data source:

```
if (($name === 'state') || ($name === 'cc_state')) {
   $data = array('AL' => 'Alabama', 'AK' => 'Alaska', 'AZ' =>
   ➥'Arizona', 'AR' => 'Arkansas', 'CA' => 'California', 'CO'
   ➥=> 'Colorado', 'CT' => 'Connecticut', 'DE' => 'Delaware',
   ➥'FL' => 'Florida', 'GA' => 'Georgia', 'HI' => 'Hawaii',
   ➥'ID' => 'Idaho', 'IL' => 'Illinois', 'IN' => 'Indiana',
   ➥'IA' => 'Iowa', 'KS' => 'Kansas', 'KY' => 'Kentucky', 'LA'
   ➥=> 'Louisiana', 'ME' => 'Maine', 'MD' => 'Maryland', 'MA' =>
   ➥'Massachusetts', 'MI' => 'Michigan', 'MN' => 'Minnesota',
   ➥'MS' => 'Mississippi', 'MO' => 'Missouri', 'MT' => 'Montana',
   ➥'NE' => 'Nebraska', 'NV' => 'Nevada', 'NH' => 'New
   ➥Hampshire', 'NJ' => 'New Jersey', 'NM' => 'New Mexico',
   ➥'NY' => 'New York', 'NC' => 'North Carolina', 'ND' => 'North
   ➥Dakota', 'OH' => 'Ohio', 'OK' => 'Oklahoma', 'OR' =>
```

*(continues on next page)*

```
➥'Oregon', 'PA' => 'Pennsylvania', 'RI' => 'Rhode Island',
➥'SC' => 'South Carolina', 'SD' => 'South Dakota', 'TN'
➥=> 'Tennessee', 'TX' => 'Texas', 'UT' => 'Utah', 'VT' =>
➥'Vermont', 'VA' => 'Virginia', 'WA' => 'Washington', 'WV' =>
➥'West Virginia', 'WI' => 'Wisconsin', 'WY' => 'Wyoming');
```

The only difference among the four select menus used in this chapter will be their names and their data sources. For each menu, a different data source is defined as the **$data** array. Two form menus, named *state* and *cc_state*, will use this list of US states.

8. If an expiration month menu is being created, define that data source:

```
} elseif ($name === 'cc_exp_month') {
   $data = array(1 => 'January', 'February', 'March', 'April',
   ➥'May', 'June', 'July', 'August',  'September', 'October',
   ➥'November', 'December');
```

For the credit card's expiration month, a select menu will display the month name but use the numbers 1 through 12 as the values.

9. If an expiration year menu is being created, define that data source:

```
} elseif ($name === 'cc_exp_year') {
   $data = array();
   $start = date('Y');
   for ($i = $start; $i <= $start + 5; $i++) {
      $data[$i] = $i;
   }
} // End of $name IF-ELSEIF.
```

For the credit card's expiration year, a list of years will be presented. This list will always start with the current year and then display five more from there. The combination of the **date()** function, to return the current year, and a **foreach** loop will populate the array.

**tip**

If the server's time zone isn't set in PHP, you'll need to set it using **date_default_timezone_set()** prior to calling any date-related function.

10. Create the opening **SELECT** tag:

```
echo '<select name="' . $name  . '"';
```

11. Add the **error** class, if applicable, and close the opening tag:

```
if (array_key_exists($name, $errors)) echo ' class="error"';
echo '>';
```

If an error exists for this element, the **error** class is added to the opening tag. The effect will be the element outlined in red (in accordance with the definition of the **error** class in the CSS file).

12. Create each option:

```
foreach ($data as $k => $v) {
   echo "<option value=\"$k\"";
   if ($value === $k) echo ' selected="selected"';
   echo ">$v</option>\n";
}
```

A **foreach** loop iterates through the data source, creating an OPTION tag for each element. If there's an existing value, that will be selected as well (**Figure 10.4**).

```
<option value="MS">Mississippi</option>
<option value="MO">Missouri</option>
<option value="MT">Montana</option>
<option value="NE" selected="selected">Nebraska</option>
<option value="NV">Nevada</option>
<option value="NH">New Hampshire</option>
```

**Figure 10.4**

13. Complete the tag:

```
echo '</select>';
```

14. Add an error message, if one exists:

```
if (array_key_exists($name, $errors)) {
   echo '<br /><span class="error">' . $errors[$name] .
   ➥'</span>';
}
```

The error message is displayed on the line after the menu.

15. Complete the function:

```
   } // End of primary IF-ELSE.
} // End of the create_form_input() function.
```

16. Save the file.

## Creating the Procedures

This chapter requires five new stored procedures. Each one applies to an important part of the checkout process:

- The customer
- The shopping cart
- The order
- The order's contents
- The payment transaction

Three of these are simple, one isn't too complicated, and one is, well, complicated. Let's look at the easy ones first.

### CLEARING THE SHOPPING CART

After the customer has completed a purchase, the shopping cart needs to be emptied of its contents. That stored procedure is short and simple:

```
DELIMITER $$
CREATE PROCEDURE clear_cart (uid CHAR(32))
BEGIN
  DELETE FROM carts WHERE user_session_id=uid;
END$$
DELIMITER ;
```

This procedure takes one argument: the customer's cart session ID. The procedure then runs a **DELETE** query on the **carts** table.

### ADDING TRANSACTIONS

The **transactions** table stores a record of every call to the payment gateway: what order the transaction was tied to and what the response was. All this information will also be available through the Merchant Interface, but it'd be nice to have it on this server as well: When it comes to databases, it's always better to store more information. There's nothing of a sensitive nature in the transaction data (that is, no billing information), so storing it doesn't constitute a security risk.

The **transactions** table has nine columns: **id**, **order_id**, **type**, **amount**, **response_code**, **response_reason**, **transaction_id**, **response**, and **date_created**. Most of these columns, and their values, will be explained

**tip**

If you can't—or don't want to—use stored procedures, you can implement the same logic using standard PHP and MySQL queries.

**tip**

You can download all the book's SQL commands from www.LarryUllman.com.

**tip**

As a reminder, the lines that change the delimiter aren't part of the stored procedure itself, but they're necessary in order to use semicolons within the definition.

**tip**

If you're looking for a good third-party tool for MySQL development, check out Toad (www.quest.com). It's available for free for Windows.

later in the chapter when the payment response is covered in detail. But for now, seven of these values need to be provided when the procedure is called. Here's that definition:

```
DELIMITER $$
CREATE PROCEDURE add_transaction (oid INT, trans_type VARCHAR(18),
➥amt INT(10), rc TINYINT, rrc TINYTEXT, tid BIGINT, r TEXT)
BEGIN
   INSERT INTO transactions VALUES (NULL, oid, trans_type, amt, rc,
   ➥rrc, tid, r, NOW());
END$$
DELIMITER ;
```

**note**

The argument names used in a stored procedure shouldn't be the same as any table's column names or as any MySQL keyword.

## ADDING CUSTOMERS

The stored procedure for adding a customer isn't that complicated, but it uses a new stored procedure concept: *outbound arguments* (new in that they haven't been discussed previously in this book). Stored procedures can be written to take arguments, just like a function in PHP. By default, all procedure arguments are *inbound*, meaning that values are assigned to the arguments when the procedure is called. You can also create *outbound arguments*. Outbound arguments are assigned values within the procedure itself, not when the procedure is called. The values assigned within the procedure can then be available outside of the procedure, after it has been called.

As a practical example of how outbound arguments might be used, take this next stored procedure, which inserts a record into the **customers** table. The rest of the checkout process will need the new record's ID value (the new customer's ID), so using an outbound argument is appropriate. Here's the procedure's definition:

**tip**

Chapter 8 provides instructions on using the command-line **mysql** client or the browser-based phpMyAdmin to create stored procedures.

```
DELIMITER $$
CREATE PROCEDURE add_customer (e VARCHAR(80), f VARCHAR(20),
➥l VARCHAR(40), a1 VARCHAR(80), a2 VARCHAR(80), c VARCHAR(60),
➥s CHAR(2), z MEDIUMINT, p INT, OUT cid INT)
BEGIN
   INSERT INTO customers (email, first_name, last_name, address1,
   ➥address2, city, state, zip, phone) VALUES (e, f, l, a1, a2, c,
   ➥s, z, p);
   SELECT LAST_INSERT_ID() INTO cid;
END$$
DELIMITER ;
```

tip

Since the default parameter type is inbound, the **IN** keyword declaring them as such is optional.

tip

Stored procedures can also have **INOUT** arguments, which can be used for both inbound and outbound purposes.

tip

Because the **get_order_contents()** procedure will be used to confirm to customers what they just purchased, the query doesn't retrieve any of the customer data.

tip

If you want to fetch the order total and shipping cost, it must be selected as part of each returned row, or a second **SELECT** query would be required and the procedure's results would be that much harder to handle.

The first nine arguments are typical inbound ones. They represent the customer's email address, first name, last name, street address, additional street address, city, state, zip code, and phone. The argument names are cryptic, but they aren't referenced more than once within the procedure, and more important, they don't conflict with the table's actual column names this way. These nine arguments are used as the values for the **INSERT** query.

The tenth argument, **cid**, is defined as outbound, thanks to the **OUT** keyword. The last thing the procedure does is call the **LAST_INSERT_ID()** function, which returns the primary key value for the previously run **INSERT**. This value is selected and assigned to **cid**.

## RETRIEVING ORDER CONTENTS

After the order has been completed, many site pages will need to retrieve the details of an order. For example, the PHP script that generates a receipt will need to fetch those order details, as will an administrative script. Doing so only requires the order ID, which can then be used to query the **order_contents** table. The **order_contents** table stores the number of items purchased, the quantity, and the price. By performing a **JOIN** from this table to the various product-related tables, similar to the **JOIN**s in the **get_shopping_cart_contents()** procedure, you ensure that each product's descriptive name can also be retrieved. The query also joins in the **orders** table so that it may select the order total and shipping cost.

```
DELIMITER $$
CREATE PROCEDURE get_order_contents (oid INT)
BEGIN
   SELECT oc.quantity, oc.price_per,
   (oc.quantity*oc.price_per) AS subtotal, ncc.category, ncp.name,
   o.total, o.shipping
   FROM order_contents AS oc
   INNER JOIN non_coffee_products AS ncp ON oc.product_id=ncp.id
   INNER JOIN non_coffee_categories AS ncc
   ON ncc.id=ncp.non_coffee_category_id
   INNER JOIN orders AS o ON oc.order_id=o.id
   WHERE oc.product_type="goodies" AND oc.order_id=oid
   UNION
   SELECT oc.quantity, oc.price_per, (oc.quantity*oc.price_per),
   gc.category,
   CONCAT_WS(" - ", s.size, sc.caf_decaf, sc.ground_whole),
   o.total, o.shipping
   FROM order_contents AS oc
```

```
    INNER JOIN specific_coffees AS sc ON oc.product_id=sc.id
    INNER JOIN sizes AS s ON s.id=sc.size_id
    INNER JOIN general_coffees AS gc ON gc.id=sc.general_coffee_id
    INNER JOIN orders AS o ON oc.order_id=o.id
    WHERE oc.product_type="coffee" AND oc.order_id=oid;
END$$
DELIMITER ;
```

**Figure 10.5** shows the result of executing this procedure.

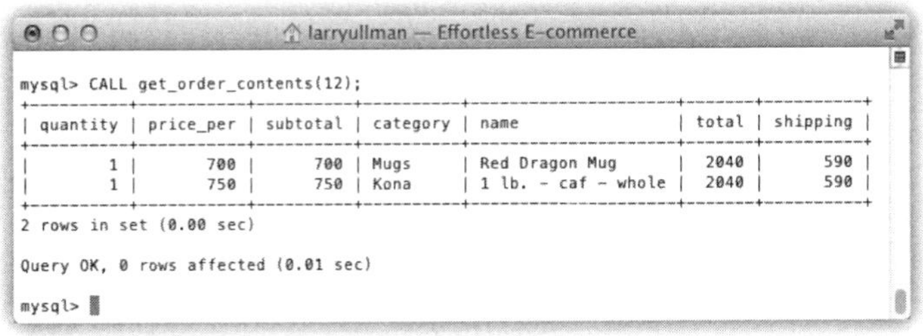

```
larryullman — Effortless E-commerce

mysql> CALL get_order_contents(12);
+----------+-----------+----------+----------+----------------------+-------+----------+
| quantity | price_per | subtotal | category | name                 | total | shipping |
+----------+-----------+----------+----------+----------------------+-------+----------+
|        1 |       700 |      700 | Mugs     | Red Dragon Mug       |  2040 |      590 |
|        1 |       750 |      750 | Kona     | 1 lb. - caf - whole  |  2040 |      590 |
+----------+-----------+----------+----------+----------------------+-------+----------+
2 rows in set (0.00 sec)

Query OK, 0 rows affected (0.01 sec)

mysql>
```

**Figure 10.5**

## ADDING ORDERS

The final stored procedure for this chapter is perhaps the most complicated one in the book. At its core, the procedure needs to add a new order to the database. This involves populating both the **orders** and **order_contents** tables. Let's look at the queries and the process separately, before revealing the complete procedure definition.

Adding records to the **orders** table is easy: The **INSERT** just requires the customer ID, the total, the shipping cost (which is also part of the total), the last four digits of the credit card number (for the customer's reference), and the date of the order. That query looks like this:

```
INSERT INTO orders (customer_id, shipping, credit_card_number,
➥order_date) VALUES (cid, ship, cc, NOW());
```

For now, let's ignore the **total** column, because that value is unknown without adding up all the items in the order.

Next, the order ID will be required to populate the **order_contents** table. That information will need to be selected into a variable:

```
SELECT LAST_INSERT_ID() INTO oid;
```

This is exactly how the customer ID value is retrieved in the **add_customer()** stored procedure.

The **order_contents** table is going to store the order ID, the product type (**coffee** or **goodies**), the product ID, the quantity, and the price being paid for each. The interesting thing is that all this information is readily available to the **add_order()** procedure without it being passed as arguments. And that's where things get complicated.

The order ID was just created, so that's not a problem. The product type, product ID, and quantity can come from the **carts** table, assuming that this procedure can access the user's cart ID. But to determine the price to be paid, factoring in sale prices, requires a **JOIN** across **carts**, **sales**, and either **non_coffee_products** or **specific_coffees**. Because this last **JOIN** is across one of two tables, a **UNION** is required, just like the **get_shopping_cart_contents()** procedure uses.

Fetching the product's information and the correct price for just non-coffee products requires this **SELECT** statement (**Figure 10.6**):

```
SELECT c.product_type, c.product_id, c.quantity,
IFNULL(sales.price, ncp.price)
FROM carts AS c
INNER JOIN non_coffee_products AS ncp ON c.product_id=ncp.id
LEFT OUTER JOIN sales ON (sales.product_id=ncp.id AND
➥sales.product_type='goodies' AND
((NOW() BETWEEN sales.start_date AND sales.end_date) OR (NOW( ) >
➥sales.start_date AND sales.end_date IS NULL)) )
WHERE c.product_type="goodies" AND c.user_session_id=<user_cart_id>
```

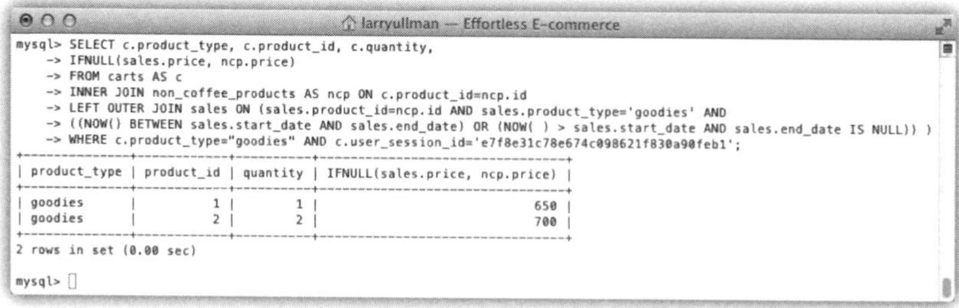

```
mysql> SELECT c.product_type, c.product_id, c.quantity,
    -> IFNULL(sales.price, ncp.price)
    -> FROM carts AS c
    -> INNER JOIN non_coffee_products AS ncp ON c.product_id=ncp.id
    -> LEFT OUTER JOIN sales ON (sales.product_id=ncp.id AND sales.product_type='goodies' AND
    -> ((NOW() BETWEEN sales.start_date AND sales.end_date) OR (NOW( ) > sales.start_date AND sales.end_date IS NULL)) )
    -> WHERE c.product_type="goodies" AND c.user_session_id='e7f8e31c78e674c098621f830a90feb1';
+--------------+------------+----------+--------------------------------+
| product_type | product_id | quantity | IFNULL(sales.price, ncp.price) |
+--------------+------------+----------+--------------------------------+
| goodies      |          1 |        1 |                            650 |
| goodies      |          2 |        2 |                            700 |
+--------------+------------+----------+--------------------------------+
2 rows in set (0.00 sec)

mysql>
```

Figure 10.6

For the price, the query uses the **IFNULL()** construct, which selects the first value if it's not **NULL** and the second value if the first value is **NULL**. Thus, **IFNULL(sales.price, ncp.price)** will select **sales.price** if it exists, and select **ncp.price** otherwise. You can confirm this by also selecting the two prices to see the results (**Figure 10.7**).

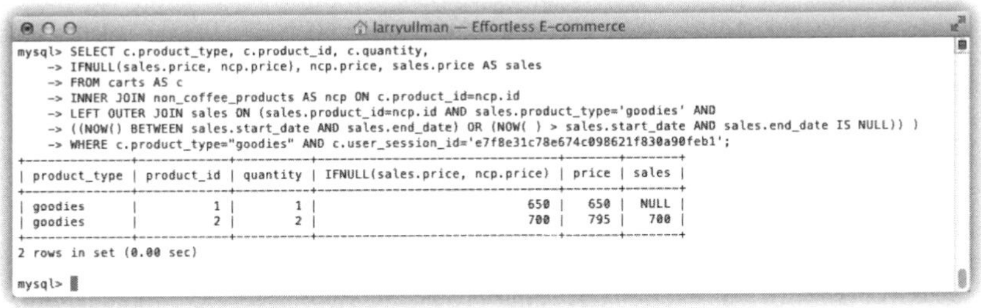

```
larryullman — Effortless E-commerce
mysql> SELECT c.product_type, c.product_id, c.quantity,
    -> IFNULL(sales.price, ncp.price), ncp.price, sales.price AS sales
    -> FROM carts AS c
    -> INNER JOIN non_coffee_products AS ncp ON c.product_id=ncp.id
    -> LEFT OUTER JOIN sales ON (sales.product_id=ncp.id AND sales.product_type='goodies' AND
    -> ((NOW() BETWEEN sales.start_date AND sales.end_date) OR (NOW( ) > sales.start_date AND sales.end_date IS NULL)) )
    -> WHERE c.product_type="goodies" AND c.user_session_id='e7f8e31c78e674c098621f830a90feb1';
+--------------+------------+----------+--------------------------------+-------+-------+
| product_type | product_id | quantity | IFNULL(sales.price, ncp.price) | price | sales |
+--------------+------------+----------+--------------------------------+-------+-------+
| goodies      |          1 |        1 |                            650 |   650 |  NULL |
| goodies      |          2 |        2 |                            700 |   795 |   700 |
+--------------+------------+----------+--------------------------------+-------+-------+
2 rows in set (0.00 sec)

mysql>
```

Figure 10.7

Now that you (hopefully) understand how the **SELECT** query works, consider that the **SELECT** query can be used immediately to provide the values for an **INSERT** query, thanks to the **INSERT...SELECT** construct. The **INSERT** for **order_contents** is

```
INSERT INTO order_contents (order_id, product_type, product_id,
➥quantity, price_per) VALUES (...
```

Putting together the **INSERT** and **SELECT** queries, the entire query becomes

```
INSERT INTO order_contents (order_id, product_type, product_id,
➥quantity, price_per)
SELECT oid, c.product_type, c.product_id, c.quantity,
IFNULL(sales.price, ncp.price)
FROM carts AS c
INNER JOIN non_coffee_products AS ncp ON c.product_id=ncp.id
LEFT OUTER JOIN sales ON (sales.product_id=ncp.id AND
➥sales.product_type='goodies' AND
((NOW() BETWEEN sales.start_date AND sales.end_date) OR (NOW() >
➥sales.start_date AND sales.end_date IS NULL)) )
WHERE c.product_type="other" AND c.user_session_id=<user_cart_id>
UNION
SELECT oid,...
```

Adding the selection of the **oid** variable ensures that the value can be inserted into **order_contents** at the same time.

Moving on in the procedure, the last step is to update the **orders** table for the order total. The total can be determined by running an aggregating query on **order_contents** for the current order:

```
SELECT SUM(quantity*price_per) INTO subtotal FROM order_contents
➥WHERE order_id=oid;
```

And now the **orders** table can be updated:

```
UPDATE orders SET total = (subtotal + ship) WHERE id=oid;
```

Finally, the order total will be necessary outside of the procedure (as part of the payment processing). To make that possible, the total should also be assigned to an outbound argument:

```
SELECT (subtotal + ship) INTO total;
```

The complete stored procedure looks like this:

```
DELIMITER $$
CREATE PROCEDURE add_order (cid INT, uid CHAR(32), ship INT(10),
➥cc MEDIUMINT, OUT total INT(10), OUT oid INT)
BEGIN
   DECLARE subtotal INT(10);
   INSERT INTO orders (customer_id, shipping, credit_card_number,
   ➥order_date) VALUES (cid, ship, cc, NOW());
   SELECT LAST_INSERT_ID() INTO oid;
   INSERT INTO order_contents (order_id, product_type, product_id,
   ➥quantity, price_per) SELECT oid, c.product_type, c.product_id,
   ➥c.quantity, IFNULL(sales.price, ncp.price) FROM carts AS
   ➥c INNER JOIN non_coffee_products AS ncp ON c.product_id=ncp.id
   ➥LEFT OUTER JOIN sales ON (sales.product_id=ncp.id AND
   ➥sales.product_type='goodies' AND ((NOW() BETWEEN
   ➥sales.start_date AND sales.end_date) OR (NOW() >
   ➥sales.start_date AND sales.end_date IS NULL)) ) WHERE
   ➥c.product_type="goodies" AND c.user_session_id=uid UNION
   ➥SELECT oid, c.product_type, c.product_id, c.quantity,
   ➥IFNULL(sales.price, sc.price) FROM carts AS c INNER JOIN
   ➥specific_coffees AS sc ON c.product_id=sc.id LEFT OUTER JOIN
   ➥sales ON (sales.product_id=sc.id AND sales.product_type='coffee'
   ➥AND ((NOW() BETWEEN sales.start_date AND sales.end_date) OR
   ➥(NOW() > sales.start_date AND sales.end_date IS NULL)) ) WHERE
   ➥c.product_type="coffee" AND c.user_session_id=uid;
   SELECT SUM(quantity*price_per) INTO subtotal FROM order_contents
   ➥WHERE order_id=oid;
   UPDATE orders SET total = (subtotal + ship) WHERE id=oid;
   SELECT (subtotal + ship) INTO total;
END$$
DELIMITER ;
```

The procedure takes the customer ID, the customer's cart ID, the shipping amount, and the credit card number (the last four digits) as inbound arguments. There are two outbound arguments: **total** and **oid**. Within a **BEGIN** block, a local variable named **subtotal** is defined. Next, the record is added to the **orders** table, and the just-created ID is selected and assigned to **oid**. After that, the **order_contents** table is populated, using the **INSERT...SELECT UNION SELECT** query.

The last three lines calculate the subtotal of the order, update the **total** column in the **orders** table, and assign the total order value to the **total** variable.

**note**

Remember that variables in stored procedures don't use a dollar sign like PHP variables.

## STORED PROCEDURES REVISITED

The modestly complex **add_order()** stored procedure demonstrates the security and performance benefits that can be had by using stored procedures. The procedure takes just four arguments—the customer ID, the customer's cart session ID, the shipping cost, and the credit card representation—and does a lot of work with that little information. The procedure could even be cut down to just two inbound arguments if the shipping were to be calculated by a database-stored function and the credit card numbers were omitted (both values will be stored in the **transactions** table anyway). From a performance standpoint, there's very little information that PHP needs to send to the database, and more critically, the PHP script needs to execute only a single query—the procedure call itself. Since query executions are one of the most demanding things a PHP script does, limiting those can have a huge performance gain (although that burden is subsequently moved to the database server).

From a security standpoint, much of the key information—like the price a product is sold for—never leaves the database, making it that much harder to be manipulated. And no PHP script directly accesses any of the database tables, adding a layer of obfuscation.

I should add that you might logically use transactions in this stored procedure, which stored procedures do support. If you use transactions, every query would have to work properly or the entire process would be reverted. Such an approach prevents an incomplete order from being recorded. Still, I opted not to use transactions, because they would further complicate an already complicated process.

# TAKING THE SHIPPING INFORMATION

Once the customer is finished shopping and is ready to purchase items, she will click a button on the shopping cart page that takes her to **checkout.php** (over HTTPS). The checkout page needs to do the following:

1. Take the customer's shipping information.
2. Validate the provided data.
3. If the data is valid, store the data and send the customer on to the next step in the checkout process.

   If the data is invalid, redisplay the form with errors.

In terms of displaying and validating the form, **checkout.php** behaves like **register.php** from Chapter 4. But there are some additional considerations that make this script more complicated than that one. Let's first define the PHP script, then the two view files it uses.

## Creating the PHP Script

**tip**

The **.htaccess** modifications in Chapter 7, "Second Site: Structure and Design" ensure that **checkout.php** is accessible only over HTTPS.

The PHP script should be accessed at least twice: originally as a GET request, at which point the form should be shown, and as a POST request, when the form is submitted. The latter action demands about 100 lines of validation, which is the bulk of the script.

Unlike the shopping area of the website, the checkout process will use PHP sessions. This is necessary because multiple scripts will all need access to some of the same information.

1. Create a new PHP script in your text editor or IDE to be named **checkout.php** and stored in the web root directory.
2. Include the configuration file:

   ```
   <?php
   require('./includes/config.inc.php');
   ```

3. Check for the user's cart ID, available in a cookie:

   ```
   if ($_SERVER['REQUEST_METHOD'] === 'GET') {
      if (isset($_COOKIE['SESSION']) && (strlen($_COOKIE['SESSION'])
      ➥=== 32)) {
         $uid = $_COOKIE['SESSION'];
   ```

To access the customer's shopping cart, this script needs the user's shopping cart session ID, stored in a cookie in the user's browser. This script first confirms that a session value was passed along in a cookie. If so, it's assigned to the **$uid** variable for later use.

4. Use the cart ID as the session ID, and begin the session:

```
session_id($uid);
session_start();
```

The shopping part of the site purposefully does not use sessions (in order to give longevity to the customer's cart and wish list), but the checkout process will. For continuity, and because the shopping cart ID will be required by the checkout process, the user's existing cart ID will be used as the session ID. This can be arranged by providing a session ID value to the **session_id()** function prior to calling **session_start()**.

The net result will be two cookies in the user's browser: **SESSION**, sent over HTTP, and **PHP_SESSION_ID**, sent over HTTPS. Both will have the same value.

5. If no session value was present in a cookie (for a GET request), redirect the user:

```
} else {
    $location = 'http://' . BASE_URL . 'cart.php';
    header("Location: $location");
    exit();
}
```

There's no point in checking out if there's nothing to purchase. And without a cart session ID, there will be nothing to purchase! In that case, the customer is redirected back to **cart.php**, over HTTP. That page will display the checkout button only if the cart isn't empty.

6. If the request method isn't GET, start the session and retrieve the session ID:

```
} else { // POST request.
    session_start();
    $uid = session_id();
}
```

This **else** clause will apply when the customer submits the form for validation. In that case, the session needs to be started. The session ID would've already been set the first time this script was accessed, so that value can be retrieved (by calling **session_id()** with no arguments) to be used later in this script.

7. Include the database connection and create an array for validation errors:

```
require (MYSQL);
$shipping_errors = array();
```

8. If the form was submitted, validate the first and last names:

```
if ($_SERVER['REQUEST_METHOD'] === 'POST') {
   if (preg_match ('/^[A-Z \'.-]{2,20}$/i',
   ➥$_POST['first_name'])) {
      $fn = addslashes($_POST['first_name']);
   } else {
      $shipping_errors['first_name'] = 'Please enter your first
      ➥name!';
   }
   if (preg_match ('/^[A-Z \'.-]{2,40}$/i', $_POST['last_name'])) {
      $ln  = addslashes($_POST['last_name']);
   } else {
      $shipping_errors['last_name'] = 'Please enter your last
      ➥name!';
   }
```

The validation routines for the customer's first and last names match those from **register.php** in Chapter 4. To make the values safe to use in the stored procedure call, each value is run through **addslashes()**.

If there's a chance that Magic Quotes may be enabled on your server (because you're using an older version of PHP), you'll also need to apply **stripslashes()** prior to validation:

```
if (get_magic_quotes_gpc()) {
   $_POST['first_name'] = stripslashes($_POST['first_name']);
   // Repeat for other variables that could be affected.
}
```

If Magic Quotes is enabled, a valid last name, such as *O'Toole*, will become *O\'Toole*, which won't pass the regular expression test. But when the stored procedure is invoked, the query will be **CALL add_customer('$fn', '$ln', . . .)**, in which case **addslashes()** must be applied to the query data to prevent the apostrophe in *O'Toole* from breaking that procedure call: **CALL add_customer('Peter', 'O'Toole', . . .)**.

**tip**

As a formality, you could add **isset()** to each validation conditional, as in **if (isset($_POST['var']) ➥&& preg_match(....**

9. Validate the street addresses:

```
if (preg_match ('/^[A-Z0-9 \',.#-]{2,80}$/i',
➥$_POST['address1'])) {
   $a1  = addslashes($_POST['address1']);
 } else {
```

```
    $shipping_errors['address1'] = 'Please enter your street
    ➥address!';
}
if (empty($_POST['address2'])) {
    $a2 = NULL;
} elseif (preg_match ('/^[A-Z0-9 \',.#-]{2,80}$/i',
➥$_POST['address2'])) {
    $a2 = addslashes($_POST['address2']);
} else {
    $shipping_errors['address2'] = 'Please enter your street
    ➥address!';
}
```

Addresses are trickier to validate because they can contain many characters besides alphanumeric ones. The regular expression pattern allows for any letter, any number, a space, an apostrophe, a comma, a period, the number sign, and a dash.

The second street address (for longer addresses) is optional, so it's only validated if it's not empty.

**10.** Validate the city:

```
if (preg_match ('/^[A-Z \'.-]{2,60}$/i', $_POST['city'])) {
    $c = addslashes($_POST['city']);
} else {
    $shipping_errors['city'] = 'Please enter your city!';
}
```

**11.** Validate the state:

```
if (preg_match ('/^[A-Z]{2}$/', $_POST['state'])) {
    $s = $_POST['state'];
} else {
    $shipping_errors['state'] = 'Please enter your state!';
}
```

There's no need to apply either **stripslashes()**, with Magic Quotes enabled, or **addslashes()** to this variable, because a valid value can contain exactly two capital letters.

**tip**

All address and phone number validation routines would need to be altered if the site is serving non-US customers.

**12.** Validate the zip code:

```
if (preg_match ('/^(\d{5}$)|(^\d{5}-\d{4})$/', $_POST['zip'])) {
    $z = $_POST['zip'];
} else {
    $shipping_errors['zip'] = 'Please enter your zip code!';
}
```

The zip code can be in either the five-digit or five-plus-four format (12345 or 12345-6789).

13. Validate the phone number:

```
$phone = str_replace(array(' ', '-', '(', ')'), '',
➥$_POST['phone']);
if (preg_match ('/^[0-9]{10}$/', $phone)) {
   $p  = $phone;
} else {
   $shipping_errors['phone'] = 'Please enter your phone
   ➥number!';
}
```

The phone number must be exactly 10 digits long, which is easy to check. But as users commonly enter phone numbers with and without spaces, hyphens, and parentheses, any of those characters that may be present are first removed via **str_replace()**. Its first argument is an array of values to find—space, hyphen, opening parenthesis, closing parenthesis; its second argument is the replacement value (here, an empty string).

**tip**

The **str_replace()** function is a faster alternative to **preg_replace()**, usable when fancy pattern matching isn't required.

14. Validate the email address:

```
if (filter_var($_POST['email'], FILTER_VALIDATE_EMAIL)) {
   $e = $_POST['email'];
   $_SESSION['email'] = $_POST['email'];
} else {
   $shipping_errors['email'] = 'Please enter a valid email
   ➥address!';
}
```

Thanks to the **filter_var()** function, this is the most straightforward of all these validation routines. If your PHP installation doesn't support the Filter extension, you can search online for the Perl-compatible regular expression (PCRE) pattern to use instead.

Unlike every other variable, the customer's email address will be stored automatically in the session so that a receipt can be sent to the customer once the order has gone through.

15. Store the data in the session if the shipping information matches the billing:

```
if (isset($_POST['use']) && ($_POST['use'] === 'Y')) {
   $_SESSION['shipping_for_billing'] = true;
   $_SESSION['cc_first_name']  = $_POST['first_name'];
```

```
    $_SESSION['cc_last_name'] = $_POST['last_name'];
    $_SESSION['cc_address'] = $_POST['address1'] . ' ' .
    ➥$_POST['address2'];
    $_SESSION['cc_city'] = $_POST['city'];
    $_SESSION['cc_state'] = $_POST['state'];
    $_SESSION['cc_zip'] = $_POST['zip'];
}
```

The checkout form will present the customer with a check box to select if she wants the shipping information to be used as the billing address too (**Figure 10.8**). In that case, the customer's name and address need to be stored in the session for use in the next PHP script. Also, a value is stored in the session indicating this choice.

Authorize.net takes the customer's street address as a single item, so the two potential street addresses are concatenated together in the session.

**note**

Fraudulent credit card charges often use different shipping and billing addresses. If your site allows for this, make sure your payment gateway has stringent fraud protection tools.



**Figure 10.8**

**16.** If no errors occurred, add the user to the database:

```
if (empty($shipping_errors)) {
    $r = mysqli_query($dbc, "CALL add_customer('$e', '$fn',
    ➥'$ln', '$a1', '$a2', '$c', '$s', $z, $p, @cid)");
```

To add the customer to the database, the **add_customer()** stored procedure is invoked. The first nine arguments are the PHP variables assigned during the validation process. The tenth is a MySQL user-defined variable. This will match up with the outbound parameter in the stored procedure, to be further explained in the next step.

**17.** If the procedure worked, retrieve the customer ID:

```
if ($r) {
    $r = mysqli_query($dbc, 'SELECT @cid');
    if (mysqli_num_rows($r) == 1) {
        list($_SESSION['customer_id']) = mysqli_fetch_array($r);
```

To get the customer ID generated by the stored procedure, a second query must select **@cid**. This query is run, then the results of the query are fetched into **$_SESSION['customer_id']**. If you find this concept confusing, it may help to think about this in MySQL terms, as if the procedure were being called from the command-line **mysql** client (**Figure 10.9**), not a PHP script.

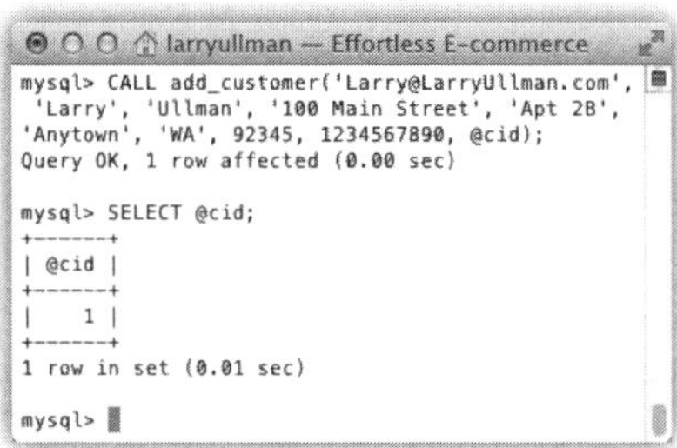


**Figure 10.9**

The first query itself is a call to a MySQL stored procedure. When the query is executed, a reference to a user-defined variable—**@cid**—is created. This is a variable that exists within MySQL but outside of the stored procedure (variables in MySQL outside of stored procedures begin with **@**). Within the stored procedure, a value is assigned to the internal variable **cid**, as explained earlier in the chapter. This variable is associated with **@cid**, thanks to the procedure call and the outbound argument. When the procedure call is complete, **@cid** still exists (because it's outside of the procedure), but it will now have a value. But **@cid** only exists within the MySQL world; to get it to a PHP script, you must select and fetch it.

**18.** Redirect the customer to the billing page:

```
$location = 'https://' . BASE_URL . 'billing.php';
header("Location: $location");
exit();
```

At this point, the customer can be sent to **billing.php**, where the billing information will be requested and processed.

**19.** If there was a problem, indicate an error:

```
    }
}
trigger_error('Your order could not be processed due to a system
➥error. We apologize for the inconvenience.');
```

The two closing brackets complete the two query-related conditionals. If the customer got to this point in the script, it means that she did everything right but the system isn't working. In that case, you should log the error, email the administrator—pretty much panic—and let the customer know that a problem occurred through no fault of her own. The site's support team or administrator would be able to contact the customer immediately, as both the customer's email address and phone number would be stored in the error log.

**20.** Complete the **$shipping_errors** and request method conditionals:

```
   } // Errors occurred IF.
} // End of REQUEST_METHOD IF.
```

This concludes the end of the form validation process. The rest of the script will apply to the initial GET request. It will also apply should there be errors in the form data after the POST request.

**21.** Include the header file:

```
$page_title = 'Coffee - Checkout - Your Shipping Information';
include('./includes/checkout_header.html');
```

Note that this script includes the new **checkout_header.html** file, not the original **header.html**.

**22.** Retrieve the shopping cart contents:

```
$r = mysqli_query($dbc, "CALL
➥get_shopping_cart_contents('$uid')");
```

The customer's shopping cart ID is necessary at this point in order to retrieve and later display what the customer is purchasing. This is the same stored procedure used by **cart.php** in Chapter 9, "Building a Shopping Cart."

**23.** Complete the script:

```
if (mysqli_num_rows($r) > 0) {
   include('./views/checkout.html');
} else { // Empty cart!
   include('./views/emptycart.html');
}
```

If the stored procedure returned some records, then the **checkout.html** view file will be included (this will be a new file, to be written shortly). If the stored procedure didn't return any records, the **emptycart.html** file will be included instead. It was defined in Chapter 9. Its inclusion means that the customer won't be able to continue the checkout process, which is entirely appropriate when there are no items in the customer's cart.

**24.** Finish the page:

```
include('./includes/footer.html');
?>
```

The checkout process scripts include the standard footer.

**25.** Save the file.

## Creating the View Files

The **checkout.php** script uses three view files:

- **checkout.html**
- **checkout_cart.html**
- **emptycart.html**

The first file is included if products exist in the shopping cart. The second file is included by the first (which is why there's no reference to it in **checkout.php**). The third has already been defined.

Let's begin with **checkout_cart.html**.

### CREATING CHECKOUT_CART.HTML

The **checkout_cart.html** view file displays the contents of the cart—what the customer is about to purchase (**Figure 10.10**). It's defined as its own script so that it can be used by both of the first two steps of the checkout process. Unlike the **cart.html** view file, this one doesn't allow the customer to update the quantities, remove items, or move items to the wish list. More important, this script needs to watch out for situations in which the customer is attempting to purchase an item that is insufficiently stocked. In such cases, the original shopping cart page recommends that customers update the quantity of the item or move it to their wish list (see Figure 9.6). This script will forcibly move the item to the wish list if it's still in the cart but can't be fulfilled.

Your Shopping Cart

| Item | Quantity | Price | Subtotal |
|---|---|---|---|
| Mugs::Pretty Flower Coffee Mug | 1 | $6.50 | $6.50 |
| Mugs::Red Dragon Mug | 2 | $7.00 | $14.00 |
| Kona::1 lb. - decaf - whole | 1 | $7.00 | $7.00 |
| | | **Shipping & Handling** | $7.95 |
| | | **Total** | $35.45 |

**Figure 10.10**

1. Create a new HTML page in your text editor or IDE to be named **checkout_cart.html** and stored in the **views** directory.

2. Begin the HTML box and the cart table:

```
<?php
echo BOX_BEGIN;
echo '<h2>Your Shopping Cart</h2>
<table border="0" cellspacing="8" cellpadding="6" width="100%">
  <tr>
    <th align="center">Item</th>
    <th align="center">Quantity</th>
    <th align="right">Price</th>
    <th align="right">Subtotal</th>
  </tr>';
```

3. Include the product functions file:

```
include('./includes/product_functions.inc.php');
```

   The **product_functions.inc.php** script was begun in Chapter 8 and expanded in Chapter 9. It defines a couple of necessary functions for displaying the shopping cart.

4. Initialize a variable to represent the order total:

```
$total = 0;
```

5. Create an array for identifying problematic items:

```
$remove = array();
```

   With the site as written, it's possible that the customer is still trying to purchase items that aren't available. You can handle this in a couple of ways. First, you could remove those items from the cart and place them in the wish list, as this page will do. Alternatively, you could allow the sale to go through with the thinking that the item would be available relatively soon. The risk of such a policy depends on what's being sold and how readily it's available. This site won't charge a customer's card until a product ships, so allowing an order to go through that may not be fulfilled at that moment isn't fraudulent.

   In any case, the **$remove** array will be used to store insufficiently stocked products found in the customer's cart so that they can later be removed.

6. Fetch each product:

```
while ($row = mysqli_fetch_array($r, MYSQLI_ASSOC)) {
```

**tip**

You could also write logic that will sell a partial order: If the customer wants four of something and only three are available, sell three and move one to the wish list. Or the site could ask the customer how they want the item to be handled.

7. If the quantity of the item in the cart is greater than the stock on hand, make a note of the item:

```
if ($row['stock'] < $row['quantity']) {
   echo '<tr class="error"><td colspan="4" align="center">
   ➥There are only ' . $row['stock'] . ' left in stock of the ' .
   ➥$row['name'] . '. This item has been removed from your cart
   ➥and placed in your wish list.</td></tr>';
   $remove[$row['sku']] = $row['quantity'];
```

If the store doesn't have enough of an item in stock to cover the number in the cart, a message is added to the table indicating the problem to the customer (**Figure 10.11**). Then, the problematic item is added to the **`$remove`** array, using the syntax *SKU* `=>` *`quantity`*.

**Figure 10.11**

8. If the stock is fine, display the item:

```
} else {
   $price = get_just_price($row['price'], $row['sale_price']);
   $subtotal = $price * $row['quantity'];
   echo '<tr><td>' . $row['category'] . '::' . $row['name'] . '
   ➥</td>
      <td align="center">' . $row['quantity'] . '</td>
      <td align="right">$' . $price . '</td>
      <td align="right">$' . number_format($subtotal, 2) . '</td>
   </tr>
   ';
   $total += $subtotal;
}
```

This code is similar to that in **`cart.html`**, except for the particulars of each table row: The quantity can't be altered and there are no links to remove or move the item.

9. Complete the loop and add the shipping:

```
$shipping = get_shipping($total);
$total += $shipping;
echo '<tr>
   <td colspan="2"> </td><th align="right">Shipping &amp;
   ➥Handling</th>
   <td align="right">$' . number_format($shipping, 2) . '</td>
</tr>
';
```

Again, this code is largely similar to that in **cart.html**. Figures 10.9 and 10.10 show the result.

10. Add the shipping to the session:

```
$_SESSION['shipping'] = $shipping;
```

The shipping cost is calculated by the **get_shipping()** function, defined in **product_functions.inc.php**. Because the shipping amount will be needed by the next PHP script, it's now stored in the session (at this point the order itself has been finalized, so the shipping can be finalized, too).

11. Display the total:

```
echo '<tr>
   <td colspan="2"> </td><th align="right">Total</th>
   <td align="right">$' . number_format($total, 2) . '</td>
   <td> </td>
</tr>
';
```

12. If the **$remove** array isn't empty, remove the problematic items:

```
if (!empty($remove)) {
   mysqli_next_result($dbc);
   foreach ($remove as $sku => $qty) {
      list($sp_type, $pid) = parse_sku($sku);
      $r = mysqli_multi_query($dbc, "CALL add_to_wish_list
      ➥('$uid', '$sp_type', $pid, $qty);CALL remove_from_
      ➥cart('$uid', '$sp_type', $pid)");
   } // End of FOREACH loop.
} // End of $remove IF.
```

If the **$remove** array isn't empty, then at least one product in the customer's cart needs to be moved to her wish list. You can accomplish that by parsing the SKU, then calling the **add_to_wish_list()** and **remove_from_cart()** stored procedures for each item. That's what the **foreach** loop accomplishes.

**tip**

If when using stored procedures you see a "commands out of sync" error message, it means that stored procedure results exist that haven't been retrieved.

But before the loop, there's a line of code that prevents a problem with how stored procedure calls work in PHP. The **get_shopping_cart_contents()** stored procedure, like any procedure that runs a **SELECT** query, returns two sets of results: the **SELECT** results and results indicating the success of running the procedure. These latter results must be addressed before calling another stored procedure or you'll see errors. The invocation of the **mysqli_next_result()** function will take care of that. It clears this secondary result set.

To execute the two stored procedures, the **mysqli_multi_query()** function is used instead of two executions of **mysqli_query()**. This function, as its name implies, allows more than one query to be executed with a single database call.

**13.** Complete the page:

```
echo '</table>';
echo BOX_END;
```

**14.** Save the file.

## CREATING CHECKOUT.HTML

The **checkout.html** view file is included by **checkout.php**. It must include **checkout_cart.html** and then display the form for obtaining the customer's shipping information (**Figure 10.12**).

**Figure 10.12**

1. Create a new HTML page in your text editor or IDE to be named **checkout.html** and stored in the **views** directory.

2. Add the progress indicator:

```
<div align="center"><img src="/images/checkout_indicator1.png" />
➥</div>
<br clear="all" />
```

   To make the checkout process clear to the customer, and where she is in that process, a *progress indicator* or *progress tracker* will be used (see Figure 10.3).

3. Include the **checkout_cart.html** view:

```
include('./views/checkout_cart.html');
```

   This includes the script just created. The file reference is relative to **checkout.php**, which is including this **checkout.html** view file (which is why the code is **./views/checkout_cart.html** instead of just **checkout_cart.html**).

4. Begin the HTML box and the form:

```
echo BOX_BEGIN;
?>
<h2>Your Shipping Information</h2>
<p>Please enter your shipping information. On the next page,
➥you'll be able to enter your billing information and complete
➥the order. Please check the first box if your shipping and
➥billing addresses are the same. <span class="required">*
➥</span> Indicates a required field. </p>
<form action="/checkout.php" method="POST">
```

   Before the form are some simple instructions to the customer. Then the form is begun, which will be submitted to **checkout.php**. If you've placed your files within a subdirectory, you'll need to change this path accordingly.

5. Include the form functions:

```
<?php include('./includes/form_functions.inc.php'); ?>
```

   The **form_functions.inc.php** script defines the **create_form_input()** function written earlier in the chapter. The function will be used repeatedly by this form.

6. Create the Use Same Address for Billing check box:

```
<fieldset>
  <div class="field"><label for="use"><strong>Use Same Address
  ➥for Billing?</strong></label><br /><input type="checkbox"
```

*(continues on next page)*

```
➥name="use" value="Y" id="use" <?php if (isset($_POST['use']))
➥echo 'checked="checked" ';?>/></div>
```

If the customer selects this check box, she won't need to enter her address on the next page, because her shipping address will be stored in the session. To make the check box sticky, a PHP conditional is added within the input.

7. Create the first name input:

```
<div class="field"><label for="first_name"><strong>First Name
➥<span class="required">*</span></strong></label><br />
➥<?php create_form_input('first_name', 'text', $shipping_errors);
➥?></div>
```

The DIV is used by the template to style form elements. Then comes the label, along with an indication that this is a required field. After a break, the `create_form_input()` function is called, creating a text box with a name of `first_name`. The `$shipping_errors` array is passed to the function. When the page is first loaded, `$shipping_errors` will be empty (it's initialized in `checkout.php`); if an error occurs, the error will be stored in it.

8. Create the last name, addresses, and city inputs:

```
<div class="field"><label for="last_name"><strong>Last Name <span
➥class="required">*</span></strong></label><br /><?php create_
➥form_input('last_name', 'text', $shipping_errors); ?></div>
<div class="field"><label for="address1"><strong>Street Address
➥<span class="required">*</span></strong></label><br /><?php
➥create_form_input('address1', 'text', $shipping_errors); ?>
➥</div>
<div class="field"><label for="address2"><strong>Street
➥Address, Continued</strong></label><br /><?php create_form_
➥input('address2', 'text', $shipping_errors); ?></div>
<div class="field"><label for="city"><strong>City <span
➥class="required">*</span></strong></label><br /><?php
➥create_form_input('city', 'text', $shipping_errors); ?></div>
```

These four inputs are repetitions of the first name input, except that the second address field isn't required.

9. Create the state select menu:

```
<div class="field"><label for="state"><strong>State <span
➥class="required">*</span></strong> </label><br /><?php
➥create_form_input('state', 'select', $shipping_errors); ?></div>
```

To create the select menu using the **create_form_input()** function, the second argument just needs to be **select**. The data used in the menu is based on the element's name.

10. Create the zip code, phone number, and email address inputs:

```
<div class="field"><label for="zip"><strong>Zip Code <span
➥class="required">*</span></strong></label><br /><?php
➥create_form_input('zip', 'text', $shipping_errors); ?></div>
<div class="field"><label for="phone"><strong>Phone Number
➥<span class="required">*</span></strong></label><br />
➥<?php create_form_input('phone', 'text', $shipping_errors); ?>
➥</div>
<div class="field"><label for="email"><strong>Email Address
➥<span class="required">*</span></strong></label><br />
➥<?php create_form_input('email', 'text', $shipping_errors); ?>
➥</div>
```

11. Complete the form:

```
  <br clear="all" />
<div align="center"><input type="submit" value="Continue onto
➥Billing" class="button" /></div></fieldset></form>
```

As mentioned earlier, this button, which continues the checkout process, needs to be impossible to miss.

12. Complete the page:

```
<?php echo BOX_END; ?>
```

13. Save the file.

Now you can test the **checkout.php** process. If you fill out the form *incorrectly*, it will be displayed again (**Figure 10.13**). If you fill it out correctly, you'll be sent to **billing.php**, which will be written next.

Figure 10.13

# TAKING THE BILLING INFORMATION

After the customer has properly provided her shipping information, the site will ask for the customer's billing information. When accepting credit cards to be processed by Authorize.net, the billing information equates to the customer's credit card data plus the billing address. This is the most sensitive information requested and handled by any script in the entire book. This is therefore the most complex and important script in the book (well, coupled with the next two). The entire billing process is reflected in **Figure 10.14**.

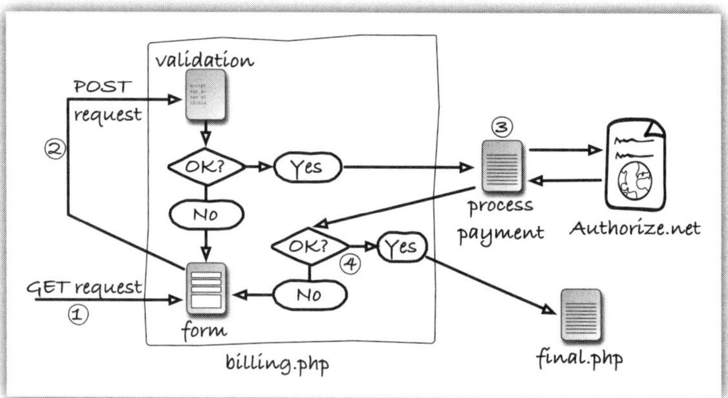


**Figure 10.14**

To make this script easier to comprehend, let's look at it piecemeal: the GET part (that displays the order contents and the form), the POST part (that validates the form data), and the payment processing part.

## Creating the Basic PHP Script

To start, the basic PHP script will address all of the GET functionality. It's similar to **checkout.php** and short (without all the form validation and billing processing stuff).

1. Create a new PHP script in your text editor or IDE to be named **billing.php** and stored in the web root directory.

2. Include the configuration file:

```
<?php
require('./includes/config.inc.php');
```

3. Begin the session and retrieve the session ID:

```
session_start();
$uid = session_id();
```

This page will be able to access the same session data as **checkout.php**. The session ID needs to be assigned to the **$uid** variable so that it can be used many times over in this page (to access the user's cart).

4. Redirect invalid users:

```
if (!isset($_SESSION['customer_id'])) {
   $location = 'https://' . BASE_URL . 'checkout.php';
   header("Location: $location");
   exit();
}
```

If **$_SESSION['customer_id']** isn't set, the user hasn't come to this page via **checkout.php**, meaning her order can't be completed. In that case, the customer is redirected back to the checkout page to begin again.

5. Require the database connection and create an array for storing errors:

```
require (MYSQL);
$billing_errors = array();
```

6. Include the header file:

```
$page_title = 'Coffee - Checkout - Your Billing Information';
include('./includes/checkout_header.html');
```

Again, the newer, custom **checkout_header.html** file is included, not the older **header.html**.

7. Get the shopping cart contents:

```
$r = mysqli_query($dbc, "CALL get_shopping_cart_contents('$uid')");
```

8. Include the view files:

```
if (mysqli_num_rows($r) > 0) {
   if (isset($_SESSION['shipping_for_billing']) &&
   ➥($_SERVER['REQUEST_METHOD'] !== 'POST')) {
      $values = 'SESSION';
   } else {
      $values = 'POST';
   }
   include('./views/billing.html');
} else { // Empty cart!
   include('./views/emptycart.html');
}
```

You've already seen most of this code several times; the difference is the conditional that checks for the **$_SESSION['shipping_for_billing']** element. This conditional is necessary because the HTML form in the view file could be prepopulated with values in two situations.

In the first case, the customer selected the check box (on **checkout.php**) to use her shipping information as her billing information. If so, the values already stored in **$_SESSION** should be used for the form elements.

The second situation in which there will be values to display in the form is when the customer submitted the form but errors occurred. If so, the values should come from **$_POST**. Note that even if the user opted to use the same information for shipping and billing, once she's submitted the form only the posted values will count. This way, if the customer altered any of the prepopulated values, the changes will be reflected when the form is redisplayed. Still, if the customer didn't alter the original session-based values, those same values will be used again after any errors.

9. Complete the page:

```
include('./includes/footer.html');
?>
```

10. Save the file.

## Creating the View File

The next step is to create the **billing.html** view file. Like **checkout.html**, this script should include **checkout_cart.html** (to display the cart) and then create an HTML form, primarily using the **create_form_input()** function (**Figure 10.15**).

1. Create a new HTML page in your text editor or IDE to be named **billing.html** and stored in the **views** directory.

2. Add the progress indicator:

```
<div align="center"><img src="/images/checkout_indicator2.png" />
➥</div>
<br clear="all" />
```

The progress indicator for this page uses a different image showing that this is the second step in the process (I'd include a figure here, but the changes are too subtle in black and white).

3. Include the **checkout_cart.html** view:

```
<?php
include('./views/checkout_cart.html');
```

This is the same view file included by **checkout.html**.

Figure 10.15

4. Begin the HTML box and the form:

```
echo BOX_BEGIN;
echo '<div class="inner">
<h2>Your Billing Information</h2>
<p>Please enter your billing information below. Then click
➥the button to complete your order. For your security, we will
➥not store your billing information in any way. We accept Visa,
➥MasterCard, American Express, and Discover.</p>';
echo '<form action="/billing.php" method="POST"
➥id="billing_form">';
```

   Again, there are some simple instructions, plus an indication that the customer's data will be safe. The instructions also indicate what card types are accepted. You may choose to make this more prominent or use images to represent the accepted cards.

   The form gets submitted back to **billing.php**. Again, change the reference to that file if you've placed your scripts within a subdirectory.

5. Include the form function file and complete the PHP block:

```
include('./includes/form_functions.inc.php');
?>
```

6. Create the credit card number input:

```
<fieldset>
   <div class="field"><label for="cc_number"><strong>
   ➥Card Number</strong></label><br /><?php
   ➥create_form_input('cc_number', 'text', $billing_errors,
   ➥'POST', array('autocomplete' => 'off')); ?></div>
```

   The element for taking the customer's credit card number is just a text input. The potential existing value for this input can come only from POST, because the credit card number will never be stored in the session.

   The input uses the extra HTML **autocomplete="off"**, which is a necessary security measure. If you don't use this attribute, and the user's browser is set to remember the customer's form data, then the browser will record the user's credit card number in plain text on the customer's computer. That's not good. (It may still happen because of less diligent e-commerce sites, though.)

**note**

You don't have to ask the customer what type of card she's using; the card number is indicative of the card type.

7. Create the expiration date elements:

```
<div class="field"><label for="exp_date"><strong>Expiration
➥Date</strong></label><br /><?php create_form_input('cc_
➥exp_month', 'select', $billing_errors); ?><?php create_form_
➥input('cc_exp_year', 'select', $billing_errors); ?></div>
```

   The expiration date is generated using two select menus. The first is the expiration month and the second is the year. Because the fourth argument to the **create_form_input()** function—for indicating where existing values come from—isn't provided, the default (**$_POST**) will be used.

**tip**

You could add a little help button next to the CVV input that creates a pop-up window indicating where customers can find their CVV number.

8. Create the card verification value (CVV) input:

```
<div class="field"><label for="cc_cvv"><strong>CVV</strong>
➥</label><br /><?php create_form_input('cc_cvv', 'text',
➥$billing_errors, 'POST', array('autocomplete' => 'off')); ?>
➥</div>
```

   The CVV code is an extra security measure used to limit fraud. What the customer should enter here are the three digits on the back of Visa, MasterCard, and Discover cards or the four digits on the front of American Express cards. This is an extremely sensitive piece of information, so like the card number input, the **autocomplete="off"** code will be added to the input HTML. And, as with the card number, the value can only come from **$_POST**.

**tip**

The term *CVV* is generally used interchangeably with CVC, among others.

9. Create the first and last name inputs:

```
<div class="field"><label for="cc_first_name"><strong>First Name
➥</strong></label><br /><?php create_form_input('cc_first_name',
➥'text', $billing_errors, $values); ?></div>
<div class="field"><label for="cc_last_name"><strong>Last Name
➥</strong></label><br /><?php create_form_input('cc_last_name',
➥'text', $billing_errors, $values); ?></div>
```

The rest of this form is largely like the shipping form, except that each input is prefaced with *cc_*. An important addition is that each call to **create_form_input()** includes the fourth argument. The fourth argument indicates where an existing value should exist: in **$_SESSION** or **$_POST**. The value of the **$values** variable will have been determined in the **billing.php** script (as you've already seen).

10. Create the address input:

```
<div class="field"><label for="cc_address"><strong>Street
➥Address </strong></label><br /><?php create_form_input(
➥'cc_address', 'text', $billing_errors, $values); ?></div>
<div class="field"><label for="cc_city"><strong>City </strong>
➥</label><br /><?php create_form_input('cc_city', 'text',
➥$billing_errors, $values); ?></div>
<div class="field"><label for="cc_state"><strong>State
➥</strong></label><br /><?php create_form_input('cc_state',
➥'select', $billing_errors, $values); ?></div>
<div class="field"><label for="cc_zip"><strong>Zip Code
➥</strong></label><br /><?php create_form_input('cc_zip',
➥'text', $billing_errors, $values); ?></div>
```

These are just like the inputs on the shipping information form, plus the additional fourth argument indicating the source of the value. If the customer selected the Use Shipping for Billing check box, these inputs will be prepopulated with data from the session the first time the page is loaded. If the form is redisplayed, the values will come from **$_POST**.

There is only one street address field, though, because Authorize.net is set up to accept only a single street address.

11. Complete the form:

```
   <br clear="all" />
<div align="center" id="submit_div"><input type="submit"
➥value="Place Order" class="button" /></div></fieldset></form>
```

12. Complete the page:

```
<div>By clicking this button, your order will be completed and
➥your credit card will be charged.</div>
<?php echo BOX_END; ?>
```

The instructions make it clear that the act of clicking the button completes the order.

13. Save the file.

Now you can load the billing page in your web browser, although submitting the form will have no effect.

## Validating the Form Data

Now that the shell of the script has been written, as has the view file for creating the form, it's time to add the code that processes the form data. This is largely like the validation in **checkout.php**, with additional validation of the credit card data. Needless to say, it's very important that you treat that credit card data with the utmost security. For example, you might think it's safe to store such information in the session, even temporarily:

```
$_SESSION['cc_number'] = $_POST['cc_number'];
```

But that one, seemingly harmless line just stored the customer's credit card number in a plain text file, in a publicly available directory on the server! Fortunately, the way this next script is written, all the ultimately sensitive information will exist only on the server (in memory) for the time it takes this script to execute.

1. Open **billing.php** in your text editor or IDE, if it isn't already open.

2. After creating the **$billing_errors** array, but before including the header file, check for the form submission:

```
if ($_SERVER['REQUEST_METHOD'] === 'POST') {
```

Again, if Magic Quotes might be enabled on your server, you'll need to add code applying **stripslashes()** to some of the variables at this point:

```
if (get_magic_quotes_gpc()) {
   $_POST['cc_first_name'] = stripslashes(
   ➥$_POST['cc_first_name']);
   // Repeat for other variables that could be affected.
}
```

3. Validate the first and last names:

```
if (preg_match ('/^[A-Z \'.-]{2,20}$/i',
➥$_POST['cc_first_name'])) {
    $cc_first_name = $_POST['cc_first_name'];
} else {
    $billing_errors['cc_first_name'] = 'Please enter your first
    ➥name!';
}
if (preg_match ('/^[A-Z \'.-]{2,40}$/i',
➥$_POST['cc_last_name'])) {
    $cc_last_name  = $_POST['cc_last_name'];
} else {
    $billing_errors['cc_last_name'] = 'Please enter your last
    ➥name!';
}
```

These regular expressions are the same as those used in **checkout.php**. Unlike in the **checkout.php** script, **addslashes()** doesn't need to be applied to any values, because no strings will be used in any stored procedure calls.

4. Remove any spaces or dashes from the credit card number:

```
$cc_number = str_replace(array(' ', '-'), '',
➥$_POST['cc_number']);
```

As with the phone number in **checkout.php**, the first step in validating the credit card number is to remove any spaces or numbers from the submitted credit card number. This allows customers to enter the number however they prefer.

tip

You may want to add to the form an indicator as to how the credit card number can be entered (for example, #### #### #### ####).

5. Validate the card number against allowed types:

```
if (!preg_match ('/^4[0-9]{12}(?:[0-9]{3})?$/', $cc_number)
➥// Visa
&& !preg_match ('/^5[1-5][0-9]{14}$/', $cc_number) // MasterCard
&& !preg_match ('/^3[47][0-9]{13}$/', $cc_number) // American
➥Express
&& !preg_match ('/^6(?:011|5[0-9]{2})[0-9]{12}$/', $cc_number)
➥// Discover) {
    $billing_errors['cc_number'] = 'Please enter your credit card
    ➥number!';
}
```

All credit card numbers adhere to a specific formula, based on the type of credit card. For example, all Visa cards start with 4 and are either 13 or 16 characters long. All American Express cards start with either 34 or 37 but must be exactly 15 characters long. These four patterns can confirm that the supplied credit card number matches an allowed pattern. By checking that the number follows an acceptable format, the script won't attempt to process clearly unacceptable credit cards.

Note that nothing else is done with the card number at this point; however, an error message is created if the number doesn't match one of the four patterns.

6. Validate the expiration date:

```
if ( ($_POST['cc_exp_month'] < 1 || $_POST['cc_exp_month'] >
➥12)) {
   $billing_errors['cc_exp_month'] = 'Please enter your
   ➥expiration month!';
}
if ($_POST['cc_exp_year'] < date('Y')) {
   $billing_errors['cc_exp_year'] = 'Please enter your expiration
   ➥year!';
}
```

The expiration date consists of two parts: the month and the year. The month must be between 1 and 12, and the year can't be before the current year.

As an added check, you could confirm that if the expiration year is the current year, the expiration month isn't before the current month (meaning that the card hasn't already expired).

7. Validate the CVV:

```
if (preg_match ('/^[0-9]{3,4}$/', $_POST['cc_cvv'])) {
   $cc_cvv = $_POST['cc_cvv'];
} else {
   $billing_errors['cc_cvv'] = 'Please enter your CVV!';
}
```

The CVV will be either three or four digits long.

8. Validate the street address:

```
if (preg_match ('/^[A-Z0-9 \',.#-]{2,160}$/i',
➥$_POST['cc_address'])) {
   $cc_address  = $_POST['cc_address'];
} else {
   $billing_errors['cc_address'] = 'Please enter your street
   ➥address!';
}
```

Since the billing form uses a single street address, the maximum length is doubled from those in the shipping form.

9. Validate the city, state, and zip code:

```
if (preg_match ('/^[A-Z \'.-]{2,60}$/i', $_POST['cc_city'])) {
   $cc_city = $_POST['cc_city'];
} else {
   $billing_errors['cc_city'] = 'Please enter your city!';
}
if (preg_match ('/^[A-Z]{2}$/', $_POST['cc_state'])) {
   $cc_state = $_POST['cc_state'];
} else {
   $billing_errors['cc_state'] = 'Please enter your state!';
}
if (preg_match ('/^(\d{5}$)|(^\d{5}-\d{4})$/',
➥$_POST['cc_zip'])) {
   $cc_zip = $_POST['cc_zip'];
} else {
   $billing_errors['cc_zip'] = 'Please enter your zip code!';
}
```

10. If no errors occurred, convert the expiration date to the correct format:

```
if (empty($billing_errors)) {
   $cc_exp = sprintf('%02d%d', $_POST['cc_exp_month'],
   ➥$_POST['cc_exp_year']);
```

Authorize.net can accept the expiration date in several formats: *MMYY*, *MM-YY*, *MMYYYY*, *MM/YYYY*, and so on; this site will submit it as *MMYYYY*. The year will already be four digits long, but the month could be either one or two digits. To turn the month into a two-digit value, use the **sprintf()** function. Its first argument is the formatting pattern: **%02d%d**. The **%02d** will format an integer as two digits, adding extra zeros as necessary. The subsequent **%d** just represents an integer without any additional formatting. The second and third arguments in this **sprintf()** call are the values to be used for the two placeholders. The end result will be values like 012015 or 102015.

11. Check for an existing order ID in the session:

```
if (isset($_SESSION['order_id'])) {
   $order_id = $_SESSION['order_id'];
   $order_total = $_SESSION['order_total'];
```

The next bit of code needs to create a new order ID, which is a new set of records in the **orders** and **order_contents** tables. However, the billing form could be submitted more than once, so the script shouldn't automatically call the associated stored procedure to do that.

For example, if the payment gateway reported a problem with the provided credit card, the customer would correct that information (in the form) and resubmit the form. In such a case, the site shouldn't create a second, duplicate order. To prevent that from happening, the script will look in the session for a previously stored order ID. If one is found, the previously stored ID and total will be assigned to local variables, to be used by the payment process.

12. If there's no existing order ID, get the last four digits of the credit card number:

```
} else {
   $cc_last_four = substr($cc_number, -4);
```

The site will store, in the **orders** table, the last four digits of the credit card number used. This is a safe and common practice that provides a reference to the card used without storing the actual credit card number (which would be very bad).

13. Store the order:

```
$shipping = $_SESSION['shipping'] * 100;
$r = mysqli_query($dbc, "CALL add_order({$_SESSION['customer_
➥id']}, '$uid', $shipping, $cc_last_four, @total, @oid)");
```

**note**

The code that invokes the **add_order()** stored procedure will be executed only once, no matter how many times the billing form has to be resubmitted.

If all the user-supplied data is valid, the script needs to store the order information in the **orders** table. Doing so before calling the payment gateway means that the order's ID number can be sent along as part of the payment gateway transaction. More important, the **add_order()** procedure calculates the order total, which is required for the payment gateway request as well.

Even though the complete order will now be stored in the database—prior to authorizing the payment—the site won't treat this order as successful, because, as you'll see in the next chapter, the success of an order also depends on the transaction record found in the **transactions** table.

One thing to note here is that the shipping amount stored in the session is in dollars, but the shipping amount (in fact, all amounts) in the database is in cents. Thus, the shipping amount is multiplied by 100 before being used in the query.

**14.** Retrieve the total and order ID:

```
if ($r) {
   $r = mysqli_query($dbc, 'SELECT @total, @oid');
   if (mysqli_num_rows($r) == 1) {
      list($order_total, $order_id) = mysqli_fetch_array($r);
```

To retrieve the order total and ID, select those two user-defined MySQL variables. This is similar to how the customer ID was selected after calling the **add_customer()** procedure.

**15.** Store the order ID and total in the session:

```
$_SESSION['order_total'] = $order_total;
$_SESSION['order_id'] = $order_id;
```

Should the billing form be submitted a second time, the conditional defined in Step 11 will be true, thanks to these lines.

**16.** If the order ID and total couldn't be retrieved, trigger an error:

```
} else { // Could not retrieve the order ID and total.
   unset($cc_number, $cc_cvv, $_POST['cc_number'],
   ➥$_POST['cc_cvv']);
   trigger_error('Your order could not be processed due to a
   ➥system error. We apologize for the inconvenience.');
}
```

As with the **checkout.php** script, if the PHP code gets to the **trigger_error()** point, it means that the customer did everything right but the system failed. That is one of the worst things that could happen (and really shouldn't on a live, tested site). I've only included the **trigger_error()** call, but you should make sure that something significant—like emailing the administrator—happens in this case so that the problem gets fixed immediately. Fortunately, the customer's contact information—name, phone number, and email address—are stored in the session, making them available to any error logging that **trigger_error()** does.

On that note, *because the error-handling function, as defined, records every variable that existed at the time of the error, the customer's credit card number and CVV value would be sent in an unsecured email or stored in a plain text log file*. Such an occurrence would be a terrible security violation and a failure to abide by PCI DSS standards. *To prevent this, before triggering the error, the* **unset()** *function deletes those variables.*

**note**

The error handling function will send an email when an error occurs on a live site.

**note**

Think about what might happen to any customer-supplied data should an error occur at any point in the checkout process!

tip

For these errors, you'd also want to indicate to the customer what will happen next: The customer shouldn't resubmit the order, she'll be contacted shortly, and so forth.

**17.** If the **add_order()** procedure failed, trigger an error:

```
} else { // The add_order() procedure failed.
   unset($cc_number, $cc_cvv, $_POST['cc_number'],
   ➥$_POST['cc_cvv']);
   trigger_error('Your order could not be processed due to a
   ➥system error. We apologize for the inconvenience.');
}
```

This is a replication of the code in Step 16, applicable if the **add_order()** procedure call doesn't return a positive result.

**18.** Complete the form-handling conditionals:

```
      } // End of isset($_SESSION['order_id']) IF-ELSE.
   } // Errors occurred IF.
} // End of REQUEST_METHOD IF.
```

**19.** Save the file.

Now you can test the **billing.php** script as long as you purposefully create errors (because the payment-processing aspect hasn't been defined yet).

# PROCESSING CREDIT CARDS

The next step in the checkout sequence is to process the payment (this is number 3 in Figure 10.14). To process the payment, the customer information, payment data, and order specifics need to be sent to the payment gateway, and the returned response needs to be confirmed. With the Authorize.net system, this task isn't that difficult. In fact, since the first edition of the book was written, this process was made even easier thanks to Authorize.net's new PHP library.

I'll first walk you through downloading and installing that library. Then you'll update **billing.php** to use it.

## Installing the SDK

The Authorize.net SDK provides some classes that make interacting with the Authorize.net system a breeze. You can even download some sample code to use as a basis for your own projects. The worst thing I can say about the SDK is that it doesn't seem to be well documented (a statement that applies to many libraries you find online).

1. In your browser, head to http://developer.authorize.net/downloads/.
2. In the Language SDKs section, click Download under PHP (**Figure 10.16**).

   You'll need to agree to the terms of service, too. You can even read them if you want.

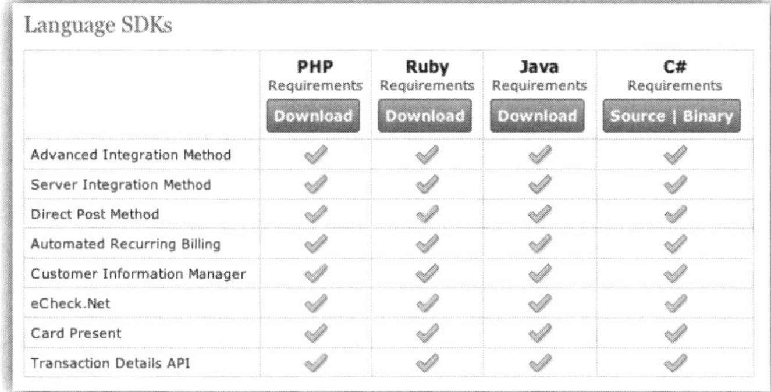

Language SDKs

| | PHP Requirements Download | Ruby Requirements Download | Java Requirements Download | C# Requirements Source \| Binary |
|---|---|---|---|---|
| Advanced Integration Method | ✓ | ✓ | ✓ | ✓ |
| Server Integration Method | ✓ | ✓ | ✓ | ✓ |
| Direct Post Method | ✓ | ✓ | ✓ | ✓ |
| Automated Recurring Billing | ✓ | ✓ | ✓ | ✓ |
| Customer Information Manager | ✓ | ✓ | ✓ | ✓ |
| eCheck.Net | ✓ | ✓ | ✓ | ✓ |
| Card Present | ✓ | ✓ | ✓ | ✓ |
| Transaction Details API | ✓ | ✓ | ✓ | ✓ |

**Figure 10.16**

3. Unzip the downloaded file.

   The downloaded file will have a name like **anet_php_sdk-1.1.8**. Unzip it to create a folder of items.

4. Copy, or move, the resulting folder to your website's folder.

   The uncompressed folder will have the name **anet_php_sdk**. Copy or move it to the directory where you have your website. I also recommend that you put this folder in a logical subdirectory, such as one named **vendor**, perhaps placed within the **includes** directory (since that's already been created to store includable files).

**tip**

From that same page, also download the Sample Applications if you want to see different uses of the SDK.

## Using the SDK

Using the Authorize.net SDK begins by including the **AuthorizeNet.php** file, which is included in the **anet_php_sdk** folder. If you've placed that folder within a **includes/vendor** directory, the inclusion path would be

```
require('includes/vendor/anet_php_sdk/AuthorizeNet.php');
```

Next, you'll create an object of type **AuthorizeNetAIM**:

```
$aim = new AuthorizeNetAIM(API_LOGIN_ID, TRANSACTION_KEY);
```

Even if you haven't done much object-oriented programming, this process will be easy to follow and use.

**tip**

The SDK includes classes for other Authorize.net integration approaches, not just the AIM approach being used in this book.

When creating the object, you'll need to pass your Authorize.net login ID and transaction key. These are provided when you register for test accounts (Figure 10.2), and they're available in your Merchant Interface for live accounts. I would recommend assigning these values to constants in your configuration file.

Next, the payment gateway needs to receive a large number of name-value pairs in each request. These pairs communicate to the gateway everything required to process the transaction:

- The customer's credit card data
- The customer's billing address
- The order information
- Anything else you'd like to associate with the transaction

When using the SDK, you identify the name-value pairs by assigning values to the public properties of the object:

```
$aim->card_num = $cc_number;
$aim->exp_date = $cc_exp;
$aim->card_code = $cc_cvv;
$aim->first_name = $first_name;
```

The possible properties weren't easy to find (in my opinion; I had to go looking through the SDK code), but I'll present the most important ones in this chapter. You can also pass any piece of information along using the **setCustomField()** method of the object:

```
$aim->setCustomField('thing', 'value');
```

That code allows you to associate whatever data you want with the transaction. Authorize.net will record that data on its end, and it will be passed back to your site after the transaction is made.

Finally, you invoke the right method to perform the type of request you want:

- `authorizeOnly()`
- `priorAuthCapture()`
- `void()`
- `authorizeAndCapture()`

For example:

```
$response = $aim->authorizeAndCapture();
```

As in that code, you'll always want to assign the result of the transaction to a variable for use later on. I'll return to that issue in a couple of pages. But first, in case you're not familiar with how charges are handled, it's a two-step process: *authorization* and *capturing*. The authorization step is where confirmation is made that a charge is possible. In other words, is the payment information valid and can it be charged the given amount? If so, then a *hold* is placed on the card for that amount.

Different card companies will reserve authorized funds for different lengths of time, anywhere from three days to some months.

The details can vary depending on the type of card used, but the hold is normally kept for around seven days, at which point in time the hold is released. Understand that merely placing a hold—authorizing a charge—doesn't get you any money.

The actual charge is processed in the *capture* phase. Assuming your business has a hold on a card (a hold was created that hasn't yet expired), you can capture up to that held amount. At that point, the money is transferred from the customer to your business (more specifically, to your merchant account).

When the customer is charged for their order is a policy decision that each business will need to make.

With some businesses, you'll want to perform both steps—authorize and capture—at the same time. This would be the case in physical stores, where the customer is purchasing items at that moment, or when a website delivers digital goods instantaneously. With a site such as the Coffee example, I've chosen to authorize the payment on the public side but capture payment on the administrative side, when the order is ready to be shipped.

## Examining the Server Response

Before updating the billing script to use the SDK, let's take a quick look at the Authorize.net response. When you use AIM, the server response will be a long string of data in this format:

```
|1|,|1|,|1|,|This transaction has been approved.|,|K2TQ8W|,|Y|,...
```

You can make use of this response in a couple of ways. In the first edition, I used the **explode()** function to convert that string into an array. When using the SDK, you can treat the **$response** variable as an object, which is far cleaner and easier. For example, one of the most important pieces of the response is the **approved** status. This is a Boolean, so it can be used as the basis of a conditional:

```
if ($response->approved) {...
```

To find out what properties exist in the **$response** variable, I did this:

```
echo '<pre>' . var_dump($response) . '</pre>';
```

**Figure 10.17** shows part of the result.

```
public 'approved' => boolean true
public 'declined' => boolean false
public 'error' => boolean false
public 'held' => boolean false
public 'response_code' => string '1' (length=1)
public 'response_subcode' => string '1' (length=1)
public 'response_reason_code' => string '1' (length=1)
public 'response_reason_text' => string 'This transaction has been approved.' (length=35)
public 'authorization_code' => string '67P395' (length=6)
public 'avs_response' => string 'Y' (length=1)
public 'transaction_id' => string '2198162976' (length=10)
public 'invoice_number' => string '12' (length=2)
public 'description' => string '' (length=0)
public 'amount' => string '20.40' (length=5)
public 'method' => string 'CC' (length=2)
public 'transaction_type' => string 'auth_only' (length=9)
public 'customer_id' => string '3' (length=1)
public 'first_name' => string 'Larry' (length=5)
public 'last_name' => string 'Ullman' (length=6)
public 'company' => string '' (length=0)
public 'address' => string '100 Main Street' (length=15)
public 'city' => string 'Anytown' (length=7)
public 'state' => string 'ME' (length=2)
public 'zip_code' => string '23905' (length=5)
public 'country' => string '' (length=0)
public 'phone' => string '' (length=0)
public 'fax' => string '' (length=0)
public 'email_address' => string 'larry@larryullman.com' (length=21)
public 'ship_to_first_name' => string '' (length=0)
public 'ship_to_last_name' => string '' (length=0)
public 'ship_to_company' => string '' (length=0)
public 'ship_to_address' => string '' (length=0)
public 'ship_to_city' => string '' (length=0)
public 'ship_to_state' => string '' (length=0)
public 'ship_to_zip_code' => string '' (length=0)
public 'ship_to_country' => string '' (length=0)
public 'tax' => string '' (length=0)
public 'duty' => string '' (length=0)
public 'freight' => string '' (length=0)
public 'tax_exempt' => string '' (length=0)
public 'purchase_order_number' => string '' (length=0)
public 'md5_hash' => string 'F8F3254FE50A9165CC3F5E60576D4594' (length=32)
public 'card_code_response' => string 'P' (length=1)
public 'cavv_response' => string '2' (length=1)
public 'account_number' => string 'XXXX6811' (length=8)
public 'card_type' => string 'MasterCard' (length=10)
public 'split_tender_id' => string '' (length=0)
public 'requested_amount' => string '' (length=0)
public 'balance_on_card' => string '' (length=0)
public 'response' => string '|1|,|1|,|1|,|This transaction has been approved.|,|67P395|,|Y|
```

**Figure 10.17**

The full breakdown of these properties and what they mean is available in the Authorize.net manual. The most important of these is the **approved** status. If it has a value of **true**, then the transaction succeeded. If not, then a problem occurred. The specific type of problem will be reflected by the *response reason code* and the *response reason text*. Again, the Authorize.net AIM manual and online documentation lists all the possible codes and messages.

## Updating billing.php

With an introduction to the SDK in place, and an explanation of the response you'll get, it's time to use that code in the billing script. But first, you'll need to define your API login ID and transaction key as constants in your configuration file:

tip

Your login ID and transaction key must be kept safe. Having this information, hackers could credit their cards from your account.

```
define('API_LOGIN_ID', '29hxJ9Ge');
define('TRANSACTION_KEY', '8EKf5a673hC3jqD2');
```

These two pieces of information uniquely identify you to the Authorize.net system

With that done, and the SDK on your site, you can incorporate some of the code already explained into **billing.php** to process the customer's payment. After that, the transaction should be recorded in the database and the script should respond accordingly (item number 4 in Figure 10.14).

1. Open **billing.php** in your text editor or IDE, if it isn't already open.
2. After **isset($_SESSION['order_id']) if-else**, check that the order ID and total are set:

   ```
   if (isset($order_id, $order_total)) {
   ```

   The **if-else** conditional that should precede this line creates these two variables either by retrieving them from the session or by executing the stored procedure. As long as both variables exist, the payment request can be processed.
3. Include the Authorize.net SDK file:

   ```
   require('includes/vendor/anet_php_sdk/AuthorizeNet.php');
   ```

   You'll have to change the reference to the script so that the path is accurate for your setup.
4. Create the Authorize.net AIM object:

   ```
   $aim = new AuthorizeNetAIM(API_LOGIN_ID, TRANSACTION_KEY);
   ```

   This code has already been explained and assumes that you've defined the constants in the configuration file. If your constants use values associated with a test account, a test transaction will be performed. If your constants use values associated with a real account, a real transaction will be performed.

5. Set the amount to be charged:

```
$aim->amount = $order_total/100;
```

Authorize.net expects the charge to be in dollars, so the order total here must be divided by 100.

6. Set the invoice and customer numbers:

```
$aim->invoice_num = $order_id;
$aim->cust_id = $_SESSION['customer_id'];
```

It's not required to pass along these values as part of the transaction, but by doing so, you'll make it easier to reconcile transactions (because Authorize.net will store your references, too).

7. Set the credit card information:

```
$aim->card_num = $cc_number;
$aim->exp_date = $cc_exp;
$aim->card_code = $cc_cvv;
```

8. Set the billing address:

```
$aim->first_name = $cc_first_name;
$aim->last_name = $cc_last_name;
$aim->address = $cc_address;
$aim->state = $cc_state;
$aim->city = $cc_city;
$aim->zip = $cc_zip;
```

9. Set the customer's email address:

```
$aim->email = $_SESSION['email'];
```

This is not required for payment processing purposes but helps to tie the orders on your site to transactions processed through Authorize.net. Also, Authorize.net is able to automatically send out receipts to customers when provided with an email address (**Figure 10.18**).

**Figure 10.18**

**10.** Perform the request:

```
$response = $aim->authorizeOnly();
```

Again, the request is only authorizing the charge; the payment won't be captured at this stage.

**11.** Add slashes to two of the text values:

```
$reason = addslashes($response->response_reason_text);
$full_response = addslashes($response->response);
```

The reason text and the full response could have problematic characters (namely, the single quotation mark), so **addslashes()** must be applied before you use these values in the stored procedure.

**12.** Record the transaction in the database:

```
$r = mysqli_query($dbc, "CALL add_transaction($order_id,
➥'{$response->transaction_type}', $order_total, {$response->
➥response_code}, '$reason', {$response->transaction_id},
➥'$full_response')");
```

To record the transaction in the database, call the **add_transaction()** stored procedure. Its first argument is the order ID. The second is the transaction type. The third is the amount involved. The fourth argument is the response code. The next argument is the transaction ID. This is a value returned by Authorize.net that reflects this transaction in their system. Finally, the entire transaction response, as a string, is stored in the table. Admittedly, this response contains all this other information, but in a less accessible way.

**13.** If the transaction was a success, store the response code in the session:

```
if ($response->approved) {
   $_SESSION['response_code'] = $response->response_code;
```

The response code value will be required by the last script in the process.

**14.** Redirect the user:

```
$location = 'https://' . BASE_URL . 'final.php';
header("Location: $location");
exit();
```

The **final.php** script is the last page in the checkout process. It should indicate the success to the customer, send an email, create a receipt, and so on.

**15.** If the transaction wasn't a success, respond accordingly:

```
} else {
   switch ($response->response_code) {
      case '2': // Declined
         $message = $response->response_reason_text . ' Please
         ➥fix the error or try another card.';
         break;
      case '3': // Error
         $message = $response->response_reason_text . '  Please
         ➥fix the error or try another card.';
         break;
      case '4': // Held for review
         $message = "The transaction is being held for review.
         ➥You will be contacted ASAP about your order. We
         ➥apologize for any inconvenience.";
         break;
   }
} // End of $response_array[0] IF-ELSE.
```

For each possible response code, numbered 2 through 4, a message is created. In the first two cases, the message includes the textual reason from the response. Some example reasons are:

- The credit card number is invalid.
- The credit card has expired.
- The merchant doesn't accept this type of credit card.

In any of these cases, the billing form will be shown again (because the user isn't being redirected).

**16.** Complete the `isset($order_id, $order_total)` conditional:

```
} // End of isset($order_id, $order_total) IF.
```

This line should come just before the curly bracket that closes the `if (empty($billing_errors)) {` conditional.

**17.** Save the file.

Lastly, `billing.html` needs to be updated to display a message if it exists. To do so, add this code after the instructions but before the form is begun:

```
if (isset($message)) echo "<p class=\"error\">$message</p>";
```

**Figure 10.19** shows how this might look.

Your Billing Information

Please enter your billing information below. Then click the button to complete your order. For your security, we will not store your billing information in any way. We accept Visa, MasterCard, American Express, and Discover.

The credit card has expired. Please fix the error or try another card.

Card Number

4222222222222

**Figure 10.19**

# COMPLETING THE ORDER

The **final.php** script is the last page in the checkout process. It should be accessed only after a completed sale. In terms of the database, the script should clear the **carts** table, since now those items have been purchased. In terms of the customer, the script should

- Indicate completion of the order
- Offer a receipt
- Send an email confirmation
- Tell the customer what will happen next

This last item is important: Just because the customer has already given you money doesn't mean he couldn't use a little extra reassurance about that decision. The site should provide a sense of when the order will be processed and even ship, if possible.

You could also use the **final.php** script to take user feedback, attempt to sell other products, and so forth.

Let's start with the PHP script, and then create the view file. The code for generating an HTML email receipt will be created separately in Chapter 13, "Extending the Second Site."

## Creating the PHP Script

The PHP script is the simplest of those in this chapter, but let's still walk through it explicitly.

1. Create a new PHP script in your text editor or IDE to be named **final.php** and stored in the web root directory.

2. Include the configuration file:

```
<?php
require('./includes/config.inc.php');
```

3. Begin the session and get the session ID:

```
session_start();
$uid = session_id();
```

   This code is the same as in **billing.php**.

4. Validate that the page is being accessed appropriately:

```
if (!isset($_SESSION['customer_id'])) {
   $location = 'https://' . BASE_URL . 'checkout.php';
   header("Location: $location");
   exit();
} elseif (!isset($_SESSION['response_code']) ||
➥($_SESSION['response_code'] != 1)) {
   $location = 'https://' . BASE_URL . 'billing.php';
   header("Location: $location");
   exit();
}
```

   The first conditional is the same as in **billing.php** and implies that the user attempted to skip the **checkout.php** page. If so, the customer is redirected back to it. The second conditional implies that the user skipped the **billing.php** page and redirects the browser there.

5. Require the database connection:

```
require (MYSQL);
```

6. Clear the shopping cart:

```
$r = mysqli_query($dbc, "CALL clear_cart('$uid')");
```

   Now that the order has been completed, the contents of the user's shopping cart should be cleared. This is accomplished by calling the **clear_cart()** stored procedure.

7. Include the header file:

```
$page_title = 'Coffee - Checkout - Your Order is Complete';
include('./includes/checkout_header.html');
```

8. Include the view:

```
include('./views/final.html');
```

9. Clear the session:

```
$_SESSION = array();
session_destroy();
```

Clearing the session prevents a second immediate order by the same customer from conflicting with the order just submitted. That may not be a common occurrence, but without this code, if the customer does go back and purchase something else, the existing order ID will be erroneously used.

10. Complete the page:

```
include('./includes/footer.html');
?>
```

11. Save the file.

## Creating the View File

The view file can be as simple or as complex as you want it to be; just ensure that the site conveys appreciation to the customer for the order, and communicates everything the customer should know. For **final.html**, stored in the **views** directory, a couple of messages are printed, providing the customer with the order ID and total, along with an indication of what will happen next (**Figure 10.20**).

**tip**

You may want to add to the final checkout page an obvious link back to the shopping area.

Your Order is Complete

Thank you for your order (#14). Please use this order number in any correspondence with us.

A charge of $37.22 will appear on your credit card when the order ships. All orders are processed on the next business day. You will be contacted in case of any delays.

An email confirmation has been sent to your email address. Click here to create a printable receipt of your order.

**Figure 10.20**

```
<?php echo BOX_BEGIN; ?>
<h2>Your Order is Complete</h2>
<p>Thank you for your order (#<?php echo $_SESSION['order_id']; ?>).
➥Please use this order number in any correspondence with us.</p>
<p>A charge of $<?php echo number_format($_SESSION['order_total']
➥/100, 2); ?> will appear on your credit card when the order ships.
➥All orders are processed on the next business day. You will be
➥contacted in case of any delays.</p>
<p>An email confirmation has been sent to your email address.
➥<a href="receipt.php">Click here </a>to create a printable receipt
➥of your order.</p>
<?php echo BOX_END; ?>
```

In the view, a link exists to **receipt.php**, which is created in Chapter 13. Such a file is just a combination of the order information and the shopping cart information, without any extra HTML, images, and so forth.

# TESTING THE SITE

With all the code written, you can fully test the site. You could use your own information—including credit card data—to test the payment gateway, but that's not the best of ideas. Here are syntactically valid test credit card numbers:

- 370000000000002, American Express
- 6011000000000012, Discover
- 5555555555554444, MasterCard
- 4007000000027, Visa

Those numbers will work, regardless of the address and CVV values used with them. If you want to make them fail, one option is to use an expiration date in the past.

Authorize.net has its own method for triggering specific responses. If you use the faux-Visa number 4222222222222, the **amount** value can trigger a specific error response. For example, the response reason code of 6 means the credit card number is invalid. If you process a test transaction using that Visa number and an amount of 6, the returned response will be that the transaction was declined because of an invalid credit card number.

Because the amount used in the payment process isn't an editable, dynamic value (which, for security purposes, is for the best), you'll have to manually alter the **billing.php** script accordingly:

```
$aim->amount = 6;
```

# GOING LIVE

Once you're happy with the site and it's time to go live, here's all you need to do:

1. Make sure you have an actual Authorize.net account associated with your merchant bank.
2. Use your actual Authorize.net login ID and transaction key in the **config.inc.php** script.
3. Set the site to live in the configuration file:

   ```
   if (!defined('LIVE')) DEFINE('LIVE', true);
   ```

   By changing the value of the **LIVE** constant, the site will hide all errors.
4. Test the site a couple of more times, just to be safe.

   Unless you go into the Merchant Interface to change your account mode, even a real Authorize.net account begins in test mode. This round of tests just confirms that your account information is working with the live Authorize.net information.
5. Use the Merchant Interface to take your account live.
   a. Log in to the Merchant Interface at https://account.authorize.net.
   b. Click Account in the main toolbar.
   c. Click General Security Settings > Test Mode.
   d. Click Turn Test Off.
6. Run one or two real transactions, as an extra precaution.

   You can test the site by purchasing something inexpensive, just to be safe. Then you can go into the Merchant Interface and quickly void the transaction. (You can easily find the transaction under Search > Unsettled Transactions.)

**tip**

Authorize.net, like all payment gateways, completes the processing of all transactions at a particular time each day.

# 11 SITE ADMINISTRATION

The last requirement of the Coffee site is the ability to administer it. I won't discuss and develop every administrative feature, but this chapter will walk through the most important and complex ones. Chapter 13, "Extending the Second Site," will have additional thoughts, examples, and recommendations for the Coffee site as well.

The site administration pertains to three categories of information:

- Products
- Sales
- Orders

For each of these, the chapter will present one or more scripts to view and manipulate the respective data, such as adding new products, defining sales, increasing inventory, viewing orders, and so on.

The administrative pages will use neither the MVC approach nor the stored procedures that the public side does. Instead of using stored procedures, the chapter will use prepared statements, providing you with a different approach for working securely with a database. Without the stored procedures, the MVC design approach will be somewhat undermined, and because the administrative side won't have the performance and maintenance demands of the public side, it makes sense to use a single, complete PHP script for each task.

# SETTING UP THE SERVER

At this point, after all the work completed in the preceding four chapters, there's not much server setup to be performed. The administrative site can use the same configuration file and database connection file as the public side. It can also use the same CSS, footer, and images.

The most important setup involved is the creation of an HTML header appropriate for what the administrator will need to do. Also, a few lines of code have to be added to the **`create_form_input()`** function. Before that, though, I want to restate the need for folder-based authentication.

tip

Even if you wanted the extra security of having the administrator connect to the database as a MySQL user with different privileges, that can still be accomplished using only a single PHP connection script and some logic.

## Requiring Authentication

Unlike the "Knowledge Is Power" example, in which administrators use the same integrated login system as the customers, the Coffee site places all the administrative scripts within their own directory. Since the administrative pages will allow access to some customer information—name, address, email address, and phone number (but no billing data)—it's imperative that the administrative directory be secure. To start, give the directory a unique name, or better yet, put the administrative files in a subdomain such as `http://`***`admin`***`.example.com` (again, using a more original value in lieu of ***`admin`***).

Second, the admin pages should be available only via HTTPS. Chapter 7, "Second Site: Structure and Design," walks through a mod_rewrite definition (for the Apache web server) that can enforce this constraint.

Third, the administrative directory must be password protected. Chapter 7 talks about how you might use a host-provided control panel for performing this task. With the directory protected, users will be prompted for a username and password when they attempt to access any of the administrative directory's content (see Figure 7.8).

## Creating a Template

Naturally, the administrative pages will use a different template than the public side, as there are different scripts with different purposes. The admin template is just a modified version of the public template (**Figure 11.1** on the next page). It features:

- Different primary links
- No background image behind the content
- A wider area for the content

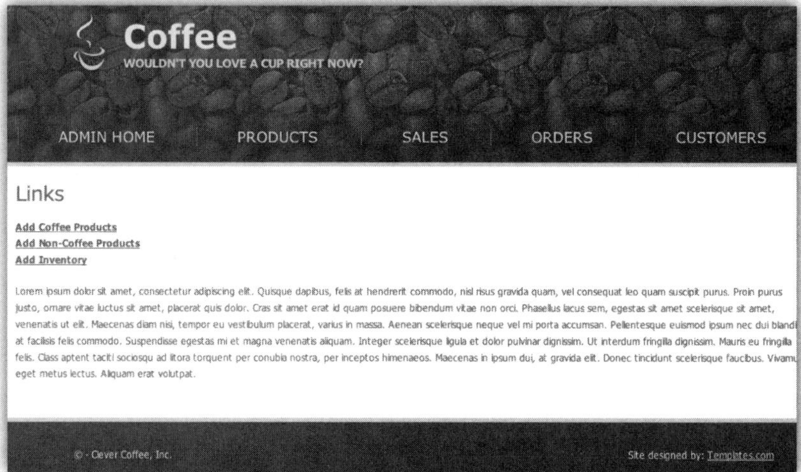


Figure 11.1

Almost all these changes can be made by creating a new header file (you'll see the new, full header code shortly).

The primary links represent the three main content areas—products, sales, and orders, plus customers (although no customer-related script will be created in this chapter). For now, the main products links will be written into the home page. In Chapter 14, "Adding JavaScript and Ajax," you'll add some JavaScript to create a "suckerfish" menu for the products links. With a suckerfish menu, when the mouse hovers over a single link, sublinks appear as a drop-down menu (if you search online for the term, you'll find thousands of results). **Figure 11.2** shows the effect.

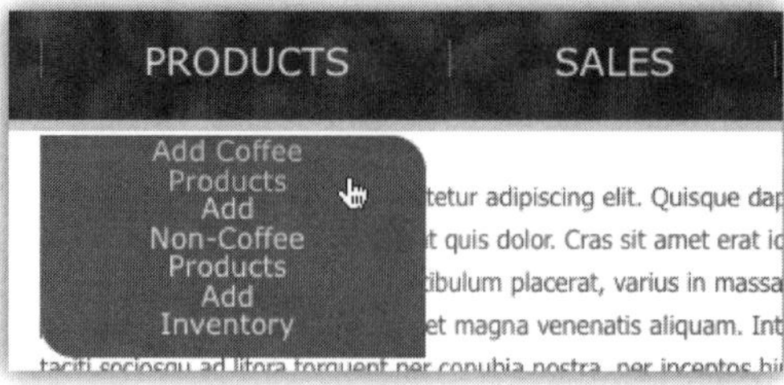


Figure 11.2

To remove the background image behind the content, you need to override the CSS for the **#content** DIV. Otherwise, the admin pages can use the same CSS as the public ones.

To make a larger usable content area, the template needs to drop the following two DIV tags from the public template:

```
<div class="container">
  <div class="inside">
```

tip

All the code is available from www.LarryUllman.com.

## CREATING THE HEADER

Along with the features of the template just discussed (which are primarily implemented in the header), the header file will also begin the session (sessions will be used in a few spots as a convenience). Here's the complete administrative header:

```
<?php session_start(); ?><!DOCTYPE html PUBLIC "-//W3C//
➥DTD XHTML 1.0 Strict//EN" "http://www.w3.org/TR/xhtml1/DTD/
➥xhtml1-strict.dtd">
<html xmlns="http://www.w3.org/1999/xhtml" xml:lang="en" lang="en">
<head>
<title><?php // Use a default page title if one wasn't provided...
if (isset($page_title)) {
  echo $page_title;
} else {
  echo 'Coffee - Administration';
}
?></title>
<meta http-equiv="Content-Type" content="text/html; charset=utf-8" />
<link href="/css/style.css" rel="stylesheet" type="text/css" />
<style type="text/css" media="screen">
  #content { background: #fff; width:100%; padding:20px 100px
  ➥30px 0px; }
  #header .nav li ul a { color:#ffe7be; text-decoration:none;
  ➥text-transform:none; font-size: .75em; }
</style>
<!--[if lt IE 7]>
  <script type="text/javascript" src="/js/ie_png.js"></script>
  <script type="text/javascript">
    ie_png.fix('.png, .logo h1, .box .left-top-corner, .box
    ➥.right-top-corner, .box .left-bot-corner, .box .right-
    ➥bot-corner, .box .border-left, .box .border-right, .box
    ➥.border-top, .box .border-bot, .box .inner, .special dd,
    ➥#contacts-form input, #contacts-form textarea');
  </script>
```

(continues on next page)

```
<![endif]-->
</head>

<body id="page1">
  <!-- header -->
  <div id="header">
    <div class="container">
      <div class="wrapper">
        <div class="logo"><h1><a href="/index.php">Coffee</a>
        ➥<span>Wouldn't you love a cup right now?</span></h1>
        ➥</div>
      </div>
      <ul class="nav sf-menu">
      <!-- MENU -->
      <li><a href="index.php">Admin Home</a></li>
      <li><a href="#">Products</a></li>
      <li><a href="create_sales.php">Sales</a></li>
      <li><a href="view_orders.php">Orders</a></li>
      <li><a href="#">Customers</a></li>
      <!-- END MENU -->
      </ul>
    </div>
  </div>
  <!-- content -->
  <div id="content">
    <div class="container">
```

As you can see in the highlighted code, the session is begun as the first step.

After the site's primary CSS file (from the public directory) is included, the `#content` and `#header .nav li ul a` formatting is overwritten. The latter change will make the cascading (suckerfish) menu items smaller when it comes time to add that functionality.

## CREATING THE FOOTER

The footer file simply needs to complete the template:

```
      </div>
    </div>
  </div>
  <!-- footer -->
  <div id="footer">
```

```
        <div class="container">
            <div class="indent">
                <div class="fleft"> &copy; - Clever Coffee, Inc.</div>
                <div class="fright">Site designed by: <a href="http://
                ➥www.templates.com">Templates.com</a></div>
            </div>
        </div>
    </div>
</body>
</html>
```

## CREATING THE HOME PAGE

Right now, there's nothing for the home page to do, because all the key functionality is in other scripts. However, until the suckerfish menu is added, links to the products pages will be helpful. I'll put those within the body of the home page, along with some filler text.

```
<?php
require('../includes/config.inc.php');

$page_title = 'Coffee - Administration';
include('./includes/header.html');

?>
<h3>Links</h3>
<ul>
<li><a href="add_specific_coffees.php">Add Coffee Products</a></li>
<li><a href="add_other_products.php">Add Non-Coffee Products</a></li>
<li><a href="add_inventory.php">Add Inventory</a></li>
</ul>

<?php include('./includes/footer.html'); ?>
```

# Updating create_form_input( )

The **create_form_input()** function, first defined in Part 2, "Selling Virtual Products," then redefined in Chapter 10, "Checking Out," will be used in the administrative pages, too. As currently defined, the function works well for the public side, creating the text inputs and different select menus used by the checkout process. The administrative pages will have some forms that also require textareas, so that functionality needs to be added to the function.

As written in Chapter 10, the structure of the function is as follows:

```
if ( ($type === 'text') || ($type === 'password') ) {
   // Lots of code.
} elseif ($type === 'select') {
   // Lots more code.
} // End of primary IF-ELSEIF.
```

To support textareas, add the following code before the closing **IF-ELSEIF** curly bracket:

```
} elseif ($type === 'textarea') {
   if (array_key_exists($name, $errors)) echo ' <span class=
   ➥"error">' . $errors[$name] . '</span><br />';
   echo '<textarea name="' . $name . '" id="' . $name . '" rows="5"
   ➥cols="75"';
   if (array_key_exists($name, $errors)) {
      echo ' class="error">';
   } else {
      echo '>';
   }
   if ($value) echo $value;
   echo '</textarea>';
```

For an explanation of this code beyond the inline comments, see Chapter 4, "User Accounts."

# ADDING PRODUCTS

**tip**

This chapter doesn't include scripts for adding general coffee or goodie types, although each would be easy to create. Turn to my support forums if you need help implementing either.

The e-commerce site sells two types of products: coffee and other (aka goodies). The two products are treated differently in the database and in the catalog, so the administrative scripts for adding each will differ, too.

## Adding Non-Coffee Products

Non-coffee products—books, mugs, and so on—are represented as records in the **non_coffee_products** table. For each item, there is a **non_coffee_category_id** (a reference to the values in the **non_coffee_categorties** table), a name, a description, an image, a price, and the quantity in stock (**Figure 11.3**). Handling most of these values is straightforward, although the file upload is a bit tricky, requiring code similar to that used for working with PDFs in Chapter 5, "Managing Site Content."

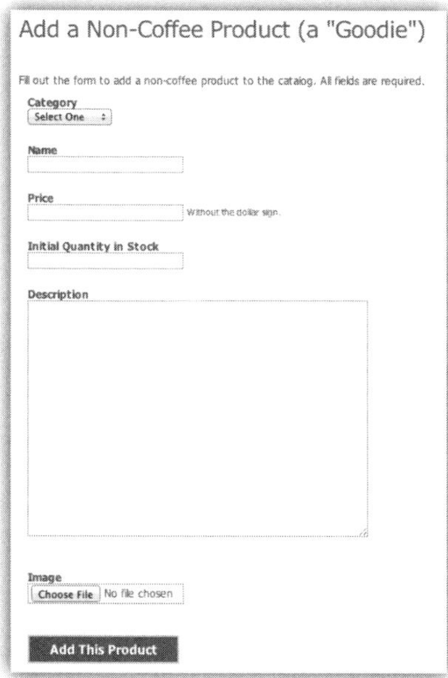


Figure 11.3

1. Create a new PHP script in your text editor or IDE to be named **add_other_products.php** and stored in the administrative directory.

2. Include the configuration file, the header, and the database connection:

```
<?php
require('../includes/config.inc.php');
$page_title = 'Add a Goodie';
include('./includes/header.html');
require(MYSQL);
```

3. Define an array for storing errors:

```
$add_product_errors = array();
```

4. Check for a form submission:

```
if ($_SERVER['REQUEST_METHOD'] === 'POST') {
```

5. Validate the product's category:

```
if (!isset($_POST['category']) || !filter_var($_POST['category'],
➥FILTER_VALIDATE_INT, array('min_range' => 1))) {
   $add_product_errors['category'] = 'Please select a category!';
}
```

tip

A page for creating new non-coffee categories would be a slimmed-down version of the ***add_other_products.php*** script, taking just a category name, description, and an image file.

tip

Using prepared statements for database queries changes the way query values will be treated, as you'll see in Step 12.

The product's category value should come from a select menu. It needs to be an integer with a value of at least 1. If those criteria aren't met, an error is added to the errors array. Unlike validation routines seen elsewhere in the book, nothing else is done with the validated value at this point.

6. Validate the price and quantity in stock:

```
if (empty($_POST['price']) || !filter_var($_POST['price'],
➥FILTER_VALIDATE_FLOAT) || ($_POST['price'] <= 0)) {
   $add_product_errors['price'] = 'Please enter a valid price!';
}
if (empty($_POST['stock']) || !filter_var($_POST['stock'],
➥FILTER_VALIDATE_INT, array('min_range' => 1))) {
   $add_product_errors['stock'] = 'Please enter the quantity in
   ➥stock!';
}
```

The price must not be empty and must be a float (a decimal) that's not less than or equal to 0. The quantity in stock must be an integer greater than or equal to 1. You could change the **min_range** to 0 if you wanted to allow the administrator to add products whose inventory will be increased later.

7. Validate the name and description:

```
if (empty($_POST['name'])) {
   $add_product_errors['name'] = 'Please enter the name!';
}
if (empty($_POST['description'])) {
   $add_product_errors['description'] = 'Please enter the
   ➥description!';
}
```

These two values can't be empty.

**tip**

Because the images on the site are relatively small, the maximum size could reasonably be restricted to less than 100 KB.

8. Begin validating the image:

```
if (is_uploaded_file($_FILES['image']['tmp_name']) &&
➥($_FILES['image']['error'] === UPLOAD_ERR_OK)) {
   $file = $_FILES['image'];
   $size = ROUND($file['size']/1024);
   if ($size > 512) {
      $add_product_errors['image'] = 'The uploaded file was too
      ➥large.';
   }
```

This code is similar to that used in Chapter 5 to validate uploaded PDF files. The image's maximum size is 512 KB.

**9.** Validate the file's type:

```
$allowed_mime = array ('image/gif', 'image/pjpeg', 'image/jpeg',
➥'image/JPG', 'image/X-PNG', 'image/PNG', 'image/png',
➥'image/x-png');
$allowed_extensions = array ('.jpg', '.gif', '.png', 'jpeg');
$fileinfo = finfo_open(FILEINFO_MIME_TYPE);
$file_type = finfo_file($fileinfo, $file['tmp_name']);
finfo_close($fileinfo);
$file_ext = substr($file['name'], -4);
if ( !in_array($file_type, $allowed_mime) ||
➥!in_array($file_ext, $allowed_extensions) ) {
  $add_product_errors['image'] = 'The uploaded file was not
  ➥of the proper type.';
}
```

Again, this is similar to the process for uploading PDFs explained in Chapter 5. First, an array of allowed MIME types is defined. Then an array of allowed extensions is defined (as an extra check). Third, the **Fileinfo** extension is used to check the file's type to a high degree of accuracy.

Fourth, the last four characters in the uploaded file's name are retrieved, in order to be compared against the allowed extensions (as an extra precaution).

The code then creates an error if any of two conditions are false. The first checks that the file's MIME type is appropriate. The second checks that the file's extension is on the approved list.

**10.** Move the file to its final destination:

```
if (!array_key_exists('image', $add_product_errors)) {
  $new_name = sha1($file['name'] . uniqid('',true));
  $new_name .= ((substr($ext, 0, 1) != '.') ? ".{$ext}" : $ext);
  $dest =  "../products/$new_name";
  if (move_uploaded_file($file['tmp_name'], $dest)) {
    $_SESSION['image']['new_name'] = $new_name;
    $_SESSION['image']['file_name'] = $file['name'];
    echo '<h4>The file has been uploaded!</h4>';
  } else {
    trigger_error('The file could not be moved.');
    unlink ($file['tmp_name']);
  }
} // End of array_key_exists() IF.
```

If no image-related error exists, a new name for the image is created, starting with the application of **SHA1()** to the combination of the file's current name and a unique ID. This will generate a 40-character-long random name. Then the existing extension is appended. Finally, the file is moved to its final resting place, within the ***<web root directory>*/products** folder.

The image's new name and its original filename are both stored in the session for use later.

Note that applying **sha1()** to the output of **uniqid()** makes the result less likely to be unique and also less secure (that is, easier to crack). For a password or other user identifier, that would be a mistake. With this particular use, where I just need to create a reasonably random name of a consistent length, this isn't a problem.

**11.** If a file upload error occurred, determine what it was:

```
} elseif (!isset($_SESSION['image'])) {
   switch ($_FILES['image']['error']) {
      case 1:
      case 2:
         $add_product_errors['image'] = 'The uploaded file was
         ➥too large.';
         break;
      case 3:
         $add_product_errors['image'] = 'The file was only
         ➥partially uploaded.';
         break;
      case 6:
      case 7:
      case 8:
         $add_product_errors['image'] = 'The file could not be
         ➥uploaded due to a system error.';
         break;
      case 4:
      default:
         $add_product_errors['image'] = 'No file was uploaded.';
         break;
   } // End of SWITCH.
} // End of $_FILES IF-ELSEIF-ELSE.
```

Yet again, this is all similar to that in the PDF upload script. First, the **switch** will be checked only if there's no file already represented in the session. This is necessary because it's possible that the administrator uploaded an image correctly the first time, but had another error in the form. In that case, when the administrator resubmits the form, the existing image upload should be used.

**12.** If there were no errors, add the record to the database:

```
if (empty($add_product_errors)) {
   $q = 'INSERT INTO non_coffee_products (non_coffee_category_id,
   ➥name, description, image, price, stock) VALUES (?, ?, ?, ?,
   ➥?, ?)';
   $stmt = mysqli_prepare($dbc, $q);
   mysqli_stmt_bind_param($stmt, 'isssii', $_POST['category'],
   ➥$name, $desc, $_SESSION['image']['new_name'], $price,
   ➥$_POST['stock']);
   $name = strip_tags($_POST['name']);
   $desc = strip_tags($_POST['description']);
   $price = $_POST['price']*100;
   mysqli_stmt_execute($stmt);
```

As explained in Chapter 7, to use prepared statements, the first step is to define the query, using placeholders (the question marks) in lieu of actual values. Then the statement is *prepared*. Next, the placeholders are bound, by type, to PHP variables. The second argument to the **mysqli_stmt_bind_param()** function indicates that the first placeholder is an integer, the next three are strings, and the fifth and sixth are integers.

Note that the price should come in as a decimal (for example, 4.25), which is more logical for the administrator, but it must be submitted to the database as an integer in cents (425).

Four of the values to be used in the query come from **$_POST** and **$_SESSION** directly. The other two values will come from local variables, after the **strip_tags()** function is applied.

If you have problems when executing this script, you can use the following line (after preparing the statement) to see what the problem is:

```
if (!$stmt) echo mysqli_stmt_error($stmt);
```

**13.** If the query created a new record, print a message and perform some cleanup:

```
if (mysqli_stmt_affected_rows($stmt) === 1) {
   echo '<h4>The product has been added!</h4>';
   $_POST = array();
   $_FILES = array();
   unset($file, $_SESSION['image']);
```

If one row was affected, a message will be printed, and the variables will be reset (because the form will be shown again, and it shouldn't display the previous values).

14. If there was a problem, trigger an error:

```
} else {
   trigger_error('The product could not be added due to a system
   ➥error. We apologize for any inconvenience.');
   unlink ($dest);
}
```

When a problem occurs, because of a database or query error, a message is displayed to the administrator and the uploaded file is removed (to prevent deadwood from cluttering the **products** directory).

15. Complete the errors array and request method conditionals:

```
   } // End of $errors IF.
} else {
   unset($_SESSION['image']);
} // End of the submission IF.
```

The final unsetting of the session variable would apply if the administrator uploaded a file but incompletely filled out the form, and then, for some reason, clicked the link in the header to return to this page, thereby starting the process anew.

16. Include the form functions script:

```
require('../includes/form_functions.inc.php');
```

The **create_form_input()** function is defined in this script, in the public **includes** folder, so it must be included here.

17. Begin the form:

```
?><h3>Add a Non-Coffee Product (a "Goodie")</h3>
<form enctype="multipart/form-data" action="add_other_products.
➥php" method="post" accept-charset="utf-8">
   <input type="hidden" name="MAX_FILE_SIZE" value="524288" />
   <fieldset><legend>Fill out the form to add a non-coffee
product to the catalog. All fields are required.</legend>
```

To handle the file upload, the form must use the **enctype** attribute, and it should include the **MAX_FILE_SIZE** hidden input (which recommends a maximum upload file size to the browser). That value is in bytes.

**18.** Create the category menu:

```
<div class="field"><label for="category"><strong>Category</
strong></label><br /><select name="category"<?php if
➥(array_key_exists('category', $add_product_errors)) echo
➥' class="error"'; ?>>
<option>Select One</option>
<?php
$q = 'SELECT id, category FROM non_coffee_categories ORDER BY
➥category ASC';
$r = mysqli_query($dbc, $q);
while ($row = mysqli_fetch_array ($r, MYSQLI_NUM)) {
   echo "<option value=\"$row[0]\"";
   if (isset($_POST['category']) && ($_POST['category'] ==
   ➥$row[0]) ) echo ' selected="selected"';
   echo '>' . htmlspecialchars($row[1]) . '</option>';
}
?>
</select><?php if (array_key_exists('category',
➥$add_product_errors)) echo ' <span class="error">' .
➥$add_product_errors['category'] . '</span>'; ?></div>
```

I choose not to have the **create_form_input()** function generate this select menu, because the menu's options require a database query (unlike the menus currently created by that function). Therefore, all the error-handling code has to be inline. Other than that, this code should be pretty straightforward by now.

**19.** Create the name, price, and stock elements:

```
<div class="field"><label for="name"><strong>Name</strong>
➥</label><br /><?php create_form_input('name', 'text',
➥$add_product_errors); ?></div>
<div class="field"><label for="price"><strong>Price</strong>
➥</label><br /><?php create_form_input('price', 'text',
➥$add_product_errors); ?> <small>Without the dollar sign.
➥</small></div>
<div class="field"><label for="stock"><strong>Initial Quantity
➥in Stock</strong></label><br /><?php create_form_input('stock',
➥'text', $add_product_errors); ?></div>
```

These are all basic text inputs.

20. Create the description element:

```
<div class="field"><label for="description"><strong>Description
➥</strong></label><br /><?php create_form_input('description',
➥'textarea', $add_product_errors); ?></div>
```

The description is a textarea.

**tip**

For more explanation of the image file input's code, see how PDFs are handled in Chapter 5.

21. Begin the image file input:

```
<div class="field"><label for="image"><strong>Image</strong>
➥</label><br /><?php
if (array_key_exists('image', $add_product_errors)) {
   echo '<span class="error">' . $add_product_errors['image'] .
   ➥'</span><br /><input type="file" name="image" class=
   ➥"error" />';
```

If an image-related error exists, the error message is first displayed; then the file input is created, with an assigned **error** class.

22. Complete the image file input:

```
} else { // No error.
   echo '<input type="file" name="image" />';
   if (isset($_SESSION['image'])) {
      echo "<br />Currently '{$_SESSION['image']['file_name']}'";
   }
} // end of errors IF-ELSE.
?></div>
```

If no image-related error exists, then the file input has no additional class. If a value exists in **$_SESSION['image']**, the already uploaded file's name is indicated to the administrator.

23. Complete the form:

```
   <br clear="all" />
   <div class="field"><input type="submit" value="Add This
   ➥Product" class="button" /></div>
   </fieldset>
</form>
```

24. Complete the PHP page:

```
<?php include('./includes/footer.html'); ?>
```

25. Save the file and test it in your browser.

    The script does not restrict the uploaded image to a given pixel size, nor does it resize the image to the proper dimensions (96 pixels wide by 76 pixels tall), so it's up to the administrator to use an image that's sized appropriately.

    Any errors in using the form will be reflected inline (**Figure 11.4**).

**tip**

You can have PHP resize images; it just requires external libraries and a bit more code.

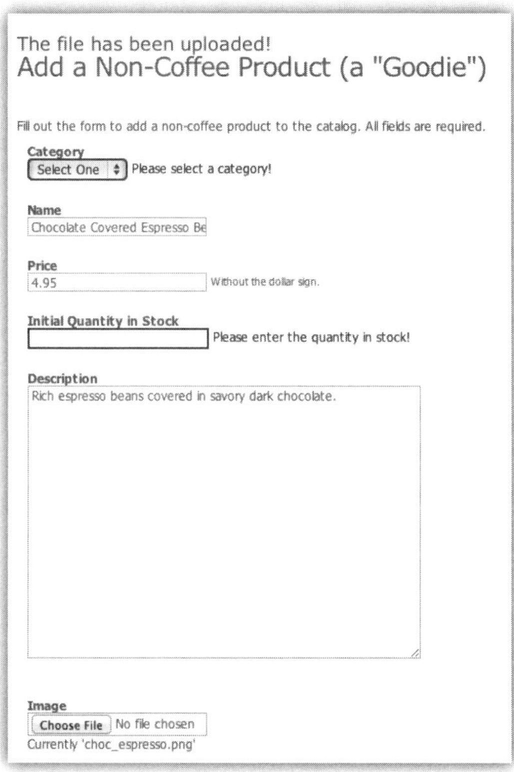


Figure 11.4

# Adding Coffee Products

For non-coffee products, each product a customer might purchase is associated with a particular non-coffee category. For coffee products, each specific product is associated with a particular type of coffee: Dark Roast, Kona, Original Blend, and so on. For each coffee type, there can be a number of specific products available: Given five initial size options, there are already 20 possible combinations of sizes, ground beans versus whole, and caffeinated versus decaffeinated. Therefore, the fastest way for the administrator to add specific coffee products is to present multiple options as part of one form (**Figure 11.5**).

**Figure 11.5**

Unlike the **add_other_products.php** script, this form won't use the **create_form_input()** function or perform any error reporting. The form is easy enough to use that errors shouldn't be a problem, and the method of generating the form in this script is different enough that using **create_form_input()** would overly complicate matters. Of course, you can add error reporting and automate the form generation if you'd like an extra challenge.

1. Create a new PHP script in your text editor or IDE to be named **add_specific_coffees.php** and stored in the administrative directory.

2. Include the configuration file, the header, and the database connection:

```
<?php
require('../includes/config.inc.php');
$page_title = 'Add Specific Coffees';
include('./includes/header.html');
require(MYSQL);
```

3. Identify how many records might be created at once:

```
$count = 10;
```

   The **$count** variable is the basis for how many specific coffee products can be created with each use of the page. Changing this number will alter the number of form rows generated in the table.

4. Check for a form submission:

```
if ($_SERVER['REQUEST_METHOD'] === 'POST') {
```

5. Check for a category:

```
if (isset($_POST['category']) && filter_var($_POST['category'],
➥FILTER_VALIDATE_INT, array('min_range' => 1))) {
```

If the administrator didn't select a coffee category (using the select menu at the top of the form), there's no need to continue. For this reason, the category value is validated first. The category should be an integer greater than or equal to 1.

6. Define the query and prepare the statement:

```
$q = 'INSERT INTO specific_coffees (general_coffee_id,
➥size_id, caf_decaf, ground_whole, price, stock) VALUES
➥(?, ?, ?, ?, ?, ?)';
$stmt = mysqli_prepare($dbc, $q);
```

This script, which will execute the same query up to **$count** times (using different values for each execution), is an excellent place to use prepared statements. The query needs to be prepared only once, its usage can be cached by the database, and the only thing that needs to be transmitted to MySQL for each query execution are the actual values (as opposed to the whole query).

7. Bind the variables:

```
mysqli_stmt_bind_param($stmt, 'iissii', $_POST['category'],
➥$size, $caf_decaf, $ground_whole, $price, $stock);
```

Six values need to be present in variables when the query is executed. The first two—the category and size values—will be integers, as will the last two (the price and the quantity in stock). The third and fourth values—caffeinated/decaffeinated and ground/whole beans—will be strings.

The first of these values will be the same for each query, and will come from **$_POST['category']**. The rest of the values will be determined within a **foreach** loop.

8. Begin looping through the submitted values:

```
$affected = 0;
for ($i = 1; $i <= $count; $i++) {
```

A **for** loop needs to run through **$count** iterations, matching the number of items that may be submitted. Prior to that, the **$affected** variable is initialized to 0. It will be used to track the total number of affected rows by all the executed queries.

9. Validate the required values:

```
if (filter_var($_POST['stock'][$i], FILTER_VALIDATE_INT,
➥array('min_range' => 1))
&& filter_var($_POST['price'][$i], FILTER_VALIDATE_FLOAT)
&& ($_POST['price'][$i] > 0) ) {
```

The initial quantity in stock and the item's price will be entered by the administrator into text inputs (see Figure 11.5). For each product submission, both values are validated using the Filter extension, ensuring that the stock value is an integer greater than or equal to 1 and that the price is greater than 0.

10. Assign the values to variables:

```
$size = $_POST['size'][$i];
$caf_decaf = $_POST['caf_decaf'][$i];
$ground_whole = $_POST['ground_whole'][$i];
$price = $_POST['price'][$i]*100;
$stock = $_POST['stock'][$i];
```

To be used in the query, each value must be assigned to a variable identified in the binding call (in Step 7). Again, the price needs to be multiplied by 100 to change the decimal to an integer.

11. Execute the query:

```
mysqli_stmt_execute($stmt);
$affected += mysqli_stmt_affected_rows($stmt);
```

First the query is executed, and then the number of affected rows is added to the existing count.

12. Complete the control structures and print the number of affected rows:

```
  } // End of IF.
} // End of FOREACH.
echo "<h4>$affected Product(s) Were Created!</h4>";
```

The script ignores any incomplete submissions rather than generating errors. By using this approach, the administrator isn't told that a problem exists simply because they only added six new items instead of the full ten (or whatever value **$count** has).

13. Complete the form submission conditionals:

```
  } else {
    echo '<p class="error">Please select a category.</p>';
  }
} // End of the submission IF.
```

The **else** clause applies if no category was selected.

**14.** Begin defining the form:

```
?><h3>Add Specific Coffees</h3>
<form action="add_specific_coffees.php" method="post"
➥accept-charset="utf-8">
  <fieldset><legend>Fill out the form to add specific coffee
  ➥products to the site.</legend>
```

**15.** Create the category select menu:

```
<div class="field"><label for="category"><strong>General Coffee
➥Type</strong></label><br />
<select name="category"><option>Select One</option>
<?php
$q = 'SELECT id, category FROM general_coffees ORDER BY
➥category ASC';
$r = mysqli_query($dbc, $q);
  while ($row = mysqli_fetch_array ($r, MYSQLI_NUM)) {
    echo '<option value="' . $row[0] . '">' .
    ➥htmlspecialchars($row[1]) . '</option>';
  }
?>
</select></div>
```

The list of coffee categories will be derived from a database query. This is a static query—it will never change—so there's no need to use prepared statements. To prevent XSS attacks, the string category value is run through `htmlspecialchars()` first.

**16.** Define a table:

```
<table border="0" width="100%" cellspacing="5" cellpadding="5">
  <thead>
    <tr>
      <th align="right">Size</th>
      <th align="right">Ground/Whole</th>
      <th align="right">Caf./Decaf.</th>
      <th align="center">Price</th>
      <th align="center">Quantity in Stock</th>
    </tr>
  </thead>
  <tbody>
```

The form for adding specific products uses table rows to present a series of form elements: one for each possible product quality.

17. Determine the size options:

```
<?php
$q = 'SELECT id, size FROM sizes ORDER BY id ASC';
$r = mysqli_query($dbc, $q);
$sizes = '';
while ($row = mysqli_fetch_array ($r, MYSQLI_NUM)) {
  $sizes .= '<option value="' . $row[0] . '">' .
  ➥htmlspecialchars($row[1]) . '</option>';
}
```

Each of the **$count** number of form elements will contain three select menus. Since the values for these menus will be the same for each row, it's best to define those menu options once, rather than query the database for each generated menu. To start, the **$sizes** variable will be assigned a series of option tags (as a string of HTML), based on the values retrieved from the **sizes** table.

18. Determine the grind and caffeine options:

```
$grinds = '<option value="ground">Ground</option><option
➥value="whole">Whole</option>';
$caf_decaf = '<option value="caf">Caffeinated</option><option
➥value="decaf">Decaffeinated</option>';
```

Both of these qualities have two possible options. Again, just the option tags are defined. The select tags will be given unique names for each row.

**tip**

The two text inputs in this form have **class="small"** attributes. Thanks to the CSS, this makes them not quite so wide as a standard input.

19. Create one table row of form elements for each number in **$count**:

```
for ($i = 1; $i <= $count; $i++) {
  echo '<tr>
  <td align="right"><select name="size[' . $i . ']">' . $sizes
  ➥. '</select></td>
  <td align="right"><select name="ground_whole[' . $i . ']">' .
  ➥$grinds . '</select></td>
  <td align="right"><select name="caf_decaf[' . $i . ']">' .
  ➥$caf_decaf . '</select></td>
  <td align="center"><input type="text" name="price[' . $i .
  ➥']" class="small" /></td>
  <td align="center"><input type="text" name="stock[' . $i .
  ➥']" class="small" /></td>
  </tr>
';
} // End of FOR loop.
```

Each table row contains five columns, each of which contains a form element. The name of each form element is an array, using the current count number as its index. The result will be an array named **$_POST['size']**, indexed from 1 to **$count**, another named **$_POST['ground_whole']**, indexed from 1 to **$count**, and so on.

20. Complete the PHP block and the table:

```
?></tbody>
</table>
```

21. Complete the form:

```
        <div class="field"><input type="submit" value="Add These
        ➥Products" class="button" /></div>
    </fieldset>
</form>
```

22. Complete the page:

```
<?php include('./includes/footer.html'); ?>
```

23. Save the file and test it in your browser (**Figure 11.6**).

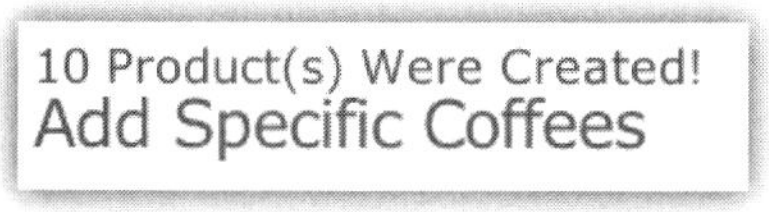

10 Product(s) Were Created!
Add Specific Coffees

**Figure 11.6**

# ADDING INVENTORY

In an e-commerce site that sells physical products, inventory management is an important feature. As you'll see later in this chapter, the inventory of an item is reduced when the item *ships* (you could alternatively choose to reduce the quantity on hand when the item *sells*). There needs to be a way to increase the inventory, too.

As I imagine it, the administrator might daily or weekly review the sales and the current inventory, then order more quantities of products to replenish the business's stock. When that shipment arrives, the added inventory needs to be reflected on the site.

To accomplish this, the administrator will be presented with a list of every product available for sale. Each will have a text input wherein the administrator enters the number just received (**Figure 11.7**).

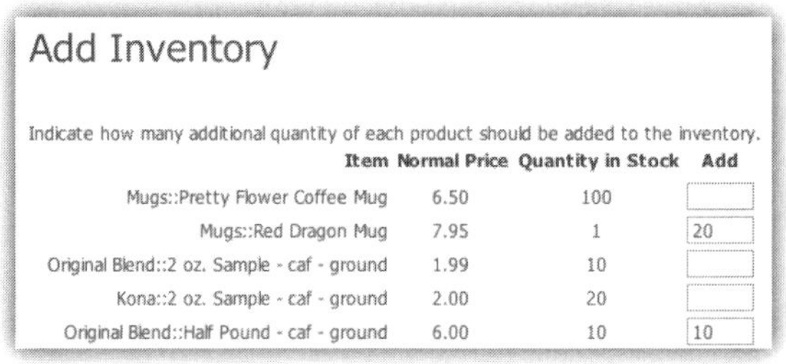

Add Inventory

Indicate how many additional quantity of each product should be added to the inventory.

| Item | Normal Price | Quantity in Stock | Add |
|---|---|---|---|
| Mugs::Pretty Flower Coffee Mug | 6.50 | 100 | |
| Mugs::Red Dragon Mug | 7.95 | 1 | 20 |
| Original Blend::2 oz. Sample - caf - ground | 1.99 | 10 | |
| Kona::2 oz. Sample - caf - ground | 2.00 | 20 | |
| Original Blend::Half Pound - caf - ground | 6.00 | 10 | 10 |

**Figure 11.7**

1. Create a new PHP script in your text editor or IDE to be named **add_inventory.php** and stored in the administrative directory.

2. Include the configuration file, the header, and the database connection:

```
<?php
require('../includes/config.inc.php');
$page_title = 'Add Inventory';
include('./includes/header.html');
require (MYSQL);
```

3. Check for a form submission:

```
if ($_SERVER['REQUEST_METHOD'] === 'POST') {
   if (isset($_POST['add']) && is_array($_POST['add'])) {
      require('../includes/product_functions.inc.php');
```

   This script's form will submit an array of values in **$_POST['add']**. The only initial validation is that **$_POST['add']** is set and that it is an array. If so, the **product_functions.inc.php** file (from the web root's **includes** directory) is required, because the script will need to use the **parse_sku()** function defined in it.

4. Define two queries:

```
$q1 = 'UPDATE specific_coffees SET stock=stock+? WHERE id=?';
$q2 = 'UPDATE non_coffee_products SET stock=stock+? WHERE id=?';
```

   This script will execute two different **UPDATE** queries: one to update the stock values in the **specific_coffees** table and another to update the stock values in the **non_coffee_products** table. Each is assigned to a separate variable here. The placeholders in each represent the number to be added to the inventory and the ID value (that is, which product is being updated).

5. Prepare the statements:

```
$stmt1 = mysqli_prepare($dbc, $q1);
$stmt2 = mysqli_prepare($dbc, $q2);
```

Each query is prepared separately, assigning the results to different variables.

6. Bind the variables:

```
mysqli_stmt_bind_param($stmt1, 'ii', $qty, $id);
mysqli_stmt_bind_param($stmt2, 'ii', $qty, $id);
```

For both statements, variables are bound to the parameters. As you can see, the same variables will be bound to both queries. However, for each submitted value, only one of the two queries will be executed.

7. Loop through each submitted value:

```
$affected = 0;
foreach ($_POST['add'] as $sku => $qty) {
```

First, a variable is initialized at 0, in order to count the number of affected rows. Then a **foreach** loop will go through the **$_POST['add']** array. For each item in that array, the index is assigned to **$sku** and the value to **$qty**. This is the same **$qty** variable that's been bound to the prepared statements.

8. Validate the quantity to be added:

```
if (filter_var($qty, FILTER_VALIDATE_INT, array('min_range'
➥=> 1))) {
```

The first requirement is that the number of items being added is an integer greater than or equal to 1.

9. Parse the SKU:

```
list($type, $id) = parse_sku($sku);
```

The **parse_sku()** function will turn a value such as **C23** into a type of **coffee** and an ID of 23, necessary for the queries. This **$id** variable has already been bound to the prepared statements.

10. Execute the correct prepared statement based on the type:

```
if ($type === 'coffee') {
   mysqli_stmt_execute($stmt1);
   $affected += mysqli_stmt_affected_rows($stmt1);
} elseif ($type === 'goodies') {
   mysqli_stmt_execute($stmt2);
   $affected += mysqli_stmt_affected_rows($stmt2);
}
```

If the current item's type equals **coffee**, the first prepared statement will be executed, updating a record in the **specific_coffees** tables. If the type equals **goodies**, the second prepared statement will be executed, updating a record in the **non_coffee_products** table. The number of affected rows is added to the existing count in both cases.

**11.** Complete the quantity validation **IF** and the **foreach** loop. Print the results:

```
    } // End of IF.
} // End of FOREACH.
echo "<h4>$affected Items(s) Were Updated!</h4>";
```

**12.** Complete the form submission conditionals:

```
    } // End of $_POST['add'] IF.
} // End of the submission IF.
```

**13.** Begin the form:

```
?><h3>Add Inventory</h3>
<form action="add_inventory.php" method="post"
➥accept-charset="utf-8">
    <fieldset><legend>Indicate how many additional quantity of
    ➥each product should be added to the inventory.</legend>
```

**14.** Create a table:

```
<table border="0" width="100%" cellspacing="4" cellpadding="4">
<thead>
    <tr>
        <th align="right">Item</th>
        <th align="right">Normal Price</th>
        <th align="right">Quantity in Stock</th>
        <th align="center">Add</th>
    </tr></thead>
<tbody>
```

The table will list the current products. For each product, the table shows the item's name, its normal price (as an additional point of reference), the current quantity in stock, and an input for adding more.

**tip**

This query is rather similar to the **UNION** queries used on the public side of the site. See those chapters for detailed explanations of the SQL.

**15.** Fetch every product:

```
<?php
$q = '(SELECT CONCAT("G", ncp.id) AS sku, ncc.category,
➥ncp.name, FORMAT(ncp.price/100, 2) AS price, ncp.stock FROM
➥non_coffee_products AS ncp INNER JOIN non_coffee_categories
➥AS ncc ON ncc.id=ncp.non_coffee_category_id ORDER BY category,
```

```
➥name) UNION (SELECT CONCAT("C", sc.id), gc.category,
➥CONCAT_WS(" - ", s.size, sc.caf_decaf, sc.ground_whole),
➥FORMAT(sc.price/100, 2), sc.stock FROM specific_coffees
➥AS sc INNER JOIN sizes AS s ON s.id=sc.size_id INNER JOIN
➥general_coffees AS gc ON gc.id=sc.general_coffee_id ORDER BY
➥sc.general_coffee_id, sc.size, sc.caf_decaf, sc.ground_whole)';
$r = mysqli_query($dbc, $q);
```

The query is a **UNION** of two **SELECT** queries, retrieving every product from the **non_coffee_products** and **specific_coffees** tables. The query returns each item's SKU, category and name, price, and current stock.

**16.** Create a table row for each product:

```
while ($row = mysqli_fetch_array ($r, MYSQLI_ASSOC)) {
   echo '<tr>
   <td align="right">' . htmlspecialchars($row['category']) .
   ➥'::' . htmlspecialchars($row['name']) . '</td>
   <td align="center">' . $row['price'] .'</td>
   <td align="center">' . $row['stock'] .'</td>
   <td align="center"><input type="text" name="add[' .
   ➥$row['sku'] . ']"  id="add[' . $row['sku'] . ']" size="5"
   ➥class="small" /></td>
   </tr>';
}
```

The first three columns in the row print literal values. The fourth column is a text input, whose name will be *add[*SKU*]*.

**17.** Complete the PHP block and the table:

```
?> </tbody></table>
```

**18.** Complete the form:

```
   <div class="field"><input type="submit" value="Add The
   ➥Inventory" class="button" /></div>
   </fieldset>
</form>
```

**19.** Complete the page:

```
<?php include('./includes/footer.html'); ?>
```

**20.** Save the file and test it in your browser (**Figure 11.8**).

2 Items(s) Were Updated!
Add Inventory

**Figure 11.8**

**tip**

The updated quantity should be reflected when the page reloads.

# CREATING SALES

The site allows the administrator to put any product on sale, for a definite or indefinite amount of time. From the perspective of the database, all that's required is the insertion of a new record into the **sales** table. To manage this process, the **create_sales.php** script will function much like **add_inventory.php**, except that rather than indicating additional quantities of each product, the administrator indicates the sale price, the start date, and, optionally, the end date for each product the site sells (**Figure 11.9**).

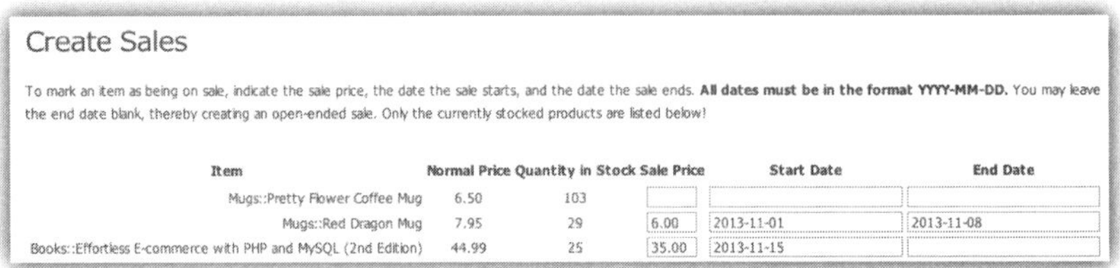


**Figure 11.9**

For now, the administrator will have to enter the dates the hard way: manually typing values in the format **YYYY-MM-DD**. In Chapter 14, the jQuery Datepicker plug-in will be applied. That plug-in will create a pop-up calendar, making the page easier to use and more reliable.

1. Create a new PHP script in your text editor or IDE to be named **create_sales.php** and stored in the administrative directory.

2. Include the configuration file, the header, and the database connection:

```
<?php
require('../includes/config.inc.php');
$page_title = 'Create Sales';
include('./includes/header.html');
require (MYSQL);
```

3. Check for a form submission:

```
if ($_SERVER['REQUEST_METHOD'] === 'POST') {
```

4. Confirm that the three required variables exist:

```
if (isset($_POST['sale_price'], $_POST['start_date'],
➥$_POST['end_date'])) {
```

The form will post back to this page three arrays, representing prices, start dates, and end dates.

5. Require the product functions:

```
require('../includes/product_functions.inc.php');
```

Again, as with the add inventory page, the **parse_sku()** user-defined function will be required.

6. Prepare the query to be run:

```
$q = 'INSERT INTO sales (product_type, product_id, price,
➥start_date, end_date) VALUES (?, ?, ?, ?, ?)';
$stmt = mysqli_prepare($dbc, $q);
mysqli_stmt_bind_param($stmt, 'siiss', $type, $id, $price,
➥$start_date, $end_date);
```

The query inserts into the **sales** table a record consisting of the product's type, ID, sale price, start date, and end date. Three of these values, including the two dates, will technically be strings. The product ID and price will be integers.

7. Loop through each submitted value:

```
$affected = 0;
foreach ($_POST['sale_price'] as $sku => $price) {
```

The script should receive three arrays: **$_POST['sale_price']**, **$_POST['start_date']**, and **$_POST['end_date']**. It doesn't matter which array the code loops through, but price is a logical selection. Each array is indexed using the product's SKU.

8. Validate the price and start date:

```
if (filter_var($price, FILTER_VALIDATE_FLOAT)
&& ($price > 0)
&& (!empty($_POST['start_date'][$sku]))
&& (preg_match('/^(201)[3-9]\-[0-1]\d\-[0-3]\d$/',
➥$_POST['start_date'][$sku]))
){
```

The new sale price must be a decimal (aka, a float) greater than 0. The starting date is checked that it's not empty, and that it matches a regular expression. The expression supports the years 2013 through 2019, the months 01 through 19 (limiting the months to just 12 overly complicates the expression), and the days from 01 to 39 (ditto).

**tip**

A stricter validation would check that the starting date and ending date (if provided) are valid. You could also confirm that the start date isn't before today and that the end date is after the start date.

9. Parse the SKU:

```
list($type, $id) = parse_sku($sku);
```

I'm sounding like a broken record here but...the **parse_sku()** function is invoked here as it is in the add inventory page, creating the **$type** and **$id** variables in the process. These same variables have already been bound to the prepared statement.

10. Associate the dates with variables:

```
$start_date = $_POST['start_date'][$sku];
$end_date = (!empty($_POST['end_date'][$sku]) &&
➥preg_match('/^(201)[3-9]\-[0-1]\d\-[0-3]\d$/',
➥$_POST['end_date'][$sku])) ? $_POST['end_date'][$sku] : NULL;
```

The starting date is available in the **$_POST['start_date']** array. For the current iteration of the **foreach** loop, the specific date to use is in **$_POST['start_date'][$sku]**. The end date is optional, so if the associated **$_POST** value isn't empty and matches the same regular expression, the administrator-provided value will be used. Otherwise, **NULL** is assigned to the **$end_date** variable.

11. Convert the price to cents and then execute the query:

```
$price = $price*100;
mysqli_stmt_execute($stmt);
$affected += mysqli_stmt_affected_rows($stmt);
```

12. Complete the price and start date validation, plus the **foreach** loop:

```
    } // End of price/date validation IF.
} // End of FOREACH loop.
```

13. Indicate the results and complete the form submission conditionals:

```
        echo "<h4>$affected Sales Were Created!</h4>";
    } // $_POST variables aren't set.
} // End of the submission IF.
?>
```

14. Begin the form:

```
<h3>Create Sales</h3>
<p>To mark an item as being on sale, indicate the sale price,
➥the date the sale starts, and the date the sale ends. <strong>
➥All dates must be in the format YYYY-MM-DD.</strong> You may
➥leave the end date blank, thereby creating an open-ended sale.
➥Only the currently stocked products are listed below!</p>
<form action="create_sales.php" method="post" accept-charset=
➥"utf-8">
    <fieldset>
```

This form begins with some instructions, because the use of the dates could be confusing.

**15.** Begin a table:

```
<table border="0" width="100%" cellspacing="4 cellpadding="6">
  <thead>
  <tr>
    <th align="center">Item</th>
    <th align="center">Normal Price</th>
    <th align="center">Quantity in Stock</th>
    <th align="center">Sale Price</th>
    <th align="center">Start Date</th>
    <th align="center">End Date</th>
  </tr>
  </thead>
  <tbody>
```

**16.** Retrieve every product that's currently in stock:

```
<?php
$q = '(SELECT CONCAT("G", ncp.id) AS sku, ncc.category,
➥ncp.name, FORMAT(ncp.price/100, 2) AS price, ncp.stock FROM
➥non_coffee_products AS ncp INNER JOIN non_coffee_categories
➥AS ncc ON ncc.id=ncp.non_coffee_category_id WHERE ncp.stock
➥> 0 ORDER BY category, name) UNION (SELECT CONCAT("C", sc.id),
➥gc.category, CONCAT_WS(" - ", s.size, sc.caf_decaf,
➥sc.ground_whole), FORMAT(sc.price/100, 2), sc.stock FROM
➥specific_coffees AS sc INNER JOIN sizes AS s ON s.id=sc.size_id
➥INNER JOIN general_coffees AS gc ON gc.id=sc.general_coffee_id
➥WHERE sc.stock > 0 ORDER BY sc.general_coffee_id, sc.size,
➥sc.caf_decaf, sc.ground_whole)';
$r = mysqli_query($dbc, $q);
```

This `UNION` query is essentially the same as that on the add inventory page, with the addition of a `WHERE` *`table`*`.stock > 0` clause. The thinking there is that the administrator would want to create sales only for products currently in stock.

**17.** Print each item as its own row:

```
while ($row = mysqli_fetch_array ($r, MYSQLI_ASSOC)) {
  echo '<tr>
    <td align="right">' . htmlspecialchars($row['category']) .
    ➥'::' . htmlspecialchars($row['name']) . '</td>
    <td align="center">' . $row['price'] .'</td>
    <td align="center">' . $row['stock'] .'</td>
```

*(continues on next page)*

```
        <td align="center"><input type="text" name="sale_price[' .
        ➥$row['sku'] . ']" class="small" /></td>
        <td align="center"><input type="text" name="start_date[' .
        ➥$row['sku'] . ']"/></td>
        <td align="center"><input type="text" name="end_date[' .
        ➥$row['sku'] . ']"/></td>
    </tr>';
}
```

The first three columns display values returned by the query. The last three columns each define a text input. The name of each input is an array, using the product's SKU as its index.

**18.** Complete the table and the form:

```
    </tbody></table>
    <div class="field"><input type="submit" value="Add These
    ➥Sales" class="button" /></div>
    </fieldset>
</form>
```

**19.** Complete the page:

```
<?php include('./includes/footer.html'); ?>
```

**20.** Save the file and test it in your browser.

# VIEWING ORDERS

The scripts to this point affect the product catalog and what the customer can purchase. Once customers have completed their orders, the administrator needs a way to view and handle those orders. This will be a three-step process:

- Viewing every order
- Viewing the particulars of a single order
- Processing an order

The processing part is when the business will get its money. Chapter 10 authorized payment for an order (that is, created a *hold*). Once the order has been reviewed and processed, using the following scripts the payment will be captured (that is, transferred).

To understand how the orders are represented in the database, you may want to review the checkout process, specifically **billing.php**, before looking at these scripts. You'll notice that the database may reflect orders that haven't been finalized (that is, orders for which payment wasn't processed). The corresponding administrative system can indicate to the administrator if funds couldn't be captured for an order, but as an extra precaution, nonfinalized orders won't be listed by this next script.

## Listing Every Order

The PHP script for listing every order is short and simple: The only thing complicated about it is the query it runs (as can often be the case). **Figure 11.10** shows what the heart of the page looks like.

View Orders

| Order ID | Total | Customer Name | City | State | Zip | Left to Ship |
|---|---|---|---|---|---|---|
| 14 | $37.22 | Ullman, Larry | Anytown | ID | 75860 | 2 |
| 13 | $59.64 | Ullman, Larry | Anytown | PA | 39056 | 3 |
| 12 | $20.40 | Ullman, Larry | Anytown | ME | 23905 | 18 |
| 11 | $19.20 | Ullman, Larry | Anytown | PA | 12345 | 2 |

**Figure 11.10**

**note**

This script is named **view_orders.php** (with an "s" after "order"). The next script will be the singular **view_order.php**.

1. Create a new PHP script in your text editor or IDE to be named **view_orders.php** and stored in the administrative directory.

2. Include the configuration file, the header, and the database connection:

```
<?php
require('../includes/config.inc.php');
$page_title = 'View All Orders';
include('./includes/header.html');
require (MYSQL);
```

3. Create a table:

```
echo '<h3>View Orders</h3><table border="0" width="100%"
➥cellspacing="4" cellpadding="4">
<thead>
  <tr>
    <th align="center">Order ID</th>
    <th align="center">Total</th>
    <th align="right">Customer Name</th>
    <th align="right">City</th>
    <th align="center">State</th>
    <th align="center">Zip</th>
    <th align="center">Left to Ship</th>
  </tr></thead>
<tbody>';
```

The HTML table reflects the information to be displayed about each order. This includes the order ID; the order total; the customer's name, city, state, and zip code; and a count of how many items are left to be shipped in this order. This count will act as an indicator of which orders have been completed and which have not.

**4.** Define and execute the query:

```
$q = 'SELECT o.id, FORMAT(total/100, 2) AS total, c.id AS cid,
➥CONCAT(last_name, ", ", first_name) AS name, city, state, zip,
➥COUNT(oc.id) AS items FROM orders AS o LEFT OUTER JOIN
➥order_contents AS oc ON (oc.order_id=o.id AND oc.ship_date
➥IS NULL) JOIN customers AS c ON (o.customer_id = c.id) JOIN
➥transactions AS t ON (t.order_id=o.id AND t.response_code=1)
➥GROUP BY o.id DESC';
$r = mysqli_query($dbc, $q);
```

The query needs to join the **orders**, **order_contents**, **customers**, and **transactions** tables. To retrieve the count of items left to ship in an order, the query uses a **LEFT OUTER JOIN** between **orders** and **order_contents** where the order ID matches, but the **ship_date** is **NULL**. The effect of this condition is that only **order_content** records without ship dates will be matched to orders. This is strictly for the purpose of indicating unfulfilled orders; viewing any particular order will show the complete contents, whether they've shipped or not.

Only orders that have a corresponding transaction response code of 1, indicating a successful request of the payment gateway, will be returned.

The orders are listed starting with the newest.

**5.** Print each record in the table:

```
while ($row = mysqli_fetch_array ($r, MYSQLI_ASSOC)) {
  echo '<tr>
    <td align="center"><a href="view_order.php?oid=' .
    ➥$row['id'] . '">' . $row['id'] . '</a></td>
    <td align="center">$' . $row['total'] .'</td>
    <td align="right"><a href="view_customer.php?cid=' .
    ➥$row['cid'] . '">' . htmlspecialchars( $row['name'])
    ➥.'</a></td>
    <td align="right">' . htmlspecialchars($row['city']) .
    ➥'</td>
    <td align="center">' . $row['state'] .'</td>
    <td align="center">' . $row['zip'] .'</td>
```

```
        <td align="center">' . $row['items'] .'</td>
    </tr>';
}
```

The order ID is linked to the **view_order.php** script (to be written next), passing along the order ID in the URL. The customer ID is linked to the **view_customer.php** script, passing along the customer ID in the URL. That script isn't written in this book, but it should be something you wouldn't have a problem implementing.

6. Complete the table:

```
echo '</tbody></table>';
```

7. Complete the page:

```
include('./includes/footer.html');
?>
```

8. Save the file and test it in your browser.

   You'll have to have some orders in the database in order for the results to be meaningful.

**note**

I've not added pagination or table sorting to the list of orders. This is something you should be able to do yourself, or you can see Chapter 14 for how to implement these features using JavaScript.

## Viewing One Order

The **view_order.php** script receives the order ID in the URL and displays all the order's details (**Figure 11.11**). The administrator can then click a button to mark the order as shipped. At that point, the order cycle will be complete.

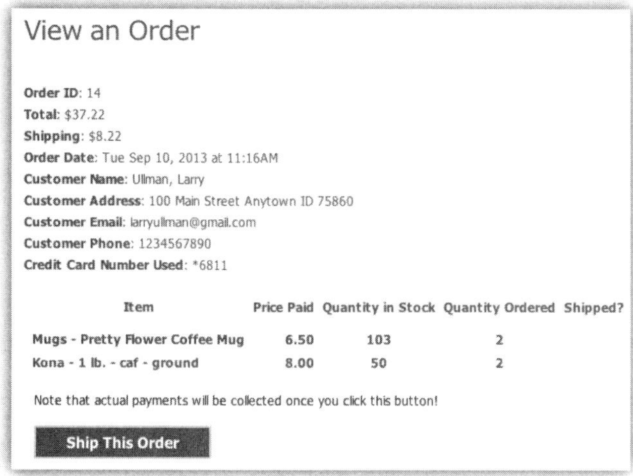


**Figure 11.11**

To start this process, the next series of steps will explain how to display the order's contents. Subsequently, you'll see how to mark an order as shipped.

1. Create a new PHP script in your text editor or IDE to be named **view_order.php** and stored in the administrative directory.

2. Include the configuration file and the header:

```
<?php
require('../includes/config.inc.php');
$page_title = 'View An Order';
include('./includes/header.html');
```

3. Validate the order ID:

```
$order_id = false;
if (isset($_GET['oid']) && (filter_var($_GET['oid'],
➥FILTER_VALIDATE_INT, array('min_range' => 1))) ) {
   $order_id = $_GET['oid'];
   $_SESSION['order_id'] = $order_id;
} elseif (isset($_SESSION['order_id']) &&
➥(filter_var($_SESSION['order_id'], FILTER_VALIDATE_INT,
➥array('min_range' => 1))) ) {
   $order_id = $_SESSION['order_id'];
}
```

The script can't function at all if it doesn't have access to a valid order ID (an integer greater than or equal to 1). The first time this page is accessed, it should receive an order ID in the URL (from the link on **view_orders.php**). If that's the case, the local **$order_id** variable is created for use in a query later in the script, and the order ID is stored in the session for use when the page is submitted back to itself.

If the order ID isn't in the URL but is in the session, that order ID value is assigned to a local variable and will be used by the page instead. This would be the case when the administrator clicks the Ship This Order button.

4. Stop the page if the **$order_id** isn't valid:

```
if (!$order_id) {
   echo '<h3>Error!</h3><p>This page has been accessed in
   ➥error.</p>';
   include('./includes/footer.html');
   exit();
}
```

If the page doesn't have a valid order ID, there's no point in continuing. An error will be printed, the footer included, and the script terminated.

**5.** Require the database connection:

```
require(MYSQL);
```

**6.** Define and execute the query:

```
$q = 'SELECT FORMAT(total/100, 2) AS total, FORMAT
➥(shipping/100,2) AS shipping, credit_card_number,
➥DATE_FORMAT(order_date, "%a %b %e, %Y at %h:%i%p") AS od,
➥email, CONCAT(last_name, ", ", first_name) AS name,
➥CONCAT_WS(" ", address1, address2, city, state, zip) AS address,
➥phone, customer_id, CONCAT_WS(" - ", ncc.category, ncp.name)
➥AS item, ncp.stock, quantity, FORMAT(price_per/100,2) AS
➥price_per, DATE_FORMAT(ship_date, "%b %e, %Y") AS sd FROM orders
➥AS o INNER JOIN customers AS c ON (o.customer_id = c.id) INNER
➥JOIN order_contents AS oc ON (oc.order_id = o.id) INNER JOIN
➥non_coffee_products AS ncp ON (oc.product_id = ncp.id AND
➥oc.product_type="goodies") INNER JOIN non_coffee_categories
➥AS ncc ON (ncc.id = ncp.non_coffee_category_id) WHERE o.id=' .
➥$order_id . '
UNION
SELECT FORMAT(total/100, 2), FORMAT(shipping/100,2),
➥credit_card_number, DATE_FORMAT(order_date, "%a %b %e, %Y
➥at %l:%i%p"), email, CONCAT(last_name, ", ", first_name),
➥CONCAT_WS(" ", address1, address2, city, state, zip), phone,
➥customer_id, CONCAT_WS(" - ", gc.category, s.size, sc.caf_decaf,
➥sc.ground_whole) AS item, sc.stock, quantity, FORMAT(
➥price_per/100,2), DATE_FORMAT(ship_date, "%b %e, %Y") FROM
➥orders AS o INNER JOIN customers AS c ON (o.customer_id =
➥c.id) INNER JOIN order_contents AS oc ON (oc.order_id = o.id)
➥INNER JOIN specific_coffees AS sc ON (oc.product_id = sc.id AND
➥oc.product_type="coffee") INNER JOIN sizes AS s ON (s.id=sc.
➥size_id) INNER JOIN general_coffees AS gc ON (gc.id=sc.
➥general_coffee_id) WHERE o.id=' . $order_id;
$r = mysqli_query($dbc, $q);
```

This query is similar to those in Chapter 9, "Building a Shopping Cart," in that it requires a **UNION** of two **SELECT** statements. Unlike that chapter's queries, this query must also join in the **customers**, **orders**, and **order_contents** tables. **Figure 11.12** (on the next page) shows the result of running this query.

```
larryullman — Effortless E-commerce
*************************** 1. row ***************************
           total: 37.22
        shipping: 8.22
credit_card_number: 6811
              od: Tue Sep 10, 2013 at 11:16AM
           email: larryullman@gmail.com
            name: Ullman, Larry
         address: 100 Main Street  Anytown ID 75860
           phone: 1234567890
     customer_id: 7
            item: Mugs - Pretty Flower Coffee Mug
           stock: 103
        quantity: 2
       price_per: 6.50
              sd: NULL
*************************** 2. row ***************************
           total: 37.22
        shipping: 8.22
credit_card_number: 6811
              od: Tue Sep 10, 2013 at 11:16AM
           email: larryullman@gmail.com
            name: Ullman, Larry
         address: 100 Main Street  Anytown ID 75860
           phone: 1234567890
     customer_id: 7
            item: Kona - 1 lb. - caf - ground
           stock: 50
        quantity: 2
       price_per: 8.00
              sd: NULL
2 rows in set (0.00 sec)

mysql>
```

Figure 11.12

**tip**

In Chapter 13, you'll see how the form might be expanded to allow for the shipping of individual items.

**7.** If rows were returned, start a form:

```
if (mysqli_num_rows($r) > 0) {
   echo '<h3>View an Order</h3>
   <form action="view_order.php" method="post"
   ➥accept-charset="utf-8">
      <fieldset>';
```

The form posts back to this same page and only contains, as written, a submit button.

**8.** Fetch the first returned row and display the general information:

```
$row = mysqli_fetch_array($r, MYSQLI_ASSOC);
echo '<p><strong>Order ID</strong>: ' . $order_id .
➥'<br /><strong>Total</strong>: $' . $row['total'] .
➥'<br /><strong>Shipping</strong>: $' . $row['shipping'] .
➥'<br /><strong>Order Date</strong>: ' . $row['od'] .
➥'<br /><strong>Customer Name</strong>: ' .
➥htmlspecialchars($row['name']) . '<br /><strong>Customer
➥Address</strong>: ' . htmlspecialchars($row['address']) .
➥'<br /><strong>Customer Email</strong>: ' .
➥htmlspecialchars($row['email']) . '<br /><strong>Customer
➥Phone</strong>: ' . htmlspecialchars($row['phone']) .
➥'<br /><strong>Credit Card Number Used</strong>: *' .
➥$row['credit_card_number'] . '</p>';
```

The query will return the general order and customer information once for each item in the order (see Figure 11.13). To display the general information only once, and first, the first returned row is immediately fetched, outside of any loop. You'll see how and why this works shortly.

9. Create the table:

```
echo '<table border="0" width="100%" cellspacing="8"
➥cellpadding="6">
<thead>
  <tr>
    <th align="center">Item</th>
    <th align="right">Price Paid</th>
    <th align="center">Quantity in Stock</th>
    <th align="center">Quantity Ordered</th>
    <th align="center">Shipped?</th>
  </tr>
</thead>
<tbody>';
```

The table lists the ordered items, along with the price paid, the quantity currently in stock, the quantity ordered, and when the item has shipped, if applicable.

**tip**

As a fraud prevention technique, you could retrieve the billing address from the payment transaction and compare it to the shipping address, looking for suspicious differences.

10. Create a flag variable to track if the order has already shipped:

```
$shipped = true;
```

The administrator is going to be given the option of processing the payment for this order only if it hasn't already shipped. The assumption will be that it has, and later code will change this setting if that's not the case.

11. Print each item:

```
do {
  echo '<tr>
    <td align="left">' . $row['item'] . '</td>
    <td align="right">' . $row['price_per'] . '</td>
    <td align="center">' . $row['stock'] . '</td>
    <td align="center">' . $row['quantity'] . '</td>
    <td align="center">' . $row['sd'] . '</td>
  </tr>';
```

Because one row has already been fetched, the less common **do...while** loop will be used to navigate the remaining query results. This construct performs some actions first and checks the conditional last, thereby guaranteeing that the code within the loop will be executed at least one time. Within the loop, each value is displayed within a table row.

12. Update the shipping status:

```
if (!$row['sd']) $shipped = false;
```

If `$row['sd']` is `NULL` (for any item in the order), then the entire order hasn't been shipped yet, and the flag variable should indicate that.

13. Complete the loop and the table:

```
} while ($row = mysqli_fetch_array($r));
echo '</tbody></table>';
```

After the contents of the loop are executed, the condition is checked. The specific condition is the fetching of another array from the query results. If another array can be found, the loop will be repeated again.

14. If the order hasn't entirely shipped, create the submit button:

```
if (!$shipped) {
   echo '<div class="field"><p class="error">Note that actual
   ➥payments will be collected once you click this button!
   ➥</p><input type="submit" value="Ship This Order"
   ➥class="button" /></div>';
}
```

For orders that have completely shipped, no submit button will exist (**Figure 11.13**).

**Figure 11.13**

15. Complete the form:

```
echo '</fieldset>
</form>';
```

16. Complete the `mysqli_num_rows()` conditional:

```
} else {
   echo '<h3>Error!</h3><p>This page has been accessed in
   ➥error.</p>';
```

```
    include('./includes/footer.html');
    exit();
}
```

This **else** clause applies if no records were returned by the query.

17. Complete the page:

```
include('./includes/footer.html');
?>
```

18. Save the file and test it in your browser.

    At this point, clicking the submit button will have no effect, however.

# PROCESSING PAYMENT

To complete the **view_order.php** script, the functionality for processing completed orders has to be integrated. This entire process involves these steps:

1. Requesting actual payment for the order
2. Recording the payment request transaction in the database
3. Updating the **order_contents** table
4. Updating the catalog inventory
5. Reporting on the results

Although there are many steps, the code itself isn't that complicated, largely thanks to the work that's already been done for the public side of the site.

The code for processing the payment capture is about 70 lines long, well spaced, and with comments. You can place it all within an includable file, or just add it to **view_order.php**, as in these next steps:

1. Open **view_order.php** in your text editor or IDE, if it isn't already open.

2. After including the database connection, check for a form submission:

```
if ($_SERVER['REQUEST_METHOD'] === 'POST') {
```

3. Retrieve the customer ID, order total, and transaction ID:

```
$q = "SELECT customer_id, total, transaction_id FROM orders AS
➥o JOIN transactions AS t ON (o.id=t.order_id AND t.type=
➥'auth_only' AND t.response_code=1) WHERE o.id=$order_id";
$r = mysqli_query($dbc, $q);
```

At this point in the script, **$order_id** has already been validated to be an integer greater than or equal to 1, meaning it's safe to use in a query (you could use prepared statements, if you'd rather). The query selects three pieces of information from the **orders** and **transactions** tables.

Each order can be represented in the **transactions** table multiple times, but only once in an **auth_only** status. That's the status returned when an authorization (but not capture) request succeeds (in **billing.php**).

Along with that check, the order is only valid—and its amount should only be captured—if the **response_code** for that previous transaction equals 1, meaning that the authorization request worked.

If this query returns a record considering those criteria, the order can be captured and shipped.

4. If one row was returned, get the selected values:

```
if (mysqli_num_rows($r) === 1) {
  list($customer_id, $order_total, $trans_id) =
  ➥mysqli_fetch_array($r, MYSQL_NUM);
```

If the query in Step 3 returned one record, then the customer's ID, the total of the order, and, most important, the transaction ID can be fetched.

5. Check for a positive order total:

```
if ($order_total > 0) {
```

As a safety check, only positive payment requests will ever be made.

6. Include the Authorize.net SDK and create the **AuthorizeNetAIM** object:

```
require('../includes/vendor/anet_php_sdk/AuthorizeNet.php');
$aim = new AuthorizeNetAIM(API_LOGIN_ID, TRANSACTION_KEY);
```

This code is the same as that in **billing.php**, except for adjusting the path to the SDK library.

**tip**

The order total is only required if less than the original, authorized amount, but it's best to be thorough and include it.

7. Capture the payment:

```
$response = $aim->priorAuthCapture($trans_id, $order_total/100);
```

Rather than calling the **authorizeOnly()** method, as **billing.php** did, this script calls the **priorAuthCapture()** method. Its first argument is the transaction ID. The second is the amount to capture. That amount is in dollars.

8. Record the transaction results:

```
$reason = addslashes($response->response_reason_text);
$full_response = addslashes($response->response);
$r = mysqli_query($dbc, "CALL add_transaction($order_id,
```

```
➥'{$response->transaction_type}', $order_total,
➥{$response->response_code}, '$reason',
➥{$response->transaction_id}, '$full_response')");
```

This code is exactly like that in **billing.php**.

9. If the request was successful, create a message:

```
if ($response->approved) {
   $message = 'The payment has been made. You may now ship the
   ➥order.';
```

As explained in Chapter 10, if the **approved** attribute of the returned response has a true value, the request succeeded. If so, a message is assigned to a variable for use later in the script.

10. Update the **order_contents** table:

```
$q = "UPDATE order_contents SET ship_date=NOW() WHERE
➥order_id=$order_id";
$r = mysqli_query($dbc, $q);
```

To reflect that the order has shipped (or can be shipped now), the **order_contents** table needs to be updated for every row with the current order ID.

11. Update the site's inventory:

```
$q = 'UPDATE specific_coffees AS sc, order_contents AS oc SET
➥sc.stock=sc.stock-oc.quantity WHERE sc.id=oc.product_id AND
➥oc.product_type="coffee" AND oc.order_id=' . $order_id;
$r = mysqli_query($dbc, $q);
$q = 'UPDATE non_coffee_products AS ncp, order_contents AS oc
➥SET ncp.stock=ncp.stock-oc.quantity WHERE ncp.id=oc.product_id
➥AND oc.product_type="goodies" AND oc.order_id=' . $order_id;
$r = mysqli_query($dbc, $q);
```

Now that the items in the order have officially been purchased and can head out the door, the site's inventory needs to reflect the sold items. This means that for every item in the **order_contents** table (for the current order), the corresponding records in the **specific_coffees** and **non_coffee_products** tables have to be updated.

In case this syntax looks a bit confusing to you, MySQL allows you to perform a **JOIN** on an **UPDATE** query. In this case, two queries can update the entire inventory, no matter how many records are present in the **order_contents** table. Each query may make more sense if viewed as a standard **SELECT JOIN**:

**tip**

The comma between the table names in the queries is equivalent to the word **JOIN**.

```
SELECT sc.stock, oc.quantity FROM specific_coffees AS sc,
➥order_contents AS oc WHERE sc.id=oc.product_id AND
➥oc.product_type="coffee" and oc.order_id=X
```

Rather than *selecting* the two values—stock and quantity—in matching rows, the one value is used to update the value in the other.

**12.** If the payment request didn't succeed, create an error:

```
} else { // Do different things based upon the response:
   $error = 'The payment could not be processed because: ' .
   ➥$response->response_reason_text;
} // End of payment response IF-ELSE.
```

As in Chapter 10, **$response->response_reason_text** contains a textual description of the problem. This will be safe to reveal to the administrator.

**13.** Complete the order total **IF-ELSE**:

```
} else { // Invalid order total!
   $error = "The order total (\$$order_total) is invalid.";
} // End of $order_total IF-ELSE.
```

If the order total wasn't a positive number, that message is assigned to an error variable, along with the actual total.

**note**

You'll need to use relatively recent orders to test this process; the authorization for older orders may have since been revoked.

**14.** If no matching order was found, indicate that:

```
} else { // No matching order!
   $error = 'No matching order could be found.';
} // End of transaction ID IF-ELSE.
```

**15.** Report any messages or errors:

```
echo '<h3>Order Shipping Results</h3>';
if (isset($message)) echo "<p>$message</p>";
if (isset($error)) echo "<p class=\"error\">$error</p>";
```

**Figures 11.14** and **11.15** show these lines in action.

Order Shipping Results

The payment has been made. You may now ship the order.

**Figure 11.14**

Order Shipping Results

The payment could not be processed because: A valid referenced transaction ID is required.

**Figure 11.15**

**16.** Complete the form submission **IF**:

```
} // End of the submission IF.
```

**17.** Save the page and test it in your browser.

# PART FOUR
## EXTRA TOUCHES

# 12 EXTENDING THE FIRST SITE

The goal of this book is to teach sound e-commerce code and methodologies. In thinking of the two sites I'd develop in this book to achieve that goal, I tried to come up with examples that best portray the breadth of what e-commerce can be. Being who I am, however, I also dreamed up about three dozen other ideas for each one that actually made it into the book. Rather than discard good brainstorming, I thought I'd create an entire chapter dedicated to the various ways you could expand the "Knowledge Is Power" site.

I've grouped my suggestions into three categories:

- Public additions
- Security improvements
- Administrative features

Separate from those groups, I'm also going to introduce and explain how to use PayPal's PDT (Payment Data Transfer) for a slightly improved user experience.

A few of the ideas in this chapter will be discussed in theory, without using code. Other thoughts will be explained in some detail and will include a sufficient amount of code. A few more suggestions will be fully realized.

Also keep in mind that you could add components from any other section of the book to the "Knowledge Is Power" site. For example, you could

- Use Stripe as the payment processor (see Chapter 15, "Using Stripe Payments")
- Integrate Ajax (see Chapter 14, "Adding JavaScript and Ajax")
- Create an administrative interface for viewing orders (see Chapter 11, "Site Administration")

As with most anything in web development, the only limitation is in deciding what's most appropriate for your site and its customers.

**tip**

Some of these ideas may also be developed (to varying degrees) in the downloadable scripts available at www.LarryUllman.com.

# NEW PUBLIC FEATURES

You can add a number of features to the public side that I think users would appreciate. The "Knowledge Is Power" site is an example of a content management system (CMS), so everything the user does with the site involves viewing content. To improve that experience, I've come up with four good features you can easily add:

- Recording viewing history
- Note taking
- Marking pages as favorites
- Rating content

There are two great benefits to implementing these features. First, they get users to return, and in e-commerce, returning users generate more money. Second, these features allow your users to provide qualitative feedback on the content you provide. That feedback will make the site better for other users, thereby creating more customers.

## Logging History

One addition you can make is to log all the pages people visit. Your web server is probably already doing this, but the logging I'm talking about would focus solely on what content is viewed. This type of logging wouldn't count the images, CSS pages, and other items.

## ADDING A SEARCH ENGINE

An internal search engine (one built into the site, as opposed to a public search engine like Google) is a logical and good addition to the "Knowledge Is Power" site. There are three relatively easy ways to implement a search engine that I discuss in an article I wrote for Peachpit.com. You can find it at www.peachpit.com/articles/article.aspx?p=1802754.

Those solutions can work well for the database-driven content. To also index the PDF content, you'll need to turn to a third-party library, such as a framework component that's capable of reading PDFs.

More and more sites these days are creating professional search engines using Solr (http://lucene.apache.org/solr/) or elasticsearch (www.elasticsearch.org). Both are built upon the popular Lucene (http://lucene.apache.org) search engine. These tools work quite well, but they require additional software to be installed and running on your web server. I recommend that you investigate elasticsearch in particular, but only when you find yourself with a couple of days to spend on that particular aspect of the project.

To log a history of visits, you first need to create a **history** table:

```
CREATE TABLE history (
`id` INT UNSIGNED NOT NULL AUTO_INCREMENT,
`user_id` INT UNSIGNED NOT NULL,
`type` ENUM('page', 'pdf'),
`item_id` INT UNSIGNED DEFAULT NULL,
`date_created` TIMESTAMP NOT NULL DEFAULT CURRENT_TIMESTAMP,
PRIMARY KEY (`id`),
KEY (`type`, `item_id`)
) ENGINE=InnoDB DEFAULT CHARSET=utf8;
```

Because all of the HTML content is viewed through **page.php**, you only need to have that one script record the HTML viewing history. The **page.php** script will add a new record to the **history** table every time the page is loaded (by an active user). Here's what that query looks like:

```
INSERT INTO history (user_id, type, item_id) VALUES ($user_id,
➥'page', $page_id)
```

This query runs once you've already validated the user ID (stored in the session) and page ID values. Presumably, you'd execute this query only for active users. As written, one record is created for each page view. Later in the chapter you'll see how to design the table and write the query if you only want to record a single viewing for each user and page.

The **view_pdf.php** page executes the same query but changes the type to **pdf** and uses the **id** value from the **pdfs** table for the **item_id**.

These changes have no visible impact to the user, but the **history** table will then be able to provide the user with a history of every page and PDF she's seen:

```
SELECT DISTINCT(pa.id) AS page_id, pa.title AS page_title FROM pages
➥AS pa JOIN history AS h WHERE pa.id=h.item_id AND h.type='page'
➥AND h.user_id=X
UNION
SELECT DISTINCT(pdfs.id) AS pdf_id, pdfs.title AS pdf_title
➥FROM pdfs JOIN history AS h WHERE pdfs.id=h.item_id AND
➥h.type='pdf' AND h.user_id=X
```

This table will also provide the administrator with indications of the most popular pages. That information can also be used on the public side, perhaps to display the ten most popular articles on the home page (**Figure 12.1**). Here's the **JOIN** query that returns the ten most frequently viewed pages:

Most Popular Pages
1. This is a Common Attack Article.
2. This is another Common Attack Article
3. Using a Firewall

Figure 12.1

```
SELECT COUNT(history.id) AS num, pages.id, pages.title FROM pages,
➥history WHERE pages.id=history.item_id AND history.type='page'
➥GROUP BY (history.item_id) ORDER BY num DESC LIMIT 10
```

## Recording Favorites

To make the site easier to use, especially as you create more content, you can give users the ability to bookmark their favorite pages. Doing so for the HTML pages is simple. First, create this table:

```
CREATE TABLE favorite_pages (
`user_id` INT UNSIGNED NOT NULL,
`page_id` MEDIUMINT UNSIGNED NOT NULL,
`date_created` TIMESTAMP  NOT NULL,
PRIMARY KEY (`user_id`, `page_id`)
) ENGINE=InnoDB DEFAULT CHARSET=utf8;
```

This is a *junction* table, used to manage the many-to-many relationship between **users** and **pages**. It has only three columns, and the first two together constitute the primary key (that is, it's a *compound primary key*). Each favorite for each user will be represented by one record in this table.

Next, create an image displayed with the content that, when clicked, passes the page ID along in the URL (**Figure 12.2**):

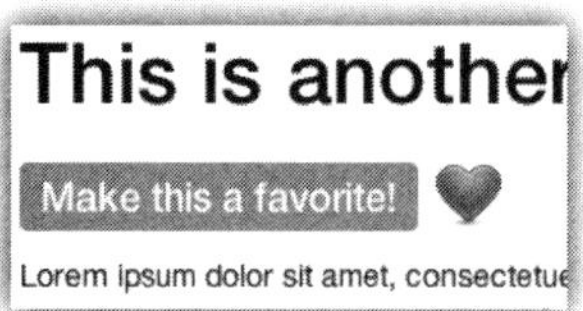


**Figure 12.2**

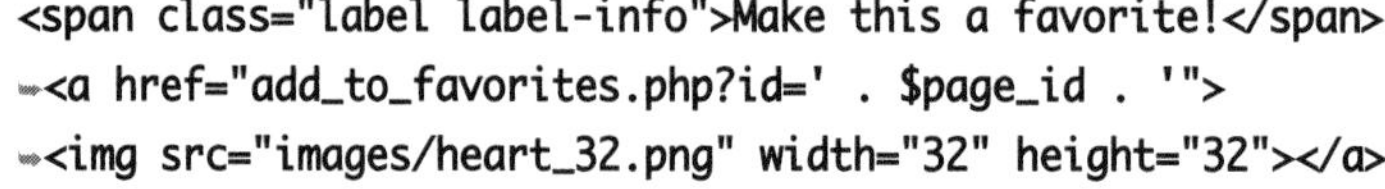

```
<span class="label label-info">Make this a favorite!</span>
➥<a href="add_to_favorites.php?id=' . $page_id . '">
➥<img src="images/heart_32.png" width="32" height="32"></a>
```

**tip**

If you want to store only one record for each viewed page, the **history** table would use the same structure as **favorite_pages**.

On the **add_to_favorites.php** page, you would store in the **favorites** table the user's ID from the session and the page ID from the URL:

```
INSERT INTO favorite_pages (user_id, page_id) VALUES ($user_id,
➥$page_id)
```

You can then create a **favorites.php** page that displays all of the user's favorites. It needs to perform a **JOIN** to get the favorite content (**Figure 12.3**):

```
SELECT id, title, description FROM pages LEFT JOIN favorite_pages
➥ON (pages.id=favorite_pages.page_id) WHERE favorite_pages.user_id='
➥. $user_id . ' ORDER BY title';
```

**tip**

You can also mark the user's favorites next to each item in a history page.

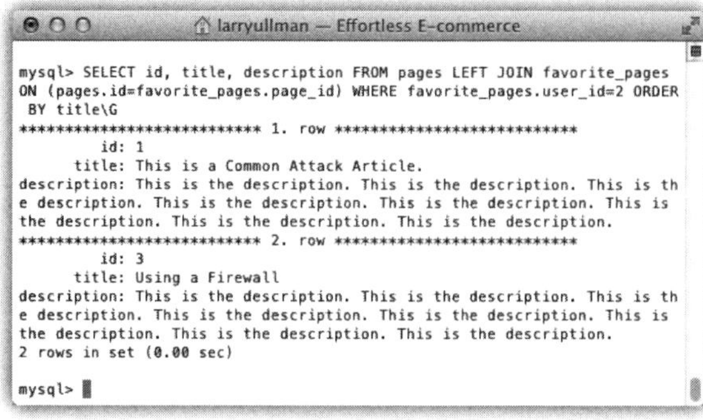

```
larryullman — Effortless E-commerce
mysql> SELECT id, title, description FROM pages LEFT JOIN favorite_pages
ON (pages.id=favorite_pages.page_id) WHERE favorite_pages.user_id=2 ORDER
 BY title\G
*************************** 1. row ***************************
         id: 1
      title: This is a Common Attack Article.
description: This is the description. This is the description. This is th
e description. This is the description. This is the description. This is
the description. This is the description. This is the description.
*************************** 2. row ***************************
         id: 3
      title: Using a Firewall
description: This is the description. This is the description. This is th
e description. This is the description. This is the description. This is
the description. This is the description. This is the description.
2 rows in set (0.00 sec)

mysql>
```

**Figure 12.3**

On each content page, you can replace the "Make this a favorite!" code with a check to see whether the page is already in the user's favorites. If it is, you display text and an image indicating that. Perhaps clicking another link removes it from the user's favorites by sending the page ID along to **remove_from_favorites.php** (Figure 12.4):

```
$q = 'SELECT user_id FROM favorite_pages WHERE user_id=' .
➥$user_id . ' AND page_id=' . $page_id;
$r = mysqli_query($dbc, $q);
if (mysqli_num_rows($r) === 1) {
   echo '<h3><img src="images/heart_32.png" width="32" height="32">
   ➥<span class="label label-info">This is a favorite!</span>
   ➥<a href="remove_from_favorites.php?id=' . $page_id . '">
   ➥<img src="images/close_32.png" width="32" height="32"></a></h3>';
} else {
   echo '<h3><span class="label label-info">Make this a favorite!
   ➥</span> <a href="add_to_favorites.php?id=' . $page_id . '">
   ➥<img src="images/heart_32.png" width="32" height="32"></a></h3>';
}
```

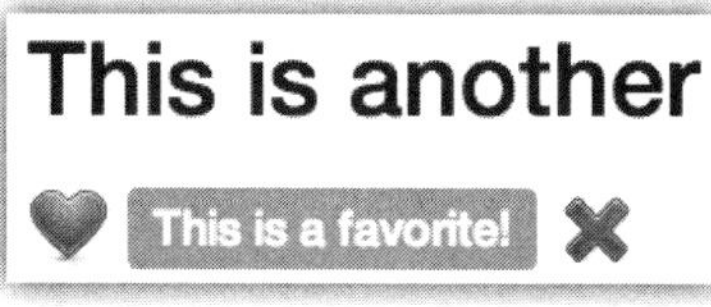


Figure 12.4

Making a note of favorite PDFs requires a bit more thought. You can't easily add links to the PDF itself, so you'd have to put the "Add to Favorites" link somewhere else, like on the page that lists all the PDFs. This means the user would have to read the PDF, then go back to that page to flag it. As for storing favorite PDFs in the database, you can create a **favorite_pdfs** table, just like **favorite_pages**, or create a **favorites** table that stores both, like the history example.

## Rating Content

Continuing on this same theme, to be even more precise you can let users indicate a rating of each page. You store the rating in a table:

```
CREATE TABLE page_ratings (
`user_id` INT UNSIGNED NOT NULL,
`page_id` MEDIUMINT UNSIGNED NOT NULL,
`rating` TINYINT UNSIGNED NOT NULL,
`date_created` TIMESTAMP  NOT NULL,
PRIMARY KEY (`user_id`, `page_id`)
) ENGINE=InnoDB DEFAULT CHARSET=utf8;
```

**tip**

The user experience for marking pages as favorites can be greatly enhanced using Ajax, as you'll learn in Chapter 14.

**tip**

The images used in this example are freely available at www.woothemes.com/2009/09/woofunction-178-amazing-web-design-icons/.

Unlike with the **history** table, where you may want to record every time the user visited a page, you want each user to be able to rank a page only once. You accomplish that using this query:

```
REPLACE INTO page_ratings (user_id, page_id, rating) VALUES
➥($user_id, $page_id, $rating)
```

As for the query itself, the **REPLACE INTO** SQL statement is a gem of a command. If a record with the given primary key already exists, an **UPDATE** query will be performed. If no such record exists, an **INSERT** will be performed. With the **page_ratings** table, the primary key is the combination of the user's ID and the page ID. If those two values are the same as an existing record, the rating value will be updated.

**tip**

An even better addition is to use Ajax to submit the user's rating to the server behind the scenes and immediately update the page to reflect the rating.

The rating will be an integer, from, say, 1 to 5, and it has to be validated as such. The easiest way to submit the rating is to use a drop-down menu in a form that posts the rating back to **page.php**. The **page.php** script then needs an extra block at the top of the script that checks for a POST request and adds the record to the database if all the data successfully passes the validation tests.

The ratings can then be displayed to the user on his favorites and history pages. The ratings can also be used by the administrator to see the best reviewed content, which again may be turned into a listing on the home page (**Figure 12.5**):

Highest Rated Pages
4.3 This is a Common Attack Article.
4.0 This is another Common Attack Article
3.5 Using a Firewall

Figure 12.5

```
SELECT ROUND(AVG(rating),1) AS average, pages.id, pages.title FROM
➥pages, page_ratings WHERE pages.id=page_ratings.page_id GROUP BY
➥(page_ratings.page_id) ORDER BY average DESC LIMIT 10
```

You can also do this for the PDFs, but you'd have to add the logic to the **pdfs.php** script.

## Making Notes

Allowing users to make notes on pages is another service you can add. The required table looks like this:

```
CREATE TABLE notes (
`user_id` INT UNSIGNED NOT NULL,
```

```
`page_id` INT UNSIGNED NOT NULL,
`note` TEXT NOT NULL,
`date_updated` TIMESTAMP NOT NULL DEFAULT CURRENT_TIMESTAMP ON
➥UPDATE CURRENT_TIMESTAMP,
PRIMARY KEY (`user_id`, `page_id`)
) ENGINE=InnoDB DEFAULT CHARSET=utf8;
```

Once you've created that table in your database, you can update the **page.php** script to allow for note taking. Let's walk through that code:

1. Open **page.php** in your text editor or IDE.

2. After displaying the content, check for a form submission:

   ```
   if ($_SERVER['REQUEST_METHOD'] === 'POST') {
       if (isset($_POST['notes']) && !empty($_POST['notes'])) {
         $notes = $_POST['notes'];
   ```

   There are a couple of things to understand about this code. First, you want to show the note-taking form only for active users, so I recommend both creating the form and handling its submission, just after the page content has been shown:

   ```
   if (isset($_SESSION['user_not_expired'])) {
     echo "<div>{$row['content']}</div>";
     // New code here.
   ```

   This way, the form's submission is checked only if the user is active. In keeping with my standard approach, when one script both displays and handles a form the script will first attempt to handle the form and then display it.

   As for the validation, in a site like this where the content may be technical, it's possible, if not probable, that the user will submit notes with code in it. For this reason, I'm not applying **strip_tags()** to the submitted notes, but I'll absolutely want to make sure the notes are escaped properly when outputted.

**tip**

The downloadable code from www.LarryUllman.com will reflect the added code.

3. Store the notes in the database (**Figure 12.6** on the next page):

   ```
   $q = "REPLACE INTO notes (user_id, page_id, note) VALUES
   ➥($user_id, $page_id, '" . escape_data($notes, $dbc) . "')";
   $r = mysqli_query($dbc, $q);
   if (mysqli_affected_rows($dbc) > 0) {
     echo '<div class="alert alert-success">Your notes have been
     ➥saved.</div>';
   }
   ```

As an extra security measure, considering the lack of good validation or tag stripping, you may want to use prepared statements here. I'll talk more about prepared statements later in the chapter.

I'm also presuming that the user ID and page ID variables have already been validated by the script by this point.

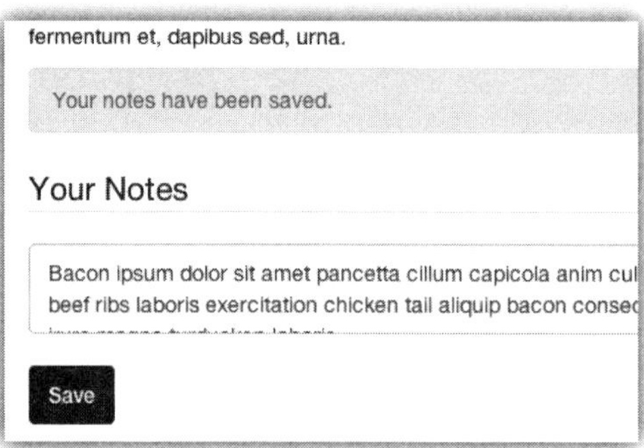


**Figure 12.6**

To verify a positive result, you need to make sure that the number of affected rows is positive. When you perform a **REPLACE** query, unlike with an **INSERT** query the number of affected rows may not be 1 (it's a MySQL quirk).

4. Complete the form submission conditionals:

```
   }
}
```

I'm not doing any error reporting on the form's submission. If the form is submitted with an empty notes field, the submission is just ignored.

5. Retrieve the user's current notes for that page:

```
if (!isset($notes)) {
   $q = "SELECT note FROM notes WHERE user_id=$user_id AND
   ➥page_id=$page_id";
   $r = mysqli_query($dbc, $q);
   if (mysqli_num_rows($r) === 1) {
      list($notes) = mysqli_fetch_array($r, MYSQLI_NUM);
   }
}
```

The **$notes** variable will be set if the form was just submitted. In that case, there's no need to pull the notes from the database. If that variable is *not* set, then the notes should be retrieved from the database for the current user and the current page.

6. Begin a form and a textarea:

```
echo '<form action="page.php ?id=' . $page_id . '" method="post"
➥accept-charset="utf-8">
<fieldset><legend>Your Notes</legend>
<textarea name="notes" class="form-control">';
```

Notice that the form's **action** attribute must pass along the page ID in the URL; otherwise, access will be denied when the form is submitted (because the script needs to receive a page ID in the URL).

7. Display the current notes (**Figure 12.7**):

```
if (isset($notes) && !empty($notes)) echo
➥htmlspecialchars($notes);
```

The user's current notes, if there are any, will be placed between the textarea tags.

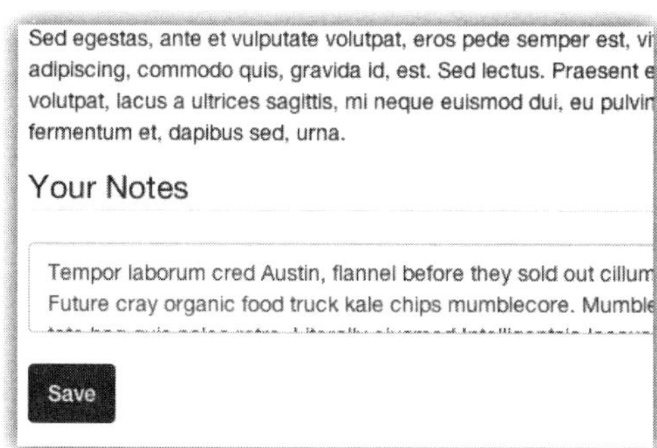


**Figure 12.7**

8. Complete the form:

```
echo '</textarea><br>
<input type="submit" name="submit_button" value="Save"
➥id="submit_button" class="btn btn-default" />
</fieldset>
</form>';
```

9. Save the script and test in your browser.

## SEARCH ENGINE OPTIMIZATION

Search engine optimization (SEO) is a big topic, but I want to mention one suggestion here. A logical change to how this site's content is displayed comes from changing the URLs for the content pages. As it stands, the site's URLs will look like **category.php?id=1**, **category.php?id=2**, **page.php?id=49**, **page.php?id=1239**, and so forth. These URLs are functional but not descriptive. From a search engine's perspective, it'd be much better if you were to put the title of the content in the URL, as the URL can have a weight in calculating the content's search engine relevance. But the site will still need those ID values, so the ideal URLs might look like (with each preceded by *www.example.com/*)

- category/id/1/General-Web-Security
- category/id/2/PHP-Security
- page/id/49/Using-Firewalls
- page/id/1239/Preventing-XSS-Attacks

You can easily create links in this format by using the proper PHP code:

```
echo "<div><h4><a href=\"page/id/{$row['id']}/" . urlencode($row['title'])
➥. "\">{$row['title']}</a></h4>...
```

This creates links in a better format, but the web server needs to be told how to read these links. That's accomplished using mod_rewrite (for the Apache web server). When you define certain mod_rewrite rules, behind the scenes the web server can turn **category/id/1/General-Web-Security** into **category.php?id=1&title=General-Web-➥Security**. This script will then still have access to **$_GET['id']** but the user—and search engines—see prettier URLs. Creating pretty URLs using mod_rewrite is covered in Chapter 7, "Second Site: Structure and Design."

The big catch relative to search engines and this site is that almost all of the content is behind a paywall: the content is only visible to paid viewers. It's not possible for Google, or any other search engine, to index your site's content. If you search online, you'll find various discussions as to how you can handle this particular situation.

# SECURITY IMPROVEMENTS

As I explained in Chapter 2, "Security Fundamentals," you have to find the right level of security for the application at hand. Implicit in this statement is that you can always make a site more secure. To that end, I want to put forth two security improvements you can make to bump up the level of security in the "Knowledge Is Power" site. The first is to make the switch to using prepared statements for all your queries. The second is a different way of handling forgotten passwords. Both changes are ones I recommend you consider implementing in any project you have.

## Using Prepared Statements

The code in Part 2, "Selling Virtual Products," builds up queries by interspersing SQL and PHP variables. If done properly—if you validate data and run strings through an escaping function like **mysqli_real_escape_string()**—this approach can be perfectly secure. However, if you make a mistake you leave yourself vulnerable to SQL injection attacks.

An alternative approach is to use prepared statements whenever potentially unsafe data might be used in a query. Prepared statements are not inherently more secure than the alternative, but they're much more forgiving. With prepared statements, you should still properly validate your data, but if you make a mistake or get careless, your database will remain protected.

Chapter 7 explains how prepared statements are executed in PHP. If you need more of an explanation of the mechanics, see that chapter. Here, let's quickly look at how you'd convert some of the "Knowledge Is Power" queries to use prepared statements.

**note**

Chapter 11 specifically uses prepared statements on the administrative side of the site, if you'd like to see other examples.

When the user registers (using **register.php**), the following code is executed:

```
$q = "INSERT INTO users (username, email, pass, first_name,
➥last_name, date_expires) VALUES ('$u', '$e', '"  .
➥password_hash($p, PASSWORD_BCRYPT) .  "', '$fn', '$ln',
➥SUBDATE(NOW(), INTERVAL 1 DAY) )";
$r = mysqli_query($dbc, $q);
if (mysqli_affected_rows($dbc) === 1) {
```

To convert that to a prepared statement, replace all references to variables with question marks:

```
$q = "INSERT INTO users (username, email, pass, first_name,
➥last_name, date_expires) VALUES (?, ?, ?, ?, ?, SUBDATE(NOW(),
➥INTERVAL 1 DAY) )";
```

Next, you prepare the query:

```
$stmt = mysqli_prepare($dbc, $q);
```

Then you associate the PHP variables with the placeholders (the question marks in the query):

```
mysqli_stmt_bind_param($stmt, 'sssss', $u, $e, $pass, $fn, $ln);
```

Finally, you execute the query and confirm the results:

```
$pass = password_hash($p, PASSWORD_BCRYPT);
mysqli_stmt_execute($stmt);
if (mysqli_stmt_affected_rows($stmt) === 1) {
  mysqli_stmt_close();
  // Other code
```

Hopefully this should be fairly straightforward. All of the data will have been previously validated and assigned to variables (that code would be unchanged). The prepared statement uses five question marks in place of these variables. (As a reminder, the question marks are not placed within quotes, even those that represent string values.) The variables are then bound to the parameters. As the password needs to be hashed, that's addressed next, assigning the result to the corresponding bound variable. Finally, the statement is executed, its number of affected rows is checked, and the statement is closed.

These lines of code do not constitute a big change, and prepared statements are more protective should you have an oversight in your code (such as in a validation routine). If you have any trouble getting this, or any prepared statement, to work, you can use this line of code to see if any errors occurred:

```
mysqli_stmt_execute($stmt);
if (!$stmt) echo mysqli_stmt_error($stmt);
```

As another example, the administrator's **add_page.php** script uses both strings and an integer:

```
$q = "INSERT INTO pages (categories_id, title, description, content)
➥VALUES ($cat, '$t', '$d', '$c')";
$r = mysqli_query($dbc, $q);
if (mysqli_affected_rows($dbc) === 1) {
```

Here's the conversion of that:

```
$q = " INSERT INTO pages (categories_id, title, description,
➥content) VALUES (?, ?, ?, ?)";
$stmt = mysqli_prepare($dbc, $q);
mysqli_stmt_bind_param($stmt, 'isss', $cat, $t, $d, $c);
mysqli_stmt_execute($stmt);
if (mysqli_stmt_affected_rows($stmt) === 1) {
   mysqli_stmt_close();
   // Other code
```

Hopefully this simple code switch should make perfect sense.

As a final example, let's look at the login process. The query executed there uses potentially unsafe data in a **SELECT** query. When the user logs in, the following code is executed (from `login.inc.php`):

```
$q = "SELECT id, username, type, pass, IF(date_expires >= NOW(),
➥true, false) AS expired FROM users WHERE email='$e'";
$r = mysqli_query($dbc, $q);
if (mysqli_num_rows($r) === 1) {
   $row = mysqli_fetch_array($r, MYSQLI_ASSOC);
```

Using prepared statements, it would now begin like this:

```
$q = "SELECT id, username, type, pass, IF(date_expires >= NOW(),
➥true, false) AS expired FROM users WHERE email=?";
$stmt = mysqli_prepare($dbc, $q);
mysqli_stmt_bind_param($stmt, 's', $e);
mysqli_stmt_execute($stmt);
mysqli_stmt_store_result($stmt);
if (mysqli_stmt_num_rows($stmt) === 1) {
```

The use of the `email` variable in that query is an *inbound* parameter: a variable's value is used in a SQL command. All of the other examples to this point have *also* used inbound parameters. But this query fetches results, so you can use *outbound* parameters to get those results into PHP variables. Here's what would come next, after checking that one row was returned:

```
mysqli_stmt_bind_result($stmt, $user_id, $username, $type, $pass,
➥$expired);
mysqli_stmt_fetch($stmt);
mysqli_stmt_close($stmt);
```

After those lines of code have been executed, you can use the **$user_id**, **$username**, **$type**, **$pass**, and **$expired** variables.

## Resetting Passwords More Securely

In Chapter 4, "User Accounts," the **forgot_password.php** script was developed. The script emails users a new, temporary password when they can't get into the site. As mentioned at the time, there are a couple of downsides to that approach. First, it allows anyone to reset anyone else's password simply by submitting an email address to the form. Second, it transmits the temporary password via email, which is less secure.

An alternative, and more secure, approach is not to touch the user's current password at all. Instead, offer to the user a temporary, onetime access code that gets the user into the site, at which point the user can change her password. If the user didn't make the "forgot password" request, or made it in error, the email message can be ignored.

To implement this approach, begin by creating a new database table:

```
CREATE TABLE access_tokens (
`user_id` INT UNSIGNED NOT NULL,
`token` CHAR(64) NOT NULL,
`date_expires` DATETIME NOT NULL,
PRIMARY KEY (`user_id`),
UNIQUE (`token`)
) ENGINE=InnoDB DEFAULT CHARSET=utf8;
```

This table will store access tokens. Each token must be unique, will be associated with a specific user, and will be good only for a short amount of time.

Next, you'll need to make a series of changes to the **forgot_password.php** script. Let's walk through those changes:

1. Open **forgot_password.php** in your text editor or IDE.

2. Delete all the code that creates a new password and emails it to the user.

   You'll be replacing all the code between these two lines:

   ```
   if (empty($pass_errors)) { // If everything's OK.
   } // End of empty($pass_errors) IF.
   ```

3. Within the now empty block (referenced in Step 2), begin by creating a token:

   ```
   $token = openssl_random_pseudo_bytes(32);
   $token = bin2hex($token);
   ```

   The **openssl_random_psuedo_bytes()** function, added to PHP in version 5.3, creates a reasonably random string of bytes. Its first argument is the length, in bytes, that the output should be. I'm using 32 for that value, which equates to a string 64 characters long after running the bytes through **bin2hex()**. That function is necessary because **openssl_random_pseudo_bytes()** returns binary data, which is not usable in the email to be sent to the user.

4. Store the token in the database:

   ```
   $q = 'REPLACE INTO access_tokens (user_id, token, date_expires)
   ➥VALUES (?, ?, DATE_ADD(NOW(), INTERVAL 15 MINUTE))';
   $stmt = mysqli_prepare($dbc, $q);
   mysqli_stmt_bind_param($stmt, 'is', $uid, $token);
   mysqli_stmt_execute($stmt);
   if (mysqli_stmt_affected_rows($stmt) === 1) {
   ```

   The token then needs to be stored in the database, associated with the user's ID, and set to last for a short interval. You'll see that I used a prepared statement to do that. The **REPLACE** command ensures that only one token can exist per user.

   Previous to this code, the user's ID was already fetched using the submitted email address from the form.

5. Create the reset URL:

   ```
   $url = 'https://' . BASE_URL . 'reset.php?t=' . $token;
   ```

   The URL will be something like https://example.com/reset.php?t= 47466 1eee4ea561d483e5bda313e7067a150be399f7d828ce9bd3d2733f94d69. This is the page the user will be taken to after clicking a link in an email (should the password reset be needed).

6. Send the email:

   ```
   $body = "This email is in response to a forgotten password reset
   ➥request at 'Knowledge is Power'. If you did make this request,
   ➥click the following link to be able to access your account:
   $url
   For security purposes, you have 15 minutes to do this. If you do
   ➥not click this link within 15 minutes, you'll need to request a
   ➥password reset again.
   ```

   *(continues on next page)*

```
If you have _not_ forgotten your password, you can safely ignore
➥this message and you will still be able to login with your
➥existing password. ";
mail($email, 'Password Reset at Knowledge is Power', $body,
➥'FROM: ' . CONTACT_EMAIL);
```

Now that the token has been stored in the database, it needs to be emailed to the user. The email provides clear instructions, including the fact that the user can also ignore this email (**Figure 12.8**).

Figure 12.8

7. Display a message and complete the page (**Figure 12.9**):

```
echo '<h1>Reset Your Password</h1><p>You will receive an access
➥code via email. Click the link in that email to gain access
➥to the site. Once you have done that, you may then change your
➥password.</p>';
include('./includes/footer.html');
exit();
```

# Reset Your Password

You will receive an access code via email. Click the link in that email to gain access to the site. Once you have done that, you may then change your password.

Figure 12.9

8. Complete the conditional begun in Step 3:

```
} else { // If it did not run OK.
   trigger_error('Your password could not be changed due to a
   ➥system error. We apologize for any inconvenience.');
}
```

**9.** Save the script and test in your browser.

The last step is to create **reset.php**. Its logic will be a bit more complex because it has to do the following:

- Verify the token received in the URL
- Present a form to change the password
- Handle the change password form

Let's walk through that script in detail:

**1.** Create a new PHP script in your text editor or IDE to be named **reset.php**.

**2.** Begin with the standard stuff:

```
<?php
require('./includes/config.inc.php');
require(MYSQL);
$page_title = 'Reset Your Password';
include('./includes/header.html');
```

**3.** Create two variables for storing errors:

```
$reset_error = '';
$pass_errors = array();
```

The **$reset_error** variable will be used to represent an error specifically related to the reset part of the process. For example, it'll indicate if no, or an invalid, token is received by the script. The **$pass_error** array will be used for the validation of the change password form.

**4.** Check for the token in the URL:

```
if (isset($_GET['t']) && (strlen($_GET['t']) === 64) ) {
   $token = $_GET['t'];
```

The very first time this script is accessed, it will be passed a token in the URL (after the user has clicked the link in the email). This conditional checks for the presence of that variable. As an additional but simple test, it also confirms that the variable's value is 64 characters long.

**5.** Fetch the user ID:

```
$q = 'SELECT user_id FROM access_tokens WHERE token=? AND
➥date_expires > NOW()';
$stmt = mysqli_prepare($dbc, $q);
mysqli_stmt_bind_param($stmt, 's', $token);
mysqli_stmt_execute($stmt);
```

*(continues on next page)*

```
mysqli_stmt_store_result($stmt);
if (mysqli_stmt_num_rows($stmt) === 1) {
   mysqli_stmt_bind_result($stmt, $user_id);
   mysqli_stmt_fetch($stmt);
```

A prepared statement is being used to fetch the stored user ID that matches the given token. Notice that two conditions apply in the query: The token has to exist in the table and the token's expiration date must be after the current time. This process uses both inbound and outbound parameters.

In theory, a hacker could attempt to get into the site by requesting a password reset and then trying to guess the random, 64-character long string. Although this is unlikely to be a problem, for extra security, you can have the reset page prompt the user with a predetermined security question before allowing her in.

**6.** Regenerate the session ID and store the user ID in the session:

```
session_regenerate_id(true);
$_SESSION['user_id'] = $user_id;
```

**7.** Clear the token from the database:

```
$q = 'DELETE FROM access_tokens WHERE token=?';
$stmt = mysqli_prepare($dbc, $q);
mysqli_stmt_bind_param($stmt, 's', $token);
mysqli_stmt_execute($stmt);
```

Now the token can't be reused.

**8.** If the query did not retrieve a user ID, create an error message:

```
} else {
   $reset_error = 'Either the provided token does not match that
   ➥on file or your time has expired. Please resubmit the "Forgot
   ➥your password?" form.';
}
```

This **else** clause applies if the conditional in Step 5 is false. That could be because the token doesn't exist in the database or because it exists but has expired (**Figure 12.10**).

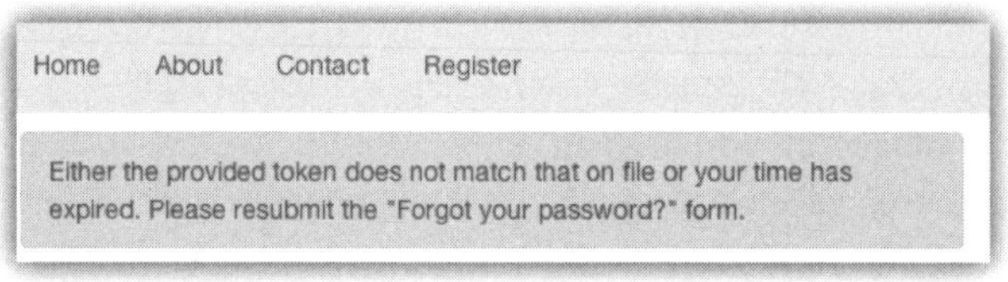

**Figure 12.10**

9. Complete the `$_GET['t']` conditional:

```
} else { // No token!
   $reset_error = 'This page has been accessed in error.';
}
```

If no `$_GET['t']` exists, or its value isn't 64 characters long, this **else** clause applies. This is an import default case for the page, since the `$reset_error` variable will be used as an indicator later in the script as to whether it's safe to show the change password form.

10. Check for the form submission:

```
if (($_SERVER['REQUEST_METHOD'] === 'POST') &&
➥isset($_SESSION['user_id'])) {
   $reset_error = '';
```

This conditional should apply after the user has submitted the change password form (on this same page). As an extra safety check, the conditional also confirms that the user's ID has previously been stored in the session. That check prevents someone from trying to submit form data to this script without having previously gone through the reset process.

If both conditions are true, the `$reset_error` variable is cleared. This change will mean it's safe to display the form (in case the user has submitted the form but has made a mistake).

11. Validate the passwords:

```
if (preg_match('/^(\w*(?=\w*\d)(?=\w*[a-z])(?=\w*[A-Z])\w*)
➥{6,}$/', $_POST['pass1']) ) {
   if ($_POST['pass1'] == $_POST['pass2']) {
      $p = $_POST['pass1'];
   } else {
      $pass_errors['pass2'] = 'Your password did not match the
      ➥confirmed password!';
   }
} else {
   $pass_errors['pass1'] = 'Please enter a valid password!';
}
```

This code is the same as in `change_password.php`.

12. If there were no errors, update the password in the database:

```
if (empty($pass_errors)) {
   $q = 'UPDATE users SET pass=? WHERE id=? LIMIT 1';
   $stmt = mysqli_prepare($dbc, $q);
```

*(continues on next page)*

```
mysqli_stmt_bind_param($stmt, 'si', $pass,
➥$_SESSION['user_id']);
$pass = password_hash($p, PASSWORD_BCRYPT);
mysqli_stmt_execute($stmt);
```

This code is similar to that already explained for using prepared statements in the registration process. You'll notice that the password is hashed, and assigned to the **$pass** variable, before being stored.

**13.** If the query worked, complete the page (**Figure 12.11**):

```
if (mysqli_stmt_affected_rows($stmt) === 1) {
   echo '<h1>Your password has been changed.</h1>';
   include('./includes/footer.html');
   exit();
```

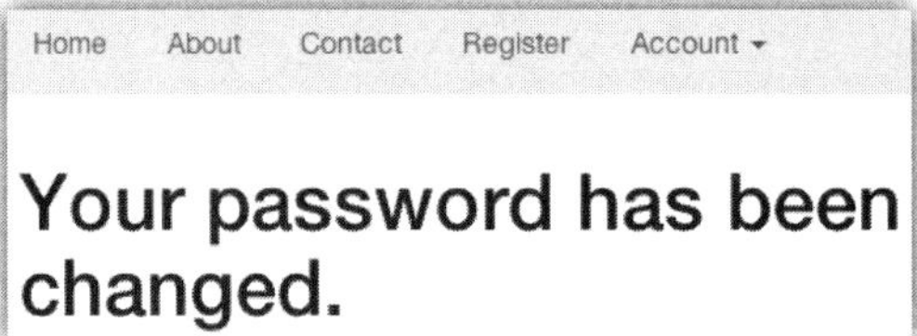


**Figure 12.11**

The page is completed so that the form isn't shown again. You might want to also send an email to the user confirming the change (as a security precaution).

**14.** Complete the remaining conditionals:

```
      } else { // If it did not run OK.
         trigger_error('Your password could not be changed due to
         ➥a system error. We apologize for any inconvenience.');
      }
   } // End of empty($pass_errors) IF.
} elseif ($_SERVER['REQUEST_METHOD'] === 'POST') {
   $reset_error = 'This page has been accessed in error.';
} // End of the form submission conditional.
```

The first **else** clause applies if the **UPDATE** query failed. The **elseif** applies if the method is POST but no user ID exists in the session. That would be the case if a hacker submitted data to the site without having gone through the reset process first.

**15.** If it's safe to change the password, begin the form:

```
if (empty($reset_error)) {
   require_once('./includes/form_functions.inc.php');
   echo '<h1>Change Your Password</h1>
   <p>Use the form below to change your password.</p>
   <form action="reset.php" method="post"
   ➥accept-charset="utf-8">';
```

The **$reset_errors** variable is being used to indicate whether the user should be allowed to change her password. If this variable still has an empty value—if it hasn't been assigned an error message—then the form will be shown. The form itself will be exactly like that in **change_password.php**, without requiring the original password (**Figure 12.12**).

**Figure 12.12**

**16.** Complete the form:

```
create_form_input('pass1', 'password', 'Password',
➥$pass_errors);
echo '<span class="help-block">Must be at least 6 characters
➥long, with at least one lowercase letter, one uppercase letter,
➥and one number.</span>';
create_form_input('pass2', 'password', 'Confirm Password',
➥$pass_errors);
echo '<input type="submit" name="submit_button" value="Change
➥&rarr;" id="submit_button" class="btn btn-default" />
</form>';
```

17. Complete the conditional begun in Step 15:

```
} else {
   echo '<div class="alert alert-danger">' . $reset_error .
   ➥'</div>';
}
```

This is where any reset-related error would be shown (as in Figure 12.10).

18. Complete the page:

```
include('./includes/footer.html');
?>
```

19. Save the script and test it in your browser.

You'll need to begin the process by first completing the "forgot password" form. Then click the link in the email.

## ADDING USER INFORMATION TO PDFS

The PDF content displayed on the site presumably took some work to put together. Fortunately, it's only available to be read by paid subscribers, so the business will get some money back for its effort. Unfortunately, a PDF being viewed in the user's web browser can also be downloaded to the user's machine (technically, it's already on the computer). This means less ethical users can pass your PDFs along to others or put them online where anyone can read them. That would be a copyright violation, of course, but you'd have to know it happened to catch it, and then you'd have to legally pursue the matter.

You can dissuade users from doing this by embedding the user's personal information in the PDF itself. For example, when the user views a PDF, you could write her email address and name at the top and bottom of each page. This way, if the user felt like sharing the PDF with others, she'd have to be comfortable with whoever receives the PDF seeing her name and address. Plus, you'd have clear proof of who violated the terms of the agreement.

On the other hand, the honest users may not like this, and it'll require much more programming and server processing to write the user information to each PDF displayed on the fly. Also, tricks like these can be circumvented, so even all this effort won't necessarily be foolproof.

# ADMINISTRATIVE CHANGES

As written, there's not much to the administration of the site: An administrator can add HTML content and PDFs. The chapters don't show how to update or delete content, because both are simple concepts. Updating content is very similar to the sticky forms, except that the first time the form is loaded, it must validate the ID received in the URL and retrieve the current values from the database.

I also haven't implemented a system for viewing user information, although that's easily done (just perform the authentication for the administrator, and then run a **SELECT** query on the **users** table). Be careful about what user information is viewable by whom, though, as your user's data is one of the most sensitive pieces of information used in this example.

There are four other possible additions that I'm going to explain in a bit more detail, however.

## Making Recommendations

Implementing a recommendations system is a fantastic way to encourage people to use your site and increase your business. Whether it's something like Netflix— which recommends titles based on your body of ratings and viewing history—or like Amazon—which recommends related and alternative products to those you're looking at, that are in your cart, or that you just purchased—there's a lot you can do with recommendations. Designing the logic for a recommendations system may take some effort, though.

**tip**

Check out some of the public recommendations in this chapter for how you can use customer feedback to present extra value to other customers.

In one such implementation, you can have the administrator making the recommendations: For each page, the administrator uses a drop-down menu (which allows for multiple selections) to associate related content. You then create a **recommendations** table that stores for each page an ID of other recommended pages:

```
CREATE TABLE recommendations (
`page_a` INT UNSIGNED NOT NULL,
`page_b` INT UNSIGNED NOT NULL,
PRIMARY KEY (`page_a`, `page_b`)
) ENGINE=InnoDB DEFAULT CHARSET=utf8;
```

Using that table structure, each related (recommended) pair of pages will need to be recorded only once. Logically, if page Y is recommended when you're reading page X, then page X will likely be a good recommendation when you're reading page Y.

To get the recommended pages for the current page, use this query (**Figure 12.13**):

```
SELECT p.id, p.title FROM pages AS p, recommendations AS r WHERE
(r.page_a = $page_id AND r.page_b=p.id) OR
(r.page_b = $page_id AND r.page_a=p.id)
```

```
larryullman — Effortless E-commerce
mysql> SELECT p.id, p.title FROM pages AS p,
    -> recommendations AS r WHERE
    -> (r.page_a = 1 AND r.page_b=p.id) OR
    -> (r.page_b = 1 AND r.page_a=p.id);
+----+--------------------------------------+
| id | title                                |
+----+--------------------------------------+
|  2 | This is another Common Attack Article |
|  3 | Using a Firewall                     |
+----+--------------------------------------+
2 rows in set (0.00 sec)

mysql>
```

**Figure 12.13**

**note**

Allowing for recommendations across content types requires a more complex table structure.

In short, that query says: If the current page ID equals the **page_a** column in the **recommendations** table, then find the matching **page_b** records. If the current page ID equals the **page_b** column in the **recommendations** table, then find the matching **page_a** records.

An alternative way to implement a recommendation system is to base recommendations on the current user's rankings and the rankings of other users. For example, if user Alice gave page X five stars and page Y four stars, and user Bob gave page Y four stars, Bob *might* really like page X as well. Such a recommendation system can be more accurate than the administrator-created one, but it relies extensively on lots of data, sound logic, and filtering. The more accurately you can equate Bob's tastes to other users' tastes, the better you can make recommendations to Bob. This is what Netflix does, and it does so very well.

## Placing HTML Content in Multiple Categories

Just like a blog can file posts under multiple categories (and multiple tags), you may decide that some of your HTML content should be listed in multiple categories, too. That requirement would result in a many-to-many relationship between the **pages** and the **categories** tables. To address that new relationship, you have to take the **category_id** out of the **pages** table and use a junction table instead. That table is defined as

```
CREATE TABLE pages_categories (
`page_id` INT UNSIGNED NOT NULL,
`category_id` SMALLINT UNSIGNED NOT NULL,
PRIMARY KEY (`page_id`, `category_id`)
);
```

In this table you store one record for every unique combination of page and category.

In terms of the PHP code, you won't need to change the header file, which links to every category. The **SELECT** query there will still work. But the **category.php** page will now have to perform a join across **pages_categories** and **pages**:

```
SELECT id, title, description FROM pages, pages_categories WHERE
➥pages.id=pages_categories.page_id AND pages_categories.
➥category_id=' . $cat_id . ' ORDER BY date_created DESC
```

The **add_page.php** script will need to allow for multiple categories to be selected. That's accomplished by making the drop-down menu create an array (**Figure 12.14**):

```
<select name="category[]" class="form-control" multiple size="5">
```



**Figure 12.14**

Then, the handling part of the script has to validate that **$_POST['category']** has a **count()** greater than 0. And after the record is added to the **pages** table, you insert one record into **pages_categories** for each selected category.

**tip**

You'll also need to change the code that makes the categories menu sticky to allow for **$_POST['category']** being an array.

## Allowing for Content Drafts

Most CMS systems, such as WordPress, support the ability to create drafts of content. Drafts allow administrators to create new content within the system, without that content having to be live.

It's easy to convert the site as it stands to support drafts. First, add a **status** column to the **pages** table:

```
ALTER TABLE pages ADD COLUMN status ENUM('draft', 'live') AFTER
➥categories_id;
UPDATE pages SET status='live';
```

(The **UPDATE** query will be for the existing pages that are live.)

Next you want to add a status drop-down menu (or just a "live" checkbox) to the **add_page.php** form (**Figure 12.15**):

```
<div class="form-group">
<label for="status" class="control-label">Status</label>
<select name="status" class="form-control"><option
➥value="draft">Draft</option>
<option value="live">Live</option>
</select></div>
```

**Figure 12.15**

You use the value of that form element in the **INSERT** query (after validating all the data, of course):

```
INSERT INTO pages (categories_id, status, title, description,
➥content) VALUES ($cat, '$status', '$t', '$d', '$c')
```

Finally, change all your public-side queries so that they include only live content. That's accomplished by adding a **WHERE status='live'** clause to your queries. Here's the modified query for **category.php**:

```
SELECT id, title, description FROM pages WHERE categories_id=' .
➥$cat_id . ' AND status='live' ORDER BY date_created DESC
```

Note that this structure allows for multiple types of statuses, if that's helpful to you. For example, you can use **draft**, **pending**, **edited**, and **live**.

If you've also implemented the ability to associate content with multiple categories, add the **status** clause to that modified query instead.

## Supporting Multiple Types of Administrators

The site supports any number of administrators, but it doesn't do much in the way of acknowledging individual administrators. For example, the site doesn't reflect who authored a page of content. If you have multiple administrators, you may want to add a **user_id** column to the **pages** and **pdfs** tables to store which administrator added that content to the system. You might then allow only the original creator of some content to update or delete it.

If you want to support multiple *types* of administrators, you'll need to make more changes. First, change the structure to create a separate table that lists the possible user types:

```
CREATE TABLE user_types (
`id` SMALLINT UNSIGNED NOT NULL,
`type` VARCHAR(20) NOT NULL,
PRIMARY KEY (`id`),
UNIQUE (`type`)
) ENGINE=InnoDB DEFAULT CHARSET=utf8;
```

I haven't set the primary key column as an auto-increment there, because I'll likely set it on a per-type basis:

```
INSERT INTO user_types VALUES
(1, 'member'),
(50, 'author'),
(100, 'editor'),
(150, 'admin');
```

The numeric values there will be significant, and by spacing them out, you'll be able to add shades of user types later on (such as variations of members or authors).

Next, change the **users** table:

```
ALTER TABLE users MODIFY type SMALLINT UNSIGNED NOT NULL;
```

Then, update all your user records to make every user the right type.

Turning to the code, you'll first want to record the user level in the session upon login (from **login.inc.php**):

```
$q = "SELECT id, username, type, pass, IF(date_expires >= NOW(),
➥true, false) AS expired FROM users WHERE email='$e'";
$r = mysqli_query($dbc, $q);
if (mysqli_num_rows($r) === 1) {
   $row = mysqli_fetch_array($r, MYSQLI_ASSOC);
   if (password_verify($p, $row['pass'])) {
      $_SESSION['user_type'] = $row['type'];
```

Next, create a new function that denies access to content if a minimum type level is not reached. With the current site implementation, **redirect_invalid_user()** just checks for the existence of certain session variables to deny or allow access to content, so that function isn't suitable for checking user levels.

Here's how I define such a function:

```
function is_valid_user_type($user_level = 0, $required = 50) {
   if ($user_level >= $required) {
      return true;
   } else {
      return false;
   }
}
```

On a script such as **page.php**, any user can access that page (although only active users can view the content). No change is required in scripts like **page.php**.

**tip**

Creating constants for the various user levels allows you to get rid of the "magic numbers" like 50 in the **is_valid_user_type()** call.

However, the **add_page.php** script will be restricted to authors and above:

```
if (is_valid_user_type($_SESSION['user_type'], 50)) {
   // Safe.
} else {
   // Redirect or show error and terminate.
}
```

If you create an **edit_page.php** script, you can use this function to allow any editor or administrator to view the page. You also want to grant access to the author of the page being edited:

```
if (is_valid_user_type($_SESSION['user_type'], 100) ||
➥($author_id === $_SESSION['user_id'])) {
   // Safe.
} else {
   // Redirect or show error and terminate.
}
```

That code does assume that you've pulled the author ID (associated with the page record) from the database as well.

# IMPLEMENTING PAYPAL PDT

One more way you could improve the "Knowledge Is Power" site is to implement PayPal's Payment Data Transfer (PDT) feature. PDT is a secure way to fetch the details of an order from PayPal. It's quite similar to the Instant Payment Notification (IPN) process already in use by the site, in theory, but when and how you'd use PDT does differ slightly.

**note**

Remember that IPN is used only if you've provided an IPN URL in your PayPal account.

With IPN, a PHP script on your server is accessed when transactions occur involving your PayPal account. Because PayPal's request of the IPN script occurs behind the scenes (neither you nor the customer sees it), it's a great way to validate that an order succeeded. The possible downside to just using IPN is that when the customer is returned to your site after making the purchase at PayPal, you cannot immediately confirm the purchase with the customer (and credit the account). You can resolve that issue by using PDT to confirm the transaction on the customer's destination page.

The PDT process is much the same as the IPN process. First you verify that a transaction ID was received. Then you make a cURL request of PayPal, providing certain values (including the transaction ID). The request returns the details of the transaction. You can then use that information to show it to the customer, update the database, or whatever.

I'll explain the complete process in this update of the **thanks.php** script. That's the page that the customer will be returned to after visiting PayPal. A PDT script will be created that confirms an order and immediately updates the database, just in case the IPN hasn't taken place yet.

First, though, you have to enable PDT.

## Enabling PDT

As with everything related to PayPal, these steps are subject to change.

To use PDT, you must first tell PayPal you intend to use it:

1. Log in to the PayPal Sandbox or actual PayPal.

   If you're in test mode, you'd log into the Sandbox. If you're live, head to real PayPal.

2. Click Profile > My Selling Tools.
3. Click the Update link for the Website preferences.
4. On the subsequent page, make sure Auto Return For Website Payments is on.

   PDT requires this option to be on.

5. Provide a return URL (**Figure 12.16**).

   This value should point to your **`thanks.php`** script.

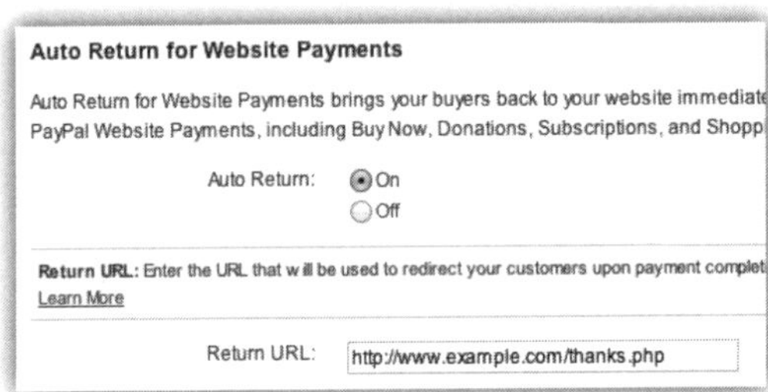


Figure 12.16

6. Further down the page, turn Payment Data Transfer on (**Figure 12.17**).

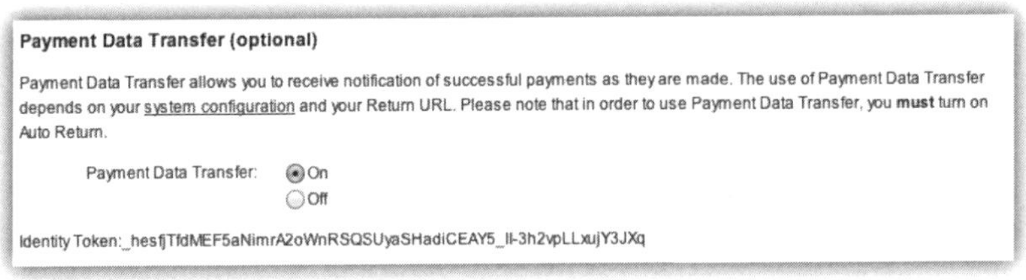

**Payment Data Transfer (optional)**

Payment Data Transfer allows you to receive notification of successful payments as they are made. The use of Payment Data Transfer depends on your system configuration and your Return URL. Please note that in order to use Payment Data Transfer, you **must** turn on Auto Return.

Payment Data Transfer: On / Off

Identity Token: _hesfjTfdMEF5aNimrA2oWnRSQSUyaSHadiCEAY5_lI-3h2vpLLxujY3JXq

Figure 12.17

7. Click Save at the bottom of the page.

8. Return to the Update Website preferences page and make note of your identity token value, under Payment Data Transfer (see Figure 12.17).

   This value is generated when you enable PDT. You'll need this when you create the script.

## Using PDT

Now that PDT is enabled, you can write a script that makes use of it. To keep things clean, you'll write a separate script and then have **thanks.php** include it. The purpose of this new script is to verify the order and update the database for that order, if it hasn't been updated already. In other words, either the IPN script or the PDT script—whichever is called first—will record the order in the database.

1. Create a new PHP script in your text editor or IDE to be named **pdt.php** and stored in the **includes** folder:

   ```
   <?php
   ```

   This script will be included by **thanks.php**, so it won't need to include the configuration or other files itself.

2. Check that a transaction ID was provided in the URL:

   ```
   if (isset($_GET['tx'])) {
      $txn_id = $_GET['tx'];
   ```

   This script needs a transaction ID, which PayPal will pass in the URL, in order to function.

3. Initialize a cURL request handler:

   ```
   $ch = curl_init();
   ```

   Most of the cURL stuff will be quite similar to that in **ipn.php**.

4. Configure the cURL request:

   ```
   curl_setopt_array($ch, array (
      CURLOPT_URL => 'https://www.sandbox.paypal.com/cgi-bin/webscr',
      CURLOPT_POST => true,
      CURLOPT_POSTFIELDS => http_build_query(array (
         'cmd' => '_notify-synch',
         'tx' => $txn_id,
         'at' => PAYPAL_IDENTITY_TOKEN,
         )),
      CURLOPT_RETURNTRANSFER => true,
      CURLOPT_HEADER => false
   ));
   ```

 **tip**

Alternatively, you could define the live and test URLs in the configuration file so the URL is automatically changed when the site goes live.

As with IPN, these lines dictate the behavior of the cURL request. First, the **CURLOPT_URL** option is where you set the URL to be requested. In this case, the URL is the file on PayPal's system to which the confirmation request must be made. In test mode, that value is https://www.sandbox.paypal.com/cgi-bin/webscr. When the site goes live, the request will be made to just https://www.paypal.com/cgi-bin/webscr.

Second, setting **CURLOPT_POST** to **true** indicates that a POST request is to be made (that is, this script will make a POST request back to PayPal).

The third option, **CURLOPT_POSTFIELDS**, is where you provide data to be posted as part of the request (data to be sent to PayPal). For PDT, you must provide a **cmd** value of **_notify-synch**. You also need to provide the transaction ID and your unique identifier. Your unique identifier can be stored in a constant in your configuration file. As in the IPN script, I'm using the **http_build_query()** function to convert the array of values to a string of data.

The fourth setting, **CURLOPT_RETURNTRANSFER**, is set to **true**, indicating that the result of the cURL request should be returned as a string, not immediately displayed.

Finally, **CURLOPT_HEADER** is set to **false** to indicate that the header shouldn't be included in the output (the result of the request).

5. Perform the cURL request:

```
$response = curl_exec($ch);
```

   This is where the actual request of PayPal is performed. The result of that request will be assigned to the **$response** variable.

6. Get the status code of the cURL response:

```
$status = curl_getinfo($ch, CURLINFO_HTTP_CODE);
```

   To verify the response, the script will look at the HTTP status code returned by PayPal. That value is fetched using this code.

7. Close the cURL request:

```
curl_close($ch);
```

8. Check that the status code was 200:

```
if ($status === 200) {
```

   The HTTP status code is checked to confirm that the PayPal communication worked. If the status code was 404 or some such, the wrong URL was most likely used.

9. Start converting the response to a usable array:

```
$lines = explode("\n", urldecode($response));
$data = array();
$data['result'] = array_shift($lines);
```

If you just dump out the value of **$response**, you'll see that it's a long string, over multiple lines (**Figure 12.18**). To begin the conversion of that string to a more usable format, the string is turned into an array of lines by breaking the original string on the newline character. The **$lines** array, which is mostly of the format **name=value**, will still need to be turned into a more usable format.

```
SUCCESS
transaction_subject=Knowledge+is+Power+Membership
payment_date=13%3A06%3A13+Sep+26%2C+2013+PDT
txn_type=subscr_payment
subscr_id=I-4EBG76KS3LL5
last_name=User
residence_country=US
item_name=Knowledge+is+Power+Membership
payment_gross=10.00
mc_currency=USD
business=seller_1281297018_biz%40mac.com
payment_type=instant
protection_eligibility=Ineligible
payer_status=unverified
payer_email=buyCC_1281297278_per%40mac.com
txn_id=1SR14990Y82068008
receiver_email=seller_1281297018_biz%40mac.com
first_name=Test
payer_id=6EFB727KZ7R56
receiver_id=MAGDFTY3H6XU8
payment_status=Completed
payment_fee=0.59
mc_fee=0.59
mc_gross=10.00
custom=38904
charset=windows-1252
```

**Figure 12.18**

But before that's done, the first line is the SUCCESS/FAIL message. I'm going to take this line from the array, using the **array_shift()** function. That function returns the first value of an array and removes it from the array. This returned value is assigned to **$data['result']**.

10. Convert the rest of the response to array elements:

```
foreach ($lines as $line) {
   if (stristr($line, '=')) {
      list ($k, $v) = explode('=', $line);
      $data[$k] = $v;
   }
}
```

The next step (**Figure 12.19**) is to loop through the rest of the **$lines** array and convert each **name=value** to **$data['name'] = value**.

```
Array
(
    [result] => SUCCESS
    [transaction_subject] => Knowledge is Power Membership
    [payment_date] => 13:12:06 Sep 26, 2013 PDT
    [txn_type] => subscr_payment
    [subscr_id] => I-DB81K36L6F8T
    [last_name] => User
    [residence_country] => US
    [item_name] => Knowledge is Power Membership
    [payment_gross] => 10.00
    [mc_currency] => USD
    [business] => seller_1281297018_biz@mac.com
    [payment_type] => instant
    [protection_eligibility] => Ineligible
    [payer_status] => unverified
    [payer_email] => buyCC_1281297278_per@mac.com
    [txn_id] => 0HR654900J034221F
    [receiver_email] => seller_1281297018_biz@mac.com
    [first_name] => Test
    [payer_id] => 6EFB727KZ7R56
    [receiver_id] => MAGDFTY3H6XU8
    [payment_status] => Completed
    [payment_fee] => 0.59
    [mc_fee] => 0.59
    [mc_gross] => 10.00
    [custom] => 38904
    [charset] => windows-1252
)
```

**Figure 12.19**

11. Check for the right values:

```
if ( ($data['result'] === 'SUCCESS')
&& isset($data['payment_status'])
&& ($data['payment_status'] === 'Completed')
&& ($data['receiver_email'] === 'seller_1281297018_biz@mac.com')
&& ($data['mc_gross'] == 10.00)
&& ($data['mc_currency'] === 'USD')
) {
```

As on the IPN script, just looking for a response of SUCCESS isn't sufficient. For the transaction to be official enough to warrant updating the site's database, several other qualities should exist. For starters, **payment_status** needs to equal **Completed**, because there will be other possible statuses that don't warrant changes (such as **Pending**). You should confirm that the payment was received by the proper email address (the one that matches the e-commerce site's merchant PayPal account). This check prevents the site from taking action based on a payment that didn't go to that merchant (because someone attempted a hack).

**note**

Make sure you use your actual PayPal-associated email address for the **receiver_email** comparison.

Next, the **mc_gross** and **mc_currency** values should match the gross cost and currency for the transaction.

This bit of code, and much of that to follow, closely mimics the IPN script.

**tip**

If you change any of your site's parameters, such as the cost of a subscription, you'll need to change this script, too.

**12.** Check for this transaction in the database:

```
$q = "SELECT id FROM orders WHERE transaction_id='$txn_id'";
$r = mysqli_query($dbc, $q);
if (mysqli_num_rows($r) === 0) {
```

This is a very important step here because the IPN script may or may not have already recorded the order and updated the database. You don't want to do that twice!

**13.** Add this transaction to the **orders** table:

```
$uid = (isset($_POST['custom'])) ? (int) $_POST['custom'] : 0;
$amount = (int) ($_POST['mc_gross'] * 100);
$q = "INSERT INTO orders (user_id, transaction_id,
➥payment_status, payment_amount) VALUES ($uid, '$txn_id',
➥'{$data['result']}', $amount)";
$r = mysqli_query($dbc, $q);
if (mysqli_affected_rows($dbc) === 1) {
```

The query is essentially the same as that in **ipn.php**. First, two values are made safe to use in a query. You'll see here a reference to **$_POST['custom']**, which is the user's ID originally stored in the **register.php** script, then passed to PayPal, and now returned as part of the transaction.

The **orders** table also records the transaction ID, payment status, and payment amount. Note that the payment amount in the database is stored in cents, so the received amount must be multiplied times 100.

**14.** Update the **users** table:

```
if ($uid > 0) {
   $q = "UPDATE users SET date_expires = IF(date_expires >
   ➥NOW(), ADDDATE(date_expires, INTERVAL 1 YEAR),
   ➥ADDDATE(NOW(), INTERVAL 1 YEAR)), date_modified=NOW()
   ➥WHERE id=$uid";
   $r = mysqli_query($dbc, $q);
   if (mysqli_affected_rows($dbc) !== 1) {
      trigger_error('The user\'s expiration date could not be
      ➥updated!');
   }
} // No user ID.
```

By this point, the script is ready to update the user's account, assuming a valid user ID was provided. To do that, an **UPDATE** query is run, providing a new value for both the **date_expires** column and **date_modified**. Again, this query is the same as that in **ipn.php**.

If one row wasn't affected by the query, an error is triggered. This is important, as it implies that a payment went through but no user was credited. And because the order was already recorded, if the IPN script is called after this one, it won't attempt to update the user's account.

**15.** Complete several conditionals:

```
            } else { // Problem inserting the order!
               trigger_error('The transaction could not be stored
               ➥in the orders table!');
         } // The order has already been stored, nothing to do!
      } // Not valid response.
   } // Can't confirm the PDT.
} // No $_GET['tx'].
```

In almost all of these cases, no further action is required. Remember that this is really a backup to the IPN script, which also watches for and handles the various potential problems.

**16.** Complete the script:

```
?>
```

**17.** Save the file.

To use this file, include it in **thanks.php**:

```
include('./includes/pdt.php');
```

You can include that line anywhere after the database connection script has been included.

# 13 EXTENDING THE SECOND SITE

As I explained at the beginning of Chapter 12, "Extending the First Site," I want this book to present the widest possible range of what e-commerce can be. To that end, I came up with a slew of possible topics. I selected the most appropriate ones to be used and explained in Part 3 of the book. In this chapter, I want to mention a few other ways you can extend and enhance the Coffee site.

I've organized these ideas into three categories:

- Public
- Administrative
- Structural

The majority of the chapter looks at the public side of the site, however. Although I haven't dedicated a section to security enhancements—security was treated quite seriously in this example already—you'll find a few more security-related suggestions scattered about. As with Chapter 12, some of these ideas will be explained in theory, others will be discussed along with a bit of code, and a few more will be fully implemented.

Finally, as I also mentioned in Chapter 12, remember that you can add components from any other chapter to the Coffee site. You can

- Decide to use PayPal, perhaps in conjunction with another payment provider (see Chapter 6, "Using PayPal")
- Allow for user management (see Chapter 4, "User Accounts")
- Develop support for multiple administrative types (see Chapter 12)

It all comes down to choosing the features and structure that match what you, or your client, imagine the site to be.

# PUBLIC SUGGESTIONS

Even though the public side of the Coffee site is well developed and feature-rich, there are still plenty of ways you could improve it. To start, let's look at receipts. If your payment provider isn't sending receipts for you, you ought to create that process yourself. Two ways receipts are commonly presented to customers are

- As a stripped-down web page that can be printed or saved
- As an email (normally an HTML one)

Let's go ahead and implement both of these procedures.

## Creating a Receipt Page

Most sites do offer a "printable" version of a receipt. All web pages are "printable," of course; what I'm talking about here is just a version of the HTML page that omits anything not germane to the receipt itself: images, links, JavaScript, and so forth. With the Coffee site, the receipt page should be something like what `view_order.php` displays (see Figure 11.13), but without the fancy header and footer. Let's create an in-browser receipt page now (**Figure 13.1**):

**tip**

You can also create a "printer-friendly" page by using a print-specific CSS stylesheet.

**Your Order**

**Order ID**: 14

**Order Date**: Tue Sep 10, 2013 at 11:16AM

**Customer Name**: Ullman, Larry

**Shipping Address**: 100 Main Street Anytown ID 75860

**Customer Email**: larryullman@gmail.com

**Customer Phone**: 1234567890

**Credit Card Number Used**: *6811

| Item | Quantity | Price | Subtotal |
|---|---|---|---|
| Mugs - Pretty Flower Coffee Mug | 2 | $6.50 | $13.00 |
| Kona - 1 lb. - caf - ground | 2 | $8.00 | $16.00 |
| | | **Shipping** | $8.22 |
| | | **Total** | $37.22 |

Figure 13.1

### MAKING THE CUSTOMER COMFORTABLE

One of the best general things you can add to the Coffee site is several obvious ways to contact the site's administrator or support team. You can do so by using a combination of a contact form, a help menu, a FAQ page, or a direct phone number. Make it easy, and as immediate as possible, for the customer to get help and answers to her questions.

1. Begin a new PHP script in your text editor or IDE to be named **receipt.php**.

2. Include the configuration file:

```
<?php
require('./includes/config.inc.php');
```

3. Validate the required parameters:

```
if (!isset($_GET['x'], $_GET['y']) || !filter_var($_GET['x'],
➥FILTER_VALIDATE_INT, array('min_range' => 1)) ||
➥(strlen($_GET['y']) !== 40) ) {
    $location = 'https://' . BASE_URL . 'index.php';
    header("Location: $location");
    exit();
} else {
    $order_id = $_GET['x'];
    $email_hash = $_GET['y'];
}
```

The **final.php** script terminates and wipes out the customer's session, so this script can't access any of the customer's information from the session. My solution is to pass to this page two values: the order ID and a hashed version of the customer's email address. Just passing the order ID wouldn't be sufficiently secure, as that would allow any user to view anyone else's order. For that reason, I'm also passing the customer's email address: the combination of the two is required to retrieve the order information. However, passing the email address in plain format would also be bad, so I use a simple **SHA1()** hash of it instead.

For a bit of obfuscation, the two values are passed in the URL as **x** and **y**.

This code performs a bit of basic validation on these two values and redirects the browser should the criteria not be met. The ultimate validation will be whether the two values match those already stored in the database.

4. Include the database connection and the header:

```
require(MYSQL);
include('./includes/plain_header.html');
```

You'll notice that this script includes a new header file, to be created in a couple of pages.

5. Define the query:

```
$q = 'SELECT FORMAT(total/100, 2) AS total, FORMAT(shipping/100,2)
➥AS shipping, credit_card_number, DATE_FORMAT(order_date, "%a
➥%b %e, %Y at %h:%i%p") AS od, email, CONCAT(last_name, ", ",
➥first_name) AS name, CONCAT_WS(" ", address1, address2, city,
➥state, zip) AS address, phone, CONCAT_WS(" - ", ncc.category,
➥ncp.name) AS item, quantity, FORMAT(price_per/100,2)
➥AS price_per FROM orders AS o INNER JOIN customers AS c
➥ON (o.customer_id = c.id) INNER JOIN order_contents AS oc
➥ON (oc.order_id = o.id) INNER JOIN non_coffee_products AS ncp
➥ON (oc.product_id = ncp.id AND oc.product_type="goodies")
➥INNER JOIN non_coffee_categories AS ncc ON (ncc.id =
➥ncp.non_coffee_category_id) WHERE o.id=? AND SHA1(email)=?
UNION
SELECT FORMAT(total/100, 2), FORMAT(shipping/100,2),
➥credit_card_number, DATE_FORMAT(order_date, "%a %b %e, %Y
➥at %l:%i%p"), email, CONCAT(last_name, ", ", first_name),
➥CONCAT_WS(" ", address1, address2, city, state, zip), phone,
➥CONCAT_WS(" - ", gc.category, s.size, sc.caf_decaf,
➥sc.ground_whole) AS item, quantity, FORMAT(price_per/100,2)
➥FROM orders AS o INNER JOIN customers AS c ON (o.customer_id
➥= c.id) INNER JOIN order_contents AS oc ON (oc.order_id = o.id)
➥INNER JOIN specific_coffees AS sc ON (oc.product_id = sc.id
➥AND oc.product_type="coffee") INNER JOIN sizes AS s ON
➥(s.id=sc.size_id) INNER JOIN general_coffees AS gc ON
➥(gc.id=sc.general_coffee_id) WHERE o.id=? AND SHA1(email)=?';
```

This query is a more stripped-down version of the query run on the **view_order.php** script. Unlike that query, this one doesn't retrieve the customer's ID number, the number of each item in stock, or the shipping date.

I'll use prepared statements for this query, in the **WHERE** clauses. One condition is a matching order ID. The second condition is that the **SHA1()** hash of the stored email address must match the provided email hash.

**note**

You can heighten the security of this process by choosing a more secure hashing algorithm than SHA1.

**Figure 13.2** shows the result of the query when run in the **mysql** client.

```
larryullman — Effortless E-commerce
*************************** 1. row ***************************
             total: 37.22
          shipping: 8.22
credit_card_number: 6811
                od: Tue Sep 10, 2013 at 11:16AM
             email: larryullman@gmail.com
              name: Ullman, Larry
           address: 100 Main Street  Anytown ID 75860
             phone: 1234567890
              item: Mugs - Pretty Flower Coffee Mug
          quantity: 2
         price_per: 6.50
*************************** 2. row ***************************
             total: 37.22
          shipping: 8.22
credit_card_number: 6811
                od: Tue Sep 10, 2013 at 11:16AM
             email: larryullman@gmail.com
              name: Ullman, Larry
           address: 100 Main Street  Anytown ID 75860
             phone: 1234567890
              item: Kona - 1 lb. - caf - ground
          quantity: 2
         price_per: 8.00
2 rows in set (0.00 sec)

mysql>
```

**Figure 13.2**

6. Prepare and execute the query:

```
$stmt = mysqli_prepare($dbc, $q);
mysqli_stmt_bind_param($stmt, 'isis', $order_id, $email_hash,
➥$order_id, $email_hash);
mysqli_stmt_execute($stmt);
```

Each variable is used twice in the query, so each must be bound twice.

7. Confirm the number of results returned:

```
mysqli_stmt_store_result($stmt);
if (mysqli_stmt_num_rows($stmt) > 0) {
   echo '<h3>Your Order</h3>';
```

Remember that you have to call the **mysqli_stmt_store_result()** function before calling **mysqli_stmt_num_rows()** when using prepared **SELECT** statements.

8. Bind the results to PHP variables and fetch the first row:

```
mysqli_stmt_bind_result($stmt, $total, $shipping, $cc_num,
➥$order_date, $email, $name, $address, $phone, $item, $quantity,
➥$price);
mysqli_stmt_fetch($stmt);
```

Except for the particulars of the prepared statement, most of the logic and code mimics that in **view_order.php**.

9. Display the general order information:

```
echo '<p><strong>Order ID</strong>: ' . $order_id . '</p>
➥<p><strong>Order Date</strong>: ' . $order_date . '</p>
➥<p><strong>Customer Name</strong>: ' . htmlspecialchars($name)
➥. '</p><p><strong>Shipping Address</strong>: ' .
➥htmlspecialchars($address) . '</p><p><strong>Customer Email
➥</strong>: ' . htmlspecialchars($email) . '</p><p><strong>
➥Customer Phone</strong>: ' . htmlspecialchars($phone) . '</p>
➥<p><strong>Credit Card Number Used</strong>: *' . $cc_num . '
➥</p>';
```

10. Create a table for showing the order details:

```
echo '<table border="0" cellspacing="3" cellpadding="3">
   <thead>
      <tr>
         <th align="center">Item</th>
         <th align="center">Quantity</th>
         <th align="right">Price</th>
         <th align="right">Subtotal</th>
      </tr>
   </thead>
   <tbody>';
```

**note**

Arguably, the table should be updated to use CSS, not HTML attributes, for its formatting.

11. Print each item:

```
do {
   echo '<tr>
      <td align="left">' . $item . '</td>
      <td align="center">' . $quantity . '</td>
      <td align="right">$' . $price . '</td>
      <td align="right">$' . number_format($price *
      ➥$quantity, 2) . '</td>
   </tr>';
} while (mysqli_stmt_fetch($stmt));
```

This is the same construction used in **view_order.php**. I'm adding the subtotal column here, though.

12. Add the shipping and the total:

```
echo '<tr>
   <td align="right" colspan="3"><strong>Shipping</strong></td>
   <td align="right">$' . $shipping . '</td>
</tr>';
```

*(continues on next page)*

```
echo '<tr>
   <td align="right" colspan="3"><strong>Total</strong></td>
   <td align="right">$' . $total . '</td>
</tr>';
```

13. Complete the table:

```
echo '</tbody></table>';
```

14. If no rows were returned, print an error:

```
} else {
   echo '<h3>Error!</h3><p>This page has been accessed in
   ➥error.</p>';
}
```

This will be the case if the provided values are incorrect, most likely because the values have been manipulated by a hacker.

15. Complete the page:

```
include('./includes/plain_footer.html');
?>
```

The **plain_footer.html** file, not the normal footer file, is included here.

16. Save the file.

You can't test this script yet, since the header and footer files don't exist. As for those, I went extremely minimal here. This is my plain header file:

```
<html><head><title>View Your Receipt</title><style type="text/css"
➥media="all">
  body {font-family:Tahoma, Geneva, sans-serif; font-size:100%;
  ➥line-height:.875em; color:#70635b;}
</style></head><body>
```

There's a reason I opted to combine all this HTML into one compressed format, with the CSS inline. I'll explain shortly.

The footer file just completes the body and HTML:

```
</body></html>
```

Create both of these and save them in the **includes** directory.

The last step is to update **final.html** (the view page that the customer sees as the last step) to create a proper link to **receipt.php** (**Figure 13.3**). You'll need to modify that code to pass along the correct values to the receipt page:

```
<a href="receipt.php?x=<?php echo $_SESSION['order_id'] . '&y=' .
➥sha1($_SESSION['email']); ?>">Click here</a>...
```

```
<h2>Your Order is Complete</h2>
n any correspondence with us.</p>
der ships. All orders are processed on the next business day. You will be contact
href="receipt.php?x=14&y=3f2a26679ca26f5e1696b1c6034f97862a7927bb">Click here</a>
```

Figure 13.3

You can reference the session at that point in the code because the session data isn't wiped out until after that view file is used.

Now you can test **receipt.php** in your browser by completing an order and then clicking the link to view the receipt.

## Emailing Receipts

The second type of receipt to be added is an email receipt. Because a lot of information could be in this receipt (itemizing multiple products), sending an HTML receipt is a logical choice. Considering that some people like HTML email and others don't, the professional solution is to send an email that's viewable in either HTML (**Figure 13.4**) or plain text format (**Figure 13.5**). That's what **email_receipt.php** will do. This script will be included by **final.php**.

tip

Most payment providers can send out confirmation emails, too, but you can't control the format as easily.

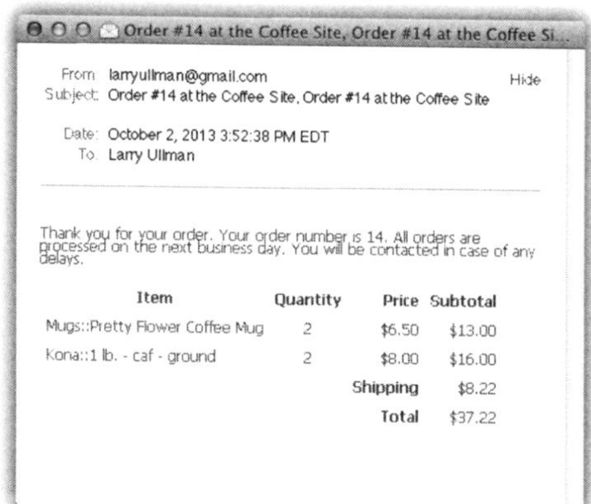


Figure 13.4

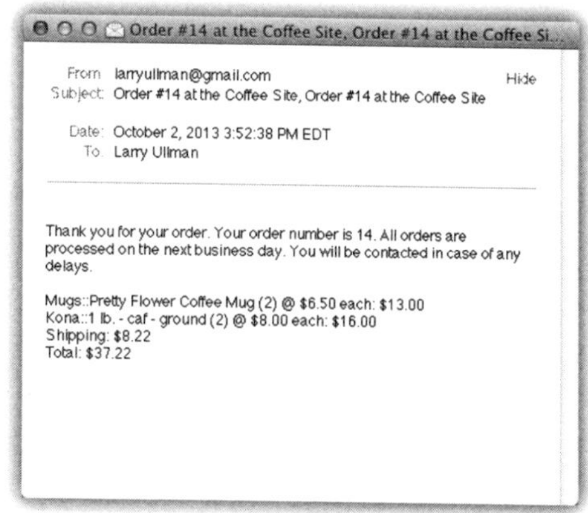


Figure 13.5

In theory, you can generate a multipart email (one that's readable in both formats) by just creating the proper body and headers that adhere to the email standard. In my experience, that's much, much easier said than done. A better solution is to use a third-party library that will guarantee accurate and reliable results. For **email_receipt.php**, let's turn to the Zend Framework (http://framework.zend.com).

tip

You can also use the PEAR **Mail_Mime** class to send out HTML email.

## INSTALLING THE ZEND FRAMEWORK

**tip**

If you do a lot of PHP development, you ought to be familiar with the Zend Framework, even if you don't routinely use it.

The Zend Framework, created by key PHP developers, has a module for just about anything you'll want to do with PHP. The framework is fairly well documented and established. One of the best features of the framework is that you can use pieces of it as needed, without having to adopt or incorporate the entire library. In other words, a site like this one can use just **`Zend\Mail`** without the entire site being Zend Framework based.

To use the Zend Framework on the site, including parts of the Zend Framework, you'll need to install the needed framework files first. As of version 2 of the Zend Framework, installation is easily handled using Composer (http://getcomposer.org). Composer is an excellent *dependency manager* for PHP. If you haven't used Composer, or any dependency manager, before, it works like this: You tell Composer what requirements you have for your site and Composer will make sure those requirements are met by downloading whatever libraries are missing.

To install the Zend Framework, you must first install and configure Composer. This will require some command-line work:

1. Access your computer from a command-line interface.

   This is the Terminal application on Mac OS X, or a command or DOS prompt on Windows (aka a console window).

2. Move to a logical destination directory for Composer:

   ```
   cd /path/to/dir
   ```

   You can install Composer anywhere; you don't necessarily need to install it within your project directory (arguably, you shouldn't). On Windows, I might install Composer within my home directory or in the XAMPP folder, if I've installed that. The resulting command is **`cd C:\xampp`**. On Mac OS X, I might install Composer in my Sites folder: **`cd ~/Sites`**.

3. Execute the following command (**Figure 13.6**):

   ```
   curl -sS https://getcomposer.org/installer | php
   ```

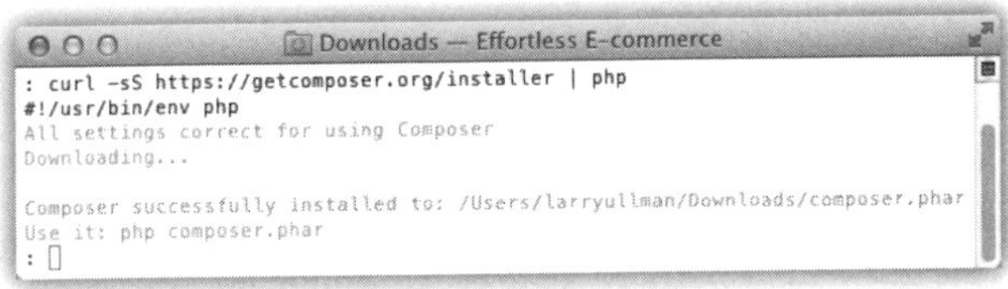


**Figure 13.6**

That line will use cURL to download the Composer installer, and then use your local version of PHP to run the installer. If you get an error message about not being able to find or recognize PHP, you'll need to change the end of that command to include a full path to your PHP executable (such as **C:\xampp\php\php.exe**).

That takes care of the installation of Composer (assuming the process worked). You should find in the folder you used (in Step 2) **composer.phar**. That script will do the work of installing dependencies.

You need to install Composer only once, not once for each site.

Next, you need to identify the dependencies for the project. That's accomplished by creating a file of JSON (JavaScript Object Notation) data named **composer.json**. Put this in your site's **includes** directory. Here are the contents of that file for this project:

```
{
   "repositories": [
      {
      "type": "composer",
      "url": "https://packages.zendframework.com/"
      }
   ],
   "require":
      {
      "zendframework/zend-mail": "2.0.*"
      }
}
```

If you haven't worked with JSON before, the syntax may seem quite strange, but that's JSON for you. The **"require"** section is where you identify the dependencies for the project. For this project, the only dependency is a 2.0 or higher version of **Zend\Mail**. To tell Composer where to find this package, the **"repositories"** section identifies the Zend Framework's repository as a place to also look for packages.

With Composer installed and the dependencies for the project identified, the final step is to have Composer install the dependencies. For this, you again turn to the command line:

1. Access your computer from a command-line interface.

   This is the Terminal application on Mac OS X, or a command or DOS prompt on Windows (aka a console window).

2. Move to your site's **includes** directory:

   ```
   cd /path/to/dir
   ```

   You want to move to the directory for your project where you created the **composer.json** file. If you followed my instructions, this is wherever your other includable files are.

**tip**

Ideally, you should add your PHP executable to your environment's path. Look online to find instructions for your operating system.

3. Execute the following command (**Figure 13.7**):

   ```
   php /path/to/composer.phar install
   ```

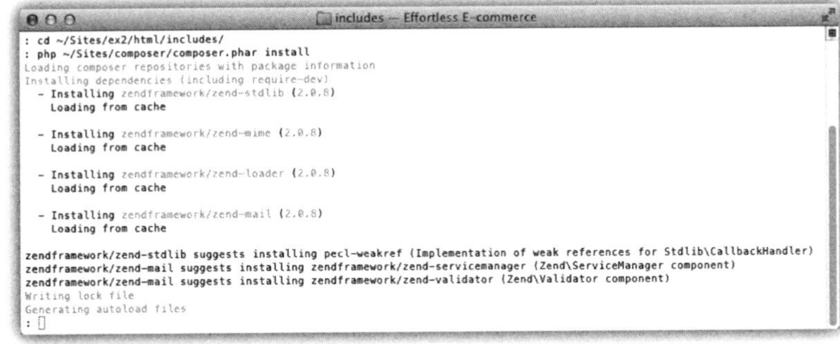


**Figure 13.7**

This line uses the **composer.phar** script to install the necessary dependencies. Depending on your setup and your operating system, you'll most likely need to explicitly set the path to the PHP executable and/or the path to **composer.phar**.

4. Look within the **includes** directory to find the newly created **vendor** folder (**Figure 13.8**).

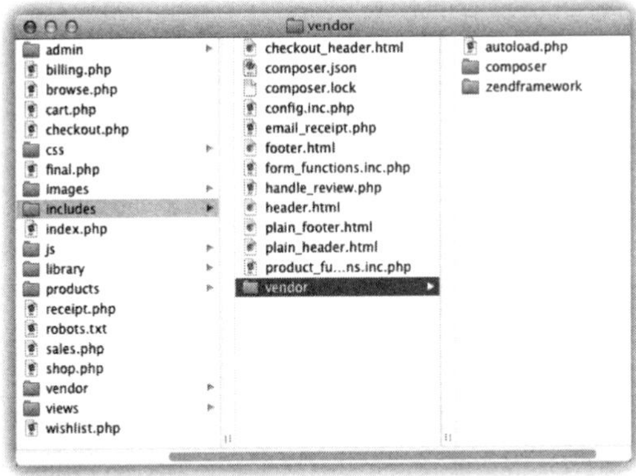


**Figure 13.8**

Composer should create the **vendor** folder and place the necessary components within it.

With the Zend Framework components installed, you can now create the PHP script that will send the email receipt.

## CREATING THE PHP SCRIPT

The **email_receipt.php** page has to send out an email available in two versions: plain text and HTML. This means the script needs to create two separate email bodies:

1. Create a new PHP script in your text editor or IDE to be named **email_receipt.php** and stored in the **includes** directory.

```
<?php
```

2. Begin the plain text version of the body:

```
$body_plain = "Thank you for your order. Your order number is
➥{$_SESSION['order_id']}. All orders are processed on the next
➥business day. You will be contacted in case of any delays.\n\n";
```

   The plain text version starts by thanking the customer, indicating the order number and stating what's to be expected next.

3. Begin the HTML version of the body:

```
$body_html = file_get_contents('includes/plain_header.html');
$body_html .= '<p>Thank you for your order. Your order number
➥is ' . $_SESSION['order_id'] . '. All orders are processed
➥on the next business day. You will be contacted in case of
➥any delays.</p>
<table border="0" cellspacing="3" cellpadding="3">
  <tr>
    <th align="center">Item</th>
    <th align="center">Quantity</th>
    <th align="right">Price</th>
    <th align="right">Subtotal</th>
  </tr>';
```

   The HTML version of the body starts with the beginning HTML code: to create an HTML email, you create an entire HTML page, as if it were to be viewed in a web browser. You can even include CSS, as you would in a standard HTML page. When sending HTML in email, it's best to include inline CSS, not external style sheets. For ease of maintenance, I've created the HTML header as a separate file (already used on the **receipt.php** page). The contents of that file will be the initial part of the **$body_html** string.

   The body then begins with the same message as in Step 2, plus the start of a table definition.

4. Retrieve the order contents:

```
$r = mysqli_query($dbc, "CALL get_order_contents({
➥$_SESSION['order_id']})");
while ($row = mysqli_fetch_array($r, MYSQLI_ASSOC)) {
```

The **get_order_contents()** stored procedure returns the details about what products, and in what quantities and at what price, are associated with a given order number. The procedure doesn't return anything regarding the customer, which is fine in this situation.

5. Add each item to both versions of the body:

```
$body_plain .= "{$row['category']}::{$row['name']}
➥({$row['quantity']}) @ \$" . number_format($row['price_per']/100,
➥2) . " each: $" . number_format($row['subtotal']/100, 2) . "\n";
$body_html .= '<tr><td>' . $row['category'] . '::' . $row['name']
➥. '</td>
<td align="center">' . $row['quantity'] . '</td>
   <td align="right">$' . number_format($row['price_per']/100, 2)
   ➥. '</td>
<td align="right">$' . number_format($row['subtotal']/100, 2)
   ➥. '</td>
</tr>
';
```

For the plain text version, the item's name, quantity, price, and subtotal is listed on a single line. For the HTML version, a table row is created listing the same information.

6. Store the shipping and order total for later use:

```
$shipping = number_format($row['shipping']/100, 2);
$total = number_format($row['total']/100, 2);
```

After the loop has completed—after every item has been added to the email—the cost of shipping and the total should be appended to the email body. To make those values available after the execution of the loop, they're assigned to other variables here.

7. Complete the loop and clear the next results:

```
} // End of WHILE loop.
mysqli_next_result($dbc);
```

Because the **get_order_contents()** stored procedure performs a **SELECT** query, an extra set of results will be returned. These results should be addressed so that other stored procedures that are run later (by **final.php**, if applicable) won't cause problems. Invoking the **mysqli_next_result()** function will mitigate the potential complication.

**8.** Add the shipping:

```
$body_plain .= "Shipping: \$$shipping\n";
$body_html .= '<tr>
   <td colspan="2"> </td><th align="right">Shipping</th>
   <td align="right">$' . $shipping . '</td>
</tr>
';
```

I'm using double quotation marks in assigning plain text values because I want to conclude most lines with a newline (**\n**). The **\$$shipping** construct prints a literal dollar sign (the first dollar sign is escaped), followed by the value of **$shipping**. If you tried to use **$$shipping** instead, you'd create a *variable variable*, and PHP would try to insert the value of, say, **$11.24**, which wouldn't work.

For the HTML version, another table row is added. To create the HTML, single quotes are used so as not to conflict with all the double quotes around the attributes.

**9.** Add the total:

```
$body_plain .= "Total: \$$total\n";
$body_html .= '<tr>
   <td colspan="2"> </td><th align="right">Total</th>
   <td align="right">$' . $total . '</td>
</tr>
';
```

**10.** Complete the HTML body:

```
$body_html .= '</table></body></html>';
```

At this point, both email bodies have been generated and the email can be created and sent. (You can also use the **plain_footer.html** file as the end of the page here.)

**11.** Include the **autoload.php** script:

```
require('includes/vendor/autoload.php');
```

Composer creates the **autoload.php** script within the **vendor** directory. Including this one script will provide a way for the script to automatically include every other file it needs.

The path value here is relative to **final.php**, which includes **email_receipt.php**.

12. Include the Zend Framework namespaces:

```
use Zend\Mail;
use Zend\Mime\Message as MimeMessage;
use Zend\Mime\Part as MimePart;
```

Zend Framework 2 is namespace based, so the above syntax is needed to bring in the classes to be used.

**tip**

This is a good example how object-oriented programming (OOP) allows you to use existing class definitions without knowing much about OOP yourself.

13. Create the two parts of the email:

```
$html = new MimePart($body_html);
$html->type = "text/html";
$plain = new MimePart($body_plain);
$plain->type = "text/plain";
$body = new MimeMessage();
$body->setParts(array($plain, $html));
```

I found this code online for creating multipart (plain text and HTML) emails using Zend Framework 2. First, two **MimePart** objects are created, one for each content type. Then the two parts are used as the body of a new **MimeMessage**.

**tip**

Using **Zend\Mail**, you can send a single email to as many recipients as you want, and you can also use Cc and Bcc.

**note**

To catch possible errors when using **Zend\Mail**, you could wrap the code within a **try...catch** block.

14. Establish the email parameters:

```
$mail = new Mail\Message();
$mail->setFrom('admin@example.com');
$mail->addTo($_SESSION['email']);
$mail->setSubject("Order #{$_SESSION['order_id']} at the Coffee
➥Site");
$mail->setEncoding("UTF-8");
$mail->setBody($body);
$mail->getHeaders()->get('content-type')->setType('multipart/
➥alternative');
```

The **from** address should be something appropriate for the site. The **to** address is the customer's email, stored in the session on **checkout.php**. The subject includes the order ID. All of this code is covered in the Zend Framework documentation and elsewhere online.

**tip**

The Zend Framework manual has more on **Zend\Mail**, including how to use a specific SMTP server to send the message.

15. Send the email:

```
$transport = new Mail\Transport\Sendmail();
$transport->send($mail);
```

16. Save the file.

You can now test the script by completing an order. When you get to **final.php**, the email receipt should be sent.

## Paginating the Catalog

One feature I haven't incorporated into this site is *pagination*: making a list of items appear in smaller groupings—like 10 to 20 at a time—over multiple pages. One reason I haven't incorporated pagination is that the script for listing every coffee product does so using a single drop-down menu. No pagination is required there. As for the non-coffee products, the site would have to get fairly large for it to require pagination. But should you want to add that feature, it's quite simple to implement. If you don't already know how, I discuss the concept in detail in my *PHP and MySQL for Dynamic Web Sites: Visual QuickStart Guide* (Peachpit Press, 2011), or you can simply ask how in my support forums (www.LarryUllman.com/forums/).

With the Coffee site, there may be two complications to using pagination, depending on what structure you used: the pretty URLs and the stored procedures. As for the first, if you're using mod_rewrite, you'll need to modify the **.htaccess** rules so that they recognize and handle the pagination variables that get passed along in the URL.

For example, the **browse.php** page is the most likely candidate for pagination. Here's the original **.htacess** rule for that script:

```
RewriteRule ^browse/(coffee|goodies)/([A-Za-z\+\-]+)/([0-9]+)/?$
➥browse.php?type=$1&category=$2&id=$3
```

And here's how it looks with the additional two parameters:

```
RewriteRule ^browse/(coffee|goodies)/([A-Za-z\+\-]+)/
➥([0-9]+)(/([0-9]+)/([0-9]+))?/?$ browse.php?type=$1
➥&category=$2&id=$3&s=$5&np=$6
```

In the pattern, one larger grouping has been added: **(/([0-9]+)/([0-9]+))?**. That entire grouping is optional, since the first time the browser page is loaded no pagination values would be appended to the URL. If present, the syntax must be a slash, followed by one or more numbers, followed by another slash, followed by one or more numbers. Thus, a valid URL includes both **/browse/goodies/Mugs/6** and **/browse/goodies/Mugs/6/10/3**.

If the URL is of the latter format, the first new number is associated with the **$_GET['s']** variable, short for "starting point." The second new number is associated with the **$_GET['np']** variable, short for "number of pages." Those two variables are all that's required to paginate a page.

The URLs that the script creates for the pagination links need to pass along these values and adhere to the syntax the **.htacess** rule is expecting:

```
<a href="/browse/goodies/Mugs/6/10/3">Next</a>
```

In terms of the stored procedures, the **select_products()** stored procedure is the only one affected by pagination. One way to convert it for pagination purposes is to create new logic in that procedure. You have the procedure accept two new parameters: the offset for the query and the number of records to fetch. These parameters are then used in a **LIMIT** clause. However, that **LIMIT** clause is applied only to the "goodies" query (the coffees aren't paginated because they're already shown as a select menu). Moreover, you also need to write the query so that it *doesn't* use a **LIMIT** clause if the passed values are 0 (in other words: fetch all the records). As you can tell, the stored procedure can quickly get even more complicated.

An alternative solution is to break the one procedure into three:

- **select_coffees()**
- **select_all_goodies()**
- **select_page_goodies()**

With this arrangement, no elaborate logic has to be written in the stored procedures. Instead, the **browse.php** script will call the right stored procedure based on whether the script is displaying coffee or goodies, and whether it's displaying every goodie or just a page of them.

If you're not using stored procedures or mod_rewrite, implementing pagination becomes even easier, because you can use the standard approach. Regardless of your situation, if you have any questions or problems with how to incorporate pagination, you can always ask about it in my support forums.

## Highlighting New Products

You may want to highlight new products to make the site look fresh and busy. You can do so by

- Showing the most recent three or four products on the home page
- Displaying the most recent three or four products in a given category on the **shop.php** page
- Creating a separate "New Items" page that lists the *X* most recently added products

You've already created the paradigm for implementing any of these features: It's essentially the same code and queries used to display sale items. But this time, you don't use the **`sales`** table and you order the results by the creation dates.

## Making Recommendations

Part of a good shopping cart—at least prior to the customer completing the sale—is recommending other products to purchase. Recommendations offer an additional benefit to the customer, because he truly may be interested in other items and appreciate those items being brought to his attention. (And it could mean more money for your business!)

There are two broad types of recommendations:

- **Upselling:** Recommending similar products that are better and more expensive
- **Cross-selling:** Recommending additional related products that the customer may want

Upselling in this particular site is simple: If a customer has a one-pound bag of coffee in their cart, recommend the two-pound bag. Or if your site sells audio-visual equipment, you might recommend other models (like a receiver or DVD player) by the same manufacturer.

Cross-selling has a larger potential—not everything can be upsold—but requires more thought. When a site doesn't have that many products or that large of an order history, you can implement recommendations by creating a system whereby the administrator makes associations among products. If the site sells a lot of stuff, this strategy could become impractical, so if you have a number of orders in the system, you can create automatic recommendations based on what other customers have purchased. The premise, and the underlying code, is simple: If a customer has, say, a bag of Kona coffee in his cart, recommended products would be those things that other customers purchased in addition to Kona coffee. You can even define the strength of a recommendation based on how often it's purchased along with the original product.

**tip**

See Chapter 12 for more thoughts and code for implementing recommendations.

## Adding Customer Reviews

In my opinion, customer reviews are one of the greatest reasons to shop online. Certainly not all reviews are valid, or even legitimate, but customer reviews provide potential buyers with more input for making a decision. More input can mean more sales, which is good for your site.

With the Coffee site, how reviews are implemented is a bit tricky because of the nature of the products and how they're shown on the site. For example, a review of just a coffee type—such as Kona—is probably more useful than reviewing individual coffee products: Kona in a one-pound, decaffeinated, whole bean package. The review system to be added in this chapter reflects just a coffee type (**Figure 13.9**).

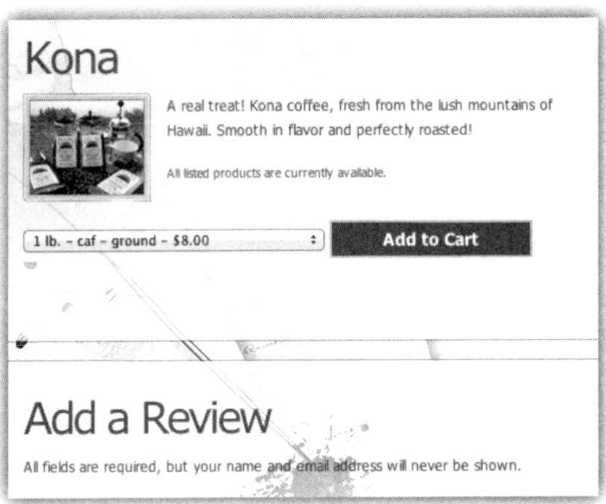

**Figure 13.9**

**tip**

Apropos of nothing, if you like this book, please take the time to review it online!

Conversely, reviews for the non-coffee products should be specific to each item: The Red Dragon Mug is different than the Pretty Flower Coffee Mug. Two books are even more dissimilar.

The complication with the non-coffee products is that there's no individual listing page, which is where reviews would be shown. In the following pages, I'll demonstrate how to implement a review system for the coffees. The code you'd use would be virtually the same for the non-coffee products, but you'd first want to create a page for displaying individual non-coffee items.

Because of the structure of the site, you must take four separate steps to implement a review system:

1. Change the database.
2. Modify the **browse.php** script.
3. Create the view file for showing the review form and existing reviews.
4. Create the PHP script that will handle a review form submission.

I'll walk through each of these steps in order.

## DATABASE CHANGES

To support reviews, you create a new table:

```
CREATE TABLE `reviews` (
  `id` INT(10) UNSIGNED NOT NULL AUTO_INCREMENT,
  `product_type` ENUM('coffee','goodies') NOT NULL,
  `product_id` MEDIUMINT(8) UNSIGNED NOT NULL,
  `name` VARCHAR(60) NOT NULL,
  `email` VARCHAR(80) NOT NULL,
  `review` TEXT NOT NULL,
  `date_created` TIMESTAMP NOT NULL DEFAULT CURRENT_TIMESTAMP,
  PRIMARY KEY (`id`),
  KEY `product_type` (`product_type`,`product_id`),
  UNIQUE (`email`, `product_type`, `product_id`)
) ENGINE=InnoDB  DEFAULT CHARSET=utf8;
```

The **reviews** table stores the product type and ID. For the ID value, with non-coffee products, this will be a specific ID. For the coffee products, this will be the generic coffee type ID value (for example, Kona coffee is 3). The reviewer's name, email address, and review are also stored. The name and email address won't be publicly viewable, but the email address will be used as a basic check to prevent one person from submitting multiple reviews for the same product (using the same email address).

For better security, you could add a "status" column and set all reviews to "pending." Then an administrator can manually inspect and approve every review.

The Coffee site relies heavily on stored procedures. If you keep that approach, you must create two new procedures. The first adds records to the **reviews** table:

```
CREATE PROCEDURE add_review (type VARCHAR(7), pid MEDIUMINT, n
➥VARCHAR(60), e VARCHAR(80), r TEXT)
BEGIN
INSERT INTO reviews (product_type, product_id, name, email, review)
➥VALUES (type, pid, n, e, r);
END$$
```

The second new procedure retrieves records from the table:

```
CREATE PROCEDURE select_reviews(type VARCHAR(7), pid MEDIUMINT)
BEGIN
IF type = 'coffee' THEN
```

(continues on next page)

```
SELECT review FROM reviews WHERE type='coffee' AND product_id=pid
➥ORDER by date_created DESC;
ELSEIF type = 'goodies' THEN
SELECT review FROM reviews WHERE type='goodies' AND product_id=pid
➥ORDER by date_created DESC;
END IF;
END$$
```

By this point, both of these procedures (or how you'll execute the same queries without stored procedures) should hopefully be comfortable for you. After creating both, you can test them in your database before getting to the PHP scripts (**Figure 13.10**).

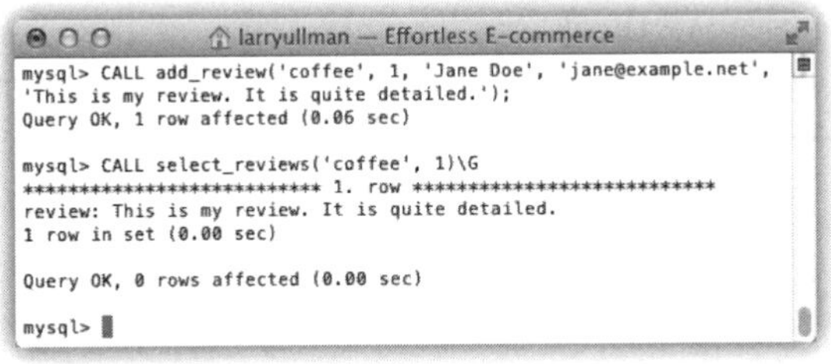

```
larryullman — Effortless E-commerce
mysql> CALL add_review('coffee', 1, 'Jane Doe', 'jane@example.net',
'This is my review. It is quite detailed.');
Query OK, 1 row affected (0.06 sec)

mysql> CALL select_reviews('coffee', 1)\G
*************************** 1. row ***************************
review: This is my review. It is quite detailed.
1 row in set (0.00 sec)

Query OK, 0 rows affected (0.00 sec)

mysql>
```

**Figure 13.10**

## UPDATING BROWSE.PHP

With the MVC-like structure used by the Coffee site, lots of separate files are created and included. For the coffee products, the **browse.php** script displays a specific type of coffee. The original code looks like this:

```
} elseif ($type === 'coffee') {
  include('./views/list_coffees2.html');
}
```

After validating the variables required by the page and executing the **select_products()** stored procedure, the proper view file is included in the above code. That part of the process remains unchanged to incorporate the reviews. After the inclusion of the view file, you have to add several more lines of code. Here's the new result, which I'll explain:

```
} elseif ($type === 'coffee') {
  include('./views/list_coffees2.html');
  mysqli_next_result($dbc);
  include('./includes/handle_review.php');
  $r = mysqli_query($dbc, "CALL select_reviews('$type', $sp_cat)");
  include('./views/review.html');
}
```

First, after including the display view file, you need to clear the remaining stored procedure results. As I explained earlier in this chapter, this is required when you're running another stored procedure after having executed a **SELECT** procedure.

Next, the script for handling the review submission is included. That script will be created as the last step.

After that, the stored procedure for selecting reviews is called. It's passed two variables that have already been validated.

Finally, the view file for showing the review form and existing reviews is included. Let's write that file next.

## CREATING THE VIEW FILE

After the stored procedure in **browse.php** executes, control is passed to the view file. It has two jobs: displaying the form for adding a review and showing the existing reviews. Thanks to the **create_form_input()** function, creating the form is a breeze. Thanks to the **select_reviews()** stored procedure, displaying existing reviews is easy as well.

1. Begin a new script in your text editor or IDE to be named **review.html** and stored in the **views** directory:

   ```
   <?php
   ```

2. Begin a box and display a message, should a **$message** variable exist:

   ```
   echo BOX_BEGIN;
   if (isset($message)) echo "<p>$message</p>";
   ```

   The **message** variable will be assigned a value in **handle_review.php** when a review is added. It just needs to be displayed if it is set (**Figure 13.11**).

   **Figure 13.11**

3. Begin the form:

   ```
   echo '<h2>Add a Review</h2><p>All fields are required, but your
   ➥name and email address will never be shown.</p><form action="/
   ➥browse/' . $type . '/' . urlencode($category) . '/' . $sp_cat .
   ➥'" method="post">';
   ```

The form will be submitted back to this same page. The catch is that **browse.php** must receive several values in the URL; simply using **browse.php** as the action value won't work.

If you're not using mod_rewrite, you can change the action to this format: **browse.php?type=$type&category=$category&id=$sp_cat**.

4. Create the name and email inputs:

```
echo '<div class="field"><label for="name"><strong>Name</strong>
➥</label><br />';
include('./includes/form_functions.inc.php');
create_form_input('name', 'text', $review_errors);
echo '</div>
<div class="field"><label for="email"><strong>Email</strong>
➥</label><br />';
create_form_input('email', 'text', $review_errors);
```

I'm using the function already created to make these inputs.

5. Create the review element:

```
echo '</div>
<div class="field"><label for="review"><strong>Review</strong>
➥</label><br />';
create_form_input('review', 'textarea', $review_errors);
```

6. Complete the form and the box:

```
echo '</div><input type="submit" value="Submit" class="button" />
➥</form>';
echo BOX_END;
```

This completes the section of the page that shows the "add a review" form.

7. Begin the **Reviews** section:

```
echo BOX_BEGIN;
echo '<h2>Reviews</h2>';
```

The rest of the code will show the existing reviews for the product.

8. If reviews exist, display them:

```
if (mysqli_num_rows($r) > 0) {
   while ($row = mysqli_fetch_array($r, MYSQLI_ASSOC)) {
      echo '<p>' . htmlspecialchars($row['review']) . '</p>
      ➥<hr />';
   } // End of WHILE loop.
```

9. If reviews don't exist, display that message (**Figure 13.12**):

```
} else {
   echo '<p>There are currently no reviews for this product.</p>';
}
```

Figure 13.12

10. Complete the HTML box:

```
echo BOX_END;
```

11. Save the file.

If you want, you can load **browse.php** in your browser now. The only thing left to do is add the code for handling the form submission.

## CREATING THE HANDLING SCRIPT

The final script in the process handles the form submission (and is also included by **browse.php**). This script has to validate the form data and insert the review into the database.

1. Begin a new script in your text editor or IDE to be named **handle_review.php** and stored in the **includes** directory:

```
<?php
```

2. Create an array for storing errors:

```
$review_errors = array();
```

3. Check for a form submission:

```
if ($_SERVER['REQUEST_METHOD'] === 'POST') {
```

4. Validate the name:

```
if (preg_match ('/^[A-Z \'.-]{2,60}$/i', $_POST['name'])) {
   $name  = $_POST['name'];
} else {
   $review_errors['name'] = 'Please enter your name!';
}
```

For each invalid element, an error is added to the array.

5. Validate the email address:

```
if (filter_var($_POST['email'], FILTER_VALIDATE_EMAIL)) {
   $email = $_POST['email'];
} else {
   $review_errors['email'] = 'Please enter a valid email
   ➥address!';
}
```

6. Validate the review:

```
$review = strip_tags($_POST['review']);
if (empty($review)) {
   $review_errors['review'] = 'Please enter your review!';
}
```

To validate the review, I first strip any tags from it, and then ensure that the remaining string isn't empty.

7. If no errors occurred, add the review to the database:

```
if (empty($review_errors)) { // If everything's OK...
   $r = mysqli_query($dbc, "CALL add_review('$type', $sp_cat,
   ➥'$name', '$email', '$review')");
```

To add the review to the database, you only need to call the stored procedure.

8. Confirm that the procedure worked:

```
if (mysqli_affected_rows($dbc) > 0) {
   $message = 'Thank you for your review!';
}
```

I've chosen to ignore failed submissions, but you could trigger an error here instead.

9. Clear the POST array:

```
$_POST = array();
```

This is necessary so that the form does not redisplay the values.

10. Complete the conditionals:

```
   } // Errors occurred IF.
}
```

11. Save the script and test it in your web browser.

## Creating "Add to Wish List" Links

A simple change you can make to the site is to include "Add to Wish List" links beside products, just like the "Add to Cart" links. With the **wishlist.php** script as written, you just need to create an "add" action conditional, like the one in **cart.php**:

```
if (isset($pid, $type, $_GET['action']) && ($_GET['action'] ===
➥'add') ) {
   $r = mysqli_query($dbc, "CALL add_to_wish_list('$uid', '$type',
   ➥$pid, 1)");
} elseif (isset($type, $pid, $_GET['action']) && ($_GET['action']
➥=== 'remove') ) { // Remove it from the cart.
// And so on.
```

## Improving the Cart's Display

The success of the site will depend, in some small part, on the user's reaction to the shopping cart. If it's nice and inviting and makes the customer comfortable, she's more likely to complete the sale. With that in mind, you may want to put some effort into improving that interface. For example, consider creating links from the products in the cart to the product's image and description in the site. Customers often like being able to revisit what it is that they're buying.

**tip**

If you create a page for viewing individual items, you can add a review functionality to it.

Second, you can add messages to the cart page to indicate the result of the latest action. The message can range from something as simple as "The cart has been updated" to something more specific like "Mugs::Red Dragon has been removed from your shopping cart." To do this, the HTML view file has to check for and display a message:

```
if (isset($message)) echo $message;
```

Then the PHP script assigns a value to **$message** for each action:

```
if (isset($pid, $type, $_GET['action']) && ($_GET['action'] ===
➥'add') ) {
   $r = mysqli_query($dbc, "CALL add_to_cart('$uid', '$type',
   ➥$pid, 1)");
   $message = 'The item has been added.';
```

If you want to refer to specific products by name, you'll also need to create a stored procedure (or direct query) that retrieves the product information for a given product type and ID. Such a procedure can then be called after an **INSERT**, **UPDATE**, or **DELETE** query is executed.

### Checking Order Status Online

Even though customers don't have a true account with the site (that is, the ability to log in and log out), it'd be nice if they could check the status of an order. To do that, you create a form where customers supply their email address and order number, easily found on the original receipt (shown in the browser or the confirmation email).

When the form is submitted, the page confirms that the email address matches the order number. You can modify the **get_order_contents()** procedure so that it also returns the shipping status (the date each item shipped), thereby revealing this information to the customer online.

You can also add a comments field to the **orders** table, where the administrator can make notes for the customer to see regarding the order as a whole. Another comments field can be added to **order_contents**, for notes particular to a given product.

## ADMINISTRATIVE SUGGESTIONS

Although most of the suggestions in this chapter focus on the public side, there are many ways to expand the administrative side as well. I'll run through a few recommendations over the next few pages.

### Home Page Additions

The home page as written does nothing but present a few links. What you might put there depends on the site and, frankly, what the administrator wants to see on that page. Information that might logically be displayed includes the ten most recent orders or any product whose inventory is running low.

To do the former, just re-create the **view_orders.php** script but have the query only return ten (or so) records. To do the latter, run a **UNION** query that retrieves every product whose stock value is less than whatever number is appropriate (say, five or ten, depending on the site's activity level).

## Shipping Alternatives

Shipping, like the choice of payment processor itself, is such a big topic that I could arguably dedicate an entire chapter to the myriad ways to handle this part of an order. The simplest, but clearly not the best, approach to handle shipping is to not charge anything additional at all: Just factor enough profit into each item sold to cover the expense. The site that does this will run the risk of losing business to other sites that overtly charge less for the same item, even though those sites will later add in shipping charges. Also, this approach wouldn't allow for different shipping options (such as the speed of delivery) or easy adjustments to the cost of shipping as they change over time.

The Coffee site as written implemented the second simplest way to calculate shipping: a proportional amount dictated by the order total. This approach is easy to manage, easy to change, and reasonable both for the business and for the customer.

To calculate shipping based on the weight of the order, you need to modify the database so that the weight of items is recorded along with the other product details. Depending on what you're selling, it's best to represent all weights in the same unit: grams, kilograms, ounces, pounds, what have you. The shopping cart will then retrieve the weight for each product, generate a weight total, and calculate the shipping using the total weight.

On a similar note, you can create an additional shipping cost representative column in the database. This could be a column added to the specific products tables (**non_coffee_products** and **specific_coffees**, accordingly), in which case you can expect a lot of **NULL** values, which is not ideal. Alternatively, you can create a new table that represents as one row each product that has an additional shipping cost:

```
CREATE TABLE `extra_shipping` (
   `id` INT UNSIGNED NOT NULL AUTO_INCREMENT,
   `product_type` ENUM('coffee','goodies') NOT NULL,
   `product_id` MEDIUMINT UNSIGNED NOT NULL,
   `extra_charge` MEDIUMINT UNSIGNED NOT NULL,
   `date_created` TIMESTAMP NOT NULL DEFAULT CURRENT_TIMESTAMP,
   `date_modified` TIMESTAMP NOT NULL DEFAULT '0000-00-00 00:00:00',
   PRIMARY KEY (`id`),
   KEY `product_type` (`product_type`,`product_id`),
) ENGINE=InnoDB  DEFAULT CHARSET=utf8;
```

Unfortunately, this means another table joined into many of the **SELECT** queries.

The most complicated way of calculating shipping is based on the distance (and possibly the weight or size as well). To pull this off, you'd need the customer's postal code and, for international orders, country. You then tie into the system developed by your shipping company of choice. For example, UPS and FedEx both have Application Programming Interfaces (APIs) available through which you can get exact prices on shipping based on the distance, weight, size, and delivery speed. These APIs work quite similarly to the payment gateway API. For more information, see the documentation for the shipping company of your choosing.

## Viewing Customers

**tip**

A bigger change you can make to the site is to give customers the option of registering and logging in.

Because the site doesn't require that customers register, the order is the most important and atomic record stored in the database. For this reason, browsing by or searching for specific customers becomes less useful (for example, the same customer, if active, might be represented multiple times on the site). If you want to create the ability to find customers, you can easily apply the **view_orders.php** and **view_order.php** functionality to the **view_customers.php** and **view_customer.php** pages.

## Shipping Partial Orders

The Authorize.net payment gateway, like many others, supports the capturing of partial payments. For example, a customer might make an order that totals $100. You can easily modify the site so that a partial order can be shipped and the corresponding part of the payment is captured at that time.

To do this in terms of the **view_order.php** script, you need to create checkboxes for each item so that the administrator can indicate which should be shipped. Logically, you can place each checkbox in the "Shipped?" column, in cases where no ship date exists. Each checkbox should use the **order_contents** table ID as its value.

**tip**

The Authorize.net Advanced Integration Method (AIM) manual covers partial payments in more detail.

When the **view_order.php** form is submitted back to the page, the script will need to use all the selected **order_contents** IDs to create an order total. You must also decide when the shipping charge will be captured. The easy solution is to charge it in entirety the first time a partial order is shipped, and then not charge it at all on subsequent shipments.

After the payment is processed, the **ship_date** in the **order_contents** table will have to be set to **NOW()** for only those selected items. The same applies to the inventory updates.

## Viewing Incomplete Orders

The site as written may record some incomplete orders in the database. This occurs if the customer gets all the way to the point of submitting the `billing.php` form but fails to use a valid payment method (and never resubmits the form). The administrator shouldn't see such orders in the same way as orders that have been approved (that is, the administrator shouldn't ship out orders for which payment hasn't been authorized), but being aware of such incomplete orders is beneficial.

For example, a high number of incomplete orders might be an indication of a logistical problem with the site or the payment request process. The administrator may also want to follow up with customers who didn't complete their order, as a customer service (and sales) technique. To list incomplete orders, use a query similar to that in `view_orders.php`, but check for a response code that's not `1`.

### IMPROVING THE SECURITY

The security measures taken in this site are fairly tight, and I can recommend using the code and functionality in good conscience. Because all form data is thoroughly validated using regular expressions, most of the functionality remains within the database, and the payment request is made behind the scenes, so it's fairly secure.

Outside the website itself, one recommendation I make, which Authorize.net also suggests, is that you change your Authorize.net identifying information regularly. This includes the user API login ID and the transaction key. These values can be changed easily (in the Merchant Interface). After you change the login ID and transaction ID, only two lines in `config.inc.php` need to be updated to account for the changes.

# STRUCTURAL ALTERATIONS

The last topic I want to discuss is possible structural alternations you can make to the site. In other words, if you'd rather not use the MVC approach and stored procedures, what can you do instead?

## Using Prepared Statements

The Coffee site relies extensively on stored procedures. There are numerous benefits to this approach; the most critical are

- Greatly improved security
- Better performance
- Compartmentalization of code

With the first edition of the book, I discovered a percentage of readers who either didn't have the ability to use stored procedures or simply didn't want to.

**tip**

You can find more examples on my blog (www.LarryUllman.com).

For the most part, switching from stored procedures to prepared statements should be fairly easy. With the Coffee site, switching to prepared statements won't impact your data validation at all, because the stored procedures can be treated like prepared statements in that regard (for example, you don't have to escape strings).

To demonstrate how you'd write some of the scripts using prepared statements, let's take a look at the **select_categories()**, **select_products()**, and **add_customer()** procedures. Rewriting any of the others is similar.

The **shop.php** script in Chapter 8, "Creating a Catalog," uses a stored procedure named **select_categories()**. This procedure takes one argument: a string with a value of **coffee** or **goodies**. The procedure then fetches either all the coffee types or the non-coffee categories accordingly.

To use **shop.php** without the stored procedure, replace this line:

```
$r = mysqli_query($dbc, "CALL select_categories('$type')");
```

with direct queries:

```
if ($type == 'coffee') {
   $r = mysqli_query($dbc, 'SELECT * FROM general_coffees ORDER by
   ➥category');
} elseif ($type == 'goodies') {
   $r = mysqli_query($dbc, 'SELECT * FROM non_coffee_categories
   ➥ORDER by category');
}
```

And that's all there is to it! In this case, you don't need to use prepared statements at all. No need to even change the view file.

The next stored procedure, **select_products()**, takes two arguments: a string with a value of **coffee** or **goodies**, and an integer representing the coffee or non-coffee category ID. The procedure, called by **browse.php**, expects to receive both the broad type—coffee or goodies—in the URL, along with the specific category ID. To change this to a nonstored procedure version, you again need to replace this line:

```
$r = mysqli_query($dbc, "CALL select_products('$type', $sp_cat)");
```

with the following:

```
if ($type === 'coffee') {
   $q = 'SELECT gc.description, gc.image, CONCAT("C", sc.id) AS sku,
   CONCAT_WS(" - ", s.size, sc.caf_decaf, sc.ground_whole,
   CONCAT("$", FORMAT(sc.price/100, 2))) AS name, sc.stock
   FROM specific_coffees AS sc INNER JOIN sizes AS s ON
   ➥s.id=sc.size_id
   INNER JOIN general_coffees AS gc ON gc.id=sc.general_coffee_id
   WHERE general_coffee_id=? AND stock>0
   ORDER by name ASC';
} elseif ($type === 'goodies') {
   $q = 'SELECT ncc.description AS g_description, ncc.image AS
   ➥g_image,
   CONCAT("G", ncp.id) AS sku, ncp.name, ncp.description, ncp.image,
   CONCAT("$", FORMAT(ncp.price/100, 2)) AS price, ncp.stock
   FROM non_coffee_products AS ncp INNER JOIN non_coffee_categories
   ➥AS ncc
   ON ncc.id=ncp.non_coffee_category_id
   WHERE non_coffee_category_id=? ORDER by date_created DESC';
}
$stmt = mysqli_prepare($dbc, $q);
mysqli_stmt_bind_param($stmt, 'i', $sp_cat);
mysqli_stmt_execute($stmt);
```

Both queries use the PHP variable **$sp_cat**, which is the integer, so the one variable can be bound after the query is defined.

When turning to prepared statements, you need to bind the outbound parameters (that is, bind the query results to PHP variables). You also have to change the view file to use **mysqli_stmt_fetch()** and the bound variables instead of **mysqli_fetch_array()** and the **$row** variable.

Chapter 10, "Checking Out," has the most complicated—and important—stored procedures, so the PHP scripts there will need to be reworked more than those from the other chapters.

The first procedure in Chapter 10 is **add_customer()**, called in the **checkout.php** script after the customer has successfully completed the shipping form. The code in the PHP script calls the procedure, which will add a record to the **customers** table. The procedure also returns the customer ID via an outbound argument named **@cid**. This value needs to be stored in the session for later use. Here's the original code:

```
$r = mysqli_query($dbc, "CALL add_customer('$e', '$fn', '$ln',
➥'$a1', '$a2', '$c', '$s', $z, $p, @cid)");
if ($r) {
   $r = mysqli_query($dbc, 'SELECT @cid');
   if (mysqli_num_rows($r) == 1) {
      list($_SESSION['customer_id']) = mysqli_fetch_array($r);
```

Without a stored procedure, you replace that code with the following:

```
$q = 'INSERT INTO customers (email, first_name, last_name,
➥address1, address2, city, state, zip, phone) VALUES
➥(?, ?, ?, ?, ?, ?, ?, ?, ?)';
$stmt = mysqli_prepare($dbc, $q);
mysqli_stmt_bind_param($stmt, 'sssssssis', $e, $fn, $ln,
➥$a1, $a2, $c, $s, $z, $p);
mysqli_stmt_execute($stmt);
if (mysqli_stmt_affected_rows($stmt) === 1) {
   $_SESSION['customer_id'] = mysqli_stmt_insert_id($stmt);
```

And that's all you'd need to do.

If you have trouble converting any of the stored procedures to prepared statements, check out my explanations of prepared statements in Chapter 7, "Second Site: Structure and Design," the explanations in Chapter 12, or the PHP manual. If you're still having problems, just ask in my support forums.

### DROPPING THE MVC APPROACH

The MVC approach I take in Part 3 is really more like MVC-ish. I've separated the site's components into three parts:

- PHP scripts, which act as controllers
- Stored procedures, which act as models
- Files containing mostly HTML, which act as the views

The result is better separation of presentation and logic than you'd have in a traditional approach (such as in Part 2). But if you've already dropped the stored procedures, or if you just don't care for working with so many disparate files, you can re-entangle the components with ease.

The site already uses header and footer files for most of the presentation. I would never change that approach. But you could forgo the included view files and just take that combination of presentation and logic and put it directly within the main PHP script (where the files would've been included). The result will be a bit messier, and perhaps harder to maintain. On the other hand, it will be more apparent how, for example, query results are displayed on a page.

## Tweaking the Database

The foundation of the website is the database, so I'd be remiss not to mention alternatives there. To start, the system as written will create a lot of flotsam: wish list and shopping cart items never to be purchased. You likely want to create a PHP (or command-line) script that routinely rids the database of old stuff. A record is old if its modification date is more than, say, six months old or if its creation date is more than six months old and its modification date is still 0000-00-00 00:00:00, meaning the record has never been updated.

**tip**

On *nix systems, **cron** can be used to automatically execute a PHP script at periodic intervals. Such a script can be used to perform maintenance.

Second, if you're using the stored procedures and like how they work, you should probably read up on how to handle errors in stored procedures. Though handling errors in stored procedures isn't hard to do, the topic is large and technical enough that I had to omit it from the book to avoid taking away from the more important points.

Finally, you can get much better performance from the database by taking advantage of **VIEW** tables. A **VIEW** table is a memorized **SELECT** query that you can run other queries on as if it were a real table. The syntax for creating a **VIEW** is

```
CREATE VIEW view_name AS <SELECT QUERY>
```

As an example, the **UNION** used in the procedures for retrieving every shopping cart or wish list item is quite demanding. You can create a **VIEW** that performs all the **JOIN**s, effectively replacing the **product_type** and **product_id** values from the database tables with the actual information you want to display in the browser. The view can also store the associated user session ID values.

```
CREATE VIEW cart_view AS
SELECT user_session_id, CONCAT("G", ncp.id) AS sku, c.quantity,
➥ncc.category, ncp.name, ncp.price, ncp.stock, sales.price AS
➥sale_price FROM carts AS c INNER JOIN non_coffee_products AS ncp
➥ON c.product_id=ncp.id INNER JOIN non_coffee_categories AS ncc
➥ON ncc.id=ncp.non_coffee_category_id LEFT OUTER JOIN sales
➥ON (sales.product_id=ncp.id AND sales.product_type='goodies'
➥AND ((NOW() BETWEEN sales.start_date AND sales.end_date)
➥OR (NOW() > sales.start_date AND sales.end_date IS NULL)) )
➥WHERE c.product_type="goodies"
UNION
SELECT user_session_id, CONCAT("C", sc.id), c.quantity,
➥gc.category, CONCAT_WS(" - ", s.size, sc.caf_decaf,
➥sc.ground_whole), sc.price, sc.stock, sales.price FROM carts
➥AS c INNER JOIN specific_coffees AS sc ON c.product_id=sc.id
➥INNER JOIN sizes AS s ON s.id=sc.size_id INNER JOIN general_coffees
➥AS gc ON gc.id=sc.general_coffee_id LEFT OUTER JOIN sales
➥ON (sales.product_id=sc.id AND sales.product_type='coffee'
➥AND ((NOW() BETWEEN sales.start_date AND sales.end_date) OR
➥(NOW() > sales.start_date AND sales.end_date IS NULL)) ) WHERE
➥c.product_type="coffee";
```

To be clear, the **SELECT...UNION...SELECT** query is the same as the one in the **get_shopping_cart_contents()** stored procedure, except that the **user_session_id** value is now part of the selection instead of part of the **WHERE** condition. **Figure 13.13** shows two **SELECT** queries run on this **VIEW** table, with the latter automatically reflecting changes in the **carts** table (due to customer actions).

```
larryullman — Effortless E-commerce
mysql> SELECT * FROM cart_view;
+-----------------------------------+-----+----------+----------+---------------------------+-------+-------+------------+
| user_session_id                   | sku | quantity | category | name                      | price | stock | sale_price |
+-----------------------------------+-----+----------+----------+---------------------------+-------+-------+------------+
| 679297987524cc02beaca70.07316888  | G1  |        1 | Mugs     | Pretty Flower Coffee Mug  |   650 |   100 |       NULL |
| 83567636524cc039e9ac42.13299731   | G1  |        1 | Mugs     | Pretty Flower Coffee Mug  |   650 |   100 |       NULL |
| 1163898945524cc0adbb4562.1924379  | G1  |        1 | Mugs     | Pretty Flower Coffee Mug  |   650 |   100 |       NULL |
| 1051516577524cc0339c3193.0370946  | C1  |        1 | Kona     | 2 oz. Sample - caf - ground |   200 |    20 |       NULL |
| 1163898945524cc0adbb4562.1924379  | C4  |        1 | Kona     | 1 lb. - caf - ground      |   800 |    48 |       NULL |
+-----------------------------------+-----+----------+----------+---------------------------+-------+-------+------------+
5 rows in set (0.00 sec)

mysql> SELECT * FROM cart_view;
+-----------------------------------+-----+----------+----------+---------------------------+-------+-------+------------+
| user_session_id                   | sku | quantity | category | name                      | price | stock | sale_price |
+-----------------------------------+-----+----------+----------+---------------------------+-------+-------+------------+
| 679297987524cc02beaca70.07316888  | G1  |        1 | Mugs     | Pretty Flower Coffee Mug  |   650 |   100 |       NULL |
| 83567636524cc039e9ac42.13299731   | G1  |        1 | Mugs     | Pretty Flower Coffee Mug  |   650 |   100 |       NULL |
| 1163898945524cc0adbb4562.1924379  | G1  |        2 | Mugs     | Pretty Flower Coffee Mug  |   650 |   100 |       NULL |
| 1051516577524cc0339c3193.0370946  | C1  |        1 | Kona     | 2 oz. Sample - caf - ground |   200 |    20 |       NULL |
| 1163898945524cc0adbb4562.1924379  | C4  |        1 | Kona     | 1 lb. - caf - ground      |   800 |    48 |       NULL |
| 1163898945524cc0adbb4562.1924379  | C7  |        1 | Kona     | 1 lb. - decaf - whole     |   800 |    19 |        700 |
+-----------------------------------+-----+----------+----------+---------------------------+-------+-------+------------+
6 rows in set (0.00 sec)

mysql>
```

**Figure 13.13**

Once this view is defined, the **get_shopping_cart_contents()** query will only need to do a **SELECT** on this one table, with a single condition: matching the user's session ID:

```
SELECT * FROM cart_views WHERE user_session_id=uid;
```

**tip**

**VIEW** tables were added to MySQL in version 5.0.

# 14 ADDING JAVASCRIPT AND AJAX

Part 4, new in this edition, is largely about ways you can improve the two example sites and enhance the customer experience. One of the absolutely best ways you can improve any online user's experience is by incorporating JavaScript. Most of this chapter will explain and demonstrate how you can enhance some of the existing features by applying the world's most popular scripting language. But the chapter will also introduce a couple of new concepts that can only be accomplished using JavaScript.

Instead of breaking the chapter into those ideas that pertain to the "Knowledge Is Power" site, or the Coffee site, or dividing the content up into public, administrative, security, and so forth, I'll start with some relatively basic JavaScript enhancements. Then the chapter will describe those techniques that use Ajax specifically.

If you aren't comfortable with JavaScript, you should still be able to follow along in this chapter, although you might have problems should things not work as you expect. Further, if you aren't comfortable with JavaScript and you are a web developer, I strongly recommend that you take on learning JavaScript as the next thing you do—after finishing this book, that is.

### PROPER JAVASCRIPT USAGE

Although some 97 percent of users have JavaScript enabled, you should not assume that JavaScript will always be available. The only exception is the case in which what you want to accomplish can only be done using JavaScript and you don't mind leaving some users behind. Other than that, the preferred approach (for quite some time now) is to employ *progressive enhancement*.

Progressive enhancement is a technique in which you first implement baseline functionality and appearance: a site that will work for any browser on any device. Then you enhance the baseline functionality and appearance using JavaScript and CSS, but only for browsers that can support those enhancements.

Progressive enhancement may sound complicated, but it's actually quite easy to do. In fact, the two projects in this book are already on the progressive enhancement path, as all of the functionality has been implemented without requiring JavaScript. Most of the code added in this chapter will be enhancements of existing functionality. In the rare situations where that's not the case, I'll make a specific note of the exception and how you might code the example differently.

**tip**

If you need to learn JavaScript, I've heard great things about the book *Modern JavaScript: Develop and Design (New Riders, 2012)*, written by someone named Larry Ullman.

# ADDING JQUERY

All of the examples in this chapter will use the jQuery JavaScript framework as opposed to hand-coded JavaScript or a different framework or library. I've made this decision for a couple of reasons. First, thanks to the Twitter Bootstrap framework, the "Knowledge Is Power" site already uses jQuery. This line, in the **footer.html** file, includes it:

```
<script src="//ajax.googleapis.com/ajax/libs/jquery/1.10.2/
➥jquery.min.js"></script>
```

A second reason is that jQuery is extremely reliable in terms of browser support, having been well tested across all the standard browsers. Third, you can find jQuery information and resources in abundance online, which is good, because this chapter will only get you started.

The "Knowledge Is Power" site is all ready to begin using jQuery. Any new code you'd add would be placed in a script tag after the inclusion of jQuery. In order to use jQuery on the Coffee site, you'll need to include the jQuery library there, too.

**tip**

Loading JavaScript near the end of the page can help the page to load faster in web browsers.

Generally speaking, I recommend including JavaScript files near the end of the script. With the Twitter Bootstrap framework, this is the default:

```
<script src="//ajax.googleapis.com/ajax/libs/jquery/1.10.2/
➥jquery.min.js"></script>
<script src="js/bootstrap.min.js"></script>
</body>
</html>
```

**note**

You can download the jQuery library, install it on your server, and include it using a local reference instead.

In this chapter, I'll recommend linking to jQuery in your header files instead. Doing so will greatly simplify where you can write any page-specific JavaScript.

For the examples that use the "Knowledge is Power" site, you should move the inclusion of the jQuery library to your header file. I'd place mine after the title tag. The inclusion of **`bootstrap.min.js`** can remain in the footer.

For the Coffee site, you'll need to include the jQuery library in three header files:

- `/includes/header.html`
- `/includes/checkout_header.html`
- `/admin/includes/header.html`

I'll reiterate these requirements when the time comes.

With the jQuery library included, specific bits of JavaScript for each enhancement will be added using script tags for the page in question. On a complete site, depending on how it's implemented, I might be inclined to combine all of those bits of JavaScript into one external JavaScript file that is also included by the header or footer.

# PREVENTING DUPLICATE ORDERS

In the Coffee site, the **`billing.php`** script can take a few moments to execute once the form is submitted. The potential delay comes from the script's need to send a request to the gateway and await a response. This extra pause could give the customer the impression that the form was not submitted, causing him to perhaps click the submit button again to "correct" the problem. With the site as written, this won't create two orders, because the gateway will reject duplicate submissions within a default time period of two minutes. Still, it'd be better to avoid this problem entirely. And it'd be better to give an indication to the customer that the order is being processed and that a delay is to be expected. Although this is a valuable approach, I purposefully omitted it from the **billing.php** script because implementing all that requires JavaScript and I didn't want to further confuse an already complex system.

Given the fact that the form is present in a view file, and the jQuery library is included in the header, you can simply add the necessary JavaScript code to **billing.html** after the form. The following steps assume you've already added jQuery to **checkout_header.html**.

1. Open **billing.html** in your text editor or IDE.

2. At the end of **billing.html**, add a script block and watch for the document to be ready:

   ```
   <script type="text/javascript">
   $(function() {
      // Subsequent code goes here.
   });
   </script>
   ```

   The JavaScript code that does the work for this page will go within these two tags. Within that block, you first add this construct:

   ```
   $(function() {
   });
   ```

   The very basic JavaScript being executed is just **$();**. This is magic jQuery-speak for "when the document is ready, do the following." The code to be executed when the document is ready is defined in an *anonymous function* (a function without a name). The code in the following steps will be added between those two lines.

3. Watch for a form submission:

   ```
   $('#billing_form').submit(function() {
   });
   ```

   This is more jQuery magic. The **$('#billing_form')** part is a way of selecting an element on the page, specifically the element with an ID value of **billing_form**. The **.submit()** says that when the selected element is submitted, the inline function should be executed. That function's code comes next.

4. Within the curly brackets added in Step 3, disable the submit button:

   ```
   $('#billing_form').submit(function(){
      $('input[type=submit]', this).attr('disabled', 'disabled');
   });
   ```

**tip**

Alternatively, the submit button can be selected by giving it a unique ID and referring to `$('#submit_id_value')`.

**tip**

I chose to format the processing message using the same button class because it's prominent, but you might want to use a style that looks distinct from the original button.

The `$('input[type=submit]', this)` part selects all inputs found within the `#billing_form` element (represented by the special keyword `this`) whose type is `submit`. The `.attr('disabled', 'disabled')` code adds the `disabled` attribute to the selected element (the submit input) with a value of `disabled`. In sum, when the form is submitted JavaScript will dynamically turn the submit button's HTML into this:

```
<input type="submit" value="Place Order" class="button"
➥disabled="disabled" />
```

5. On the next line, but before the `});` bit, add the following:

```
$('#submit_div').html('<p class="button">Processing...</p>');
```

You may be picking up on this already: `$('#submit_div')` selects the element on the page with an ID value of `submit_div`. The `.html()` method, applied to that selection, can be used to assign new HTML to the element. The specific HTML to be assigned is the paragraph tag. The effect of this line will be the replacement of the submit button with the "Processing..." message (**Figure 14.1**).

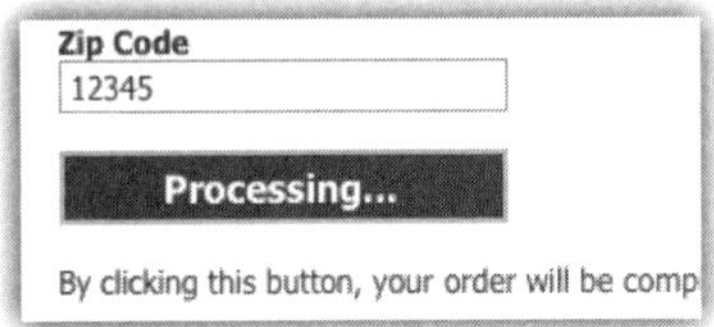


**Figure 14.1**

6. Make sure the billing form has an ID attribute with a value of `billing_form`:

```
<form action="/billing.php" method="POST" id="billing_form">
```

This should already be in place (in `billing.html`), but the JavaScript won't work without the ID value, so it's best to check again.

7. Add an ID attribute with a value of `submit_div` to the DIV that contains the submit button:

```
<div align="center" id="submit_div">
```

Again, this may already be present if you followed the exact instructions in Chapter 10, "Checking Out," but you should double-check.

8. Save the file.

9. Test in your browser.

   If you already had the **`billing.php`** page open, you'll need to reload the page to enable the added JavaScript.

   If it doesn't work, check your browser's error console for possible problems (**Figure 14.2**).

Figure 14.2

**tip**

Debugging JavaScript can be tedious for the novice. If you have problems, look online for answers or post a question in my support forums.

# USING SUPERFISH

The *suckerfish* style of cascading menus has been around for years and has become one of the de facto navigation approaches for today's sites. All suckerfish menus are based on a group of nested, unordered lists that get dynamically converted into cascading menus (**Figure 14.3**). A number of tools are available for creating suckerfish menus, but because the Coffee site will already use jQuery in some other places, I've turned to a jQuery-based plug-in called *Superfish* (http://plugins.jquery.com/superfish/) here.

**note**

The Twitter Bootstrap framework supports drop-down menus without using a plug-in.

Figure 14.3

In the following steps, I'll explain how to create a suckerfish menu for the administrative side of the Coffee site. Originally, several links were thrown onto the home page; now they'll be moved to the primary navigation, where they belong.

1. Download the latest version of Superfish.

2. Expand the downloaded file.

   The download will be a ZIP file that needs to be extracted in order to get at its good parts.

3. Copy the **`hoverIntent.js`** and **`superfish.js`** scripts from the Superfish download's **`src/js`** directory to the site's **`js`** directory.

After expanding the downloaded file, the result will be a folder named something like **joeldbirch-superfish-0d3a5f4**. Within the **src** subfolder, you'll find a **js** folder, which contains the pertinent JavaScript files.

The **hoverIntent.js** library isn't technically part of Superfish, but Superfish can use it for a better menu experience. For consistency, all the JavaScript for the entire site is being placed within the public **js** folder (these new files won't go within **admin**).

4. Copy the **superfish.css** file from the Superfish download's **src/css** directory to the site's **css** directory.

   This CSS file styles the Superfish menu. Again, all CSS goes into the public **css** directory.

5. Open **admin/includes/header.html** in your text editor or IDE.

6. Change the menu options to:

```
<ul class="nav sf-menu">
<!-- MENU -->
<li class="first"><a href="#">Products</a><ul>
   <li><a href="add_specific_coffees.php">Add Coffee Products
   ➥</a></li>
   <li><a href="add_other_products.php">Add Non-Coffee Products
   ➥</a></li>
   <li><a href="add_inventory.php">Add Inventory</a></li>
   </ul></li>
<li><a href="create_sales.php">Sales</a></li>
<li><a href="view_orders.php">Orders</a></li>
<li><a href="#">Customers</a></li>
<!-- END MENU -->
</ul>
```

   There are two important changes here. First, before the closing LI tag for the products link, another unordered list is added. This list contains links to three pages. Second, an additional class of **sf-menu** (short for suckerfish menu) is added to the parent unordered list.

**tip**

To apply multiple CSS classes to a single element, separate the class names with a space.

7. After including the site's primary CSS file, include the Superfish CSS file:

```
<link href="/css/superfish.css" rel="stylesheet"
➥type="text/css" />
```

   Again, the reference to the CSS file assumes it will be found in the ***web root directory*/css** folder. If your site is not in the web root directory, you'll need to change the reference accordingly.

## DIRECTLY LINKING TO PRODUCT CATEGORIES

One reasonable concern with the Coffee site's design is that, except for the sale items, the customer must click through two pages to get to actual products she can purchase (first the shop page, then browse). An easy fix would be to change the navigation so that it allows for direct access to the specific categories. You can do that by applying the suckerfish technique to the public navigation.

To start, you convert the main navigation menu into a nested unordered list. Use PHP to generate the sublists, but the desired HTML will look like this:

```
<ul class="nav sf-menu">
<li><a href="/shop/coffee/">Coffee</a>
  <ul>
    <li><a href="/browse/coffee/Dark+Roast/2">Dark Roast</a></li>
    <li><a href="/browse/coffee/Kona/3">Kona</a></li>
    <li><a href="/browse/coffee/Original+Blend/1">Original Blend
    ➥</a></li>
  </ul>
</li>
<li><a href="/shop/goodies/">Goodies</a></li>
<li><a href="/shop/sales/">Sales</a></li>
<li><a href="/wishlist.php">Wish List</a></li>
<li><a href="/cart.php">Cart</a></li>
</ul>
```

You would take the same steps to create comparable HTML for the categories of goodies, too.

Finally, apply the same combination of CSS and JavaScript that you used on the administrative pages to convert this into a suckerfish menu.

8. Include jQuery, and then the **hoverIntent** and Superfish JavaScript files:

```
<script src="//ajax.googleapis.com/ajax/libs/jquery/1.10.2/
➥jquery.min.js" charset="utf-8"></script>
<script src="/js/hoverIntent.js" type="text/javascript"
➥charset="utf-8"></script>
<script src="/js/superfish.js" type="text/javascript"
➥charset="utf-8"></script>
```

Make sure you include the scripts in this order. Also change the references to the files to be correct for your setup.

**tip**

If the Superfish menu doesn't work for you, use a good JavaScript debugging tool, such as Firebug for the Firefox browser, to see what might be wrong.

**tip**

The **ul.sf-menu** code selects every unordered list with a class of **sf-menu**, but the template has only one.

**note**

I also tweaked some of the CSS to make the menu look marginally better.

9. In a separate script block, apply Superfish:

```
$(function() {
   $('ul.sf-menu').superfish({
      autoArrows: false,
      speed: 'fast'
   });
});
```

This code enables the Superfish menu. Within the anonymous function that is executed when the document is ready, the unordered list with a class of **sf-menu** is selected. To that selection, the **superfish()** method is applied. Two attribute-value pairs are passed to the **superfish()** method: one disables arrows that indicate submenus exist; the other sets the Superfish speed to **fast**.

10. Save the file and test it in your browser by viewing any administrative page.

# ADDING A CALENDAR

As you'll recall, in Chapter 11, "Site Administration," you wrote the **create_sales.php** script. Sales rely on a starting, and optional ending, date. With the original script, it was up to the administrator to enter these values in the proper format. A much improved solution is to present a pop-up calendar the administrator can use to select the dates (like you see everywhere online). The result will be more intuitive for the administrator and more reliable in terms of the data returned.

To add a calendar to the **create_sales.php** script, I'll turn to the jQuery User Interface (jQuery UI) library. jQuery UI is an extension of jQuery that provides a wealth of features and possibilities. For the purpose of this example, I recommend you create and install a custom version of jQuery UI specific to this need.

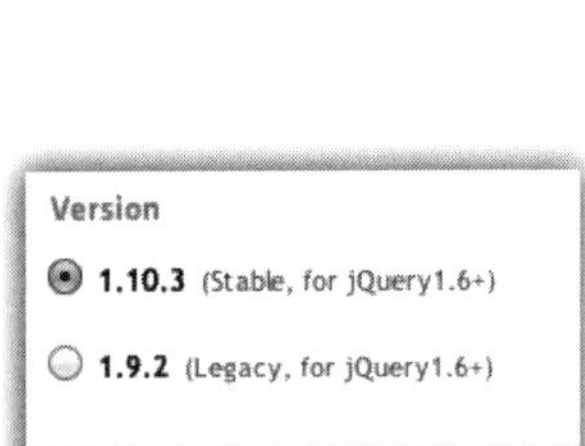


**Figure 14.4**

1. Head to http://jqueryui.com/.
2. Click Custom Download.
3. On the Custom Download page, first toggle everything off (**Figure 14.4**). The default is to download the entire library, which isn't necessary.

4. Select Datepicker in the Widgets section (**Figure 14.5**).

   The page will automatically select the other components that are required to use Datepicker.

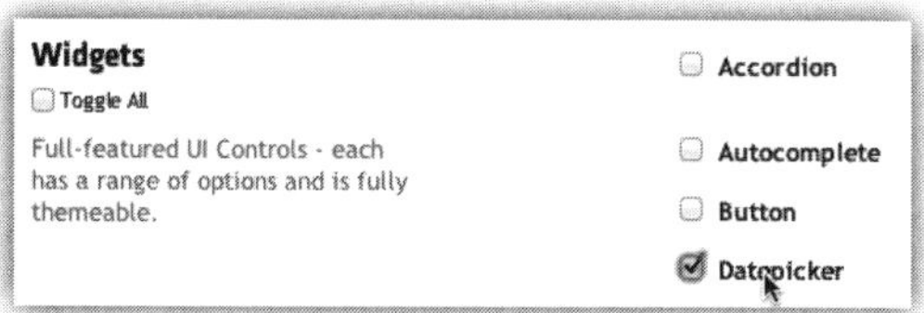


**Figure 14.5**

5. At the bottom of the page, select a theme (**Figure 14.6**).

   The jQuery Datepicker tool will use one of jQuery's User Interface themes for its formatting. I'll be using UI-Lightness, but you can choose whatever you like.

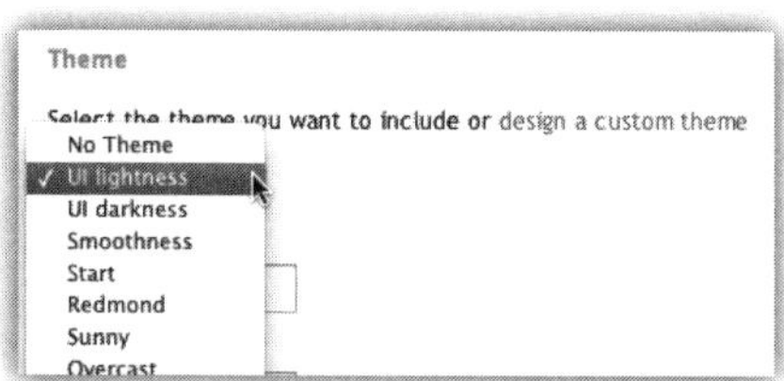


**Figure 14.6**

There are many other jQuery UI themes available (see http://jqueryui.com/), or you can roll your own.

6. Click Download.

7. Expand the downloaded folder.

   The download will have a name like **jquery-ui-1.10.3.custom.zip**.

8. Copy the contents of the **css/*theme*** folder to your site's **css** folder.

   For example, if you chose the UI-Lightness theme, copy the contents of **css/ui-lightness** to your CSS folder. This will include an images folder and the CSS files.

9. Open **create_sales.php** in your text editor or IDE.

10. At the end of the page, before the inclusion of the footer, include the UI-Lightness theme CSS file and the jQuery UI library:

```
<link href="/css/jquery-ui-1.10.3.custom.min.css"
➥rel="stylesheet" type="text/css" />
<script src="/js/jquery-ui-1.10.3.custom.min.js"
➥type="text/javascript" charset="utf-8"></script>
```

11. Add the **calendar** class to the two date inputs:

```
<td align="center"><input type="text" name="start_date[' .
➥$row['sku'] . ']" class="calendar" /></td>
<td align="center"><input type="text" name="end_date[' .
➥$row['sku'] . ']"  class="calendar" /></td>
```

The two date inputs have an additional **class** attribute, with a value of **calendar**. This class value will be used to apply the jQuery Datepicker to these inputs.

12. After the inclusion of the jQuery UI library, convert the two date columns into Datepickers:

```
<script type="text/javascript">
$(function() {
   $(".calendar").datepicker({dateFormat: "yy-mm-dd",
   ➥minDate:0});
});
</script>
```

The **$();** syntax in jQuery is a way of executing some JavaScript once the page has been loaded. The specific code to be executed is placed within an anonymous function.

The anonymous function selects every element on the page that has a class of **calendar**. To that selection, the **datepicker()** method is invoked, converting the elements into Datepickers. Two properties are passed to the **datepicker()** method. The first, **dateFormat: "yy-mm-dd"**, specifies the format that the selected date should be in. This format matches what is usable in the database queries. The second property, **minDate:0**, indicates that the earliest date that can be selected is the current date (zero days from now).

13. Save the file and test it in your browser (**Figure 14.7**).

| Start Date | End Date |
|---|---|

| Su | Mo | Tu | We | Th | Fr | Sa |
|---|---|---|---|---|---|---|
| | | 1 | 2 | 3 | 4 | 5 |
| 6 | 7 | 8 | 9 | 10 | 11 | 12 |
| 13 | 14 | 15 | 16 | 17 | 18 | 19 |
| 20 | 21 | 22 | 23 | 24 | 25 | 26 |
| 27 | 28 | 29 | 30 | 31 | | |

October 2013

**Figure 14.7**

# PAGINATION AND TABLE SORTING

The **view_orders.php** script purposefully does not include pagination, nor does it include a way for the administrator to sort by column (that is, by the customer's last name or zip code). But you can add both of these features—and many, many more—to the page by using one of the available table plug-ins for jQuery. For example, I've used DataTables before with great success (www.datatables.net). In the next series of steps, let's integrate DataTables into the **view_orders.php** script.

1. Download the latest version of DataTables from www.datatables.net.
2. Expand the downloaded folder.

   The result will be a folder named something like **DataTables-1.9.4**.
3. Copy the **media/js/jquery.dataTables.min.js** script to your site's **js** folder.

   This one script will do all the work, although you can also copy over the CSS and images if you'd like.
4. Open **view_orders.php** in your text editor or IDE.
5. After completing the table, exit the PHP section and include the DataTables script:

   ```
   ?>
   <script src="/js/jquery.dataTables.min.js" type="text/javascript"
   ➥charset="utf-8"></script>
   ```
6. Apply DataTables:

   ```
   <script type="text/javascript">
   $(function() {
      $("#orders").dataTable();
   });
   </script>
   ```

   That code selects the page element with an ID value of **orders**. The **dataTable()** function is applied to this selection. That's all you need to do (in terms of the JavaScript).
7. Re-engage PHP for the footer inclusion:

   ```
   <?php
   ```

8. Add the ID to the table:

```
<table border="0" width="100%" cellspacing="4" cellpadding="4"
➥id="orders">
```

9. Save the file and test it in your browser (**Figure 14.8**).

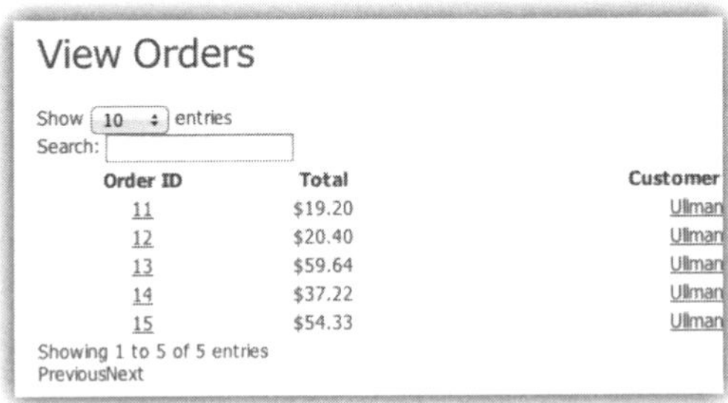


**Figure 14.8**

The changes will likely be subtle, but for starters, if you click the column headings now, the rows will be sorted by that column (**Figure 14.9**).

View Orders

Show 10 entries
Search:

| Order ID | Total | Customer |
|---|---|---|
| 13 | $59.64 | Ullman |
| 15 | $54.33 | Ullman |
| 14 | $37.22 | Ullman |
| 12 | $20.40 | Ullman |
| 11 | $19.20 | Ullman |

Showing 1 to 5 of 5 entries
PreviousNext

**Figure 14.9**

10. See the DataTables documentation for ways to customize the behavior and appearance.

# APPLYING AJAX

The remaining examples in this chapter will use Ajax. If you've never used Ajax before, it's about time you started. Ajax is a great way of enhancing the user's experience, and it's regularly implemented on the most popular sites. Using Ajax, what would otherwise require an overt request of the server, a redrawing of the web page, and perhaps even the loading of a different web page can now be accomplished behind the scenes while the browser stays put (so to speak).

If you're unsure of what, exactly, Ajax is, it can most simply be described as having JavaScript, behind the scenes, make a request of a server-side resource. For example, instead of having the entire browser submit form data to the server, wait for the server response, and redraw the page, you can use JavaScript to send the form data to the server and await the response while the user's browser remains unchanged.

tip

Ajax is just a label given to a combination of tools that have been around for years.

Applying Ajax is a multistep process:

1. Create the basic functionality.
2. Create the server-side script that JavaScript will request.
3. Add the JavaScript that invokes the server-side script.
4. Handle the server-side script's response.

Note that the Ajax resources (the server-side scripts) do not need to create complete HTML pages. In this chapter, these scripts will create only a bit of text. In more complicated examples, the server-side resources might create JavaScript Object Notation (JSON) data, or chunks of HTML to be displayed on the page (but, again, not entire HTML pages).

If you've never used Ajax before, the remaining part of the chapter will be either an eye-opening experience or overwhelming and frustrating. If you have problems with the following examples, the first thing you should do is directly run your server-side PHP script in the browser to confirm that it's working. Next, use your browser's network monitoring tools (**Figure 14.10**) to determine that

- The Ajax request is being made
- Data is being passed to the Ajax request (and what that data is)
- Data is being returned by the server-side script (and what that data is)

tip

As always, watch for JavaScript errors in your browser's console.

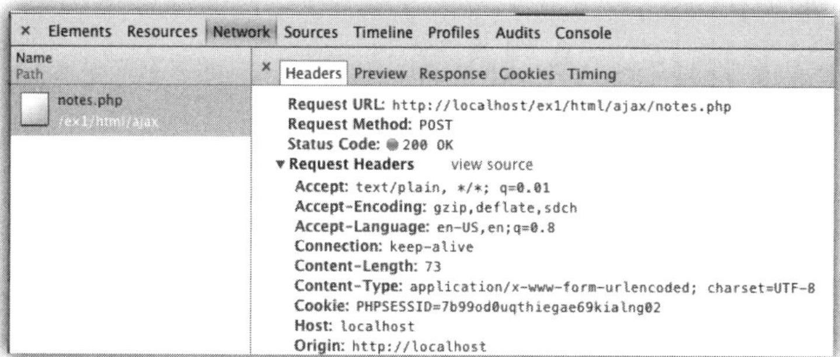


**Figure 14.10**

With this information, you should be able to identify the cause of the problem. Of course, be sure to take the time to formally learn JavaScript and Ajax. It will do you a world of good.

### MORE PROFESSIONAL AJAX

In this chapter, I'm creating the Ajax processes in a very ad hoc manner. Each server-side resource and section of JavaScript is being created on its own. Taking this approach makes it easy for you to follow and abides by the piecemeal take this book has on e-commerce. You can use what you want without too many integration issues. But in a complete site, I'd likely develop the Ajax side a bit differently.

The biggest change I'd make would be from creating individual, specialized Ajax-related PHP scripts to using a formal application programming interface (API). The adoption of consistent and powerful APIs has been critical to today's web. Once you've written a great API for your site, you'll have created a valuable tool that can be used in many ways. But the process of developing a formal and complete API is beyond what's practical for this book or chapter.

# WORKING WITH FAVORITES

For the first Ajax example, let's update the "Knowledge Is Power" site so that pages can be marked, or removed, as favorites without leaving the page. The ability to support favorites was explained in Chapter 12, "Extending the First Site." If you have not yet implemented that code and created the underlying database table, you'll need to do so first.

The code in Chapter 12 creates one of two blocks of HTML, depending on whether the page is currently listed as a favorite. If the page is a favorite, this HTML is added (**Figure 14.11**):

```
<h3><img src="images/heart_32.png" width="32" height="32">
➥<span class="label label-info">This is a favorite!</span>
➥<a href="remove_from_favorites.php?id=X"><img src=
➥"images/close_32.png" width="32" height="32"></a></h3>
```

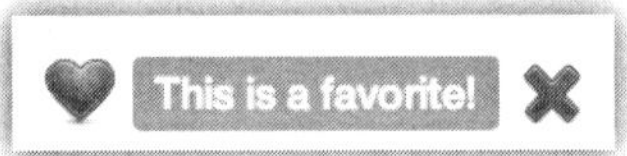


**Figure 14.11**

If the page is not a favorite, the user sees **Figure 14.12**:

```
<h3><span class="label label-info">Make this a favorite!</span>
➥<a href="add_to_favorites.php?id=X"><img src="images/heart_32.png"
➥width="32" height="32"></a></h3>
```

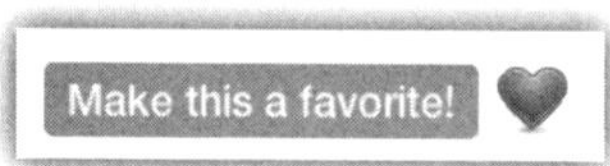


**Figure 14.12**

If the page is not listed as a favorite, a link is presented to mark it as so. If the page is listed as a favorite already, the user is given the option of deselecting it as a favorite. To "Ajax-ify" this process, when the user clicks one of those links, JavaScript will invoke the server-side script that adds or removes the favorite for that user in the database. The JavaScript will also need to update the page's HTML to reflect the changing status.

First, let's create the server-side resource that updates the database. Then I'll return to **page.php** to create the JavaScript code that will perform the Ajax request in lieu of sending the user to **add_to_favorites.php** and **remove_from_favorites.php**.

## Creating the Server-Side Resource

A single PHP script can be written so that it both adds and removes items from the user's list of favorites. To pull that off, the script needs three pieces of information:

- The page ID
- The user's ID
- The desired action (add or remove)

After performing some validation, the script will update the database. I'm writing this script so that it only returns a simple string: **true** or **false**, indicating whether or not the action succeeded. You'll see how this string is used in the JavaScript that invokes this script. For optimal security, this script will use prepared statements.

1. Create a new script in your text editor or IDE to be named **favorite.php** and stored in the **ajax** directory.

   ```
   <?php
   ```

   I recommend creating a new directory where all server-side resources for your Ajax processes go.

2. Require the configuration script:

```
require('../includes/config.inc.php');
```

This page will need the configuration script in order to access the database and the user's session.

3. Validate the required variables:

```
if (isset($_GET['page_id'], $_GET['action'], $_SESSION['user_id'])
   && filter_var($_GET['page_id'], FILTER_VALIDATE_INT,
   ➥array('min_range' => 1))
   && filter_var($_SESSION['user_id'], FILTER_VALIDATE_INT,
   ➥array('min_range' => 1))
   ) {
```

These are the three pieces of required information. Two will be passed in the URL and one will exist in the session. You can access the user's session here because the Ajax request, from the server's perspective, is being made by the user's browser as if the user were directly accessing this page (instead of the JavaScript actually doing so).

4. Define the query based on the desired action:

```
if ($_GET['action'] === 'add') {
   $q = 'REPLACE INTO favorite_pages (user_id, page_id)
   ➥VALUES (?, ?)';
} elseif ($_GET['action'] === 'remove') {
   $q = 'DELETE FROM favorite_pages WHERE user_id=? AND
   ➥page_id=?';
}
```

If the **$_GET['action']** value equals **add**, a **REPLACE** query is being executed. If the variable equals **remove**, a **DELETE** query will be run. Two placeholders represent the user's ID and the page ID.

5. Execute the query:

```
if (isset($q)) {
   require(MYSQL);
   $stmt = mysqli_prepare($dbc, $q);
   mysqli_stmt_bind_param($stmt, 'ii', $_SESSION['user_id'],
   ➥$_GET['page_id']);
   mysqli_stmt_execute($stmt);
```

If the **$q** variable was created, which means that **$_GET['action']** had a valid value, then the database connection script is included, the statement is prepared, the variables are bound, and the query is executed.

6. If a row was affected, print **true**, and terminate the script:

```
if (mysqli_stmt_affected_rows($stmt) > 0) {
   echo 'true';
   exit;
}
```

Printing **true** will be taken as an indication that the action succeeded.

7. Complete the conditionals and the script:

```
   }
} // Invalid values or didn't work!
echo 'false';
```

If the script did not succeed for any reason, it prints **false**.

8. Save the page.

If you want, you can already test it in your browser. You should see the word *false*. To make it work properly, append the two required values to the URL and execute the script while logged in:

http://www.example.com/ajax/favorite.php?action=add&page_id=18

Alternatively, you can just add this code to the script before the validation conditional:

```
$_GET['action'] = 'add';
$_GET['page_id'] = 18;
$_SESSION['user_id'] = 293;
```

(You can use any values you want for the last two; the page and user don't technically have to exist to test this.)

## Creating the Client Side

With the Ajax script written and tested, you can add the JavaScript to **page.php** that will call that PHP script. To keep the code cleaner, let's add the JavaScript in two steps. First, the **page.php** script needs to perform a simple task and then include the **favorite.js** JavaScript file. The **favorite.js** script will do all the remaining work. The basic functionality is relatively simple, but implementing that completely, handling all possible situations, takes a bit of thought.

1. Implement all of the favorite functionality (from Chapter 12), if you have not already.

   You'll also need to create the database table, also outlined in Chapter 12.

2. Open **page.php** in your text editor or IDE.

3. At the end of the page, before including the footer, add

```
echo '<script type="text/javascript">
var page_id = ' . $page_id . ';
</script>
<script src="js/favorite.js"></script>';
```

The first part creates a new script block containing one line of JavaScript:

```
var page_id = 2;
```

The remaining JavaScript will need access to the page ID value. You could get that from the URL using JavaScript, but since PHP already knows this value, I've chosen to have PHP assign it to a JavaScript variable. The result is a global JavaScript variable named **page_id**, with the proper value.

Next, the code includes **favorite.js**, to be written subsequently.

**note**

There are always reasonable arguments against using global variables, but the global **page_id** variable solves a problem easily and reliably.

4. Give your favorites-related elements unique ID values:

```
if (mysqli_num_rows($r) === 1) {
   echo '<h3 id="favorite_h3"><img src="images/heart_32.png"
   ➥width="32" height="32"> <span class="label label-info">
   ➥This is a favorite!</span> <a id="remove_favorite_link"
   ➥href="remove_from_favorites.php?id=' . $page_id . '">
   ➥<img src="images/close_32.png" width="32" height="32">
   ➥</a></h3>';
} else {
   echo '<h3 id="favorite_h3"><span class="label label-info">
   ➥Make this a favorite!</span> <a id="add_favorite_link"
   ➥href="add_to_favorites.php?id=' . $page_id . '"><img src=
   ➥"images/heart_32.png" width="32" height="32"></a></h3>';
}
```

These ID values will be required by the JavaScript. Make sure the links have the ID values **add_favorite_link** and **remove_favorite_link**. The H3 tag also has an ID value that will be necessary later.

5. Save the file.

If you want, you can reload the page in your browser. You should see an error—the **favorite.js** script does not yet exist—but you should also see the creation of the **page_id** variable (**Figure 14.13**).

```
</form>
<script type="text/javascript">var page_id = 2;</script>
<script src="js/favorite.js"></script>
```

**Figure 14.13**

With that done, you should create **favorite.js** next.

1. Create a new JavaScript file in your text editor or IDE to be named **favorite.js** and stored in the **js** directory.

2. Define the jQuery function that watches for the page to be ready:

   ```
   $(function() {
   });
   ```

   Everything else will go between these two lines.

3. Add a click event handler to the "add favorite" link:

   ```
   $('#add_favorite_link').click(function(){
      manage_favorites('add');
      return false;
   });
   ```

   This code first selects the item with an ID value of **add_favorite_link** and then assigns a click event handler to it. Within the function, the **manage_favorites()** function (a JavaScript function, to be defined shortly) will be called when this event occurs, passing along the value **add**. The **return false** line prevents the browser from following the link.

4. Repeat the process for the "remove favorite" link:

   ```
   $('#remove_favorite_link').click(function(){
      manage_favorites('remove');
      return false;
   });
   ```

   The code is the same except this event will result in **remove** being passed to **manage_favorites()**.

5. Begin defining the **manage_favorites()** function:

   ```
   function manage_favorites(action) {
   ```

   This function will be called when the click event happens. (Well, technically, the anonymous function is called, which then calls this one.) The **action** value, **add** or **remove**, will be used shortly.

   The purpose of this function is to perform the Ajax request.

6. Perform the Ajax request:

```
$.ajax({
    url: 'ajax/favorite.php',
    type: 'GET',
    dataType: 'text',
    data: {
        page_id: page_id,
        action: action
    },
    success: function(response) {
        if (response === 'true') {
            update_page(action);
        } else {
            // Do something!
        }
    } // Success function.
}); // Ajax
```

There's a lot going on here, and I'll explain it in detail. First, the **ajax()** function is jQuery's most general tool for performing Ajax requests. It takes as an argument an object of values that configure the request. That object is defined within **{}**. The syntax for a generic JavaScript object is **name: value**. An alternative way to write this code is

```
var options = {
    url: 'ajax/favorite.php',
    // And so on
};
$.ajax(options);
```

The first named item in the configuration object is **url**, which points to the server-side resource to be requested. The **type** value is the type of request to perform, normally GET or POST. The **dataType** item indicates what kind of data is expected back from the request.

Next, the **data** property is used to send data as part of the request. This is where you can pass values to the server-side script. For this particular request, two variables must be passed: **page_id** and **action**. The values of both come from JavaScript variables. Because the Ajax request uses the GET method, thanks to this **data** object the server-side PHP script will receive **$_GET['page_id']** and **$_GET['action']**.

Finally, to the **success** item you assign the function to be called when the request is successfully made. An anonymous function is being used here.

It checks the response from the server-side script. That response will be a simple string: **true** or **false**. If the response is **true**, the database was updated and the JavaScript **update_page()** function can be called.

If the response is **false**, nothing happens right now. Almost certainly the only reason for a **false** response is that you've programmed something incorrectly. You shouldn't see this on a live site. But in the **false** case, you could indicate an error to the user, or add JavaScript that lets the click process actually go through.

**7.** Complete the function:

```
} // End of manage_favorites() function.
```

**8.** Begin defining the **update_page()** function:

```
function update_page(action) {
  if (action === 'add') {
```

This function will be called after the Ajax process. Its job is to update the page's HTML to reflect the changing status. The first thing the function does is check the value of **action**. This will be either **add** or **remove**.

**9.** Update the HTML:

```
$('#favorite_h3').html('<img src="images/heart_32.png"
➥width="32" height="32"> <span class="label label-info">
➥This is a favorite!</span> <a id="remove_favorite_link"
➥href="remove_from_favorites.php?id=' + page_id + '"><img src=
➥"images/close_32.png" width="32" height="32"></a></h3>');
```

The HTML within the H3 tag is changed out from its original contents to new contents that mark this page as a favorite. The new content also has a link to remove the item from being a favorite. That link uses the global **page_id** variable.

This link allows the user to remove it as a favorite, in case she changed her mind or clicked "add favorite" by mistake.

**10.** Add an event handler for the new link:

```
$('#remove_favorite_link').click(function(){
➥manage_favorites('remove'); return false; });
```

The first time the user loads the page, only the "add favorite" link will exist. The line that adds the click event handler to the "remove favorite" link won't do anything in that case. So the add event handler code needs to be duplicated now to give this new link the same functionality.

**11.** Complete the function:

```
    } else {
        $('#favorite_h3').html('<h3 id="favorite_h3"><span class=
        ➥"label label-info">Make this a favorite!</span>
        ➥<a id="add_favorite_link" href="add_to_favorites.php?id='
        ➥+ page_id + '"><img src="images/heart_32.png" width="32"
        ➥height="32"></a></h3>');
        $('#add_favorite_link').click(function(){
        ➥manage_favorites('add'); return false; });
    }
} // End of update_page() function.
```

This is a replication of the code in Steps 9 and 10, although now creating the “add favorite” HTML and event handler.

**12.** Save and test in your browser.

You should be able to toggle the HTML back and forth by clicking the links. You can simultaneously watch your database to see the changes, or you can reload the page to confirm the changing status.

To debug any problems, keep an eye on the error console and the network monitor.

# RECORDING NOTES

Another feature added to the “Knowledge Is Power” site in Chapter 12 is the ability for users to take notes on a page (**Figure 14.14**). That process required a form submission to save the entered notes. It’d be nice if the saving could be done via Ajax as well.

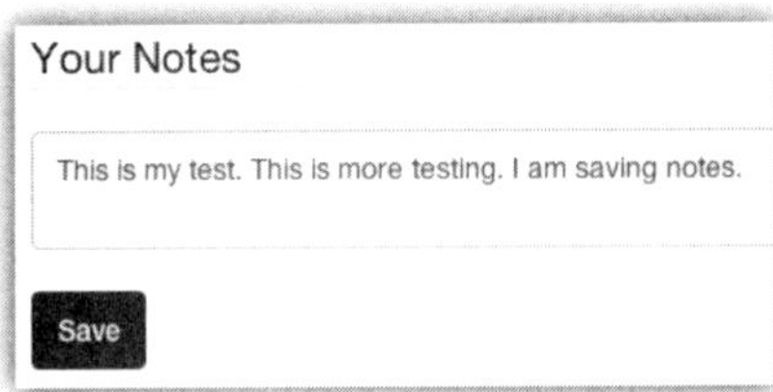


**Figure 14.14**

As with the previous example, I’ll first create the server-side PHP script and then turn to the client side.

## Creating notes.php

The server-side PHP script will expect to receive three pieces of information:

- The page ID
- The user's ID
- The notes

After performing some validation, the script will update the database. If the notes value is empty, a **DELETE** query will be run. Otherwise, an **INSERT** or **UPDATE** will be executed. As with **favorites.php**, this script will return a simple string: **true** or **false**, indicating whether or not the action succeeded. Again, prepared statements will be used.

1. Create a new script in your text editor or IDE to be named **notes.php** and stored in the **ajax** directory:

```
<?php
```

2. Require the configuration script:

```
require('../includes/config.inc.php');
```

3. Validate the required variables:

```
if (isset($_POST['page_id'], $_POST['notes'],
➥$_SESSION['user_id'])
   && filter_var($_POST['page_id'], FILTER_VALIDATE_INT,
   ➥array('min_range' => 1))
   && filter_var($_SESSION['user_id'], FILTER_VALIDATE_INT,
   ➥array('min_range' => 1))
   ) {
```

These are the three pieces of information that are required. One will exist in the session. The other two will be POSTed to the script.

4. Include the database connection:

```
require(MYSQL);
```

5. If no notes were provided, create a **DELETE** query:

```
if (empty($_POST['notes'])) {
   $q = 'DELETE FROM notes WHERE user_id=? AND page_id=?';
   $stmt = mysqli_prepare($dbc, $q);
   mysqli_stmt_bind_param($stmt, 'ii', $_SESSION['user_id'],
   ➥$_POST['page_id']);
```

**note**

From a philosophical perspective, scripts that cause database changes should use POST (arguably, **favorite.php** should).

If the notes value is empty, then a **DELETE** query will be run. Because the two queries this script executes differ in the number of parameters used, they must be prepared and bound to variables separately.

6. If notes were provided, update or insert the record:

```
} else {
   $q = 'REPLACE INTO notes (user_id, page_id, note)
   ➥VALUES (?, ?, ?)';
   $stmt = mysqli_prepare($dbc, $q);
   mysqli_stmt_bind_param($stmt, 'iis', $_SESSION['user_id'],
   ➥$_POST['page_id'], $_POST['notes']);
}
```

7. Execute the query:

```
mysqli_stmt_execute($stmt);
```

8. If more than one row was affected, print **true** and terminate the script:

```
if (mysqli_stmt_affected_rows($stmt) > 0) {
   echo 'true';
   exit;
}
```

9. Complete the conditionals and the script:

```
} // Invalid values or didn't work!
echo 'false';
```

If the script did not succeed for any reason, it prints **false**.

10. Save the page.

If you want, you can already test it in your browser. You should see the word *false*. To test it for proper usage, add this code before the validation conditional:

```
$_POST['page_id'] = 18;
$_POST['notes'] = 'Lorem ipsum dolor sit amet, consetetur
➥sadipscing';
$_SESSION['user_id'] = 293;
```

## Creating the Client-Side Materials

With the Ajax script written and tested, you can add the JavaScript to **page.php** that will call that PHP script. The **page.php** script already has one JavaScript block that creates a global variable that will also be required here:

```
<script type="text/javascript">
var page_id = 2;
</script>
```

The JavaScript file that interacts with **notes.php** will be added after that code. But first, let's make sure that **page.php** has the right HTML elements and values. You'll also need to have implemented all of the notes functionality (from Chapter 12), if you haven't already done so. Those steps include creating the database table.

1. Open **page.php** in your text editor or IDE, if it isn't already open.
2. Give the form for adding notes, and the notes textarea, unique ID values:

   ```
   echo '<form id="notes_form" action="page.php?id=' . $page_id . '"
   ➥method="post" accept-charset="utf-8">
   <fieldset><legend>Your Notes</legend>
   <textarea name="notes" id="notes" class="form-control">';
   ```

   The ID values will be used by the JavaScript.
3. Include the **notes.js** file:

   ```
   echo '<script type="text/javascript">
   var page_id = ' . $page_id . ';
   </script>
   <script src="js/favorite.js"></script>
   <script src="js/notes.js"></script>';
   ```

   This is an update of the **echo** statement previously added. It doesn't matter in which order you include **favorite.js** and **notes.js**.
4. Save the file.

With that done, you should create **notes.js**:

1. Create a new JavaScript file in your text editor or IDE to be named **notes.js** and stored in the **js** directory.
2. Define the jQuery function that watches for the page to be ready:

   ```
   $(function() {
   });
   ```

   Everything else will go between these two lines.
3. Get a reference to the form:

   ```
   var notes_form = $('#notes_form');
   ```

   The form will be accessed twice by the code, so it'll be useful to create one reference to it.

4. Begin defining a submit event handler:

```
notes_form.submit(function(){
```

All of the remaining code will go within this anonymous function.

5. Begin the Ajax request:

```
$.ajax({
   url: 'ajax/notes.php',
   type: 'POST',
   dataType: 'text',
   data: {00
      page_id: page_id,
      notes: $('#notes').val()
   },
```

Again, the **ajax()** method needs to receive a JavaScript object of information. First, the URL is defined. Next, the **type** is the type of request to make. This time, it's a POST request. The data type expected in return is **text**. Next, the **data** property is used to send information to the server-side script. One piece of information is the page ID. The second piece is the text entered into the notes textarea. The **val()** method can be used to retrieve the value of any form element.

6. Define the success function:

```
success: function(response) {
   if (response === 'true') {
      var notes_message = $('#notes_message');
      if (notes_message.length !== 0) {
         notes_message.html('Your notes have been saved again.');
      } else {
         notes_form.prepend('<p id="notes_message" class="alert
         ➥alert-success">Your notes have been saved.</p>');
      }
   } else {
      // Do something!
   }
} // Success function.
```

This is a bit more complicated than that in **favorite.js**, although the general structure is the same. First, the code checks that the response equals **true**. If so, a simple "Your notes have been saved" message should be added to the page (**Figure 14.15**). However, the second time the user clicks submit, the message will already exist; you wouldn't want to add it again. To prevent that, this code first tries to select the element with an ID value of **notes_message**. If such an element exists (which you can test for by checking the variable's **length** property), its HTML is simply updated (**Figure 14.16**). If no such element exists, a paragraph with that ID value is prepended to the form. This means it'll be added as the first child of the form.

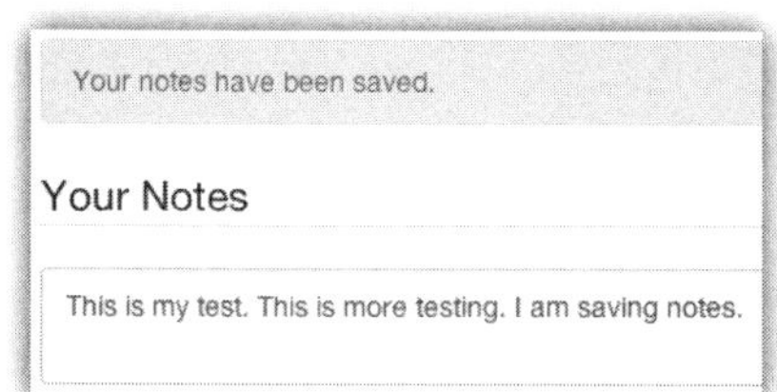


**Figure 14.15**

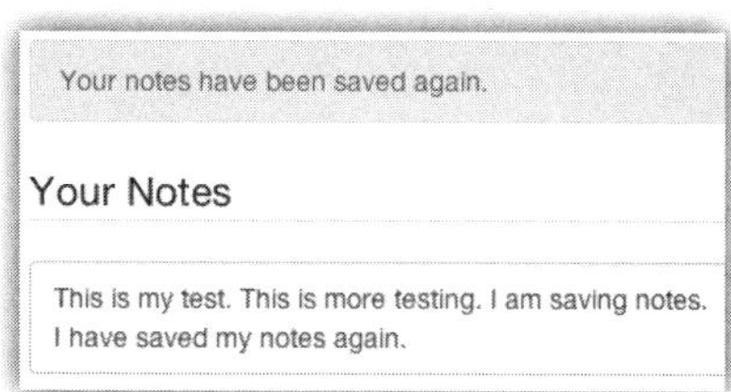


**Figure 14.16**

Again, you may want to add code that does something should the result not be **true**, although that's most likely due to a programming error on your part and shouldn't occur on a live site.

**tip**

Another feature you can add is a timer that invokes the Ajax request every couple of minutes to automatically save the user's notes.

7. Complete all of the functions:

```
        }); // Ajax
        return false;
    }); // End of submit() function.
}); // Main anonymous function
```

8. Save and test in your browser.

# BETTER CART MANAGEMENT

Another good use of Ajax involves managing the cart for the Coffee site. First, you can use Ajax to dynamically add items to the cart without the user leaving the page she's currently viewing (in other words, without being taken to **cart.php**). To support that, write the server-side Ajax script to function exactly like **cart.php**. The script will need to receive an SKU and an action. The script can then fetch the customer's session ID from a cookie, or create one if none exists. After validating the received data, the Ajax script will then call the stored procedure to add the item to the shopping cart table in the database.

Moreover, if you exactly mimic the logic of the original **cart.php**, you can create an Ajax script that can be used to

- Add items to the cart
- Remove items from the cart
- Update the quantities in the cart

Subsequently, with all that logic in place, you can Ajax-ify all of these pages:

- **browse.php**
- **cart.php**
- **wish_list.php**

You can also replicate this work to Ajax-ify the wish list management.

In terms of the JavaScript required, along with making the Ajax request, the JavaScript will need to notify the user of whatever change was made. The only tricky scenarios would be updates on the **cart.php** and **wish_list.php** pages. On those pages, changes made to the cart or wish list via Ajax would need to be made dynamically using JavaScript. This would be a matter of adding or removing table rows.

If you feel like pursuing any of these ideas and need assistance, just post a message in my support forums (www.LarryUllman.com/forums/).

# TAKING CUSTOMER FEEDBACK

Chapter 13, "Extending the Second Site," added a way for users to review products on the Coffee site. At the time, the review was a simple form, taking the user's name, email address, and the review itself. Let's now look at three better ways to take customer feedback, making use of JavaScript in general and Ajax in particular

## Submitting Reviews

Just like the note-taking ability in the "Knowledge Is Power" site, the reviews are submitted to the site by formally reloading the **browse.php** page. That's absolutely fine, but the experience can be slightly better if reviews are submitted via Ajax.

The basic principle and functionality generally match that already explained with the **notes.js** script. The only significant difference is that the reviews form provides (and requires) three form elements. Each needs to be validated. This also means the JavaScript needs to be written to handle errors on each of these.

Start by creating a form submission event handler in jQuery:

```
$(function() {
   var reviews_form = $('#reviews_form');
   reviews_form.submit(function(){
   });
})
```

Within the event handler, you should first validate the form elements. Here's how that looks; it's just checking for nonempty values:

```
var okay = true;
var name = $('#name').val();
if (name.length == 0) {
   okay = false;
   // Add CSS formatting and warning text.
}
```

As you can see there, I'm using a flag variable to determine whether or not the form was properly filled out. If any element is empty, then **okay** will become `false`.

For each empty input, you'll want to add a CSS class to highlight the offending field, and add a text message to the page indicating the problem.

**tip**

For more precision, you can first trim the form value of empty spaces before checking its length.

Once all of the validation has been performed, if no error occurred you perform the Ajax request, passing the data to a server-side script. That will look a lot like the JavaScript and PHP used in the note-handling process.

Finally, upon the successful completion of the Ajax process, replace the entire review form with a message indicating the successful submission:

```
reviews_form.html('<p>Thank you for your review!</p>');
```

## Marking Reviews as Helpful

Another addition is to allow users to mark reviews as helpful. This is a great "meta" feature that ensures that the better reviews bubble to the top and are always the most readily available (well, that's the theory anyway).

One way of creating such a feature is to start with a database table like this:

```
CREATE TABLE review_votes (
`id` INT UNSIGNED NOT NULL AUTO_INCREMENT,
`review_id` INT UNSIGNED NOT NULL,
`vote` TINYINT UNSIGNED NOT NULL,
PRIMARY KEY (`id`),
KEY (`review_id`)
) ENGINE=InnoDB DEFAULT CHARSET=utf8;
```

The table has a foreign key to the **reviews** table. Each vote for a review as being helpful is recorded as a 1. Unhelpful review votes are recorded as 0. The most helpful reviews are either those with the most 1's or the highest average, depending on how you'd prefer to rank them.

I've selected the vote average in the query in Figure 14.17 so that you can see how it works.

This query can pull the reviews for a product in the order of most helpful to least helpful (**Figure 14.17**):

```
SELECT review FROM reviews LEFT JOIN review_votes ON
➥reviews.id=review_votes.review_id GROUP BY review_id
➥ORDER BY AVG(vote) DESC
```

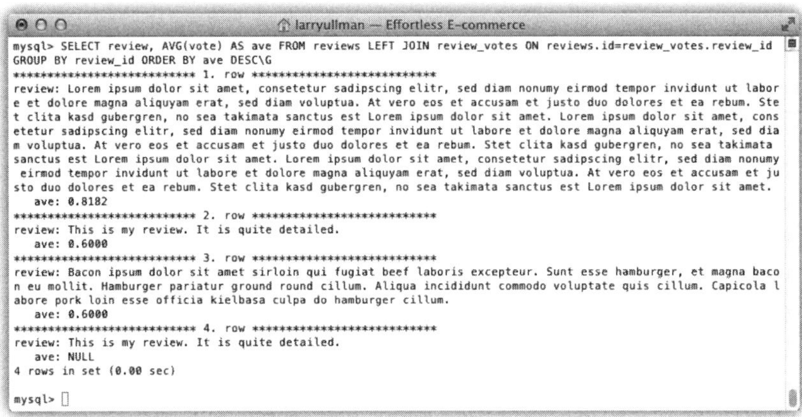



**Figure 14.17**

From the programming perspective, you can make two links:

```
Was this review helpful? <a id="helpful_yes_link" href="helpful.
➥php?vote=1&id=' . $review_id . '">Yes</a> | <a id="helpful_no_link"
➥href="helpful.php?vote=0&id=' . $review_id . '">No</a>
```

As you can see, both links are to **helpful.php**, passing along the review ID and the vote. That script records the vote in the database.

This basic functionality can easily be updated to use Ajax, just like the **favorites.js** script does. Start with that example's code as your approach if you'd like to implement this.

The problem with the structure and approach explained thus far is that it'd be extremely easy to hack. I could create a PHP script that calls the **mark_review.php** page hundreds of times in order to promote or demote the reviews I want. To prevent that kind of abuse, you need some way to associate a vote with a user.

One option is to allow only logged-in users to vote. You can then store the user's ID in the **review_votes** table and put a **UNIQUE** index on the combination of the **review_id** and the **user_id** to prevent duplicate submissions. This restriction to logged-in users would greatly and easily minimize abuse, but it would also greatly limit the number of votes received. In other words, you'd end up with less, but better quality, data.

If you don't want to restrict votes to logged-in users, you'll need another way of identifying each uniquely. If, as in the Coffee site, anonymous users still have identifying cookies, that value can be used. If the site doesn't already use cookies, you can create one for this purpose. Yes, a hacker can simply delete or assign a new value to the cookie, but that's better than nothing at all.

Another option is to use an identifier available in PHP's **$_SERVER** array. You can, for example, use the user's IP address. This value is easy to access, but doing so comes with its own problems. First, multiple users from the same large organization may all be associated with the same IP address. Second, most users' IP addresses change frequently.

Those are some of the options for identifying users, and you can find others online. You'll need to choose the approach that's best for your site and your site's users.

## ADDING RATINGS

In Chapter 13, I mentioned star ratings as another way to get good user feedback. There are several methods of implementing star ratings. The progressively enhanced version uses an HTML5 range input, or any HTML standard's select menu, as the basic interface. This is then magically converted to something stylish using CSS and JavaScript. You can find instructions online.

Since both sites in this book are already using jQuery, I recommend using a jQuery plug-in instead. The RateIt plug-in (http://rateit.codeplex.com/) is one of the most reliable and exhaustive star rating plug-ins I've seen. It's easy to use, flexible, and well maintained. You should have few problems using it, along with the information in this chapter, to add star ratings to either example project.

# 15 USING STRIPE PAYMENTS

Since I wrote the first edition of this book in 2010, an exciting new way of accepting payments online has arisen. I've labeled this the "middle way," because the approach provides all the benefits of both of the traditional methods of accepting payments. Stripe is one such "middle way" provider. I absolutely recommend using Stripe, or a "middle way" provider like Stripe, for your e-commerce projects.

In this chapter, I'll explain what Stripe is, how it works, and how you create an account there. I'll then walk you through using Stripe to process single charges (as a possible replacement for using Authorize.net) on the Coffee site. Finally, I'll explain how you can use Stripe to process recurring payments (as a possible replacement for PayPal) with the "Knowledge Is Power" example.

## ABOUT STRIPE

Stripe was created in 2010 with the goal of making it much, much easier to accept credit card payments online. At the time, accepting credit cards meant burdensome PCI compliance requirements, the need for a merchant account, and lots of fees. Stripe came onto the scene with a product that was vastly easier to implement, dead simple to understand, and extremely developer friendly.

To best understand what Stripe is, compare it to the alternative solutions. In an e-commerce site, you take a customer's billing information and pass it, along with the order information (at the very least, the total order amount), to a payment gateway such as Authorize.net. Authorize.net acts as an intermediary between the credit card companies and a *merchant account*. The payment

## MY RELATIONSHIP WITH STRIPE

I first used Stripe in 2012 as the payment provider on a client's e-commerce site (by the client's choice). I was immediately impressed. Over the course of 2012, I published a series on my blog on integrating Stripe to process payments. Going into 2013, when planning this edition of this book, I knew I would explain Stripe in the book because Stripe provides such a great solution for a complicated problem. When I made that decision, I had no other affiliation with the company; I just highly respected their product and organization, and I thought you, the reader, would do well to consider Stripe for your e-commerce projects.

Through a series of events, in the summer of 2013 I accepted a support position at Stripe. After 14 years of working for myself, this was too good an opportunity to pass up. I went to work for Stripe for the same reason I had already chosen to include Stripe in this book: It's a fantastic product that you ought to consider using.

In this chapter, I'll say many glowing things about Stripe. I'm not saying them because I work at Stripe. On the contrary, I work at Stripe and I'm covering Stripe in this book because I feel so strongly about the company and the product.

That being said, I feel equally strongly about this new "middle way" of processing payments. If you cannot, or would rather not, use Stripe, there are similar alternatives. In Europe, Paymill (www.paymill.com) is the most comparable. In the United States and many other countries, Braintree Payments (www.braintreepayments.com) is another.

gateway confirms that the charge can be made to the customer's credit card and passes that charge information to the merchant account. The payment gateway will report the results back to your site, too. The merchant account is what allows your business to accept credit card transactions. It coordinates the credit card transactions with your bank account, getting you your money (**Figure 15.1**).

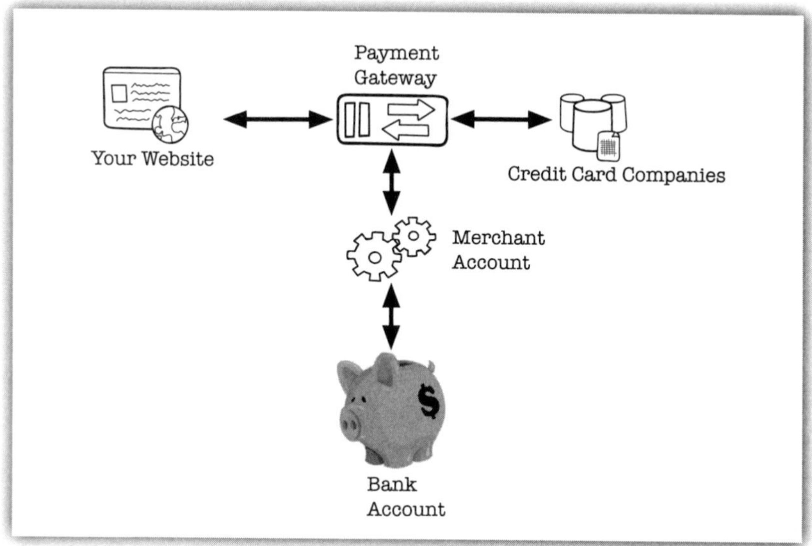


**Figure 15.1**

Your bank may also be able to act as the merchant account.

This is the basic premise of the conventional payment systems. Note that you can't just mix and match the pieces involved. Different payment gateways and merchant accounts accept different card types. And different payment gateways, merchant accounts, and bank accounts are set up to work together (or not).

Furthermore, this conventional payment system has oodles of fees. The payment gateway charges a transaction fee, and the merchant account does, too. You may also need to pay monthly fees.

So how is Stripe different? First, Stripe is a "full-stack" solution, meaning Stripe acts as both the payment gateway and the merchant account. Your website communicates the customer and order information to Stripe, Stripe clears it with the associated credit card company, and Stripe puts the money in your bank account (**Figure 15.2**). And...that's it. You don't have to do anything special with your bank account to make this happen. It just works.

Figure 15.2

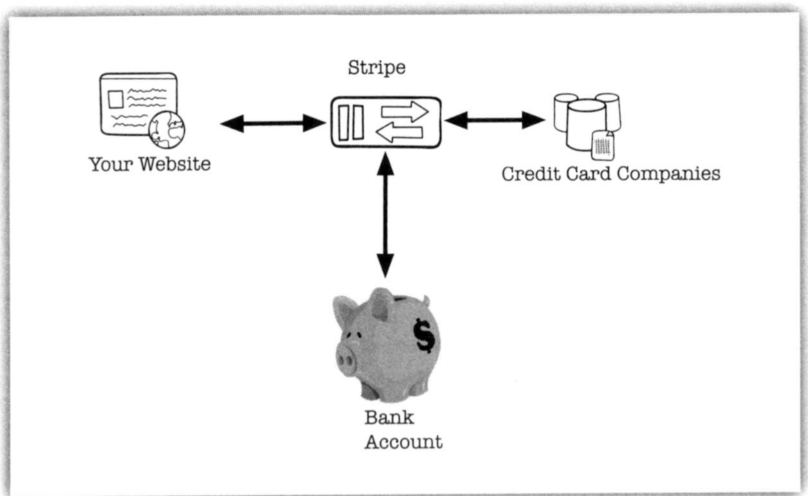


Another key difference with Stripe is that it has virtually removed the PCI requirements that exist when using a traditional payment provider. To use Stripe, you need to

- Load the payment page over HTTPS
- Include a Stripe JavaScript library
- Not assign names to key form elements

That's it for integration and PCI compliance: Just have an SSL certificate to enable HTTPS, as you would with any e-commerce site.

This brings me to why I refer to this as the "middle way" approach. Using this technique, you don't have a heavy PCI compliance burden that comes with having the customer's credit card information touch your server. And yet you also don't have to send the customer to a third-party site to complete the transaction, as you do with the conventional PayPal approach. It's truly the best of both worlds.

As mentioned in other chapters, both PayPal and Authorize.net now have "middle way"–like options.

## Why Stripe?

You have many options when it comes to processing payments, so why should you consider Stripe? First, and I cannot stress this enough, Stripe is crazy easy to use. You probably can't fully appreciate how easy Stripe is to use until you use it, but know now that being easy to use is a core principle at Stripe.

Second, from a developer's standpoint, Stripe is a real joy. They've created a clean, powerful API that allows you to utilize the Stripe system however you need to. Stripe provides a user-friendly web-based interface, but their API steals the show.

Stripe offers all the functionality you would expect (or hope for) from any payment system. Stripe can do all of the following:

- Process all the major credit cards
- Handle onetime payments
- Support subscriptions (recurring payments)
- Detect and prevent fraud
- Automatically send out email receipts
- Let you manually enter charges, if need be

All prices are in US dollars and are correct as of this writing.

Stripe also provides good libraries for interacting with the Stripe API in the most popular programming languages. And Stripe's documentation is reasonably short, understandable, and easy to look through for answers.

In terms of the financials, Stripe's fees are about as good as you'll get in the industry. For each successful transaction, you pay 2.9 percent of the total charge plus 30 cents. So a $10 charge costs you 59 cents. A $100 charge costs you $3.20. Again, these rates are fairly standard; PayPal charges the same. Stripe has no monthly fees and no setup fees, and you won't be charged for failed payments.

The minimum charge you would process through Stripe is 50 cents.

And, if you're now convinced to try Stripe, know that you can be taking real, live payments in less than an hour. Stripe has no tedious application process, and there's no long wait for your account to be approved.

## Why Not Stripe?

tip

You can be notified when Stripe is available in your country by signing up at https://stripe.com/global.

Although I can readily recommend that anyone consider using Stripe, it's not the right choice for everyone. To be fair and balanced, I'll discuss some reasons you might not use Stripe.

First, Stripe is currently only available in the United States, Canada, the United Kingdom, and Ireland. It's available in beta in a few more countries at the time of this writing, too. Stripe is expanding, but it may not be accessible to you yet.

Second, Stripe is not the most feature-rich processor. For example, if you need a built-in tax calculator, Stripe can't do that for you, although you can turn to some third-party sites for that functionality. If you need monthly statements, they aren't directly provided (although you can create your own by exporting the data you need).

Third, by default, Stripe will transfer monies to your bank account seven days after the transaction has occurred. This delay allows for refunds to be processed or fraudulent charges to be caught (and means that Stripe does not need to keep some of your funds in reserve). Most payment systems have a built-in delay, though, except for a PayPal-to-PayPal transaction (although all PayPal monies still take a couple of days to be transferred to your bank account).

tip

If you send an email to Stripe support, the response might come from me!

Finally, as of this writing, there's no support phone number you can call. Stripe's documentation is quite good, and you can get support via email or Internet Relay Chat (IRC), but if you absolutely need a number you can dial, that's not Stripe (not now, anyway).

# CREATING AN ACCOUNT

When you go to use any payment system for the first time on a project, you'll need to create a test account. As with almost every step of the process, Stripe makes this ridiculously easy.

With most payment systems, testing is done in one of two ways:

- Create a test account, which is entirely separate from the live account.
- Create a real account, but send test transactions through a separate system.

With Stripe, you'll need to create only one account. You'll use this same account for both testing and live transactions. The only difference will be the use of two API keys (one is public, one is private), as I'll explain later. You'll develop your site using the test API keys. Then, when the site is ready to go live, you swap those out for the real API keys. You don't have to change any other code, including the URL used to communicate with Stripe (which, as you'll discover, you never see anyway).

Let's start by creating your account:

1. Head to https://stripe.com.
2. Click Sign In (in the upper-right corner).
3. On the Sign In page, click Sign Up, next to "Don't have an account?"
4. Enter your email address and a password (**Figure 15.3**).

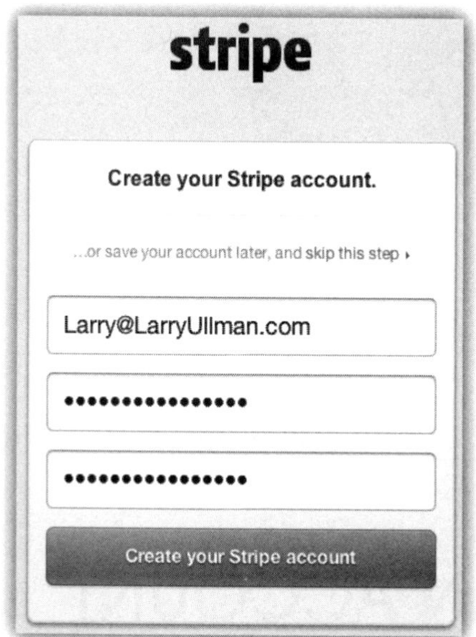


**Figure 15.3**

You can actually play around with Stripe—including taking test charges from your site—without creating an account at all. To do that, click "skip this step," and then you can access a temporary, unnamed account that can be used for testing purposes. But I think it makes more sense to go ahead and create an account that you can later return to.

5. Click "Create your Stripe account."

That's all you need to do to create a real Stripe account. You're now ready to begin integrating it. You can create and test transactions and then view those transactions within the Stripe interface. At this point, you can even start taking real payments! But in order for those payments to be transferred to your bank account, you'll need to activate your account first. I'll explain that process later in the chapter.

Before integrating Stripe into your site, you'll need your API keys, which are your unique identifiers. They're available through your Stripe dashboard, which is where you end up after first creating an account or after logging in.

1. In the dashboard, click Your Account > Account Settings.
2. In the Account Settings control panel, click API Keys.
3. Copy your test secret and test publishable keys (**Figure 15.4**).

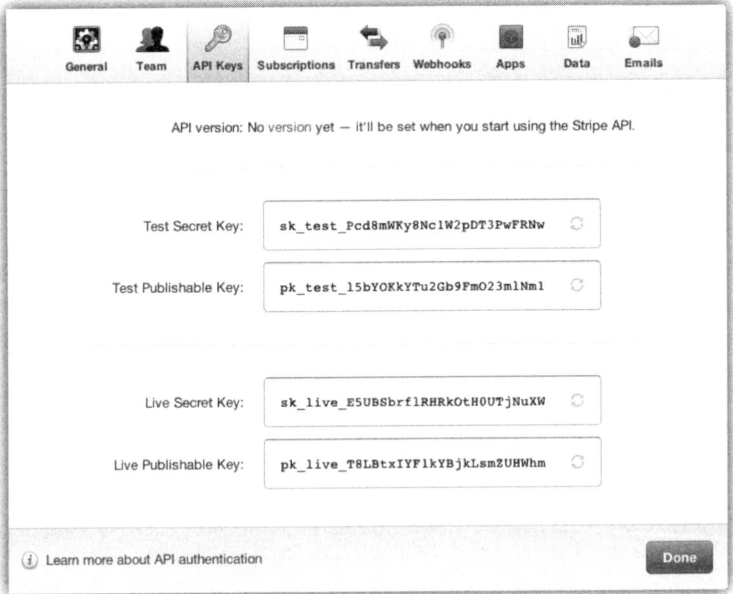


**Figure 15.4**

It's a bit confusing, but the LIVE/TEST switch in the upper-left corner only toggles what data you view. It does not change your status.

4. Click Done to leave the Account Settings panel.
5. Click Your Account > Sign Out to leave the Stripe dashboard.

   After you've implemented Stripe and run a few test charges, you can log in again to view those.

# PERFORMING SINGLE CHARGES

Before getting into the code, I should reiterate how Stripe works compared to traditional payment processing approaches. Historically, depending on the payment system in use, there were two possible workflows. In the conventional PayPal approach (and those like it), the user is sent from your site to the payment processor's site, where the payment information will be taken. The user is then hopefully returned to your site.

With Authorize.net (and others), your site takes the payment information and passes it to the payment processor behind the scenes. The user never leaves your site, but the customer's payment information does go through your server.

As I already said, Stripe has developed a great middle ground between these two approaches. Thanks to the **`Stripe.js`** JavaScript library, you can have your proverbial cake and eat it too. Using **`Stripe.js`**, the user never leaves your website *and* you aren't exposed to extra security risks, because the user's payment information won't touch your server. The process works like this:

1. You create a form on your website that accepts the payment details.
2. You include a Stripe JavaScript library on the page.
3. You write a JavaScript function that watches for the form submission.
4. When the form is submitted, the user's payment details are securely sent to Stripe via Ajax.
5. Stripe confirms that the payment information is valid and returns a *token* that uniquely identifies that payment information (for example, **`tok_1RjDrZFBkiyqTt`**).
6. The JavaScript function that handles the Ajax response stores the token in a hidden form element and actually submits the form to your server.
7. The server-side script (aka the PHP code) that handles the form's submission uses the token to process the payment.

So the customer never leaves your site, but the payment information never hits your server!

**tip**

Most of the complication of using Stripe in the Coffee example comes from adopting a process designed for Authorize.net to now use Stripe.

Let's apply this new approach to the Coffee site. You'll first create the HTML form. Then you'll create the JavaScript that validates the form data, sends it to Stripe, and handles the response. Finally, you'll write the server-side PHP script that processes the payment.

## Creating the Form

Integrating Stripe into the Coffee site begins by editing **`billing.html`**, the page that displays the final payment form. For the purposes of the JavaScript, the form and its elements will need to have proper ID values. Most importantly, to maintain the minimal PCI compliance burden, the form elements for the credit card data—number, expiration date, and CVC code—should not have name values. This is very important!

Stripe takes advantage of a little-known quality of HTML forms. The names of your form elements correspond to the names of the indexes where you can access the form data: **`$_POST['name']`**, **`$_POST['email']`**, etc. Taking this knowledge a step further, it turns out that if you don't provide a name for a form element, then that element's value won't be passed to the server. This is how you protect the user and your business: The user's payment information never gets to your website! Your server will, however, receive the Stripe-provided token, which represents the payment option (it will be stored in a hidden form element via JavaScript and DOM manipulation).

**note**

In the downloadable code available at www.LarryUllman.com, you'll find this page as **`billing_stripe.php`**.

1. Open **`billing.html`** in your text editor or IDE.

2. Make sure the form has a unique ID value:

```
echo '<form action="/billing.php" method="POST"
➥id="billing_form">';
```

If you're following this book sequentially, this will already be in there.

3. Within the form, add a place for showing errors:

```
echo '<span class="error" id="error_span"></span>';
```

Put that code just inside the opening form tag but before the fieldset. It already has the **`error`** class and a unique ID value.

4. Replace the creation of the card number input with

```
<input type="text" id="cc_number" autocomplete="off" />
```

The original code used the **create_form_input()** function to generate this form element. But that function creates a form element with a name value, which is not acceptable when using the Stripe integration (unless you still want the PCI compliance burden). And since this element won't be made sticky anyway, much of the functionality of the **create_form_input()** function is no longer required.

5. Replace the creation of the expiration date inputs with

```
<input type="text" id="cc_exp_month" autocomplete="off" />/
➥<input type="text" id="cc_exp_year" autocomplete="off" />
```

These elements are being changed from select menus to text inputs, also without names.

6. Replace the creation of the CVC input with

```
<input type="text" id="cc_cvv" autocomplete="off" />
```

7. Save the file.

If you want, you can reload the page in your browser, although you won't see anything interesting just yet, aside from the changed inputs (**Figure 15.5**).

**tip**

CVC, CVV, CVD, CVN, CVV2, CVVC, CCV, and CVC2 are all acronyms for the card security code.

Figure 15.5

## Adding the JavaScript

**tip**

When using **Stripe.js**, your only requirement to be PCI compliant is that the HTML form be loaded via HTTPS.

With the form updated, you'll now add the JavaScript that performs all the magic. But first, you need to include the **Stripe.js** library on your payment page:

```
<script type="text/javascript" src="https://js.stripe.com/v2/">
➥</script>
```

As you can see, this library is hosted on Stripe's server. You don't have to download and install it on your site—in fact, you shouldn't. Note that this library is loaded over HTTPS, and your HTML page (the one with the payment form on it) must be loaded via HTTPS, too.

Stripe recommends that this file be included in the head of the document, so add it to **checkout_header.html**:

```
<title><?php
if (isset($page_title)) {
   echo $page_title;
} else {
   echo 'Coffee - Wouldn\'t You Love a Cup Right Now? - Checkout';
}
?></title>
<script src="//ajax.googleapis.com/ajax/libs/jquery/1.10.2/jquery.
➥min.js"></script>
<script type="text/javascript" src="https://js.stripe.com/v2/">
➥</script>
```

With that library included in the header file, two script blocks should be added to **billing.html**. The first script block needs to set your public Stripe key:

```
<script type="text/javascript">
Stripe.setPublishableKey('pk_test_15bY0KkYTu2Gb9Fm023m1Nm1');
</script>
```

This code can be anywhere after you've included the **Stripe.js** library (which defines the **Stripe** object used in that block). I suggest placing it near the end of **billing.html**. The value here should be your public key, found in your Stripe account settings. Do not put your private key here!

If you want, since **billing.html** is included from a PHP page, you could store the Stripe API keys as constants in the configuration file:

```
define('STRIPE_PRIVATE_KEY', 'sk_test_PcdmWKy8Nc1W2pDT3PwFRNw');
define('STRIPE_PUBLIC_KEY', 'pk_test_15bY0KkYTu2Gb9Fm023m1Nm1');
```

Then you can have PHP print this value within the JavaScript:

```
echo '<script type="text/javascript">Stripe.setPublishableKey(
➥"' . STRIPE_PUBLIC_KEY . '");</script>';
```

By having PHP print this value, you can quickly change from testing to live mode by only editing your configuration file.

Next, the remaining JavaScript code will go into a new JavaScript file to be included by **billing.html**:

```
<script type="text/javascript" src="/js/billing.js"></script>
```

Change the reference to the JavaScript file to be correct for your server.

## Writing billing.js

Now that the stage has been set, the JavaScript that does all the work will be written in **billing.js**. Again, the JavaScript needs to

- Handle the form submission
- Validate the form data
- Perform an Ajax request to Stripe
- Store the returned token in a hidden form element
- Submit the form to the server

Let's make that happen.

**tip**

Using Stripe requires JavaScript, so you may want to add a note about that somewhere on the page.

1. Create a new JavaScript file in your text editor or IDE to be named **billing.js** and stored in the **js** directory.
2. Add an event handler on the form's submission:

   ```
   $(function() {
     $('#billing_form').submit(function() {
     });
   });
   ```

   The JavaScript is going to use jQuery, which has already been included by the header (if not, add that code now). When the document is ready, the JavaScript adds a submit event handler to the billing form. Most of the following code will go within the innermost anonymous function (between lines 2 and 3 above).

3. Create a flag variable:

```
var error = false;
```

This variable will be used for the form validation.

4. Disable the submit button:

```
$('input[type=submit]', this).attr('disabled', 'disabled');
```

This code was explained in Chapter 14, "Adding JavaScript and Ajax." It finds all the input elements with a **type** value of **submit** and applies the **disabled** attribute to them. Alternatively, you could give the submit button a unique ID value and reference that.

5. Retrieve the form values:

```
var cc_number = $('#cc_number').val(),
   cc_cvv = $('#cc_cvv').val(),
   cc_exp_month = $('#cc_exp_month').val(),
   cc_exp_year = $('#cc_exp_year').val();
```

This jQuery code fetches the values for the four relevant form elements and stores them in local variables.

6. Validate the credit card number:

```
if (!Stripe.validateCardNumber(cc_number)) {
   error = true;
   reportError('The credit card number appears to be invalid.');
}
```

You can use any amount of standard JavaScript to perform minimal validation on the form data. However, it's best to be as thorough as you can in the validation; there's no need to send an incomplete request to Stripe, only to wait for that response to return an error.

The **Stripe** object, defined in **Stripe.js**, has several validation methods built in:

- **validateCardNumber()**
- **validateCVC()**
- **validateExpiry()**

The first method will confirm that the provided number matches the right syntax for credit cards. If that method returns **false**, the **error** variable will be set to **true** and a JavaScript function named **reportError()** will be called to show the error to the user. That function will be written shortly.

7. Validate the CVC/CVV:

```
if (!Stripe.validateCVC(cc_cvv)) {
   error = true;
   reportError('The CVV number appears to be invalid.');
}
```

   This is a variation on the code in Step 6.

8. Validate the expiration date:

```
if (!Stripe.validateExpiry(cc_exp_month, cc_exp_year)) {
   error = true;
   reportError('The expiration date appears to be invalid.');
}
```

   This is another variation, although the **validateExpiry()** method takes two arguments.

9. If no error occurred, request the token from Stripe:

```
if (!error) {
   Stripe.createToken({
      number: cc_number,
      cvc: cc_cvv,
      exp_month: cc_exp_month,
      exp_year: cc_exp_year
   }, stripeResponseHandler);
}
```

   The **createToken()** method of the **Stripe** object is all you need to perform the Ajax request. Its first argument is a custom object containing the credit card information. That object should pass along the payment details. Note that you must match the names of the object attributes—**number**, **cvc**, **exp_month**, **exp_year**—exactly. You can pass along other values, such as the customer's address, using other attributes enumerated in the Stripe documentation.

   The **createToken()** method's second argument is the name of the JavaScript function to call after Stripe returns the token.

**10.** Complete the two anonymous functions:

```
        return false;
    }); // form submission
}); // document ready.
```

The submit handling function needs to return **false** to prevent the form from being submitted to the server.

**11.** Define the **reportError()** function:

```
function reportError(msg) {
    $('#error_span').text(msg);
    $('input[type=submit]', this).attr('disabled', false);
    return false;
}
```

This function is used to display errors. It receives the error message as an argument. The first thing the function does is add that error message to the error span created in the form (**Figure 15.6**). Next, the function re-enables the submit button to allow for subsequent submissions (after correcting the error).

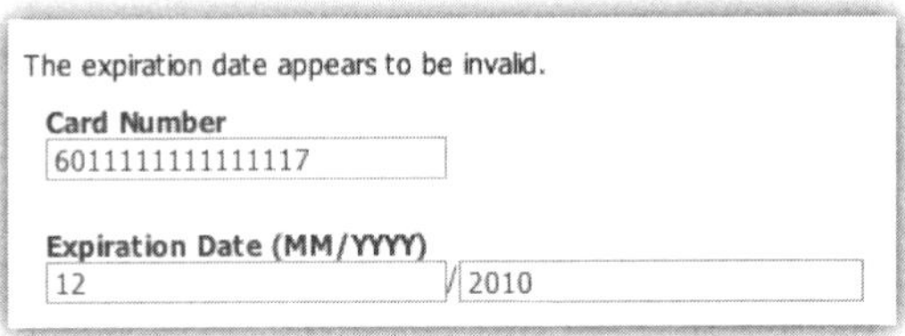


**Figure 15.6**

As written, the JavaScript displays only a single error at a time.

This function has to return **false** to also prevent the form from being submitted to the server, since this function could be called from the anonymous form submission handling function.

**12.** Begin defining the **stripeResponseHandler()** function:

```
function stripeResponseHandler(status, response) {
```

This function will be called when Stripe responds to the request for a payment token. The function receives two arguments: the status of the response and the response itself.

The **status** argument will receive the status code, which loosely emulates standard HTTP status codes. Basically, 200 is good; 400, 401, 402, and 404 generally mean you messed up; and codes in the 500s means Stripe's servers messed up. If you want to be thorough, you should check and address the status code, but I'm going to omit that step in this code and focus on the **response** value instead.

The response is going to be an object with several properties (**Figure 15.7**):

```
▼ Object
  ▼ card: Object
      address_city: null
      address_country: null
      address_line1: null
      address_line2: null
      address_state: null
      address_zip: null
      country: "US"
      customer: null
      exp_month: 12
      exp_year: 2014
      fingerprint: "0Flv2HtC1RZduMvU"
      id: "card_102jx52BAZoCjj35oO5V1r0E"
      last4: "1117"
      name: null
      object: "card"
      type: "Discover"
    ▶ __proto__: Object
    created: 1381587373
    id: "tok_102jx52BAZoCjj35V3eZSd6E"
    livemode: false
    object: "token"
    type: "card"
    used: false
  ▶ __proto__: Object
```

Figure 15.7

- **id**, which is the token identifier
- **card**, information about the card (but not the card number itself)
- **livemode**, which will be **true** or **false**
- **used**, a Boolean indicating whether this token has already been used

If an error occurred, there will be an **error** property, instead of the above (**Figure 15.8**).

```
▼ Object {error: Object}
  ▼ error: Object
      code: "invalid_cvc"
      message: "Your card's security code is invalid."
      param: "cvc"
      type: "card_error"
    ▶ __proto__: Object
  ▶ __proto__: Object
```

Figure 15.8

**13.** If an error occurred, report it:

```
if (response.error) {
   reportError(response.error.message);
```

If the **response** variable (which will be a JavaScript object; see Figure 15.8), has an **error** property, that needs to be shown to the customer. This could be an indication of an invalid credit card number, for example. The specific error will be found within **response.error.message**, which can be directly passed to the **reportError()** function to display it on the page (**Figure 15.9**).

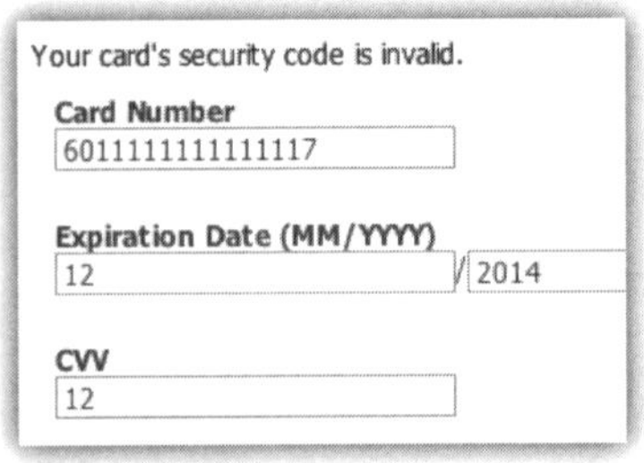

Your card's security code is invalid.
Card Number
6011111111111117
Expiration Date (MM/YYYY)
12 / 2014
CVV
12

Figure 15.9

**14.** If no error occurred, add the token to the form:

```
} else {
   var billing_form = $('#billing_form');
   var token = response.id;
   billing_form.append("<input type='hidden' name='token'
   ➥value='" + token + "' />");
```

First, a reference is made to the form. Next, the token is grabbed from the **response** object. The token value can be found in the **id** property. Third, a new hidden input is added to the form, with a name of **token** and the token value.

**15.** Submit the form and complete the function:

```
   billing_form.get(0).submit();
}
```

Now the form needs to be submitted to the handling script. Because there's an event handler watching for form submissions, this somewhat obtuse code must be used to submit the form without triggering the submission event.

**16.** Save the file.

If you want, you can test it in your browser to verify that the error reporting is working. If you remove the form submission line from the **stripeResponseHandler()** function, you can even test the Stripe process when using correct information. If you look at the updated page source, you'll see the Stripe token stored in the form upon successful completion (**Figure 15.10**).

```
▼<form action="/billing_stripe.php" method="POST" id="billing_form">
   <span class="error" id="error_span"></span>
  ▶<fieldset>…</fieldset>
   <input type="hidden" name="token" value="tok_102jxG2BAZoCjj35cvru4JES">
 </form>
```

**Figure 15.10**

## STRONGER VALIDATION

Stripe does not have a set validation requirement; it will pass along whatever information you provide to the appropriate bank. If you pass Stripe the CVC number, that will be validated along with the other credit card information. If you don't pass the CVC number, that won't be included in the validation. The same goes for the user's name and billing address.

It's entirely up to you how much information you want to take and validate. I argue for passing along more information, though. Doing so improves the opportunity of spotting fraud and minimizes the chance of wrongly being rejected for legitimate charges.

To add the user's name and billing information in this example, you simply update the JavaScript so that it also passes along those values as part of the first object in the **createToken()** method call. You can find the proper object names to use in the Stripe documentation (such as **address_city**, **address_line1**, and so forth).

For even better security and validation, you can enable CVC and zip code checks in your Stripe dashboard (under Account Settings). Checking those options will tell Stripe to reject a card for either a CVC or zip code match failure. Surprisingly, rejecting charges under these circumstances is not something banks always do.

## Database Changes

The original database had one table—**transactions**—defined explicitly based on the information returned when using Authorize.net. That table won't work when using Stripe for a few reasons, most particularly the fact that Stripe uses strings for the charge IDs, whereas Authorize.net uses large integers. To use Stripe for the e-commerce site, first add this table:

```
CREATE TABLE `charges` (
  `id` INT(10) UNSIGNED NOT NULL AUTO_INCREMENT,
  `charge_id` VARCHAR(60) NOT NULL,
  `order_id` INT(10) UNSIGNED NOT NULL,
  `type` VARCHAR(18) NOT NULL,
  `amount` INT(10) UNSIGNED NOT NULL,
  `charge` TEXT NOT NULL,
  `date_created` TIMESTAMP NOT NULL DEFAULT CURRENT_TIMESTAMP,
  PRIMARY KEY (`id`),
  KEY `order_id` (`order_id`),
  KEY `charge_id` (`charge_id`)
) ENGINE=InnoDB  DEFAULT CHARSET=utf8;
```

If you're using stored procedures, you'll need to add the following, which will add a record to that table:

```
DELIMITER $$
CREATE PROCEDURE add_charge (charge_id VARCHAR(60), oid INT,
➥trans_type VARCHAR(18), amt INT(10), charge TEXT)
BEGIN
  INSERT INTO charges VALUES (NULL, charge_id, oid, trans_type,
  ➥amt, charge, NOW());
END$$
DELIMITER ;
```

There's also one more niggling issue. The **billing.php** script as written uses the last four digits of the credit card number in a stored procedure:

```
$cc_last_four = substr($cc_number, -4);
$shipping = $_SESSION['shipping'] * 100;
$r = mysqli_query($dbc, "CALL add_order({$_SESSION['customer_id']},
➥'$uid', $shipping, $cc_last_four, @total, @oid)");
```

Originally, the script received the credit card number and could easily access the last four digits. With Stripe, that information is not immediately available. For now, you can use a temporary value:

```
$cc_last_four = 1234;
```

Later in the chapter you'll see how the last four digits of the card number become available again after processing the charge with Stripe.

## Writing the PHP Code

If your JavaScript code is working properly, and the customer's payment information is correct, a representative token will be stored in a hidden form input (see Figure 15.10) and the form will be submitted to the server. (But the payment information won't be provided to the server, because those form elements have no name attributes.) The server can now use **$_POST['token']** to process the payment.

The Stripe.js library does not make a payment; it just creates a token associated with a payment method.

The PHP script that handles the form data now needs to

- Validate that a token was received from the form
- Validate all of the other form data (everything required by your site; not by Stripe)
- Make the charge request of Stripe
- Handle Stripe's response
- Handle any errors

Let's walk through all of these steps in detail (except for the other form validation, which already exists). First, though, you'll want to download and install the Stripe PHP library:

1. Head to https://stripe.com.
2. Click Documentation.
3. On the documentation page, click API libraries.
4. Download the PHP library.
5. Expand the downloaded file.

   The downloaded file will have the name **stripe-php-latest.zip** (or **.tar.gz**).

 **tip**

The Stripe library can also be installed using Composer. See Chapter 13, "Extending the Second Site," for more on Composer.

6. Copy the **Stripe.php** file and the **Stripe** folder from the downloaded file to your site's directory.

   Both items can be found within the **lib** folder of the download. I recommend that you place them within your public **includes** folder, or within a subdirectory such as **includes/lib**. Note the path to the **Stripe.php** file.

With the Stripe library installed, you can use your PHP script to process the charge:

1. Open **billing.php** in your text editor or IDE.

2. Remove the validation of the user's credit card information.

   This validation is no longer necessary because the credit card information has already been validated by Stripe. And the credit card information won't be received by this script anyway!

   Note that all of the other form data still ought to be validated. The other information won't be used by Stripe, but it will be used by the site.

3. Add validation for the Stripe token:

```
if (isset($_POST['token'])) {
   $token = $_POST['token'];
} else {
   $message = 'The order cannot be processed. Please make sure
   ➥you have JavaScript enabled and try again.';
   $billing_errors['token'] = true;
}
```

   If **$_POST['token']** is set, it's assigned to a local variable for easy reference. If **$_POST['token']** is not set, then the order can't be processed. This could be because

   - You made a mistake in the JavaScript
   - Someone is trying to be tricky
   - A user has just disabled JavaScript

   In any case, the script needs to let the user know

   - That an error occurred
   - That she hasn't been charged yet
   - What the user should do next

The error message created here will be shown later in the form thanks to this code, which is already present (**Figure 15.11**):

Your Billing Information

Please enter your billing information below. Then click the button to complete your order. For your security, we will not store your billing information in any way. We accept Visa, MasterCard, American Express, and Discover.

The order cannot be processed. Please make sure you have JavaScript enabled and try again.

**Figure 15.11**

```
if (isset($message)) echo "<p class=\"error\">$message</p>";
```

The **`$billing_errors`** element also has to be created to prevent the order from being completed later in the script. (This construct is necessary since there's no dedicated place in the form to display token-related errors.)

4. Remove all of the code that pertains to using Authorize.net. This includes everything between

   ```
   if (isset($order_id, $order_total)) {
   ```

   and

   ```
   } // End of isset($order_id, $order_total) IF
   ```

   That code will be replaced with code specific to Stripe.

   You'll also need to remove this line, found earlier in the script:

   ```
   $cc_exp = sprintf('%02d%d', $_POST['cc_exp_month'],
   ➥$_POST['cc_exp_year']);
   ```

5. Where you just removed all the Authorize.net code, begin a **`try`** block:

   ```
   try {
   ```

   The Stripe library throws an exception when a problem occurs, so you should execute all of the Stripe code within a **`try...catch`** block.

6. Include the Stripe library:

   ```
   require_once('path/to/Stripe.php');
   ```

   You need to include the **`Stripe.php`** file, found wherever you stored it earlier. Obviously change the **`path/to`** part to match where you stored the Stripe items.

**note**

Keep your private API key private!

7. Set your secret API key:

```
Stripe::setApiKey(STRIPE_PRIVATE_KEY);
```

This is where you use the other Stripe API key. My earlier recommendation was to store this as a constant in a configuration file, which you could now use here.

8. Create the charge:

```
$charge = Stripe_Charge::create(array(
    'amount' => $order_total,
    'currency' => 'usd',
    'card' => $token,
    'description' => $_SESSION['email'],
    'capture' => false
    )
);
```

The **create()** method of the **Stripe_Charge** class creates new Stripe charges. It takes an array as an argument. As for what goes in the array, the full Stripe API lists all the possible options, but at the very least you want these array indexes and values:

**tip**

Stripe supports the ability to pass metadata along with your charges, allowing you to associate more pieces of meaningful site data with your Stripe transactions.

- **amount**: The amount needs to be an integer in *cents*. This is easy to miss. If you have a decimal, say $1.95, just multiply that times 100. With the Coffee site, all of the amounts are in cents already.
- **currency**: The currency is a three-letter ISO code, such as **usd** or **cad**. In other words, what currency are you being paid in (regardless of what the customer's native currency is)?
- **card**: The card should be the token.

You can optionally provide a **description** value. This is an easy way to associate other information with the charge. The recommended and logical choice is to provide a unique customer identifier with the description, such as the customer's email address.

**note**

You can capture payments for up to 7 days after they were authorized.

Finally, the **capture** element is given a value of **false**. Just as in the Authorize.net example, the payment is first authorized on the public side and can then be captured when the item is shipped.

Behind the scenes, Stripe will use cURL to perform the request.

**9.** Test the success of the operation:

```
if ($charge->paid == 1) {
```

Within the **try** block, after the invocation of **create()** you can use the **$charge** object to test the success of the operation (assuming no exceptions occurred). The charge object will have many attributes (**Figure 15.12**), including

- **amount**, the amount charged
- **id**, a unique identifier
- **livemode**, a Boolean (no value, as in Figure 15.12, means **false**)
- **card**, an object that stores information about the card charged (but nothing too revealing beyond the address and the last four digits of the card)
- **currency**, the ISO code
- **paid**, a Boolean
- **description**, the description you provided

To confirm that the charge went through, and that you were paid, you can check the **paid** attribute. (Even in authorization mode, **paid** will equal 1 or **true**.)

```
Stripe_Charge Object
(
    [_apiKey:protected] => sk_test_cyFiWIBiAhaZiW2WiURm4MNw
    [_values:protected] => Array
        (
            [id] => ch_102jyI2BAZoCjj35RP3QgGkT
            [object] => charge
            [created] => 1381591844
            [livemode] =>
            [paid] => 1
            [amount] => 3722
            [currency] => usd
            [refunded] =>
            [card] => Stripe_Card Object
                (
                    [_apiKey:protected] => sk_test_cyFiWIBiAhaZiW2WiURm4MNw
                    [_values:protected] => Array
                        (
                            [id] => card_102jyI2BAZoCjj357Kflz0yL
                            [object] => card
                            [last4] => 1117
                            [type] => Discover
                            [exp_month] => 12
                            [exp_year] => 2014
                            [fingerprint] => 0Flv2HtClRZduMvU
                            [customer] =>
                            [country] => US
                            [name] =>
                            [address_line1] =>
                            [address_line2] =>
                            [address_city] =>
                            [address_state] =>
                            [address_zip] =>
                            [address_country] =>
                            [cvc_check] => pass
                            [address_line1_check] =>
                            [address_zip_check] =>
                        )
```

Figure 15.12

For added protection, you could confirm that the **livemode** is **true** (when you are live), that the **currency** is your currency, that the **amount** is the expected amount, and so forth. But if **paid** is **true** (or 1), and all the other conditions you want to test are correct, the customer has paid and you should consider the order completed.

10. Store the transaction in the database:

```
$full_response = addslashes(serialize($charge));
$r = mysqli_query($dbc, "CALL add_charge('{$charge->id}',
➥$order_id, 'auth_only', $order_total, '$full_response')");
```

These two lines store the charge information in the database, using the new table and stored procedures created for Stripe.

11. Add the transaction info to the session:

```
$_SESSION['response_code'] = $charge->paid;
```

The **final.php** script will expect **$_SESSION['response_code']** to exist and have a value of 1.

12. Redirect the customer to the next page:

```
$location = 'https://' . BASE_URL . 'final.php';
header("Location: $location");
exit();
```

13. If no charge was made, alert the customer:

```
} else {
   $message = $charge->failure_message;
}
```

This code probably won't often be executed, since a failure to create a paid charge will normally trigger an exception (to be caught later in the script). But just in case, the **failure_message** property will reflect any particular error.

14. Catch any card errors:

```
} catch (Stripe_CardError $e) {
   $e_json = $e->getJsonBody();
   $err = $e_json['error'];
   $message = $err['message'];
```

The Stripe library will throw an exception if the charge was declined. In that case, you need to use this code to parse the error message out of the response. Stripe assures that the value (**`$error['message']`** in the above) will be informative and presentable to the customer (**Figure 15.13**). Some actual values are as follows:

- The card number is incorrect
- The card number is not a valid credit card number
- The card's expiration month is invalid
- The card's expiration year is invalid
- The card's security code is invalid
- The card has expired
- The card's security code is incorrect
- The card was declined

**tip**

Arguably, the error message should be made more obvious to the customer than what is shown in Figure 15.13.

You may wonder how the charge attempt could fail when the **`Stripe.js`** library provides a handy-dandy way to securely handle the payment information. The **`Stripe.js`** process does only two things:

- Transmits the payment information to Stripe in a secure way (limiting your liability)
- Verifies that the payment information *looks* usable

In terms of watching for errors, it's this second factor that comes into play. Stripe will confirm that the card information looks valid, but that doesn't mean it can be used for a payment. Only when the charge is attempted will Stripe, and you, discover that the shopper is using a debit card with insufficient funds or a credit card that's over the limit. These are the kinds of errors you must now watch for.

**Figure 15.13**

**tip**

Stripe supports webhooks, which will ping a script on your server when events occur.

15. Catch any other exceptions:

```
} catch (Exception $e) {
   trigger_error(print_r($e, 1));
}
```

This is the final fallback, designed to catch any other non-card error, and it won't be triggered often. There are other specific exceptions you could try to catch, including a **Stripe_ApiConnectionError** or a **Stripe_InvalidRequestError**. See the Stripe documentation for details.

16. Save the file.

# TESTING STRIPE

To test what you've created, you can use your own credit card without concern (so long as you're using the test keys). Or you can use some of the sample credit card numbers listed in Stripe's documentation (see https://stripe.com/docs/testing).

To emulate specific failures, there are special numbers (also listed in the Stripe documentation):

- 4000000000000101 will fail based on an invalid CVC
- 4000000000000002 will be declined (as if there were insufficient funds; see Figure 15.13)
- 4000000000000069 will be declined as an expired card
- 4000000000000119 will be declined for a generic processing error (**Figure 15.14**)

Your Billing Information

Please enter your billing information below. Then click the button to complete your order. For your security, we will not store your billing information in any way. We accept Visa, MasterCard, American Express, and Discover.

An error occurred while processing your card. Try again in a little bit.

**Figure 15.14**

You can also trigger declines by using an invalid month value, a year in the past, or a two-digit CVC number (correct numbers are three or four digits long). Providing a non-integer amount for the charge will trigger an invalid amount failure, since the amount must be an integer (in cents).

One thing you ought to know about testing is that these numbers will have these effects only when in test mode (that is, when you're using the testing public and private keys). When you use these numbers on a live site, Stripe will just report that the card was declined, because those are invalid numbers.

In addition, the validations you want to test will depend on what information you'll take. For example, if you don't take the customer's address information, there's no point in testing the address or zip code verifications.

After running some test charges, log in to your Stripe account to view them (**Figure 15.15**). Click any individual charge attempt to see even more details (**Figure 15.16**).

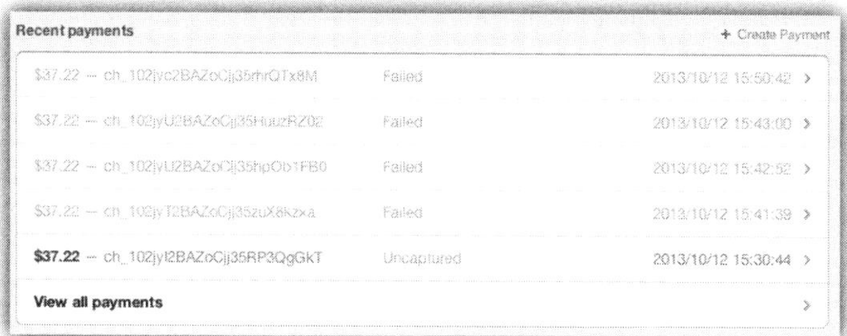


Figure 15.15

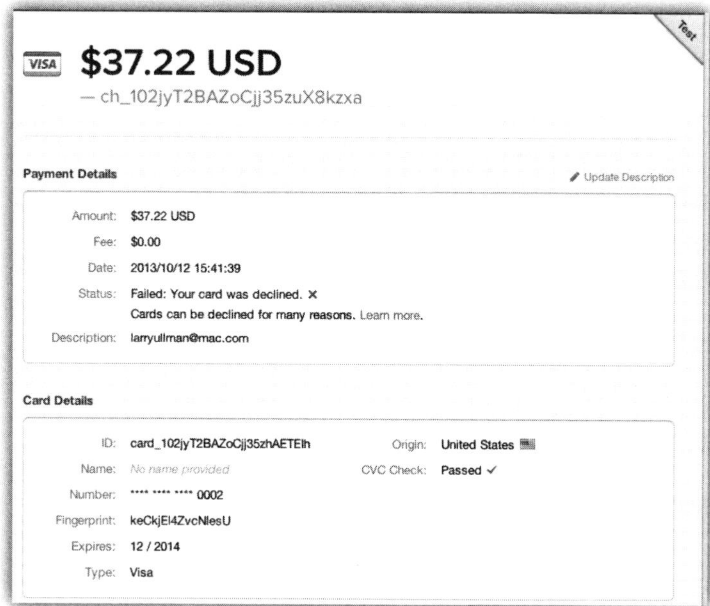


Figure 15.16

# GOING LIVE

When you're ready to go live, there are a couple of things you need to do. First, swap out your test API keys for the live API keys (in both the JavaScript and the PHP script). Second, activate your account. You don't have to activate your account in order to process real charges, but your account must be active before Stripe can send funds to your bank.

To activate your account, you can either toggle your dashboard to the live view (in the upper-left corner) to be prompted, or you can select Your Account > Activate Account.

On the resulting page, you'll need to fill out a form, providing the following information (**Figure 15.17**):

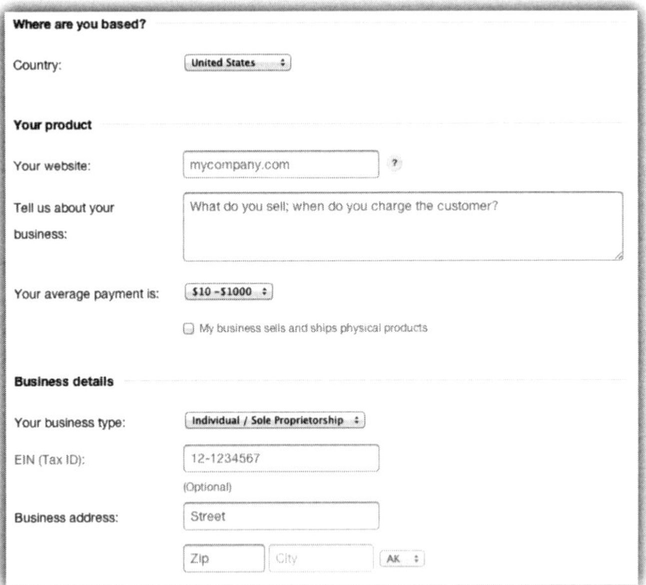


**Figure 15.17**

- A description of your product/business (what you sell, what your URL is, how much business you expect to do, etc.)
- Your business's legal details (country, business type, legal name, tax ID number, and address)
- Your personal and contact information
- Your bank details (where the money should go)

Stripe takes this seriously: They will validate you and your company's identification. On the other hand, Stripe won't randomly lock your account once it's been activated because some transaction raised a flag in their automated system of blind checks (unlike, say, PayPal).

Going forward, I have a few more recommendations. First, keep an eye on your server logs. Make sure no sensitive data is being stored there (or being sent via email). Because the payment information won't be hitting your server, you should be safe, but it's best not to make assumptions. You'll also want to regularly rotate your logs, just so they don't become unwieldy.

Second, every few months or so go into your Stripe account and change your keys. This is a good general practice for any e-commerce site, just as it's best for everyone to change their login passwords regularly. You can change your keys in the Stripe dashboard, under Your Account > Account Settings > API Keys. There's a refresh icon ("Roll Key") to click (**Figure 15.18**). Changing your private key is what really counts since the public key is already, well, public. Stripe, in its brilliance, will give you the option of continuing to support the old key for 12 hours (**Figure 15.19**). This provides a little leeway in case an order comes through in the time between when you roll the key and when you change it on the site (or if you fail to change the key in all your code—but if you use a constant, that shouldn't happen).

**tip**

If your secret API key has been comprised, change it and block the old one immediately.

**Figure 15.18**

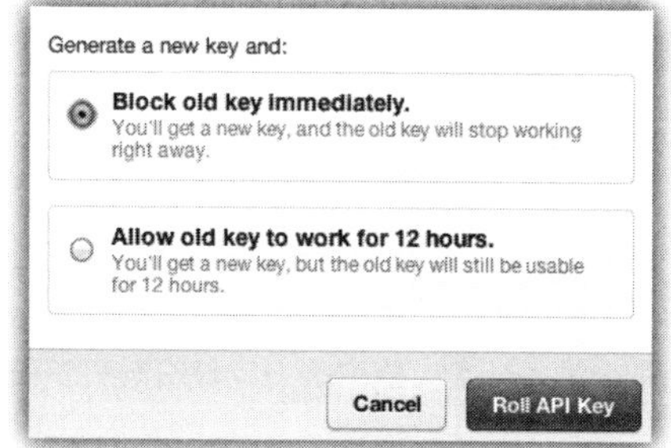


**Figure 15.19**

Third, while you are on the API Keys page, check the API version in use (**Figure 15.20**). When your site interacts with Stripe, Stripe will make note of the API version you're using (the version of the PHP library). Stripe makes regular updates to its libraries, and you should keep yours up to date. But Stripe will continue to support whatever version you're using. Periodically, you should check your API version against the current version. Then download the latest version of the Stripe library and upload it to your site. Once that's done, click the Upgrade button on the API keys page to complete the upgrade.

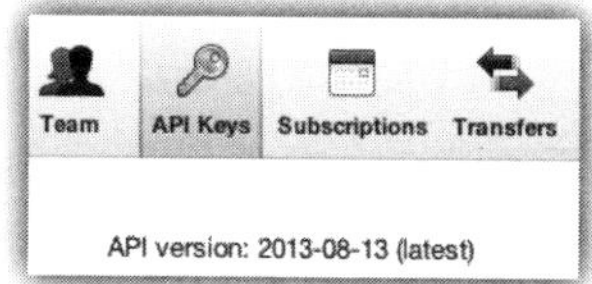


**Figure 15.20**

Finally, enable two-step verification in your Stripe account (Account Settings > General). By doing so, you can log in to your Stripe account only after you've entered your correct email address and password and a verification code is sent to your mobile phone. Yes, you'll need a mobile phone with the Google Authenticator app installed to do this, but I highly recommend enabling this extra level of verification. That way, no one can get into your Stripe account and make a huge mess of things without your email address, password, and physical access to your mobile phone.

# CAPTURING CHARGES

In the Coffee site, the public billing form only *authorizes* charges. The actual charges are processed, and you get your money, once the charges are *captured* on the administrative side.

Given the code explained thus far in this chapter, here are the steps for capturing a previously authorized charge:

1. Retrieve the charge ID from the database.

   The query is similar to the one originally in **view_order.php**:

   ```
   SELECT customer_id, total, charge_id FROM orders AS o JOIN
   ➥charges AS c ON (o.id=c.order_id AND c.type='auth_only')
   ➥WHERE o.id=$order_id
   ```

   Let's assume you've executed that query and fetched the charge ID into a variable named **$charge_id**.

2. Include the Stripe library and set your API key:

   ```
   require_once('path/to/Stripe.php');
   Stripe::setApiKey(STRIPE_PRIVATE_KEY);
   ```

3. Retrieve the charge using the charge ID:

   ```
   $charge = Stripe_Charge::retrieve($charge_id);
   ```

   The **retrieve()** method of the **Stripe_Charge** class fetches a charge object from Stripe using the charge ID.

4. Capture the charge by calling the **capture()** method:

   ```
   $charge->capture();
   ```

   That's all you have to do.

5. Check the **paid** property to confirm that the charge was captured:

   ```
   if ($charge->paid == 1) {...
   ```

Again, take these steps within a **try...catch** block in case any exceptions are thrown.

If you view the captured charge in your Stripe dashboard, you can see all of the events involving it within the payment's logs section. **Figure 15.21** shows the initial request for a payment token, the initial charge (which was an authorization), and the final capture.

Click any particular log item to view the details.

Logs

| | | |
|---|---|---|
| 200 | POST /v1/charges/ch_102jyl2BAZoCjj35RP3QgGkT/capture | 2013/10/12 16:15:53 > |
| 200 | POST /v1/charges | 2013/10/12 15:30:44 > |
| 200 | POST /v1/tokens | 2013/10/12 15:30:43 > |

**Figure 15.21**

# PERFORMING RECURRING CHARGES

The previous set of explanations works great for the Coffee site, where a onetime charge must be made. But on the "Knowledge Is Power" site, recurring payments are involved. This is possible in Stripe, too, and I'll explain the process now, with a sufficient amount of code.

Recurring charges in Stripe are a combination of three things:

- Plans
- Customers
- Subscriptions

You can create several different types of plans. They can last for different durations or reflect different costs (such as membership levels).

You can create plans programmatically using the API, but you can also do so in your dashboard:

1. Log in to Stripe.
2. Click Plans on the left.

**tip**

If you've already created a plan, make another by clicking New in the upper-right corner.

3. On the resulting page (**Figure 15.22**), click Create Your First Plan.

**Figure 15.22**

4. Complete the pop-up form (**Figure 15.23**).

**Figure 15.23**

The ID value needs to be unique and ought to be short. It'll be used by the API. The name should be friendly. Then enter an amount and interval.

**tip**

Stripe supports trial periods for plans.

5. Click Create Plan.

Once you've created a plan, you can associate customers with it. You'd likely do that programmatically.

With the "Knowledge Is Power site," first you want to create a payment form, just as I explained for the Coffee site. Make sure you don't assign name values to the credit card elements! The form should also take whatever other customer information you want: email address, name, and so forth. For "Knowledge Is Power," this means you can just add the billing form elements to the registration page.

Next, you can use the same JavaScript already explained with the Coffee site for handling the form's submission, verifying the payment information, and retrieving a token from Stripe. If you use the same unique IDs for your form elements, the existing **billing.js** will work without modification.

On the server side, upon the form's submission, you first validate that a token exists, as already explained. Then you validate the other form data. If all of the data passed the tests, you then include the Stripe library and set your API key:

```
require_once('path/to/Stripe.php');
Stripe::setApiKey(STRIPE_PRIVATE_KEY);
```

Next, you create a new **Stripe_Customer** (not a **Stripe_Charge**):

```
$customer = Stripe_Customer::create(array(
   'description' => "Customer $email",
   'email' => $email,
   'card' => $token,
   'plan' => 'kip_basic'
));
```

And that's all there is to it. This code will create a new customer object in your Stripe account. The customer's credit card information will be associated with that customer. And the customer will be subscribed to that plan. If the plan is billed monthly, then every month Stripe will automatically generate an invoice and attempt to pay that invoice using the customer's credit card information on file. You'd want to make use of the Stripe webhooks feature so that your site is notified when invoices are paid. With each paid invoice, you update that customer's access to your site.

# INDEX

## SYMBOLS



## A

## B



## C

## D

## E

## T



## U